Power and Popular Protest

Power and Popular Protest

Latin American Social Movements

Updated and Expanded Edition

EDITED BY

Susan Eckstein

CONTRIBUTORS

Manuel Antonio Garretón M. • Daniel H. Levine
Cynthia McClintock • Scott Mainwaring
Maria Helena Moreira Alves • June Nash • Marysa Navarro
John Walton • Timothy Wickham-Crowley • León Zamosc

UNIVERSITY OF CALIFORNIA PRESS
Berkeley   Los Angeles   London

University of California Press
Berkeley and Los Angeles, California

University of California Press, Ltd.
London, England

© 2001, 1989 by
The Regents of the University of California

LIBRARY OF CONGRESS
Library of Congress Cataloging-in-Publication Data

Power and popular protest: Latin American social movements / edited by Susan Eckstein.
  p. cm.
  ISBN 0-520-22705-0 (alk. paper)
  1. Latin America—Politics and government. 2. Government, Resistence to—Latin
America. 3. Social movements—Latin America.
  I. Eckstein, Susan, 1942–
  F1410.P76 1988
  320.98—dc 19

                    88-2465
                    CIP

Printed in the United States of America

09 08   07   06   05   04   03   02
9   8   7   6   5   4   3   2

CONTENTS

LIST OF TABLES AND FIGURES / *vii*
CONTRIBUTORS / *ix*
PREFACE TO THE SECOND EDITION / *xiii*
PREFACE TO THE FIRST EDITION / *xv*

Chapter 1. Power and Popular Protest in Latin America
Susan Eckstein / 1

Chapter 2. Peru's Sendero Luminoso Rebellion: Origins and Trajectory
Cynthia McClintock / 61

Chapter 3. Peasant Struggles of the 1970s in Colombia
León Zamosc / 102

Chapter 4. Winners, Losers, and Also-Rans: Toward a Comparative Sociology
of Latin American Guerrilla Movements
Timothy P. Wickham-Crowley / 132

Chapter 5. Cultural Resistance and Class Consciousness in Bolivian
Tin-Mining Communities
June Nash / 182

Chapter 6. Religion and Popular Protest in Latin America: Contrasting
Experiences
Daniel H. Levine and Scott Mainwaring / 203

Chapter 7. The Personal Is Political: Las Madres de Plaza de Mayo
Marysa Navarro / 241

Chapter 8. Popular Mobilization and the Military Regime in Chile:
The Complexities of the Invisible Transition
Manuel Antonio Garretón M. / 259

Chapter 9. Interclass Alliances in the Opposition to the Military in Brazil:
Consequences for the Transition Period
Maria Helena Moreira Alves / 278

Chapter 10. Debt, Protest, and the State in Latin America
John Walton / 299

Chapter 11. Poor People Versus the State and Capital: Anatomy of a
Successful Community Mobilization for Housing in Mexico City
Susan Eckstein / 329

Epilogue. Where Have All the Movements Gone?
Latin American Social Movements at the New Millennium
Susan Eckstein / 351

INDEX / *407*

LIST OF TABLES AND FIGURES

TABLES

2.1 Regional Inequalities in Peru / *66*

2.2 Living standards, Ayacucho versus Cuzco / *69*

2.3 The Impact of Agrarian Reform in Highlands Peru / *74*

2.4 Electoral Trends in Selected Regions of Peru, 1978–85 / *86*

2.5 Attitudes toward Democracy in Lima, 1982–86 / *88*

4.1 Changes in Latin American University Enrollments, 1955–75 / *142*

4.2 Degree of Peasant Support for Guerrilla Movements / *145*

4.3 Land Tenure Systems and Peasant Support / *148*

4.4 Social Conditions Favoring or Disfavoring Transfer of Mass Loyalties to Insurgents in Latin America / *174*

10.1 Latin American Debt by Country / *302*

10.2 Summary by Country of Latin American Austerity Protests, 1976–87 / *310*

E.1 Latin American Strike Activity / *369*

E.2 Consumer Price Increases: Food and Fuel/Electricity / *376*

FIGURES

3.1 Colombian Agrarian Structures, Main Class Sectors, and Their Demands (1960s) / *110*

4.1 Trajectories of Latin American Guerrilla Movements, 1955–85 / *136*

4.2 Social Conditions for Expansion and Success of Guerrilla Movements / *144*

CONTRIBUTORS

Susan Eckstein is professor of sociology at Boston University. In 1997–98 she served as president of the Latin American Studies Association. She is the author of *Back from the Future: Cuba under Castro, The Poverty of Revolution: The State and Urban Poor in México, El estado y la pobreza urbana en México*, and *The Impact of Revolution: A Comparative Analysis of Mexico and Bolivia*, as well as numerous articles on political, social, and economic developments in Latin America.

Manuel Antonio Garretón is professor at the University of Chile. Previously, he was research professor at FLACSO-Chile and visiting professor and researcher at various Latin American, European, and U.S. universities. He is the author of a number of books and articles on culture, politics, and society in Chile and other Latin American countries, including *La faz sumergida del iceberg: Estudios sobre la transformación cultural, Dimensiones actuales de la sociología* (coeditor), and *Hacía una nueva era política: Estudio sobre las democratizaciones*. In 2000 he served as president of the Committee on Class and Social Movements of the International Sociological Association.

Daniel Levine is professor of political science at the University of Michigan. He has published widely on religion, society, and politics and on democracy and democratization in Latin America. Among his most recent books are *Voces populares en el catolicismo Latinoamericano* and *Constructing Culture and Power in Latin America*. Previous books include *Religion and Politics in Latin America: The Catholic Church in Venezuela and Colombia*, and the edited volume *Religion and Political Conflict in Latin America*. In addition, he has published articles on religion and politics in Latin America.

Scott Mainwaring is director of the Kellogg Institute and Eugene Conley Professor of Government at the University of Notre Dame. His latest books are *Rethinking Party Systems in the Third Wave of Democratization: The Case of Brazil; Presidentialism and Democracy in Latin America*, coedited with Matthew

Shugart; and *Building Democratic Institutions: Party Systems in Latin America,* coedited with Timothy R. Scully. In addition, he is the author of *The Catholic Church and Politics in Brazil, 1916–1985,* and coeditor of *A igreja nas bases em tempo de transiçao.* He has also published articles on social movements and transitions to democracy in Latin America.

Cynthia McClintock is professor of political science and international affairs at George Washington University. Her books include *Revolutionary Movements in Latin America: El Salvador's FMLN and Peru's Shining Path, Peasant Cooperatives and Political Change in Peru,* and, *El Gobierno Militar/The Peruvian Experiment Reconsidered* (coeditor). In addition, she has published numerous articles in scholarly journals. During 1994–95 she was president of the Latin American Studies Association.

Maria Helena Moreira Alves currently lives and does research in Chile. She has taught political science and Latin American studies at the University of the State of Rio de Janeiro (UERJ), Amherst College, the University of Wisconsin–Madison, and the University of New Mexico. She has worked in popular education programs with the Central Único dos Trabalhadores (CUT) and with unions and grass-roots groups in Brazil, Central America, and Chile. She is the author of *State and Opposition in Military Brazil* and has written extensively on popular movements, human rights, and the history of the Brazilian labor movement.

June Nash is Distinguished Professor of Anthropology Emeritus at the City College of the City University of New York. She is the author of *In the Eyes of Ancestors: Belief and Behavior in a Maya Community,* the award-winning *We Eat the Mines and the Mines Eat Us, From Tank Town to High Tech: The Clash of Community and Industrial Cycles;* coeditor of *Sex and Class in Latin America, Women, Men, and the International Division of Labor,* and *Women and Change in Latin America;* and editor of *Crafts in the World Market.* She has written articles on peasants, miners, industrial workers, and artisans in Latin America and the United States.

Marysa Navarro is Charles Collis Professor of History and chair of the Latin American, Latino, and Caribbean Studies Program at Dartmouth College. She is the author of *Los nacionalistas, Evita,* and numerous articles. She is also coeditor, with Wilma Mankiller, Wendy Mink, Barbara Smith, and Gloria Steinem, of the *Reader's Companion to U.S. Women's History.*

John Walton is professor of sociology and anthropology at the University of California at Davis. He has written about development, urbanization, political economy, social-cultural history, and collective action in such books as *Elites and Economic Development: Labor, Class and the International System* (coauthor), *Reluctant Rebels: Comparative Studies of Revolution and Underdevelopment, Free Markets and Food Riots: The Politics of Global Adjustment* (coauthor), and *Western Times and Water Wars: State, Culture, and Rebellion in*

California. He is currently at work on a history of California focused on collective memory.

Timothy Wickham-Crowley is associate professor of sociology and member of the Center for Latin American Studies at Georgetown University. He is the author of *Exploring Revolution* and *Guerrillas and Revolution in Latin America.* His current research interests focus on development and underdevelopment in the Americas since 1500.

León Zamosc is professor of sociology at the University of California at San Diego. He has written widely on social development, the informal economy, agrarian structures, peasant struggles, and indigenous movements in Colombia, Ecuador, and El Salvador. He is currently doing research on rural redefinitions in Spain.

PREFACE TO THE SECOND EDITION

Since the publication of the first edition of *Power and Popular Protest,* Latin America and the world in general have changed. The Cold War has ended, and in turn U.S. Latin American political interests and policies have changed. As a consequence, U.S. military support subsided, except to the drug economies of the region. Latin America was, from Washington's vantage point, safe for democracy. And that is what Latin Americans had pressed for, often courageously, in the 1970s and 1980s, as the contributors to this book so ably describe and analyze.

Capitalism as well has emerged victorious. The demise of the Soviet Union and the Soviet Bloc discredited socialism as we knew it. The former Eastern Bloc countries embraced market reforms. On a lesser scale, so too did the remaining Communist countries. But with the new world order came a new economic model that the United States, as well as the multilateral institutions with which it is associated, used their power to impose: neoliberalism. Governments in Latin America joined the neoliberal bandwagon, albeit to varying degrees depending on domestic resistance and their own priorities. They lowered barriers to trade, they eliminated or reduced price subsidies, they privatized their economies, they encouraged exports and policies to make their export sectors more competitive, and they reduced social expenditures. The reforms were designed to privilege market forces, to make for greater economic efficiency and greater profits (including for foreign capital), and to minimize the state's role in the economy. They were intended to remove market "fetters" associated with the now-discredited economic model, import substitution. Import substitution had included institutional barriers to the free mobility of land, labor, and capital, to the benefit especially of domestic capital but, in limited ways, also workers and sometimes the peasantry.

Whatever logic the reforms had, and however they helped to address fiscal and other economic problems rooted in import substitution, they were not politically popular among the many victims of the new measures. Those able to compete in the new globalized and unapologetically pro-business environment did well by the reforms, whereas many urban and rural poor, factory workers, public sector employees, and others were hard hit by some, if not all, the changes. Laborers faced new insecurities, and typically also new deprivations. While the social movements of the 1970s and 1980s helped to pave the way for the political, if not economic, changes of the 1990s and to open up certain opportunities for previously excluded groups, new economic and sometimes even new political institutions became bases of new movements of resistance and change.

The new edition of *Power and Popular Protest* provides a unique opportunity to reflect on the movements of the 1960s to 1980s and examine their long-term effects. In the Epilogue, written especially for this edition I discuss not only the impact of all the movements analyzed in the first edition but also new movements that arose on the heels of the old, in the changed macro economic and political milieu. Nowhere else can be found as systematic and comprehensive an overview of the Latin American social movement landscape at the dawn of the millennium. In continuing to seek redress and press new claims, disadvantaged groups demonstrate that they still have faith that they can be actors and not mere subjects of history. And their aspirations came to be influenced by new global as well as local conceptions of individual and collective rights. The changes will be shown to broaden the Latin American social movements repertoire, both in its social base and goals.

The new edition of *Power and Popular Protest* also includes a new chapter that focuses on the dynamics of one of the most effective non-squatter-based housing movements in the region, in Mexico after the mid-1980s earthquake. It discusses not merely how a poor people's movement succeeded against all odds in getting a government to rebuild a neighborhood for its longtime residents. It also examines how macro political and economic dynamics of the 1990s affected the long-term effects of the movement. Poor people's housing, in Mexico as in the other mushrooming cities of Latin America, remains terribly inadequate. The Mexican example illustrates how through collective efforts new solutions may come about.

I could not have written the epilogue without the assistance of the contributors to the first edition of this book. They provided me with new information on their respective case studies as well as on other regional movements. Their insights were invaluable, and I am indebted to them.

Susan Eckstein
Boston, Massachusetts

PREFACE TO THE FIRST EDITION

North Americans tend to equate protest, especially in the Third World, with guerrilla wars or communist movements. Such a conception is misleading. It is too narrow. Defiance is much more widespread than such movements would indicate. It takes many forms, and it may articulate a broad spectrum of ideologies. Defiance may take the form of foot-dragging, pilfering, and passive noncompliance as well as participation in strikes, street demonstrations, land seizures, and revolutionary or other opposition movements. The outcomes of defiance may be equally varied. Outcomes depend only partially on the rage, ideology, and tactics of protesters; they depend very much on elite responses, class alliances, and global economic and geopolitical forces.

Both the variety of expressions and variety of outcomes of defiance are patterned by historical and structural forces that the actors themselves do not necessarily comprehend. The empirically detailed and analytically grounded essays in this book contribute to an understanding of that patterning.

The essays focus on Latin American experiences, but the theoretical and political implications of the studies are much broader. Ideally, this book will enlighten readers not only about the causes and consequences of protest and resistance movements in Latin America but also about ways in which, and reasons why, the patterning of defiance in Latin America contrasts with that in other regions of the world. Our understanding of the historically specific and generalizable features of protest movements will accordingly be improved.

Seen "from above," defiance is bothersome. It threatens the economic and political order and the interests that benefit from it. Seen "from below," defiance is risky. Protesters often accomplish little, and elites may fire, imprison, exile, or kill them for not complying with rules and expectations. Because of the risks, subordinate groups often opt to acquiesce, or defy conditions they dislike in subtle ways. When they publicly challenge the status quo, it is not because they are predisposed to make trouble. It is because they have limited alternative means to voice their views and press for change, and because they consider conditions unjustifiable or intolerable.

This book should contribute to a better understanding of the concerns of the politically and economically weak. Perhaps it will also inspire privileged groups to reduce inequities and injustices so that oppressed groups need not be defiant before their concerns are addressed.

Susan Eckstein

CHAPTER ONE

Power and Popular Protest in Latin America

Susan Eckstein

Why do city-dwellers take to the streets and not to ballot boxes to express dissatisfaction with government policies under democratic as well as authoritarian governments? Why do the same angry workers sometimes support revolutionary movements and at other times express their outrage through foot-dragging, strikes, and rituals? Why do some peasants acquiesce to rural conditions not to their liking while others do not? Moreover, why do similar types of protest movements produce different outcomes in different countries? Neither political science paradigms of regime types nor theories of social movements that focus merely on the grievances, organization, and leadership of defiant groups adequately account for the conditions inducing common folk to resist and protest exploitation, degradation, and poverty, the range of ways in which they express dissatisfaction with their lot, and the outcomes of their defiance.

This chapter and those that follow highlight the diversity of expressions of defiance and, most important, the range of outcomes of defiance in Latin America. Timothy Wickham-Crowley and Cynthia McClintock deal with the common origins, but varying fates, of rural guerrilla movements; Leon Zamosc examines how and explains why the ideology, activities, and accomplishments of a peasant movement changed over time even when its social base did not; and June Nash focuses on miner protests that combine primordial beliefs, customs, and rituals with twentieth-century revolutionary and reactionary politics. Daniel Levine and Scott Mainwaring describe how, and explain why, lower-class movements simi-

My thanks to Jack Goldstone, Daniel Levine, Scott Mainwaring, Cynthia McClintock, June Nash, Frances Piven, James Scott, Theda Skocpol, John Walton, Timothy Wickham-Crowley, and León Zamosc for comments on an earlier version of this chapter. I would like also to thank the Center for International Affairs at Harvard and the Boston University Graduate School for institutional support during the period in which I wrote the chapter.

1

larly grounded in liberation theology have differed in their involvements, depending on specific national and local conditions. Manuel Antonio Garretón, Maria Helena Moreira Alves, and Marysa Navarro, by contrast, focus on multiclass movements based on common opposition to repressive governments that have failed to resolve national economic problems, Navarro dealing specifically with defiance organized and led by women. John Walton examines protests in a number of countries by the middle and "popular" classes against austerity measures imposed by governments to mitigate their foreign debts, as well as government defiance of policies imposed by international creditors.

The chapters cover movements that span the continent—from Mexico in the north to Argentina and Chile in the south. They represent a mere sampling of the ways in which Latin Americans have, often courageously, defied conditions they find intolerable. Protesters in many countries in the region have been thrown out of work, imprisoned, tortured, exiled, or killed. Latin American elites have at their command substantial repressive resources, which they all too frequently have deployed to defend their political and economic interests when challenged "from below."

While the collection intentionally includes studies of the gamut of groups that have engaged in protest activity in recent decades, it includes neither the entire universe of groups and movements nor a representative sampling of them. Rather, the book is designed to uncover common patterns in movements with different social bases and different goals, movements in different sociopolitical contexts, and defiance that is diversely expressed. Our current knowledge of Latin America is painfully inadequate and centered primarily on elite concerns and perspectives. As a consequence, we know much more about state structures, political parties, and interest groups than about the lives and preoccupations of "popular" groups. Usually it is only when U.S. interests and dominant class hegemony have been challenged, as in Central America in the 1980s, that attention has shifted to subordinate groups.

Our limited empirical and analytic understanding of Latin American protest also reflects disciplinary biases and fads. When social science research on Latin America "took off" in the 1960s, it was heavily influenced by modernization theory and its behavioralist assumptions, according to which individuals would be economically mobile and countries would develop economically and become more democratic politically when the population assimilated Western values and participated in modern institutions. However, democracy would be undermined by "extremist" politics if individuals were uprooted from their traditional way of life without being absorbed into modern institutions or if their expectations did not materialize.

The fact that massive urbanization and marginality did not give rise to revolutionary movements forced more and more (though certainly not all) scholars to abandon behavioralist analyses. The focus of concern shifted from society to the state, to analyses of bureaucratic authoritarianism and corporatist views of state-society relations. The emphasis turned to order and social control rather than mobilization, defiance, and protest. At the same time, the "dependency school of thought" challenged the evolutionary, cultural, and individualistic assumptions on which modernization theory was premised, arguing instead that Latin American development must be understood in the context of global economic dynamics. However, in emphasizing how global dynamics constrained Latin American options, "dependency" writers found little room for voluntarism and left conflicts grounded in noneconomic relationships unexplained.

Latin Americans have been more defiant than the available literature would lead us to believe, even if less so than we might expect, given existing injustices and inequities. The pervasiveness of protest does not, however, signify that global political and economic dynamics are inconsequential. Several of the authors in this volume highlight ways in which global forces directly and indirectly shape the outbreak and outcome of protest movements. But the impact of such forces must be understood in the context of local structures, local social arrangements, and local cultural traditions. Similar colonial heritages and similar postcolonial subjugation to global economic and political powers cannot account for the diversity of the ways Latin Americans have opposed conditions they dislike, even when subject to the same set of external constraints.

The analytic lenses through which contributors to this book view protest and resistance movements are somewhat eclectic. The diversity reflects the methodological and theoretical biases of the authors and their disciplines, which include sociology, political science, anthropology, and history. Differences among them notwithstanding, the authors share a historical-structural perspective. They show ideology, values, traditions, and rituals to be of consequence and trace the importance of culture to group, organizational, and community dynamics and to other features of social structure. Yet they never presume that protest is mechanically determined by social structure. They show the patterning of defiance to be contingent on historical circumstances.

Social structure is of consequence because the unequal distribution of power, wealth, and prestige generates disparate interests among people differently situated in group hierarchies. Those who control the means of physical coercion and the means of producing wealth have power over those who do not. This power can involve control over ideas as well as material resources. When the poor and working classes rebel, it is not because they are intrinsically troublemakers. They rebel because they have limited alternative means to voice their views and press for change.

The case studies in this book show economic relationships, especially *changing* economic relationships, to be the principal cause of protest and pressure for change. The means of protest chosen, however, will be shown to hinge on contextual factors: on cross-class, institutional, and cultural ties; state structures; and real, or at least perceived, options to exit rather than rebel. The analyses also demonstrate that politics and religion, as well as concerns based on race, ethnicity, and gender, independently and in combination with economic forces, may be sources of disgruntlement that stir defiance.

The historical-structural approach that the authors employ differs from analyses that explain collective action at the level of the individual. Psychological explanations emphasize character traits and stressful states of mind that dispose individuals to rebellion. Persons with authoritarian personalities (Hoffer 1951, Lipset 1981) and persons who are alienated and anomic (Kornhauser 1959), who feel frustrated and deprived relative to others with whom they compare themselves (Davies 1962, Feierabend and Feierabend 1971, Gurr 1970), and who are attracted to new norms and values (Smelser 1963) have all been portrayed as defiant types. Such persons have typically been portrayed as nonrational or irrational in rebelling.

Rational-choice theorists (see, for example, Olson 1965; Popkin 1979), also explain defiance at the level of the individual. However, they argue that mobilization is a calculated response, based on individual assessments of the costs and benefits of noncompliance with the status quo. Olson posits that rational, self-interested individuals are disinclined to assume the risks of mobilization for "collective goods" because they can "ride free." He contends that collective defiance is likely only when actors receive selective rewards for their participation in anti–status quo movements and when nonparticipants are penalized for their lack of involvement.

Rational-choice theory cannot account for the ways group solidarities, moral commitment to the collectivity, and other nonrational values may mobilize people to act independently of individual self-interest. What is rational for the individual is not always consistent with the politically or culturally inspired choices of groups. Moreover, group involvements and cultural features pattern self-perceptions and how individuals defy conditions they dislike. Accordingly, even when defiance reflects individual self-interest, what individuals consider their self-interest can only be understood in the context of broader social and cultural forces.

Explanations on the individual level, in turn, often cannot account for the impact acts of defiance have, since the actual outcome of an act often differs from the envisioned outcome that motivated rebellion. That is, the patterned *range of ways* individuals and groups respond to conditions they consider unsatisfactory and the *range of outcomes* of defiant acts hinge not merely on psychological attributes, states of mind, and individual rational decision making. Cultural and structural forces influence individual and group perceptions, sentiments, and actions, sometimes in ways that are not necessarily obvious to the actors. Such cultural and structural forces influence the extent to which any given situation is believed to be intolerable, whether grievances are expressed overtly or by covert defiance, and whether the aggrieved seek individual or collective solutions to their plight.

The studies in this book point both to specific features of social structure that condition the ways subordinate groups address their plight and to elite responses. The authors show the patterning of defiance to be shaped by structural features independently of whatever rage and psychological attributes might have predisposed people to protest. The authors also trace the impact of defiance to elite responses and macro political and economic conditions, which cannot necessarily be deduced from the factors inducing individuals to defy the status quo. Rebels may usher in consequences they had not intended. The analyses accordingly show that features of social structure must theoretically and empirically be part of any full understanding of protest and resistance.

We are obviously not the first to posit a historical-structural perspective. Marx and his disciples have argued that antagonistic economic interests generate conflict and defiance. This chapter and the analyses that follow build on certain Marxist traditions: on Marxist analyses that highlight the importance of market as well as production relations, changing and not merely well-established economic relations, and injustices rooted in noneconomic as well as economic relations. People's lives are heavily influenced by their economic "location," but by other forces as well. Economic relations do not mechanistically determine whether, how, and when persons in subordinate positions rebel. Marx himself, it should be remembered, recognized that class politics vary with historical circumstances.

Non-Marxists have also argued a relationship between social structure and protest movements. There is a large body of literature in the United States that interprets social movements from a structural perspective. Much of it is not historically grounded, however, and some is too abstract to account for important nuances of movements. Neil Smelser (1963), for example, claims that determinants of collective defiance include structural conduciveness (the permissiveness of social arrangements to the generation of social movements), structural strain (the existence of ambiguities, deprivations, tensions, and conflicts in society), and the breakdown of social controls. But which features of social structure condition the array of responses to strains, and which pattern outcomes of defiance? His thesis does not adequately specify an answer to these questions.

While Smelser's thesis may have validity on an abstract level, the essays

in this volume illustrate why such abstract theorizing is not very enlightening: it leaves much unexplained. The strength of the essays lies
not only or primarily in their implicit or explicit theoretical grounding
but also in their subtle understanding of historical variability. Smelser's
thesis, by contrast, provides us with no framework for understanding,
for example, why the austerity programs described by John Walton in
his essay resulted in different types of protest movements and movements with different outcomes in different Latin American countries. It
also does not help explain why the Colombian peasant movement that
Zamosc analyzes began as a state-initiated reform movement, subsequently broke with the state and became radicalized, and then later became conservative and inconsequential. Nor can Smelser's approach account for the varied ways in which Bolivian tin miners have articulated
class-based grievances: their grievances have at different times been
channeled into rituals rooted in their peasant heritage, into revolutionary movements, and into support for reactionary politicians.

Resource-mobilization theory is perhaps the most well formulated
non-Marxist school of thought that explains social movements at the organizational, not individual, level (see Jenkins 1983 and McAdam, Mc-
Carthy, and Zald 1987 for excellent reviews of the resource-mobilization
"school"). Proponents of this perspective argue that grievances are endemic to social structure, and that grievances therefore cannot themselves account for the emergence of social movements. Like rational-
choice theorists, they see movement actions as rational responses to the
costs and rewards of different lines of action. However, they emphasize
that movements are contingent, above all, on resources, group organization, and opportunities for collective action. They have noted that economic, communication, and human resources (e.g., organizational and
legal skills and the unspecialized labor of supporters) can be of consequence, and that the degree of preexisting group organization affects
the mobilization potential of groups as well. Resource-mobilization theorists have posited that when groups share strong distinctive identities
and dense interpersonal networks, members are readily mobilizable:
both the identity and the networks provide a base for collective incentives. They have also argued that outside organizers or movement entrepreneurs can be critical for mobilizing movements, especially among deprived groups with minimal political and organizational experience.

Piven and Cloward (1979) also explain protest at the structural, not
individual, level. Yet they do not agree with the resource-mobilization
theorists who attribute social movement potential primarily to organizational features and organizational resources. They see organization, especially over time, as undermining possibilities for subordinate groups
to bring about change. They argue that poor people are most likely to
bring about change through disruption, and that disruption can be mo-

bilized without formal organization. In their view, organizations are vulnerable to internal oligarchy and to external cooptation, and organizations that develop within movements tend to blunt the main source of movement influence, militancy. In arguing that formal organization is necessarily incompatible with mobilization, they overstate their case. Piven and Cloward correctly note that there are conservatizing tendencies to most organizations, but organizations may also bring people together and instill values that stir defiance, intentionally or not.

Still other studies of social movements have noted that the origin and fate of defiance cannot be understood merely, or even mainly, either at the level of organization and group unruliness or at the level of the individual. Skocpol (1979) and Walton (1984), for example, highlight how state structures and macro economic influences shape rebellions. Such macro forces can pattern protest in ways that are not necessarily apparent to the people involved. We shall see below how such macro forces can influence the manner in which grievances are expressed and the success that defiance is likely to have.

While building on an already existent structural tradition, this book aims to specify, as no work has to date, the institutional and cultural features that pattern responses to grievances and influence outcomes of protest and resistance movements in Latin America. This chapter provides a framework for comprehending the varied forms defiance assumes, their varied origins, and their varied outcomes. In it I describe how and explain why economic relations and economic conditions are the principal cause of defiance, but also how conflicts rooted in political, gender, race, and ethnic relations may also be of consequence. The focus of the chapter then shifts to contextual factors shaping responses to grievances—namely, local institutional arrangements, class alliances, popular cultures of resistance, and state structures. Afterwards, structural features shaping outcomes of defiance are examined, including the impact of diverse, but structurally rooted, elite responses. The chapter ends with a brief summary of some of the distinctive features of Latin America's heritage that have patterned defiance in the region differently than in other parts of the world.

The remaining chapters illustrate propositions made in this introductory essay, and, indeed, provide some of the case material for some propositions I advance. Since the studies are few in number and not randomly selected, they do not in themselves provide evidence to prove an overarching theory of the causes and consequences of protest and resistance. The analyses are nonetheless interesting in their own right, and they contribute to our understanding of how the aggrieved try to alleviate their plight and how and why their success varies.

Precisely because the causes and consequences of defiance are complex (but patterned), this book has modest objectives. No theory can adequately account for, and predict, the full range of ways in which groups in civil society express anger and the effects defiance has. Yet improved comprehension of the factors shaping movements of defiance and de-tailed studies of specific protests can contribute to more enlightened "theories of the middle range," to borrow Merton's (1961) phrase.

Despite the level of detail in the essays, this book should also be of interest to those who are not specialists in the area. Aside from the historical significance of the movements that the authors describe, knowledge of Latin American experiences can contribute to a better understanding of the universal and the historically specific features of protest movements. Much of the U.S. literature on social movements tends to generalize from the U.S. experience to all social movements. Consequently, the studies in this volume can indirectly help us better understand the historically rooted and contextual features that shape movements in the industrial world, while directly enlightening us about movements in Latin America.

THE VARIED FORMS OF PROTEST

Large-scale rebellions, let alone revolutions, are rare, and when they occur they are often either crushed or give rise to states that subordinate the interests of the rebels to those of dominant and ruling groups. Expressions of defiance that fall short of revolution in intent and effect are much more frequent. The range of ways in which people express defiance is delimited by social structure just as socially more accepted behavior is so delimited.

James Scott (1986) correctly and insightfully argues that peasants frequently engage in everyday forms of resistance—such as foot-dragging, passive noncompliance, deceit, pilfering, slander, sabotage, and arson—that stop short of outright collective defiance. There is reason to believe that other economically subordinate groups may resist conditions imposed by dominant groups in roughly similar ways, depending on circumstances. For people in structurally disadvantaged positions such "everyday forms of resistance" may accomplish more, in both the short and long run, than publicly organized protests; this is especially likely when the risks of repression are great. Their defiance may require little or no coordination, and it may not *directly* challenge elite domination and norms. While such quiet forms of defiance rarely result in major change, they can, on occasion, undermine government legitimacy and productivity to the point where political and economic elites feel the need to institute significant reforms.

In addition to such "everyday forms of resistance," there exist more direct and explicit ways in which the aggrieved have historically protested conditions they dislike and tried to bring about change: strikes, land seizures, demonstrations, riots, rebellions, and protests. In these instances the amount of coordination is generally greater.

These varied expressions of defiance have at least one important feature in common. They involve efforts of the politically and economically weak to resist conditions they consider unjust through noninstitutionalized channels.

Even when subordinate groups collectively and publicly defy conditions they dislike, they typically do not resort to violence, especially initially. If violence ensues, it usually is initiated by more powerful groups to coerce the weak back into docility. In Latin America, for example, the military and police have been responsible for many more injuries and deaths than have guerrilla bands.

The case studies in this book focus primarily on coordinated and overt nonviolent forms of defiance. However, most of the groups under investigation combine overt with more subtle forms of resistance and defiance, and a few have combined violent with nonviolent protest. In her discussion of the Peruvian Sendero Luminoso guerrilla movement, for example, Cynthia McClintock highlights how peasants who were not sufficiently committed to the movement to join quietly collaborated with the rebels in ways that contributed to an erosion of government legitimacy. Peasants in the area where Sendero initially operated tacitly lent support to the guerrillas by refusing to help officials hunt down cadres and by providing militants with food, shelter, and information; they also sabotaged elections, not by attacking the political system publicly, or, in Gramsci's (1971) terminology, frontally, but by quietly and individually invalidating their ballots in large numbers. Once it had gained a footing in the highland region of Ayacucho, Sendero was able to spread its base to other regions of the country as well.

The relationship between overt confrontational and more subtle forms of defiance is also addressed in several of the other essays. June Nash shows how Bolivian miners, through their regular participation in centuries-old rituals rooted in their agricultural past, have reinforced a spirit of rebellion that has given impetus to strikes, protests, and even a revolution when conditions have been "ripe." The rituals are deep-rooted and provide the bedrock upon which explicitly political protests have built. The rituals and overtly political acts build on shared grievances. In their article on religion and protest Daniel Levine and Scott Mainwaring, in turn, discuss how participation in nominally nonpolitical church-sponsored "base communities" may (or may not) lay the bases for political protest movements.

While the same groups and individuals may engage in overt and more subtle forms of resistance, the repertoire of collective action on which groups draw tends to be limited and heavily influenced by social structural features and historic traditions. It is no accident that some people rebel by refusing to work or refusing to work at full capacity, while others loot, and still others demonstrate in the streets or turn to electoral sabotage. Factory workers strike because they can thereby defy rules of the workplace and restrict their bosses' profits. Workers in the informal sector, by contrast, seize land sites to erect dwellings and protest against increases in their cost of living. However unhappy they may be with their work and earnings, their work setting is not conducive to collective defiance: they are employed in small businesses with no job security or are self-employed.

Different groups not only draw on different forms of defiance. Over time, societal repertoires have also changed. Charles Tilly (1978) and his associates (Tilly and Tilly 1981; Shorter and Tilly 1974; and Tilly, Tilly, and Tilly 1975) argue, for example, that in Western Europe the repertoire shifted from food riots, resistance to conscription, rebellion against tax collectors, and organized invasions of fields and forests to demonstrations, protest meetings, strikes, and electoral rallies between the eighteenth and nineteenth centuries. In the twentieth century, lengthy proactive activities by large-scale special-purpose associations have become more common. Tilly and his colleagues trace the changes to increased economic concentration and proletarianization on the one hand and the growing power of the nation state and the institutionalization of liberal democracy on the other. As the loci of power in society shifted, ordinary people's interests, opportunities, and capacities to act together altered.

Yet historical traditions, as well as institutional arrangements, influence how people respond to conditions they dislike. People learn repertoires of defiance partly in reaction to dominant group responses. The Latin American repertoire has been shaped—as we shall see later—by dependence on foreign trade, technology, and capital, a bureaucratic centralist tradition, and a distinctive, Catholic-inspired worldview.

Latin America is more of a "living museum" than Europe. New forms of defiance have appeared on the scene there, while old forms have persisted. Centuries-old types of protest, such as food riots and rural land seizures, appear alongside strikes, demonstrations, and protest meetings. The broader Latin American repertoire is no doubt rooted in the more partial nature of the region's industrial transformation, the restricted economic opportunities associated with "dependent development," and the more limited power of the nation-state over ordinary people's lives. Economically, Latin American industrialization has produced a proletariat. However, factory workers account for only a minority of the labor force in most countries in the region. The majority of laborers continue to work in agriculture or are self-employed or employees in small-scale paternalistic enterprises.

Latin America's broader repertoire is also rooted in its distinctive political history. Twentieth-century Latin American history has been punctuated by shifts between authoritarian and democratic rule. By contrast, with some exceptions, Western Europe experienced progressive democratization. As Latin American regime conditions have oscillated, so too has the nature of political strife; for this reason, the basis of political conflict has not evolved from one form to another, as historically in Europe.

Despite some shared political and economic experiences, Latin American countries have not had entirely parallel histories. National variations in levels of industrialization, the timing and extent of unionization, economic wealth, and political repression, for example, make for some patterned differences in contemporary expressions of defiance among Latin American countries. The different modes of "popular" defiance against unpopular austerity measures described by Walton—riots in Jamaica, street demonstrations in Chile, and strikes in Andean nations— are at least partially rooted in different traditions of protest that have evolved over the years in countries with distinctive political and economic histories. Nonviolent demonstrations are a typical Chilean form of protest. As Garretón notes, Chileans turn to demonstrations not only to defy austerity measures that have caused their living standards to plunge but also to defy political injustices of the repressive Pinochet government. Yet aggrieved groups have turned to the streets to press for change under democratically elected governments as well as under military rule. The "popular" classes have most typically done so. However, when the socialist government of Salvador Allende favored the lower and working classes, the middle classes mobilized through extra-institutional channels as well: housewives with their pots and pans, truckdrivers with their vehicles (which they used to block traffic and the delivery of goods). Indeed, pots and pans have since been added to the symbolic repertoire of protest in Chile. Opponents of Pinochet's military government bang them at designated times.

Within Latin America the Bolivian repertoire also stands out. When dissatisfied with policies, peasants and city-dwellers there, more than elsewhere in the region, block roads. In a country with a poorly developed road system, this disruptive tactic can be quite effective.

Defiance, whether overt or covert, presumes intent. Defiance must therefore be analytically distinguished from noncompliance grounded in ignorance or confusion about expected and appropriate behavior. Nonetheless, both intentional and unintentional noncompliance may generate the same social consequences, including an erosion of elite legitimacy.

The intent of defiance may be defensive, restorative, or offensive; in Tilly's terms, it may be *reactive* or *proactive*, designed to deny claims made by superordinate groups or to press new claims. While defiance is deliberate, it may usher in changes the actors never intended. The failure to account analytically for the ways in which the outcomes of defiance may differ from intent is a serious shortcoming of much of the existing literature on protest and social movements. In the Mexican revolution, for example, Zapatistas protested against the agents of agrarian capitalism who violated their ancestral property claims. Their movement was anticapitalist and restorative in spirit. Yet their quiescence once their poor-quality parcels of land were returned facilitated capitalist development in the rest of the country. Similarly, Nash shows in chapter 5 how Bolivian miners have supported revolutionary movements and populist military coups d'état only to usher into office governments that turned on them. While people of all classes tend to have a limited understanding of the forces of history, the subordinate position of the politically and economically weak limits their ability both to understand the full ramifications of their actions and to counter the power of superordinate groups, including groups they had not envisioned would be of consequence.[1] Subordinate groups tend to direct their defiance against local targets, but national and even international structures and circumstances can influence what their acts accomplish. I shall examine factors shaping the outcomes of defiance after discussing how social bases and contextual factors shape the patterning of protest.

THE SOCIAL BASES OF DEFIANCE

Domination and subordination are common features of institutional life, and they give rise to certain contradictory interests. Top positions incline the occupants toward preserving the status quo, while bottom positions incline their occupants toward change to improve their lots. Structurally rooted inequities and injustices may be tolerated by subordinates, but obviously not always. Given the importance of working for a livelihood and employer extraction of surplus from laborers, there are structural reasons why conflict has frequently focused on wage and work conditions. This is true even in socialist enterprises in socialist societies. However, the nature of the conflicting interests of people differently situated in institutional hierarchies and the responses of persons in subordinate positions to such conflicting interests are shaped by organizational settings and by the broader society in which the organizations are embedded. Below I discuss how production and market, but also gender, political, racial, ethnic, and religious relationships, may be sources of contention and foci of defiance.

1. As Mills (1959:185) notes: "Some men have the power to act with much structural relevance and are quite aware of the consequences of their actions; others have such power but are not aware of its effective scope; and there are many who cannot transcend their everyday milieu by their awareness of structure or effect structural change by any means of action available to them."

Conflicts Rooted in Relations of Production

People experience deprivation within concrete settings. Laborers' anger typically is directed at their bosses, who they believe to be oppressing them, not at broad invisible forces like capitalism or distant agents of capitalism, like banks, which may ultimately be responsible for their plight.

Marx gave us reason to believe that industrial workers would be more defiant than peasants, not because their work conditions are worse, but because large numbers of them experience their misery collectively. Since Latin American governments in the post–World War II era have promoted industry, initially for domestic consumption and more recently for export, Marx's logic would lead us to expect that societal strife should have intensified as the productive bases of the countries shifted.

There was added reason to believe that industrialization in Latin America would stir unrest: factory workers in the region earn little compared to their equivalents in the highly industrial countries. Yet the response of Latin American factory workers to their work situations must be understood in the context of their respective countries. They are a relatively privileged group. They rank among the minority who earn at least the official minimum wage and who qualify for unemployment, health, and social security benefits. Industrial workers have succeeded in winning such concessions in part because they are comparatively few in number, but also because their work has been considered central to their countries' economic advancement and because industrialists initially sought labor support in their struggle against entrenched oligarchies for control of the state. Under the circumstances, governments and private employers granted concessions to the proletariat, though often only in response to real or threatened strike activity.

Although wildcat strikes sometimes occur, unions organize most strikes. We see here how defiance and organization can be closely linked. However, the impact of unionization on strike activity will be shown subsequently to be contingent on state/union relations, and not on organization per se.

While strike activity reflects underlying conflicting interests between labor and capital, its absence does not necessarily imply worker satisfaction. Discontent is least likely to be expressed in overt, coordinated work stoppages under nondemocratic regimes where strike activity is outlawed and so likely to be repressed that the costs are often perceived to outweigh possible gains. This cost/benefit interpretation of strike activity is consistent with rational-choice theory. Where strikes are outlawed, workers who strike may even run the risk of being fired. Yet rational-choice theory does not sensitize us to the variety of ways in which workers might, under the circumstances, undermine elite interests without directly confronting the powers that be: for example, through foot-dragging, absenteeism, and pilferage. Such quiet defiance will minimally undermine employers' ability to generate surplus, and will possibly also bring some material gains to workers as well. The varied expressions of defiance cannot be explained at the level of the individual, on which rational-choice theory is premised.

The nature of workers' grievances can be expected to differ some-what in socialist and capitalist enterprises, with different inequities in the distribution of power, wealth, and prestige in the two types of organiza-tional hierarchies and different expectations about justice and enterprise objectives in the two types of societies. Cuba, for example, claims to be a "proletarian state," and most units of production in the country are state-owned. Yet the state's public identification with workers has not eliminated tensions between workers and managers. Instead, the revolu-tion has changed the nature of workers' grievances and how grievances are articulated. Since Cuban workers are not free to strike and since unions are politically controlled, workers have turned to quieter and more covert forms of defying work conditions they dislike. They have, on occasion, quite effectively expressed resentment with their hands and feet in poor on-the-job performance and high absenteeism. Their low level of compliance, for example, compelled the revolutionary leadership to modify policies implemented in the late 1960s. At the time, workers had been asked to work long hours, and, in the case of the sugar harvest, without additional pay. Meanwhile, material living standards plunged as the government stressed exports and investments in basic industries. Al-though asked to work for "moral" reasons, out of a commitment to com-munism, workers resented the demands on their time and the deteriora-tion in their living standards. They expressed their resentment through poor work performance in the absence of institutional channels to voice their discontent. Productivity plunged, and the economic crisis received much international publicity. Pressed to alter its accumulation strategy, the government not only reintroduced material incentives and expanded the supply of consumer goods but also granted labor greater partici-patory rights in enterprise, union, and government decision making. Ideally, of course, labor should be free to organize. Yet in the Latin American countries where it enjoys organizational and strike rights, la-bor has rarely had as great an impact on state policy and won such eco-nomic and political concessions as the seemingly uncoordinated acts and publicly unarticulated complaints of Cuban workers in the late 1960s.

Employers (in Cuba, the state) are probably most responsive to pres-sures "from below" when labor resistance, however expressed, results in a sudden decrease in productivity, when alternative sources of labor are unavailable (because of labor regulations, skill requirements, or full em-ployment), and when repression to enforce conformity is too politically or economically costly. By contrast, when pilfering, foot-dragging, and other forms of quiet resistance persist at long-established levels, employers probably either tolerate the costs to their profit maximization or try to modify work conditions in small ways to induce greater output.

Not merely conditions of industrial employment but the loss of such employment may provoke protest. Garretón notes, for example, that as many Chilean workers have lost their jobs under the right-wing government of Pinochet, the base of mobilizations shifted from the "classes" to the "masses": that is, from the more organized, formal sector of society to the more economically marginal sectors. They mobilize, though, through neighborhood, not work-based, groups. In contrast, unionized Chilean workers have been relatively quiescent, despite their history of militancy. They fear losing their jobs if they protest. Also, the military has been better able to regulate the activity of union organizations than that of the large, amorphous nonunionized population.

Yet in Latin America labor defiance has by no means been confined to urban settings. Marx argued that the relations of production made peasants a conservative political force, but recent studies of revolution have shown that peasants should not be politically dismissed.[2] Peasants, Marx noted (1959: 338), do similar but uncoordinated work: in contrast to factory workers who work side by side in related activities, peasants, he asserted, were a "simple addition of homologous magnitudes, much as potatoes in a sack form a sack of potatoes." They often also own "the means of production," de facto if not de jure. Such structural constraints notwithstanding, in Latin America peasants have played a critical role in the Mexican, Bolivian, and Cuban revolutions. However, the role of the peasantry should not be exaggerated. While agrarian rebellions in regions of each country helped bring down the anciens régimes, peasants' "social location" restricted what they attempted to accomplish through defiance and what they actually accomplished. In no country did peasants bring down the state on their own. Moreover, they helped "make" the revolutions more by seizing lands, disrupting production, and creating disorder than by participating in movements inspired by revolutionary ideology.

But even when peasants are outwardly passive, deferential, and quiescent, they can, as noted earlier, defy conditions they dislike by withholding production or by keeping crucial information from their superiors. Such subtle forms of defiance of exploitation and abuse are undoubtedly more common than outright rebellion. Peasants generally only take on the risks of direct confrontation when injustice is perceived to be intolerable, when the demands made of them increase suddenly (rather than incrementally), and when local and national institutional and cultural conditions (discussed below) incline them to seek redress collectively.

Peasant grievances, however expressed, vary with property and labor

2. Although their arguments differ see, for example, Moore 1966; Wolf 1969; Scott 1976; Migdal 1974; Paige 1975; Skocpol 1979; and Popkin 1979.

relations. For this reason, the concerns of tenant farmers, sharecroppers, smallholders, and wage laborers differ. Rural wage laborers are preoccupied with wage and work conditions, propertied peasants with the prices of the products they market and the goods and services they consume, and tenant farmers and sharecroppers with the demands on their labor (or the product of their labor).

The impact of tenancy arrangements on peasant rebellion is a subject of great debate. Wolf (1969) argues that the global economy devastates the moral economy of the peasantry and radicalizes the "middle peasant" in particular. Paige (1975), by contrast, argues that sharecroppers and migratory estate laborers are the principal base of revolutionary movements, owing to specific conditions rooted in their relationship to noncultivators. According to him, agrarian rebellions will range from reformist protests over commodity prices and working conditions to nationalist and socialist revolutionary movements, depending upon particular combinations in the organization of land, capital, and wages. When cultivators depend on wages and noncultivators on land for income, conflict is most likely to produce revolutionary movements. Both Wolf and Paige base their studies on twentieth-century peasant experiences around the world.

Contemporary Latin American history suggests that peasant grievances vary with forms of land tenure, but that economic dislocations, and not land-tenure patterns in themselves, fuel agrarian rebellion. Wickham-Crowley shows in chapter 4, for example, that guerrilla movements (begun typically by educated university students) have won greatest peasant backing in regions populated heavily by sharecroppers, squatters, and migratory laborers. Yet he finds that dislocations that erode peasants' sense of security, and not merely rural class relations, contribute to agrarian radicalization. Peasants embroiled in change are more likely to support revolutionary movements than either peasants who remain secure in possession of land or rural wage workers where agrarian capitalism has been in place for some time. Similarly, in chapter 2 McClintock suggests that the Sendero Luminoso guerrilla movement secured a peasant base among smallholders in the Ayacucho region of Peru in the late 1970s and early 1980s because of a subsistence crisis there;[3] her findings imply that the dislocations and insecurities that incline agriculturalists to support a guerrilla movement may involve no actual or threatened change in land tenancy arrangements. Peasant claims to land were not challenged, but the meaning of land to peasants' livelihood changed. Yet McClintock's study also shows that peasant perceptions, and not merely their objective economic conditions, influence their stance toward guerrilla movements. Sendero's support in Ayacucho

3. On subsistence crises as a source of peasant rebellion, see Scott 1976.

waned when Alan García, a charismatic left-leaning national leader, began to promise change.

Rural responses to economic conditions may be further complicated by the diversity of economic relations in which agriculturalists engage. Although various land-tenancy and labor relations can be analytically distinguished, concretely agriculturalists may engage in multiple work relationships. Peasants with communal or individual land rights may work part-time or seasonally as wage laborers, for instance, within or outside the farm sector. Those involved in two or more job situations may be expected to respond differently to conditions they dislike than those involved in only one. Smallholders who do supplementary low-paying wage work, for example, may tolerate the exploitation more than landless laborers. The very participation of agriculturalists in multiple economic relations should be viewed as a mode of adaptation to unsatisfactory economic conditions and a structured response that itself must be explained. The impact of work diversification, and the conditions under which it is likely to occur, will be discussed in greater detail below.

Market-based Tensions

Studies of worker and, to a lesser extent, peasant protest have tended to focus on conflicts rooted in production relations. Yet market relations can be an independent source of tension.

Both rural and urban populations experience the market as consumers and producers of goods and services. However, groups differ in their ability to structure market relations in their favor owing to their different economic and political clout. Market-based grievances are also structurally rooted, but in the society at large, not conditions at work.

The rural work force experiences the market through interactions with government agents and businessmen, including persons who commercialize and tax their production and control their access to financing.[4] Just as factory workers typically perceive their bosses, and not capitalism in the abstract, to be the source of their problems, here too government and private agents are the target of anger, not the invisible market or distant high-level bureaucrats who make, but do not implement, state policies affecting local market operations. Increased costs imposed by such agents—for example, property and market taxes and transportation rates—particularly enrage rural small landholders who "own the means of production," for they incur the increased expenses directly. Because such petits bourgeois, unlike the bourgeoisie, have weak market and political power, they often cannot pass newly imposed costs on to

---

4. Market relationships can here be seen to be shaped by politics and administration. Market dynamics are not a force sui generis.

consumers of their labor through higher prices. Generally, competition limits the amount they can charge, or the government restricts the prices they can get for their goods. Since World War II many governments in the region have regulated the prices of basic foods, even in the market economies, to keep down the cost of living for the politically more influential urban population.

Market-rooted tensions are destined to become ever more important in Latin America, as both producer and consumer relations are increasingly commodified and as independent market-oriented employment expands. Simultaneously with the progress of agrarian and industrial capitalism, self-employment has increased in both the cities and the countryside throughout much of the region. Proletarianization is not the only, and often not the primary, consequence of the "deepening" of capitalism. And, as just noted, owners of the "means of production" experience the impact of market forces directly. In rural regions, land concentration and capital-intensive agriculture, combined with population growth, have created a landless labor force. Some of the landless are employed as wage workers on agricultural estates, but most are not. To minimize the size of the landless population somewhat in regions ill-suited to large-scale capital-intensive production, governments have institutionalized smallholding land rights. Governments promulgated land reforms initially only in response to revolutionary pressure "from below." However, in the aftermath of the Cuban revolution, they have done so also to avert radical movements, partly under pressure from the United States.

Yet Latin America's "incomplete" proletarianization is not merely a by-product of state policy. It also reflects peasants' resistance to loss of control over their labor. Peasants often opt to engage in labor-intensive small-scale commerce and petty commodity production rather than work for a wage. While they thereby avoid direct subjugation to capitalist exploitation within their immediate work setting, they remain extremely vulnerable to unfavorable and fluctuating market forces owing to their weak market power.

Market tensions may be rooted in global as well as domestic processes. Paige's study of agrarian protest, the most systematic quantitative and theoretically grounded study to date, focuses specifically, for example, on conflict in the export sector. Yet he does not analyze *how* global market dynamics shape agrarian movements independently of their effect on domestic class relations. Wickham-Crowley builds on Paige's argument in showing that peasant support for guerrilla movements in the 1960s was concentrated in places where a decline in world commodity prices reduced peasant earning power; however, the same was not true in the 1970s and early 1980s. The implications of Wickham-Crowley's findings are that adverse global market conditions may attract peasants to guerrilla movements, but that they do not always do so. Peasant responses are contingent on contextual factors, to be discussed below.

Much of the literature on revolutions presumes that state-class transformations resolve rural conflicts, especially when peasants gain legal rights to much-desired private plots. Yet land ownership may generate new tensions after revolution owing both to government policies and market dynamics that peasant beneficiaries of land reforms come to experience directly. Depending on how the market is experienced and on government tax, credit, and pricing policies, postrevolutionary peasant concerns will vary. Not all peasants who gained land rights as a result of the 1952 revolution in Bolivia, for example, have remained quiescent. They have since protested when angered about a variety of circumstances. Land-reform beneficiaries have set up roadblocks to deprive city-dwellers of farm products, to pressure haulers and truckers to rescind transport price increases, and to press the government to retract price hikes on basic foods that they must purchase. Bolivian smallholders have also defied government regulations and engaged in lucrative contraband and illegal coca production (for cocaine) when there were considerable profits to be made thereby; they are even known to have captured and mutilated officials who obstructed their activity. Their deliberate evasion of the law reflects an effort to maximize their own economic advantage, as the rational peasant thesis would lead us to expect (see Popkin 1979); they are not, by nature, predisposed toward criminality and disorder. Yet their manner of defiance is culturally patterned in part. Roadblocks, as previously noted, form part of the distinctive Bolivian repertoire of protest.

Even under socialism, market dynamics can be a source of conflict. When private economic activity is proscribed, the very presence of market activity represents a form of quiet defiance of the law; in this context, conflict is not rooted in market relations, but market activity expresses protest against the state or, more accurately, against specific state policies. In Cuba, market involvements have varied with official economic options. Small farmers who have been angry about the low prices the state procurement agency pays, for example, have kept their output down or diverted production to the more lucrative black market. It became apparent that their low productivity was deliberate, and not the result of laziness and incompetence, when the government improved their (legitimate) market opportunities. Private farmers' output rose immediately in the early 1980s when the state procurement agency raised the prices it paid producers for their crops and when the government allowed growers to sell privately whatever they produced above their obligation to the state.

Throughout Latin America, market dynamics have been a source of tension in the cities as well. Since urban wage and salaried jobs have not expanded commensurately with the rate of growth of the urban labor force, ever more city-dwellers, as well as propertied peasants, seek to eke out a living through petty entrepreneurial ventures. Like smallholders in the countryside, they have little market power and so cannot structure market relations in their favor. The urban self-employed rarely defy conditions rooted in their work situation directly. Instead, their protests focus on the economic impact of their weak earning power on their purchasing power. They have sought, in particular, to reduce the costs of goods and services that they consume.

As in the countryside, in the city some protests must be understood in the context of global, and not merely domestic, market dynamics. For example, chapter 10 highlights how debt-ridden Latin American governments have implemented austerity programs that eliminate food and transport subsidies, freeze wages (despite inflation), and dismantle state-owned enterprises. They have done so largely under pressure from foreign creditors (above all, the IMF), although often with the support of at least certain segments of the local bourgeoisie. International creditors, with their own fiscal interests in mind, have made their loans conditional on reforms whose political consequences Latin American governments have had to bear. The austerity measures have prompted street demonstrations, riots, strikes, looting, political rallies, attacks on government buildings, and street violence, especially in the cities. Yet the defiance has not been mechanistically determined by world economic forces and institutions. Walton argues in chapter 10 that the varied forms of defiance have not been purely spontaneous but involved some degree of organization, and that austerity protests have their own moral economy, much as eighteenth-century English food riots did (Thompson 1971). Protesters make it clear that austerity is not socially workable or just. Typically, the protests have been ignited by sudden government-initiated price increases that cut deeply into the capacity of the urban poor to address their subsistence needs. The salaried middle class, who have had to cope not only with a rise in their cost of living but also with unemployment caused by cutbacks in public-sector activity, have also not always quietly accepted their sudden loss of status and means of livelihood.[5]

Such market-based protests may, indeed, prove to be more problematic to governments in the 1980s than grievances rooted in the relations of production. The latter can more easily be contained and countered

5. Middle-class protests sparked by loss of state-sector jobs are, of course, expressions of defiance against market intrusions in the world of work, not consumption. The IMF has pressured debt-ridden countries to dismantle state enterprises and to reduce public service employment. Many of the jobs had been created for political reasons: to employ labor that would otherwise have been unemployed, or not employed at a level considered commensurate with education and skill. The jobs thereby tied middle-class people to the state. They reflected a state effort to *counter* market tendencies that limited the demand for labor.

through paternalistic or bureaucratic manipulation of labor-management relations. Moreover, market forces that are global in scale cannot be readily controlled by local elites, who are—in the international arena—relatively weak.

Socialist governments may actually be more vulnerable to urban consumer defiance than governments in capitalist countries. Although socialist governments may be subject to less direct pressure from international financiers to reduce food subsidies, they have their own fiscal needs. Socialist countries turned to Western financing in the mid 1970s when interest rates were low and demand for their exports was quite high. The loans became an important source of capital financing, particularly since they allowed the governments to purchase Western goods and services. Yet when interest rates rose and export prices fell in the latter 1970s, governments in the socialist as well as the market economies incurred large Western debts. To address their fiscal needs, they too have been pressed to reduce state-provided subsidies. Because they administer the prices of many more goods and services than do nonsocialist governments, price changes affect many more consumers concomitantly. As noted above, sudden changes that hit many people at once often stir collective defiance. In Poland, for example, prices became the key to public order in the early 1980s. In Cuba, the government avoided the problem for nearly two decades; it kept the prices of rationed goods at levels set in the early 1960s. When the government finally sought to reduce the fiscal burden of the food subsidy, it pursued a less directly explosive strategy than the Polish regime. Rather than merely raise official prices of consumer goods, the Castro leadership allowed more and more goods to be sold off of rationing. By privatizing and deregulating distributive allocations, the Cuban government avoided becoming a target of consumer revolts, in contrast to the Polish government; but it did so at the cost of "socialist distributive principles." The market opening led to severe distortions in the remaining state sector and to such heavy profiteering, at consumers' expense, that the government closed the private markets in the mid 1980s. The state-regulated market distributive system resolved certain problems while generating others.

Market dynamics have also created problems for the Sandinista government in Nicaragua. However, there the government—to date— has been faced more with defiance of commercial regulations than with consumer protests over official prices. Government efforts to enforce "socialist distributive principles" have been undermined by middlemen who seek to profit from illegal trade. Scarcities have given rise to profitable illegal marketing, with adverse consequences for production promoted by the state in the legal economy. Licensed merchants defy price controls, and many Nicaraguans have quit their jobs in the productive sector or frequently absent themselves to engage in more lucrative unlicensed commerce. Rather than mobilize for higher wages, which is difficult to do because unions are government-controlled, dissatisfied workers turn to illicit, not easily controlled, commercial activity. As a consequence, the loci of conflict have shifted from "relations of production" to the realm of distribution, and from tension between labor and capital to tension between a new petite bourgeoisie (or part-time petite bourgeoisie) and the state.

Urbanization in the capitalist countries of the Third World has provoked tumult over the issue of housing as well. This has been especially true in Latin America, where an urban bias has contributed to massive migration to the cities. The high cost of professionally built housing that is commercially available has induced many of the low-income urban-dwellers to seize land illegally en masse in outlying urban areas and build their own dwellings on the plots they occupy. The termination of rent freezes has also stirred protests in older inner-city areas; this occurred, for example, in São Paulo in 1987. Most land "invasions" are organized—often with the tacit support of political parties or government officials. While the organizers of the invasions generally move on after the land occupation, the squatters typically continue to mobilize subsequently for collective services, including water, electricity, roads, markets, and legal rights to land.

Residents of the mushrooming urban squatter settlements were typically portrayed in the 1960s and 1970s as politically quiescent because they generally supported incumbent governments and rarely parties of the left (except where, as in Allende's Chile, the left held political office and organized land invasions). But radical politics is not the only or the most frequent expression of defiance. Squatters' electoral support for mainstream parties should not obscure the fact that their illegal land seizures are an expression of consumer defiance: a form of protest against the high cost and low supply of shelter in the formal housing market. Aspiring home owners have staked out property claims in defiance of the market, which prices shelter beyond their pocketbooks.

Democratic and nondemocratic governments in the capitalist countries in the region have put up some resistance to the land invasions. They have bulldozed and burned squatters' huts, and arrested and violently attacked squatters who have refused to leave. However, they have also tolerated many of the land seizures, especially when they have occurred on publicly owned property. The governments have allowed such invasions for economic and political reasons. Economically, cheap shelter has helped keep down the wage employers need to pay employees to subsist in the city. It has thereby aided industrialization, which Latin American governments have encouraged since World War II.[6] Politi-

6. Cheap shelter should therefore be viewed as a subsidy to capital as well as to labor.

cally, a permissive stance has won politicians allies among the urban poor; also, in the process of legitimizing squatters' land claims, officials succeeded in regulating (and minimizing) the issues around which the poor subsequently mobilized (Eckstein 1977).

While mobilizations for a narrow range of goods and services were the norm in the 1960s and early 1970s, the recessions of the mid 1970s and early 1980s and the repressive policies of certain of the governments then in power generated some new types of urban movements. In a few countries—for example, in Nicaragua, El Salvador, Chile, and Peru—large numbers of the urban poor began to support parties of the left and the distributional policies those parties stood for; however, even in countries where they did not, the urban poor began to mobilize around new issues, and their manner of defiance at times changed. Protests against the cost and quality of goods and services increased, such as when austerity programs were implemented. Yet neighborhood associations also began to break with entrenched governments and press for what they considered rights, not favors. In the north of Mexico and in the periphery of Mexico City, neighborhood groups deliberately rejected state help in order to resist state cooptation; they preferred instead to steal materials and illegally obtain water, electricity, and other urban services (Castells 1983). Some low-income neighborhood groups—for example, in Chile, Mexico, and Brazil—even began to press for a popular economy, in opposition to the officially sponsored one (Portes and Johns 1986): they mobilized for collective purchase, preparation, and consumption of food, collective housing improvements, and collective child care. Whether such autonomous and collectivistic movements will become more widespread, and whether they will be able to accomplish much within existing class and political systems, remains to be seen.

Racial and Ethnic Conflict

Although injustices rooted in class and market relations are the main sources of contemporary conflict in Latin America, on occasion ethnicity and race have been independent bases of mobilization for change. While most racial and ethnic protest movements are grounded in economic grievances, they should be considered analytically distinct when they involve only racially or ethnically defined segments of socioeconomic classes and when they focus on ethnic and racial, not merely or necessarily class-related, issues.

In Latin America, race and ethnicity tend to be defined in social and cultural, not biological terms. Consequently, many have presumed that the importance of race and ethnicity would wane as Indians and blacks learned Spanish and Portuguese, dressed in Western-style clothes, moved to the cities, and took jobs in the modern sector. Yet even when such cultural assimilation and social integration have occurred, Latin Americans have mobilized along ethnic and racial lines and pressed for ethnic and racial rights. This has occurred largely when people with distinctive cultural identities and physical features have also been socially segregated (de facto, not, in Latin America, de jure), when they experienced deprivations as a group, and when established social controls have broken down. However, it is changes in the absolute or relative standing of racial and ethnic groups and competition among different racial and ethnic groups for scarce privileged positions that stir such movements, not deprivation per se.[7] In the impoverished Bolivian highlands, for example, peasants who fought violently at the turn of the century for class interests—namely, for the restoration of communal lands that had been taken from them—pressed for Aymaran rights (including through their own political parties) in the 1980s. The ethnic-based movement gained momentum because of several concomitant factors (including the types of contextual factors that will be shown below to pattern defiance): peasants in the region experienced a deterioration in their economic situation, and migration became a less viable option owing to a severe national economic recession; a democratic opening, under the government of Siles Zuaso, allowed for group mobilizations throughout civil society; members of the urban intelligentsia supported the movement; and a charismatic leader who had been crippled in earlier struggles with a military government appealed to the ethnic heritage of peasants in the region. In Guatemala, racially rooted tension has also become more manifest in recent decades. There, tension between Indians and Ladinos has unified previously divided and separate Indian groups; the tension increased as market-oriented production undermined preexisting rural relationships. In Brazil, in turn, blacks mobilized against racial, cultural, and social domination in the 1970s, despite (and partly because of) the society's claims to being a racial democracy; their mobilizations increased at the same time that opposition to the military government gained momentum.

Relatively little is known about these and other racial and ethnic movements, partly because they are less consequential in Latin America than in some other regions of the world, but also because the dominant ideology in Latin America obscures the issue. Since race is claimed to be a social and cultural, not biological, phenomenon, deprivations are presumed to be an individual, not group, problem; people purportedly can "pass" if they adopt the culture and partake in the institutional life of the nation-state. This ideology has influenced much social-science thinking on the matter: in particular, analyses premised on the modernization paradigm, which dominated the literature in the United States through

---

7. Wagley (1969), for example, discusses how race becomes an issue in Brazilian communities only when there is competition for upper-class status.

the mid 1970s. Marxist analyses do not suffer from the same individual reductionism, but Marxist emphasis on class solidarities and class conflict provides no analytical basis for understanding how, when, and why racial identities may become meaningful in their own right. This is unquestionably a topic on which more theory and empirical work needs to be done.

Gender-based Resistance

Women's interests are defined by a combination of their individual and family class standing in the economy, and by their position within the family as determined by the household division of labor. As is well known, women occupy a subordinate position within the family, and generally, if they work, within the economy as well. They suffer not merely because they hold subordinate statuses in both settings, but also because men use their dominant positions to their own advantage (Bourque and Warren 1981). Men generally control access to crucial resources and cultural justifications of why that should be so.

Women's isolation within the home and their economic marginality have allegedly contributed to quiescence on their part. Yet women often defy male domination without directly confronting men. Their weak position within the family and the economy limits the ways in which they can defy conditions not to their liking, but they can undermine male authority somewhat through gossip, slander, and the informal power that they wield within the domain of the household (Lamphere 1974).

In Latin America, women's economic marginalization has had certain positive economic and political effects on households, if not on women's standing within the family. This has been especially true in illegal squatter settlements. Many women in these settlements remain in their neighborhoods during the day while their men work elsewhere, both because they are responsible for the children and the hearth and because they are limited in their job options. They are therefore in a position to defend family claims to land. They can help fend off police, tax assessors, and other state agents. In Mexico City, for example, women in the city's largest shantytown have protected their community against land developers attempting to evict families and against police who attempted to arrest participants in a local organization that used militant tactics, including physical violence, to defend local interests (Vélez-Ibañez 1983: 119–22). In São Paulo, in turn, women in charge of household consumption were the main force behind the Cost of Living Movement and efforts to form communal shopping groups in the late 1970s (Singer 1982).

Such women in squatter settlements defend class-based consumer interests. Yet women of different classes in the 1970s and 1980s also united for shared concerns, including, in essence, rights of motherhood. Poor and rich housewives alike have publicly defied military governments in

Argentina, Chile, El Salvador, and Guatemala that kidnapped and killed their children and grandchildren. In these instances as well, women's economic marginalization was a factor in their mobilization. Because fewer women hold jobs, they have had more time than their spouses to search for children who have "disappeared"; they also have not thereby risked being fired from work for challenging the regime, as might their employed spouses. Women's previous political marginalization, moreover, has worked to their advantage, for they were not as suspect when first mobilizing politically.

Men as well as women obviously share a concern about children. However, in Latin America where motherhood is glorified and women are exalted as domestic beings—as reflected in Marianismo, the counterpart to machismo (Stevens 1973)—women feel a particularly strong sense of loss when their children "disappear." Under the circumstances, motherhood creates a bond and sense of solidarity from which women have drawn the strength to defy bans on protest and to challenge, in effect, the legitimacy of repressive regimes.

The movement of politically inexperienced women in defense of the "disappeared" was particularly effective in Argentina. There, women protested—as chapter 7 describes—when few men dared. The Argentinian military tried to dismiss and discredit the women. However, the women's persistent, silent, nonviolent street demonstrations and hunger strikes helped bring down the repressive government, especially after the loss of the war with Britain over the Falkland Islands severely discredited the armed forces.

These examples illustrate that gender may, analytically, be of consequence in two distinct ways: as a social base of mobilization and resistance and as a set of issues around which men as well as women can press for change. Concretely, of course, the two may be interrelated. However, while women often mobilize for men's and household concerns, men infrequently mobilize for issues defined as women's concerns. If anyone struggles for "women's issues," it is generally only women.

From an analytical perspective, the women's mobilizations in defense of housing and other consumer claims, as well as in defense of "the disappeared," call for another important revision of orthodox Marxist thinking. As we have seen, women's noninvolvement in the production process has made it easier for them to defy the established order; Marx, as we know, presumed that the seeds of protest were rooted, above all, in conflicting interests embedded in relations of production.

Politically Grounded Defiance

The antigovernment protests by the relatives of the disappeared in Argentina, Chile, El Salvador, and Guatemala show not only that women may collectively resist conditions they dislike but also that political institutions and political processes may be sources of grievances and targets of defiance independently of class- and market-rooted tensions. Political protest may be grounded in the desire of politically excluded groups to be incorporated into the body politic, in dissatisfaction among enfranchised groups with existing political arrangements, and in opposition to the way political power is exercised, as reflected in specific state policies. For these reasons, political defiance may be designed to bring about change in political or other institutional spheres.

Struggles that focus explicitly on political rights and political justice often become more intense and more broadly based when groups also feel economically aggrieved and when the economic performance of regimes is questionable. Tilly (1978) adds that political conflict is especially likely when the balance of economic, military, and organizational resources among groups shifts. It would appear that shifts in control over symbolic and ideological resources may also be of consequence, and that the critical changes in the balance of resources that stir "mass" defiance may center at the elite level (not between elites and the "masses").

Dissatisfaction with political arrangements may be expressed through extra-institutional defiance and through participation in left-wing movements that challenge the status quo. However, it may also be expressed through deliberate nonparticipation in elections, ballot destruction, and refusal to participate in political and civic activities. What passes for apathy may reflect quiet dissatisfaction with, and defiance of, existing political options. To the extent that this is true, the potential base for political change is much greater than politically articulated grievances suggest.

Twentieth-century Latin American history, as previously noted, has been punctuated by oscillations between military and democratically elected governments. Although the citizenry have often accepted, however grudgingly, their loss of political rights as a result of coups d'état, such rights have subsequently often come to be foci of political mobilizations. Chapters 8 and 9 document how rich and poor have turned to the streets to press together for the restoration of electoral and other political rights.

Even when a populace enjoys formal political rights, conflict is not necessarily contained within routinized legitimate political channels. Formal rights may incite protest if citizens feel elections to be fraudulent or electoral choices limited. Especially where states are weak and civilian groups are politicized, as in Bolivia, electoral manipulation by government parties has been met with public protests. In 1978, for example, peasants refused to allow (right-wing) government-backed candidates to make public appearances. They also set up roadblocks and fought police and soldiers who attempted to arrest government opponents. Although political options subsequently improved, seven years later elections were also nearly undermined by "mass" defiance. Peasant leaders threatened to disrupt the economy with roadblocks again to register their opposition to the elections; they felt the government tried to weaken the peasant vote by not adequately facilitating rural voter registration. Even in Mexico, where the state is stronger and groups in civil society weaker, elections sparked violent and nonviolent protests in the 1980s, especially (but not only) in the northern industrial region. As the country's economic crisis caused living standards to plunge, the middle class as well as the poor (for somewhat different reasons) became less tolerant of government corruption and electoral fraud.

Electoral defiance has a particularly long history in Argentina. There, citizens have for decades expressed opposition to their political options quietly at the ballot box. Such electoral defiance peaked in 1960, when about 20 percent of all voters cast "blank" votes. Many of these voters who chose to "waste" their vote were Peronistas: they resented the fact that their party had been outlawed and registered their resentment at the polls.

The deliberate use of the ballot as an instrument of political defiance is also well illustrated in the Ayacucho region of Peru when Sendero Luminoso had a strong base there. In the early 1980s most peasants abstained from voting, annulled their ballots, or cast blank votes as an expression of hostility to their political options. The guerrilla militants saw the franchise as an important institution to challenge, and sympathizers in the region helped undermine state legitimacy by denying the regime electoral support. By contrast, fewer peasants in the region rejected the electoral system in 1985, when the left-leaning presidential candidate, Alan García, gave them reason for optimism.

While somewhat distinctive conditions, traditions, and histories have given rise to variations in expressions of politically rooted defiance among Latin American countries, throughout the region the same socioeconomic classes have tended to express political grievances in roughly similar ways under both democratic and nondemocratic regimes. Economically subordinate groups protest most frequently in the streets, for their ability to influence decision making through formal or nontumultuous informal political channels is limited, despite their strength of numbers. In Latin America, real power is rarely vested in formal political institutions, and even when peasants, workers, and the urban poor enjoy formal political rights, they lack access to the effective, informal channels of influence.

Businessmen and other segments of the so-called middle class (who in Latin America rank among top income earners) rarely take to the streets, because they generally can rely on effective behind-the-scenes informal political channels of influence to which the "popular" classes have no access. However, when elite groups are unable to defend their interests through either formal or informal means, they too have taken to the streets; for this reason, the antimilitary mobilizations in Brazil and Chile had some middle-class support.

The middle classes do not only protest for democracy, however. They have, on occasion, defied democracy to the point where they have backed military coups d'état, and, in extreme instances, financed their own militias. They have supported antidemocratic coups and militias when democracy failed, in their view, to restrain sufficiently worker and lower-class demands. While the middle classes tend to be favorably predisposed toward democracy, when their economic interests have thereby been jeopardized, they have sacrificed their political rights. Changing class dynamics and economic conditions accordingly explain why the same middle-class groups that pressed for democracy in Brazil and Chile in the 1980s backed military extralegal usurpations of power in the 1960s. And in El Salvador in the early 1980s, members of the bourgeoisie defied democracy to the point of financing right-wing death squads. They did so to subvert moderate government-backed social reforms and to quell a broadly based guerrilla movement that threatened their class interests.

While political defiance often masks underlying economic grievances, the "relative autonomy" of politics sometimes results in classes turning "inward" on themselves. In hierarchically structured societies—which Latin American countries have historically been—electoral contests may turn factions of classes against each other when elites are themselves divided; this may occur even when class-rooted economic grievances lie at the base of the politicization. The most notorious Latin American example of intraclass warfare occurred in Colombia in the 1940s during the period known as La Violencia, when peasants, many of whom had been economically uprooted during the Depression, turned on one another in support of the political party with which their *patrón* was affiliated.

In sum, politically based defiance has been expressed in a variety of ways, ranging from guerrilla activity, support of left-wing parties, and public defiance of the law to more subtle and covert activity, including the political equivalent of foot-dragging, electoral sabotage. Socioeconomic groups tend to express their grievances differently politically, owing to the different channels of effective influence open to them; the middle classes will turn to the same disruptive tactics as the poor when informal as well as formal channels of influence fail them. Yet the absence of politically articulated defiance does not necessarily signify satisfaction with existing political arrangements and the likelihood of continual quiescence. Persons who are politically discontented may feel that the costs of "going public" are too great. When they perceive the risks accordingly, they may turn to covert expressions of defiance or withdraw from politics and deny the regime electoral legitimacy. The "popular" classes need not be offered selective incentives, as rational-choice theory posits, to defy political arrangements in quiet ways. To focus merely on manifest expressions of defiance gives a false impression of regime support and legitimacy.

Religion: Not Just an Opiate

Religion has been thought to be an atavism likely to disappear with modernization, epiphenomenal, and an irrational alternative to politics. Yet in recent decades new religious values and new religious activity have stirred conflict, not only within religious hierarchies, but within the societies in which they are embedded.

In Latin America, the Catholic church has been one of the pillars of the established order for centuries. That is no longer always the case. Since the 1960s grass-roots ecclesial base communities (CEBs) inspired by Vatican II–grounded "liberation theology" have nurtured dissent, contributed to a delegitimation of established structures and leaders, and laid a foundation for new kinds of leaders and solidarities. In so doing, they have created tension within the church itself, at the national and international levels, and within local polities (Levine 1986).

The new theology stresses issues of justice and equality and calls for a "preferential option for the poor." Advocates accordingly see religious values and symbols as a reason for poor people to mobilize against immoral social structures. Injustices once claimed to be divinely ordained are now portrayed as social inventions that can be altered. The new theology has taken hold especially where economic dislocations have prepared the ground by dismantling traditional social bonds between classes; this has been especially true in Central America, but also in Chile and Brazil.

The nature of CEB involvements varies considerably by country, even though the groups are grounded in the same religious doctrine and the same organizational hierarchy. CEBs have been a force behind protests against unjust policies, such as austerity programs in the Dominican Republic (see chapter 10), revolutionary movements in Nicaragua and El Salvador, and mass pressure for democratization in Brazil, Chile, and Haiti. Yet in other settings they have reinforced and strengthened conservative regimes. Levine and Mainwaring argue in chapter 6 that CEB involvements vary with interpretations of religious doctrine by the clergy and their sociopolitical role on the one hand and according to broader church-state relations on the other.

CEBs exemplify the potential linkages between protest and organization. The grass-roots CEB organizations sometimes stir defiance, disproving theories that posit that disruption thrives in the absence of intermediary organizations. CEBs provide an institutional nexus whereby people with similar deprivations meet regularly, recognize that their problems are shared, and, on occasion, attempt to change their lot. Moreover, people may be mobilized through their involvements in CEBs even when they did not initially affiliate with this end in view. CEBs have also become an important arena in which lay people have developed leadership skills, especially in those societies where organization in civil society is restricted. This was especially true in Nicaragua under Somoza.

Clergy have been leading critics of repressive regimes in the region. They have challenged governments when few others dared, because their sacred calling provided them with some immunity from "this-worldly" abuse. Yet as clergy increasingly partake in the realm of the "profane," they seem to be losing some of their sacred aura. While clergy who spoke out against torture and repression in Brazil and Chile between the mid 1960s and the mid 1970s experienced minimal reprisals, Archbishop Romero was subsequently shot in San Salvador while delivering a sermon and other priests and missionaries have been murdered in El Salvador and Guatemala.

CEBs represent not merely a church-based response to injustices in civil society. They represent a response to a crisis within the church itself. Because the church had failed to be sufficiently responsive to its membership in recent decades, lay involvement in church life had declined. Catholics increasingly "defected" to Protestantism, and the hierarchy had difficulty recruiting clergy. Catholics, in essence, expressed their dissatisfaction with the church with their feet; they did not directly confront the hierarchy and press for change. Under the circumstances, the hierarchy saw CEBs as a means to strengthen its base at the grassroots level. Some CEBs have, however, become forces unto themselves, challenging the hierarchy and church beliefs on the one hand and pressing for change in diverse institutional spheres on the other.

The vast majority of Latin Americans continue to consider themselves Catholic, whether or not they actively partake in CEBs or more traditional church activity. Nonetheless, Protestantism has been winning growing numbers of converts in recent decades. Protestantism has made its greatest inroads where economic dislocations have weakened long-established patterns of authority and control and the Catholic church has failed to respond to the changed conditions. Latin Americans have turned to Protestantism out of discontent with life under the established order at least as much as out of an understanding of the new religious doctrine and a belief in its superiority. Lower-class converts, in particular, often know little about the content of their newly acquired affiliation. Yet their new religion generally is very meaningful to them. As a minority religion in the region, Protestantism is sectlike in structure and mentality.

Although Protestantism reflects religious defiance of Catholic hegemony in the region, its political impact tends to be conservative. Since it is "other worldly" in orientation, it is tolerant of "this worldly" social injustices. Moreover, some of the missionary work has been financed by conservative U.S. groups, and it has served as a vehicle for implanting U.S. anticommunist and religious views (Hvalkof and Aaby 1981).

Yet the political import of religion hinges not merely on the doctrines the groups espouse. Both Protestants and Catholics have been agents of change when they have challenged long-standing patterns of domination. In the Guatemalan highlands, for example, Catholic and Protestant missionaries alike have broken the hold of folk Catholicism and the social order it legitimated (see Brintnall 1979). The pride that accompanied conversion fostered change. Indian converts founded peasant leagues, challenged Ladino political domination, and broke with the Indian structure of civil-religious power. We see here how religion's impact on society rested not merely or necessarily on its manifest content but—as Weber argued—on the predispositions it inspired. Yet the new religions captured the hearts and minds of Indians only once national and local changes provided them with new economic opportunities; earlier missionary efforts had failed. Religious revolts that transform social relations seem most likely to arise when the old order has already begun to crack.

Precisely because the impact of religion lies not merely in its manifest content, even centuries-old folk religions have served as a bedrock on which protest and resistance movements have built. Indian cults that have survived the conquest and Westernization by adapting to and incorporating Christian and modern features provide no explicit mandate for political defiance. Yet, as June Nash documents, folk practices can keep a spirit of defiance alive when they bring people of similar social standing together; under conditions described below, such cultures of resistance may contribute to political protest even when people do not partake in the rituals with such an end in view. In Brazil, Afro-American movements similarly build on remnants of the African religions that former slaves brought with them. Even Cuba's Marxist-dominated revolution has not obliterated the hold of African-rooted beliefs. Syncretic religions that involve cultural resistance to white domination have played a particularly central role in racial and ethnic-based movements in the region.

In sum, in recent decades religious institutions and religious values have stirred defiance, intentionally and unintentionally. Dissatisfaction with Catholicism, for centuries the hegemonic religious force in Latin America, has taken many forms. On occasion, the church has responded in ways that have won back lay loyalty. By involving the laity more in church activity, and thereby altering relations within religious institutions, the church has, at times, become a locus of mobilizations for change in other institutional realms as well; the hierarchy has not necessarily sanctioned "this worldly" activity, even when it has been supported by priests on the local level. The significance of religion derives from the meanings followers ascribe to their belief systems; these meanings are not determined merely by the formal content of religion.

CONTEXTUAL FACTORS SHAPING RESPONSES TO GRIEVANCES

Class and market relations, gender, politics, and religion may be sources of rage, but we have seen that the ways discontent is expressed may vary considerably. Historical evidence suggests that local institutional structures and cultural milieux, interclass ties and alliances, and perceived options all condition whether and how shared grievances are defied and resisted. Only when "conditions are ripe" will people publicly protest en masse conditions they believe to be unjust.

Local Institutional Relations, Class Alliances, and Popular Cultures of Resistance

When institutions bring people together in similarly structured situations, individuals are likely to feel that their private grievances are collectively shared and collectively soluble. Collective defiance is a particularly likely response to shared grievances if rituals and "popular" beliefs reinforce a culture of resistance. Under such circumstances, disgruntled persons are likely to turn to collective, rather than individual, adaptive strategies; this is particularly so when—as detailed below—macro political conditions are also conducive.

Agriculturalists who maintain ties through community-based cultural and social institutions, and not merely or even necessarily through production, tend to perceive grievances as commonly shared. The more local social and cultural ties are mutually reinforcing, and the greater the history of community protest on which to build, the more likely villagers are to engage in collective defiance. Although it is widely believed that agrarian capitalism undermines village solidarities, market relations may generate new resources that strengthen local institutions where local ties are already strong and where individuals who share common grievances are linked by kinship, ethnicity, and cultural bonds. When, in addition, communities are differentiated socially and economically into two distinct camps, commonly shared injustices are likely to be collectively resisted. By contrast, the more complex the local class structure, the less likely it is that grievances will be perceived to be collectively shared and collectively correctable. When kinship, patronage, and ritual ties cross-cut class lines, collective solidarity is rare.

In places where village solidarities are strong, family members who migrate to address class- and market-based problems may unwittingly reinforce local cultural and institutional bonds at the same time as they turn to individual and household solutions to situations considered intolerable. Where population pressure is great, for example, some family members may migrate but return for fiestas, rituals, and labor-intensive stages of the agricultural cycle. They thereby maintain ties with their former community and contribute to its economic and social base. Moreover, migrants reduce pressure on the land that might otherwise divide the community. Yet by bringing urban ideas back with them, they may stir village dissatisfaction with the status quo.[8] Migrants who pursue private solutions to their socioeconomic problems may spark village-based strife at the same time as they reinforce village solidarity. Wolf (1969: 292, 294) argues that the middle peasant plays a pivotal role in revolutions precisely because he retains a footing in village life at the same time as members of his family migrate and are exposed to urban, industrial political ideas. According to him, it is the very attempt of peasants to remain traditional that makes them revolutionary, with villagers venting their force outward to secure more living space for their customary corporate way of life.

Different village structures help account for different peasant responses to abuse and exploitation (see Skocpol 1979; Wolf 1969; Migdal 1974). In the Latin American context, village structures have shaped revolutionary movements and influenced how aggrieved rural people have responded to "revolutionary situations." Zapata's peasant rebellion centered in the region of Mexico where corporate village life prevailed, and his followers fought for the restoration of collective land rights and the preservation of their communities. The sugar economy had eroded "inwardly" oriented communities in Cuba long before Castro organized his rural guerrilla movement. Consequently, Castro's initial rural support came from peasant squatters to whom he promised *individual* land rights; he based his guerrilla movement in an area where land security was an issue, but agrarian capitalism had not proletarianized the labor force.

Village structures can contribute to collective acts of defiance even in the aftermath of revolution, especially when local solidarities are strengthened by the state/class transformation. The previously described Aymaran movement in the Bolivian highlands in the 1980s, for example, was grounded in a deteriorating rural economy and increased rural-urban ties. Yet peasants sought collective ethnically based solutions to their plight partly because revolutionary land, labor, and political reforms had previously strengthened village solidarities. In postrevolu-

8. The return not only of cityward migrants but also of international migrants may unwittingly ignite protest. The discontent that led many Cubans to storm foreign embassies and seek to emigrate to the United States in 1980 has been partially attributed to islander contact with visiting émigrés in the latter 1970s. In this case, though, the defiance was rooted more in national than in village institutional life.

tionary Mexico, village structures have to date not sparked much collective defiance among economically hard-pressed peasants. There, local groups have lost much of their autonomy through incorporation into national government and party institutions, and local leadership has been coopted through patronage into national institutional structures (discussed in greater detail below). Thus, the experience of Mexico and Bolivia suggests that agrarian revolutions that both strengthen village ties and preserve local institutional autonomy are more likely than those that do not to spark subsequent village-based mobilizations.

Collective defiance is especially probable when the cultural climate is conducive to mobilization efforts as well (Gamson 1986). Because mass media coverage may be decisive in informing elites and mass publics about movement actions as well as in forming the morale and self-image of movement activists, the mass media are important actors in political conflicts. The media can become a channel through which alternative views, symbols, and meanings get expressed. This implies that media discourses frame issues for the public, and that the media may become an arena in which groups struggle over the definition and construction of social reality. For these reasons, the ruling classes in Latin America, especially, but not exclusively, under military regimes, have often exercised tight control over what views get expressed. Illiteracy and poverty have further limited these media functions in the region. Nonetheless, the media have been of consequence to protest and resistance movements in the region. The women protesting the "dirty war" in Argentina, for example, benefited from media coverage, including coverage abroad. Also, in Bolivia the Aymaran movement benefited from an Aymaran radio station that both reinforced ethnic identity and communicated ethnic concerns.

The significance of the media may lie not only in enabling contesting groups to air their views, but also in exposing people to alternative ways of life and thought, and in so doing mobilizing the previously uninformed to seek change. McClintock argues, for example, that modern communications made peasants in the Ayacucho region of Peru more aware of their relative deprivations, which in turn fueled their sympathies for the guerrilla movement organizing in their region.

In communities where cultural traditions reinforce a common identity and a spirit of resistance, collective defiance against commonly held grievances is likely even in the absence of media access. Culture is an area of life over which subordinate groups often have some control. It therefore may provide a realm where subordinate groups can nurture moral dissent against domination. No doubt cultural expressions of defiance have their greatest hold where deprivations have been collectively experienced for generations, and where institutional life brings similarly situated people together. Commemorations of past struggles, public funerals to honor friends and relatives who have died in pursuit of common causes, folk heroes and ballads, and rituals that include symbolic protest all help create and reinforce cultural expressions of resistance. Wickham-Crowley, for example, finds that guerrilla movements disproportionately take hold in areas with histories of popular rebellion against central authority and often fail where such cultures are absent.

While cultures of resistance make collective defiance more probable, they are rarely the spark that ignites protest. Sendero Luminoso, for example, established its initial social base in a region with a rebellious cultural tradition, Ayacucho. Yet Ayacucho lent little support to guerrilla efforts two decades earlier, and a neighboring region, Cuzco, with an equally strong, if not stronger, rebellious cultural tradition, but a more viable economic base in the 1970s and 1980s, did not respond to Sendero's destabilizing efforts. A rebellious tradition may contribute to collective efforts to bring about change when groups feel shared grievances. However, the root cause of protest tends to rest with inequities and injustices that are structural in origin.

Cultures of resistance may remain meaningful to people even after the conditions that gave rise to them are no longer of consequence. Such cultures are likely to persist when people with a common background continue to share common grievances and to retain contact with one another. Nash shows that Bolivian miners, who are among Latin America's most militant laborers, are deeply influenced by primordial beliefs and rituals rooted in their agrarian past. Preconquest peasant-based beliefs, which are perpetuated and reinforced through rituals, contribute to a continued collective identity and a sense of when the collectivity has been mistreated. The miners' cultural heritage has accordingly influenced both the timing and the place of protests addressing their deplorable current conditions of work. The rituals are not a charter for behavior. Indeed, the political action inspired by the rituals has ranged, with circumstances, from reaction to revolution. Nash shows sacred festivities not to be a substitute for social change, but a base on which labor and political defiance has built. Sometimes gatherings that began as ritual events turned into political protests, and not always at the miners' own initiative; on occasion, authorities who feared worker get-togethers repressed the activities and in so doing sparked miner protests. Such repression unwittingly politicized the occasions, and the massacres have since been incorporated into the symbolic significance miners attach to the rituals.

The impact of cultural values and norms on defiance can thus be very different from what Kornhauser (1959) and other "mass society" theorists posited. Kornhauser argued that the breakdown of norms stirred unrest. Yet we have stressed the opposite: that cultural traditions may spark protest. In the absence of cultural (and group) bonds, disgruntled individuals are likely to accept their lot, however grudgingly, or turn to individual, not collective, efforts to address their plight.

Support by More Privileged Individuals and Groups

Local institutional arrangements and cultural traditions are not, however, the only contextual features to influence whether aggrieved people seek individual or collective, overt or covert, solutions to conditions they dislike. In both the city and the countryside, economically subordinate groups are more likely to defy conditions they dislike collectively if they have the support of more advantaged individuals or groups. This strategic support may come from the more economically well-to-do, political parties of considerable standing, or religious leaders.

Protest movements do not necessarily and inevitably emerge out of the contradictions in economic or other structural arrangements, even when subordinate groups perceive their situation to be unsatisfactory and unjust. Better-situated individuals help arouse the masses and shape the demands of the aroused in such a way that individual discontent is collectively channeled.

The better situated may be of consequence for several reasons. For one, they may induce lower-status people to consider as unacceptable conditions that they otherwise might tolerate. Second, they may provide ordinary folk with leadership skills and material resources they otherwise might lack. Third, their very involvement may minimize elite use of force against the tumultuous, because elites are much more reluctant to use repression against the middle than the "popular" classes. Therefore, with the protection of more privileged individuals and groups, the "popular" classes may be more willing to defy conditions they dislike and more successful in pressing for change.

Yet "well-situated" individuals rarely succeed in inciting rebellion when subordinate groups do not already feel aggrieved. Instead, their importance rests with the direction and coordination they give to rebellious sentiments.

Several of the movements previously discussed probably would not have arisen, even though "underlying" economic conditions were conducive, had it not been for the support of better-situated individuals. The movements among the urban poor that resisted cooptation and pressed for new claims, for example, were initiated by outside groups: by clergy, student militants, and political parties. Catholic "base communities" that have stirred unrest occurred under the aegis of prelates outraged by economic and political conditions. The autonomous movements in the north of Mexico were led by student militants who took advantage of major tensions between the Monterrey bourgeoisie and local functionaries of the ruling party. The mobilizations of entire *campamentos* (squatter settlements) in Allende's Chile occurred under the sponsorship of political parties. Wickham-Crowley and McClintock also high-light how important outside leadership was in the guerrilla movements they studied. Most founders of guerrilla movements have been univer-sity students and faculty, though most of the movements failed precisely because the leadership did not appeal to the peasantry in meaningful ways. Sendero's success in Ayacucho—as McClintock details—derived from the leadership's ability to identify with its social base and address local concerns; when the militants failed to do so, peasant support for the movement waned.

Outside leadership is of particular consequence in turning localized rural rebellions into nationally coordinated revolutionary movements. Peasants typically engage in revolutionary activity when a revolutionary elite adds a new layer of leadership and doctrine to peasant life. In all Latin American revolutions, cultivators rebelled against intolerable *local* conditions; their support for *national* movements hinged on alliances with the urban intelligentsia.

Movements "from below" may benefit from the support of other classes, or factions of classes, and not merely from the support of better-situated individuals. Working- and lower-class opposition to the military governments in Brazil and Chile gained particular momentum when sup-ported by important segments of the middle class. Zamosc traces the ori-gin of the Colombian peasant movement ANUC to the strategic support of the industrial bourgeoisie. ANUC collapsed when industrialists' politi-cal and economic interests shifted, causing them to turn on the peasantry.

Privileged individuals do not, however, always channel "ordinary people's" grievances in ways that effectively bring about change. Their visions may be imperfect, and their self-interest may stand in the way. Garretón argues, for example, that mass protests against the repressive Pinochet regime in Chile failed to force the military back to the barracks even when supported by middle-class groups, because the political par-ties, for their own opportunistic as well as ideological reasons, competed for control of the opposition movement. In so doing, the parties under-mined the collective strength of the opposition. By contrast, in Brazil, where political parties have historically been much weaker, multiclass-based protests resulted in a successful partial restoration of political rights. However, once the military relinquished power, class differences within the opposition movement came to the fore, which weakened the movement and marginalized the working class politically.

In highlighting the role that "well-situated" individuals may assume in stirring and channeling dissent, it is obvious that protest and resistance movements are not mechanistically determined by structural and cul-tural forces alone. Leadership—as many of the chapters that follow show—can have a decisive impact. However, its impact is not under con-ditions of its own choosing.

State Structures

State institutional arrangements and policies, as noted above, benefit groups unequally, and the felt injustices that they generate are an obvious source of conflict. Yet state institutional arrangements may also be a contextual factor, influencing responses to grievances. The democratic versus exclusionary nature of regimes on the one hand, and state material, symbolic, and organizational resources on the other, influence whether and how discontent is articulated. They affect whether people turn to collective or individual, formal or informal, strategies to improve conditions they dislike.

Democratic governments often are faced with more public protests than exclusionary military regimes. This is so even though people tend to be better off under democracy and even though democratic regimes offer at least some access to legitimate channels of political expression. Protest is more likely in politically "open" societies because the risks are less and the prospects of reward are greater. The very perception of regime responses influences how the aggrieved respond to their plight. Since democratic governments claim to rule in the name of their citizenry and since they must regularly hold elections, they must be somewhat responsive to "popular" demands; otherwise, the electorate may subsequently shift their allegiance to an opposition party.

To argue that democracy may unwittingly stir unrest when it relies on minimal use of force to rule turns rational-choice theory "on its head." That is, aggrieved persons may be inclined to rebel not so much because they are presented with incentives (a "carrot") as because they are not constrained by dominant group control (a "stick"). The *dis*incentives for *not* rebelling generally are fewer under democratic than under authoritarian regimes.

Democratic regimes that identify with the laboring classes are particularly vulnerable to pressure "from below." Workers' movements in Chile—for example, among textile workers—have followed national elections that laborers perceived as leftist victories (Winn 1986). Under leftist and populist governments, workers obviously feel that their prospects of winning concessions through mobilization are good.

State/labor relations in turn condition responses to grievances, somewhat independently of regime commitment to democracy and to the laboring classes in particular. To illustrate, strike activity varies in Latin America with state/labor relations. For this reason, strikes have been less frequent in Mexico, where labor shares formal political power through corporate status in the governing party, than in pre-Allende Chile, where labor enjoyed organizational rights but no institutional ties to the state (Zapata 1977). The different strike patterns cannot be attributed to objective differences in the economic status of workers in the two countries.

Different patterns of state/labor relations also help account for vary-ing cross-national responses to similar austerity measures. Mexico's cor-poratist system contributed to much greater public tolerance of the measures there than in many other countries in the region. Because "popular" groups are formally incorporated into the government-party apparatus in Mexico, they cannot easily oppose state policies without breaking with the regime. Moreover, the leadership of state-affiliated groups often benefits economically and politically from the state affilia-tion even when rank and file do not.

In the absence of a well-instituted corporatist system, divisions among elites, as well as between elites and laboring groups, may spark defiance. The ruling class usually has a vested collective interest in preserving the status quo. But social and economic change may affect elite groups dif-ferently, to the point where they do not remain equally committed to the status quo. Elites competing for dominance may seek the support of the lower classes, and in so doing both raise poor people's hopes that change is possible and weaken the legitimacy of the institutions that oppress them. Competing political elites may even unwittingly stir up tumult when candidates and parties that command political loyalty raise rank-and-file hopes and aspirations. In Colombia, both La Violencia and the politics of the alliance between the industrial bourgeoisie and the peas-antry that led to the formation of ANUC were rooted in economic and political tensions among factions of the dominant class. In their quest for votes, competing candidates appealed to the urban and rural poor in ways that aroused mass mobilizations, land seizures, and other forms of unrest. Similarly, the restoration of democracy in Bolivia in the 1980s resulted in political competition, which in turn precipitated demonstra-tions, roadblocks, and strikes; indeed, protest became the modal manner in which groups pressed for their interests and contested power.

The Bolivian experience highlights another way in which state struc-tures shape protest activity independently of the policies states imple-ment: state resource capabilities. Relevant state resources include the ability to maintain unity within the state apparatus itself and material and symbolic resources with which to mystify constituencies and coopt opposition. The weaker a government and the more internally divided it is, the more state institutions will fall prey to domestic and foreign pres-sures that stir defiance; this is likely under both democratic and non-democratic regimes.[9]

Walton suggests in chapter 10 that not merely the state's formal struc-ture—its democratic or authoritarian form—but also the ability of a

---

9. The reformist junta in El Salvador (1979–82), for example, was divided on the issue of agrarian reform. The different military factions mobilized civilians, some in favor, others in opposition to land redistribution.

"power bloc" to maintain hegemony will influence responses to unpopular policies. Aggrieved groups are especially likely to defy conditions they dislike in intensely politically divided societies. Walton notes, for example, that while democratic and authoritarian governments alike have implemented austerity programs, protests against the programs have been greatest in countries where political divisiveness and power struggles have prepared the ground.

The material and symbolic resources that may diffuse (or defuse) potential unrest include patronage and subsidies. Such resources may be administered so as to cultivate relations of the patron-client type, and thereby deference and dependence. Economically subordinate groups can often be appeased with minor material benefits and their leadership with economic and political spoils. By skillfully making use of limited material resources, states can minimize "popular" unrest while ruling primarily in the interests of bureaucrats and the dominant class. The "bulkier," or larger, the state apparatus and the greater the state's revenue base, the more easily resources can be used to generate clientelistic relationships.

While contemporary Latin American regimes have relied on and cultivated patronage politics, their capacity to continue to do so contracted with their fiscal crises in the 1980s. Moreover, the IMF has insisted on state-sector cutbacks as a prerequisite for debt refinancing. Thus, at the very time when increased unemployment and deteriorating standards of living make the need for relief greater, governments are less able to address civilian needs through patronage and other subsidies. Protests may well increase with the retrenchment of the state's presence in society.

State symbolic resources may, however, diffuse protest, when material resources do not. Democratically elected governments may, for example, successfully convey the impression that they are responsive to "popular" concerns and in so doing induce quietude. Alan García in Peru and Raul Alfonsín in Argentina, for example, benefited from charismatic and populist appeal. On a more institutional level, the ideology of Mexico's dominant party has contributed—along with the material resources it commands—to the regime's long-standing stability. The party stresses its roots in the country's revolution. Though ruling primarily in the interests of the middle and upper classes, the party has propagated a populist ideology that deprives the left of symbolic "space."

Studies suggest that the state structures to which revolutions give rise minimize the likelihood of subsequent defiance. Based on the French, Soviet, and Chinese experiences, Skocpol, for example, argues that states become more bureaucratized and centralized, and more autonomous of domestic groups and foreign powers, as a result of revolutionary transformations. She implies that the structural changes decrease the probability of subsequent protest activity. Irrespective of the type of state to which they give rise, new regimes—she claims—are better able to regulate society administratively, ideologically, and coercively than the regimes they displace. The impact of revolutionary movements on state structures is discussed below, but it is important to note here that even if revolutions do give rise to more centralized and bureaucratic states, they give rise to states that *modify* how grievances are articulated; they do not eliminate conflict. The more centralized the state and the greater its repressive capacity, the more likely discontent is to be expressed in covert ways; this is true of all regimes, whether or not they are born of revolution.

In Latin America, revolutions have modified state structures in ways that have influenced subsequent responses to grievances. The patterning of postrevolutionary protest has varied, in part, with the nature and strength of the states to which the upheavals have given rise. In Cuba, the revolution gave rise to a stronger, more hegemonic, state than had previously existed. Although ostensibly a "workers' state," it has not always ruled in the workers' interests, and workers have, as previously noted, resisted policies they dislike. Yet because public protest is risky under Castro, people rely on covert forms of defiance when discontented. The revolution has not eliminated conflict; it has merely changed the nature of grievances and the way grievances are expressed.

In Mexico, the prerevolutionary state was already highly centralized. However, the revolution was consolidated in a manner that tied military and civilian groups to the state apparatus on a functional and territorial basis. The restructuring gave diverse groups a stake in the status quo, albeit to different degrees and in different ways. The stakes, in turn, have inclined aggrieved groups to comply with the "rules of the game" and seek change "from within." When overt defiance has occurred, it has generally been isolated and localized.[10] As a consequence, significant multiclass protest movements did not emerge until the 1980s, when an earthquake dislocated many lower- and middle-class families already hard-hit by the country's economic crisis. Then, *damnificados* (the damned)—as earthquake victims are called—from rich and poor areas of Mexico City together protested for new housing.

Yet even when Mexicans have been seemingly quiescent, covert forms of defiance have been rampant, and tolerated by the governing class. The law is continually violated behind the scenes, not publicly in the streets. The regime, in particular, thrives on corruption. For decades such everyday defiance of the law enhanced the regime's stability; all

10. The confrontation between students and the state in Mexico City in 1968 is the one major exception. Precisely because the state's brute use of force then was so visible, it contributed more than any other incident to erosion of the regime's legitimacy.

groups had some stake in noncompliance with rational-bureaucratic rules. However, with the economic contraction and fiscal crisis of the 1980s, the material base for corruption dried up; the fiscal constraints may explain why the government "chose" to launch an anticorruption campaign at the time and why electoral support for the "official" party then became problematic. As fewer benefit from payoffs and patronage, the inducement to collaborate with elites will decline and electoral and other forms of defiance are likely to increase.

In Bolivia, by contrast, the revolution has probably given rise to more public protest than the old regime. The new regime never achieved internal unity. Groups previously excluded from the body politic have come to feel entitled to new benefits, while the state's resource base has not expanded sufficiently to address the new claims, and the potential gains from defiance under civilian governments (above all, between 1952 and 1964 and under Siles Zuaso in the early 1980s) have often out-weighed the potential costs. Therefore, growth in state presence in so-ciety, including after revolution, does not necessarily result in greater quiescence. State institutional arrangements and state resource capaci-ties influence how disgruntled people respond to conditions they dislike, whether or not governments are grounded in revolution.

While state structures condition the likelihood and forms of protest, they are not static entities. They may change, including in response to pressure "from below." This is obvious in the context of revolution, but true also in its absence. Even revolutionary regimes may begin as moder-ate reform governments. As state institutional arrangements change, so too should the impact of the political apparatus on subsequent defiance.

That resources are of consequence to protest movements has, of course, been well documented by resource-mobilization theorists. Yet we have stressed much more than resource-mobilization theorists how macro social and cultural forces condition defiance and the varied ways in which it is expressed. Our approaches are not inconsistent, but we pro-vide a basis for understanding how contextual factors pattern the broad range of ways in which resources are utilized.

Options to Exit

The options people have, and consider themselves to have, also influ-ence responses to felt injustices. The greater the diversity of options, the less dissatisfaction with conditions in any one setting will spark overt col-lective defiance.[11]

11. Our concern here is with economic options. However, perceived political options may influence responses just as economic options do. When legitimate politics provide ag-grieved individuals and groups with effective channels of interest articulation, for ex-ample, protest is unlikely.

In any given social and cultural milieu, the more attractive economic alternatives are, the more likely it is that people will "exit" rather than rebel. It therefore is essential to understand the conditions under which people turn to such individual adaptive strategies rather than collective defiance to address conditions they dislike.

There are several economic options that disgruntled individuals may consider. They may migrate seasonally or permanently, change jobs, or take on additional jobs. For decades in Latin America, migration has offered sufficient promise that rural laborers have more often than not "exited" rather than rebelled when rural conditions seemed intolerable.

As an individual adaptive strategy, economic role diversification has ramifications in each job sphere. Laborers with a single income source who collectively experience deprivations may be more apt than diversely employed workers to try overtly or covertly to change work conditions they dislike, unless the risks of reprisal and job loss are very high. However, employers who rely on workers with diverse economic commitments may find their labor force to be unreliable; such laborers are more likely to miss work because of competing claims on their time, and they may use their varying jobs to their own advantage. Wage workers, for example, may quit or absent themselves from work during periods important to the agricultural cycle and they may pilfer materials from their place of employment for "sideline" jobs. From the employers' vantage point, such uncoordinated economic "sabotage" may be harder to discipline than union activity.

The Cuban government has experienced the complex consequences of diversified economic options for workers. As previously noted, around 1980 the government began to allow farmers to sell surplus that they produced above their state quota at the price the market would bear; new "farmers' markets" were set up for them in the cities. At the same time, the government also permitted state employees to do small-scale private contract work in their off-hours. The reforms were designed to increase productivity and make the economy more responsive to consumer demand, for low (but quite equitable) living standards had contributed to dissatisfaction with the regime in the late 1960s. However, workers manipulated the reforms to their own advantage. Farmers delivered their poorest-quality goods to the state in order to maximize their earnings on the more lucrative "free market," and an illegal stratum of middlemen arose to profit from the new market opportunities. Workers also absented themselves from their formal jobs to profit from sideline activities, and they pilfered supplies from their state jobs to use in the sideline activities (*Granma Weekly Review* 11 March 1984, p. 4). Thus, in diversifying labor's economic options to resolve productivity and political problems, the government created new bases for quiet worker defiance of state regulations. Because of the severity of the distortions caused by the "market opening," the government closed the private markets in 1986 and launched a "rectification" campaign.

Chapter 3, moreover, highlights the ramifications of multiple employment for organizers of protest movements. The leadership of ANUC in Colombia had difficulty mobilizing agriculturalists partly because its rural base was so heterogeneous, but also because individual agriculturalists were involved in multiple class relationships with opposing interests. When ANUC tried to organize the rural proletariat, for example, it met with part-time wage workers who were constantly on the move; the workers were also smallholders, with property as well as proletarian interests.

When alternative opportunities objectively exist and people do not take advantage of them, it should not be assumed a priori that laborers are content with their lot if they are quiescent. Noneconomic considerations—such as kinship and community ties—may make dissatisfied laborers reluctant to "exit" and take advantage of jobs elsewhere. Meanwhile, the contextual factors previously discussed may incline aggrieved individuals to accept conditions as unchangeable or to defy conditions they dislike in quiet and minimally coordinated ways.

Businessmen seeking cheap labor for industry and agriculture have faced the problem of inducing poor peasants, especially subsistence smallholders, to accept wage work, even when the workers' financial situation would thereby improve. In the sparsely populated Bolivian lowlands, for example, military recruits were called in to harvest cotton in the 1970s; impoverished peasants in the highlands refused to respond to the call for labor. The economic reward was considered insufficient to offset the personal costs that migration would entail.

Political elites who have offered material incentives to encourage peasants in highly politicized regions to migrate have also encountered similar problems. This occurred in Bolivia as well. The Bolivian government, with U.S. backing, had sponsored "colonization projects" to resettle peasants from the densely populated valley and highland areas after the 1952 revolution. The programs were designed both to promote much-needed food production for the domestic market and to reduce turbulence in the areas of peasant concentration. While the "colonizers" could benefit economically from resettling, the prospects were not sufficient to induce them to break with their village way of life. Only when coca growing for the foreign cocaine market became very profitable in the colonization areas were highland peasants willing to make the break, but then in *defiance* of the government, which, under U.S. pressure, outlawed cocaine-related activity there. Paradoxically, the *new* areas that were intended to reduce rural strife became centers of clashes between peasants, middlemen, and law enforcement agents once coca became a very lucrative crop in the 1980s.

Thus, alternative options influence how aggrieved persons respond to their lot. The alternatives that they will consider vary with their values, commitments, and social ties, and not merely or necessarily with the actual range of alternatives that exist. Aggrieved workers are likely to "exit" if options objectively exist and if their ties to their existing employment or community are not strong. Friendships and tradition make for employment commitment even when work conditions are oppressive and when the risks of mobilizing to improve work conditions are high. Peasants must often migrate to improve their lot because local options are so limited, but among equally impoverished peasants, those with weakest community ties are most apt to give up their village way of life.

Nonrational as well as rational factors, in essence, condition responses to injustices, including whether disgruntled people exit or rebel. The nonrational factors can be understood if the social and cultural milieux are taken into account; they cannot, however, be understood solely at the level of the individual.

THE IMPACT OF PROTEST

Despite much attention to the origins of defiance, its impact has rarely been studied. The outcome depends only partially on the rage, ideology, and tactics of protesters; it depends very much on whether the "subversive" acts seriously undermine the legitimacy and economic base of elites. The way powerful groups respond to pressure "from below" is of great consequence to the outcome of defiance. The classes allied in protest movements and global economic and political forces may also be of consequence.

Elite Responses

Dominant group responses cannot be mechanically predicted a priori. At the state level, military and civilian governments alike have met popular uprisings with reform as well as repression. However, democratic regimes that depend on mass legitimacy are more likely to address protest with reform, especially if they have the resource capability to do so. Governments' responses will thus hinge on their repressive and administrative resources and their bias toward repression versus reform.

Elites perceive public protest as threatening because it is highly visible and may cause "contagion." Yet quiet forms of defiance such as foot-dragging, pilfering, and ballot destruction may be of equal concern to them if elite claims to profits or legitimation are thereby challenged.

When elites respond to protest with force, the opposition movement may actually be strengthened. Force may increase anger against elites and increase solidarity among people with shared grievances. However, extreme levels of terror may—as Wickham-Crowley notes—have the historically "successful" impact of dampening rebellion; this is an especially likely outcome when protesters consider themselves to have no options. Extreme terror seems to have been the undoing of a number of urban guerrilla movements in the 1970s, for example, the Tupamaros in democratic Uruguay.

Repression rarely quells movements when the state itself is internally divided, when tumult is widespread, and when protesters enjoy tactical mobility. Latin American governments do not have the material capability of employing force on a large scale unless financed from abroad, and the democratic countries in the region cannot, for ideological reasons, rely on prolonged and extensive use of force to rule. As long as the state's repressive capabilities are limited (for material or ideological reasons) and the tumultuous can and are willing to move their bases of operation, force will not curtail opposition movements. In Peru, for example, government repression against Sendero Luminoso in the southern highlands (along with reforms by the populist president, Alan García) weakened the movement's support there in the mid 1980s. However, rather than accept defeat the guerrilla movement moved to other regions of the country and diversified its support base in the process.

That state responses shape outcomes of tumult is shown in chapter 10. Although the protests Walton studied were similarly sparked by austerity measures, they varied considerably in their effect. Government responses, in turn, were structurally grounded: they were contingent on state resources and state/society relations. Insurgents typically won some concessions. However, under weak and unpopular regimes, the ramifications of the defiance were often considerable; the protests caused governments to be deposed or further weakened. By contrast, some of the stronger governments were able to turn the uprisings to their own advantage. For fear that hemispheric disorder might otherwise ensue, the U.S. government and international creditors have allowed the more powerful countries to repay their debts on more favorable terms when rocked by protest.

Elite responses have also had a great bearing on the outcomes of guerrilla movements. Wickham-Crowley shows that guerrilla movements are less apt to expand their bases of support and more likely to be limited in their accomplishments when governments are somewhat responsive to popular concerns. The two Latin American guerrilla movements that succeeded in seizing power occurred in countries where highly personalized dictatorships responded to revolutionary challenges with inflexibility. Conversely, the only two Central American countries—Costa Rica and Honduras—that experienced no major guerrilla movements in the 1970s and 1980s had governments that were somewhat responsive to mass grievances.

Although prolonged protest movements may in themselves undermine state legitimacy, successful extralegal seizures of power are generally contingent on internal disunity within the state apparatus. Military desertion has been critical to revolutionary victories.

Outcomes of conflicts rooted in economic relations are contingent, in turn, on dominant class responses. In industrial settings, partial concessions from management may reduce labor militancy, and the acceptance of collective bargaining may routinize defiance to the point where its disruptive impact and costs to profits are minimized. In the case of agriculture, Paige (1975) has argued that rural social movements and their outcomes hinge partly on elite bases of wealth. Agrarian elite are least apt to respond to pressure "from below" with reform when their main source of wealth derives from land (versus capital). If laborers also depend on land (versus wages) for their livelihood, landowners' inflexibility is likely to induce a revolutionary movement among the discontented rural labor force.[12]

In the context of revolution, changing state dynamics pattern subsequent protest. As noted above, Skocpol shows how, and explains why, bureaucratic exigencies make for similar state tendencies in such ideologically dissimilar revolutions as the French on the one hand and the Soviet and Chinese on the other. Yet she provides no analytic basis for understanding how modes of economic organization, and associated class and political relations, shape revolutionary outcomes. She implies that bureaucratic exigencies are more decisive than class and ideological forces in shaping new regime policy.[13]

It would appear that class and ideological, as well as bureaucratic, forces influence the effects of revolution. My study of the social welfare outcomes of Latin American revolutions (see Eckstein 1982) documents, for example, how the class base of the new regimes and the dominant mode of economic organization shape allocative policies after revolution. I found the dominant mode of production under the new order to have a decisive bearing on patterns of land and income distribution and health welfare.[14] In Latin America, socialism has allowed certain allocative options that capitalism has not, although the greatest gains for the lower classes in Cuba occurred when the new regime first consoli-

12. Paige, however, premises his argument incorrectly on the assumption that outcomes of social movements flow from the goals of the movements.

13. Skocpol notes, however, that different surviving agrarian structures and differing revolutionary state-builder relations with the peasantry affect the outcomes of the upheavals.

14. Kelley and Klein (1980), by contrast, argue that all revolutions give rise to inequality in the long run because of human capital differences that are unaffected by class-state upheavals. While human capital differences have an impact on distributive allocations after revolution, the authors fail to take into account political forces that shape access to human capital resources; this access, and the significance of access, varies among postrevolutionary societies.

dated power. Yet the postrevolutionary Cuban government is the least tolerant of dissent. Postrevolutionary states differ in their allocative and participatory policies in accordance with their class biases, political openness, and resources.

Class Alliances

The more diversified the base of resistance, the more difficult it is for a state to address the varied grievances of groups concomitantly through force or reform. While elite responses are of consequence, so too are the responses of other groups in civil society. Revolutionary movements succeeded in Mexico, Bolivia, Cuba, and Nicaragua when not only "popular" groups but also sectors of the middle class—including professionals, educators, and certain businessmen—defied the old regime. By contrast, when the urban middle classes have not joined in, agrarian movements have never ushered in regime transformations.[15] Governments are much less likely to use force against the middle classes; therefore, movements involving the middle classes are much less likely to be repressed. The diverse socioeconomic groups that rebelled in Mexico, Bolivia, Cuba, and Nicaragua had different reasons for defying the government in power, but the net effect of their combined defection was a breakdown of the existing political and economic order. Class alliances proved possible because the leadership of the opposition movements in each country emphasized moderate political goals, such as the ouster of a dictatorship or the restoration of democracy; the leadership did not press for socialism, even when, as in Cuba and to a lesser extent in Nicaragua, the new regimes subsequently became committed to socialism.

For the laboring classes, alliances with the middle classes typically are a mixed blessing. In the long run, the middle class tends to dominate multiclass movements for its own ends. In Mexico, for example, an alliance between some urban middle-class groups and agrarian Zapatistas resulted in an agrarian reform that the peasants were unable to obtain on their own and the middle-class revolutionaries had initially opposed. Yet, as noted above, the anticapitalist reform ultimately helped usher in a procapitalist regime. The middle class dominated the newly formed state, which it used primarily for its own advantage. In Bolivia, middle-class attempts to depose the land- and mine-based oligarchy failed in the early 1940s; only when the middle-class reformers allied themselves with the increasingly militant labor movement did they succeed. Initially after the 1952 revolution, labor benefited from the alliance: the oligarchy was deposed and labor gained organizational rights, veto power in the mines, and the right to name vice-presidential and congressional candidates and the heads of several ministries. However, once the ruling-class fac-

15. The failure of the guerrilla movement in El Salvador to date, for example, rests in part on its inability to win over key segments of the bourgeoisie.

tion came to consider labor a liability and received foreign military and economic aid, it turned on the very class with which it had brought down the old order. Labor lost nearly all the gains it had made in the early years of the revolution.

As the examples above illustrate, neither classes nor states are static entities. When the priorities of powerful groups change, the stance toward movements "from below" may also change; such changes can affect both the state's role as a contextual factor shaping how grievances are articulated and state responses to protest when it occurs. State priorities may shift with economic and political exigencies (which involve global market and geopolitical, as well as domestic accumulation and legitimation, considerations), changes in the basis of the dominant class's wealth, and state-class relations. Zamosc, for example, argues that the Colombian industrial bourgeoisie and the state repressed and divided a peasant movement they had created when dominant class relations and state priorities shifted. In Bolivia, the middle class turned on labor when the basis of its wealth altered after the revolution. With access to new sources of wealth through the state and commercial agriculture in a previously undeveloped region of the country, it no longer "needed" labor.

Global Economic and Geopolitical Forces

Global economic and political forces can also have a decisive impact on the outcome of defiance. The responses of powerful international actors are contingent on their interests, their capacity to defend those interests, and global economic conditions.

By the 1980s foreign economic interests in the Third World centered not only on supplies of raw materials and overseas markets but also on offshore plants producing for the home market. Yet the responses of powerful international actors have depended not solely on their interests but also on "world time" (Walton 1984). The "same" practices (e.g., trade, manufacturing) may have different meanings and consequences depending upon when they occur. Moreover, the "acceptable" ways in which powerful international actors can assert their interests have changed over time. Direct military intervention, for example, is considered increasingly unacceptable. Consequently, world powers currently rely much more on counterinsurgency and economic blockades, which are not always as effective.

The responses of powerful international actors do not merely depend on their economic interests. Geopolitical considerations that cannot be entirely explained in terms of "underlying" economic interests may also be of consequence. Cold War politics have had a substantial impact on foreign responses to Third World struggles.

With specific reference to Latin America, because countries in the region occupy a weak position within the world economy, global conditions often influence the outcome of domestic tumult, including tumult rooted in seemingly nationalistic concerns. External groups may aid contesting groups in ways that affect each side's material and symbolic strength. Yet global dynamics may shape the outcome of domestic struggles even in the absence of specific foreign intervention. The timing of protest in this respect can be critical. In Mexico, for example, peasants won major land claims only after twenty years of civil strife. Their victory came with the Great Depression. The United States was too concerned at the time with its own internal problems to intervene, and when prices for exports plunged, landowners' ability and motivation to resist expropriation weakened. Under the circumstances, the state "chose," and was able to, redistribute land to restore order to the countryside. Similarly, in Peru, the populist military government of General Velasco Alvarado faced little elite opposition to its sweeping agrarian reform in 1969 because of the timing of the new law. Low world commodity prices at the time made domestic commercial farming unprofitable (especially in the sugar sector), and elite interests since World War II had shifted considerably from agriculture to industry. Therefore, the oligarchy had a limited interest in defending their land-holdings.

Global geopolitical dynamics have, in turn, shaped resistance movements in Latin America. The fear of communism at our backdoor has influenced U.S. responses to progressive nationalist movements in Cuba, Chile, Nicaragua, and other Central American countries, countries in which the United States has had relatively little economic interest. While the United States has deployed a variety of tactics to undermine left-wing movements in each of these countries, it has not always succeeded in its efforts despite its global preeminence. The Cuban experience demonstrates that U.S. foreign policy may have the opposite effect than intended: in attempting to stifle Castro's nationalist populist movement by imposing an economic blockade, the United States helped push Cuba into the Soviet camp.

In highlighting how elite responses, disunity within the dominant class and the state apparatus, multiclass alliances, and global market and geopolitical dynamics all shape outcomes of defiance at least somewhat independently of the motives that spark defiance and the form defiance assumes, the shortcomings of most explanations of protest and social movements become apparent. Outcomes often cannot be deduced from why people rebel. The conditions under which broader forces influence the patterning of defiance and its accomplishments can be studied and analytically incorporated into a theory of protest and resistance. However, the conjunctural nature of certain of these forces and the fact that power can be used in diverse ways (including not at all!) means that no mechanistic or abstract theory will do. There will always be historical variability, and the best studies will always be historically grounded.

LATIN AMERICAN PROTEST IN COMPARATIVE PERSPECTIVE

The studies in this volume suggest that certain distinctive features, as well as more universal ones, pattern protest in Latin America. From a global perspective, the countries are weak politically and economically. They are all dependent on foreign technology, capital, and trade, although the way they are linked to the world economy has shifted somewhat over the years and the linkages differ somewhat among the countries in the region. Their economic dependence has in turn made them vulnerable to shifting dominant power concerns. The dependence has shaped the extent and nature of opportunities for local groups, the types of grievances groups have, whether and how groups defy conditions they dislike, and the outcome of defiance. Of course, the way the countries are linked to the world economy and geopolitics are not the only factors of consequence. However, they are of sufficient importance that it cannot be assumed a priori that economic groups have the same set of grievances and their acts of defiance have the same effects in Latin America as in the more industrial countries.

Latin American countries also share a common Iberian heritage, which includes a bureaucratic centralist tradition premised on hierarchy and inequality and a Catholic-inspired worldview (see Véliz 1980). This heritage has been exploited and perpetuated by dominant groups who benefit from it. Many of the studies in this volume show, implicitly if not explicitly, how this heritage weighs on the living, shaping both the movements directed toward change and the pressures that resist change. Even rebellious groups do not break entirely with the social order they oppose.

Catholic symbols, beliefs, and organizations have in different ways influenced movements in Latin America as diverse as the mothers protesting the "disappearance" of their children in Argentina, protests against government-initiated austerity measures designed to address debt crises, and such successful guerrilla movements as that of the Sandinistas in Nicaragua. Catholic theology, through the groups and clergy it has inspired, has directly stirred defiance. However, the influence of Catholicism is more typically indirect. At a very fundamental level, Catholicism forms part of Lain Americans' worldview, including feelings about rights and justice. Because Catholicism continues to have such a hold, defiant groups often incorporate religious symbols into their movement even when they are not motivated by specifically religious concerns.

The Catholicism in question, however, is a distinctively Latin American variant, especially among the "popular" classes. Lower-class Catholicism incorporates indigenous beliefs and rituals, and it centers around saints—including mestizo and black saints—not Jesus Christ. Véliz (1980) aptly refers to Latin American Catholicism as latitudinarian. Such latitudinarianism is especially apparent among the rebellious tin miners described by Nash in chapter 5. The miners' protests cannot be understood merely in terms of their "class location" and economic deprivation. Primordial beliefs onto which Catholicism has been welded have influenced when and how the miners have defied their oppressive economic lot. The miners do not merely mirror and mimic the beliefs and actions of fellow miners in the industrial world, even when Marxism and other Western ideologies have made their way into the mines.

Catholicism, moreover, has not imposed a single ideological stamp on protest movements in the region. It has been associated with movements ranging from the "right" to the "left" of the political spectrum. In the Mexican revolution, the Catholic hierarchy played a major role in the counterrevolution, while rebellious Zapatistas relied on the brown-skinned Virgin of Guadalupe, patron saint of Mexico, to lead and assist them in their struggle against landowners and local authorities for land rights. In Nicaragua, Sandinistas acquired inspiration and organizational skills from the Catholic church prior to the fall of Somoza, and the hierarchy has been a basis of opposition to the new regime. At still other times, Catholicism has influenced protest movements that are not identified with any particular ideology. The Argentine *madres,* for example, who incorporated Catholic symbolism into their protest movement, deliberately refused to identify themselves with any political movement or party.

The latitudinarian tradition helps explain why race has rarely been a basis of protest, even though many countries in the region are racially heterogeneous, racial inequities exist, and people are very aware of racial differences. While people are sensitive to such physical differences as skin color, according to the dominant ideology, race is a cultural, not biological, matter in Latin America. Racial and ethnic minorities can, to some extent, therefore "pass." This conception of race differs most strikingly from South Africa's. The difference helps explain why racial groups are more apt to mobilize along class lines in Latin America and along racial lines in South Africa. Since the conquest, the church has granted Indians a place in the social order, albeit an inferior one.

Latin America's bureaucratic centralist tradition, in turn, undoubtedly also patterns protest in the region. It probably has minimized overt movements against authority and given many movements a statist component. The bureaucratic centralist heritage, for example, undoubtedly accounts for the nature of defiance in the mushrooming capital cities of Latin America. We have seen that protests in the cities typically focus on such ostensibly nonpolitical issues as rights to property, better wages, and the quality and cost of goods and services. Urban movements rarely challenge government authority directly.

In line with the hierarchical, centralist, latitudinal tradition, protest movements in the region have been inspired more by indignation over

injustice than inequality. The "popular" classes, as we have seen, have
sought to redress unjust land allocations and unjust prices. Nowhere in
Latin America, for example, have peasants pressed for an egalitarian
distribution of land. More egalitarian societies may have resulted from
the defiant acts of rebels, but concern over equality has not been the
motor force behind protests in the region.

The bureaucratic centralist latitudinarian heritage distinguishes Latin
America from other regions of the world, whereas "dependent development" characterizes other regions of the Third World as well. "Dependent development" makes for some distinctive labor force characteristics, with ramifications for protest. Latin America's more limited
industrialization, and the more privileged position of its small proletariat
relative to the growing urban "informal sector" masses and large remaining peasantry, has tended to make for greater labor quiescence
than in European countries when they initially industrialized. Yet Latin
America must be distinguished from other parts of the Third World in
its urban bias; the bias against the peasantry has exacerbated migration,
shifting the loci of conflict, with time, to the cities. It is the urban "informal sector" laborers, not the industrial proletariat, who constitute the re-
serve army in Latin America.

The strongest industry-based labor movements in Latin America have
been centered in the most industrial nations in the region, Argentina
and Chile. However, even in these countries, the demands of labor have
differed from those of their European and U.S. counterparts. Juan
Perón, who led the most consequential labor movement in Argentina's
history, mobilized workers around issues of social justice in a manner
that contributed to bureaucratic centralism. Whereas workers in Europe
pressed historically for political, economic, and social equality, Peronism
built on workers' concerns for state-guaranteed employment and social
security benefits. Peronism strengthened workers' ties to the state. Radical movements that aim to break with the statist tradition and to transform the state have rarely found a home among industrial workers in
Latin America. Industrial workers did not play a leading role in the
Cuban revolution, and in Chile miners—isolated, subject to extremely
hazardous conditions, and producers of the country's main source of foreign exchange—have generally been more militant than factory workers.
The corporatist bent of most labor movements in Latin America reflects
the centralized statist nature of Latin American societies.

In summarizing the distinctive features of Latin American defiance,
national and subnational differences should not be overlooked. State
and village structures, bases of production, and race and ethnicity vary
within and among countries in the region in ways that pattern conflicts.
Indigenous beliefs and solidarities are of greatest consequence in those
countries and regions of countries where village structures have sur-

vived (even if in modified form) into the modern era. The latitudinal tradition allows modernization to build on, and not necessarily displace, long-standing village customs and practices.

Precisely because defiance builds on historical traditions, it needs to be studied in its social context. Defiance is not mechanically patterned merely by people's "social location." The detailed studies in this book contribute to a better understanding of the unique and generalizable features of protest movements.

TASKS OF THE PAPERS

The chapters that follow do not present repeated efforts to address the same set of questions concerning the origins and outcomes of protest movements. They also do not in sum portray the region's entire array of protest movements. Urban and middle-class movements, for example, are noticeably underrepresented. Generalizations about the patterning of protest in Latin America that can be extrapolated from these essays must therefore be considered provisional. The contribution of the studies lies more on the level of description, albeit analytically grounded description, than on the level of theory.

The authors base their arguments on both retrospective and prospective analyses, although some do so more explicitly than others. Retrospective analyses focus on causes and conditions that are shown to generate particular historical outcomes, while prospective analyses begin with a particular historical condition and specify the paths leading to alternative outcomes. Levine and Mainwaring, for example, examine how church-linked base communities, inspired by liberation theology, have had different effects depending on the commitments of the local leadership of the groups and church-state relations; Wickham-Crowley traces the factors accounting for the different political outcomes of guerrilla movements; and Walton shows how and explains why similar austerity measures have been met with different types of responses depending on different political, organizational, and cultural conditions. In documenting the different trajectories of guerrilla movements, Wickham-Crowley suggests that there is nothing intrinsic to the initial ideology, organization, and social base of the movements that itself determines movement outcomes.

Zamosc combines a retrospective with a prospective analysis. The conditions accounting for the rise of a Colombian peasant movement, its radicalization, and ultimate demise are shown to be somewhat different. Zamosc's study of ANUC, like Wickham-Crowley's of guerrilla movements, informs us that there is no necessary relationship between the base of a movement, its ideology, and its impact. While maintaining a common base, the movement went through several stages: reformist, radical, and conservative. The evolution of the movement hinged in part on changing macro political and economic conditions, quite independent of the needs and wants of ANUC's peasant base.

Recurrent themes in this volume do not in themselves constitute evidence that the most important features of Latin American protest movements have been delineated. They may merely reflect a common set of biases among the contributors. I selected contributors not merely because they were very knowledgeable about particular movements, but also because I knew they would address a similar range of structural concerns. Nonetheless, recurrent themes cannot be attributed to a single overarching theory that induced the authors to focus on certain features to the exclusion of others: the chapters were not written to prove a predefined theory.

Seen together, these essays provide convincing evidence that a historical-structural approach is fruitful. They do not, however, in themselves provide a basis for fully discrediting and dismissing alternative interpretations of protest movements, for the authors did not specifically test the validity of alternative theories and find the alternatives to be wanting. Although *I* have indicated instances in which a historical-structural approach can account for the patterning of protest in ways that other approaches cannot, no analytic perspective can explain all that is relevant about the causes and consequences of protest. In some respects, explanations at the individual and structural levels are actually complementary. A historical-structural approach, for example, cannot account for why, under a given set of social conditions, any one individual might or might not defy conditions he or she dislikes, or for psychological factors that predispose certain individuals to assume leadership positions in protest movements; it can only account for the conditions that prompt groups of people, in the aggregate, to act as they do. To the extent that the different explanations call for different types of evidence, data that verify one explanation do not automatically discredit others. Therefore, we must ask not which theory or theoretical perspective is true and which is false, but which leads to more interesting hypotheses and which explains more. The studies in this volume, I believe, rather convincingly highlight the value of historical-structural analyses.

In emphasizing the importance of social structure, the authors do not deny or belittle the role of culture. Instead, the studies exemplify how culture assumes meaning through group, organizational, and institutional life. For this very reason, the same set of beliefs and customs can sometimes be associated with compliant behavior and at other times with defiance.

The essays are ordered according to the socioeconomic base of the movements the authors describe, since economic relations are so central to people's lives and to the patterning of protest. Peasant movements are discussed first, then mining and urban lower-, working-, and middle-class movements. Among movements drawing on similar social bases, the studies that focus on localized protests within a single country are presented first, then localized protests that focus on two or more countries. These chapters are followed by analyses of movements that are multiclass and national in scope, but focus on a single country, and then by broadly based cross-national studies. The chapters are therefore ordered in a manner that can contribute readily to theory building. Individual case studies are followed by multicase studies, analyses of movements with restricted social bases are followed by analyses with cross-class appeal.

These essays are of political as well as theoretical significance. Although not necessarily written with a political agenda in mind, they all suggest that the life of the urban and rural poor is not mechanistically determined by economic forces or formal institutional politics. In stressing the importance of class alliances and the support of more advantaged folk in poor people's protest movements, the authors show that the economically disadvantaged are not necessarily doomed to a life of deprivation and degradation. A better understanding of the concerns of the weak and the limits of current institutional politics will, it may be hoped, contribute to a more enlightened and just use of power in the years to come.

REFERENCES

Bourque, Susan, and Kay Warren
    1981   *Women of the Andes: Patriarchy and Social Change in Two Peruvian Towns.* Ann Arbor: University of Michigan Press.
Brintnall, Douglas
    1979   *Revolt against the Dead: The Modernization of a Mayan Community in the Highlands of Guatemala.* New York: Gordon & Breach.
Castells, Manuel
    1983   *The City and the Grass-Roots.* Berkeley and Los Angeles: University of California Press.
Davies, James
    1962   "Toward a Theory of Revolution." *American Sociological Review* 27 (February): 5–19.
Eckstein, Susan
    1977   *The Poverty of Revolution: The State and Urban Poor in Mexico.* Princeton, N.J.: Princeton University Press.
    1982   "The Impact of Revolution on Social Welfare in Latin America." *Theory and Society* 11 : 43–94.
Feierabend, Ivo, and Rosalind Feierabend
    1971   "Aggressive Behaviors within Polities, 1948–1962." In *When Men Revolt and Why: A Reader in Political Violence and Revolution,* edited by James Davies, pp. 229–49. New York: Free Press.

Gamson, William
   1986   *Political Discourse and Collective Action.* Boston College, Social Economy and Social Justice Program, Working Paper 4.
Gramsci, Antonio
   1971   *Selections from the Prison Notebooks.* Ed. and trans. Quinten Hore and Geoffrey Nowell Smith. London: Lawrence & Wishart.
Gurr, Ted
   1970   *Why Men Rebel.* Princeton, N.J.: Princeton University Press.
Hoffer, Eric
   1951   *The True Believer: Thoughts on the Nature of Mass Movements.* New York: Harper & Row.
Hvalkof, Soren, and Peter Aaby, eds.
   1981   *Is God an American? An Anthropological Perspective on the Missionary Work of the Summer Institute of Linguistics.* Copenhagen: International Work Group for Indigenous Affairs and Survival International.
Jenkins, J. Craig
   1983   "Resource Mobilization Theory and the Study of Social Movements." *Annual Review of Sociology* 9:527–53.
Kelley, Jonathan, and Herbert Klein
   1981   *Revolution and the Rebirth of Inequality: A Theory Applied to the Bolivian National Revolution.* Berkeley and Los Angeles: University of California Press.
Kornhauser, William
   1959   *The Politics of Mass Society.* Glencoe, Ill.: Free Press.
Lamphere, Louise
   1974   "Strategies, Cooperation, and Conflict among Women in Domestic Groups." In *Woman, Culture & Society,* edited by Michelle Rosaldo and Louise Lamphere, pp. 97–112. Stanford, Calif.: Stanford University Press.
Levine, Daniel H., ed.
   1986   *Religion and Political Conflict in Latin America.* Chapel Hill: University of North Carolina Press.
Lipset, S. M.
   1981   *Political Man: The Social Bases of Politics.* Baltimore: Johns Hopkins University Press.
McAdam, Doug, John McCarthy, and Mayer Zald
   1988   "Social Movements and Collective Behavior: Building Macro-Micro Bridges." In *Handbook of Sociology,* edited by Neil Smelser and Ron Burt. Beverly Hills, Calif.: SAGE, forthcoming.
Marx, Karl
   1959   "The Eighteenth Brumaire of Louis Bonaparte." In *Marx & Engels.* edited by Lewis Feuer, pp. 318–48. Garden City, N.Y.: Doubleday.
Merton, Robert
   1961   *Social Theory and Social Structure.* New York: Basic Books.
Migdal, Joel
   1974   *Peasants, Politics, and Revolution.* Princeton, N.J.: Princeton University Press.

Mills, C. Wright
1959   *The Sociological Imagination.* New York: Oxford University Press.
Moore, Barrington, Jr.
1966   *Social Origins of Dictatorship and Democracy.* Boston: Beacon Press.
Olson, Mancur, Jr.
1965   *The Logic of Collective Action.* Cambridge, Mass.: Harvard University Press.
Paige, Jeffery
1975   *Agrarian Revolution: Social Movements and Export Agriculture in the Underdeveloped World.* New York: Free Press.
Piven, Frances, and Richard Cloward
1979   *Poor People's Movements: Why They Succeed, How They Fail.* New York: Vintage Books.
Popkin, Samuel
1979   *The Rational Peasant.* Berkeley and Los Angeles: University of California Press.
Portes, Alejandro, and Michael Johns
1986   "Class Structure and Spatial Polarization: An Assessment of Recent Urban Trends in Latin America." *Journal of Economic and Social Geography* 77:378–88.
Scott, James
1976   *The Moral Economy of the Peasant: Rebellion and Subsistence in Southeast Asia.* New Haven, Conn.: Yale University Press.
1986   *Weapons of the Weak: Everyday Forms of Peasant Resistance.* New Haven, Conn.: Yale University Press.
Shorter, Edward, and Charles Tilly
1974   *Strikes in France, 1830–1968.* New York: Cambridge University Press.
Singer, Paul
1982   "Neighbourhood Movements in São Paulo." In *Towards a Political Economy of Urbanization in Third World Countries.* Delhi, India: Oxford University Press.
Skocpol, Theda
1979   *States and Revolution: A Comparative Analysis of France, Russia, and China.* New York: Cambridge University Press.
Smelser, Neil
1963   *Theory of Collective Behavior.* New York: Free Press.
Stevens, Evelyn
1973   "Marianismo: The Other Face of Machismo." In *Female and Male in Latin America,* edited by Ann Pescatello, pp. 89–102. Pittsburgh: University of Pittsburgh Press.
Thompson, E. P.
1971   "The Moral Economy of the English Crowd in the Eighteenth Century." *Past and Present* 50 (February): 76–136.
Tilly, Charles
1978   *From Mobilization to Revolution.* Reading, Mass: Addison-Wesley.
Tilly, Charles, Louise Tilly, and Richard Tilly
1975   *The Rebellious Century.* Cambridge, Mass.: Harvard University Press.

Tilly, Charles, and Louise Tilly, eds.
  1981   *Class Conflict and Collective Action*. Beverly Hills, Calif.: SAGE.
Vélez-Ibañez, Carlos
  1983   *Rituals of Marginality*. Berkeley and Los Angeles: University of Cali-
            fornia Press.
Véliz, Claudio
  1980   *The Centralist Tradition of Latin America*. Princeton, N.J.: Princeton
            University Press.
Wagley, Charles
  1969   "From Caste to Class in North Brazil." In *Comparative Perspectives in
            Race Relations*, edited by Melvin Tumin, pp. 47–62. Boston: Little,
            Brown.
Walton, John
  1984   *Reluctant Rebels*. New York: Columbia University Press.
Winn, Peter
  1986   *Weavers of Revolution: The Yarur Workers and Chile's Road to Socialism*.
            New York: Oxford University Press.
Wolf, Eric
  1969   *Peasant Wars in the Twentieth Century*. New York. Harper & Row.
Zapata, Francisco
  1977   "Strikes and Political Systems in Latin America." Paper presented
            at the Latin American Studies Association Meeting, Houston,
            November.

CHAPTER TWO

Peru's Sendero Luminoso Rebellion: Origins and Trajectory

Cynthia McClintock

In mid 1982, Edith Lagos, a 19-year-old Peruvian guerrilla commander, died in a battle with the police in the small, remote southern highlands city of Ayacucho. More people turned out for her funeral than for any other event in recent Ayacucho history. The crowd was estimated at between 15,000 and 30,000 people in a city of only about 70,000. Hand-carved statuettes of Lagos sold briskly in the Ayacucho market.

Lagos was a leader of the Sendero Luminoso (Shining Path) guerrillas. To most analysts, Sendero Luminoso is the ugliest guerrilla movement that has ever appeared in Latin America. Savage, sectarian, and fanatical, it is compared to Pol Pot's Khmer Rouge rather than to the Sandinistas or the Farabundo Martí National Liberation movement (FMLN) in El Salvador. Without military provocation, Sendero initiated armed struggle in 1980 against an elected government considered democratic by most criteria. Sendero labels every past and present Peruvian government "fascist" and "reactionary," though virtually all other analysts see many differences among these governments and consider some of them to have been reformist and progressive. Claiming to be Maoist, it has refused to work with other Marxist groups in the country, and it has assassinated officials from Marxist and social democratic parties as readily as those from conservative parties.

Sendero repudiates not only the United States but also the Soviet Union and, perhaps most virulently, the current Chinese leadership. Until recently, it rarely sought to explain its actions or its vision of Peru's

I would like to thank Susan Eckstein for her many helpful comments on the drafts of this article. I am also grateful to the Graduate School of Arts and Sciences and the School of Public and International Affairs at George Washington University for their support of my summer research in Peru in 1985 and 1986, which was crucial to the collection of data for this study.

future. Yet for several years Sendero Luminoso apparently enjoyed the support of a majority of the people in Ayacucho. The primary concern of this chapter is to understand how this apparent anomaly happened—how guerrillas considered "lunatic" and "terrorist" not only by conservatives but also by many Peruvian Marxists could have gained substantial popular backing in one region of the country. Core support has come from various "provinces" (the rough equivalent of counties in the United States) in the Ayacucho "department" (the rough equivalent of a state in the United States). About sixteen provinces in Ayacucho and the neighboring departments of Apurímac and Huancavelica have been classified as an "emergency zone," where the military has been put in control and many constitutional rights have been suspended in an effort to defeat Sendero.

The evidence of popular support for Sendero is virtually irrefutable and comes from various sources. Consider, for example, electoral data for the region. In the May 1980 national elections and the November 1980 municipal elections, abstention rates were higher in Ayacucho than in any other department. The rate was almost 50 percent in November 1980, about twenty percentage points higher than the national average (Tuesta Soldevilla 1983:61). While abstention might have reflected fear of Senderista retaliation, null and blank voting would not have, and the percentage of null and blank votes was also extraordinarily high in the emergency zone departments. In the May 1980 election the null and blank vote was 42 percent of the total cast in Ayacucho; the rate nationwide was 27 percent (Presidencia de la República 1981:101–7). Such patterns were new for Ayacucho.[1] Amid fears of violence, the November 1983 municipal elections were not even held in most of Ayacucho. In the one province where balloting was possible, abstention was over 50 percent, and 56 percent of all votes were null or blank. The victorious party, PADIN, was the only party to promise amnesty for the guerrillas; it won 19 percent of the vote (González 1984:34).

Journalists have also reported support for Sendero from their interviews in the region. In mid 1982 a journalist asked "all those who wanted to converse" in Ayacucho whether or not they thought Sendero was a peasant movement and whether or not it counted on support from the population; according to the journalist, the response was virtually unanimous: "It's a movement supported by the youngest peasants. The older ones are resigned to their lot, but they do back their kids" (González 1982:47). Also in the early 1980s, an Ayacucho police chief estimated

1. In 1963, for example, the abstention rate was only 18 percent, not a great deal higher than the national average of 11 percent; the percentage of null and blank votes was apparently below 1 percent (Larson and Bergman 1969:383–84). Although there were many new voters in the 1980s elections, who were more likely to be illiterates with a tendency to spoil their ballots, this was the case throughout Peru, not just in Ayacucho.

that "80 percent of the townspeople of Ayacucho sympathize with Sendero" (*Andean Report,* March 1984, p. 47).

Through 1982, most Ayacucho peasants refused to report on Senderistas in the vicinity, whom they supplied with food and shelter.[2] Government intelligence personnel were rarely able to secure information from the emergency zone peasantry about Senderista leaders.

The Sendero guerrillas themselves are currently estimated to number between 2,000 and 15,000; an intermediate estimate is most common.[3] At first, most militants were young, and many were students or former students, often from peasant backgrounds; by 1986, however, recruits came from diverse age and occupational groups.[4] The number of actual peasant combatants is small.

The toll of the guerrilla war has been very high. Between 1980 and 1987, political violence took more lives in Peru than in any other Latin American nation save El Salvador, Nicaragua, and Colombia. According to official figures, the toll between May 1980 and December 1987 was 10,541 lives.[5] Among the dead were 283 civilian authorities and 568 security personnel.[6] Most of the rest were ordinary folk, especially Andean peasants and Senderista suspects.

The violence has gradually affected more people and more parts of the country. Between May 1980 and December 1987, a total of 9,534 attacks were recorded.[7] During the first four years of the violence, almost one-third of all attacks took place in the department of Ayacucho, versus 23 percent in Lima.[8] In contrast, in 1985–87, the largest number of attacks (more than 30 percent) occurred in Lima and the second largest percentage in Ayacucho.[9] In the early 1980s, the only provinces declared

2. Informal interviews with peasant leaders (not from Ayacucho) during various periods in the early 1980s.

3. The 15,000 maximum figure is Sendero's own. See Sandra Woy-Hazleton and William A. Hazleton, "International Human Rights Concerns: The Challenge of Guerrilla Terrorism in Peru" (Paper presented at the International Studies Association Meeting, April 15–18), p. 2. For the government's estimates, which average about 5,000, see *New York Times,* 23 April 1987; *In These Times,* 1–7 April 1987, p. 11.

4. According to data provided by the Dirección General de Inteligencia of the Interior Ministry, of the 1,765 persons arrested on charges of terrorism between January 1986 and October 1986, slightly fewer than half were under twenty-five years of age; 34 percent were workers, 21 percent were unemployed, 18 precent were students, and 11 percent were white-collar employees. Similar figures for earlier years showed a larger representation for students; see *El Comercio,* 4 April 1985, p. A8.

5. *Peru Report,* vol. 1, no. 2, p. 42, and *Caretas,* no. 987, 30 December 1987, p. 28.

6. *Caretas,* no. 884/885, 30 December 1985, pp. 32–35; *Caretas,* 29 December 1986, pp. 17–19; *Caretas,* 30 December 1987, p. 28.

7. *Idem.*

8. *Caretas,* no. 807, 9 July 1984, p. 10.

9. *Caretas,* no. 884/885, 30 December 1985, p. 34; *Caretas,* 29 December 1986, p. 17; and Diego García-Sayan, "Violencia Política y Pacificación en el Perú" (unpublished paper, Lima). 1987 data are January–June only.

as "emergency zones" were in the southern highlands; by late 1987, the number was over thirty provinces—more than double the early 1980s figure—including Lima, Callao, and provinces in the northern upper-jungle coca-growing region (Americas Watch 1987: 5).

As the violence expanded, its context and character changed. In early 1983 the state launched a massive counterinsurgency campaign in Ayacucho, repressing the rebellion to a considerable degree. It is likely that more than one Sendero subsequently emerged. Some Senderistas went to the nearby southern highlands area of Puno, especially to the provinces of Azangaro and Melgar, where they sought to establish the kind of peasant base they had enjoyed in Ayacucho, but their success was limited (González 1986; *Latin America Regional Reports, Andean Group,* 31 July 1986, pp. 2–3). Another Sendero may be in the cities now, especially in Lima, building support in squatter settlements and public universities. Yet another Sendero, one that takes advantage of political and economic opportunities presented by Peru's drug trade, is active in the northern upper-jungle coca-growing region.

The analysis in this chapter draws on various sources. First, it draws on my own interviews in Lima, Huancayo, and Trujillo at numerous intervals between 1980 and 1987. Economic data and electoral data are culled from numerous publications. For information on the role of Sendero in the Ayacucho university, the works of Palmer (1985) and (1986) and Degregori (1986) have been especially important. Also, I have been carrying out research on an agrarian cooperative in Peru's central highlands since 1973 and have gained the confidence of a number of people there who are familiar with the problems of Ayacucho and Sendero. Members of my original 1973 research team have from time to time carried out informal surveys in parts of this cooperative; one site in the department of Huancavelica, which we have called "Varya," has allegedly become a pro-Senderista community. The surveys are "informal" in the sense that they were nonrandom and are relatively small.

SENDERO'S ESTABLISHMENT OF A SOCIAL BASE IN THE SOUTHERN HIGHLANDS, PRE-1983

Ideally, a social science analysis of a revolutionary movement would determine the precise importance of various economic, political, and social factors. This scholarly task is difficult, however, as revolutionary movements are not, of course, laboratory experiments where specific contingencies may be manipulated. For the relatively few cases of real-world revolutionary movements, the scholar cannot always isolate economic, political, and social factors from one another. Yet the southern highlands region that provided Sendero's original support has economic, political, and social characteristics that are *all* different from those of Peru's other regions and that would *all* be considered to make backing for guerrilla groups more likely.

Nor can the scholar readily measure "revolutionary leaders' skill"—in this case, the effectiveness of Sendero's strategies. Certainly, in comparison to the guerrillas of the 1960s, Sendero was much more successful in building mass support in the southern highlands. A rigorous assessment of Sendero's effectiveness is, however, impossible. There were rival Marxist groups to Sendero in the southern highlands in the 1970s and 1980s, but not rival guerrilla groups, and so it cannot be shown that citizens preferred Sendero to another band. Also, after 1982, as peasants became more aware of many characteristics of Sendero—especially its dogmatism and brutality—they withdrew their support. Furthermore, Sendero has not to date achieved the same kind of success—broad and deep support among peasants and students—in any other rural area. Sendero's strategy may thus only have been appropriate in a small, unusual part of the country at a particular time. Sendero's approach may have facilitated gaining mass support in one region, but not winning state power nationwide.

Thus, I cannot provide here a rank-order of conditions important to the emergence of Sendero Luminoso. I think, however, that it is possible by various techniques to identify a set of factors that all seem to have been necessary to the growth of support for Sendero through 1982. First, the "emergency zone" where mass support emerged—first Ayacucho and then Huancavelica and Apurímac in the southern highlands—may be contrasted to other areas. Second, changes in economic, political, and social factors, as well as in the character of guerrilla organization, can be assessed from the period of the 1960s, when revolutionary groups were defeated rather quickly, to the 1980s, when they have not been.

My analysis below identifies four factors as necessary to the development of popular support for Sendero in the southern highlands prior to 1983: (1) absolute economic decline and a real threat to subsistence; (2) politicization of various groups during the 1970s leading more peasants to blame their plight on the government; (3) shrewd organizational strategies on the part of Sendero; and (4) a weak and inappropriate response by the Peruvian state. As all these conditions applied at the same time, no one can be singled out as most important, or sufficient. I believe that all four were necessary, and all together sufficient.

The following subsections deal in turn with each of these four factors. The final subsection discusses factors that cannot now be empirically demonstrated to have influenced popular support in the southern highlands—in particular, cultural factors and the rise.of a new cash crop,

TABLE 2.1 Regional Inequalities in Peru

	Annual Farm Income Per Capita (thousands of soles, 1961)	Life Expectancy (years at birth, 1979)	Adult Illiteracy (percentage, 1981)	Without Potable Water (percentage, 1981)	Population Per Physician (1981)	Caloric Intake (percentage of FAO requirements, 1980)
Southern Highlands[a]	3.8	51	45	84	18,000	—
Ayacucho	3.3	51	45	85	16,779	—
Northern and Central Highlands[b]	8.1	57	28	76	8,236	72[e]
Coast[c]	11.2	63	13	48	1,749	—
Lima	30.2	70	5	26	525	96
Poor Southern African Nations[d]	—	50	57	—	21,124	92

SOURCES: Consejo Nacional de Población 1985; except potable water figures from Banco Central de Reserva 1986a:22, farm income per capita from Webb 1977:119–29, and caloric intake from World Bank 1981:35.

[a] Averages for the five poorest southern highlands departments: Ayacucho, Huancavelica, Cuzco, Apurímac, and Puno.

[b] Averages for the three exclusively highlands departments: Junín, Pasco, and Cajamarca.

[c] Averages for the five main coastal departments: Piura, Lambayeque, La Libertad, Lima, and Ica.

[d] Averages for low-income nations in Africa south of the Sahara, from World Bank 1983: vol. 2, 152–55. Estimates were the most recent available, generally late 1970s or early 1980s.

[e] Figure is for "northern highlands" only. Exact area is unspecified.

coca. (Subsequently, coca has clearly been an important factor in other regions, not so much because of the emergence of the coca industry as because of U.S.-backed attempts at its eradication).

Economic Decline and Threat to Subsistence

In the early 1980s peasants in Peru's southern highlands faced what was possibly the most serious threat to their subsistence of the twentieth century. Living standards plummeted throughout the nation; in Ayacucho, Apurímac, and Huancavelica, where living standards were already much lower than in the rest of the country, the decline meant virtual starvation. Poverty was both relative to other regions and absolute. Scott (1976) has emphasized threats to subsistence as the sine qua non of peasant rebellion, and the Peruvian case bears out his argument well.

Table 2.1 shows that Peru's southern highlands are a region as poor as some of the poorest countries in the world. In 1961 agricultural incomes in the southern highlands were less than half those in the northern and central highlands, and less than one-seventh of incomes in Lima. Agricultural incomes in three Ayacucho provinces of early core support for Sendero—Huanta, Huamanga, and Cangallo—were lower than for all but 9 of Peru's 155 provinces (Webb 1977:119–29). There are about thirty-five times as many people per doctor in the southern highlands as in Lima. The lack of physicians was a major reason for life expectancy rates that were as low as in sub-Saharan Africa.

The major reason for the poverty in the southern highlands is that the departments are heavily agricultural in a region ill-suited to agriculture. In Ayacucho, Huancavelica, and Apurímac, over three-quarters of the labor force was employed in agriculture as of 1961 (Larson and Bergman 1969:324–25). Yet it is estimated that in Ayacucho only 4 percent of the total land area of the department is used for agriculture (Gitlitz 1984a). Most of the rest of the land is too arid, too stony, too precipitous, or too high. Ayacucho's land/family ratio is probably one of the worst among Peruvian departments, and Peru's ratio as a whole is the second worst in Latin America, after El Salvador (Martínez and Tealdo 1982:39).

The central highlands (Junín and Pasco) and the northern highlands (Cajamarca) seem better off than the southern highlands because there are more alternatives to farming. The greater prosperity of the central highlands, with per capita farm incomes at about 9,000 soles in 1961, is probably due to the mining and commerce in the region (Webb 1977:119–29). In the northern highlands, where per capita resident farm incomes were about 6,400 soles in 1961, the greater prosperity seems due to easier access to the coast and a prosperous dairy industry in the department's capital (Gitlitz 1984b:7).

Living standards in Ayacucho, Apurímac, and Huancavelica are also below those in Cuzco, the southern highlands department that has not been severely affected by guerrilla actions. In the government's 1972 and 1981 maps of poverty, Apurímac, Ayacucho, and Huancavelica were the three poorest departments in both eras; Cuzco was the eighth poorest in 1972 and the sixth in 1981, of twenty-four (Banco Central de Reserva 1982 and 1986b).[10] Further data are reported in table 2.2. It should also be noted that tourism has boomed in Cuzco since the early 1970s, and that some of the income from tourism is not reported in Cuzco. Cuzco has benefited in recent years not only from increased tourism but also from a more significant agrarian reform and better access to the coast.

Not only are peasants in Ayacucho, Apurímac, and Huancavelica poor relative to other Peruvians, but they became poorer in the past decade. Per capita highlands farm income dropped from an index figure of 106 for 1950 and 1961 to 100 for 1972 and further to 82 for 1980 (McClintock 1984: 59–61). Whereas per capita incomes were estimated to be about U.S. $100 annually in Ayacucho in 1961, by 1979 they were about $60 or $70, and they were even lower by the early 1980s (Gitlitz 1984a:2).

Many peasants perceived a crisis. For example, in Varya, the allegedly pro-Sendero community in Huancavelica that I studied, peasants were very negative about their community's progress. In my research team's informal survey, 84 percent of twenty-five respondents said in 1980 that the community's progress in recent years had been "bad."[11] Varya peasants were also asked, "What have been the achievements in your community in recent years?" Despite the optimistic phraseology, 92 percent of the respondents replied, "None." I asked the same questions in 1980 at two other sites, one a coastal cooperative and the other a prosperous central highlands peasant community. Of fifty-five respondents in these areas, only 7 percent said that progress had been "bad."

Subsistence became threatened in the southern highlands. As of 1980, daily caloric intake was estimated at below 70 percent of minimum FAO requirements in the southern highlands (McClintock 1984:58–59). In a study made by the Peruvian government, daily per capita intake among lower-class people throughout the country was found to have plummeted from 1,934 calories per capita in 1972 to 1,486 in 1979 (Fernández Baca 1982:89–90). Most disturbing of all are some official data for particularly poor zones in the southern highlands. As of roughly 1980,

10. In the 1972 map Cajamarca was tied for third place with Huancavelica, but this finding is atypical. See, for example, the 1972 ENCA (Encuesta Nacional de Consumo de Alimentos) study, reported in Havens et al. 1983:20.

11. This was a nonrandom application, primarily to men, of a brief questionnaire. For further information on the nature of these surveys and a description of Varya, see McClintock 1981:102–5.

TABLE 2.2 Living Standards, Ayacucho versus Cuzco

	Ayacucho	Cuzco
Gross domestic product (per capita, in real intis, 1979)[a]	54	99
Gross domestic product (per capita, in real intis, 1984)	45	99
Illiteracy rate, 1961	73%	67%
Illiteracy rate, 1972	56	48
Illiteracy rate, 1981	45	37
Without potable water, 1972	93	89
Without potable water, 1981	85	76
Population per physician, 1981	16,779	5,904

SOURCES: For gross domestic product data in 1979 and 1984, Instituto Nacional de Estadística 1987: 94; for 1961, Larson and Bergman 1969:364; for 1972, Amat y León 1981:37–39; for 1981, illiteracy and potable water, Banco Central de Reserva 1986a:22, 24; population per physician, Consejo Nacional de Población 1985.
[a] Intis became the official currency in 1985.

individuals in these zones were apparently consuming as little as 420 calories a day (González 1982:43).

The World Bank characterized the nutritional situation in 1980 as "bad" (World Bank 1981:35). By 1983, a year in which the Sendero movement grew considerably, it was even worse. Minimal subsistence conditions were reduced further by natural disasters. Warm ocean currents (El Niño) brought floods to Peru's northern coast and drought to Peru's southern highlands. While the southeastern highlands department of Puno was the one most devastated by the drought, almost all the southern highlands region, including Ayacucho, was seriously affected.[12] In the country as a whole, 1983 agricultural production fell by about 15 percent, and potato production more; in the southern highlands, potato production can be estimated to have fallen between 40 and 50 percent.[13] The Ecumenical Committee on the Andes described the situation in the following terms:

> In the southern Andes, severe drought completely destroyed the harvest, forcing peasants to consume surplus seed intended for this year's planting. Starvation is rampant among subsistence farmers; illness, particularly tuberculosis, has spread alarmingly. The price of basic foodstuffs rose dramatically in regional and national markets, affecting the urban

12. See *Andean Focus* (a publication of the Ecumenical Committee on the Andes), no. 2 (November–December 1983), and *Latin America Weekly Report* (WR-83-23), 26 August 1983, p. 9.
13. Calculated from *Latin America Weekly Report* (WR-84-02), 13 January 1984, p. 11; *Latin America Weekly Report* (WR-83-23), 26 August 1983, p. 9; and *Latin American Regional Reports, Andean Group* (RA-84-02), 2 March 1984, p. 6.

poor. Unemployment increased in the agricultural sector (subsistence farmers traditionally work as paid laborers at harvest time). . . . News reports documented cases of peasants selling their children for $25.(*Andean Focus,* November–December 1983, p. 1)

While many peasants sought to migrate, the vast majority failed to find jobs. Unemployment was very high. Nationwide, unemployment and underemployment, which had been less than 50 percent of the work force in the early 1970s, skyrocketed to about 59 percent in 1983 (World Bank 1981:6; Panfichi 1984:70). Peasants had long depended on seasonal employment to supplement their agricultural incomes, but the work was less and less available, and wages were lower (see below).

Employment in coca cultivation and production was probably the most lucrative alternative, but insufficient jobs were available even in this new boom industry, which in any case was centered in the northern, rather than southern, highlands. Overall, a much smaller percentage of peasants in Peru seem to have participated in the benefits from coca production than in Bolivia, where the crop has had a substantial positive effect on peasant incomes (Healy 1985). "Guesstimates" are in the range of 5 percent of peasants participating in Peru versus 10 percent in Bolivia.[14]

Politicization in the Southern Highlands

During the 1960s and 1970s political life was transformed in Peru's southern highlands. For most of the twentieth century, peasants in the area did not see their problems in a national political context. They were illiterate and isolated from the national political arena, dominated by a traditional elite who owned the haciendas and mines of the area. Suddenly, however, for various reasons these conditions changed: young people from the area were able to secure an education and learn about the wider world, and they became more sensitive to the gross social and economic inequalities in Peru; they were also able to communicate their perceptions to the Ayacucho peasants.

Until the 1960s very few people in Ayacucho were able to gain an understanding of Peru's society and economy. In 1961 illiteracy affected over 70 percent of the adult population in Ayacucho, Huancavelica, and Apurímac—the highest rate in the country (Larson and Bergman 1969: 364). Contact with the coast was much more limited for Ayacucho and Apurímac than for any other highlands department. Ayacucho was not connected directly with the coast until the mid 1960s, when the Vía de los Libertadores (Highway of the Liberators) was built to Pisco (Palmer

14. Interviews with Kevin Healy, Roldolfo Osores, Luis Deustua, and other analysts in 1986.

1986:134). At this time, there were only two buses for local transportation in Ayacucho and fewer than a hundred cars and trucks (Palmer
1986:133).

Not only did peasants and townspeople thus rarely travel out of the
region, but people from the coast rarely reached Ayacucho. In particular, political activists did not seek to mobilize the people of this region. In
the 1963 presidential election, the percentage of the total population
that voted was lower—at between 6 and 8 percent—in Ayacucho, Apurímac, and Huancavelica than in any other department in the country;
the rates were slightly higher in Cuzco and Puno, and much higher in
the northern and central highlands (Larson and Bergman, 1969:383).
In much of the northern and central highlands—Cajamarca and Pasco—
the political party APRA (American Popular Revolutionary Alliance)
worked successfully to build a popular base, capturing solid majorities
at the polls in the early 1960s (Larson and Bergman 1969:381, 384; Gitlitz 1984b). In the southern highlands, however, APRA was relatively
inactive.

Union organizers and Marxist political leaders were rare throughout
Peru during this period. When they sought to mobilize peasants in highland regions, they were usually identified quickly by hacienda authorities
and barred from the vicinity (Cotler 1970; McClintock 1981:64–83).
While there were fewer large haciendas in the Ayacucho area than in
most of the highlands, the traditional landed elite, in alliance with the
Catholic church, seemed to maintain a conservative political hegemony
in much of the area (Palmer 1986:133–34; Degregori 1986: 237–38).

Change began after 1959. In that year the National University of San
Cristóbal of Huamanga was reopened in Ayacucho (it had been closed
since 1885). The university grew rapidly, with an open admissions policy; by 1970 it employed at least 300 faculty and enrolled perhaps as
many as 15,000 students (Palmer 1986:136). At this time, about 70 percent of the students came from the department of Ayacucho itself; many
were the children of peasants, the first in their families to gain a higher
education (Palmer 1986:138).

The implications of the university's emergence were numerous and important, and they illustrate why—as Timothy Wickham-Crowley notes in
his comparative study in chapter 4—guerrilla movements have emerged
in countries with expanding university systems. With the arrival of many
leftist scholars, the traditional hegemony of the landed and religious
elite eroded, and political debate intensified, primarily among various
groups of leftists. The opportunity to gain a higher education greatly
raised students' professional expectations, but, as a result of Peru's
post-1975 economic depression, very few of them were able to realize
these expectations. Jobs were scarce, and a graduate of a provincial high-

lands university was rarely competitive. Commented one student: "No one gets a job anywhere with a degree from the University of Huamanga" (González 1982:46).

A considerable number of the university's graduates became teachers. Ironically, as Palmer (1986) emphasizes, education was the only major program not slighted by the Peruvian government during this period. By 1981 there were 4,741 teachers and 1,450 schools in the department of Ayacucho (Palmer 1986:138). In 1961 literacy stood at a mere 21 percent among persons aged seventeen and older; by 1981 it was 56 percent of persons of fifteen and older (Larson and Bergman 1969:363–64; Palmer 1985:84). This percentage is still increasing (Palmer 1986:138).

Understanding of the national political arena also increased as a result of improvements in transportation and communication, as well as migration. The new road to the coast greatly facilitated transport. In 1974 electrical supply was improved in the city of Ayacucho, and television arrived shortly thereafter. Migration rates out of Ayacucho, Apurímac, and Huancavelica have traditionally been among the highest in the country, presumably because of the poverty in these departments (Larson and Bergman 1969:309; Presidencia de la República 1981:475). In the 1970s, as a result of the economic depression in the country as a whole, some of these migrants began to return to Ayacucho, and apparently brought with them a more radical worldview.[15]

Another very important factor in the politicization of the Ayacucho peasants was the character of agrarian reform in the area. During the 1960s and 1970s agrarian reform was the banner of two successive governments—the democratically elected Belaúnde government (1963–68) and the reformist military government under General Juan Velasco (1968–75). Ultimately, however, the economic promise of the reform was not fulfilled in the emergency zone departments. Although interpretations of the reform in the area certainly vary and have not been fully documented, many citizens seemed to decide that reform had not succeeded in the region and that a more revolutionary approach would be necessary.

In the early 1960s the Acción Popular political party and its presidential candidate, Fernando Belaúnde Terry, won the popular vote in the southern highlands departments, to a considerable degree on the basis of his promise of agrarian reform. At this time, many politically attuned peasants spurned guerrillas in the belief that agrarian reform was a better option than revolution (Handelman 1975; Craig 1969; Tullis 1970). This promise went almost totally unfulfilled during Belaúnde's

15. Conversation with Billie Jean Isbell, who said that a study by Teodoro Altamirano is reporting results of this nature.

five years in office. In Ayacucho, a mere fifty-four families benefited from the government's reform (Palmer 1973:191).

Agrarian reform was also a key promise of the Velasco military government later in the decade; under this administration, a sweeping reform was, in fact, implemented in most of the country. By many criteria the Velasco government's reform was the most ambitious in Latin America save Cuba; virtually all large haciendas were swept from the countryside (McClintock 1981). In Ayacucho, however, the impact of the reform was more limited than in almost any other part of the country (see table 2.3).

Why was the impact of the reform scant in Ayacucho? Primarily because there were very few prosperous estates in the department. The value of the property expropriated and transferred to peasant beneficiaries in the Ayacucho Agrarian Zone (which included parts of Huancavelica and Apurímac as well as Ayacucho) was a mere 4,900 soles per family, or less than U.S. $250, compared to twice as much in Cuzco, four times as much in Junín, twelve times as much in Puno, and thirty-two times as much in Lima (McClintock 1984:66). The absolute number of haciendas that could be transformed into viable peasant cooperatives was also small. By and large, such haciendas had been expropriated and restructured by 1976; as table 2.3 shows, in Ayacucho the number of enterprises in this category was smaller than anywhere else in the Peruvian highlands. The number of beneficiaries was also modest—barely more than 10 percent of the rural population.

Unfortunately, precise data comparing peasant families in Ayacucho to peasant families elsewhere in terms of their landowning status are not available. Calculation is complicated by the fact that agrarian reform zones did not correspond to departments. However, it seems that the number of reform-based cooperative workers was small in Ayacucho, and the number of families in indigenous peasant communities high (Palmer 1973:192–94; Bonilla 1986:5).

Yet, although the material impact of the reform was slight in Ayacucho, its political impact was large. As mentioned previously, the traditional *hacendados* had been able to maintain political hegemony in the region and to control access to much of the countryside, barring leftist political organizers. With the agrarian reform, the *hacendados* and their staff left. Land titles, which previously had often been disputed between haciendas and peasant communities, became secure. The feudal services that many hacienda managers had required from peasants, again in both haciendas and communities, no longer applied. Many peasants throughout the Peruvian highlands felt autonomous for the first time. From the guerrillas' perspective, tactical mobility was greatly enhanced. A large new political space was opened to political organizers.

TABLE 2.3 The Impact of Agrarian Reform in
Highlands Peru

	Reform Beneficiaries (percentage of rural population)	Number of Cooperatives as of December 1975
Ayacucho	11%	9
Apurímac	14	20
Huancavelica	36	11
Cuzco	39	50
Puno	15	30
Junín	37	24
Cajamarca	6	25
North Coast[a]	54	54

SOURCES: Number of family beneficiaries by department from "Reforma agraria en cifras," Documento de Trabajo no. 11, 1975, from the Ministry of Agriculture. This number is multiplied by five to indicate the total number of beneficiaries, and then divided by rural population figures for 1972 given in Presidencia de la República 1984:629.
[a] Averages for La Libertad and Lambayeque.

In the case of previous Latin American agrarian reforms, governments have been able to establish new political institutions in the countryside to channel demands and coopt unrest. For example, during the 1930s and 1940s, the Mexican government forged the strong grass-roots links of its ruling party, the PRI; during the 1960s, the Venezuelan government achieved a similar political base for the political party Acción Democrática. In contrast, the Velasco government failed to build such a political institution.

The Velasco regime tried: in mid 1971 the "social mobilization" agency SINAMOS was launched. In many respects, SINAMOS was to have fulfilled the traditional role of the progovernment political party; yet it survived for only a few years. The reasons for the failure of the military government's political plan are various and complex (McClintock and Lowenthal 1983). One problem was military factionalism, which led to ideological and organizational confusion at the grass roots. Also, by 1976 Peru was in the midst of a grave economic crisis, and resources were no longer available for rural organization.

While the government did not succeed in mobilizing the peasantry, other political groups were able to operate more effectively in the highlands. Two peasant confederations became active. The National Agrarian Confederation (CNA) was established in 1974 under official auspices; it claimed to include as many as twenty departmental federations and 144 provincial agrarian leagues during the mid 1970s, with a total membership of about 170,000 peasants (Matos Mar and Mejía 1978: 120). Some top military government officials had apparently hoped that the CNA would provide a vehicle for government control over the peasantry, but the CNA resisted such a role. After a leftist peasant leader from Cuzco was elected CNA president in 1977 and the confederation began to criticize the government more vehemently and call for further land redistributions, the government dissolved the CNA. The CNA continued on its own, however, and established close ties to the Partido Socialista Revolucionario (PSR), a pro-Velasquista party that is currently a member of the Izquierda Unida (United Left) coalition. A second confederation, the Peruvian Peasant Confederation (CCP) also grew a great deal during the 1970s. The CCP, which was tied to the Marxist Vanguardia Revolucionaria in the 1970s, is generally considered to be to the left of the CNA, although many policy positions of the two federations have been similar. In 1978 the CCP claimed 250,000 members (Matos Mar and Mejía 1980:120).

Unfortunately, there is no major study of these two peasant confederations. From the work of Handelman (1981), García-Sayan (1982), and Bejar and Franco (1985), some characteristics of the two federations are evident, however. Both were active in demanding a more radical agrarian reform and, to this end, in supporting land invasions. The regions of greatest activity seem to have been Cuzco, Cajamarca, Piura, and the Andahuaylas province of Apurímac.

The messages of the two peasant confederations were of considerable interest to the people of the southern highlands. In part as a result of recruitment by the two confederations, the vote for the Marxist left skyrocketed in the Peruvian highlands. Whereas a Marxist left had barely existed in the elections of the early 1960s, in the 1978 Constituent Assembly elections (the first to be held since 1963), the Marxist left tallied almost 40 percent of the vote in most southern highlands departments, versus 29 percent nationwide (McClintock 1984:56). In 1980, in an election that was essentially a contest between the center-right Acción Popular and the center-left APRA parties, the vote for the Marxist left declined in the southern highlands; yet, in Ayacucho the Marxist tally was still 27 percent, greater than in any other department of the country except for two tiny mining departments on the southern border (McClintock 1984:56).

Was the overall effect of the peasant confederations to orient the highlands peasantry toward electoral politics and away from violent protest? The answer to the question is unclear. They may have in some areas, especially Cuzco; it is also interesting to note that they were unusually inactive in Ayacucho—perhaps because entry to the region was prohibited by Sendero, or perhaps simply because of the remoteness of

Ayacucho and the small number of haciendas there. On the other hand, militants of the large and militant Andahuaylas peasant federation, led by Julio César Mezzich in the department of Apurímac, are widely believed to have joined Sendero in the early 1980s (Berg 1986).

Certainly, however, by the 1970s peasants and students were much more inclined to ponder their lot and to criticize social injustice in Peru. They were much more attuned to the nature of government policies toward agriculture, and they correctly perceived that these policies, never very advantageous to the peasantry, were becoming ever more adverse (see below). More than ever before, peasants and students blamed their abject poverty on the government.

For example, in my informal surveys of the early 1980s, peasants were almost unanimous in criticizing the government for "not helping at all" (McClintock 1984:72–73). Thus, in one central highlands community in 1981, for example, 94 percent of seventeen respondents said that the government "did not help at all," versus a much smaller 37 percent in 1975. In two coastal cooperatives, the figures were 95 percent in 1983, versus 30 percent in 1974. Peasants' complaints were vehement, often full of rage and despair:

> There's no help from the government. On the contrary, everything costs more. Living has just become impossible and every day it's more difficult, especially when you have kids and depend solely on your land. Here, they've always forgotten us. There's no help. Exactly the opposite—the cost of everything has risen too much, and that's not the way to help. They're killing the poor people.

The Organizational Strategies of Sendero Luminoso

Sendero Luminoso was much shrewder and more dedicated than Peru's 1960 guerrillas, and much more effective in building an alliance between its militants and the peasantry. Sendero was correct in thinking that conditions were ripe for armed struggle. Although most Ayacucho communities that provided Sendero with its original base of support were unfamiliar with other Marxist groups, many communities in Huancavelica and Apurímac that were quickly attracted to Sendero were familiar with them, and apparently did prefer Sendero. However, during the 1980–82 period, peasants did not seem to anticipate a strong reaction from the state; we cannot know what their choices would have been if they had foreseen the post-1982 counterinsurgency offensive. Also, peasants have come to reject many Senderista characteristics.

As Gott (1971), Chaplin (1968), and Wickham-Crowley (in chapter 4 of this volume) have pointed out, Peru's revolutionary activists of the early 1960s were naive and impatient intellectuals. Generally of middle- to upper-class origin and from the coastal cities, these guerrillas knew very little about highlands Peru or its people. They were familiar neither with the Indian language nor with indigenous customs. Persuaded by the example of the 1959 Cuban revolution that they could mobilize the Andean peasantry relatively quickly and easily, they did not establish a political base in one place. Rather, they fanned out to different parts of Peru's central and southern mountains and jungle fringe, for the most part roving from place to place.

The guerrillas failed to realize that wandering, unprotected guerrilla bands, led by undisguised non-Indians, would be readily spotted by government authorities. The revolutionaries overlooked the differences between the Cuban Sierra Maestra and the Peruvian highlands; the Peruvian mountains are quite bare and thus provide little protection, especially against aerial surveillance. While these dangers were apparently not weighed by the guerrillas, they were by peasants in the area. Probably only a few hundred highlands peasants were recruited to the guerrilla cause at this time. Most actual recruits seem to have been jungle Indians, many of whom proved to be politically fickle. The military defeated the guerrillas in about two years; several thousand people were arrested, and about five hundred were killed.

Sendero's strategies were very different. Sendero's strategies diverged also from those of the other Marxist groups of the 1980s, which rejected guerrilla war in favor of participation in the new democratic system. Many Marxist parties continued to be dominated by upper-middle-class intellectuals and developed neither the commitment nor the resources for grass-roots organization that have characterized Sendero Luminoso.

Sendero's patience, dedication, and long-term perspective have been virtually unique among Peruvian revolutionary groups. Abimael Guzmán, the original leader of Sendero, was a political activist in Ayacucho for more than fifteen years before the start of violent actions. Guzmán came to Ayacucho in 1962 from the university at Arequipa, a large city off Peru's south coast, where he had earned degrees in philosophy and law with theses on the "Kantian Theory of Space" and "The Bourgeois Democratic State." He taught as a philosophy professor in the university's education department.

Until the late 1960s Guzmán's primary focus was mobilizing support in the Ayacucho university itself. Guzmán was reportedly charismatic and popular as a teacher. He devoted large amounts of time to political meetings and discussions at his home in Ayacucho. At first, Guzmán was a member of the Communist Party, which was pro-Soviet; in 1964, following the Sino-Soviet split, he as well as many other Communist Party members broke away to join Bandera Roja (Red Flag), one of Peru's first Maoist groups. In 1966, in the wake of steep cuts in the university budget, pro-Guzmán radicals won control of the university council and took various initiatives that garnered support for the Guzmán group among Ayacucho's urban population (Palmer 1986; Gitlitz 1984a; Degregori 1986).

Guzmán's decision to transform university students into revolutionary militants was not unique among Peruvian Marxists, but his effort was particularly shrewd and intensive. The focus upon the university's education program was truly brilliant, as many students would ultimately become teachers in the Ayacucho peasant communities, giving lessons not only in reading or mathematics but also in politics. As previously mentioned, there were almost 5,000 teachers in Ayacucho by 1981, perhaps as many as half of whom had studied in the Sendero-controlled education program in the university. Also, for about two years in the mid 1970s, Sendero controlled the large high-school education program at the university (Degregori 1986:250–59). The Guzmán group's success with the students was probably in part because they were inclined to radicalism owing to their origins in impoverished Ayacucho and their own slim chances of upward mobility; but the band's commitment to the students' radicalization was also important.

In the late 1960s the Guzmán faction was expelled from the Bandera Roja, apparently because Guzmán was demanding more immediate preparations for armed struggle. In 1970 the group commonly known as Sendero Luminoso, officially named the Communist Party of Peru, was established. At about the same time, much more intensive efforts were begun to build support among peasant communities in Ayacucho. Sendero militants fanned out from Ayacucho to the surrounding villages. Many worked as teachers, some took up odd jobs in their native communities, and perhaps a few became social workers or the like. In contrast to most Peruvian revolutionaries from middle-class backgrounds, the Senderistas were prepared to live austerely for many years in remote, bleak places. They learned the Indian language if they did not already know it, and they often married into the communities.

Sendero was also unique among Peruvian Marxist groups in its openness to young provincial militants as leaders. At its inception, Sendero included a substantial number of white, cosmopolitan intellectuals from the coast or large cities; but, by 1980, with the exception of Guzmán himself, the leadership was largely Ayacucho-born (Degregori 1986:248). The Senderistas were often considered "country bumpkins" by other Peruvian Marxists (Palmer 1986:128). It was apparently these young Ayacucho-born militants, such as Edith Lagos, who pressed the decision to begin armed struggle in 1980 (Degregori 1986:249).

Sendero was also much more careful than other guerrilla groups to provide its peasant allies with material benefits. Often in coordination with university extension programs, Senderistas provided regular paramedical services and agricultural advice, as well as education, to many Ayacucho communities for more than a decade. Between 1980 and 1982, too, it appears that Senderistas utilized violence selectively and that some of their violent actions at this time benefited the peasantry. During this period, Sendero blacklisted relatively well-to-do landowners, shopkeepers, and intermediaries, killing them or causing them to flee. Sendero would then distribute their property among villages, and debts to them would be cancelled. To recruits Sendero offered basic subsistence.

During this period Sendero was also careful to protect its peasant allies as well as its cadres. As early as the 1970s, government officials trying to enter Senderista territory were shot (Palmer 1985:81); a decade later assassinations and assassination threats against civilian authorities were so common that almost none remained in the area. Of course, if no government officials were in the region, they could not monitor organizations or individuals. However, during this period, Sendero was not confronting a counterinsurgency effort; when this effort was begun in 1983, Sendero was unable to protect its allies, and thus lost a great deal of support. It does not appear that Sendero planned its response to the counterinsurgency offensive carefully.

Sendero reduced risks from detection to its militants in other ways too.[16] Most important, in contrast to the 1960s guerrillas, Senderistas were indigenous to the region and thus did not stand out physically from the rest of the population. Also, members' identities have been carefully concealed. All members use aliases, and during terrorist actions they are masked with large woolen hoods. Few Senderistas know more than four others: each guerrilla cell has a maximum of five members; one is the leader, joining the committee at the next higher level. If one Senderista is captured, the entire cell is usually disbanded. Infiltration of top Sendero ranks is virtually impossible, as Sendero has not allowed any new members into key leadership groups since the early 1980s, with the possible exception of long-time peasant leader Julio Mezzich.

Weak and Inappropriate Response by the State

There has been a great deal of debate in Peru about the type of response that should be made to Sendero by the state: whether it should be primarily military or primarily economic and political. Virtually all analysts agree, however, that a response of some kind was necessary if Sendero were to be countered. For more than two years, however, the Belaúnde government chose to virtually ignore the Senderista rebellion.

Between May 1980 and December 1982, the Belaúnde government's only response to Sendero was to dispatch a special police unit, called the *sinchis*, to Ayacucho. The *sinchis* were purportedly trained in counterinsurgency techniques, but their behavior in Ayacucho gave little evidence of any professional expertise. Most were from coastal areas and felt ill at ease in the very different highlands environment. The *sinchis* were widely reported to be not only abusive but also ineffectual.

16. Interviews with Raúl González and Gustavo Gorritti in Lima, July 1986.

No special economic or political initiatives were taken to alleviate the human suffering in the southern highlands. In 1981, only 2.7 percent of all Peruvian agricultural investment was made in the highlands; over 90 percent was devoted to the coast or jungle (Abusada 1984:64). The percentage of total public investment planned for Ayacucho in 1982 was only 1 percent of total public investment—even though Ayacucho holds about 3 percent of Peru's population (Presidencia de la República 1982: 523). The 1 percent figure was only slightly more than the 0.6 percent annual average under the military governments between 1968 and 1980 (González 1982:61).

The terms of trade for agricultural products, which had not been especially favorable to peasants for many years, became more adverse in the early 1980s. In part because of Belaúnde government liberalization policies, prices for basic agricultural products rose by only about half as much as the consumer price index, and prices for potatoes—the key product in the southern highlands—rose by only about 30 percent versus roughly 150 percent for the CPI during 1981 and 1982 (McClintock 1985b:table 4). Simultaneously, the amount of real credit available declined by about 20 percent, while the cost of fertilizers and other important inputs increased (McClintock 1985b:27–29).

Why did the Belaúnde government fail to fashion a more effective response to Sendero? While a definitive analysis cannot be attempted here, some tentative explanations can be advanced. First, President Belaúnde seemed personally unwilling to focus on either Peru's mounting social and economic problems in general or on Sendero in particular. Cartoonists often portrayed the president sitting in the clouds. For about two years, Belaúnde dismissed Sendero as a band of unhinged individuals with no support, or as common criminals, or as dupes of the drug traffickers or communist foreign powers. Perhaps, Belaúnde remembered too well that he had been ousted from the presidency in 1968 by the military in part because of the officers' perceptions that he had mishandled the 1960s guerrilla problem, and he did not want the 1960s events to be repeated in the 1980s.

Nor by most accounts were the Peruvian military eager to enter Ayacucho. After all, at this time the military government had just completed a major agrarian reform, which it hoped and said had brought social progress to Peru. Leaving office in 1980, President Morales Bermúdez emphasized that the military's reforms had laid the basis for a real democracy in Peru. The military apparently did not want to believe that their interpretation of the 1970s reforms was not fully accurate. Perhaps weary of politics, and certainly divided on many political issues, the military were apparently in no mood for a major counterinsurgency offensive in one of the most remote areas of the country.[17]

17. Confidential interviews, Lima, July 1986.

Ayacucho's remoteness was itself a factor in the inadequate response of the state. While the road between the city of Ayacucho and Lima was quite good, travel to many rural communities in the department was extremely hazardous, and reaching some parts of the department from Lima could take three days. Apparently, Abimael Guzmán chose Ayacucho as his base of activities not only because of its poverty but also because of its remoteness, which he correctly perceived as a geopolitical advantage.

Other Factors That May Have Contributed to Sendero's Growth

Two additional factors may have contributed to Sendero's success. They are (1) southern highlands culture and its fit with Sendero and (2) the coca industry. Definitive evidence on the role of these factors is not available, but they will be discussed here because they are of considerable analytical interest, and are often discussed in the scholarly literature, including in Wickham-Crowley's chapter for this volume.

Has Sendero enjoyed a special resonance among the Ayacucho people for cultural reasons? "Culture" is an imprecise term, and so this question has various dimensions. Perhaps the most important dimension is whether or not Ayacucho has had a particular culture of rebellion.

Briefly, the historical record suggests that the people of Ayacucho have not been more prone to overt political protest than the people of other central and southern highlands departments. Indeed, peasant villages in Ayacucho have been less inclined to join together to fight against domination, and less successful when they have tried. First, prior to the Spanish conquest, the Ayacucho peoples had been conquered by Cuzco's Incas, who were more aggressive and more successful in battle (Degregori 1986; Bonilla 1986). The most important rebellion of the eighteenth century, led by Túpac Amaru between 1765 and 1783, was centered in Cuzco; while many provinces to Cuzco's south participated, Ayacucho did not (Golte 1980:207 and map 27). There were numerous rebellions in the Peruvian highlands during the early twentieth century, but again the major areas of protest were Cuzco and Puno, not Ayacucho (Burga and Flores Galinod 1984:111, 118, 122, 172, 173). The geographical pattern was similar during the 1960s, when peasants were demanding land reform. Cuzco and, to a lesser extent, the central highlands departments of Cerro de Pasco and Junín were the most frequent sites of land invasions and other protest activity (Handelman 1975; Tullis 1970).

One reason for the lower level of political protest in Ayacucho may have been the high level of intercommunity conflict in the area (Palmer 1973; Bonilla 1986). For example, the number of boundary disputes among peasant communities in Ayacucho has been one of the highest in Peru (Palmer 1973:198). Communities may have quarreled more frequently with each other in Ayacucho than elsewhere because there were fewer hacienda targets. The massive forced migrations ordered under Viceroy Francisco de Toledo in the sixteenth century may also have fragmented the peoples of Ayacucho (Palmer 1973 : 198–99). Various scholars believe that the intensity of intercommunity conflict in Ayacucho is a major barrier to any movement that would try to mobilize support on the basis of a broad appeal to Indian ethnicity.[18]

Certainly, in the 1980s Ayacucho peasants were angry. They interpreted their suffering in the light of their history as a conquered people and the discrimination they had long suffered as Indians in a country governed for centuries by and for whites.[19] Sendero's call for a new government run by and for Indians was indubitably very appealing.

Yet, if the basis of Sendero's appeal were primarily cultural, Cuzco should be a major locus of the movement. As noted above, Cuzco has been the center of most major Indian movements in Peru, and the "Indian-ness" of Cuzco has not changed in the past decade. So, why did Cuzco not become a social base for Sendero? The answers were suggested above. It seems that Cuzco became more prosperous in the 1960s and 1970s, and that, in the wake of substantial agrarian reform and peasant organizational activity in the department, a larger number of citizens became oriented toward electoral politics, sympathizing with the Marxist electoral coalition Izquierda Unida. While traditions of protest may incline peasants to rebel, they are not likely to spark defiance in the absence of appropriate economic and political preconditions.

Another dimension of the cultural question is religious. Recently, various analysts have noted the spread of apocalyptic and millenarian beliefs in the Peruvian highlands. While peasants who experience subsistence crises and economic dislocations may be drawn to such noninstitutional religious movements, there is no evidence that they simultaneously turn to anti-institutional guerrilla groups. On the contrary, in one of the few attitudinal studies carried out in the southern highlands, surveying miners of peasant background in Huancavelica in the late 1970s, Langton (1986 : 39) found that indigenous religious beliefs and practices (such as belief in mine spirits and participation in rituals) were associated with lower social consciousness and less participation in protest activities. Sendero's heavy recruitment among young people also suggests an appeal based more on political ideology than on religious faith.

Yet another dimension of the cultural question is Sendero's own character and its attractiveness to southern highlands people. In other words, did southern highlanders offer support to Sendero rather than other

18. Heraclio Bonilla, "Structure and Conflict in Andean Communities" (research proposal to the Tinker Foundation, 1986). Also, Billie Jean Isbell, in a guest lecture at George Washington University, April 1986.

19. Various interviews, in particular with Luis Millones, Lima, July 1986. See also Granados 1987.

Marxist groups, not because of Sendero's organizational skills, but because of its "totalitarian," "fanatical," or "brutal" nature?

First, it is not clear exactly how "totalitarian" Sendero is. Especially since 1982, it has seemed possible that there is more than one Sendero, and that the various new organizations have distinctive orientations. Also, there may not be one major leader at this time. Guzmán disappeared from public view around 1980 and he is sometimes rumored to have died. Further, when Sendero has unilaterally reached policy decisions and tried to force them on the peasantry, its approach has often backfired (see below).

Sendero's ideological fanaticism is well known. Senderistas consider themselves Gang-of-Four Maoists. They are so fanatically Maoist that they paint slogans on Andean village walls proclaiming "Death to the Traitor Deng Xiaoping," despite the fact that most Ayacucho peasants have never heard of the Chinese leader. Senderistas use esoteric symbolism; for example, when they hang dead dogs from poles, it is apparently to repudiate the current Chinese leadership as the "running dogs" of imperialism. In the few pamphlets Sendero has distributed, such as *¡Desarrollemos la guerra de guerrillas!* (Let's develop the guerrilla war!) and *¡No votar! Sino, generalizar la guerra de guerrillas para conquistar el poder para el pueblo!* (Don't vote! Rather, generalize the guerrilla war to conquer power for the people!), the language is rather academic. Words such as "feudalism," "bourgeoisie," and "imperialism" are common, whereas references to the Incan past, indigenous customs, and popular anecdotes are nonexistent. Nor do such references appear frequently in Senderista posters or slogans (Salcedo 1986:64–67). The same tendency is evident in Senderista names. For example Guzmán's nom de guerre, Comrade Gonzalo, is Spanish rather than Quechua. Various Senderistas have also named their children "ILA" or "IRA," acronyms for "Inicio de la lucha armada" or "Inicio de la revolución armada" (start of the armed struggle or armed revolution).

Such ideological fanaticism must have appealed to the students and young people who became Senderista militants, but there is no evidence at all that it appealed to peasants. As Gitlitz (1984a) suggests, it was probably rarely grasped by peasants. The peasants seem to have interpreted Sendero in part in their own way, without a great deal of basis in fact. Thus, for example, peasants seem to put Sendero into a Quechua and Incan worldview (Gitlitz 1984a:17). In fact, however, as we saw above, Sendero does not commonly use Incan symbols, and Sendero has often opposed many Incan rituals (Degregori 1986).

There is also no evidence that Sendero's brutality appealed to peasants. Especially since the government's counterinsurgency offensive, the prevailing peasant attitude in Ayacucho seemed to be fear, not bloodthirstiness (Degregori 1986:256).

The effects of Peru's coca boom on peasant support for Sendero Luminoso in the southern highlands are also uncertain. Probably, the effects in this region were minor. The coca industry has expanded rapidly in Peru over the past decade. As of 1982 it was estimated that the value of Peru's drug exports was about U.S. $850 million, more than any of the country's legal exports (Lee 1985–86: 145–46). Only a decade before, Peru had produced very little coca for export. Coca grows easily on the lower altitudes of most of the eastern Andean foothills including Peru's southern highlands. However, the center of Peru's drug trade is in the northern highlands, especially in the departments of Huanuco, San Martín, and Pasco. The Upper Huallaga river valley in this area is one of the most lucrative coca production sites in the world.

A question of major theoretical importance is whether or not the coca industry dislocated the peasant smallholders in the southern highlands. As Eric Wolf (1969) first emphasized and as Wickham-Crowley discusses in this volume, capitalist expansion and concomitant peasant dislocation have often been considered important to rural protest among peasant smallholders. As noted above, the southern highlands peasants were indeed smallholders, and many can be expected to have been critical of the expansion of modern capitalist enterprises.

In the case of coca, however, there is no evidence from either Peru or Bolivia that the growth of the agroindustry alienated peasants. Amid the nation's economic crises, most peasants are pleased about the availability of some new economic opportunities (Healy 1985). In contrast to previous export commodity booms, coca has not displaced peasant smallholders. Much of the area where coca is grown had not been intensively cultivated in the past (because of poor access to these lower foothills), and coca production is predominantly by smallholders.

In one important way, however, there is a link between Sendero and the coca industry: Sendero receives money from the coca traffickers.[20] The exact nature of this relationship is unclear, and seems to vary by region and era. Sendero itself denies profiting from the drug trade, but proclaims cocaine as a weapon in the anti-imperialist struggle and a boon for Peru's peasants.

THE EROSION OF SENDERO'S SOCIAL BASE, POST-1982

First, this section describes the trends in guerrilla activities and in popular support for violent movements since 1982. These events are recent, and definitive studies of them are not available, but it appears that Sendero's social base has eroded considerably, except in coca-growing areas. Then, the section explores the various explanations for this trend, em-

---

20. González 1987; *Andean Report*, March 1987, pp. 38–39; *Wall Street Journal*, 1 May 1987, p. 23.

phasizing the impact of new military and political initiatives by the Peruvian state.

Trends in Guerrilla Violence and Popular Attitudes, 1983–86

Between 1983 and 1986, violent actions by Sendero and other groups increased. As noted above, however, the number of Sendero attacks did diminish in Ayacucho—from 1,226 in 1983 to 821 in 1984, and yet further to 495 in 1985 (González, Salcedo, and Reid 1986:45). Perhaps more important, there is substantial evidence of a decline in popular support for Sendero in Ayacucho as well as in Apurímac and Huancavelica. The electoral data in table 2.4, for example, show the drop in null and blank voting and in absenteeism in these and other departments between 1980 and 1986. In step with the nation as a whole, Ayacucho went for Alan García in 1985, giving him 50 percent of the department's valid vote (Tuesta Soldevilla 1987:200). Fear was one factor in the electoral trend, as communities with high rates of absenteeism or Marxist voting would be more likely to be charged with pro-Senderista sympathies by the military. However, the reports of journalists and human rights groups are virtually unanimous that after 1982 the prevailing political attitude to the military and Sendero in Ayacucho became "a plague on both your houses" (Americas Watch 1985; González 1983 and 1985; González, Salcedo, and Reid 1986).

Sendero was by no means defeated. Some communities continued to support Sendero (Berg 1986); null and blank voting and absenteeism remained at higher levels than in other parts of the country (see table 2.4). Sendero retained a capacity to reappear in zones that it had once left, and it increased its actions in other parts of the country, especially in Lima, as noted above. Yet, Sendero did not achieve the social base in any of these areas that it had in Ayacucho.

During 1986 the Sendero guerrillas targeted a new southern highlands department: Puno. While Sendero had been active in Puno since about 1984, its violent actions there quintupled in 1986 (*Caretas*, 31 July 1986, pp. 10–12). Sendero's decision to target Puno as a new social base was logical; Puno is one of Peru's poorest departments, and the legacy of the 1970s agrarian reform was unusually bitter there, as a relatively small number of families became members of rather prosperous and large agricultural cooperatives called SAIS. However, for various reasons to be discussed below, Sendero failed to build the kind of support that it had in Ayacucho. As table 2.4 shows, electoral trends indicate decreasing, not increasing, alienation from the democratic system in Puno. In 1987 violence was once again at relatively low levels in Puno; between January and June 1987, less than 1 percent of all terrorist actions were in Puno, and less than 3 percent of all deaths (García-Sayan 1987; *Andean Report*, March 1987).

Violent actions have increased more in Lima than in any other part of

TABLE 2.4 Electoral Trends in Selected Regions of Peru, 1978–85

| | Null and Blank Votes (percentages of total votes) | | | | | | Absenteeism (percentages of registered voters) | | | | | |
| | Presidential | | Municipal | | | | Presidential | | | Municipal | | |
	1980	1985	1983	1986			1980	1985		1983	1986
Ayacucho	42%	36%	52%	39%			27%	17%		74%	41%
Emergency Zone Departments[a]	41	33	47	37			28	19		61	36
Puno	26	25	27	24			19	9		43	21
Cuzco	30	26	31	18			22	13		45	30
Lima	17	7	11	7			15	8		26	15
Nationwide	21	14	18	15			19	10		36	22

SOURCE: Tuesta Soldevilla 1987:189–233.
[a] Averages for Ayacucho, Apurímac, and Huancavelica.

Peru. From mid 1980 to mid 1984, Lima attacks were 23 percent of the reported total, whereas during the first six months of 1987 they were 37 percent (*Caretas*, 9 July 1984, p. 10; García-Sayan 1987: 6). For various reasons, however, the spiraling violence did not indicate rising support for Sendero. First, many of the attacks were selective assassinations and bomb placements, which did not require large military contingents; in contrast, in the early 1980s in Ayacucho, Sendero coordinated major maneuvers, including the takeover of the Ayacucho prison.

Second, many of these actions have been carried out not by Sendero but by a second group, the Movimiento Revolucionario Túpac Amaru (MRTA).[21] The MRTA is a more conventional group than Sendero; MRTA's leaders seek to communicate with a broad spectrum of citizens about their goals, try to justify their actions, and engage in more "Robin Hood" actions and fewer assassinations. Typically, they take public responsibility for their attacks and are less secretive and clandestine than Sendero; in one region in 1987, MRTA leaders gave lengthy interviews to the Peruvian media and wore guerrilla uniforms. Whereas Sendero has scorned alliances with foreign guerrilla groups, the MRTA is linked to Colombia's M-19 (*Caretas*, 16 November 1987, p. 17). By late 1987, especially after the spectacular takeover of Juanjui, a town in Peru's upper-jungle coca-producing region, Sendero felt eclipsed by the MRTA. New, intense controversies over strategy and tactics emerged within the Sendero leadership; apparently, some Senderista militants believed that, to compete with the MRTA, Sendero should give new emphasis to political work in urban areas (González 1988).

Third, while the number of violent attacks increased in Lima, according to various sets of data, popular support for them did not. Table 2.4 documents the rise in electoral participation in Lima during the 1980s— a degree of participation that is excellent by any standard. The respected public-opinion firm Datum has monitored attitudes toward different regime types in Lima regularly during the 1980s; table 2.5 shows that citizens have gradually become more enthusiastic about democratic government and less inclined toward socialist revolution. An in-depth analysis of political attitudes in one poor area of Lima between 1983 and 1985, carried out by well-known, highly respected scholars loosely identified with Peru's left, found virtually no support for Sendero (Degregori, Blondet, and Lynch 1987).

Sendero has, however, established a new social base in one region: the prime coca-growing territory around the Upper Huallaga valley in the departments of Huanuco and San Martín. Many analysts were surprised at the appearance of Sendero in this zone. In contrast to the southern

21. On the MRTA, see in particular González 1988; *Sí*, 16 November 1987, pp. 13–16; *Caretas*, 16 November 1987, pp. 8–17.

TABLE 2.5 Attitudes toward Democracy in Lima,
1982–86 (*N* ≅ 400–800)

	Preferred Political Regime in Lima		
	November 1982	January 1984	June 1986
Democratic (elected)[a]	69%	72%	88%
Socialist (by revolution)	13	13	6
Military (by coup)	5	9	3
Other, don't know	14	6	4

SOURCES: Figures are from Datum polls. The question was: "Which of these types of government do you consider to be the most adequate for a country such as ours?" *Caretas*, 13 December 1982, p. 22, and 20 February 1984, p. 24. Data for 1986 from Manuel Torrado, director of Datum.
[a] In 1986 includes responses "Democratic such as the current one" and "Democratic with a harder hand."

highlands, this valley is prosperous. The people living on these lower Andean slopes are less likely to be descendants of the Incas than the people living in the southern highlands. Sendero apparently chose to recruit in the Huallaga valley to take advantage of the popular opposition in the region to the coca-eradication programs sponsored by the United States and Peruvian governments. Sendero did mobilize and support coca-growers, and became the dominant authority at several sites. However, by 1987 it was also clear that Sendero's role in this zone was problematical in various respects.[22] First, at times Sendero collaborated with drug traffickers in the area, and accordingly Sendero's puritanical image was tarnished. Second, when the MRTA also became active in the area, the competition between the two revolutionary organizations became so intense that violence erupted on more than one occasion.

Explanations for the Erosion of Sendero's Social Base, 1983–86
Why did Sendero's social base erode? Peru's economic crisis, which as we saw above was crucial to Sendero's rise, did not abate. Indeed, at least until 1986, it became more severe, exacerbated by the violence itself. Nor, in this short period of time, did citizens in the southern highlands or elsewhere become dramatically more or less politicized. With respect to the two other factors discussed above, however—the response of the state and guerrilla strategy—major changes are evident.

The most important change was in the response of the state. In December 1982–January 1983, the military went to Ayacucho, and a counterinsurgency offensive was launched. In turn, this offensive resulted in

22. González 1987 provides an excellent description and analysis. See also *Caretas*, 7 September 1987, pp. 31–39.

new tactics on the part of Sendero, many of which alienated their previous supporters. More gradually, with the inauguration of Alan García in July 1985, the state began to fashion a political and economic response to Sendero. In the view of many observers, however, the political and economic dimensions of the counterinsurgency effort were still slight.

The Military Offensive. During 1985 between 5,000 and 7,000 security-force personnel were deployed in the southern highlands emergency zone; most were from the army, but navy, air force, civil guard, republican guard and plainclothes investigative police representatives also participated (*Andean Report,* September 1985, p. 157). Another 2,500–3,000 troops were deployed in the emergency zone in the northern highlands and high jungle (*Andean Report,* June 1985, p. 94). About 10 percent of the Peruvian army was stationed in these areas. Counterinsurgency equipment included about five Bell 212 helicopters (*Andean Report,* September 1985, p. 157). In the view of many Peruvian military officers, more sophisticated counterinsurgency equipment, including, for example, new special high-altitude helicopters and night gear, would be a boon; in contrast to many Latin American governments facing guerrilla threats, Peru has enjoyed little U.S. military aid in recent years (USAID 1986:60).

The military's first priority in 1983 was to identify pro-Senderista communities and to raid them. Often, these raids were brutal and arbitrary (Americas Watch 1984). Soldiers would enter allegedly pro-Senderista communities and detain or kill the individuals whom they considered most likely to be guerrillas—teachers, high school students, leftist political leaders. Sometimes, they burned buildings and raped women. More than fifty clandestine mass graves have been discovered in various areas of the emergency zone, with about twenty bodies in each (Americas Watch 1985:8). Illegal detention and interrogation centers were set up in the zone, and numerous reports confirm that torture was common at these sites. As of mid 1985, the number of disappearances was 1,325 (Americas Watch 1985:5). At times, air raids were carried out against suspect communities. In 1983 Huancasancos was one targeted village; in 1984 Chapi was another, with a death toll of perhaps as many as 3,000 people (*Andean Focus,* April 1986, p. 10). Revelations of mass graves and air raids continued throughout 1986, suggesting that the number of victims in the struggle was considerably higher than official government statistics have indicated.

A second key strategy of the Peruvian military was the establishment of civil defense patrols among the emergency zone peasant communities. These have been called *rondas campesinas,* and alternatively *montoneras.* The theory behind their formation is that the peasant communities could then defend themselves against Senderista incursions. In practice, however, the armed forces often monitor peasants for their willingness to join the patrols and accuse those who refuse to serve of being Senderistas (Americas Watch 1985:2). Also, when the civil defense patrols were encouraged to apprehend and even kill suspected Senderistas, the patrols often took advantage of their new official mandate to charge traditional enemies—other communities, estranged relatives, and the like—with Senderista sympathies and to attack them. In many areas, violence escalated as newly armed communities tried to settle long-simmering disputes with other communities under the pretext of their being Senderistas (Degregori 1986:258–59; Americas Watch 1985:14).

Of course, such a brutal and indiscriminate counterinsurgency campaign did not build new popular support for the state; rather, it alienated citizens further. However, the campaign did greatly increase the costs of sympathy for Sendero. Most southern highlands people had not anticipated the intensity of the violence, and they blamed not only the military but also Sendero. Moaned one southern highlands peasant, for example:

> Why don't they take care of us? They got us into this problem, but they don't protect us; they ought to protect us, defend us. Why did they say that they would be at the front of the battle and us behind? Where are they? Here you don't see them. They've gotten us into this mess and now they've gone. It just can't be. (Degregori 1986:256; my translation)

After his inauguration in July 1985, in an effort to build support for the Peruvian state, President García quickly raised human rights standards. In October 1985 it was revealed that army troops had massacred as many as seventy-five civilians in two separate incidents a few months earlier. García's response, in a clear warning to the military, was to dismiss three top generals. Subsequently, Peru's human rights record improved markedly in most respects. The number of "assumed terrorists" (a classification widely believed to include a large number of innocent citizens) killed in counterinsurgency declined from 1,721 in 1984 to 390 in 1986 and 283 in 1987 (*Caretas,* 29 December 1986, p. 19, and 30 December 1987, p. 28). The number of civilians killed (many also by the military) declined from 1,750 in 1984 to 368 in 1986 and 350 in 1987 (*Caretas,* 29 December 1986, p. 19, and 30 December 1987, p. 28). During the final two and a half years of the Belaúnde administration, the number of "disappearances" averaged approximately 880 per year; during the first year and a half of the García administration, the number of "disappearances" averaged approximately 205 per year (Americas Watch 1987:29).

Of course, however, while these figures indicate an improved human rights situation, they also document the continuation of violations. The most notorious of these violations was the massacre of almost three hundred suspected Senderistas in Lima prisons by the Republican Guard and the army in June 1986. The government has failed to prosecute the responsible authorities.

As of early 1988, the Achilles heel of the Peruvian government's counterinsurgency program seemed to be the same as it had been since 1980: woefully inadequate intelligence.[23] Sendero remains virtually impervious to infiltration; the organization maintains a tight cellular structure and monitors new recruits closely, apparently limiting membership rights to those who carry out assassinations. At the same time, the intelligence efforts of the police and the military have been timid. Increasingly, however, the García government has recognized the importance of intelligence to the counterinsurgency campaign, and it has recently announced intelligence initiatives. In late 1986, for example, officials proclaimed a new program to persuade captured guerrillas to repent and disclose information about their former colleagues. In March 1987, the government established a new police intelligence outfit, the Dimin, including about 300 experienced counterinsurgency officers to be hand-picked by its new chief, who in turn was appointed by President García. According to sources, these initiatives had helped to improve the government's intelligence capability somewhat.[24]

Political and Economic Initiatives. Although democratically elected, President Belaúnde was unable to maintain popular support for his government. Amid economic decline and guerrilla war, Belaúnde seemed unable to focus on realistic policy alternatives for the country. Many citizens, contemplating the government's economic policies, began to believe that it was not even trying to encourage the economic and social development of the country as a whole; in good part for this reason, majorities in my informal surveys in the highlands and on the coast judged the Belaúnde government *not* democratic (McClintock 1985:34). In a formal survey reported in *Debate* (vol. 7, no. 32 [May 1985]: 24–28), more than half the respondents evaluated the Belaúnde government as either "a bad government" or "one of the worst governments Peru has ever had."

Fortunately for the legitimacy of the Peruvian democratic state, by 1983 a new political star appeared: Alan García. The dynamic and flamboyant García was chosen secretary-general of the APRA party in Oc-

23. *U.S. Overseas Loans and Grants, July 1, 1945–September 30, 1986* (Washington, D.C.: Agency for International Development).

24. Interviews with Raúl González, Gustavo Gorritti, and military officers, 1985–87; see also *Andean Report,* March 1987.

tober 1982, and then overwhelmingly nominated as the party's presidential candidate in February 1984. Peruvians were very impressed by García's youthful energy and charisma, and by his fervent indications of commitment to Peru and especially to the Peruvian peasantry. More than a year before the election, García was the odds-on favorite to win. García promised that, whereas the Belaúnde government had stood for "representative democracy," his government would stand for "social democracy," and that it would be much more meaningful for citizens.

In office, García did seek to ameliorate the social and economic grievances of poorer Peruvians in the southern highlands. (As Wickham-Crowley notes in chapter 4, guerrilla movements succeed in expanding their social bases only when states fail to be minimally responsive to citizens' grievances.) Perhaps the most important government initiative was to increase peasants' access to credit. Between 1985 and 1986, the total number of hectares in Peru that were worked with credit increased by 50 percent, and the total amount of money loaned increased by 68 percent (Banco Agrario del Perú 1987: 19). Loans were disproportionately favorable to the highlands region: the total number of hectares worked with credit there increased by 141 percent between 1985 and 1986, and the total amount of revenue loaned increased by 179 percent (Banco Agrario del Perú 1987 : 33). In the "Andean Trapezoid," the García government's name for the poorest highland region of the country, including Ayacucho, Apurímac, Huancavelica, Cuzco, and Puno, as well as highland areas in Arequipa, Moquegua, and Tacna, the total number of hectares worked with credit rose by 119 percent, and the total amount of money loaned rose by 112 percent (Banco Agrario del Perú 1987: 38). In the Andean Trapezoid, a majority of the loans were made at zero interest rates (Banco Agrario del Perú 1987 : 35). At the same time, the prices for most key agricultural inputs were slashed; accordingly, sales of fertilizer tripled between 1985 and 1986 (*Andean Report,* January 1987, p. 3). Farmers were also guaranteed reasonable prices for basic agricultural products by the government; in 1986, the total cost of the government's subsidies, which were paid primarily for rice, corn, and sugar, has been estimated at about $110 million (*Andean Report,* January 1987, p. 5).

The García government has also shifted public investment patterns, although not as dramatically as he had promised. Total public investment funds and the percentage of these funds allocated to the Andean Trapezoid apparently changed very little between the final years of the Belaúnde government and the first years of the García government (Instituto Nacional de Planificación 1986; 1987: 10). Some effort, however, was made by the García government to direct agricultural investment away from super-high-technology projects, considered boondoggles and white elephants by virtually all agronomists (World Bank 1986: 28; Urban 1986), toward projects that would more directly benefit the rural poor. Between 1981 and 1983, for example, the Belaúnde government assigned a whopping 67 percent of all agricultural investment to four mammoth irrigation projects (Majes, Chira-Piura, Jequetepeque-Zaña, and Tinajones), at a cost of $122 million annually; in 1986 the parallel figures for these four projects plus Chavimochic (located in the APRA party's political base) were 57 percent of the total agricultural budget and $91 million dollars (Banco Central de Reserva 1986a; Instituto Nacional de Planificación 1987 : 19). Perhaps more important than these official figures, however, was the widespread view in the provincial cities that I visited in the fall of 1987—Ayacucho, Cuzco, and Trujillo—that a greater share of the allocated funds was actually being spent on the projects rather than diverted into politicians' wallets. Whereas during the Belaúnde years I had at times found no evidence of any work on a project in the countryside that city officials had claimed was ongoing, in 1987 I was especially impressed by the intensive project efforts of the Ayacucho development corporation; when I checked the claims of development corporation authorities against the reports of numerous residents from one of the communities in the Ayacucho area, they jibed closely.

Agrarian reform was not a priority program of the García government. By and large, the government maintained that the agrarian reform that had been carried out by the military regime during the 1970s was sufficient. However, in the department of Puno, where the benefits of the agrarian reform had been particularly skewed in favor of a relatively small number of workers on ex-haciendas, where leftist political parties had been especially effective in mobilizing non-beneficiaries for a more egalitarian reform, and where Sendero was increasingly active in 1986, the government did act. In the last few months of 1986 and the first few months of 1987, approximately 750,000 hectares were distributed to nearly 400 peasant communities, benefiting some 150,000 people (*Andean Report,* March 1987, p. 41).

The García government initiated several programs that were advantageous to the poor both in Lima and elsewhere. The most important was the PAIT (Programa de Apoyo al Ingreso Temporal), a short-term public employment program. In 1986 this program gave jobs to 224,985 persons; in 1987 it employed 280,751 individuals, 30 percent of whom resided in the Andean Trapezoid (Banco Central de Reserva 1987).

A particularly innovative García program has been the "Rimanacuy," or dialogue between government officials and peasant community leaders. In 1986 and 1987 these exchanges have been held in Huancayo, Cuzco, and Puno. Apparently, government officials have learned more about peasants' needs at these meetings, and personal and political alliances have been begun.

In sum, the García government has clearly done more than its predecessor to try to build legitimacy for the democratic state among the impoverished citizens of the Andean Trapezoid. Yet it is far from clear whether or not he has done enough; it is also far from clear whether or not the government will be able to continue its most important programs, such as the dramatic increase in agrarian bank credit, through its final years in office. Even as of 1986 and 1987, boom years for the Peruvian economy, the quality of life for most Peruvians in the Andean Trapezoid probably improved marginally, if at all. One of the reasons for the marginal effect of the government's programs was Sendero's direct obstruction of them.

Senderista Organization and Strategy. Prior to 1983 and the Peruvian military's counterinsurgency offensive, Sendero's tactics were very shrewd, enabling it to win considerable popular support. Since 1983, however, the military's offensive has sparked more vicious and extremist behavior among the Senderistas. With the notable exception of the upper-jungle coca-growing areas—not incidentally the only area where Sendero has built a popular base in recent years—Sendero's actions have demonstrated little or no concern for the security or well-being of most Peruvians, including the poorest Peruvians, at least from a short- or medium-term perspective. As documented above, the Senderistas' behavior cost them popular support; more and more, young male peasants in the Andean Trapezoid fled their communities to avoid the terror of Sendero and the terror of the military (González 1988:49). By 1987 Sendero was as much or more on Peruvians' minds than it had been in the early 1980s, but Sendero itself seemed to be a very different group. Once militants with a solid social base in Peru's most destitute and remote region, not only preaching but also practising Maoism, Sendero was now based in Lima and the coca-growing regions of Peru, mostly practising acts of urban terrorism that could be carried out by twenty to thirty Senderistas.

Since 1983 Sendero has used force against peasants or against their representatives much more frequently (Degregori 1986; González 1983 and 1985). Whereas previously Senderistas had attacked only community elites, the guerrillas began to identify "traitors" among the rank-and-file peasants, and sometimes executed them. As many as twenty-four peasants considered to be working with the government have been assassinated at one time (*Resumen Semanal,* 11–17 December 1987, p. 6). At least two mayors—one from the United Left in the community San Juan de Salinas near Puno and the second from APRA in the community Huanta near Ayacucho—were killed by Sendero despite overwhelming opposition to their executions from the townspeople (Americas Watch 1987:20; Gonzales 1987:35; *Resumen Semanal,* 27 November–3 December 1987, p. 4).

In an effort to obstruct the García government's development efforts, Sendero has also targeted development workers. In Ayacucho, Sendero had killed at least thirty engineers and technicians by December 1987; the nationwide total was over forty (Americas Watch 1987:22). Not surprisingly, the government's development organizations in Ayacucho cannot fill a substantial number of its positions. Other Sendero activities exacerbating peasants' economic hardship include its destruction of transportation facilities and its attempts, primarily in the mid 1980s, to close peasant markets.

As described above, in 1986 and early 1987 Sendero fervently sought a social base in Puno, but failed in this attempt. Why, especially given the poverty of this department? First, social and political institutions were much stronger at the grass-roots in Puno than they had been in the early 1980s in Ayacucho. The Catholic church, whose leadership in Puno was much more progressive than in Ayacucho, the United Left, and peasant leaders who had benefited from the agrarian reform all collaborated to stop Sendero. This was especially the case after Sendero's assassination of the United Left mayor in the area. Second, the government's reactions were much sounder: the emphasis was on agrarian reform and on intelligence-seeking, not repression, by the military. Finally, Sendero's overall strategy was much more violent. Sendero killed numerous leaders of agrarian-reform enterprises and roughed up many peasants who refused to participate in Senderista schemes (*Latin America Regional Reports, Andean Group*, 31 July 1986, pp. 2–3).

Sendero's tactics in Lima also alienated citizens, especially in 1986. Attacks were made not only against luxury facilities frequented by elites but also on movie theaters and similar establishments visited by average citizens. In 1987–88, however, Sendero adopted new strategies in Lima, in part to compete with the more open, conventional MRTA (which has also been more discriminating in its violent attacks than Sendero). Sendero began to enter public debate, in particular by publishing the daily paper *El Diario*. Sendero sought to penetrate labor groups and participate in strikes. These new strategies might gain Sendero some new support in Lima.

CONCLUSIONS

This chapter has emphasized four conditions necessary to the emergence of Sendero Luminoso in Peru's southern highlands: poverty, politicization, shrewd guerrilla organization, and ineffectual state response. In the first two of these four factors, there has been little change during the 1980s. Since roughly 1983, however, Sendero Luminoso has seemed to err in important ways, alienating some of its supporters, whereas the government's response has become more appropriate and the state more legitimate.

The sine qua non is poverty. The relationship between regions of abysmal poverty and regions of guerrilla strength has very probably been stronger in Peru than in any other Latin American country. The southern highlands departments that are now incorporated into the emergency zone (Ayacucho, Apurímac, and Huancavelica) are worse off by almost all criteria than any other departments in the country. Moreover, in absolute terms, income has declined for the peasant families of these departments, and in recent years they have even faced a threat to subsistence—rare in Latin America by the late 1970s. In comparison, Cuzco, which had traditionally been among Peru's most protest-oriented departments, has become somewhat better off in various respects in recent years, and few of its citizens have been attracted to Sendero.

A second key factor was politicization. In the 1960s and 1970s, education expanded at every level in the Peruvian highlands. Peasants, students, and teachers became much more aware of the gross social and economic inequalities in Peru, and more aware of the Peruvian state's centuries-long abuse and neglect of the people of the Peruvian highlands. At the same time, under the military governments of the 1970s, Marxist and other leftist groups were able to organize in the highlands more readily than in previous years.

In Cuzco, Puno, and various other highlands areas, leftist organizations with ties to nationwide movements and parties gained citizens' support, and peasants became less likely to be attracted to extremely violent groups like Sendero. In Ayacucho, however, Sendero seemed to gain a virtual political monopoly in the 1970s, in large part through Guzmán's extraordinarily shrewd politicking in the Ayacucho university. Galvanizing cadres from among the education students at the university, Guzmán and Sendero were more dedicated to grass-roots activities in remote areas than any other Peruvian guerrilla group has ever been. Sendero was also extremely careful to protect its cadres, developing a clandestine cell structure that is unprecedentedly tight among Latin American guerrilla movements.

However, after the onset of the Peruvian military's counterinsurgency offensive in early 1983, Sendero's dedication seemed to become fanaticism and brutality. Apparently, Sendero refused to accept the fact that most citizens were now more afraid for their lives than they were eager for revolution. Despite new public-relations efforts such as *El Diario*, Sendero resorted more and more often to sheer terror to achieve its goals. Increasingly, young revolutionaries, especially those in Lima, were attracted to the MRTA rather than to Sendero (Americas Watch 1987:25).

The ultimate outcome of Peru's current guerrilla war will probably depend more upon the response and legitimacy of the Peruvian state than upon any other factor. If the Belaúnde government had taken more steps—militarily, economically, and politically—against Sendero in the early 1980s, it is doubtful that Sendero would have gained such strength. As Wickham-Crowley points out in chapter 4, to date no Latin American revolutionaries have succeeded in taking power from a responsive government, and it would seem that Sendero built some popular support during the early 1980s in part because citizens did not perceive the Belaúnde government as responsive. If the García government can keep its key promises, and the real social and economic grievances of many of Peru's people are gradually ameliorated, then Peru may achieve peace.

REFERENCES

Abusada, Roberto
 1984 "Política agraria en el Perú, 1980–1983." Report prepared for the U.S. Agency for International Development.
Amat y León, Carlos
 1981 *La desigualdad interior en el Perú.* Lima: Universidad del Pacifíco.
Americas Watch
 1984 *Abdicating Democratic Authority: Human Rights in Peru.* New York: Americas Watch.
 1985 *A New Opportunity for Democratic Authority.* New York: Americas Watch.
 1986 *The Central-Americanization of Colombia? Human Rights and the Peace Process.* New York: Americas Watch.
 1987 *A Certain Passivity.* New York: Americas Watch.
Banco Agrario del Perú
 1987 *Memoria 1986.* Lima: Banco Agrario del Perú.
Banco Central de Reserva [Peru]
 1982 *Resumen económico.* Lima: Banco Central de Reserva.
 1986a "Ayuda memoria." Mimeographed.
 1986b "Mapa de pobreza del Perú 1981." Mimeographed.
 1986c "Perú: Indicadores sociales." Mimeographed.
 1987 "Programa de apoyo al ingreso temporal (PAIT)." Typescript.
Bejar, Héctor, and Carlos Franco
 1985 *Organización campesina y reestructuración del estado.* Lima: CEDEP.
Berg, Ronald H.
 1986 "Sendero Luminoso and the Peasantry of Andahuaylas." Paper presented at the Latin American Studies Association meeting in Boston, October.
Bonilla, Heraclio
 1986 "Structure and Conflict in Andean Communities." Research proposal, Instituto de Estudios Peruanos.
Burga, Manuel, and Alberto Flores Galindo
 1984 *Apogeo y crisis de la república aristocrática.* 3d ed. Lima: Ediciones Rikchay Peru.
Chaplin, David
 1968 "Peru's Postponed Revolution." *World Politics* 20 (April).

98   CYNTHIA McCLINTOCK

Consejo Nacional de Población [Peru]
1985   *Perú: Guía demográfica y socioeconómica.* Lima: Consejo Nacional de Población.
Cotler, Julio
1970   "Traditional Haciendas and Communities in a Context of Political Mobilization in Peru." In *Agrarian Problems and Peasant Movement in Latin America,* edited by Rodolfo Stavenhagen, pp. 533–88. Garden City, N.Y.: Doubleday, Anchor Books.
Craig, Wesley W., Jr.
1969   "Peru: The Peasant Movement of La Convención." In *Latin American Peasant Movements,* edited by Henry A. Landsberger, pp. 274–96. Ithaca, N.Y.: Cornell University Press.
Degregori, Carlos Iván
1986   "Sendero Luminoso: Los hondos y mortales desencuentros." In *Movimientos sociales y crisis: El caso peruano,* edited by Eduardo Ballón, pp. 225–66.
Degregori, Carlos Iván, Cecilia Blondet, and Nicolas Lynch
1987   *Conquistadores de un nuevo mundo: De invasores a ciudadanos en San Martin de Porres.* Lima: Instituto de Estudios Peruanos.
Dietz, Henry A.
1982   "National Recovery vs. Individual Stagnation: Peru's Urban Poor since 1978." Paper presented at the 44th International Congress of Latin Americanists, University of Manchester, 5–10 September.
Fernández Baca, Jorge
1982   "La producción de alimentos en el Perú." *QueHacer* 17 (June).
García-Sayan, Diego
1982   *Tomas de tierras en el Perú.* Lima: DESCO.
1987   "Violencia política y pacificación en el Perú." Manuscript.
Gitlitz, John
1984a   "An Overview of Sendero Luminoso." Unpublished manuscript.
1984b   "Sendero Luminoso in Cajamarca, Perú." Paper presented at the New England Council of Latin American Studies meeting, Harvard University, October.
Golte, Jurgen
1980   *Repartos y rebeliones: Túpac Amaru y las contradicciones de la economía colonial.* Lima: Instituto de Estudios Peruanos.
Gonzales, José
1987   "¿Se despunta Sendero?" *Debate* 47 (November).
González, Raúl
1982   "Por los caminos de Sendero." *QueHacer* 19 (October).
1983   "Crónica inconclusa: Las batallas de Ayacucho." *QueHacer* 21 (February).
1984   "Ayacucho en el año de Noel." *QueHacer* 27 (February).
1985   "Sendero: Cinco años despues de Belaúnde." *QueHacer* 36 (August–September).
1986   "Puno: El corredor senderista." *QueHacer* 39 (February–March).
1987   "Coca y subversión el el Huallaga," *QueHacer* 48 (September–October).

1988   "Sendero: Los problemas del campo y de la ciudad . . . Y ademas el MRTA." *QueHacer* 50 (January–February).

González, Raúl, José María Salcedo, and Michael Reid
1986   "The Dirty War." *NACLA Report on the Americas* 20 no. 3 (June 1986): 33–45.

Gott, Richard
1971   *Guerrilla Movements in Latin America.* Garden City, N.Y.: Doubleday.

Granados, Manuel Jesús
1987   "El PCP Sendero Luminoso: Aproximaciones a su ideologiá." *Socialismo y Participación* 37 : 15–37.

Handelman, Howard
1975   *Struggle in the Andes: Peasant Political Mobilization in Peru.* Austin: University of Texas Press.
1981   "Peasants, Landlords and Bureaucrats: The Politics of Agrarian Reform in Peru." *American Universities Field Staff Reports,* no. 1.

Havens, A. E., Susana Lastarria-Cornhiel, and Gerardo Otero
1983   "Class Struggle and the Agrarian Reform Process." In *Military Reformism and Social Classes: The Peruvian Experience, 1968–1980,* edited by David Booth and Bernardo Sorj, pp. 14–39. London: Macmillan.

Healy, Kevin
1985   "Recent Effects of Foreign Cocaine Markets on Bolivia's Society and Economy: The Boom within the Crisis." Paper presented at conference, Coca and Its Derivatives: Biology, Society and Policy, Cornell University, April.

Instituto Nacional de Estadística [Peru]
1986   "Ejecución presupuestal a nivel de gastos corrientes y de capital." Typescript.
1987   "Perú: Compendio estadístico 1986." Lima: INE.

Instituto Nacional de Planificación [Peru]
1986   Data collected personally from the INP archive.
1987   "Evaluación de la Inversión Pública 1986." Mimeographed.

Inter-American Development Bank
1985   *Economic and Social Progress in Latin America.* Washington, D.C.: Inter-American Development Bank.

Langton, Kenneth P.
1986   "The Church, Social Consciousness and Protest." *Comparative Political Studies* 19 : 317–55.

Larson, Magali S., and Arlene G. Bergman
1969   *Social Stratification in Peru.* Berkeley: Institute of International Studies, University of California.

Latin American Bureau
1985   *Peru: Paths to Poverty.* Nottingham: Russell Press.

Lee, Rensselaer W., III
1985–86   "The Latin American Drug Connection." *Foreign Policy* 61 : 142–60.

McClintock, Cynthia
1981   *Peasant Cooperatives and Political Change in Peru.* Princeton, N.J.: Princeton University Press.

1984   "Why Peasants Rebel: The Case of Peru's Sendero Luminoso." *World Politics* 37:48–84.

1985a   "Democracy in Peru." Paper presented at conference, Democracy in the Third World, Hoover Institution, Stanford University, December.

1985b   "'Promises, promises . . .': Agricultural Policy-making in New Andean Democracies." Paper presented at the American Political Science Association meeting, New Orleans, August–September.

McClintock, Cynthia, and Abraham F. Lowenthal, eds.

1983   *The Peruvian Experiment Reconsidered.* Princeton, N.J.: Princeton University Press.

Martínez, Daniel, and Armando Tealdo

1982   *El agro peruano, 1970–1980: Análisis y perspectivas.* Lima: CEDEP.

Matos Mar, José, and José Manuel Mejía

1980   *Reforma agraria: Logros y contradicciones, 1969–1979.* Lima: Instituto de Estudios Peruanos.

Ministerio de Economía y Finanzas [Peru]

1986   *El presupuesto del sector público para 1986.* Lima: Dirección General del Presupuesto Público.

Morner, Magnus

1985   *The Andean Past: Land, Societies, and Conflicts.* New York: Columbia University Press.

Palmer, David Scott

1973   *"Revolution from Above": Military Government and Popular Participation in Peru, 1968–1972.* Cornell University Latin American Studies Program, Dissertation Series, no. 47. Ithaca, N.Y.

1985   "The Sendero Luminoso Rebellion in Rural Peru." In *Latin American Insurgencies,* edited by Georges Fauriol, pp. 67–96. Washington, D.C.: Georgetown University Center for Strategic and International Studies and National Defense University.

1986   "Rebellion in Rural Peru: The Origins and Evolution of Sendero Luminoso." *Comparative Politics* 18:127–46.

Panfichi, Aldo

1984   *Población y empleo en el Perú.* Lima: DESCO.

Presidencia de la República [Peru]

1981   *Peru, 1981.* Lima: Presidencia de la República.

1982   *Peru, 1982.* Lima. Presidencia de la República.

1983   *Peru, 1983.* Lima: Presidencia de la República.

1984   *Peru, 1984.* Lima: Presidencia de la República.

Rubio, Marcial C.

1985–86   "La diaria amenaza." *QueHacer* 38 (December–January).

Salcedo, José María

1986   "Con Sendero en Lurigancho." *QueHacer* 39:60–67.

Scott, James C.

1976   *The Moral Economy of the Peasant: Rebellion and Subsistence in Southeast Asia.* New Haven, Conn.: Yale University Press.

Tuesta Soldevilla, Fernando

1983   *Elecciones municipales: Cifras y escenario político.* Lima: DESCO.

1987   *Perú político en cifras.* Lima: Fundación Friedrich Ebert.

Tullis, F. LaMond
  1970   *Lord and Peasant in Peru.* Cambridge, Mass.: Harvard University Press.

Urban, Klaus
  1986   "Irrigación y desarrollo: Experiencias con grandes irrigaciones en la costa peruana." In *Priorización y desarrollo del sector agrario en el Perú,* edited by A. Figueroa Arévalo and J. Portocarrero Maisch, pp. 203–25. Lima: Fundación Friedrich Ebert.

U.S. Agency for International Development [USAID]
  1986   *U.S. Overseas Loans and Grants, July 1, 1945–September 30, 1986.* Washington, D.C.: Agency for International Development.

Webb, Richard
  1977   *Government Policy and the Distribution of Income in Peru, 1963–1973.* Cambridge, Mass.: Harvard University Press.

Wolf, Eric R.
  1969   *Peasant Wars of the Twentieth Century.* New York: Harper & Row.

World Bank
  1981   *Peru: Major Development Policy Issues and Recommendations.* Washington, D.C.: World Bank.

  1983   *World Tables.* 3d ed. 2 vols. Washington, D.C.: World Bank.

  1987   *World Bank Report on Peru, 1986.* Lima: Andean Air Mail and Peruvian Times S.A.

CHAPTER THREE

Peasant Struggles of the 1970s in Colombia

León Zamosc

The National Peasant Association of Colombia, ANUC, was created in 1967 as part of an official initiative to promote direct peasant involvement in both the delivery of state services and the agrarian reform process. But by 1971 the organization had developed a broad national appeal, breaking its dependence on the government and leading what would prove to be one of the most significant agrarian struggles in modern Latin America. Facing increasing repression, ANUC tried to resist the landlord-entrepreneurial path of rural development in Colombia. Until its eventual decline during the second half of the 1970s, the movement fought for a resolution of the agrarian question that would be favorable to the peasantry. It did so by acting as a unifying force that articulated the demands of the different peasant sectors and gave expression to their grievances on three main fronts: the struggle for land, the defense of the colonists, and the protection of the smallholders.

This chapter offers a review of the peasant struggles of the 1970s, emphasizing their significance as a salient episode in the recent social history of Colombia and, more generally, as a contemporary case of peasant mobilization to influence the patterns of agrarian development under capitalism. In specific terms, there are four issues on which relevant questions can be posed. First of all, ANUC's struggles took place against the background of important changes in the process of capitalist development in Colombia. It was a period of transition, marked by the completion of the initial stage of import-substitution industrialization and the dawn of a new phase of expanding industrial exports and tighter integration into the world capitalist economy. Since the radicalization of the peasant movement was largely a response to the counter reformist turn of the government, basic questions arise regarding the relationship between the broader socioeconomic changes and the class realignments that explain this substantial shift in state policy. Calling attention to the role of the state and the class alliances and antagonisms in which the peasants were involved, this issue highlights the importance of understanding social movements in the context of their specific macroeconomic and political conditions.

2 A second theme concerns the complex setting of the agrarian question in Colombia and ANUC's standing as representative of the aspirations of the peasantry as a whole. In the resolution of the agrarian question, the stakes have to do with the alternative between a peasant agriculture supported by wide participation in the access to land and entrepreneurial production dominated by landlords who monopolize resources and exclude the peasantry. As already said, ANUC fought for a pattern of rural development in which the free peasant economy would prevail. However, the agrarian question did not present itself as a homogeneous affair in Colombia. To the contrary, it spread out into various types of regional contradictions that involved different class sectors of the peasantry. For some of these sectors, it was necessary to gain access to land of their own. Others needed improvements in their conditions of reproduction in order to consolidate or strengthen an existing peasant economy. At the heart of this issue, therefore, is the problem of the roots and consequences of the complex composition of the peasantry as a class. This raises crucial questions on the manifold structural contradictions that propelled ANUC's struggles, the implications of class heterogeneity for the development of the peasant movement, and the overall impact of the confrontation on the agrarian question in Colombia.

3 The third issue is related to the political and ideological orientations that prevailed in the peasant movement. In the course of the conflict, reformist attitudes were swept away and replaced by revolutionary stances. At the beginning, these radical stances appeared as a direct result of ANUC's links with groups and parties on the Colombian left. But later the peasant movement tried to create its own independent political organization within the leftist camp. This evolution poses important questions about the factors that account for peasant receptivity to socialist ideology, the undercurrents of ANUC's drift toward political autonomy, and the consequences of radical politicization for the movement and its struggles. These are interesting questions for any approach to peasant political participation, but they are particularly relevant from the point of view of the experience of the left in Colombia. For once in the political history of the country, socialist ideas had a chance to exert considerable influence at grass-roots levels. The outcome deserves special attention.

4 Finally, ANUC's struggles should also be related to the broader problem of the nature of the political regime in Colombia. During the 1960s and 1970s the transition to a more advanced phase of industrialization

was accompanied by the rise of bureaucratic-authoritarian military regimes in other Latin American countries (O'Donnell 1973; Collier 1979). These regimes sought to enforce social stability by curbing the economic and political demands of previously activated popular sectors. In Colombia, however, the distinctive evolution of the political system dictated a different course. The populist upsurge of the 1940s had been aborted by factional war between the traditional Liberal and Conservative parties known as La Violencia. In 1958 the two parties bridged their differences through the National Front, a coalition pact that enabled them to share power for the following sixteen years. Behind the facade of a restricted form of democracy, the National Front regime excluded all opposition from the political arena and tailored economic policy to the shifting priorities of the dominant classes. Since popular demobilization and authoritarian civilian rule provided a propitious context for the transition to the new stage of capitalist development, Colombia was spared the extremes of the military brand of bureaucratic authoritarianism. Still, the economic and social tensions related to the transition led to growing pressures that, in turn, provoked strong coercive responses from the regime. In the countryside, repression was intended to contain the demand for agrarian reform and disarticulate the political challenge posed by the peasant movement. Consequently, the development of ANUC's struggles and the results of the agrarian conflicts of the 1970s offer an important key to the understanding of the exclusionary nature of Colombia's pattern of socioeconomic and political development. This is particularly relevant given the crisis of political legitimacy that now seems to be threatening the prospects for democracy in the country.

The materials for this study were collected during five years of research in Colombia. The fieldwork covered every region affected by the agrarian struggles of the 1970s, involving a substantial number of interviews with government officials, political activists, peasant leaders, and rank-and-file members of ANUC.[1] Because of space constraints, the central issues are here integrated into a chronological account of the evolution of the peasant movement. A sketchy overview of Colombia's historical background serves as a prelude to the more detailed subsequent analysis of the setting of the agrarian question during the 1960s. Paying special attention to the development of the land struggles, separate sections examine the factors that influenced the rise, confrontation, and decline of ANUC. The final part of the chapter summarizes the cycle of the

---

1. Altogether, the process of data collection led to the formation of a specialized archive that includes 148 interviews, 435 documents of the national and regional associations of ANUC, collections of ANUC's journals and bulletins, 84 documents of related organizations, and 742 entries corresponding to articles in Colombian newspapers and magazines. This archive has been incorporated into the library of the Centro de Investigación y Educación Popular (CINEP) in Bogotá.

movement, offering some general conclusions and comments on the main themes that have been outlined in this introduction.

HISTORICAL BACKGROUND

By the end of the nineteenth century, despite ultraliberal efforts to promote free trade, Colombians had not yet been able to find a commodity that would permit the consolidation of an export economy. Topography had contributed to the formation of enclosed regional economies characterized by traditional structures of production. At the political level, extreme federalism had brought the country to the brink of disintegration. After a number of wars, the reaction to this was the so-called Conservative Republic, a long period of strong and centralized rule by the Conservative Party (Melo 1978). It was during the Conservative Republic, and more precisely at the turn of the century, that the stable link with the international market was finally established through coffee production. Colombia was a country of haciendas and peasants, and the new crop developed both with the peasant colonization of the western ranges of the Andes and within the older structure of haciendas on the temperate slopes of the eastern mountains (Machado 1977; Palacios 1979). Coffee made possible a rapid accumulation of capital, mainly by merchants who, controlling the mills and commerce, soon started to invest in imported machinery for manufactures. To facilitate the coffee exports, an infrastructure of roads and railways was developed, which contributed to strengthening the internal links among the regions. The expansion of coffee was a watershed for the country: it brought a massive incorporation of peasants into the market and set the stage for capital accumulation, the development of industry, and the formation of a national economy (Arango 1977; Bejarano 1975).

Rapid economic change led to new types of social and political conflict by the end of the 1920s. In the cities some trade unions were created by the incipient working class under the influence of radical Liberals and the newly formed Communist Party (Tirado Mejía 1978:136–40). In the countryside there was increasing discontent, particularly on the coffee haciendas in the eastern mountains, where subordinated peasants provided the labor for the plantations (Sánchez 1977; LeGrand 1986:109–34). The peasants wanted their share of the benefits of economic expansion and demanded the right to cultivate coffee of their own. Again with the involvement of radical Liberal and Communist cadres, peasant leagues were created and conflicts over land escalated.[2]

---

2. In the coffee haciendas of the eastern Andes, the early demands were related to wages and labor conditions. However, with the creation of the peasant *sindicatos* and *ligas*, land redistribution became the main issue (Gaitán 1976).

The Conservatives responded with harsh repression to both urban and rural agitation, and against a background of growing unrest, the Liberal Party came to power in 1930.

Under the so-called Liberal Republic, popular pressures were eased to some extent by means of reforms. Trade union activity was permitted within a new framework of industrial legislation. Rural trouble was defused as the state bought the most contested coffee haciendas and sold them to the peasants (Tirado Mejía 1978:144–55; Gaitán 1976:85–100). The Liberal politicians were clearly more responsive to pressures from below, but their reforms were not radical. Both parties had originally started as landowners' parties; federations of regional bosses whose networks of clientelist control vertically incorporated the population under their red and blue banners (Leal 1984:53–94). Later, the changes related to the consolidation of the export sector and incipient industrialization had failed to polarize landowning, commercial, and industrial interests along clear-cut party lines. If anything, the fact that Liberal and Conservative entrepreneurial elites had been involved in the expansion of the coffee economy allowed for the "continued vitality" of their parties (Bergquist 1986:258, 262), both of which represented segments of every dominant class and group in Colombian society (Solaún 1980:5–7; Oquist 1980:78–79).

Given the predominance of traditional agrarian structures, the bipartisan clientelist structure was particularly strong in the countryside. In the cities, where the old ideology of "hereditary" party identification was weaker, the more "welfarist" approach of the Liberals favored their relative hegemony among the new urban groups. Still, as industrialization gained momentum during the 1930s and 1940s, the workers created a unified trade union federation, and the middle sectors began to press their demands. The Liberal Party had increasing problems in balancing the interests of the dominant groups with the demands of the subordinate classes. There was an internal split and the populist Liberal faction of Jorge Eliécer Gaitán began to command more and more popular support (Robinson, 1976:67–98). As a consequence of the Liberal division, the Conservatives returned to power in 1946 and proceeded to repress the popular movement, banning the unions and resorting to indiscriminate violence against the Liberal opposition. Finally, Gaitán was assassinated in 1948, and the country plunged into what would come to be known as La Violencia (Robinson 1976:159–83).

La Violencia, considered by some historians to be a full-blown civil war, started in the cities, but took real root in the countryside, where both parties were well entrenched by clientelism. The name Violencia reflects the bloody character of the conflict. More than 200,000 people were killed in the factional struggle, which was particularly ruthless in peasant areas.[3] Some Liberal guerrillas challenged the army, but most of the fighting took the form of direct confrontations among the people, with massacres and atrocities committed in continuous strife between Liberal and Conservative villages. La Violencia was a conflict thoroughly marked by political determination. The struggle was not waged along class lines. On the contrary, it was based upon the peasants' loyalty to political bosses on each side. In the last stages, however, it became clear that the structure of the conflict was beginning to change in the direction of class struggle. Battles for land developed amid the partisan clashes, communist cadres organized strongholds of self-defense among uprooted peasants, and banditry was becoming endemic as more and more of the political gangs started to use La Violencia for the sake of revenge and economic profit. Seeing that things were getting out of control, the Liberals and Conservatives installed a military government in 1953 to pacify the country. Pacification started, but in the process the military president, Gustavo Rojas Pinilla, developed his own populist program along the lines of Argentina's Juan Perón (Tirado Mejía 1978: 179–83; Martínez and Izquierdo 1982: 15–19). Putting pressure on their loyalists in the army, the Liberals and Conservatives had Rojas Pinilla overthrown in 1957. The parties also agreed on a constitutional amendment by which both sides would share power for sixteen years under a coalition known as the National Front. The presidency would alternate between the two parties, Congress and administration would be equally divided, and only Liberals and Conservatives would be allowed to stand as candidates in elections (Kline 1980: 71–72). When the first president of the National Front took office in 1958, there was much talk about healing the wounds of La Violencia, and part of the discussion had to do with the need for agrarian reform. This invites us to look into the realities of the agrarian question in Colombia during the 1960s.

THE AGRARIAN QUESTION IN THE 1960S

The main motives behind the debate on agrarian reform were political. Worried about the erosion of the power of the traditional parties, the architects of the National Front considered that gestures toward the peasantry would help restore social harmony. As far as the economy was concerned, only the first phase of La Violencia had really implied a total disruption. After 1953 the disturbances receded to marginal mountain-

3. The classic overall description of La Violencia is Guzmán et al. 1962. Oquist 1980 provides an analytical account based on a structural regionalization that considers different roots of social conflict in La Violencia. In a more recent work, Walton (1984) offers an alternative interpretation applying his concept of "national revolt." For excellent reviews of the Violencia literature, see Bejarano 1983 and Sánchez 1985.

ous areas. This created conditions for a rapid normalization, so much so that the late 1950s and early 1960s were a period of substantial economic growth. The industrial sector took advantage of the post war situation to make a huge leap forward in the substitution of imported manufactures. Between 1951 and 1964 (a period in which Colombia's total population grew from 11.2 to 17.4 million and the proportion of rural population fell from 61.1 to 47.2 percent of the total), industrial manpower and the real value of manufactured goods increased by 69.7 and 130.9 percent respectively (DANE 1951, 1964; Bejarano, 1978:17; Kalmanovitz 1978: 135). This acceleration of industrial growth posed serious challenges to agriculture. There was increasing demand for raw materials and food-stuffs, and agricultural exports became more essential than ever to obtain the hard currency that was needed to import industrial equipment. For a while the agricultural sector lagged behind, but the situation slowly improved. A comparison of statistical data for the early 1950s and late 1960s shows that total agricultural output increased by almost a half, that the volume of coffee exports went up by a third, and that the expansion of other lines of agricultural exports was helping to compensate for the downward trend in international coffee prices (Kalmanovitz 1978: 135, 138–40; Junguito et al. 1980:34; SAC 1978:70–71; FEDECAFE 1950–65; DANE 1965–69; FAO 1952–70).

The most conspicuous element in the agricultural recovery of the 1960s was the expansion of the previously marginal capitalist agriculture. Peasant tenants and sharecroppers were being evicted from many estates of the Magdalena and Cauca inner valleys, paving the way for the planting of cotton, rice, sugar cane, soybeans, and other crops, undertaken either by the landowners themselves or by a new breed of entrepreneurs who rented the land, used wage labor, and invested in machinery and inputs (Vélez 1974). Agrarian capitalism specialized in the crops of the valleys and plains because land concentration was higher and the terrain was suitable for mechanization. But the expansion of this large-scale agriculture was a very selective process. Side by side with the new modern enclaves, there were vast areas in the plains still characterized by the old agrarian regime: large haciendas that concentrated most of the country's agricultural land and combined traditional cattle raising with servile forms of rent and sharecropping.[4]

In the mountains it was peasant farming that prevailed. Topography ruled out the use of machinery, and small-scale production responded better to the intensive labor requirements of coffee, maize, beans, potatoes, and the other highland crops. As a whole, the peasantry was still a

4. In 1960 some 43,000 estates larger than 100 hectares (3.5 percent of the total number of farms) concentrated 66 percent of the total agricultural land. The areas of greater land concentration were the Magdalena and Cauca valleys, the eastern llanos, and the savannas of the Atlantic coast (DANE 1960).

very important sector. In the early 1960s more than a million peasant families with farms smaller than twenty hectares accounted for approximately a third of the Colombian population; and despite the fact that they controlled only 14.5 percent of the land, they were responsible for 61.3 percent of the national agricultural output (DANE 1960, 1964; Kalmanovitz 1978:138–40; Moncayo and Rojas 1978:150–55). However, given the strong population growth and the conditions of "minifundia" in the highlands, an intense process of dissolution was affecting the lower peasant strata. Between 1951 and 1964, 2.3 million people emigrated from the countryside to the cities (DANE 1951, 1964). Thousands of families were also moving to new colonization areas in the piedmont forest frontiers. The liquidation of the poorer households was weeding out the old structure of the peasant economy, leaving on their feet those who had a better chance to specialize in the crops in which small-scale farming had relative advantages.

All in all, then, it can be said that the development of agriculture in Colombia was taking place along both peasant and landlord-entrepreneurial lines, shaping a mixed pattern characterized by a double specialization in space and type of crops. However, taken as a whole, the process was turning against the peasants, because both the weeding out of small-scale farming in the Andes and the expansion of agrarian capitalism in the valleys and plains entailed the dissolution of a considerable part of the peasantry.

The agrarian question had come to the crossroads. With industrial consolidation, the crucial alternative between the peasant and landlord paths of evolution was now arising as a pertinent issue all over the country. But this general contradiction involved different types of antagonisms, according to the structures that prevailed in the different regions. This implied the existence of a plurality of peasant sectors, whose circumstances and demands were quite diverse, despite their shared aspiration for a resolution of the agrarian question that would be favorable to the free peasant economy. From the point of view of such structural regionalization, figure 3.1 presents the four patterns that dominated the Colombian countryside during the 1960s.[5]

Very briefly, the scheme identifies four basic class sectors of the peasantry. In areas of peasant economy, and in some districts of past colonization, the main sector was that of the stable peasants, whose demands were related to the conditions required to maintain or reproduce peasant farming. The consolidation of their peasant economy needed improvements: better prices, better marketing systems, better credit programs

---

5. The structural regionalization presented in figure 3.1 takes into account the prevailing agrarian patterns in the main geotopographical settings of the country. It does not imply, of course, that regions were absolutely homogeneous from the structural point of view or, conversely, that particular structures could only be found in certain regions.

FIGURE 3.1 Colombian Agrarian Structures, Main Class Sectors, and Their Demands (1960s)

Geotopographical Settings	Prevailing Agrarian Structure	Main Class Sectors	Aspiration in Relation to an Independent Peasant Economy	Necessary Condition	Main Demands	Directed toward/against
Andean ranges	peasant economy →	stable peasants	consolidate →	improvement of existing reproduction conditions	improvement of services and credit →	state
Piedmont forest frontiers in the Amazon and Orinoco basins, Pacific littoral, and other marginal areas	colonization →	precarious peasants	stabilize →	obtaining the basic reproduction conditions	access to services and credit →	state
Atlantic coast, eastern llanos, marginal areas in the Andes and the inner valleys	traditional latifundios →	landless peasants	establish →	gaining access to the means of production	land →	state, landowners
Magdalena and Cauca inner valleys	agrarian capitalism →	agricultural workers	- - - →	- - -	employment, wages and labor conditions →	agricultural entrepreneurs

and extension of services. In most regions of colonization, immigrants from the Andes were trying to develop peasant farming in a precarious situation. Although land was available, basic services were urgently needed in order to stabilize households and make the settlements permanent. It was a question not of improvements but of the very establishment of transportation services, credit programs, construction of roads and bridges, and essential assistance in health and education. In areas of traditional latifundios, there were servile relations of production, with the peasants subordinated to the landlords, and the basic contradiction involved the control of land as a means of production. The possibility of an independent peasant economy depended upon the result of the impending struggle of the landless, who had to destroy large-scale property in order to be able to emerge as free peasants on their own land. Finally, in regions of capitalist agriculture, the demands of the rural workers were typically oriented toward wage levels and working conditions. But given the recency of the proletarianization process, some groups could still try to reconstitute themselves as peasants by struggling for land of their own.

This analytical outline of the agrarian question suggests that the existing contradictions could provide sufficient structural grounds to sustain a major peasant challenge. However, any struggle in favor of a future predominance of peasant farming would have to articulate the demands of the various peasant sectors into a complex strategy of attack and defense. The landless would have to take the offensive in order to change the regime of landed property in areas of latifundios and agrarian capitalism. In the regions of peasant economy and colonization, there were defensive priorities related to the protection of already existing or newly created peasant structures. The potential for rural unrest was enhanced by the fact that the first two governments of the National Front had failed to fulfill the expectations aroused by the Agrarian Reform Law of 1961. The reform program was restricted to a few places of former Violencia, and very little attention was being paid to land redistribution and peasant needs in the rest of the country (Tobón 1972).

Still, structural potential for unrest cannot by itself tell the whole story of collective action and social conflict. The rise of a peasant movement requires more than the aggravation of the agrarian antagonisms; it also needs organizational links uniting the peasants, a strong legitimation of contentious attitudes, and the existence of allies who support and help the peasant mobilization. Owing to the legacy of La Violencia, the organizational, ideological, and political conditions were adverse for a belligerent peasant movement in Colombia (Zamosc 1986:36–39). Most of the peasant leagues formed before La Violencia had disappeared, and the years of factional struggle had left deep wounds of resentment among the peasants themselves. The popular feeling for peace had helped Liberals and Conservatives to recover part of their lost legitimacy, since they appeared as "peacemakers" who could label any opposition as "subversion." Finally, in the early 1960s all the fractions of the dominant classes supported the National Front; the trade union movement had split into Liberal, Conservative, and Communist organizations (González 1975: 50–122); and the guerrillas who tried to emulate the Cuban example in the hills were unable to recruit for what the peasants seemed to regard as a useless continuation of violence.[6] To sum up, it can be argued that although there were favorable structural conditions for an eventual peasant challenge, La Violencia had erected formidable political and ideological barriers. The main obstacles had to do with the erosion of solidarity at grass-roots level, the organizational weakness and political isolation of the peasantry as a class, and the absence of legitimation to sustain contentious attitudes after the fratricidal bloodshed. Perhaps a national peasant movement would have never emerged in Colombia without an initiative that was to come from a most unexpected quarter: the government itself.

PEASANT MOBILIZATION, 1967–70

In 1966 the Liberal Carlos Lleras Restrepo was elected as the third president of the National Front. Lleras Restrepo, who was the strongest spokesman of the reformist sector of his party, had personally chaired the congressional committee that pushed through the Agrarian Reform Law of 1961 (Gilhodes 1974:217–35). Still, the pro-peasant initiatives of his administration cannot be fully understood without taking into account the critical situation of the mid-1960s. International coffee prices had collapsed and industrial production was stagnating after reaching the limits of demand for consumer goods in the internal market (Bejarano 1978:14–46). The absorption of new workers by industry went down from a yearly average rate of 4.3 percent between 1953 and 1965 to less than 2 percent in the following years while the rate of unemployment (which had been 4.9 percent in 1964) soared to 13 percent in the four main cities during 1967 (Bejarano 1978:38, 62). Rural emigration was not being absorbed by industry, and urban discontent was propping up the populist political comeback of Rojas Pinilla, who also had some landowner financial support and planned to run for the presidency as a

6. The Ejército Nacional de Liberación (ELN), created by students in 1964, was never able to expand its activities beyond its original *foco* in the middle Magdalena region. The Fuerzas Armadas Revolucionarias de Colombia (FARC), linked to the Communist Party since the years of La Violencia, also kept a very low profile of defensive activity in marginal areas. For a discussion of these guerrilla movements, see Gott 1973:306–20, 348–55, and chapter 4 in this volume.

Conservative candidate in 1970.[7] The specter of class struggle was now hovering over the cities, and an attempt had to be made to overcome the economic and social crisis that, apart from impairing capitalist accumulation, was threatening political trouble.

Lleras Restrepo adopted aggressive policies, promoting industrial exports in order to increase the availability of foreign reserves and find new markets for the country's manufactures (Bejarano 1978:90–95). Acknowledging the dynamism of the incipient capitalist agriculture, the president pledged support to the "modernized" landowners and rural entrepreneurs. However, Lleras Restrepo still considered agrarian reform (strengthening the peasantry and fostering land redistribution in the areas of traditional latifundios) as the best strategy to stop the migratory tide, improve the rural situation, and enlarge the internal market for industry (Lleras Restrepo 1982:109–15). To give more "teeth" to the otherwise mild reform legislation, a law was passed in 1968 granting rights to tenants and sharecroppers over their plots on the haciendas. Furthermore, the Agrarian Reform Institute, INCORA, started programs of redistribution in most areas of latifundios.[8] But the landowners strongly opposed these changes, and Lleras Restrepo knew that state action would not suffice to accelerate agrarian reform. Behind the state stood the National Front, a formal coalition that expressed the common interests of the dominant classes. Since land redistribution escaped the limits of these common interests, external pressure was needed to undermine the position of the landowner class within the National Front. This pressure could only come from the peasants, who appeared as a natural ally of bourgeois reformism because they had a stake in the resolution of the agrarian question.

The president appealed to the peasantry by means of a massive participation program. In 1967 a special decree created the Asociación Nacional de Usuarios Campesinos (ANUC), which would organize the peasants as users of the state services (Escobar 1982:7–8). ANUC would represent the peasantry within the state agencies and help to implement a drastic agrarian reform. It was an invitation for pressure, and the peasants responded. The organization campaign was coordinated by the Ministry of Agriculture, and dozens of specially trained promoters vis-

7. Rojas Pinilla was making a really impressive political comeback. In just a few years his populist movement, Alianza Nacional Popular (ANAPO), had developed from being an internal faction within the Conservative Party into a significant force that included opposition sectors of the Liberal Party as well. The best account of ANAPO is Dix 1980. On ANAPO's support among the landowners, see Martínez and Izquierdo 1982:42, 47–50, 72.

8. By comparison with the period 1962–66, during Lleras Restrepo's administration (1966–70) INCORA started five times as many legal processes of expropriation, involving twice the amount of land (INCORA 1978).

ited all the municipalities to form the local associations (Suárez Melo 1969; Zamosc 1986:54–60). Local members later created the departmental associations of *usuarios* that in turn would send delegates to ANUC's national assembly. In their meetings the promoters analyzed problems with the peasants, instructing them on their rights to the land and state services, encouraging attitudes of independence toward the political bosses, and nurturing a rebellious consciousness against the injustices of the rural situation. Membership cards were distributed, the *usuarios* elected representatives, and the demands were written down as petitions. Regional delegates started to meet and an embryonic national leadership developed. The ministry published a national newspaper and paid salaries to the leaders for their full-time involvement. When the first national congress of ANUC met in 1970, there were almost one million registered *usuarios* (Miniagricultura 1971). Relative to population numbers, ANUC's membership was stronger in the regions of latifundios and colonization (Zamosc 1986:71–72), which indicated that the movement had greater appeal precisely within those agrarian structures in which the peasant sectors were facing the most difficult problems: lack of land of their own and absence of basic services.

A class alliance does not imply absolute community of interests across the board. Social classes may share interests at the economic level but not at the political level. From the point of view of the underlying class alignments, therefore, ANUC's creation can be seen as part of an attempt to forge an alliance that would further the common economic interests (defined in terms of the desirability of agrarian reform) of the peasantry and the industrial bourgeoisie, but at the same time would be subject to the control of the latter's reformist politicians. There were, of course, many political underpinnings in Lleras Restrepo's decision to organize the peasants. As already noted, it was necessary to contain the rise of populism in the cities, and the National Front would need the peasant votes in order to achieve that. External pressure was coming from the United States, whose Alliance for Progress policy wanted to prevent "another Cuba" by encouraging agrarian reform and popular participation in Latin American development programs (Bagley and Botero 1978:61). Furthermore, Lleras Restrepo also saw some cause for concern in the activities of the guerrillas, and it can even be argued that he was interested in securing a base of electoral support among the peasantry for a second presidential bid after the end of the National Front (Bagley and Edel 1980:270). However, all these political motives appeared to him as conditioned by, and therefore subordinate to, the primary goals of renewing the expansion of industry and keeping the peasants in the countryside. As has been already explained, Lleras Restrepo believed that agrarian reform was absolutely necessary to meet the most urgent priorities of Colombia's capitalism, and this belief was the main factor behind his overture toward an alliance with the peasantry.

In its first stage of mobilization, ANUC articulated the demands of all the different peasant sectors, but the main emphasis was on land redistribution. Spontaneous demonstrations and land invasions by *usuarios* took place in the Atlantic coast, eastern Llanos, and many other regions (Zamosc 1986:67). The organization of the peasantry and the activity of lNCORA had provoked a strong landowner reaction. Since the approval of the law that gave rights to tenants and sharecroppers, massive evictions were taking place on haciendas throughout the country and especially in the Atlantic coast region (Bagley and Botero 1978:67; Zamosc 1986:67,78–79). ANUC's first congress had repeated the call for a drastic agrarian reform and expressed readiness to support the Conservative government that was about to take office on condition that it would maintain and expand the programs of peasant organization and agrarian reform (ANUC 1970; Escobar 1982:11–14). Though the tone was radical, the demands were still within the spirit of reformism. The peasants had remained loyal to the National Front, and the official candidate, Misael Pastrana, had won the 1970 election thanks to rural votes that overshadowed Rojas Pinilla's victory in the cities.[9] Urban populism had again been postponed, but the peasantry was now organized as a class, and the stage was set for real pressure in the countryside.

RADICALIZATION AND CONFRONTATION, 1971–75

Misael Pastrana did not share his predecessor's enthusiasm for agrarian reform. The weight of the landowners within his Conservative party was decisive, but the peasants had been mobilized and the president preferred to remain ambiguous at the beginning. Able to coordinate its activities at different levels, ANUC increased the pressure. By contrast with the previous spontaneity, the expressions of protest were now carefully organized and included new forms of action such as massive rallies and civil disobedience (Zamosc 1986:69–70). Since the Conservative government maintained its equivocal attitude, the *usuarios* started to prepare a major showdown of force. The Communist Party had dismissed ANUC as a clientelist plot, but some activists were advising the peasant leaders on a personal basis. Trotskyite militants had also become influential among the national leadership. The plans for confrontation and leftist influences aroused objections among some loyal Liberal and Conser-

9. Rojas Pinilla's lack of support in the countryside is not surprising if one takes into account that his agrarian program did not call for land redistribution and reduced agrarian reform to the promotion of colonization (Martínez and Izquierdo 1982:49–50). For an analysis of the 1970 election results see Dix 1980:141–46.

vative peasant leaders. But the majority decided to carry on, and on February 1971 a great wave of land invasions took place. Thousands of families seized portions of hundreds of estates throughout the country, especially in the inner valleys and on the Atlantic coast.[10] The government finally adopted a definite position, freezing ANUC's budget, sacking most of the promoters and dismissing pro-peasant officials from INCORA. Under the slogan "land without masters," ANUC issued a *Mandato campesino*. This document stated that instead of begging the dominant classes for agrarian reform, the peasants should accomplish it themselves, expropriating the landowners through direct action and ignoring the legal mechanisms of the state (ANUC 1971). It was now a head-on confrontation and, by the end of the year, the *usuarios* organized a second wave of land seizures. Calls for antisubversive measures reached hysterical proportions. With the endorsement of all Conservative and Liberal sectors (including many former reformists), Congress invited both parties and the private sector to reach a national agreement on agrarian reform. According to one of the proponents of the motion, such agreement was essential "to save the country from the dreadful consequences of a red revolution in the countryside" (Escobar 1982:31). The agrarian counterreform was sealed at the town of Chicoral in January 1972. Politicians and entrepreneurs met with government officials and agreed to pass legislation hardening the legal criteria for land expropriation, increasing compensation in cases of redistribution, and providing massive credit resources for the crops of capitalist agriculture (Zamosc 1986:97–99).

Disappointment and leftist influences had clearly played a central role in ANUC's radicalization. But the ultimate causes have to be sought at the more basic level of class contradictions and alignments. Here one element was the aggravation of conflicts over land, marked by the landowners' encroachments and the peasants' resolve to resist or maintain their own offensive. The second element was the isolation of the peasantry, which had developed as a result of the defeat of reformism and the consolidation of a tight opposition front of the dominant classes. Politically, the collapse of reformism was the result of the strength of the landowner interests, fears aroused by the leftist overtones of ANUC's radicalism, and the fact that urban pressures seemed to be easing after the populist electoral defeat. Economically, the interests of landowners and financiers converged on a capitalist path of agrarian development, but the change of heart of the industrialists had to do with the redefinition

---

10. All in all, 645 land invasions took place in the course of 1971. The most affected departments were Sucre, Córdoba, Bolívar, and Magdalena on the Atlantic coast, and Huila and Tolima in the inner valleys. For a statistical analysis and regional accounts of the conflicts, see Zamosc 1986:74–91. Detailed information by municipalities is presented in Zamosc 1984:231–39.

of their priorities according to the new outward orientation of the Colombian model of capitalist accumulation (Kalmanovitz 1977). In the context of changes in the international division of labor and the incorporation of peripheral countries as suppliers of certain manufactured goods, Lleras Restrepo's efforts to promote industrial exports had been so successful that they were spearheading a renewed economic expansion. Manufactured exports, which had reached almost U.S. $100 million in 1970, grew at an annual average rate of approximately 100 percent in the early 1970s (Bejarano 1978:98). For the industrialists, repeasantization as a mechanism to enlarge the internal market became irrelevant, since the important markets were now opening abroad and in the big cities themselves as a result of the expanding industrial payroll. Furthermore, checking the rural-urban migration could have unfavorable consequences in a situation that required cheaper wages for successful international competition, particularly at a time when salaries were on the rise and the rate of new urban employment was doubling the rate of population growth in the cities (Bejarano 1978:112−13). Since agrarian reformism was no longer needed and could even become an obstacle from the standpoint of the new priorities, the industrial bourgeoisie closed ranks with the other dominant groups against the peasantry.

In order to curb the peasant movement, Pastrana adopted a double policy of divisiveness and coercion (Zamosc 1986:100−104). Taking advantage of the differences between radicals and loyalists, the government encouraged the latter to break away and set up a parallel ANUC with official support. At the same time, harsh repression was used against the radicals. Land invasions (which had previously led to negotiations on the occupied estates between INCORA, landowners, and peasants) were now severely repressed by the rural police, and a free hand was given to the landowners to organize armed gangs of their own. The radical *usuarios* were declared illegal: their petitions were rejected and their rallies harassed by the authorities.

Confrontation proceeded through the rest of Pastrana's administration. The radicalized hub of the peasant movement was clearly located in the areas of land struggle (the inner valleys and, particularly, on the Atlantic coast), where the nature of the peasants' demands rendered land invasions possible as a direct form of action. The struggle for land brought politics to the forefront because it entailed a challenge to the regime of landed property and clientelist control. This generated a great receptivity to radical ideologies, which were in fact necessary to sustain the praxis of class struggle. The *usuario* leaders had been calling for an alliance with the working class; but they rejected the bureaucratic and pro-Soviet orientations of the Communists and disagreed with the Trotskyites' concept of "socialist revolution now." They felt more attracted by the new Maoist tendencies, which postulated a democratic revolution whose main force would be the peasantry and whose leadership would correspond to the vanguard of the working class (Zamosc 1986 : 114–15). During 1972 scores of young Maoist militants left the schools and universities of Medellín, Bogotá, and Barranquilla in order to take part in what they saw as an imminent insurrection, concentrating their efforts in the main areas of land struggle, especially in the western savannas of the Atlantic coast.[11]

The land struggles had been accompanied by significant mobilizations in some areas of colonization, where the main modalities of struggle were demonstrations, marches, and rallies. Some regional capitals were paralyzed by massive civil strikes, with thousands of colonists demanding roads, bridges, control of transport prices, and basic services.[12] ANUC's performance in the Andean minifundio regions was much less impressive, being in fact reduced to demonstrations over credits and services, actions in support of the demands of Indian communities, and a single local instance of a civil strike organized to reject a new tax.[13] These contrasts were distinctly related to the differential nature of the peasant aspirations. While the struggle for land had direct political implications and fostered a radical mood, the demands for services emphasized the economic dimension and led to less belligerent attitudes. The fact that the leftist influences were mainly exerted in the areas of land struggle further reinforced these differences. All in all, it can be said that heterogeneous class content was shaping an uneven development of the peasant movement. The effects of this were clearly felt with the divisive campaign of the government. Radical ANUC maintained its hegemony in the areas of land struggle and in the more galvanized regions of colonization. The progovernment ANUC predominated in minifundio areas and in the older and more stable colonization zones.

Radical ANUC began to decline by 1974. Repression was visibly containing the belligerent impulses among the rank and file. Furthermore, the success of earlier mobilizations meant that at least the most radical

11. The main Maoist party, the Partido Comunista Marxista Leninista (PCML), had an armed detachment, the Ejército Popular de Liberación (EPL), operating in the Upper Sinú area. The militants planned to penetrate the peasant movement in the coastal departments, develop links with the Upper Sinú *foco,* and expand the guerrilla war with the peasant land struggles.

12. The most impressive civil strikes took place in Florencia (Caquetá) and Saravena (Arauca). There were less important expressions of protest in Meta, Putamayo, and along the Pacific littoral.

13. The main demonstrations and rallies corresponded to Nariño, Antioquia, and Cundinamarca. The civil strike mentioned here affected the municipality of Quinchía in Risaralda. There were some marginal land struggles on the Andes, but the only ones that had some regional relevance were those of the Comité Regional Indígena del Cauca (CRIC). The Caucan Indians tried to recover communal lands lost to neighboring landowners (Antonil 1978:229–70).

groups were likely to have satisfied their "land hunger" and were now busy securing their tenure and beginning agricultural exploitation.[14] There was, however, another factor: political factionalism. In order to ignite the spark for their expected general insurrection, the Maoist cadres were seeking to escalate the land struggles into violent confrontations. Believing that the "bourgeois tendencies" of the peasantry could undermine revolutionary potential in the countryside, they also tried to impose restrictions on production for the market, consumption patterns, and details of daily life, such as what clothing to wear and what radio programs to listen to. The approach of the Maoists provoked harsher repression from the authorities and led to more and more desertions at the grass-roots level. The leaders of ANUC, who considered this approach an extremist deviation and were consolidating their own stand as a powerful bureaucratic group, decided that the *usuarios* should have an autonomous political line. They launched a campaign to purge the regional associations of Maoist militants and finally expelled the Maoist groups in 1974.[15] That same year, ANUC's leadership set up the Organización Revolucionaria del Pueblo (ORP), a secretive caucus that would prepare the ground for a future political party. Marked by sectarian debates that escaped the understanding of the ordinary peasants, political fragmentation substantially weakened radical ANUC.

DECLINE AND RECESS OF THE PEASANT MOVEMENT, 1975–81

The new outward orientation of Colombian capitalism had boosted accumulation to unprecedented levels. Under President Pastrana the real income of industrial workers went down and the salary differential vis-à-vis the United States substantially widened (Kalmanovitz 1977 : 140–43). Trade union activity had been severely repressed, which, together with the brutal restraint enforced against the peasants, was indicative of the degree of social tension generated by the economic and policy changes. The Liberal Alfonso López Michelsen, who took over in 1974 as the first president after the National Front, had exploited the widespread discontent to win the elections with a solid majority. It immediately became apparent, however, that his administration intended to consolidate the new

14. I have estimated that in the areas most affected by the land struggles (Atlantic coast and inner valleys), 10 to 15 percent of the rural families gained access to land of their own during the first half of the 1970s (Zamosc 1986 : 149–50).

15. The political confrontation reached its climax at ANUC's third national congress (Bogotá, August 1974). This event, which started with a massive peasant demonstration unprecedented in Bogotá, was marked by its chaotic proceedings. Reacting to constant sabotage by the Maoist cadres, ANUC's leaders closed the congress and excluded all dissident groups from the peasant movement (Escobar 1982 : 64–70). For detailed analysis of the political confrontations within ANUC, see Rivera 1982 : 115–53 and Zamosc 1986 : 113–21.

scheme of capitalist accumulation while taking some corrective steps to mitigate the most undesirable social effects of the model. In the countryside the main initiative was the Integrated Rural Development Program, DRI. This program, coordinated with international financial agencies, offered credit, technical assistance, and other services to the stable sectors of the peasantry. Clearly, DRI was designed to boost the production of cheap foodstuffs (which would help to maintain low wages and increase the competitiveness of Colombian exports), set some limits to rural-urban migration, and dissipate part of the agrarian discontent of the previous years (Bejarano 1978:137–42; Grindle 1986: 164–74). Still, the millions of dollars injected into the main minifundio areas were a real concession to some sections of the peasantry. Although the coffee areas were not included among the DRI regions, the Coffee Federation was running a parallel program that, fed by an unprecedented price bonanza in the world coffee market, would bring even more benefits to the peasants than those offered by DRI.[16] But these concessions and bonanzas did not affect the landless peasants. López Michelsen considered that the valleys and plains, which had been the main setting of the agrarian struggles, had to proceed with agricultural modernization, taking advantage of higher capitalist productivity to supply raw materials for industry and increase exports (DNP 1975:41–44). Consequently, the new president openly declared his opposition to agrarian reform, warning that any land invasions would be severely punished. The only palliative was the 1975 Sharecropping Law, which, seeking to alleviate peasant pressure on the land, enabled the landowners to admit sharecroppers without risking expropriation.[17]

The leaders of radical ANUC denounced the law as an attempt to circumvent the land issue by reviving servile relations of production (ANUC 1975; Escobar 1982:77–79). Believing that the movement was still strong in the areas of land struggle, they issued a call to renew the peasant invasions. But the response was restricted to only a few municipalities on the Atlantic coast. The government answered with militarization, massive arrests, and persecution of local and regional leaders (Zamosc 1986:126–29). Nothing was gained in terms of access to land,

16. Between 1975 and 1979, DRI investments amounted to almost U.S. $280 million (including credit). During the same period the Coffee Federation spent U.S. $322 million on the extension of rural services (excluding credit). See DNP 1970:20; Grindle 1986: 166; and FEDECAFE 1975–79.

17. Under the 1968 legislation, tenants and sharecroppers could claim rights to the land they worked. This had provoked massive evictions, something that not only propelled the land struggles, but also threatened to leave the landowners without reserves of labor power. As Gómez (1975) has shown, the 1975 Sharecropping Law aimed at alleviating the peasant pressure and, at the same time, making available the seasonal labor force needed for capitalist agriculture.

and the conflicts of 1975 marked the beginning of the final recess of the land struggles. Apart from repression and the already mentioned fragmentation by political factionalism, there were other factors that also contributed to easing the pressures (Zamosc 1986:130–39). One of them was migration to the towns, which in some of the main places of land struggle involved up to 20 and even 30 percent of the rural population between the mid 1960s and the mid 1970s. A second factor had to do with new occupational alternatives that developed during the 1970s. The expansion of capitalist agriculture led to very substantial increases in the absorption of labor on the Atlantic coast and in the inner valleys. After 1974 the migration of temporary agricultural workers to Venezuela also had an enormous impact. In the eastern areas of the Atlantic coast, the development of the marijuana economy came to involve an estimated third of the rural population and led to dramatic changes: old conflicts vanished, peasants cultivated marijuana under contractual agreements with landowners, and all sectors of the population were integrated into a vertical block of classes controlled by regional mafias. Combined with the cushioning effects of the Sharecropping Law, emigration, and the partial access to land that resulted from the early waves of land invasions, these new alternatives of employment helped to defuse the previous potential for conflict in the main areas of land struggle.

Radical ANUC tried to adjust to the changing conditions. Since the struggle for land was no longer a realistic option, the main efforts in these areas took two new directions. First, an attempt was made to organize the agricultural proletariat, especially the coffee and cotton pickers (Zamosc 1986:139–45). But the seasonal workers were not "pure" proletarians. Their class definition was ambiguous because most of them were peasants who were trying to supplement the incomes of their families. Furthermore, they were constantly on the move, and piecework payment systems fostered individualism and competition. It proved extremely difficult to approach and organize them: ANUC's drive led to repeated failures and was eventually abandoned. A second focus of agitation was in the cooperative settlements that had emerged as a result of the land struggles of the past (Zamosc 1986:165–78). Here the situation seemed favorable for organizational work, because most of the settlements were facing great economic hardships and had to resist the bureaucratic pressures exerted by INCORA. However, the main problem was the dogmatic adherence of radical ANUC to unrealistic principles like the refusal to accept official land titles (because they implied payment for the land) and the rejection of government programs of credit and assistance. The frustrated *usuarios,* who were forced by their objective needs to deal with the state agencies, started to abandon the organization and defect to the progovernment ANUC.

Blind opposition to the activities of the state agencies was also the crucial factor in the decline of radical ANUC throughout the areas of colonization and established peasant economy. Attracted by programs that at least produced some results in terms of credit, services, and infrastructural improvements, the peasants paid little attention to ANUC's propaganda and dismissed the leaders when it became clear that the stances of the movement were not compatible with their perceived interests. ANUC's failure was related to what seemed to be an intrinsic difficulty in articulating economic demands and political aspirations within the radical perspectives that prevailed in the movement. This had been quite clear in the extremist leftism of the Maoists, who rejected any work on economic demands as anathema to the expected insurrection. But the problem was not solved when the *usuario* leadership developed its own political project. Indeed, by trying to transform radical ANUC into a party that would carry the torch of a future socialist revolution, the leaders were again subordinating the everyday demands of the peasantry to remote political goals. They ignored the real consciousness of the peasants, dogmatically assuming that they would readily accept a proletarian perspective of self-definition and political struggle. At the level of concrete action, these principles precluded any tasks beyond the simple denunciation of the existing regime.

An aggravating factor in the decline of radical ANUC was its bureaucratic style of leadership. A small group of leaders and advisors had entrenched themselves at the top and rejected all points of view different from their own. This led to breaks with the Indian movement and a number of regional *usuario* chapters, gradually eroding the remaining support at the grass-roots level.[18] Denying that the movement was disintegrating, the leaders brought their political line to the open under the form of the Movimiento Nacional Democrático Popular (MNDP), a party whose program featured a mixture of Maoist and populist ingredients. The MNDP joined the Maoist front for the 1978 parliamentary elections, and its total failure precipitated the final crisis (Zamosc 1986: 187–90). Arguing that the dominant classes had succeeded in cornering the peasant movement, a faction of the leadership decided that it was necessary to conciliate the bourgeoisie, stressing the demands of the "rich peasantry" and going back to the traditional parties and their clientelist trade unions. Those who tried to oppose this right-wing reaction were expelled and negotiations were opened toward an agreement with the progovernment ANUC, something that was finally accomplished when the Ministry of Agriculture sponsored a reunification congress in 1981 (Escobar 1982: 160–68). At this stage there was no longer any real sup-

18. Antonil (1978: 263–69) provides a very good and accurate account of the conflict between ANUC and the Indian movement, CRIC. See Zamosc (1986: 179–81) on the breaks between ANUC's national leaders and regional chapters of the peasant movement.

port at the grass-roots level. Still, the cooptation of the bureaucratized leaders of radical ANUC was useful to the clientelist system: it provided a final touch of legitimation for the reassertion of hegemony over the defeated peasantry.

OVERVIEW AND FINAL REMARKS

In the evolution of the peasant movement, the most outstanding element is the cycle marked by its three phases: the organization of ANUC as part of a project of reformist alliance, the confrontation based upon radical stances, and the final conservative reaction of conciliation and submission. A great deal of these dynamics is explained by the oscillations of a state policy that, after a sharp turn from reformism to counter-reform, stabilized around new orientations that implied partial concessions for some sectors of the peasantry. These shifts followed the realignments that took place among the dominant classes and reflected the changing projection of the agrarian question as the rise of industrial exports modified the model of capitalist accumulation in the country. Still, it would be a mistake to consider ANUC's evolution as a mere epiphenomenon of the policies of the dominant classes and the state. It is true that reformism organized the peasants, but the real roots of the *usuarios'* upsurge were related to the underlying agrarian antagonisms and the class aspirations of the peasantry. Similarly, radicalization was not simply an effect of relative deprivation derived from counterreform: autonomous confrontation was possible because ANUC had become a tangible objectification of the power of the peasantry as a class. And in the same vein, ANUC's final rightist turn was more than a conciliatory reaction to the concessions offered by the state, because it reflected the submissive spirit derived from the prostration of the movement. To a large extent, then, ANUC's cycle depended upon the vicissitudes of the power contest that took place in the countryside, and the factors that influenced this cycle must be seen as variables that either enhanced or undermined the class power embodied by the organization. In this sense, it can be said that in addition to the strength of the landowners, the shifts in the politics of alliances of the Colombian bourgeoisie, and the government's success in splitting and repressing the *usuarios*, the major factor was the class heterogeneity of the peasant movement. At the beginning, ANUC was able to articulate the demands of the landless, of colonists, and of stable peasants. This multisectoral class base gave a strong boost to the rise of the movement, but the disparities in aspirations and radicalism led to uneven development and internal contradictions; problems that were later aggravated by political orientations that failed to respond to the immediate economic interests of the different peasant sectors.

What were the overall effects of the peasant struggles of the 1970s? In this chapter, I have argued that ANUC projected itself as a force that tried to obtain a resolution of the agrarian question that would be favorable to the peasants. From this point of view, it can be said that the outcome was largely frustrating. It can be estimated that 66,000 families gained access to land as a result of the struggles of the 1970s, but this figure barely compensated for the overall dissolution of the peasantry during the 1960s and 1970s.[19] The adverse conditions that prevailed in the new settlements led to the failure of the peasant cooperatives and the economic strangulation of individual families (Zamosc 1986:154–65). Meanwhile, agrarian capitalism consolidated its hold over the valleys and plains, largely reducing these peasant settlements to reservoirs of temporary labor. The available studies show rapid processes of differentiation and flows of rural-urban migration in the colonization areas (Marsh 1980; Giraldo and Ladrón de Guevara 1981). In the Andean regions the coffee bonanza and state support programs benefited the more stable peasant sectors, but uprooting and migration are still proceeding at an accelerated rate among the lower peasant strata. Altogether, then, the prevailing tendencies show that ANUC's struggles failed to modify the patterns of agrarian development to the advantage of the peasantry as a whole. Peasant participation in agricultural production fell from 61 percent in 1960 to 44 percent in 1981 (Zamosc 1986:208), the dissolution of the peasantry continued, and only some of the stable sectors of the peasantry managed to improve their position. As a tentative overall assessment of ANUC's historical significance, then, it can be concluded that the *usuarios* episode represented the defeat of the peasant attempt to secure the predominance of a nonmonopolistic path of agrarian evolution under Colombian capitalism.

Regarding the politics of the peasant movement, its great receptivity to leftist influences can be explained as a result of the isolation of the peasantry. After the reformist failure, the peasant movement turned to working-class organizations in an attempt to forge an alternative alliance. However, the Colombian workers' movement was badly organized and deeply divided. In the leftist camp, only the Communists had some roots in the working class, but these roots were very superficial. The Trotskyite and Maoist groups, who considered themselves vanguards of the proletariat, were merely political elites of intellectual and student extraction. In fact, the very fragmentation of the left was a symptom of the weakness of the working class and its incapacity to join the peasantry in a

19. According to my quantitative analysis of the achievements of the peasant struggles (Zamosc 1986:146–54), the 66,000 families amounted to only 11.8 percent of what had been estimated as the total number of beneficiaries of a reasonable agrarian reform in the country. Compared to other cases in Latin America, the aggregate impact of the Colombian agrarian reform was absolutely marginal: for comparative standards, see de Janvry 1981:206–7 and McClintock 1981:61.

democratic revolution during the early 1970s. For this reason, the links between ANUC and the left have to be seen as substitutes for an impossible alliance between peasants and workers. These links provided ideological support and created the much-needed illusion of a broad plebeian struggle against the dominant classes. But from the standpoint of class alliances, the truth was that the peasants were isolated in their mobilization, and it was this isolation that gradually led the *usuarios* to try to create a political force of their own. This urge was reinforced when the Maoists tried to use ANUC for their own extravagant insurrectional plans. Still, the autonomous stances developed by ANUC were also trapped in the contradiction between revolutionary orientations and day-to-day demands. The peasant aspirations were subordinated to the straightjacket of a "proletarianist" outlook, ignoring the fact that, in the absence of a truly revolutionary conjuncture, the grievances of the peasants must be necessarily handled by reference to the prevailing correlation of political forces and the existing socioeconomic and institutional reality. This failure of leftist politicization, leading to widespread loss of support at the grass-roots level, played a preponderant role in the decline and frustration of the *usuarios*.

With the peasant defeat of the 1970s, the aspirations of the mass of the Colombian rural population were again curbed and postponed. In the process, the bureaucratic remnants of ANUC were reabsorbed into the game of the Liberal and Conservative political clienteles. From the point of view of the nature of the Colombian regime, the outcome reaffirmed that the paths of opposition were closed in the country and that the popular sectors had to acquiesce to the social and political designs of the dominant classes. This was in line with developments in the cities, where the post–National Front governments continued to use the clientelist unions to divide the working class and escalated the repression against independent unions and movements of urban protest. Outwardly Colombia may have resembled an island of democracy and stable growth amid a Latin American sea of economic instability and military dictatorships. But the internal picture was not idyllic at all: while the clientelist political system excluded popular participation, rapid economic growth was marked by increasing concentration of wealth and declining living standards among the urban and rural majorities (Bejarano 1984: 17–22). Eventually, by the end of the 1970s, the regime's crisis of political legitimacy became obvious (Bagley 1984). In a context of growing apathy toward traditional politics, widespread violence and corruption linked to the drug traffic, frequent guerrilla attacks, and an unprecedented economic crisis, the 1982 electoral victory of Belisario Betancur was seen as a mandate to introduce changes and restore political legitimacy (Hartlyn 1983).

Betancur, a Conservative with populist leanings, projected a new image of leadership by boosting the country's standing in international politics, cracking down on drug traffickers and financial speculators, and trying to negotiate a formal amnesty that would solve the chronic problem of guerrilla activity. But his government surrendered to the pressures of the International Monetary Fund and failed to introduce any significant changes in economic policy. Despite rising international coffee prices that somewhat eased the effects of the depression, the consequences of "austerity" were appalling; by the end of the Betancur administration, purchasing power had sharply declined and unemployment stood at an all-time high. On the political front, the president was unable to make convincing progress toward the much-talked-about democratization of the system. Support for the initiative was never enthusiastic among the majority of Liberal and Conservative politicians, who, deeply committed to the clientelist status quo, managed to kill or postpone the approval of reforms in Congress. The overtures to the guerrillas, which were only partially successful in terms of the demobilization of the armed groups, reinforced hawkish attitudes among the military and on both sides of the bipartisan divide. Given Betancur's mixed legacy of hope and frustration, the solid 1986 victory of the Liberal presidential candidate Virgilio Barco may still provide new impetus to the process of economic and political reform. For that, however, the new Liberal government must display a substantial degree of autonomy from the traditional political elites and, above all, show real determination in addressing the problems and demands of the popular sectors.

In the meantime, one should not lose sight of the fact that Virgilio Barco's victory did not come on the crest of an outburst of popular enthusiasm and support. It was achieved through the workings of the old clientelist machinery of his party, well tuned up by regional and local bosses who had assimilated the lessons of their 1982 electoral defeat. It is clear that the crisis of political legitimacy has not yet been solved, and that a return to the repressive ways of the pre-Betancur era is not a remote possibility. Thus, while social and political compromises seem to be consolidating democratic alternatives elsewhere in Latin America, Colombia again presents a prominent contrast. This time, however, the discordant note could have ominous reverberations, because what is being questioned in Colombia's crisis of political legitimacy is the civilian government inherited from the National Front, not a Southern Cone–style military dictatorship. The future of democracy is at stake, and the outcome will depend upon the way in which Colombians come to terms with the other heritages of their recent past: a political system that denies effective participation to the popular sectors and a pattern of capitalist development that has failed to respond to the needs and aspirations of the majority.

Finally, a word is in order on the need to project the insights derived from ANUC's case to the level of theoretical and comparative reflection. During the past few years we have seen the development of sophisticated approaches to the study of the peasant economy and its reproduction in capitalist societies, but little progress has been made in the field of peasant political participation. In Latin America we have no comparative studies on the recent experiences of peasant mobilization, and much of the discussion still revolves around the issue of the presumed "revolutionary" or "conservative" quintessence of the peasantry. One contribution of this analysis of ANUC is that it clearly shows the limitations of such an approach to the problem. The oscillation that led the movement to the adoption of reformist, revolutionary, and conservative stances within a decade tells much about the complex nature of the peasantry as a class. The peasants want the promotion of social relations and values related to the domestic rural economy; but this general aspiration will assume different forms according to the class sectors that are involved and the specificities of the historical context. In some cases, the promotion of the peasant economy implies deep structural changes aimed at the establishment or restoration of peasant farming. In other cases, promoting the peasant economy means preserving an existing reality or trying to obtain relative improvements within that reality. The character of a peasant movement and the effectiveness of its struggle seem therefore to depend upon both the type of aspirations it represents and the manner in which these peasant aspirations are articulated at the level of conflicts and alliances with other social classes.

REFERENCES

Antonil [pseud.]
  1978   *Mama Coca.* London: Hassle Free Press.
ANUC [Asociación Nacional de Usuarios Campesinos, Colombia]
  1970   "Declaración de principios del primer congreso nacional." *Carta Campesina,* no. 9 (July).
  1971   "Mandato campesino." *Carta Campesina,* no. 19 (October).
  1975   "Conclusiones de la XII junta directiva nacional." *Boletín Informativo,* no. 12 (March).
Arango, Mariano
  1977   *Café e industria, 1850–1930.* Bogotá: Carlos Valencia Editores.
Bagley, Bruce M.
  1984   "Colombia: National Front and Economic Development." In *Politics, Policies and Economic Development in Latin America,* edited by R. Wesson, pp. 124–60. Palo Alto, Calif.: Hoover Institution Press.
Bagley, Bruce M., and Fernando Botero
  1978   "Organizaciones campesinas contemporáneas en Colombia: Un estudio de la asociación nacional de usuarios campesinos." *Estudios Rurales Latinoamericanos* 1 (January–April): 59–95.

Bagley, Bruce M., and Matthew Edel
   1980   "Popular Mobilization Programs of the National Front: Cooptation
          and Radicalization." In *Politics of Compromise: Coalition Government in
          Colombia,* edited by R. A. Berry, R. G. Hellman, and M. Solaún,
          pp. 257–84. New Brunswick, N.J.: Transaction Books.
Bejarano, Jesús A.
   1975   "El fin de la economía exportadora y los orígenes del problema
          agrario." *Cuadernos Colombianos* 2 (April–June): 225–303.
   1978   *Ensayos de interpretación de la economía colombiana.* Bogotá: Editorial la
          Carreta.
   1983   "Campesinado, luchas agrarias e historia social." *Anuario Colombiano
          de Historia Social y de la Cultura* 11 : 251–98.
   1984   *La economía colombiana en la década del setenta.* Bogotá: Fondo Editorial
          CEREC.
Bergquist, Charles W.
   1986   *Coffee and Conflict in Colombia, 1886–1910.* Durham, N.C.: Duke Uni-
          versity Press.
Collier, David
   1979   "Overview of the Bureaucratic-Authoritarian Model." In *The New
          Authoritarianism in Latin America,* edited by D. Collier, pp. 19–32.
          Princeton, N.J.: Princeton University Press.
DANE [Departamento Administrativo Nacional de Estadísticas, Colombia]
   1951   *Censo nacional de población, 1951.* Bogotá: DANE.
   1960   *Censo nacional agropecuario, 1960.* Bogotá: DANE.
   1964   *Censo nacional de población, 1964.* Bogotá: DANE.
   1965–69 *Anuario de comercio exterior.* Bogotá: DANE.
De Janvry, Alain
   1981   *The Agrarian Question and Reformism in Latin America.* Baltimore: Johns
          Hopkins University Press.
Dix, Robert H.
   1980   "Political Oppositions under the National Front." In *Politics of Com-
          promise: Coalition Government in Colombia,* edited by R. A. Berry, R. G.
          Hellman, and M. Solaún, pp. 131–79. New Brunswick, N.J.: Trans-
          action Books.
DNP [Departamento Nacional de Planeación, Colombia]
   1970   *Las cuatro estrategias.* Bogotá: DNP.
   1975   *Para cerrar la brecha.* Bogotá: DNP.
Escobar, Cristina
   1982   *Trayectoria de la ANUC.* Bogotá: Editorial CINEP.
FAO [Food and Agriculture Organization, United Nations]
   1952–70 *Yearbook of Food and Agricultural Statistics.* Rome: FAO.
FEDECAFE [Federación de Cafeteros de Colombia]
   1950–65 *Boletín estadístico.* Bogotá: FEDECAFE.
   1975–79 *Informes de los Comités Departamentales de Cafeteros.* Bogotá:
          FEDECAFE.
Gaitán, Gloria
   1976   *Colombia: La lucha por la tierra en la década del treinta.* Bogotá: Tercer
          Mundo.

Gilhodes, Pierre
1974   *La Question agraire en Colombie.* Paris: Presses de la Fondation Nationales des Sciences Politiques.
Giraldo, Diego, and Laureano Ladrón de Guevara
1981   *Desarrollo y colonización: El caso colombiano.* Bogotá: Universidad Santo Tomás.
Gómez, Alcides
1975   "Política agraria de López y ley de aparcería." *Ideología y Sociedad* no. 14–15 (July–December): 47–63.
González, Fernán E.
1975   *Pasado y presente del sindicalismo colombiano.* Bogotá: Editorial CINEP.
Gott, Richard
1973   *Rural Guerrillas in Latin America.* Harmondsworth, England: Penguin Books.
Grindle, Merilee S.
1986   *State and Countryside: Development Policy and Agrarian Politics in Latin America.* Baltimore: Johns Hopkins University Press.
Guzmán, Germán, Orlando Fals Borda, and Eduardo Umaña Luna
1962   *La Violencia en Colombia.* Bogotá: Universidad Nacional.
Hartlyn, Jonathan
1983   "Colombia: Old Problems, New Opportunities." *Current History* 82 (February): 62–65, 83–84.
INCORA [Instituto Colombiano de Reforma Agraria]
1978   *Informe de labores.* Bogotá: INCORA.
Junguito, Roberto, Juan E. Araya, Juan S. Betancur, Rodrigo Losada, Hernán Jaramillo, José Vallejo, and Ricardo Villaveces
1980   *Economía Cafetera Colombiana.* Bogotá: Fondo Cultural Cafetero.
Kalmanovitz, Salomón
1977   *Ensayos sobre el desarrollo del capitalismo dependiente.* Bogotá: Editorial Pluma.
1978   *La agricultura en Colombia, 1950–1972.* Bogotá: DANE.
Kline, Harvey F.
1980   "The National Front: Historical Perspective and Overview." In *Politics of Compromise: Coalition Government in Colombia,* edited by R. A. Berry, R. G. Hellman, and M. Solaún, pp. 59–83. New Brunswick, N.J.: Transaction Books.
Leal, Francisco
1984   *Estado y política en Colombia.* Bogotá: Siglo XXI Editores.
LeGrand, Catherine
1986   *Frontier Expansion and Peasant Protest in Colombia.* Albuquerque: University of New Mexico Press.
Lleras Restrepo, Carlos
1982   *La cuestión agraria.* Bogotá: Osprey Impresores.
McClintock, Cynthia
1981   *Peasant Cooperatives and Political Change in Peru.* Princeton, N.J.: Princeton University Press.
Machado, Absalón
1977   *El café: De la aparcería al capitalismo.* Bogotá: Punta de Lanza.

Marsh, Robin R.
  1980   "Colonization and Integrated Rural Development in Colombia."
         Thesis, University of California, Los Angeles.
Martínez, Juan P., and María I. Izquierdo
  1982   ANAPO: Oposición o revolución? Bogotá: Ediciones Camilo.
Melo, Jorge O.
  1978   "La república conservadora." In Colombia Hoy, edited by M. Arrubla,
         pp. 52–101. Bogotá: Siglo XXI Editores.
Miniagricultura [Ministerio de Agricultura, Colombia]
  1971   "Resumen de trabajos realizados en organización campesina."
         Mimeographed.
Moncayo, Víctor M., and Fernando Rojas
  1978   Producción campesina y capitalismo. Bogotá: Editorial CINEP.
O'Donnell, Guillermo
  1973   Modernization and Bureaucratic-Authoritarianism: Studies in South Ameri-
         can Politics. Politics of Modernization Series, no. 9. Berkeley: Insti-
         tute of International Studies, University of California.
Oquist, Paul
  1980   Violence, Conflict and Politics in Colombia. New York: Academic Press.
Palacios, Marco
  1979   El café en Colombia, 1850–1970: Una historia económica, social, y política.
         Bogotá: Editorial Presencia.
Rivera, Silvia
  1982   Política e ideología en el movimiento campesino colombiano: El caso de la
         ANUC.Bogotá: Editorial CINEP.
Robinson, J. Cordell
  1976   El movimiento gaitanista en Colombia. Bogotá: Tercer Mundo.
SAC [Sociedad de Agricultores de Colombia]
  1978   Bases para una política agropecuaria. Bogotá: Biblioteca SAC.
Sánchez, Gonzalo
  1977   Las Ligas Campesinas en Colombia. Bogotá: Tiempo Presente.
  1985   "La Violencia in Colombia: New Research, New Questions." Hispanic
         American Historical Review 65 (November): 789–807.
Solaún, Mauricio
  1980   "Colombian Politics: Historical Characteristics and Problems." In
         Politics of Compromise: Coalition Government in Colombia, edited by R. A.
         Berry, R. G. Hellman, and M. Solaún, pp. 1–57. New Brunswick,
         N.J.: Transaction Books.
Suárez Melo, Mario
  1969   "Campaña nacional de organización campesina." Documentos del
         Seminario Internacional sobre Organización Campesina. Guate-
         mala. Mimeographed.
Tirado Mejía, Alvaro
  1978   "Colombia: Siglo y medio de bipartidismo." In Colombia Hoy, edited
         by M. Arrubla, pp. 102–85. Bogotá: Siglo XXI Editores.
Tobón, Alonso
  1972   La tierra y la reforma agraria en Colombia. Bogotá: Editorial Cáncer.

Vélez, Hugo E.
  1974   *Dos ensayos acerca del desarrollo capitalista en la agricultura colombiana.*
          Bogotá: Editorial 8 de Junio.
Walton, John
  1984   *Reluctant Rebels: Comparative Studies of Revolution and Underdevelop-
          ment.* New York: Columbia University Press.
Zamosc, León
  1984   *Los usuarios campesinos y las luchas por la tierra en los años setenta.*
          Bogotá: Editorial CINEP.
  1986   *The Agrarian Question and the Peasant Movement in Colombia.* Cam-
          bridge: Cambridge University Press.

CHAPTER FOUR

Winners, Losers, and Also-Rans: Toward a Comparative Sociology of Latin American Guerrilla Movements

Timothy P. Wickham-Crowley

The men of action and conviction have failed enough of late to warrant revers-ing a famous apothegm of Marx: philosophers have tried to change the world; now it is time to try to understand it.

—BARRINGTON MOORE, JR.

In the 1960s leftist guerrilla movements appeared throughout Latin America. Today, Nicaraguan guerrilla revolutionaries who have governed for almost a decade since the overthrow of the Somoza regime face a sustained attack by nonleftist guerrilla organizations composed largely of disaffected Nicaraguans financed in good part by the U.S. government. Elsewhere in the region, other guerrilla movements continue their assaults on incumbent governments in El Salvador, Guatemala, Peru, and Colombia.

The current eruption of rural revolution mirrors a similar upsurge in the 1960s, which followed hard on the heels of the Cuban revolution. What can the sociological lessons learned from the study of earlier move-ments reveal about more recent left-wing guerrilla activity in Latin America? Can a comparative sociological approach help us to sort out the winners, the losers, and the also-rans? We wish to understand why there have been two great surges in guerrilla activity in Latin America since 1959, one in the mid 1960s and one in the mid 1970s; why only some of those guerrilla movements successfully expanded on a base of peasant support; and why only two of *those* movements succeeded in seizing state power. Although this essay focuses primarily on movements before 1970, I shall compare them in less detail with movements of the 1970s and 1980s to further our understanding of the conditions influ-encing the varied fortunes of guerrilla-based revolution. This will fill a gap in the literature, for most previous studies have, by contrast, been journalistic or noncomparative in nature.

I would like to acknowledge my debt to Cornell University, whose summer research fellow-ship in part made this research possible, as well as my debt to a University of Rochester postdoctoral fellowship. For critical comments and suggestions on this and related writ-ings, I wish to thank Joseph A. Kahl (who also provided the title), Thomas H. Holloway, León Zamosc, and especially Susan Eckstein.

A BRIEF HISTORICAL REVIEW

Following the success and socialist transformation of the Cuban revolution, guerrilla movements appeared throughout Latin America in the 1960s, but most died an early death. A few nations have seen a strong resurgence of such activity since roughly 1975: Nicaragua, Guatemala, Colombia, El Salvador, and Peru, the first three being revivals of earlier movements. Although virtually every nation in the region experienced a 1960s movement, the existing literature throws light on few of them, with Venezuela, Colombia, Guatemala, Peru, and Bolivia the most closely scrutinized nations. Bolivia is the prototype for guerrilla failure, yet we know much about it largely because of Che Guevara and his famous diary. Other failures left only traces in the written record, too few for the close analysis required here. Since the losers are underrepresented here, my sample is nonrandom, yet the comparative nature of my argument can still contribute to our understanding of the variety of outcomes of such revolutionary action.

In Cuba, Fulgencio Batista seized power in a coup in the mid 1930s and dominated Cuban politics off and on for the next twenty-five years. In 1952 he again seized power in a coup to stave off probable electoral defeat. In response, one of the disappointed candidates, Fidel Castro, organized a 1953 attack on the Moncada military barracks. Imprisoned, but later pardoned, Castro went into exile in Mexico, where he organized an invasion of Cuba. Routed in his December 1956 landing, Castro withdrew into the hills of eastern Cuba, where he built a guerrilla movement. The 26th of July Movement (M-26), as it was known, spread and grew to several hundred rural fighters plus urban supporters by early 1958, as Batista's troops proved ineffectual in counterinsurgency. Following a failed army campaign, Castro's guerrillas began a summer offensive in 1958, eventually forcing the dictator to flee the country at year's end. Castro assumed and consolidated power, instituted reforms, and declared Cuba socialist in mid 1961 following a confrontation with the United States over the nationalization of sugar lands.

Venezuela's first experiment with direct electoral democracy began in 1945, but ended in 1948, the victim of a military coup. The military government of Pérez Jiménez ruled in an increasingly bloody fashion toward the end of the 1950s, but, after a period of widespread social unrest and opposition, especially by Communists and left-wing youth, a civilian-military coup ousted the dictator in 1958. Caracas remained in revolutionary euphoria, while the interim government sought to mitigate economic problems with massive welfare spending and subsidies. Returning from exile, former president (1945–48) Rómulo Betancourt won the presidency in late 1958, brought to power on the strength of his Acción Democrática's ties to peasant voters, which went back to the 1930s. Over the next three to four years, opposition by students and

Caracas residents grew in the face of Betancourt's austerity program, and a dialectic of government and opposition violence ensued. Guerrilla bands appeared in 1962, followed a year later by more systematic guerrilla organization with party backing: the Armed Forces of National Liberation (FALN), sponsored by the Communists, and the Movement of the Revolutionary Left (MIR), organized by a splinter group from the president's own party. From 1963 on, the guerrillas' fortunes declined as agrarian reforms, elections, public distaste, efficient repression, an improving economy, and amnesties gradually took the wind from their sails. Internal splits hastened the decline. By the late 1960s, the guerrillas had all but petered out of existence.

In Guatemala, a decade of reformist government ended with the 1954 CIA-orchestrated overthrow of Jacobo Arbenz, who had begun a major land reform. A series of dictators followed. A left-leaning military revolt on 13 November 1960 was suppressed, but two young officers escaped capture, later forming the MR-13 guerrilla movement, and later still the Rebel Armed Forces (FAR). The guerrilla groups gained substantial ground in northeastern Guatemala by 1965, but succumbed to an intense U.S.-backed counterinsurgency campaign in 1966–67. After periods of dormancy and urban terrorism, various offshoots of the FAR reemerged in the 1970s, primarily among Indians in the western highlands, as more or less thinly veiled authoritarian governments came and went. Among the later guerrilla groups were the Guerrilla Army of the Poor (EGP), the FAR (again), and the Organization of the People in Arms (ORPA). After sustained growth to 1982, a violent counterinsurgency campaign under General Ríos Montt again reversed guerrilla fortunes, although they may have restrengthened their movement slightly up until the 1985 election of civilian president Vinicio Cerezo.

In Colombia, a particularly intense period of violence accelerated with the 1948 assassination of populist Liberal Jorge Eliécer Gaitán. La Violencia, as it came to be called, claimed over 200,000 lives in the next fifteen to twenty years, mostly in rural areas. In response to the violence and to the dictatorship of Rojas Pinilla (1953–57), Liberals and Conservatives agreed to forego their internecine rivalry, and to form a pact, known as the National Front, in which they alternated in the presidency and shared ministries from 1958 to 1974. Government and military soon took notice of the "peasant republics" that had formed during La Violencia as quasi-independent zones for self-defense and self-administration in agrarian matters. A military campaign retook those areas in 1964 and 1965. The Colombian Revolutionary Armed Forces (FARC), allied to the Colombian Communist Party (PCC), rose out of the ashes of those "republics." In 1965, proto-guerrillas returning from a trip to Cuba formed the Fidelista Army of National Liberation (ELN) in Santander, while a few years later Chinese-line Communists formed their own guerrilla group, the Popular Army of Liberation (EPL), based in Córdoba and

Antioquia. The fortunes of the various groups waned toward 1970, but waxed anew in the 1970s; by the early 1980s their combined membership was in the thousands. The M-19 guerrillas emerged following the allegedly fraudulent elections of 19 April 1970, which cost the ANAPO party at least a share of power. The M-19 was a radical splinter group from ANAPO, initially solely urban, but later spreading somewhat to rural areas; it, too, grew in the early 1980s, despite strong military counterefforts. However, a downward inflection in guerrilla fortunes began with the mid-1982 election of President Belisario Betancur and subsequent amnesty offers. Since then, other guerrillas have been lured from the struggle with cease-fire armistices and the option of participating in the electoral process, which the FARC has in part accepted.

In Peru, two groups formed parallel Andean *focos* in 1965, and both failed to get off the ground. Héctor Béjar's Army of National Liberation (ELN), which split from the Communists, and Luis de la Puente's Movement of the Revolutionary Left (MIR), which split from the APRA party, both unleashed guerrilla movements in the Sierra in mid-year: the ELN in La Mar Province, Ayacucho; the MIR in three sites in Cuzco, Junín, and Piura Departments. Within six months all four had been shattered, although the fronts in Ayacucho and Junín enjoyed limited success in obtaining peasant support. In the late 1970s, however, university people organized a Maoist guerrilla group, Sendero Luminoso (Shining Path), with substantial peasant support. Beginning in Ayacucho—as Cynthia McClintock describes in chapter 2 above—Sendero spread and grew in the early 1980s, despite its extreme violence and ideological rigidity. Nonetheless, by the mid 1980s Sendero seemed to have lost some of its rural support.

Working in the wake of Bolivia's 1952 revolution and subsequent land reforms, Che Guevara organized a Cuban-led *foco* in late 1966 in eastern Bolivia despite the ultimate objections of the Bolivian Communists. Forced into premature activity and completely lacking peasant support, Guevara's guerrillas split into two groups and never reunited. The army harried each band and peasants informed on them; they were ultimately destroyed by October 1967, and Guevara himself was killed following his capture. An even more minor, student-dominated *foco* effort at Teoponte a few years later was rapidly destroyed, and many of the participants died of hunger and exposure.

In Nicaragua, opposition to the thirty-year-old Somoza family dynasty still foundered in the 1960s despite sporadic guerrilla efforts (Anastasio Somoza García was assassinated in 1956, and his sons Luis and Anastasio ruled, mostly directly, until 1979). In the early 1970s, however, the Sandinista National Liberation Front (FSLN) revitalized itself with growing peasant support in the mountainous north central region. The centrist faction cemented over a three-way split within the FSLN, appealing to their common opposition to Somoza. Middle-class and even business

FIGURE 4.1 Trajectories of Latin American Guerrilla Movements, 1955–85[a]

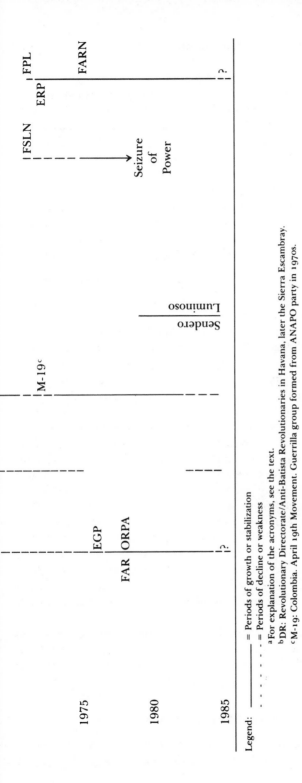

Legend: —————— = Periods of growth or stabilization

         - - - - - - = Periods of decline or weakness

[a] For explanation of the acronyms, see the text.

[b] DR: Revolutionary Directorate/Anti-Batista Revolutionaries in Havana, later the Sierra Escambray.

[c] M-19: Colombia. April 19th Movement. Guerrilla group formed from ANAPO party in 1970s.

opposition to Somoza grew as well, especially after the regime looted international relief funds sent following the 1972 Managua earthquake, and also because of Somoza's continued refusal to share real power with other social groups or parties. By 1978 civil and guerrilla opposition to Somoza finally coalesced into a semblance of unity, joining in demanding his ouster. Insurrection in various forms continued to grow until the regime fell in July 1979.

In El Salvador, an extended period of military rule since 1931 began to decay in the early 1970s. A number of guerrilla groups engaged in irregular warfare against the military, apparently unhampered by a series of internal splits. The three largest groups are the Popular Forces of Liberation—Farabundo Martí (FPL), born of a 1970 split within the Communist Party; the Revolutionary Army of the People (ERP), formed of Christians and Communists in 1971; and the Armed Forces of National Resistance (FARN), which split from the ERP in 1975. The groups gradually reached a certain *modus vivendi* and even achieved cooperation (1979–81), resulting in the joint Farabundo Martí Front for National Liberation (FMLN). At the same time, general opposition to military rule grew with the electoral frauds of 1972 and 1977 and the brutality of the Romero government (1977–79). Guerrilla and mass-organizational opposition increased even after a new "reformist" civilian-military junta seized power in late 1979. A guerrilla "final offensive" of early 1981 failed to oust the government from power, and the revolutionaries withdrew mainly to the countryside. Elections for a constituent assembly in 1982 lent some new legitimacy to the central government, as did the later legislative and presidential elections of 1984 and 1985, even though important opposition groups such as the Democratic Revolutionary Front were (self-)excluded from the elections, and despite the guerrillas' demands for boycotts. Guerrilla fortunes declined after 1982, but have since stabilized at a lower level of activity and support, keeping a dynamic stalemate with the government in recent years, with neither side able to make inroads upon the core of its opponent's strength. Peace talks, joined intermittently since late 1984, have not borne fruit, while civil opposition to President José Napoleón Duarte's government has increased somewhat since 1985.

Figure 4.1 summarizes the political trajectories of the key guerrilla movements just described. Having sketched briefly the historical background of the guerrilla movements, we may proceed to examine their origins and outcomes.

ORIGINS OF GUERRILLA MOVEMENTS

Guerrilla movements appeared in virtually every nation in Latin America in the 1960s, even in revolutionary Cuba. The cause of this sudden outpouring of revolutionary fervor was symbolic or ideological in nature, rather than material. Cuban success against U.S. opposition led to a shift in the *cultural repertoire* of collective action in the region (Tilly 1978:151–59, 224–25); it redefined revolutionary possibilities. Where communist parties had long since become inured to electoral politics and occasional agitation, a new generation of revolutionary intellectuals had their hearts and minds shaped in a new ideological crucible and soon attempted to move down "The Cuban Road." The symbolic impact of the Cuban revolution, then, exemplified Max Weber's portrait of ideas acting as historical "switchmen," which redirect the paths down which (class) interests express themselves. All Latin American revolutions since 1959 must be understood historically as post-Cuban (and now post-Nicaraguan) in nature. Since the 1960s movements cropped up throughout Latin America, one cannot hope to explain their *appearances* in terms of varying national conditions.

If Castro's victory served as an ideological switchman, soon producing a horde of 1960s imitators, few of those latter movements survived for long. By far the strongest movements of that decade grew up in Guatemala, Colombia, and Venezuela. Much weaker movements appeared in Peru, while failures abounded, most notably that of Che in Bolivia. In the 1970s strong guerrilla movements once again took hold, this time in Nicaragua, El Salvador, Guatemala, Peru, and Colombia. For both the earlier and later periods, all strong guerrilla movements gained power on a base of peasant support. Yet there is reason to believe that they struck responsive *national* chords as well, which account for the special vigor of revolutionary sentiment among the nonpeasant leadership of the movements.

For the 1960s movements, the historical conjuncture of the *international* Cuban "demonstration effect" and a frustrated *national* revolution in each nation produced powerful guerrilla movements in Venezuela, Guatemala, and Colombia. In Venezuela, the ouster of Pérez Jiménez put the nation (or at least Caracas) in a state of revolutionary euphoria for about a year. In contrast, the austerity measures imposed by the new President Betancourt, his extreme unpopularity in the capital, his unwillingness to bargain with the far left, and his repression of that left led to massive unrest in Caracas and an eventual venting of radicalism through the formation of rural guerrilla movements. In addition, the conflict deepened because the splits occurred along generational as well as ideological lines, with politicized youth strongly in the opposition camp. In Guatemala, the post-1954 reversal of the Arbenz agrarian reforms of 1952–53 amounted to a virtual agrarian counterrevolution. Peasants awakened by the promise of land reform before 1954 were slow to revert to dormancy thereafter. Finally, the social situation during and after La Violencia in Colombia has been called variously a "milieu of insurrection" and a "quasi-revolutionary situation." Peasant republics were retaken by the military in the mid 1960s, directly leading to the formation of the FARC, largest of the Colombian guerrilla groups.

The raising and dashing of revolutionary hopes distinguishes these three cases from events in Bolivia and Peru. In the former, both Che and the Teoponte guerrillas worked under the shadow of the 1953 land reforms; the peasants' main rallying concern had thus already been addressed by the 1960s. In Peru, guerrillas fared badly in La Convención valley, where a series of land seizures, beginning in 1962, had effectively eliminated the landlord class and given the peasants control of the land (Paige 1975:176–82).

In both the 1960s and the 1970s strong guerrilla movements appeared where the state was unresponsive to the revolutionaries; yet in the first period the eruption was due largely to state clampdown, while in the later period it occurred more because civil society had shifted its views of the state. Thus, if strong guerrilla movements in the 1960s appeared as a reaction to the *reimposition* of non- or counterrevolutionary governments, then their 1970s counterparts—in Colombia, Nicaragua, Guatemala, and El Salvador—appear to be responses to the *persistence* of the old regime.[1] I stress *old*, because the governments in those four nations looked increasingly archaic in a regional context, and I stress *regime* because they were also (though less) distinctive in denying real political participation to new contenders pounding at the gates of power. In the language of political science, these regimes faced "crises" of participation with which their "old" institutions were incapable of dealing, and guerrilla warfare was freshly available in the cultural repertoire as a revolutionary option. Only in Paraguay and Haiti did similar regimes persist without engendering strong guerrilla movements (although the Haitian regime has since fallen). Yet both Paraguay and Haiti have peculiar sociopolitical histories, distinguished by strong, personalistic, authoritarian control over both politics *and* society, which has worked against mass countermobilization.[2]

In Nicaragua, Guatemala, and El Salvador, personal or military dictatorships of long duration—reaching back to the 1930s in Nicaragua and El Salvador—persisted in denying any institutional share of power even

1. I borrow that final phrase from the title of Arno Mayer's book on Europe, *The Persistence of the Old Regime* (1981).

2. We might speculate about recent events in Haiti, but only in a footnote. The final fall of the Duvalier regime in Haiti may have had something to do with the final decay of the Duvalier family's authority or control over national loyalties and fears. Perhaps Duvalier *père* was unable to pass on his charismatic influence, especially over *vodoun* and the peasantry, to Duvalier *fils*. The ostentation of the "royal couple's" consumption and mass food riots were undoubtedly central to the regime's fall. As of this writing, Paraguay's Stroessner has not yet come to the problem of his succession, hence the regime there seems far more stable.

to "respectable" middle-class opposition parties, let alone the lower classes. In Colombia, political outsiders were excluded from power through 1974 by the National Front coalition, which may have retained power in 1970 through electoral fraud. Not until the 1982 elections was a "nonofficial" candidate finally chosen president. In response to a "closed" political system in all four countries, guerrilla movements were initiated in the 1970s, if not before, by disaffected intellectuals and marginal political elites.

Peru remains a special case among the later guerrilla movements: there an extremist ideology has proven a "functional alternative" to the patent political exclusivity found elsewhere in contributing decisively to the creation of revolutionary sentiment. A combination of Maoist dominance of the regional University of Huamanga and a subsistence crisis in the Andes produced the powerful guerrilla movement Sendero Luminoso, radically different in many ways from its counterparts elsewhere. The affinity between the Maoist message of peasant war against the cities, and the sierran conditions typically conducive to peasant millenarian revolt, has led to a merger of the two eschatologies in a powerful revolutionary movement with apocalyptic overtones (see chapter 2 above for more detail).

The nonpeasant founders of these revolutionary movements typically hailed from universities. Latin American intellectuals were singularly well placed (given university autonomy) and well disposed (given their history of resistance to the state) to respond to the "new ideas" of the Cuban revolution. Owing to their past history of resistance, *their* cultural repertoires, more than those of other groups, changed following Castro's victory. Perhaps they were also most sharply affected by Che's later failure in Bolivia. Most guerrilla movements, both failures and successes, were organized and led by university students and professors, or by their former peers now involved in leftist politics. Save in Bolivia when Che organized, university types were always central to leadership. I hypothesize that the rate of increase of student populations, with which expenditure probably did not keep pace, would increase the degree of radicalism in the university community as "social density" increased and student discontent grew.

In those nations where guerrillas most strongly took hold of students in the mid 1960s (see Wickham-Crowley 1982 : chaps. 2 and 3), that is, in Venezuela, Guatemala, Colombia, and Peru, table 4.1 shows a more rapid proportional rise from 1955 to 1965 in the number of students, perhaps the most revolutionary of all social groups in Latin America.

There is a clear, but imperfect, correlation in table 4.1 between university expansion and 1960s guerrilla strength, because such an upward concentration of the nations in question is unlikely to occur by chance. The correlation is less clear for the 1970s–1980s movements. From 1965

TABLE 4.1 Changes in Latin American University Enrollments,
1955–75 (in rank order by 1955–75 growth rates)

	Enrollment			Percentage Change		Rank
Country	1955	1965	1975	1955– 65	1965– 75	1965– 75
Venezuela	**7,664**	**43,477**	185,518	**467**	327	7
Peru	*16,789*	*64,541*	*186,511*	**284**	*189*	*14*
Colombia	*13,284*	*44,403*	*167,503*	**234**	277	*10*
Nicaragua	948	*3,042*	*15,579*	221	*412*	5
Panama	2,389	7,091	26,289	197	271	11
El Salvador	1,393	*3,831*	*26,909*	175	*602*	*2*
Paraguay	2,142	5,833	17,153	172	194	13
Guatemala	**3,245**	*8,459*	*22,881*	**161**	*170*	*15*
Chile	18,300[a]	43,608	149,647	138	243	12
Mexico	56,249	133,374	520,194	137	290	9
Ecuador	5,845	13,728	170,173	135	1,140	1
Costa Rica	2,537	5,824	32,483	130	458	4
Bolivia	6,280[a]	13,996	34,350	123	145	16
Brazil	72,652	155,781	1,089,808	114	600	3
Dom.						
Republic	3,161	6,606	11,773	109	78	19
Honduras	1,107	2,148	10,635	94	395	6
Haiti	859	1,607	2,467	87	54	20
Argentina	149,087	222,194	536,959	49	142	17
Uruguay	14,550	16,975	32,627	17	92	18
Cuba	24,273	20,573	82,688	−15	302	8

Boldface = Strong student-guerrilla links, 1960s.
Italics = Student-guerrilla links, 1970s–80s. The inclusion of Colombia is questionable.
SOURCES: UNESCO 1966:159–61; 1977:336–44; 1984:261–68.
[a] Interpolated estimates: for Bolivia between 1950 and 1960 data; for Chile between 1949 and 1957 data.

to 1975, while El Salvador and Nicaragua certainly ranked high (2 and 5), Colombia, Peru, and Guatemala did not (10, 14, and 15). However, the student-guerrilla connection was notably weaker in Colombia and Guatemala than elsewhere. Moreover, for Peru, the question should *not* be overall enrollments, but those at Sendero's birthplace, the University of Huamanga. Enrollments there rose very rapidly to 15,000 students— five times the capacity of the university facilities—following the radicals' 1968 victory in university elections and their subsequent adoption of open-enrollment policies (Palmer 1986:127–30). Therefore, the three nations with the *closest* student-guerrilla ties in the latter period had indeed exhibited earlier university enrollment explosions.

In summary, leftist guerrilla movements usually began as glimmers of hope in the minds of revolutionary intellectuals. Strong guerrilla movements appeared in two waves: in the 1960s in response to a reimposition of nonrevolutionary government; in the 1970s because of the persistence of old regimes. They also occurred in places with rapid enrollment-growth at universities, which typically were havens and birthplaces of guerrilla activity.

PEASANT SUPPORT AND MOVEMENT EXPANSION

In the rest of this chapter I seek to explain the causes of the *expansion* of guerrilla movements on a base of peasant support, and of the *seizure of power* in just two cases, Nicaragua and Cuba. Not all guerrilla movements succeed in moving beyond their modest beginnings; when they do so, peasant support is the *primum mobile* in the regions where they operate. Yet peasant support is a necessary, but *not* sufficient, condition for ultimate success; most movements that have garnered peasant support have failed. Those that seize power must meet two other conditions: they must be militarily strong enough to confront the government armed forces; and they must strip the incumbent government of moral authority and cloak their own movement with that aura, shifting the loyalties of the nonpeasant population to their movement. In the following sections I shall first distinguish strong guerrilla movements with peasant support (winners plus also-rans) from those which were "losers" in every sense. Then we may examine the partial success stories and examine the conditions that generated "winners" in Cuba and Nicaragua, but nowhere else. The three-variable causal model summarizing the remaining textual discussion appears as figure 4.2.

We must first consider the question of peasant support. Guerrilla movements have usually appeared as an alliance between an intellectual leadership and a peasant rank and file. The mere attempt to do so did *not* guarantee success in establishing and maintaining such an alliance: the Peruvian and Bolivian debacles of the 1960s are evidence enough to refute that thesis. How, then, can we distinguish strong, sustained peasant support from lesser degrees of assistance, or none at all? Tilly (1978: 70) provides us with theoretical guidelines, which I have adapted and extended. Three measures jointly indicate support:

(1) The *kinds* of support given by peasants to guerrillas or to the army. In increasing order we can identify the following: refusal to report on the presence of armed persons in the vicinity; supplying information; supplying food; acting as guides; acting as lookouts; occasional militia duty; and incorporation as full-time combatants.
(2) The *proportion* of peasants supplying such goods and services, again either to the guerrillas or to the soldiery.
(3) The *range of circumstances* in which such assistance is offered. Does

FIGURE 4.2 Social Conditions for Expansion and Success
of Guerrilla Movements

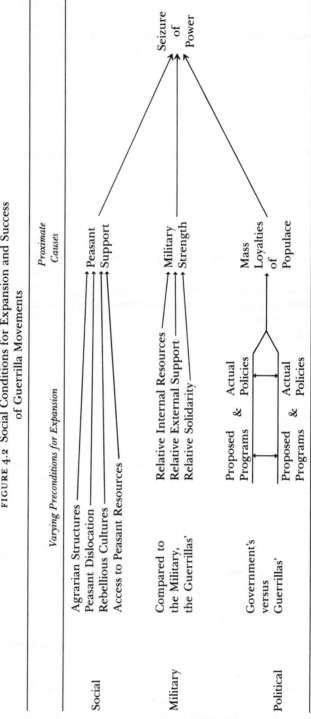

TABLE 4.2 Degree of Peasant Support for Guerrilla Movements
(by subnational region[a] and period)

Degree of Support	Before 1970	After 1970
Strong/Sustained	Cuba Venezuela I Guatemala I Colombia	Nicaragua El Salvador Guatemala III Colombia Peru III
Moderate/Short-lived	Venezuela II Peru I	Argentina Brazil
Weak/Fleeting	Guatemala II Peru II Bolivia Venezuela III Rest of Latin America	Rest of Latin America

SOURCES: Before 1970, see Wickham-Crowley 1982: chaps. 4, 8. After 1970, see Booth 1982, Montgomery 1982, Paige 1983, and chapter 2 in this volume.

[a] *Internal Locations:* The existence of multiple movements in some countries meant that the degree of support often varied by internal region; in such cases, the strong movements are usually discussed, with the exception of 1965 Peru. Locations are as follows: Cuba = Oriente, Las Villas; Venezuela I = Falcón, Lara, and parts of Portuguesa and Trujillo; Guatemala I and Colombia, see table 4.3; Venezuela II = Llanos, Eastern Fronts: Peru I = Junin, Ayacucho; Guatemala II = Huehuetenango; Peru II = Cuzco (La Convención), Piura; Bolivia = Santa Cruz–Chuquisaca border area; Venezuela III = pre-1963 bands throughout country; Nicaragua and El Salvador, see table 4.3; Guatemala III = Indian areas of central-west and north-west; Peru III = Sendero in Ayacucho, contiguous areas; Argentina = Tucumán, etc.; Brazil = Araguaia (Pará).

peasant loyalty to, and support for, one group hold up when threatened by the other group? Do peasants try to stay neutral, or do they alternately cooperate with anyone? This measure also takes into account the time during which support is given.

Given the available evidence, estimates of the extent and nature of peasant support must be qualitative rather than numerical. They are summarized in table 4.2, based on a certain consensus among chroniclers of the various movements. All of the movements listed in the "strong/sustained" category recruited hundreds of peasants as arms-bearing regulars in the 1960s, and well into the thousands in some later locales; they retained peasant support under at least moderate army pressure; and they apparently had the backing of the bulk of the civilian populace in their theaters of operation. Those in the remaining categories recruited few or no peasants to their ranks, often faced reluctant or even hostile peasants who informed on them, and could count on little or no firm support in their areas of operation (Wickham-Crowley 1982:101–11).

A few comments on table 4.2 are worth making. The reader will note that strong and sustained peasant support was far more common than was the seizure of power in either period. There is absolutely no good evidence that peasant support for the Cuban and Nicaraguan revolutionaries exceeded that in the nations with which they are grouped in table 4.2. That fact, by itself, illustrates my basic point: peasant support is not a sufficient cause of revolutionary success, but it is almost certainly a necessary one. Guerrilla movements of the 1960s in Venezuela, Colombia, and Guatemala all received peasant support rivaling that of Castro in Cuba, whether in numbers or firmness of commitment. In Venezuela and Guatemala, guerrillas provided the protective umbrella under which peasant resistance could take shape. In Colombia, La Violencia simultaneously exhausted much of the peasantry while providing a milieu of violence appropriate for guerrilla activity. While peasants' participation in *la guerrilla* of the 1960s certainly paled beside their overwhelming role in La Violencia, and while many certainly refused to participate, the numbers and protection they lent to the guerrillas justify Colombia's inclusion in the strong/sustained category of table 4.2. (Indeed, both guerrillaphile and military sources point to substantial peasant support.) After 1970 the magnitude of operations shifts upward almost everywhere in Latin America. The numbers both of guerrillas and of dead civilians soon totaled well into the thousands.

Having established variations in levels of peasant support, we wish to understand which social conditions contribute to those variations. Available evidence suggests that peasant support depends on several conditions: (1) particular types of agrarian social structures; (2) particular changes in agrarian systems; (3) the historic rebelliousness of peasants; (4) strong organizational ties linking peasants either to guerrillas or to the status quo. Much more questionable is a *possible* link between peasant support and local economic conditions: falling prices for regionally produced cash crops. Coffee was the central cash crop in most areas dominated by strong guerrilla movements in the 1960s. Evidence suggests a modest correlation in that period between price drops and increased peasant support, but data for the 1970s movements do not replicate the earlier pattern with regard either to the presence of cash crops or to the price-drop pattern (Wickham-Crowley 1982: chap. 6).

Agrarian Structure

In contrast, evidence strongly suggests that variations in agrarian structure are related to a region's receptivity to guerrilla movements. While Jeffery Paige (1975: chap. 1) argues that sharecroppers and migratory estate laborers are likely to be revolutionary, there is reason to believe that squatters, too, are likely to support guerrillas, for they share with the other two cultivators a zero-sum form of conflict with landed elites (Wickham-Crowley 1982: chap. 8). In Paige's work, such revolutionary cultivators are likely to appear where the landlord class depends solely on control of land for its income; if it instead relies largely on capital (e.g., processing or shipping equipment), then landowners can increase output through investment, and the division of income with their cultivators need not be a zero-sum game. Capital-intensive sugar plantations are a classic example of the non-zero-sum situation. As game theory suggests, zero-sum conflicts tend toward the radical, while positive-sum conflicts allow compromise. Squatters resemble sharecroppers and estate laborers in their do-or-die ties to the land, without which they would starve, surely creating a zero-sum conflict with eviction-happy landlords.

Available evidence suggests that the 1960s guerrilla strongholds had markedly higher rates of sharecropping or squatting than did the areas where there were no guerrillas, or where guerrillas got a lukewarm or hostile reception. I summarize these findings in table 4.3. The figures in row 1 compare the percentage of squatters or sharecroppers in the guerrilla department(s) (in Venezuela the states, and in Cuba the province) with that same percentage for the rest of the nation, and report the differences in percentage points between the two measures. Data in row 2 repeat the same process, but *within* each department that housed guerrillas, comparing the stronghold in each locale to the rest of the department. Data in row 3 isolate the guerrilla strongholds most precisely in their small *municipios* or districts—the equivalent of U.S. counties—and compare those few areas to the rest of each nation. Row 3 is probably the best single measure of the distinctiveness of guerrilla strongholds, but all three comparisons are instructive. In each case, a plus (+) sign indicates *more* squatters, and so forth, in the guerrilla zones than in the other areas; only those recorded in the censuses as "pure" examples are included, with mixed types falling into the residual category.

In Cuba, squatters were the key source of peasant support. They comprised more than 22 percent of all landholders in Oriente Province (home of Castro's guerrillas), but less than 3 percent in the rest of Cuba. In row 2 we see that, within Oriente, the squatters' share in the guerrilla zones was 30 percent, but only 9 percent elsewhere (Wickham-Crowley 1982 : 277–79; Ministerio de Agricultura [Cuba] 1951 : 387–93, 415–19), yielding a 21 percent difference. Che Guevara reported at best a lukewarm reception from the sugar proletariat the guerrillas encountered when they descended into the plains, in marked contrast with squatter support in the Sierra Maestra. In Venezuela, we can actually distinguish high-support areas from low-support areas, and there sharecropping is our key. In data not shown in table 4.3, we find that sharecroppers comprise 20 percent of cultivators in high-support zones scattered nationwide, versus just 5 percent in various low-support districts. Within the key guerrilla states of Falcón and Lara (row 2), we see that guerrilla strongholds in the former state enjoyed a sharecropping edge of 20 percentage points over the rest of the state, and a 12-point edge in Lara

TABLE 4.3 Land Tenure Systems and Peasant Support

	Cuba 1946	Guatemala 1964	Venezuela 1961	Colombia 1960		El Salvador 1971	Nicaragua 1963
Country Census Year Political Unit Political Subunit Type of Cultivator	Province Municipio Squatter	Department Municipio Tenant[c]	State District Sharecropper	Department Municipio[d] Sharecropper	Squatter	Department Municipio Tenant[c]	Department Municipio Squatter
Excess (+) or deficit (−) in percentage of squatters, etc., when one compares: Guerrilla-stronghold department(s), etc., to rest of the nation[a]	+20%	+8%	+1%	+10%	−13%[e]	−7%	+28%
Specific guerrilla *municipios*, etc., to the remainder of guerrilla-stronghold departments, etc., for each department[b]	+21%	+20% +12%	+13% +18%	(−8%) (−0.4%) (−11%) +1% (+14%) (−13%) (+6%)	(+2%) (−1%) (+9%) −1% (−4%) (+14%) (+8%)	−17% −16% +2% +7%	+38% +30% +41% +11%
Specific guerrilla *municipios*, etc., to the rest of each nation	+26%	+10%	+12%	+1%[e]	(−3%)[e]	−3%	+32%

SOURCES: See text, plus DANE 1962–64, 1962b, 1962c; Dirección General de Estadística y Censos [El Salvador] 1974: vol. 1, xviii, 1–5; *Newsweek*, 5 December 1983, 16 January 1984; Nuhn, Krieg, and Schlick 1975.

[a] Cuba: Oriente; Guatemala: Zacapa, Izabal; Venezuela: Falcón, Lara; Colombia: Tolima, Huila, Santander, Caldas, Valle, Antioquia, Córdoba; El Salvador: Chalatenango, Morazán, Cabañas, Usulután; Nicaragua: Matagalpa, Jinotega, Nueva Segovia, Zelaya. The second data row presents data in this same order.

[b] For details on the strongholds within departments, etc., see Wickham-Crowley 1982: 263–322.

[c] Includes sharecroppers, fixed-price tenants (and usufructuaries in Guatemala).

[d] All figures in parentheses are *estimates*, based on land area farmed; they are not highly reliable.

[e] Comparisons are in % of land area farmed; the rest of the table is in % of units held.

(Wickham-Crowley 1982:284–87; Ministerio de Fomento [Venezuela] 1967: part A, 2–9). Guatemalan data allow us only to examine undifferentiated tenancy relationships, not sharecropping by itself, yet there too we find a correlation. Combining guerrilla strongholds Zacapa and Izabal, we find an 8-point edge in tenancy (row 1) over the rest of Guatemala. The guerrilla zones within each department, more notably, were more sharply distinguished from their intradepartmental neighbors, by 20 and 12 points respectively (row 2; Wickham-Crowley 1982: 291–93; Dirección General de Estadística [Guatemala] 1968:vol. 1, 209–17, 269–86). In Colombia, the results within each department (row 2) are not as clear as elsewhere, perhaps because such widespread violence gave it a truly unique character; violence and protest may well be part of the cultural repertoire in most rural areas. If we broaden our analysis to interdepartmental comparisons (row 1), however, we do find that those places with extensive guerrilla influence in the 1960s— Tolima, Huila, Santander, Caldas, Valle, Antioquia, and Córdoba— when combined contained about 17 percent sharecroppers versus less than 8 percent in the rest of Colombia (Wickham-Crowley 1982:298– 309; DANE 1964:22–23), yielding a 10 percent difference.

Meanwhile, where sharecroppers or squatters were scarce, so too was peasant support. Such was the case, for example, in San Mateo Ixtatán in Guatemala, in La Convención valley and (perhaps) Piura Department in Peru, 1965, and in Bolivia. Efforts by the guerrilla leadership to seek peasant support failed in each of those cases. However, in those areas of Peru where there were some conflicts over land-holding (the census data fail us here), the guerrillas did receive some support from the peasants (Lamberg 1971:54; Dirección General de Estadística [Guatemala] 1968: vol. 1, 71, 121–22, 173, 274, 283; Paige 1975:176–82; Artola 1976:100).

We move now from the 1960s to the 1970s and beyond. In Nicaragua, in those departments that served as major guerrilla havens from 1963—Matagalpa, Jinotega, Nueva Segovia, and Zelaya—36 percent of the cultivators were squatters, versus but 8 percent nationwide (row 1 of table 4.3). Moreover, within each of these locales, the percentage of squatters was at least 11 points higher in the guerrilla zones than elsewhere (row 2). The only nonguerrilla zone with a high percentage of squatters was the *municipio* of Rama, in Zelaya, with over three-fourths of all squatters *not* in Zelaya's guerrilla zones. As it happens, the Sandinistas later established their eastern front there in the 1977–79 period. Overall, in row 3, we see a difference of 32 percent deriving from the fact that squatters comprised 42 percent of the cultivators in all guerrilla *municipios*, but only 10 percent elsewhere in Nicaragua (Booth 1982:117, 149; Dirección General de Estadística y Censos [Nicaragua] 1966:i–ix, 9–13).

We should also consider the revived 1970s–1980s Guatemalan guerrilla movements. The guerrilla renaissance there has been concentrated in the largely Indian areas of the western highlands, especially Chimaltenango, El Quiché, Huehuetenango, Quezaltenango, and San Marcos (Paige 1983:esp. 712–13). While these areas are not foci of sharecropping or squatting, we do find the prevalence of our third type: the migratory estate laborers, who typically leave their own villages, where land is inadequate for their needs, and migrate to harvest one or more (export) cash crops, especially coffee. Indeed, Paige himself (1983) has applied his earlier theory to illuminate the rooting of the 1970s guerrilla movements in the Guatemalan highlands. The census data do not allow us to examine this relation numerically, for migratory laborers do not appear in agrarian censuses. (They do not possess plots of land, unlike sharecroppers or squatters.)

In El Salvador, the past thirty-five years have witnessed a most thorough uprooting of the peasantry, and their increasing conversion into rural wage workers (Jung 1980:5–7). Guerrilla rooting in the peasantry may not have taken place earlier simply because the attempt was not made. The bulk of the Salvadoran peasantry seem to have become either landless or so land-poor they must do wage work to supplement family income (Deere and Diskin 1983:7–17). Furthermore, evidence suggests that they, like their Guatemalan counterparts, have largely become migratory estate laborers. In some regions, though, this transformation is still far from complete. These laborers may either live in fixed places outside cash crop zones, or continually move and migrate to those zones in high-demand periods to harvest coffee, cotton, and sugar (Jung 1980:5–7). In both Guatemala and El Salvador, one should note, the strongest peasant support for guerrillas after 1970 is found in areas not themselves centers of cash cropping; instead they are areas that certainly (Guatemala) or probably (El Salvador) provide migratory labor to other zones.

To summarize: for most of the cases reviewed here, we encounter correlations between relatively high rates of sharecropping, squatting, and migratory labor and high levels of peasant support for guerrillas. In the 1960s, for Cuba, Venezuela, and Colombia (less strongly), we find the expected connection between sharecropping or squatting and peasant radicalism, while in Guatemala tenancy is so correlated. In Peru and Bolivia we find the opposite, yet also expected, relation between secure peasant possession of land and low levels of support. In the 1970s and 1980s we can discern a clear squatter-radicalism link in Nicaragua, and a migratory labor-radicalism link in Guatemala and El Salvador, the latter less clearly. There is no such relation in the case of Peru's Sendero, based in peasant smallholder villages in the Sierra.

Peasant Dislocation

However, agrarian structure alone does not reveal all the correlates of revolutionary peasantries. Evidence suggests also that certain types of agrarian change can radicalize the peasantry, and these especially show up where our structural analysis above provides only weak confirmation (Colombia, Peru, El Salvador), but elsewhere as well. In general, assaults on the landed security of peasant cultivators lead to peasant radicalism, as in Emiliano Zapata's village in Morelos early in this century. To specify further, peasants embroiled in such changes are more likely to be revolutionary than those peasants who remain secure *or* those for whom this process is now largely an accomplished fact (e.g., the prerevolutionary sugar workers of Cuba). Thus we expect, above all, that *transitional* peasantries will be the most likely supporters of radical movements.[3]

In Cuba, the squatters of Oriente Province were not only structurally likely to be revolutionary, but also were experiencing an assault on their very landed existence, one that Oriente landlords increased in tempo after World War II. Most Cuban land-eviction court cases were centered in Oriente, and landlords were especially likely to win their cases there (Nelson 1950:20, 112; Domínguez 1978:429–33).

Outside of Cuba we encounter further evidence of revolutionary sympathies among peasantries in response to assaults on their land tenure. In 1960s Guatemala, the MR-13 guerrillas in Izabal received support in the very zone that had witnessed a major land redistribution from the United Fruit Company to peasants in the early 1950s, only to see it reversed by 1960 (Wickham-Crowley 1982:396–400; CIDA 1965:36–52). In the 1970s the transverse strip across northwest Guatemala in which the EGP guerrillas took root became known as the "Zone of the Generals" because military and civilian elites progressively displaced peasant villagers and settlers from lands that often harbored rich mineral deposits (Paige 1983:733). In both of these periods, a landed peasantry was losing ground—literally—to expropriation attempts by landed, military, government, or business elites.

While earlier scholars have found only hints of "economic" or "class" causes of La Violencia, a statistical analysis suggests that the violence between 1958 and 1963 was indeed closely related to the expansion of coffee across Colombia, with its attendant displacement of colonizer-peasants. If we regress the number of violent events, by department, on the absolute expansion of coffee production from 1932 to 1953–56, the correlation is $+ .75$ ($p < .01$). Even if some violent events themselves produced later violent events in a vendetta effect, we can control for that by substituting the natural log of the number of events in the regression equation: the results are virtually identical ($r = + .71$; $p < .01$). A multiple regression also indicates that the absolute levels of coffee production as of 1932 are not predictors of violence later on, and do not diminish the predictive

3. This thesis is closely related to the writings of James Scott, such as *The Moral Economy of the Peasant* (1976), where he has argued that peasant displacements and insecurities associated with the spread of the world (capitalist) market have tended to lead to a decay in the traditional protections afforded peasantries in Southeast Asia.

power of coffee expansion (Guzmán Campos, Fals Borda, and Umaña Luna 1962–64: vol. 2, 301–26 [events]; McGreevey 1970: 210 [coffee]). The same departments that experienced La Violencia were the birthing ground of the FARC guerrillas a few years later. Indeed, one scholar has suggested that violence stemmed from peasants' organized defense of their colonized lands.[4] Overall, this finding suggests at least a second-order effect of earlier coffee expansion on the 1960s guerrilla movements. (The relation is far from topographically neat, however, for the guerrilla groups typically retired into inaccessible hill country rather than residing in the coffee lands themselves.) As Pierre Gilhodès has argued, Colombian violence may ultimately be rooted in the expulsion of a precapitalist peasantry from possession of the land.

For El Salvador, our analysis can also have a degree of precision. Since so much proletarianization has taken place in El Salvador, we would expect to find radicalism where the number of farmers is still relatively high, and the relative number of agricultural workers (i.e., those not possessing any land) is low. Such areas are still, as it were, "in process." The ratio of agricultural workers to farmers within each department provides just such a measure: where the ratio is high (far greater than 1.0), we expect little radicalism; where the ratio is low, with the number of farmers closer to the number of wage workers in a more bifurcated agrarian structure, we expect to find more radicalism. In conformity with this hypothesis, we find a negative correlation between the worker/farmer ratio and the degree to which guerrillas control a department (measure: the percentage of each department's rural landholders living in guerrilla-controlled zones). Dropping the urban capital from the analysis, the Spearman rank correlation is − .81. The degree of departmental guerrilla control is also positively related to the *number* of farmers, and negatively related to the number of workers, whether we employ Spearman's *rho* or Kendall's *tau* (all Z-scores exceed 2.0 in absolute value).[5] This finding is cross-sectional in nature, and the data from two different census periods, yet it suggests that regions embroiled in such processes of peasant uprooting are likely to be radical "hotbeds."[6]

There exists fragmentary evidence from Nicaragua as well that similar processes may have been at work in the interior where the Sandinistas

4. The scholar in question is W. Ramírez Tobón. For this and several other ignorance-reducing comments on Colombia, I am most indebted to León Zamosc.

5. Regression is inappropriate here, for the data are both nonlinear and heteroskedastic. Data derived from Dirección General de Estadística y Censos [El Salvador] 1965: tables T-23 to T-37; id. 1974: vol. 1, 1–5; Nuhn, Krieg, and Schlick 1975: back pocket; *Newsweek*, 5 December 1983, p. 80, and 16 January 1984, p. 26.

6. More troublesome, this analysis may not be consistent with the structural analysis of the preceding section. That is, if one of these analyses is correct, it may be that the other is thereby excluded. Honduras also provides a striking contrast with El Salvador. The absence or weakness of Honduran rural revolutionary movements may be traceable to a

put down roots. Booth (1982 : 120–22) suggests that peasants in the interior were subject to regular legal and extralegal assaults upon their security, as does a commentator who pointed to the expansion of cattle ranching in eastern Matagalpa Department—a stronghold of the Sandinista National Liberation Front (FSLN)—at the expense of peasant settlers.

In the 1960s Peruvian and Bolivian failures, we would expect to find no such peasant dislocation, and consequent peasant radicalism, prior to the guerrillas' appearance. Evidence indeed suggests the opposite pattern, one of peasant *consolidation* of landholding and landownership at the expense of landlords. In Bolivia this took place following the 1952 revolution, whether through peasant land seizures, state reforms, or a mix of the two. In Peru, successful agrarian revolts in La Convención valley destroyed the landlord class there by 1964, so that the guerrillas came face to face with a new class of peasant smallholders when they arrived on the scene. Less successful agrarian revolts, or none at all, took place elsewhere in sierran Peru, in Junín and Ayacucho Departments, and there the guerrillas secured some support from land-hungry peasants (Paige 1975 : 175–82; Béjar 1970 : 58). Since that time in Peru, land reforms imposed by the military government (1968–78) have come to the Andes, yet the area that gave rise to Sendero was not well served thereby. Peasant living standards in that area of Ayacucho have fallen sharply owing to parcelization of land and declining terms of trade with the coastal areas (McClintock 1983 : 26–29). The result has been a true subsistence crisis for that Andean peasantry (McClintock 1984; see also chapter 2 above). No such evidence exists for Venezuela in the 1960s, where an extensive land reform under Acción Democrática governments touched most regions, including those where guerrillas took hold (Wickham-Crowley 1982 : 390–96).

To summarize, there is strong evidence for a process of peasant dislocation and concurrent radicalism in a number of cases: Cuba, Colombia, and Guatemala in the 1960s, and Guatemala and El Salvador for the later period. Less compelling evidence suggests a similar pattern for Nicaragua, while the peasants supporting Peru's Senderistas have undergone a subsistence crisis. In two cases where guerrillas failed to obtain peasant support, in Peru and Bolivia, we find a reverse process, peasant consolidation of control over the land. Venezuela of the 1960s fails to fit this theory, for radical hotbeds existed there despite a widespread land reform in the 1960s. As we have seen and shall see, however, other fea-

---

more secure, better-off peasantry than in El Salvador. The Honduran peasantry may have, in fact, benefited somewhat from land reforms and from some advantages gained in its political struggle with a weaker landed oligarchy than the Salvadoran peasantry faced (Ruhl 1984 : 56–60).

tures of those areas produced peasant support in the absence of such peasant dislocation.

Rebellious Cultures

Guerrillas also disproportionately took root in areas with histories of popular rebellion against federal authority, and often failed where such rebellious cultures were absent. In the Cuban case, Oriente Province, particularly the Sierra Maestra, had been the locus of slave revolts, anti-Spanish rebellions and civil wars, and antigovernment movements since the early 1800s. No other Cuban region has had such a distinctive pattern (Domínguez 1978:435–36; Wickham-Crowley 1982:373–75). In Venezuela, the guerrilla center, Falcón State, had been a haven for anti-government resistance going back at least to Bolívar. Lara State also had a rebellious past and produced a major antigovernment revolt in the 1920s, led by General José Gabaldón, father of later guerrilla chief Argimiro Gabaldón (Valsalice 1973:120–24; Gall 1973:6). Compared to certain regions of Bolivia, for example, rebellious movements are relatively scarce in Guatemalan history—yet the Sierra de las Minas, home of the FAR guerrillas in the 1960s, may indeed have had a past not unlike Cuba's Sierra Maestra (Allemann 1974:171). Colombia's sui generis history of civil war and violence has taken place largely in the coffee-growing interior, especially in departments that later became FARC guerrilla strongholds, such as Tolima and Caldas. In addition, Colombia's ELN guerrillas intentionally began operations in Santander because earlier Liberal guerrillas had operated successfully there during La Violencia (Arenas 1970:16).

We may contrast Bolivia and Peru to those cases just discussed. In the former, despite literally thousands of peasant movements in the past century, few such took place in Che Guevara's guerrilla zone near the Santa Cruz–Chuquisaca border. Thus Guevara concentrated his efforts in a region that lacked a tradition of peasant resistance to unfavorable conditions. Peasant movements in Bolivia had historically been located in the altiplano and in the Cochabamba Valley. In Peru, La Convención was an area of recent settlement and of recent struggle against land-lords, but the peasants had won that struggle by the time the guerrillas arrived. By contrast, Junín and Ayacucho Departments had exhibited the typical Andean history of sporadic peasant revolts. Guerrillas received *some* support in those places by siding with the Campa Indians in Junín, who sought the return of stolen ancestral lands, and with peasants in La Mar, Ayacucho, who had both recent and longer-term conflicts with local landlords (Béjar 1970:88–95; Artola 1976:44–79).

Moving to the 1970s and 1980s guerrilla movements, we can observe that the major centers of Sandinista support in Nicaragua were rough palimpsests of areas that had been centers of Sandino's own resistance fifty years before (Booth 1982:41–46, 116–21). Other chroniclers assure us that many residents of those regions continued to keep those memories alive, creating a culture of resistance to Somoza's National Guard. In Peru, Sendero's center of initial support lay in or near the area of Béjar's guerrilla *foco* of 1965, although it subsequently spread to other adjoining Andean regions (McClintock 1983). Thus it may well fit in with a general history of Andean peasant revolt as well as with past events peculiar to Ayacucho. In contrast, the recent Guatemalan guerrilla upsurge has taken place in the highlands, an area with a history only of cultural resistance to outsiders, not one of massive peasant revolts such as those common in Bolivia or in Cuba's Oriente.

In El Salvador and Guatemala (in the northeastern region since the 1960s), we find the opposite of the expected. The area of El Salvador's massive 1932 peasant revolt and subsequent massacre (*matanza*) in the western coffee districts has not been a center of the recent guerrilla activity. Likewise the Guatemalan east has not seen a strong recurrence of guerrilla activity since the terror of 1966–67. These findings suggest that *extreme* levels of terror against peasant movements may have the historically "successful" impact of dampening revolutionary fires.

Access to Peasant Resources

The resource-mobilization (RM) view of social movements suggests that the kind of discontent nurtured by social conditions, such as in the cases of the three just discussed, is *not* enough to generate a social movement. Discontent is always present in social systems, and the problem instead is to organize people, and to get them to commit their resources— time, money, energy, even their lives—to the goals of the movement, and not to workaday routines. Moreover, resource-mobilization theorists have noted that social movements often appear when outsiders enter a social system and begin to mobilize the resources of those who by themselves might not be able to escape the constraints of everyday life. That is, there are the mobilizers and the mobilized (McCarthy and Zald 1977).

Such a perspective has an intrinsic appeal for the study of guerrilla movements, for two reasons. First, only rarely does peasant discontent transmute itself into guerrilla war without the intervention of revolutionary intellectuals in rural areas. Second, RM theory directs our attention to the fundamental bifurcation within guerrilla movements, between the radical middle-to-upper-class mobilizers who lead such movements and the poor peasants who come to make up the rank and file. Intellectuals are free to mobilize resources for a variety of reasons: their locations within autonomous universities protect them ideologically and physically from government repression and influence; as economically privileged individuals, they have far greater resources in the first place, hence more resources are "free" to commit to nonsubsistence ac-

tivity; and their cultural repertoires were especially likely to change following the Cuban revolution, and hence they were ideologically geared
to make great sacrifices in the service of revolution. Moreover, quite
apart from mere hypothesis, we have already seen (in table 4.1) that
rapid increases in university enrollments were in fact related to the extent of student-guerrilla links.

If the mobilizers are to mobilize peasant resources in the service of
revolution, however, they must have access to the peasantry. Such access
is not a given of social structure. Instead, varied patterns of peasant-
outsider social linkages and cultural influence generate different *degrees
of access* to peasant resources. Certain features of social and cultural
structure channel the peasants and the guerrilla leaders into alliances,
while other features function as structural obstacles to such alliances.
Such features include political party influence in a region; kinship and
patron-client ties; strategic political alliances against a common enemy;
the advocacy or opposition of respected religious personnel; and (non)-
membership in minority ethnic and religious groups. Where impedi-
ments are few and facilitation great, guerrillas have generally been more
successful in securing peasant support, but not very successful where the
reverse is true. Indeed, some peasants are "available" for mobilization,
and some already in the guerrillas' camp, yet others are hostile to the
guerrillas and quite unavailable for radical mobilization (Levine 1973:
226–27). Furthermore, to put it in classic colloquial form, much depends on who "gets there firstest with the mostest": guerrillas will secure
peasant support only with difficulty where *other*, hostile political groups
have arrived earlier and themselves forged peasant alliances.[7] Guerrillas
thus fare better on virgin soil or friendly terrain than they do on occupied ground.

In Cuba, Castro's M-26 guerrilla unit gained squatter support in large
part through an alliance Fidel struck with Crescencio Pérez, a squatter
leader of the Sierra Maestra described by one (perhaps overly excitable)
chronicler as "lawyer, judge, sheriff, counsellor, and patriarch of 50,000
guajiros" (peasants in the Sierra). Pérez was a major force in organizing
Sierran *precaristas* (squatters) into anti-eviction bands *before* Castro's return from Mexican exile. Pérez placed his extensive kin and patronage
network at Castro's service *before* Castro's *Granma* landing in December
1956 (Meneses 1966:46; Barquín 1975:vol. 1, 272-F, 309, 313, 327–30).

In Venezuela, both the Falcón and Lara guerrillas were led by men
from old *latifundista* families. Most notable were Douglas Bravo, Hipólito
Acosta, and Domingo Urbina (all Falcón), and Argimiro Gabaldón (Lara).
In both states, guerrilla movements thrived in part on a social base of

7. For example, the strong links of the Liberal and Conservative parties to rural Colombia and of the reformist Acción Democrática to rural Venezuela definitely militated
against peasant support for guerrillas in those two nations.

kinship and/or patron-client relations that crossed class lines. Patron-client ties were effective here because landlord-peasant relations in these regions still retained strong elements of paternalism and affection between the classes. In part, each movement thrived as well on preexisting political loyalties and organization. FALN chief Bravo's family was a long-time opponent of the governing AD party, one of whose local gunmen had killed his father. More strikingly, the strongest guerrilla center in Venezuela thrived in certain *municipios* of Morán District in Lara State, where the residents had given the Communist Party more than 50 percent of the vote in 1958 (versus well under 10 percent nationwide). The FALN guerrillas, brought into being by the Communist Party, grew strongest in an area already firmly wedded to that party (Valsalice 1973:131, 237–58; Allemann 1974:139–40, 395; Gall 1972:13).

In Colombia, the Communist Party (PCC) had begun to establish ties to certain rural areas as far back as the 1930s. Such areas of influence spread during La Violencia, and the PCC was certainly allied with, and involved in forming, the FARC guerrilla movement in those regions (Lamberg 1971:89–91). Most important though, the FARC guerrilla leaders had no need "to go to the peasantry"—as guerrillas did elsewhere—for they were peasants themselves. While this party-guerrilla alliance was "looser" than in the Venezuelan case, the PCC link served to channel recruits and resources to the FARC.

In 1960s Guatemala, the FAR secured similar advantages through its alliance with the (Communist) Guatemalan Labor Party (PGT), benefiting from PGT influence in the Izabal guerrilla zone. The guerrillas gained other allies in Kekchí villages through Pascual Ixtapá, whose twin "residence" in both Indian and Ladino worlds gave the guerrillas a crucial channel to Indian villagers always suspicious of Ladinos (Lamberg 1971:58). Overall, however, Guatemalan guerrilla channels to the peasantry were certainly weaker than in the three previous cases.

In Peru in 1965, guerrillas had hoped to profit from the radicalization of the peasantry during the previous decade. De la Puente's MIR sought to build its *foco* in the area where the Trotskyist Hugo Blanco had earlier built his powerful peasant federation, which had carried out the first great Peruvian land invasions of the early 1960s in La Convención. De la Puente in fact sought Blanco's assistance, but failed to get his imprimatur in a brief 1962 meeting. Arriving there in 1964–65, the MIR received very modest peasant cooperation (e.g., carrying supplies), for which they paid the peasants very well, but local peasant leaders later turned against the guerrillas and led the army camp-by-camp to the MIR strongholds on the nearby Mesa Pelada. In contrast, the MIR guerrillas in Junín did get some peasant support—in the very locale where guerrilla leader Máximo Velando Gálvez had worked for several years organizing peasants, rising to a local leadership position in that office. His network of preexisting contacts provided the Junín *foco* with a peasant base superior to that of the other two MIR fronts (Béjar 1970:79–80; Allemann 1974: 196–98, 205; Artola 1976:44–45).

Guevara's ELN in Bolivia failed to establish any such channel to the peasantry, and obtained not a single peasant recruit. They even lost urban contacts after being forced prematurely into action, when deserters from the *foco* led government forces to Guevara's base camp at Ñancahuazú and the first firefight, which Guevara thought accidental. In addition, the guerrillas taught themselves the wrong Indian language, a further impediment to making contacts.

We can observe new forms of counterguerrilla influence in the period after 1970. The rural influence of parties hostile to the guerrillas had always existed, notably of AD in Venezuela and of both major parties in Colombia. In the 1970s and 1980s in Guatemala and El Salvador, however, state-formed peasant organizations gave military governments a ready channel to, and some control over, village activity. (By way of marked contrast, Colombia has been noted—except during the ANUC period, as described in chapter 3—for the weakness of its rural administrative machinery.) The Guatemalan controls are weaker and of more recent vintage than the Salvadoran, yet in both cases they gave government antiguerrilla forces "eyes," "ears," and influence in many rural areas, providing a crucial counterweight to guerrilla influence. The Somozas traditionally made use of "ears" in Nicaragua as well, but they seem to have been a less pervasive aspect of rural life.

Nonetheless, the later period also saw new forms of influence favorable to the guerrilla forces as well. Before 1970 the church hierarchy clearly supported governments in Peru, Colombia, and elsewhere (but not in Cuba, where they requested Batista's resignation in early 1958). After 1970 part of the church shifted in a manner crucial to peasant loyalty. The Medellín bishops' conference of 1968 paved the way for liberation theology, leading local priests, in particular, to view revolutionaries in a far more congenial light. Subsequently *Comunidades Eclesiales de Base* (CEBs), or base communities, helped to spread liberation theology through the region wherever Catholicism was strong. Such influence could now provide, not an impediment ("opiate") to guerrilla-peasant alliances, but rather a *nihil obstat* or even an imprimatur for revolution. That this might have destabilizing effects in the region was obvious to all. Whereas a few Protestant evangelicals had proselytized on the guerrillas' behalf in 1960s Colombia and Guatemala, now even members of the Catholic hierarchy came to denounce regime violence, as in the case of (later assassinated) Archbishop Romero in El Salvador, and Archbishop Obando y Bravo in Nicaragua. Even moderate bishops like Romero's successor in El Salvador and the conservative Guatemalan bishops were led to criticize regime violence. At the village level we can see the special role of CEBs, Maryknoll missionaries, and others in providing religious backing to peasant organizing efforts in Guatemala, El Salvador, and Nicaragua (Booth 1982:134–37; Montgomery 1982:chap. 4). These events produced bizarre political realignments, where the far right could be found assassinating an archbishop (El Salvador), and where the celebration of Catholic mass in the Guatemalan highlands came to be seen virtually as subversive activity under the rule of a Protestant evangelical general (Ríos Montt). Indeed, Guatemalan villages that went over to evangelical Christianity seemed to go over to non- or counterrevolutionary sentiment as well.

Peru's *Sendero* and the Guatemalan guerrilla renaissance garnered peasant support through a shift in organizational strategy, directly addressing a failing of their guerrilla predecessors. Indian recruitment and a partly Indian leadership comprise the key elements in that shift, made possible by a commitment to meeting the indigenous populace in their own languages, such as Quechua and Kekchí. These latter-day guerrillas have indeed built themselves from the ground up on the base of such Indian-Hispanic linkages, exemplified in Sendero's ties to Quechua villages in Ayacucho, and in the EGP and ORPA's ties to various highland Indian villages in Guatemala. In the latter place, entire villages have gone over to the guerrillas since the mid 1970s, channeled there by Indian recruits and apparently by CEBs as well. In Peru, village youth attending the regionally oriented University of Huamanga were recruited there as closet Senderistas, later returning to their villages to settle, teach, and intermarry, thus providing the basis for Sendero's deep peasant support there when it began operations in 1980 (Payeras 1983; McClintock 1983, 1984, and chapter 2 above; Palmer 1986).

To summarize, both formal and informal features of social organization blocked or facilitated attempts to build peasant-guerrilla alliances. Much as Charles Tilly (1964:191) found in his study of France's counterrevolutionary Vendée, we encounter a true mélange of such features, which do not lend themselves readily to taxonomy or summary in macrosociological terms. Political party linkages favored radical alliances through Cuba's Ortodoxos and the Guatemalan PGT; conflicting party influences both favored and disfavored guerrillas in different regions of Colombia and Venezuela in the 1960s. Linguistic barriers proved formidable to 1960s guerrillas in Guatemala, Peru, and Bolivia, yet were converted into advantages in the first two nations in the 1970s through careful work. The commitment of local rural authorities—including peasant leaders and the sons of *hacendados*—powered guerrilla organization in Cuba, Venezuela, Colombia, and parts of Guatemala and Peru in the 1960s, while slow conversion of entire villages commonly favored the process of organizing peasant support in the 1970s in Nicaragua, Guatemala, and Peru. The infiltration of villages by the eyes and ears of the authorities impeded such processes, especially in Guatemala and El Salvador, while the spread of liberation theology favored their growth.

THE IMPORTANCE OF MILITARY STRENGTH

Peasant support alone does not guarantee revolutionary success. The recent Colombian, Guatemalan, and Salvadoran cases provide especially striking evidence: by far the largest guerrilla movements Latin America has seen, numbering in the thousands, have been incapable of ousting their opponents from power. The number of combatants they can field indicates both their peasant support *and* their military strength. Military force is also a necessary component of successful revolution, but still not enough, for a mass transfer of popular loyalties must take place as well. I shall discuss military strength briefly and then mass loyalty shifts in more detail.

The collective strength of government *or* rebel armed forces depends on (1) external support, (2) internal financing, and (3) the internal solidarity of fighting forces. I shall not discuss the second element in any detail, save to note the great variation in both government financing of military activity (e.g., Venezuela gave far more resources than did Bolivia) and the resources internally available to guerrillas. Regarding the latter, post-1970 guerrillas have had far more money to spend than their predecessors, generated largely through kidnap for ransom and bank robbery.

External support varied as well. Before 1970 it was the Cuban revolutionaries who received the greatest aid, mostly coming from anti-Batista exiles and U.S. sympathizers on the mainland (Barquin 1975: vol. 1, 220, 231; Thomas 1971:986). Cuban aid to, and training of, revolutionaries was more notorious than decisive, despite its celebrity. At best, the Cubans trained a few thousand revolutionaries during the 1960s. Cuban aid has continued to Central America since 1970, at a level somewhere between that exaggerated by U.S. State Department "White Paper" advocates and minimized by their critics.

U.S. military aid for counterinsurgency has clearly been greater than that of Cuba to the region. Despite the size of such efforts in the 1960s, only in Guatemala did aid seem to shape the final outcome of the conflict, owing to the size and scope of the program, the relative weakness of the Guatemalan government, and the strength of the guerrillas. Elsewhere U.S. military aid was too minimal (Venezuela) or too superfluous (Peru) to make any difference (Wickham-Crowley 1982:169–72). Comparative evidence from the 1980s strengthens the thesis that military aid has not been all that important. The Salvadoran military crushed the 1981 guerrilla "final offensive" before the United States resumed substantial military aid, and the cut-off of U.S. aid to Guatemala did not prevent the military from facing down the guerrillas in the early 1980s.

These successes may have derived more from terrorizing the civilian populace in guerrilla zones than from sheer military capability, although previous U.S. military aid may have helped to build up the latter. Civic action by the military may well have been important in limiting guerrilla appeals in some places, and the United States certainly aided and abetted such activity as well.

Internal solidarity is the last critical element in the military outcomes of guerrilla war, whether we refer to intramilitary solidarity or to the willingness of the armed forces to stand by the regime. As Diana Russell (1974) has shown, where military forces show a high degree of loyalty to government, revolutionary movements are likely to fail. Therefore guerrilla wars are not simply battles of purses, but also of morale and solidarity. Government forces were generally fairly solidary in their campaigns against guerrillas prior to 1970, with the notable exception of Batista's troops in Cuba, who at times deserted en masse to the rebels. Venezuela experienced a pair of left-wing military revolts in 1962, but the military were highly solidary thereafter, especially following the insurgents' 1963 killing of four National Guardsmen in an attack on an excursion train. In Guatemala, the early insouciant counterinsurgency against the guerrillas (who were, after all, led by former army officers) gave way after 1966 to very nearly its opposite: violent, terror-laden, no-quarter war between rebels and government, a pattern that has continued to the present (Lartéguy 1970:88–89). Military solidarity held up well where the "total institutional" conditions of military life could provide institutional, nonclass sources of morale and support, drawing on the symbols of the military in its role as defender of the *patria,* against foreign-inspired or supported "communist subversion."

Within the insurgent forces, solidarity against the government was usually strong. Although the Colombian ELN and the Peruvian MIR's Cuzco *foco* were torn apart from within (Arenas 1970:124–36; Gall 1967:32), guerrilla bands usually held tight. Guerrilla solidarity often broke down at the organizational level, however, in the continued splintering off of more and smaller guerrilla groups, with allegations of "heresy" on either side. Only occasionally were such divisions later subordinated and effective unity restored, as in the mending of the splits among the Sandinistas (allegedly at Castro's insistence). Castro himself was faced with no such sectarian history. While the Salvadoran guerrillas announced unity in the FMLN (Farabundo Martí National Liberation Front), most of the groups continue to operate independently, as in the kidnapping of government officials by Joaquín Villalobos's ERP. Internecine violence is apparently never far from the surface, as in the 1983 icepick murder of FMLN and FPL co-leader Mélida Anaya Montes and the subsequent suicide of FPL leader Salvador Cayetano Carpio, who was at least indirectly behind the murder.

The distinctive military features of the Cuban and Nicaraguan regimes suggest a central reason for the guerrillas' success there. In both cases a personalistic dictator seized power in the 1930s and remolded the military as his personal army. The guerrillas later defeated those armed forces. Attempts by certain officers, such as the Cuban *puros*, to professionalize the army failed completely, for promotion was based in both nations on unwavering loyalty to the national *caudillo*. As such, the Cuban and Nicaraguan militaries were rendered incapable of presenting themselves as the defenders of national values and sovereignty or of the *patria* (a key source of military ideology and solidarity), for citizens knew otherwise: they were the personal tools of Batista and Somoza (Barquín 1975: vol. 1, 97–98; Bonachea and San Martín 1974: 130, 147, 271–75; Booth 1982: 52–57).

Guerrillas in those two nations also exhibited certain distinctive features. The Cuban and Nicaraguan guerrillas never splintered decisively, holding together quite well in comparison to movements elsewhere. In Cuba, the Directorio Revolucionario guerrillas never competed with Castro's M-26 for popular loyalties. In Nicaragua, the FSLN had three factions as of the mid 1970s: the Insurrectional Tendency (also known as the Terceristas), the Proletarian Tendency, and the Prolonged Popular War. The Insurrectionalists' patience and (it seems) Castro's prodding managed to pull together the other two disputatious factions of the Sandinistas. Everywhere else, guerrillas lived up to Issawi's Law of Political Fission, continually splintering due to ideological and personal differences, at times simply because of unwillingness to yield personal power (Issawi 1973: 96). Such has been the story in Colombia, Venezuela, Peru, Guatemala, and even El Salvador. The distinctive military features of Cuba and Nicaragua therefore stand out in high relief: strong and unified guerrilla forces defeated a personalized military after a more (Nicaragua) or less (Cuba) intense period of combat.

THE SHIFTING OF MASS LOYALTIES

Elements of Success: Cuba and Nicaragua

The successful Cuban and Nicaraguan revolutions were also politically like each other, yet unlike other cases in Latin America. The personal nature of the dictatorship in each case relates to a complex pattern in which that dictator responded with inflexibility and intransigence to a revolutionary challenger. In response, the revolutionary opposition secured cross-class and multi-institutional allies and support, leading to a final scenario in which a nation overthrew a dictator bereft in the end of all but decaying military support. In neither case did one or two classes "carry out" a revolution against class resistance, for in the end virtually all Cubans and Nicaraguans supported the end of the dictatorships. In

Nicaragua we saw repeated Lamberg's (1971:14) recipe for Castro's success: "moral victory among the people."

The inflexibility of the dictators may ultimately be idiosyncratic in nature. Both Batista and Somoza increasingly resisted any real sharing of political power, despite a "respectable," politically organized opposition: the Auténticos and Ortodoxos of Cuba, and first the Conservative Party and later the Broad Opposition Front (FAO) and the Democratic Liberation Union (UDEL) in Nicaragua (Thomas 1971:872–74; Booth 1982: 152–54). When U.S. support for the two regimes began to waver, then to crumble—in Cuba from the end of 1957 on, in Nicaragua from 1977 on—those regimes seemed to lose some of the basic moorings for such inflexible stances (Thomas 1971:948–49, 958, 985, 1040–41; Booth 1982:128–30).

The guerrillas in those two nations, perhaps in response to such inflexibility, proved themselves flexible enough to moderate their public programs and secure moderate allies. They ironed out with the moderates a fundamentally political, publicly broadcast accord emphasizing the dictator's ouster above all else. In Cuba, Castro always presented himself as a moderate in the mass media, and emphasized restoration of the abrogated 1940 constitution, a modest social program, and his own renunciation of any desire to seek the presidency after victory. Such views were embedded not only in his agreement with exiled ex-president Prío Socarrás but also in items intended for U.S. public consumption (e.g., Castro 1958). In Nicaragua, the FSLN's Insurrectionalists mended their internal fences while securing a broad agreement with non-Marxist groups that emphasized Somoza's ouster; it is no accident that Sandinista fortunes improved markedly after that moderate alliance was forged. The provisional government that this alliance put forth leaned in its composition toward the "respectable" opposition and away from avowed Marxist guerrillas (Booth 1982:145–81).

The guerrillas' moderate program and alliances reinforced each other. This moderate program (more so in Cuba) received substantial coverage and advocacy in the "great bourgeois" press, in particular from the *New York Times,* Cuba's *Bohemia,* and Nicaragua's *La Prensa* (Wickham-Crowley 1982:232–36; Booth 1982:103–4). Censorship of these sources was at best only sporadically effective, and guerrilla radio stations could fill in where the written press failed them (Booth 1982:160, 171; Thomas 1971:980, 996–1000).

The reinforcing effects of such moderate programs on the alliances was obvious. Especially, but not only, in Nicaragua, the urban working class was partially tied to and supported the rural guerrillas (Booth 1982: 121–25; Thomas 1971:1044–45; Bonachea and San Martín 1974), and was at its strongest in each nation's "second city," León and Santiago de Cuba, each closer to the heart of the rural insurgency than was the capital. Such working-class alliances were not decisive, however, for more striking is the allied support of "bourgeois" sectors of the populace, including not only professionals, journalists, and educators, but also segments of the capitalist class itself (Booth 1982:97–114; Bonachea and San Martín 1974:263).

The Salvadoran contrast strengthens this view. Massive guerrilla-cum-peasant resistance to government there has allied itself to often radical working-class opposition, yet has failed to come to power (Baloyra 1982:154–56). The Salvadoran business sector has either stayed firmly in the government's camp (e.g., during the 1970s), or has moved to the government's right and armed itself to resist change when the government later adopted a more moderate, even reformist, stance. Despite shifts in government policies since 1977, Salvadoran business and landlord groups remained violently opposed to the persons and programs of the guerrillas and their allies (Baloyra 1982:101–2, 143–53). Enrique Baloyra (1982:85) has argued cogently that the lack of a Somoza in El Salvador has produced a more open form of class conflict, rather than opposition to a dictatorial person. Under such conditions, at times approaching class warfare, a unified bourgeois-worker-peasant alliance against the Salvadoran government remains highly improbable. In nonclass terms, "respectable folk" (wearing white collars or holding substantial property) remain largely in the camp of the status quo ante, whereas in Cuba and Nicaragua many, if not most, of them eventually moved into open opposition to the dictatorship. The latter cases therefore fit the classic image from the *Communist Manifesto*, in which the desertion of part of the bourgeoisie is the harbinger of revolution.

In both countries as well, key institutional sectors of society provided symbolic and material backing for the guerrillas, adding color to the increasingly mass character of national resistance. I have already noted the role of the press in both nations, yet in Cuba a business civic group, the Cuban bishops, and thirteen judges separately protested and/or asked Batista to resign in early 1958 (Meneses 1966:73; Thomas 1971:982–83). Even the Cuban Santeros, Afro-Christian religious groups who had so favored Batista (the mulatto president) in the 1930s, symbolically transferred the symbols of their favor to Castro in 1958 (Bonachea and San Martín 1974:103, 131–33). Even Batista's military decayed during his second stint in office, and some soldiers resisted the deprofessionalization caused by the dictator's personal control. Most notable here is the Cienfuegos naval revolt of 5 September 1957. Universities, especially the University of Havana, were also key centers of resistance to Batista and havens for much of the underground (Bonachea and San Martín 1974:41–54, 84, 147–52). In Nicaragua institutional opposition also became apparent long before the dictator's overthrow. Church leaders and local priests, students and teachers, and various civic groups opposed Somoza, while even in Somoza's National Guard grumbling in the ranks grew and *golpista* sentiments appeared in the officer corps (Booth 1982:101–3, 108–13, 134–37).

To summarize, in Cuba and Nicaragua, guerrillas retained or forged cross-class and multi-institutional support for a program that downplayed Marxism, anti-imperialist rhetoric, and radical reforms, and instead highlighted ouster of the dictator and restoration of democracy. The program was initially more radical in Nicaragua than in Cuba, but even some Sandinista proposals were watered down to form strategic alliances with other groups (Booth 1982:145–47, 152–54; cf. Castro 1958). In each case the guerrilla-led movement overthrew a government that failed to offer counterprograms to detract from opposition strength, the dictators relying primarily on military repression and secondarily on backroom deals to retain power.

Elements of Failure: The Rest

The contrast with the losers (e.g., Peru and Bolivia) and with the also-rans (the other nations where guerrillas secured strong peasant support) now becomes clearer. In 1960s Guatemala, Colombia, and Venezuela, the guerrilla movements failed to shift mass (nonpeasant) loyalties appreciably in their direction. Outside of their rural strongholds, they never approached Trotsky's situation of "dual power," in which a substantial portion of the populace comes to regard the challenger as rightful authority. Again we can learn much by comparing the respective programs and policies of governments and their guerrilla opponents.

Government Programs: Elections and Reforms.   Let us first consider governments. In Cuba and Nicaragua, the dictators displayed little interest in, or aptitude for, mild reforms that might have made their incumbencies more popular. Batista actually snuffed out a civic action program in the Sierra Maestra begun by one of his officers in an attempt to woo the peasantry there away from support for Castro (Thomas 1971:924, 935–37, 940–41). Anastasio Somoza, Jr., too, was notable for the absence of real reforms under his rule. In contrast, guerrillas elsewhere commonly confronted elected and/or reformist governments that could tender some claims to legitimate or benevolent rule.

In unleashing his *foco* in Bolivia against René Barrientos's government (chosen in an OAS-overseen ballot two years after a coup brought him to power), Che Guevara violated his earlier thesis that guerrillas should never try to unseat elected governments; elections provide them with too much legitimacy. In his and his followers' later writings, however, such distinctions between regime types disappear, as when Régis Debray characterized as "Demo-bourgeois fascism" the Venezuelan governments elected in mass voting from 1958 on (Deas 1968:76). Peruvian guerrillas in two different periods faced an elected Fernando Belaúnde Terry. Colombian guerrillas first faced the National Front, whose advocates could point to the massively favorable 1957 plebiscite for legitimation, and later moderates such as Betancur (1982–86) and his successor. Guatemala had one relatively fair election (in 1966), and a return to electoral democracy with Cerezo's 1985 election. Guerrillas in El Salvador initially confronted dictatorships, but then confronted a government whose legitimacy improved with elections in 1982, 1984, and 1985. (Flawed as those elections may have been, privately the guerrillas acknowledged them as political defeats.) The guerrillas' lack of analysis led them to equate reformers such as Belaúnde and Venezuela's Betancourt with Batista (Lamberg 1971 : 119). Yet throughout Latin America, they generally did not face Batistas or Somozas, and they failed to adjust their actions to those differences.

Throughout the region, relatively open elections led again and again to the decline of guerrilla fortunes, often acknowledged by the revolutionaries themselves: in Venezuela following both 1960s elections, and recently in Colombia, Guatemala, El Salvador, and Peru. (Of course, corrupt or openly dishonest elections can instead trigger rebellions: cf. Mexico, 1910; Bolivia, 1952; and the Philippines in 1986; not to mention Somoza's Nicaragua.) In particular, the desertion or withdrawal of the Communists from the armed struggle, often when lured away with electoral "carrots," led directly to the decline of guerrilla fortunes in Venezuela, and certainly weakened their contemporaries in Bolivia, Guatemala, and Colombia (Lamberg 1971 : 61, 80; Maullin 1973 : 31–34). More recently, the opportunity for guerrillas themselves to participate in Colombian elections has somewhat weakened the overall militancy of the insurgency.

What kinds of reforms might the contenders for power bring to bear on the peasantry and others? Guerrillas typically provided various health, literacy, police, and administrative services to the regions they "controlled" (e.g., Raúl Castro's front for an extreme case; cf. Bonachea and San Martín 1974 : 187–97). Such activities commonly led peasants to accept the guerrillas as legitimate "governments." However, central governments could and did attempt to reduce the regional influence of guerrilla movements by competing with the insurgents for peasant loyalties, whether those governments were elected or not, and using both civilian and military organizations. They responded in kind to guerrilla welfare measures by building schools and clinics, digging wells, conducting occasional health checkups, and even carrying out local land reforms.

Whereas Batista and Somoza employed virtually no such techniques, other governments confronted with guerrillas proved themselves adept at wielding the carrot as well as the stick. The Colombian military became so practiced at directing such civic action techniques at targeted peasant populations that 1960s guerrilla spokesmen had to acknowledge the difficulties such actions created for their own recruiting (Lartéguy 1970 : 69). Whereas army violence might produce new recruits for the guerrillas, military civic action could instead produce supporters of, and collaborators with, the established order, and did seem to have some impact in reducing Colombian guerrilla activity in the 1960s (Lartéguy 1970 : 137; Maullin 1973 : 69, 79). A similar process took place in Guatemala in 1966–67, where a combination of terror tactics and civic action programs—again, by the guerrillas' own admission (Lamberg 1971 : 64; Castano 1967 : 144, 152)—led to the insurgents' loss of peasant support and even to betrayals to the government by former supporters (Allemann 1974 : 183–86; Adams 1970 : 273–74). The Peruvian armed forces used a similar combination and apparently obtained similar results in Junín in 1965, claiming to have turned the Campa Indians against their former guerrilla allies (Mercier 1969 : 177–80).

Civic action programs were less important in other nations where governments carried out more substantial social reforms. Under Rómulo Betancourt, the Venezuelan government undertook large-scale literacy campaigns, agrarian reforms, and other (often rural) reforms benefiting the peasantry and other groups whose votes had largely brought Acción Democrática to power. Even hostile chroniclers were forced to admit this, and the guerrillas conceded the government's "influence" over the peasantry and the size of the agrarian reform. Moreover, a careful statistical analysis of government "attention" to rural areas showed it responsive to pressures exerted by peasant unions (Powell 1971 : 166–70). These pro-peasant features of AD governments surely limited peasant support for guerrillas (Allemann 1974 : 146–47). Peru's Belaúnde also promised reforms, and his willingness to let stand the La Convención land invasions also undercut possible peasant support for guerrillas there (Mercier 1969 : 149). In Bolivia, the armed forces spent much of their time in civic action in the 1960s. In addition, Quechua-speaking René Barrientos (who first came to power in a coup against the revolutionary-based MNR) continued and gave a new push to the land reform program of the MNR. One analyst termed him a "peasant-hero," although he had a mixed record in such affairs (Allemann 1974 : 431).[8]

In more recent years, similar patterns have reemerged. While the Salvadoran land reform was more restricted in scope than its backers had planned, such government reforms probably had some impact in reducing the appeal of guerrilla movements in some regions. Local members of the Organización Democrática Nacionalista (ORDEN), rightist paramilitary squads used for village surveillance and counterinsurgency, could also count on special favors from the government for a time (Jung

8. For this and many other bits of information and advice, I thank Susan Eckstein.

1980:13). In addition, the Salvadoran military, known abroad chiefly for its use of terror and death-squad ties, has employed civic action techniques in guerrilla strongholds since 1985, with some successes claimed in "converting" several *municipios*. In Guatemala, the Ríos Montt government in 1982 revived the techniques of the 1960s, combining terror against civilians with a policy of *techo, tortilla, y trabajo* or *fusiles y frijoles* (roof, bread, and work or guns and beans) in an attempt to lure guerrilla supporters away with social welfare promises and policies. The government distributed some land titles, and its efforts were clearly directed to zones of guerrilla strength. The combined policies apparently had the intended effect, for guerrilla forces and activity declined from 1982 to 1984, albeit with some resurgence after 1984 (Millett 1985).

To summarize, where guerrillas have *not* succeeded in seizing power, governments improved their claims to legitimacy through elections, rural reforms and welfare measures, and/or military civic action programs, all in short supply under Batista and Somoza. Guerrilla movements remained strongest where such government activities were most restricted: Colombia from 1975 to 1982, El Salvador, and Peru from 1979 until Alan García's election as president (see chapter 2 above). The guerrillas fared worst where governments actively courted the support of the peasantry and the rest of the populace.

Governments and Guerrillas: Competing Proposals. Both governments and guerrillas indulge in the age-old political device of wooing the populace through promises of *future* benefits, such as land reforms, the building of roads, schools, clinics, and the like. Latin American guerrillas have often tried to appeal to a broad cross-section of the populace ("students, peasants, workers, and the progressive sectors of the bourgeoisie") in their public manifestos (Gott 1973). Since alliances of such groups (i.e., most of the nation) overthrew Batista and Somoza, the programs seemed well designed.

In both Cuba and Nicaragua, guerrillas downplayed their Marxist beliefs (less important in any case in Cuba) and joined with liberal groups in proposing a non-Marxist program to eliminate a dictator. Marxist language of class conflict and class analysis, anti-*Yanqui* imperialism, and overthrow of capitalism was virtually absent. While later guerrillas sought to move down the Cuban road to socialism, they often failed to examine the actual Cuban revolutionary process of 1956–58, favoring rather the post hoc analyses produced by Guevara, Debray, and Castro. By identifying with the socialist "Cuban revolution" of the 1960s, they ignored the bourgeois-democratic "Cuban revolution" of the 1950s (Lamberg 1972:108–10).

Although later guerrillas often put forth broad, classless manifestos, again and again they admitted, revealed, and even trumpeted their

Marxism, following again in Castro's footsteps; yet they did so *prior* to seizing power. Guerrilla Marxism almost naturally elicited the sustained, violent opposition of domestic and foreign (read: U.S.) anticommunist forces. In addition, the contrast between the guerrillas' public proclamations and their internal political leanings, as well as the regular formation of by-now-clichéd communist front organizations, further suggested "communist conspiracy" to opponents, as did the guerrillas' routine trips to, or training in, Cuba.

Despite their apparent strategic need for external moderate alliances, guerrilla groups also tended to splinter internally again and again, sometimes in response to "carrots" held out by governments (e.g., electoral participation, party legalization, amnesties), sometimes simply due to personal and ideological differences amounting to different degrees or types of Marxist radicalism (Lamberg 1972:112–13; Allemann 1974: 415–16; Zaid 1982).

Where the guerrillas' Marxism and/or communist alliances could be highlighted, opponents could then muster opposition based on the historical experience of revolutionary socialism. The military could point to the destruction of the government armed forces following the Cuban revolution. Governments could point to the forced collectivization of the peasantry in Russia, China, and elsewhere, and suggest to the peasants that such was the "land reform" the guerrillas really sought. The Peruvian press in 1965 termed such a future "the new *gamonalismo*" (roughly landlordism) in the service of the state. Such messages could be most effective where peasants already had or expected to acquire titles to the land they tilled (Bolivia, Venezuela, Peru's La Convención).

In Cuba, Castro retained media access to the Cuban people throughout his campaign, whether in the pages of *Bohemia*, the *New York Times*, or elsewhere (Wickham-Crowley 1982:232–36). The guerrilla movement reaped great rewards from its propaganda coups, such as the Herbert Matthews series in the *Times* (February 1957) and the extended interview with Castro published in *Bohemia* in early 1958. In Nicaragua, the opposition movement profited greatly from the sustained fire poured on the Somoza regime by Pedro Joaquín Chamorro's *La Prensa*, as well as from Somoza's media disasters, such as his National Guard's killing in cold blood of a U.S. reporter, filmed and later shown on American television (Booth 1982:103–4).

Guerrillas elsewhere lacked anything resembling a *Bohemia* or *La Prensa* from whose support they could profit. Reporting in the respected foreign press, such as the *New York Times*, also made no bones about their Marxist credentials. Their consequent lack of access to mass-distributed, friendly newspapers surely contrasts with the Cuban and Nicaraguan experiences. Both the medium and the message were therefore substantial drawbacks in their attempts to secure the mass loyalties of the populace.

In 1960s Guatemala, the guerrillas briefly received favorable domestic and foreign press coverage, but censorship soon stiffened and the 1966–67 counterinsurgency campaign snuffed out any hopes for further cultivation of mass support. Through the early 1960s in Venezuela, the Betancourt government kept the active and vocal left-wing, proguerrilla press off-balance with shutdowns, censorship, and police raids, so that the guerrillas never received sustained favorable publicity (Wickham-Crowley 1982:249–52). In Colombia, Peru, perhaps in Bolivia, and elsewhere, the large-circulation newspapers were uniformly hostile to guerrillas, and Peru's Sendero encountered hostility even from the left-wing press.

Both guerrillas and governments, then, commonly competed in both proposals and policies for the mass loyalties of the populace. Where governments refused to compete, in Cuba and Nicaragua, the dictators eventually fell. Where governments did enter the political lists, they enjoyed the distinct advantage of their incumbency plus whatever additional claims to legitimacy they could tender to the populace. Governments typically *lost* legitimacy, however, wherever military and/or death squad terror alienated the civilian populace, often producing *new* guerrillas.

The Consequences: Alliances Forged or Forgone.   While guerrillas often appeared to gain "unshaking" holds over select rural areas (Debray's remark on Venezuela), their critical links to urban areas were often sketchy, and easily broken or unraveled. Where such urban-rural linkages could be sustained—Castro's M-26 with Santiago, or the Sandinistas with León and Matagalpa—then opposition could grow in both areas, leading to coordinated rural warfare and urban insurrection, generating the mass revolutionary conditions that appeared in Nicaragua. (By itself, though, urban "terrorism" or "the urban guerrilla" has failed miserably in generating mass support, whether we refer to Red Army/Brigades activity in Europe or the Tupamaros of Uruguay, whose sharp decline began almost to the day when the military was unleashed on them. Even where mass urban opposition to a regime already exists, and explodes in uprisings unplanned by revolutionaries—Monimbó and Subtiava in Nicaragua—such revolts by themselves have been crushed. Rural revolutionaries have succeeded without substantial urban support [e.g., in China and Cambodia]; the reverse has rarely been true [Iran].)

Where urban-rural linkages were crucial for the continuation and growth of the insurrection, their loss or inadequate development led to the guerrillas' decline. In Venezuela, a series of urban shocks finally undermined the guerrilla movement: communist withdrawal from the armed struggle to pursue more conventional politics, thus depriving the rural guerrillas of supplies, networks, and cadres; the loss of Caracas *barrio* support for the urban-guerrilla Tactical Combat Units, and their resulting decline (Gall 1972 : 15 – 16); and the loss of the Central University in 1966 as arms cache and recruiting ground for the guerrillas (Lamberg 1971 : 77, 82). All these led to the left's eventual realization that "the armed struggle does not have the support of the masses," who were often already organized, with different loyalties firmly in place (Levine 1973 : 207 – 8, 227). In Guatemala, a more modest rural-urban network helped sustain the guerrillas for a time, but the guerrillas moved to urban areas as a revolutionary "terrorist" underground following the 1966 – 67 rural disaster (Allemann 1974 : 172 – 73). There as well, the populace apparently did not *want* a guerrilla solution (Lamberg 1971 : 69). In Colombia, the FARC guerrillas grew out of a congeries of peasant self-defense areas, never transcended those origins, and never approached *national* contention for power. From the late 1950s, and even earlier in places, up to the mid 1980s, the (proto-)FARC remained a regional guerrilla movement with very strong peasant support in select rural areas, but little beyond that. This regional argument applies a fortiori to the ELN and EPL guerrillas, both of whom suffered serious setbacks when their urban support groups were hit hard (Arenas 1970 : 30 – 31). Interguerrilla rivalries and attacks also weakened support as each guerrilla organization tried to dominate and/or undermine the others (Maullin 1973 : 42 – 44; Arenas 1970 : 23 – 24; Allemann 1974 : 266, 272). In Peru as well, the weakness of the 1965 guerrillas can be traced in part to their lack of urban ties, and to the indifference their *sierran focos* elicited on the coast (Allemann 1974 : 211 – 12), as well as to their Colombia-like lack of coordination. Since then, Sendero's actions have touched both rural and urban areas, but rural attacks seem to have waned as urban actions (e.g., bombing power stations) increased in the mid 1980s. Salvadoran guerrillas maintained and strengthened their urban ties for a while, but lost them for several critical years following the failed insurrection of early 1981; a partial revival may be under way.

  If a general lack of ties to urban areas weakened many guerrilla movements, then weak or absent alliances with urban social groups hurt them as well. In contrast to the guerrillas' difficulties in obtaining cross-class support for insurrection outside of Cuba and Nicaragua, governments were often successful in their own pursuit of popular legitimacy. Nowhere was this more evident than in Venezuela: "Looked at from a purely class point of view it could be said that, throughout the years 1960 – 63, the working class and peasantry were defending a moderate but active government against assault from political groups composed, for the most part, of intellectuals, students, career-politicians and people who had come down in the world" (Mercier 1969 : 106). Mercier's portrait is too sharply limned, but essentially accurate, for the working class and peasantry *largely* supported the government during the insurgent period (Lamberg 1971:73–74). Even peasant and working-class youth stayed largely with the governing party (Levine 1973:152). In the Andean nations, actual (Bolivia) or promised (Peru) land reforms generated widespread (Barrientos) or moderate (Belaúnde) peasant support in the 1960s, including electoral support, for incumbent governments faced with guerrillas. Even in Guatemala, army terror plus civic action in guerrilla zones led many peasants to adopt, in the words of one guerrilla, "a counterrevolutionary position," one reinforced by local Comisionados Militares, composed of former soldiers, which functioned in part as spy networks in the countryside (Castano 1967:152; Adams 1970:84–86).

Since 1970 elected governments in Colombia, Peru, now Guatemala, and even El Salvador have been able to make persuasive claims to popular cross-class support, even though guerrillas continued to receive strong peasant support in areas of all four nations. In Colombia and Peru such areas remained mere "oases" of the armed struggle, to use Lamberg's apt term. Belisario Betancur (1982–86) came to power based on populist and anticorruption appeals to the Colombian voters, and drew considerable support from the politically alienated, including the urban lower classes (Hartlyn 1983:62–64). Peru's Belaúnde (when reelected in 1980) and his successor Alan García also received substantial *barriada* electoral support, and the electoral participation and strength of the Peruvian left undoubtedly undercut possible Sendero support (Werlich 1981:85–86; also see McClintock, chap. 2 in this volume). The Duarte government in El Salvador has evidenced support among the middle and lower classes, including rural voters; his PDC's vote in the 1982 polls was stronger than average in the rural guerrilla strongholds of Chalatenango and Morazán (Baloyra 1982:167–84). From 1982 to 1985 the Guatemalan military governments neutralized the countryside largely through the "guns or beans" policy and village surveillance. The sharply restricted right-wing choices available to Guatemalans widened in 1985, and they elected their first civilian president in decades, Vinicio Cerezo, who promised reforms.

Outside of Cuba and Nicaragua, then, governments could regularly point to cross-class support for their right to rule, while guerrillas rarely had more than regional peasant supporters. Outside of those two nations, institutional sectors also stayed largely with incumbent governments. The military remained strongly in the governments' camp. Despite early 1960s rebellions in Guatemala and Venezuela, those armed forces later consolidated a strongly antiguerrilla attitude among the soldiery, especially in the elite units. The church generally remained on the side of the status quo as well. In Colombia and Peru, Catholic clergy publicly opposed the 1960s guerrilla movements and remained sources of conservative social control, despite the notoriety of individual exceptions such as Camilo Torres, who joined the ELN guerrillas and was killed in his first firefight. Despite, or perhaps due to the rightist assassination of his predecessor, Archbishop Romero, Salvador's Archbishop Rivera y Damas stated publicly in 1984 that the guerrillas had no support and condemned the insurgents' practice of press-ganging new recruits. However, an accurate portrait of clerical opinion in El Salvador, Guatemala, postrevolutionary Nicaragua, and elsewhere would portray a divided church, with local priests more likely to support the left, and the bishops more likely to support the right. Even in Guatemala, however, the conservative hierarchy finally criticized the government's terror tactics.

Mass Loyalty Shifts?   The preceding discussion of political influences on guerrilla success and failure requires summary. In Cuba and Nicaragua, guerrillas successfully pursued programs and proposed policies to appeal to the great majority of the national populace, and governments did not counter with their own programs of appeal. Guerrilla-led movements then secured ever greater cross-class and multi-institutional support, while governments witnessed their support base shrink to part of the military and of the upper class.

Elsewhere in the region the tale was different. Governments neutralized peasant-guerrilla ties through military civic action, or actively increased their own overall bases of support through reform programs and elections, while guerrillas pursued or revealed revolutionary socialist programs. Those programs and policies activated the violent opposition of anticommunists at home and abroad, and elicited suspicion outside the radical left, especially among moderates who had other political options to choose from. As a result, most of the other governments could reasonably claim greater and wider popular support than the insurgents they confronted, and could point to electoral and other trends suggesting that the mass loyalties of the populace were not with the guerrillas. We can attempt to summarize these differences very roughly in tabular form, giving a plus (+) or two (++) to features that favored the mass transfer of loyalty to the guerrillas, a minus (−) or two (−−) to features disfavoring such loyalty shifts, a zero (o) where the feature is neutral, and a question mark (?) if insufficient information is available.

Table 4.4 summarizes the preceding lengthy discussion of political influences and sketches in rough form the advantages enjoyed and created by the Cuban and Nicaraguan revolutionaries over their regional counterparts. Of all the other movements, the Salvadoran guerrillas have come closest to the seizure of power. Despite deeply rooted and widespread peasant support, and despite unusually strong military power, the Salvadoran guerrillas have failed to achieve their ultimate end, despite their confident claims of 1981, and have declined by the mid 1980s to a weaker position (which could change). Why?

First, Salvadoran guerrillas failed to generate a unified opposition to

TABLE 4.4 Social Conditions Favoring (+) or
Disfavoring (−) Transfer of Mass Loyalties
to Insurgents in Latin America

	Cuba 1956–58	Nicaragua 1971–79	Venezuela 1962–68	Guatemala 1962–68	Colombia 1964–70	Peru 1965	Bolivia 1967	Colombia 1975–	Peru 1979–	El Salvador 1971–	Guatemala 1975–
A) Guerrillas':											
Ideologies	++	+	−	−	−	−	−	−	− −	−	−
Rivalries (+ = none)	++	+	−(−)	−	− −	−(−)	+	− −	+	−(−)	−
Media Access	++	+	0/−[a]	0/−[b]	−?	−	− −	?	− −	+/−[c]	?
Urban Links	+	++	+/−	0	−	− −	− −	−	−	+/0	−
B) Governments':											
Elections (+ = none; fraudulent)	+	+	− −	0	−	−	−	−(−)	− −	+/0/−[d]	+
Reforms (+ = minimal)	+	++	− −	+	(+)	0/−	−	?	0	+/0[e]	+(+)
Military Civic Action (+ = absent)	++	+	0	−	−(−)	−	−	?	?	++/0[f]	−/0

Presence, Control in Rural Areas (+ = weak)	++	+	–	++	0	–	?	+	–(–)	–
C) Results of A, B:										
Guerrilla Cross-Class Support (+ = high)	++	++	0/–	0/–	–	– –	–	–	+/0[g]	0
Government Cross-Class Support (+ = low)	++	++	–/– –	+	0	0	0/–	–/0[h]	++/ 0/–[i]	+

[a] Pro-guerrilla left-wing dailies prominent early on, less so later.

[b] Favorable press in some papers, including the *New York Times*, through 1966. Censorship, less favorable press thereafter.

[c] Unfavorable press in newspapers compensated for by wide broadcast area of Radio Venceremos.

[d] Transitions from fraudulent results in 1972, 1977 to increasingly valid elections of 1982, 1984, 1985.

[e] Lack of reforms through 1979; some land reform since then.

[f] Military initially used only force with widespread abuses; recent fall in death toll, institution of civic action.

[g] Guerrillas' links to urban groups, trade unions weakened after 1981 insurrection.

[h] Belaúnde began term with diffuse popular support; ended with widespread discontent, low 1985 party vote total.

[i] Massive, cross-class discontent, 1972–77. 1979 coup reduces levels, which soon increase again. Elections after 1982 indicated cross-class acceptance of Duarte government, with some weakening after 1985.

the Salvadoran government during its weakest moments, especially 1977–80. Such unity as they have achieved came late in the game, and seems wafer-thin in contrast to the Cuban and Nicaraguan experience (Zaid 1982). Second, despite my critical comments above, we cannot rule out the importance of U.S. military aid in strengthening the government since 1981, due to the sheer size of the effort. Third, the government has strengthened its hand since 1979 with a (truncated) land reform program; with elections in 1982, 1984, and 1985, where people seemed to be voting for peace (Baloyra 1982 : 167–84); and with Duarte's attempt to distance himself (as a former victim) from army or death squad violence and torture, and even to rein it in.

Fourth, despite the government's loss of legitimacy due to terror, the guerrillas themselves have one of the greatest records of civilian terror in the region—only Peru's Sendero is comparable—with the regular execution of local "spies," the forced recruitment of new guerrillas, and even the revival of Viet Cong–style assassination of local government officials. Such activities, notably, are rather rare where the guerrillas function as the secure "government" of an area. The guerrillas, at least in the early 1980s, may have been responsible for as much as 20 per cent of the tens of thousands of civilian deaths in El Salvador, a record of violence against civilians far exceeding that of all other regional guerrillas, again possibly excepting Sendero. Guevara, Castro, and other guerrillas typically used civilian terror sparingly, but in El Salvador we have seen truly incarnate the dictum from Guevara's Bolivian diary: "Now comes the stage in which terror will be used against the peasants by both sides, although with different objectives" (Guevara 1968 : 164). The result of such two-sided terror in some regions has been a peasantry that alternately cooperates with any armed visitors, that seeks to avoid violence (often through flight), and that may embrace the adage "A plague on both your houses."

CONCLUSIONS

Figure 4.2 summarizes the preceding analyses and arguments. Only the Cuban and Nicaraguan revolutionaries achieved all three necessary conditions for revolutionary success: strong and sustained peasant support; maintenance of sufficient military strength to endure army attacks and to sustain a more general offensive; and stripping the incumbent government of all legitimacy and replacing it with their own movement as the legitimate, revolutionary alternative in the eyes of the masses. Each of these three elements was a necessary condition for the success of guerrilla-based revolution; jointly they were sufficient to seize power.

Despite their "obvious" and simple nature, these three proximate causes of revolutionary success have complex and multiple precursors.

Varying historical, structural, and cultural features of peasant life influence the propensity of regional peasantries to support revolutionary
groups. Military strength as well as mass popular loyalties depend *jointly*
on the character and actions of both the incumbent governments and
the revolutionaries, and analysis requires attention to both. Variations in
military resources and in military solidarity (especially the unity of guerrilla movements, or lack thereof) have clearly affected guerrilla fortunes
in the region. Direct competition of governments and guerrillas for mass
loyalties has tended to favor the incumbents, while government repression used in isolation has tended to favor the insurgents. The long-run
tendency, however, has been for greater government use of strategic reforms to undermine support for guerrilla movements.

Despite that trend, the story of guerrilla movements in Latin America
remains, as in the title of a recent work, "unfinished history." Confident
1967 predictions that "the guerrilla" had died with Che Guevara in a
little Bolivian schoolhouse now seem risible. Even so, later and equally
sure prophecies of "inevitable revolutions" seem to be suffering recently
as well. In January 1981 the Salvadoran FMLN predicted with certainty
that they would be in power within two weeks; a year later Tommie Sue
Montgomery (1982:xii) predicted that the government would fall within
two to five years. With the advantage of hindsight, we might suggest that
both prophets suffered from revolutionary élan, rather than benefiting
from objective analysis. More theoretically, since the political element of
mass loyalties seems to be a crucial "hinge" variable affecting revolutionary outcomes, such predictions failed to recognize the ways in which the
political system and political climate could change, ignoring the ways in
which a political system could increase its legitimacy through elections, a
point the U.S. government has understood, stressed, and pressed for.[9]
This political element is historically contingent, and not easily predict-
able from any (bourgeois or Marxist) political sociology that reduces the
political to an epiphenomenon of class relationships. The Salvadoran
political situation of 1985 was virtually unthinkable to many competent
analysts of that nation in 1980, 1981, or even 1982.

"All revolutionary regimes seem inevitable in power and impossible in
defeat," Mark Falcoff (1976:38) has noted of Allende's Chile. In recent
writings on Latin America, the success of growing revolutionary movements has to some observers seemed as inevitable as that of Falcoff's governments. Recent downswings in guerrilla fortunes in Colombia, El Salvador, Guatemala, and Peru have not, however, generated a contrary
sense of the futility of the revolutionary enterprise. This attitude seems

---

9. Of course, elections and other forms of political decompression (*distensão* in Brazil)
can have undesirable consequences from the government's point of view, as the Brazilian
military government discovered from the mid 1970s on, when fairly widespread social unrest greeted its attempts to reintroduce elections (see chapter 9 in this volume).

proper in view of my theoretical analysis, for changing government or guerrilla actions could well reverse any short-term trends, as we have seen twice in Guatemala and Colombia. If activities or inactions of both contenders can generate critical shifts in mass loyalties, then no guarantee exists for either. Nor can one predict such political changes accurately from infrastructural changes in social and economic conditions. Revolutionary politics, like politics in general, remains the art of the possible, and those possibilities are only broadly circumscribed by the social causes I have outlined here.

REFERENCES

Adams, Richard N.
1970 *Crucifixion by Power: Essays on Guatemalan National Social Structure.* Austin: University of Texas Press.
Allemann, Fritz René
1974 *Macht und Ohnmacht der Guerilla.* Munich: R. Piper.
Arenas, Jaime
1970 *La guerrilla por dentro.* Bogotá: Tercer Mundo.
Artola Azcarate, Armando
1970 *¡Subversión!* Lima: "Mas Allá."
Baloyra, Enrique
1982 *El Salvador in Transition.* Chapel Hill: University of North Carolina Press.
Barquín López, Ramón M.
1975 *Las luchas guerrilleras en Cuba.* 2 vols. Madrid: Plaza Mayor.
Béjar, Héctor
1970 *Peru 1965: Notes on a Guerrilla Experience.* New York: Monthly Review Press.
Bonachea, Ramon L., and Marta San Martín
1974 *The Cuban Insurrection, 1952–1959.* New Brunswick, N.J.: Transaction Books.
Booth, John A.
1982 *The End and the Beginning: The Nicaraguan Revolution.* Boulder, Colo.: Westview Press.
Castano, Camilo
1967 "Avec les guérillas du Guatemala." *Partisans* [Paris] 38 (July–September): 143–57.
Castro Ruz, Fidel
1958 "Why We Fight." *Coronet* 43 (February): 80–86.
CIDA [Comité Interamericano para Desarrollo Agrícola]
1965 *Guatemala: Tenencia de la tierra y desarrollo socio-económico del sector agrícola.* Washington, D.C.: Pan American Union.
DANE [Departamento Administrativo Nacional de Estadísticas, Colombia]
1962–64 *Directorio nacional de explotaciones agropecuarias (censo agropecuario), 1960: Resumen nacional.* 2 parts. Bogotá: DANE.

1962b   *Directorio nacional de explotaciones agropecuarias (censo agropecuario), 1960.* Vol. 1, *Cundinamarca.* Bogotá: DANE.

1962c   *Directorio nacional de explotaciones agropecuarias (censo agropecuario), 1960.* Vol. 2, *Caldas.* Bogotá: DANE.

Deas, Malcolm

1968   "Guerrillas in Latin America: A Perspective." *World Today* 24 (February): 72–78.

Deere, Carmen Diana, and Martin Diskin

1983   "Rural Poverty in El Salvador: Dimensions, Trends and Causes." International Labour Organization. Mimeographed.

Dirección General de Estadística [Guatemala]

1968   *II Censo agropecuario, 1964.* 2 vols. Guatemala City.

Dirección General de Estadística y Censos [El Salvador]

1965   *Tercer censo nacional de población, 1961.* San Salvador.

1974   *Tercer censo nacional agropecuario, 1971.* 2 vols. San Salvador.

Dirección General de Estadística y Censos [Nicaragua]

1966   *Censos nacionales, 1963: Agropecuario.* Managua.

Domínguez, Jorge I.

1978   *Cuba: Order and Revolution.* Cambridge, Mass.: Harvard University Press, Belknap Press.

Falcoff, Mark

1976   "Why Allende Fell." *Commentary* 62 (July): 38–45.

Gall, Norman

1967   "The Legacy of Che Guevara." *Commentary* 44 (December): 31–44.

1972   "Teodoro Petkoff: The Crisis of the Professional Revolutionary— Part 1: Years of Insurrection." *American Universities Field Staff Reports—East Coast South America Series [AUFSR-ECSAS]* 16 (January): 1–19.

1973   "Teodoro Petkoff: The Crisis of the Professional Revolutionary— Part II: A New Party." *AUFSR-ECSAS* 17 (August): 3–20.

Gott, Richard

1973   *Rural Guerrillas in Latin America.* Harmondsworth, England: Penguin Books.

Guevara, Ernesto

1968   *The Complete Bolivian Diaries of Che Guevara and Other Captured Documents.* Edited and with an introduction by Daniel James. New York: Stein & Day.

Guzmán Campos, Germán, Orlando Fals Borda, and Eduardo Umaña Luna

1962–64   *La Violencia en Colombia.* 2 vols. Bogotá: Tercer Mundo.

Hartlyn, Jonathan

1983   "Colombia: Old Problems, New Opportunities." *Current History* (February): 62–65 +.

Issawi, Charles

1973   *Issawi's Laws of Social Motion.* New York: Hawthorn Books.

Jung, Harald

1980   "Class Struggles in El Salvador." *New Left Review* 122 (July–August): 3–25.

Lamberg, Robert F.
 1971   *Die castristiche Guerilla in Lateinamerika: Theorie und Praxis eines revolu-tionären Modells.* Hannover: Verlag für Literatur und Zeitgeschehen.
 1972   "Consideraciones concluyentes en torno a las guerrillas castristas en Latinoamérica." *Aportes* 25 (July): 107–18.
Lartéguy, Jean
 1970   *The Guerrillas.* New York: World Press.
Levine, Daniel H.
 1973   *Conflict and Political Change In Venezuela.* Princeton, N.J.: Princeton University Press.
McCarthy, John D., and Mayer Zald
 1977   "Resource Mobilization and Social Movements: A Partial Theory." *American Journal of Sociology* 82 (May): 1212–41.
McClintock, Cynthia
 1983   "Sendero Luminoso: Peru's Maoist Guerrillas." *Problems of Commu-nism* 32 (September–October): 19–34.
 1984   "Why Peasants Rebel: The Case of Peru's Sendero Luminoso." *World Politics* 37 (October): 48–84.
McGreevey, William P.
 1970   "Exportaciones y precios de tabaco y café." In *Compendio de Estadísticas Históricas de Colombia,* edited by Miguel Urrutia and Mario Arrubla. Bogotá: Dirección de Divulgación Cultural.
Maullin, Richard L.
 1973   *Soldiers, Guerrillas, and Politics in Colombia.* Toronto: Lexington Books.
Mayer, Arno
 1981   *The Persistence of the Old Regime.* New York: Pantheon Books.
Meneses, Enrique
 1966   *Fidel Castro.* New York: Taplinger.
Mercier Vega, Luis
 1969   *Guerrillas in Latin America: The Technique of the Counter-State.* New York: Praeger.
Millett, Richard
 1985   "Guatemala: Progress and Paralysis." *Current History* (March): 109–13.
Ministerio de Agricultura [Cuba]
 1951   *Memoria del censo agrícola nacional, 1946.* Havana.
Ministerio de Fomento [Venezuela]
 1967   *III Censo agropecuario, 1961: Resumen general de la república.* Parts A and B. Caracas.
Montgomery, Tommie Sue
 1982   *Revolution in El Salvador.* Boulder, Colo.: Westview Press.
Nelson, Lowry
 1950   *Rural Cuba.* Minneapolis: University of Minnesota Press.
Nuhn, H., P. Krieg, and W. Schlick
 1975   *Zentralamerika: Karten zur Bevölkerungs- und Wirtschaftsstruktur.* Ham-burg: Institut für Geographie und Wirtschaftsgeographie der Uni-versität Hamburg.

Paige, Jeffery M.
1975   *Agrarian Revolution: Social Movements and Export Agriculture in the Underdeveloped World.* New York: Free Press.
1983   "Social Theory and Peasant Revolution in Vietnam and Guatemala." *Theory and Society* 12 (November): 699–737.
Palmer, David Scott
1986   "Rebellion in Rural Peru: The Origins and Evolution of Sendero Luminoso." *Comparative Politics* 18 (January): 127–46.
Payeras, Mario
1983   "Days of the Jungle: The Testimony of a Guatemalan Guerrillero, 1972–76." *Monthly Review* 35 (July–August).
Powell, John Duncan
1971   *Political Mobilization of the Venezuelan Peasant.* Cambridge, Mass.: Harvard University Press.
Ruhl, J. Mark
1984   "Agrarian Structure and Political Stability in Honduras." *Journal of Interamerican Studies and World Affairs* 26 (February): 33–68.
Russell, D. E. H.
1974   *Rebellion, Revolution, and Armed Force.* New York: Academic Press.
Scott, James
1976   *The Moral Economy of the Peasant.* New Haven, Conn.: Yale University Press.
Solari, Aldo, ed.
1968   *Estudiantes y política en América Latina.* Caracas: Monte Avila.
Thomas, Hugh
1971   *Cuba: The Pursuit of Freedom.* New York: Harper & Row.
Tilly, Charles
1964   *The Vendée.* Cambridge, Mass.: Harvard University Press.
1978   *From Mobilization to Revolution.* Reading, Mass.: Addison-Wesley.
UNESCO
1966–84 *Statistical Yearbook.* Paris and Gembloux: UNESCO.
Valsalice, Luigi
1973   *Guerriglia e politica: L'esempio del Venezuela.* Florence: Valmartina Editore. Also available in Spanish.
Werlich, David P.
1981   "Encore for Belaúnde in Peru." *Current History* (February): 66–69.
Wickham-Crowley, Timothy P.
1982   "A Sociological Analysis of Latin American Guerrilla Movements, 1956–1970." Ph.D. diss., Cornell University.
Zaid, Gabriel
1982   "Enemy Colleagues: A Reading of the Salvadoran Tragedy." *Dissent* (Winter): 13–40.

CHAPTER FIVE

Cultural Resistance and Class Consciousness in Bolivian Tin-Mining Communities

June Nash

Primordial beliefs and rituals provide deep roots for people's sense of their identity. Surviving from precolonial periods, they generate a sense of self that rejects subordination and repression. The cultural roots of resistance to alien control can generate social movements that restructure the society, influencing the choice of timing for political acts of protest as well as the place and form in which rebellion arises.

The people of the mining communities in highland Bolivia have resisted the attempts of conquerors, viceroys, governors, and populist leaders of the independence period to wipe out their own beliefs. Mining families relate to a superhuman world of saints, devils, deities, and enchanted beings with which they live in the mine, the encampment, and the region. They tend to encapsulate in a unitary worldview the widely disparate, apparently contradictory ideologies to which they have been exposed. This worldview includes primordial figures of the Quechua- and Aymara-speaking population who work in the mines; the saints and diabolical agents that have been introduced by Spanish conquerors and missionaries; and Marxist, Trotskyist, and developmentalist ideologies that inspire the political and labor movements in which they have been involved since the early part of the twentieth century.

Miners have been credited with spurring the populist revolution in 1952 that ushered in the nationalization of the mines as well as land reform liberating the peasants. Miners in the large mines owned by the tin magnates prior to the revolution share a life experience that has given them a strong identity as a community and as a class. In almost a century

Original research for this essay in 1969–71 was supported by the Social Science Research Council and the Fulbright Title V program. A return to Bolivia in 1985 made possible by the PSC City University of New York research program enabled me to check on developments brought about by the debt crisis. I am greatly indebted to Susan Eckstein for assistance in clarifying and focusing the final version of this chapter.

of industrial exploitation of the mines, they have transformed themselves from a peasant population with a localized worldview into a proletariat aware of the world market in which they buy many of their consumption needs. Although they numbered only 24,000, or 2 percent of the work force before massive layoffs in 1986, they have had a profound effect on the labor movement of the nation.

From the very beginning of industrial mining, the men and women who were drawn from the agricultural valleys of Cochabamba and the *ayllus* (land-based kinship groups) of the altiplano to the mines endured extremely hard working and living conditions. Whenever the workers joined in collective action to improve their lot, the army, quartered in barracks close to all the major mining centers, crushed their protest. The history of massacres as well as the murder and exile of their leaders have raised their consciousness of the need for political action in defense of their class interests. The imported ideologies of revolutionary action directed toward socialism have found receptive ground in the mines, where the thesis of the inevitability of class struggle and the ultimate victory of the proletariat are given meaning in the miners' present misery and their utopian visions of the future. Bolivia is one of the growing number of countries of the world where the once-repudiated Marxist thesis of the increasing misery of the working class can claim support from a measurable real decline in subsistence levels, not just a proportionate decline in earning power in relation to capitalist expropriation.

In the transition to modern industrial mining, contemporary ideologies of socialism and communism have been combined with primordial mythic forces in such a way that the people are not alienated from their cultural roots. Unlike workers in most industrial centers, they have not lost their sense of personal worth and their faith in human potential to bring about change. The Federation of Bolivian Mine Workers' Unions (FSTMB) includes leaders from all of the major ideological currents that have influenced the labor movement in the twentieth century, but it has had sufficient unity to influence national events. The FSTMB alliance with the National Revolutionary Movement (MNR) under Víctor Paz Estenssoro helped turn it into a revolutionary movement by pressing for the nationalization of the major mines and workers' control with power in the management of those mines. The federation gained the right to name and control the vice presidency and several ministries during Paz Estenssoro's first term of office because of its help in bringing the MNR to power in 1952. It split with the MNR in 1956 when Paz's successor, Hernán Siles Zuazo, introduced an International Monetary Fund–U.S.-backed stabilization plan that lowered miners' real wages in an attempt to reduce inflation. Some of the leaders of the federation supported the coup by General René Barrientos in 1964. He betrayed his promises to the workers' movement by invading the mines in 1965, repressing the labor unions, and exiling and jailing their leaders. After his death in

1969, union democracy was revived during the brief terms of office of Alfredo Ovando Candia and Juan José Torres (1969–71) only to be repressed brutally when Colonel Hugo Banzer Suárez seized power in 1971. In 1978 a fast initiated by women in the mining communities, which was joined by hundreds of political opponents of the military regime, including Christian Democrat as well as left-wing parties, brought about elections and the victory of Hernán Siles Zuazo. He was prevented from taking power by a rapid succession of military coups. The brutal repression and rank corruption of these despots was brought to an end by a series of strikes in 1982, when Siles Zuazo returned to office, this time with the support of the labor movement he had opposed in the 1950s. Yet his political base withered, including that in the mines, as the economy deteriorated because of the heavy debt incurred by the military and the declining revenues from the mines. In 1985 he was succeeded by Paz Estenssoro, who returned to power as the candidate of the post-revolutionary bourgeoisie, not the miners whom he had championed three decades earlier. In the year following his reelection, Paz Estenssoro consolidated an alliance with Banzer's party, the Democratic National Action (ADN) and proceeded to dismantle the nationalized mining sector, where the major opposition to his neoliberal economic policies was mobilized.

Considering the chronic state of crisis and the political lability of Bolivia, it seems paradoxical that mining communities retain the rituals and beliefs that link them to their agricultural past. Yet when I did my original fieldwork in Oruro from 1969 to 1971, and upon my recent return to the mining centers in 1985, I found continuous recognition of Huari, a hill spirit who has become identified with Supay, or the devil in the mines. Oruro is the capital of the department of the same name, where the major mines that were nationalized in 1952 are situated. These include Siglo XX-Catavi, Huanuni, Uncia, and Colquechaca, as well as numerous small private mines. Reflecting the continued importance of preconquest beliefs, a major sacrifice was carried out by miners in the San José mine in Oruro in the summer of 1985 when an accident took the life of a miner. Some of those who organized the ritual had been in political exile until 1982. Clearly the significance has not been lost. The integrity of this worldview that maintains contact with the past while allowing full participation in contemporary struggles is explored below.

THE BELIEF SYSTEM
AND THE SCHEDULING OF REBELLION

The ritual cycle in Oruro is structured on two axes, one dealing with agriculture, the earth, and the Pachamama (the time/space concept that is identified with Mother Earth in the hispanic tradition), the other with mining, the underground, and Supay (sometimes called Huari, the spirit of the hills). The overlay is Spanish colonial and postindependence Catholicism, but the deeper structuring derives from preconquest agricultural rites concerned with preserving the fertility of the land and maintaining harmony with the supernatural. The miners fit their industry into the old structure, maintaining equilibrium by sacrificial offerings to Supay for the mineral they extract.

Ritual time relates to the preindustrial agricultural cycles and to the spirits of the earth and hills that the farmers propitiated. The warming-of-earth ceremonies in June, with the onset of the cold dry season; the preparation of the soil in August for planting in September; and even Carnival, the season for harvests and joy, relate to farming activities.

The rituals are carried out at the four compass points, where enchanted creatures are found. These creatures relate to a myth that miners tell about Huari, the lord of the hills and the underworld, who was incensed by the failure of the agriculturalists turned miners to render him the fiestas that were his due and sent out monsters to eat them. Each of the four monsters, a toad, a water serpent, a reptile, and a hoard of ants were turned to stone or sand by the intervention of an Inca princess to whom the people prayed.

In each quarter, there are shrines devoted to the monsters that threatened to destroy the population of Uru Uru, the preconquest name for Oruro, when they first entered the mines and forgot their rituals to Huari. These stand like sentinels at the four compass points of the city of Oruro.

A giant toad sculpted out of stone greets one at the northern entrance to the city. Behind it is the rubble of the original natural stone toad, which was a meeting place of dissidents during the unpopular Chaco War with Paraguay in the 1930s, when many local miners and peasants were drafted. A general blew up the previous natural stone image in an effort to repress antiwar protest. While he succeeded in destroying the material symbol, according to local lore, he succumbed to the powers of the toad. He became paralyzed and died within a year. The toad is still given offerings on the Friday before Carnival, when hundreds of Orureños gather at the statue and celebrate *ch'alla,* an offering of food and liquor to the Pachamama.

A rocky incrustation that looks like a reptile encircling a hill on the south side of town became the site of a chapel when the priests tried to capture the power emanating in this spot, but when people attend mass here during the fiesta of the Day of the Cross on 3 May, they bring offerings of liquor and sweets for the monster. The reptile is associated with fertility, and in the recent past, I was told, newly married couples used to come to seek its blessings.

A water serpent rises in the east from what is a lake during the rainy season. At the peak of its head is a tiny chapel that was also an attempt by the Catholic church to coopt the space and its power, but the graffiti on the wall inside include messages to the serpent as well as to the Christ figure ensconced in the church nearby. At the bottom of the water serpent is a black stain that people say is the image of a priest who fought the worship of the serpent and died of paralysis.

Acres of sand dunes to the west side of town are, according to legend, the remains of ants that were sent by Huari to devour the people when they failed to render homage with the customary ceremonials. Here, too, there is a chapel with a figure of Jesus Christ, said to be a brother of the Jesus Christ figure in the church near the water serpent.

All of these enchanted figures are worshipped during the ceremonies devoted to the Christian calendar, but beyond these shrines that the missionaries tried to encapsulate, rituals devoted to pre- and postconquest deities occupy a different space as well as time. While Tuesdays and Fridays are the preferred days for the worship of Huari, the condor, the toad, the reptile, the water serpent, and the hoard of ants, Sundays and saints' days are devoted to Christ, the Lord, and the appropriate saints. The church and the plaza in front of it are appropriated by the saints, but the earth is devoted to libations to the Pachamama. Supay is the power that miners attend to below level zero, the entry level to the mines, where they never even swear in the name of the Christian saints or Jesus, although the entry to the mine has a small shrine to the patron saint of San José and a priest said a mass in the vaulted entrance during Carnival.

Although miners defer to Supay in their productive base within the mines, the cycle of Pachamama is still the most pervasive. A *ch'alla* is made to the Pachamama at all life-crisis ceremonies, inaugurations of new houses, work sites, and public buildings, as well as at most public gatherings. Alliance to the Pachamama relates the individual to life, while a contract with Supay, sometimes referred to as the devil, and more often as Tío (Uncle), brings luck and the chance windfall that might change one's circumstances but inevitably causes death in a short time. The Awicha, an old woman who lives in the mines, tempers the anger of Supay. When a thundering blast of dynamite shakes the underground and threatens a cave-in, miners call on the Awicha, who is their intermediary with Supay.

This complementarity of Pachamama and Supay is found along other dimensions of contrast. The Pachamama is a female force of continuity in subsistence production. Offering to her ensures continuity in the returns from crops and flocks. The offering of *chicha*, a fermented corn liquor sometimes mixed with alcohol, or, in some more elaborate ceremonies, the fetus of a llama, guarantees equilibrium in the productive and reproductive forces. Supay is clearly a masculine force. Offerings to him are in the form of propitiation to gain his goodwill. They are not for maintenance of a status quo, but for enrichment from the hidden treasures of the hills. A live white llama is sacrificed and its heart interred in the mines to gain his goodwill twice yearly, during Carnival and on 21 July, the eve of the month of Supay. It is both an offering to satisfy his voracious appetite so that he will not eat the men who work the mine, and a request that he yield to the workers some of the riches of the mine. Ceremonials honoring him are characterized by abandoned, passionate dancing, drinking, and chewing coca. Considering the peasants' awareness of the need to limit their flocks in order to maintain the life of the herd, it is perhaps justifiable to see in the offering of the aborted fetus to the Pachamama a recognition of the need for human intervention to assure an equilibrium between food resources and the animals that graze on her pastures. In contrast, the offering of a mature animal is a direct substitute for human lives that Supay might otherwise claim.

While celebrations of the preconquest deities are separated in the weekly calendar, the annual cycle of Christian celebrations provides a framework within which indigenous people accommodate their own ceremonies. Paralleling the opposition of the earth and the underworld is the cosmic equilibrium of the moon, as the force that generates cold, and the sun that warms the earth and the people. The conflict of the two cosmic forces comes to a climax at the time of the winter solstice, 21 June, and of the summer solstice, 21 December. Human ritual intervention at these times is necessary to ensure balance.

RITUALS OF REBELLION

Each of the ritually charged days has become identified with political events that are commemorated by the mining community. It is on these days that they express a heightened consciousness of their distinctive being as a class and as an indigenous race, alienated from their conquerors and exploiters.

The summer solstice, 21 December, was chosen as the day to stage a demonstration for higher wages in the mining encampment of Siglo XX–Catavi in 1942. The FSTMB had just been organized the year before. With rising food prices, coinciding with the inflated price of tin during World War II, the miners were determined to improve their lot by united action. A walkout staged in the second week of December was nearly coopted by the administration, until the workers retaliated. Ceferino, who started work as a child during the Chaco War in the Siglo XX–Catavi mines, told me about this event:

> Then came the strike of 1942. We had fifteen to twenty days of strike. The company announced, "The miners who do not want to work will be killed." They paid every man who went to work a bonus of two hundred

pesos. With this tip, almost all of the workers reported to work: until 21 December, when six or seven thousand workers united at ten o'clock. We were going down to the administration, calmly, without any weapons. We were a mixed lot, women, children, men. María Barzola was a delegate for the *pallires* (concentrators of mineral). When she approached the soldiers, they shot her. We were about four hundred meters from the office, and they were firing on all of us. We were surprised by the attack on us.

The celebration of the winter solstice is in conjunction with the fiesta of San Juan, 24 June. Some miners have heard the story of how San Juan entered into competition with Jesus Christ to split a rock by blowing a wind so cold it could cause frost. Campesinos celebrate the day by burning the stubble grass over their fields; in this way, they help the Pachamama maintain the balance of heat and cold. Miners to this day celebrate the eve of San Juan by lighting fires, around which they gather to drink and dance. For the campesinos, lighting the fires signifies the maintenance of fertility for their land and their flocks, and each faggot that they burn stands for the renewal of the life of one animal for the year. The miners have generalized the theme of maintaining productivity to include minerals so that life itself can continue.

For the miners, 24 June has a particular significance. It was on the eve of San Juan in 1967 that General René Barrientos sent in his troops to massacre the inhabitants, betraying the very miners who—disillusioned with the MNR since the 1956 stabilization plan—had supported his 1964 coup d'état. Barrientos cut their wages, and when they resisted, he ordered the troops into the mines. The miners chafed under military occupation until 1967, when they called a meeting of the FSTMB, scheduled for 24 June at the largest mine encampment, Siglo XX—Catavi. The meeting was deliberately scheduled for 24 June, the day of San Juan. As the miners were gathering from all the nationalized mining centers to celebrate the fiesta and welcome the delegates, the army attacked the encampment. Simón Reyes, a union leader at Siglo XX who later was jailed, described the evening's festivities:

> The enthusiasm for the night of San Juan was linked with the welcome to the delegates, demonstrating in everything a serene spirit, confident for the outcome of the meeting. The enthusiasm was prolonged until 4:30 in the morning when some people returned to their home to prepare to go to work while others continued dancing. (Reyes 1967)

Just then, the military and the national guard, armed with machine guns, mortars, and hand grenades, entered the encampment and attacked people still dancing in the streets. They fired on them with machine guns and threw grenades into houses with sleeping occupants. In the streets everything that moved was fired on, even dogs.

News of the atrocity seeped out slowly. *La Patria,* the daily newspaper of Oruro, reported on the following day that there were 16 dead and 171 wounded, and that the operation had been carried out by the mining police, the Department of Criminal Investigation (DIC), and the U.S. Rangers, with airplanes circulating overhead. Colonel Prudencia, in charge of ground operations, announced that the army had occupied the mine centers of Siglo XX and Huanuni, another nationalized mine center, to capture sympathizers of the guerrilla movement led by Che Guevara that was still operating in Santa Cruz, the eastern region of the country. Newspaper reports later revealed that at least 87 were killed, including men, women, and children, and that many more were wounded. An eyewitness at the funeral, a shopkeeper in the mining town, assured me that even more were killed. He told me that the number of caskets he saw going by looked like a stream of ants, and that there were burials in common ditches of bodies so destroyed by bazookas that they were no longer intact.

The massacre of San Juan was more destructive than any previous terror let loose in the mines. It was not designed merely to eliminate guerrilla sympathizers, as the colonel in charge claimed, or to rid the community of labor agitators, but to attack a whole class indiscriminately in order to break its resistance to the military. The genocidal attack was designed to inspire fear in the mining community, where resentment against Barrientos was pervasive. When I visited the mining encampment of Catavi on the eve of San Juan in 1985, miners celebrated the fiesta with the same devotion as when I had seen it in 1970, with perhaps even more fires burning, in memory of the massacre as well as in devotion to the Pachamama.

Another date that commemorates a seasonal transition has also been the occasion for political protest. On 21 September, the day of the spring equinox, students and workers in 1970 took to the streets to protest against the government of General Ovando. In Bolivian tradition, the day commemorates youth and love. That year the demonstration commemorated the students who had joined the remaining guerrilla troops of Che Guevara to stage an uprising in Teoponte, in the tropical zone of the Yungas, where there are plantations and a mining center. Just a few days before 21 September, Ovando had turned over the bodies of the youths, who had been brutally slain by the army when they were held in captivity. Their bodies had been destroyed by bazookas and hand grenades. The FSTMB had not formally endorsed the guerrilla movement, but its leadership saw the rally as an opportunity to discredit Ovando's regime. Shortly after the procession, the government was ousted by a right-wing junta led by General Rogelio Miranda, who had been in charge of the San Juan massacre. Miranda proved so unpopular, even with the armed forces, that the way was paved for a coup led by the populist General Juan José Torres.

RITUALS AND CLASS CONSCIOUSNESS

The meaning associated with many of the ritual observances is directly connected with class solidarity. In the enactment of these rites, fraternities of workers reinforce their common engagement in production. The dance groups and ceremonies relate them to a source of power independent of the religious and political institutions that shape their everyday existence. The political significance of the sacred festivities can be seen in Carnival and the Supay rituals.

Carnival

Carnival in February involves all local union and fraternal groups in myths and rituals that combine Christian with indigenous beliefs. Coordination depends on a municipal organizing committee, but the real impulse comes from dance groups based on occupational syndicates.

Each act of Carnival follows historical precedents relating to preconquest or early conquest days. The traditions of the indigenous and Spanish populations are interwoven as distinctive strands. Each culture contributes to the dances and dramas to interpret past and present. There are two main dramas. The first is the triumph over the monsters sent by Huari, the hill owner, which took place sometime before the conquest. Over the centuries it has assimilated postconquest spirits and powers. The second is the conquest of the Indians by the Spaniards, and the consequent subjugation of the indigenous population in the fields and mines owned by the colonists.

Dances provide the major media through which cultural messages are transmitted and continuously revitalized (Buechler 1980). The first drama is played out in the Diablada dance and in the propitiation of all the mythical monsters. The second is enacted on the plaza during Carnival Sunday by the Children of the Sun, as well as by dancing the Diablada and Morenada.

Carnival dancing is both a propitiation of supernatural forces and an assumption of the powers they represent. The magic of identification is contained in the mask. As long as dancers wear the mask, they are the figure impersonated. On Sunday the dancers remove their masks and dance under arches constructed on the plaza in front of the Church of the Mineshaft. Laden with silver, they enter the church to pray. Although the magical element is not always assumed by dancers today, a sense of transformation remains in the dance as they perform improbable feats, leaping and cavorting like devils; weaving to and fro while bearing the heavy suit of the Morenada; pole-vaulting as Tobas, Indians of the jungle. The procession advances for several miles from the north of the town to the plaza of the Church of the Mineshaft, where the Virgin is ensconced. Dancers practice arduously each Saturday from early November until Carnival, several months later.

The dances of the Diablada and the Morenada are especially important to the consciousness of laborers in relation to their work. Both dances show a movement from representation of themselves as subordinated miners or slaves, accompanied by a single devil in each group, toward a configuration of power in the form of a devil or slavedriver. The devil mask worn by Diablada dancers combines the horns of Christian figures with three serpents sprouting from the forehead. The red coverall worn by the dancers is decked with a tunic emblazoned with cut glass jewels and an apron of linked coins. Through the streets and up to the plaza, the devil dancers leap with their temptresses, men dressed as women in satin and jewels, who lure men to work for the devil.

The Morenadas represent black slaves, who once worked in the mines but were later transferred to the vineyards at low altitudes, where, it is said, they could better endure the climate. The mask they wear caricatures negroid features, with flaring nostrils, protruding lips, and bulging eyes. The lead dancer, representing the *cabecilla* (foreman), is the most elaborately dressed. He carries a pipe and cracks a whip as he leads the other dancers. They carry jeweled flasks, from which they drink the wine they were forced to produce. Their costume is like a wine cask, a synecdoche for the transformation they undergo in the dance from enslavement to the embodiment of joy made possible by the liberating effect of liquor.

The devil dance captures the essence of Carnival in Oruro. According to legend, the dance began when a miner fell asleep after the *ch'alla* to the devil in the mine. When he woke up, he saw the devil himself dancing, and he followed him, dancing out of the mine. After that, the miners continued to dance in the streets following the *ch'alla* on the Friday of Carnival. The dance evolved from being a group of miners with a devil or two in their ranks to one in which devils predominate. At first, miners danced in homage to the devil, releasing their hopes, ambitions, fears, and joys. As the dance progressed, they transformed themselves into the attractive, alluring figure. The dance is an act of devotion to the Virgin of the Church of the Mineshaft, in which dancers complain to her of their troubles, and finally give themselves up to joy as they receive her blessing.

The Morenadas reveal the deep impression made upon the indigenous population by the black slaves who were imported to work in the mines. The choreography of the many Morenada dance groups tells the legend of a rebellion against a gang leader in the Marie Antoinette vineyards. A young black woman who was the delight of the old despot attracted the attention of the slaves. Burning with desire for her, they got the *caporal* (boss) drunk and then overthrew him in a rebellion. They forced the *caporal* to stamp on the grapes and move the winch, while they ridiculed him in satiric verses (Alessandri 1968: 10). It is an incomplete rebellion, one in which the agent of oppression, not the forces of repression, is attacked and forced to take on their humble role.

Both dances assert the possibility of transformation from subordinate to superordinate positions by the enslaved proletariat. They are "primitive" forms of rebellion because they seek redemption in usurping the role of the dominant, not a collective identity in an alternative society.

Organization of dance groups provides an institutional base for important friendships and contacts, a theme that Hans Buechler highlights in his remarkable book *The Masked Media* (1980). In Oruro there are four major groups among eighteen dance societies, each representing a major occupational confederation. The railroad workers and the miners form the largest contingents. The dance groups both reinforce work-group solidarity and link them to the community.

Two separate Carnival acts, divided by time and place, but linked by common beliefs, are the *ch'alla* to the Pachamama and to Supay. The first takes place in most of the houses and yards of the townspeople at noon on the Tuesday of Carnival week. The second is performed inside the mines on Friday evening, beginning about sundown and lasting until midnight. The first brings together the members of a household and assures their health and welfare, and the productivity of whatever subsistence crops they grow in their gardens. The second reinforces the solidarity of the work group while ensuring the safety of men against accidents and their mineral yield. On the two occasions, offerings are made to gain the goodwill of the spirits of the earth and hills.

During Carnival, and on the 31st of July, the offering to Supay should include the sacrifice of a llama or sheep. The tin barons—Patiño, Hochschild, and Aramayo—used to purchase the sacrificial animal and attend the ceremonies before their mines were nationalized with the revolution of 1952. After the nationalization of the mines, some of the miners complained that these rituals were performed in excess of the Tío's needs. Juan, whose autobiography I elicited and edited (Rojas and Nash 1976), told me that going into the mine shortly after the revolution was like walking into a saloon. Such secular abuse of the ritual was curtailed in the latter part of the decade and, following military control in 1965, the rituals were entirely halted. The assault on the rituals intensified the hatred miners felt for the regime of Barrientos. The succeeding military president, Ovando, did not oppose the rituals. However, the state mining administration refused to subsidize the cost of the llama. The ritual that I observed during Carnival 1970 was limited to hot beef stew brought into the mines by workers' wives. Not until mine accidents occurred in July of that year was there a complete *k'araku*, or sacrifice of a llama in the mines.

The way that administrators respond to the rituals shapes workers' consciousness. When Patiño danced with the miners and offered each one a personal gift of a skirt or a shirt, he reduced—at least temporarily—worker alienation. The ambivalence of national mining engineers

and supervisors after the revolution of 1952 toward these autochthonous rituals created more distance between them and the workers. Since
an important part of the ritual is ensuring the continued productivity of
the mines, the men felt that it indicated a lack of their concern for the
future of the mines. Since the military did not comprehend this perspective, they opposed the rituals, and Barrientos's repression of the rituals
succeeded in transforming them into an expression of class solidarity
and opposition to the military.

The Friday before Carnival is devoted to a *ch'alla* of the serpent at the
southern end of town, and on the following Wednesday and Friday respectively, people on the north side of town honor the toad and the image of the condor. The condor is not an autochthonous mythic figure,
but he is offered a *ch'alla* during his celebration.

The special day for the serpent is the Day of the Cross, 3 May, and for
the hoard of ants, 15 July. Each celebration combines a request for material goods—a house, a truck, good health, or good fortune—with an
offering of liquor, incense, and a *mesa* (literally "table," an offering of
sugar cakes, wool, and fat). In these active cults, people reveal the intensity of their desire for material improvement in their lives and their
sense of the reciprocal balances in the universe. Most people I questioned said that they were successful in gaining the objects they requested of the enchanted images. These rituals, superficially linked with
"commodity fetishism" (Taussig 1980), at a deeper level tie workers to
the primordial past, rather than to capitalist institutions. Their sense of
dependency on the mines or other source of income is lessened as they
reckon with these other powers.

In contrast with celebrations in other countries, Oruro Carnival processions are ordered, with precise dance steps and lavish costumes. It is
not a wild excess of sex and drink, but a precise channeling of very deep
passions and sentiments. It is both an expression of, and solace for, discontent. It is a great source of pride, enabling them to rise above the
grueling poverty and despair of their everyday lives.

Along the main street on Carnival Sunday, a drama group of miners,
friends, and residents of the San José encampment—who call themselves Sons of the Sun—present a play depicting the conquest. Pro-
tagonists include Pizarro; Diego Almagro and his cohort; the priest
Vicario Hernando Luque; the king of Spain; Atahualpa, the king of the
Incas; Hualla Huisa as chief diviner; and fifteen *ñustas*, or Inca maidens.
The conquistadores are heavily bearded. The Spanish king and his
priest wear pink gauze masks with brightly rouged cheeks and widely
staring blue eyes. This contrasts with the unmasked faces of actors playing their Inca forebears, who need no falsification.

In the enactment of the death of Atahualpa, players reenact their
own conquest and subjugation. The actors keep alive the spirit of rebel-

lion by repeating Pizarro's outrageous betrayal of his promise to release Atahualpa after he had received the royal treasure. The dialogue in Quechua is an assertion of their own cultural survival in the face of Spanish domination. The effect of the drama is to reinforce resistance by enacting a moral triumph over unjust domination.

Carnival is often regarded as the drama of good over evil. After witnessing eight days of ceremonial offerings, processions, displays of faith in the Pachamama, the Virgin, the devil, and the enchanted images, my own view was that good and evil become totally blended. Participants believe that appeals to the devil make fortune, power, riches, sex, and strength possibilities. But they recognize that the success of their appeals depends on the intermediacy of the Virgin, who now acquires her own court of devils as well as guardian angels. She, too, combines good and evil. According to local lore, her existence in the Church of the Mineshaft was due to a thief, Nena Nena, who by his veneration was able to transubstantiate her. Somewhat like Robin Hood, Nena Nena, the unemployed miner, was forced to steal for a living, robbing the rich. Unlike Robin Hood, he sold his goods to the poor, albeit only for a modest profit. When one of his would-be victims turned upon him and stabbed him, he returned to his cave hollowed out of the mine hill and there prayed to the Virgin. As he lay dying, she came to him in the form in which she can still be seen in the life-sized wooden painting housed at the altar of the church over the very opening of the mineshaft.

The events of the Carnival follow a similar pattern from one year to another, but there are always special features that reflect current events. In recognition of the flight to the moon in 1970, an astronaut danced with an American flag emblazoned on his space suit and a machine gun in his hand. Carnival is always a time for cultivating one's luck and overcoming the destiny to which one is assigned. It is a time for pursuit of the ordinarily unattainable. Good fortune is available to the lowliest. The only investment is faith, plus a certain amount of ritual expenditure to secure the *aini*, or reciprocal offering, due to the devout. The past is assessed, and credits for the future are chalked up.

Why has Carnival not merely survived but also grown more elaborate over the years? Whenever people spoke about political repression and revolution, they concluded by asking me, "But have you ever been here during Carnival?" and proceeded to describe past processions and their role in them. I sensed that it was not a shift in the dialogue, but an extension of it. Carnival is an expression of people's view of their history and an account of how they have transmuted their defeat into a triumphant statement of the value of survival and self-determination. Josermo Murillo Vacareza, an Oruro lawyer whose avocation was that of a folklorist, says:

The Diablada is a splendid transformation of the disenchantment that permeates the spirit of the pueblo, releasing the frustration from those forces that falsify its inner vitality. The daring and impetuous dance is the hidden impulse, equal to that of their ancestors, to demolish, fight, and subvert that which they oppose themselves to, whether to subjugation or inferiority; the epochal music is a stimulus to an insurgent movement, as a trumpet of continuity; its rich and beautiful clothing derives from a system of impoverishment, as if to say in the hyperbole of fired imagination, that we dare to believe that there is an end to it. (Murillo Vacareza 1969:9)

It would be simplistic to say that Carnival is a substitute for revolution. It is more accurate to say that it is a reminder to the people of the necessity for revolt when the historical conditions are appropriate, just as it is a denial of the misery and drabness of their everyday lives, and an expression of what they aspire to.

The Month of Supay

The month of August is the time for the preparation of the land for planting in September. It is a time to propitiate the power of the hills, which is identified with both Supay and Huari, sometimes called Supay's father. Among the miners, the two beings are treated as one. It is simultaneously a time to recognize the Pachamama, since one must avoid the destructive potential of Huari at the same time as one wins the benefits of the earth's fertility. It is a time to ask for both fertility of the fields and mineral wealth from the mines.

The Barrientos government forbade Supay- as well as Carnival-related activities. In early July of 1970 when I lived in the San José encampment, three young miners were killed inside the mines. The workers asserted that the deaths were due to the failure to keep up the ritual sacrifice of a llama to Supay. The ritual allegedly fed the spirit of the hills and satisfied his appetite so that he would not eat the workers. Consequently, a delegation of workers urged the superintendent of the San José mine to permit them to carry out the ritual on the customary night, 31 July, which was that very month. The superintendent agreed to this and offered to pay for the llamas when he saw that the men were reluctant to return to work. However, unlike Patiño, he refused to participate in the celebration. When I attended the festivity, a miner informed me: "the *k'araku* is held in order that there be some development in the mine, or so that we might discover a vein that would benefit the company. If they [the managers] had come, we workers would want to work with greater enthusiasm and will. Here we are waiting for some improvement to take place so that we all can benefit. But what benefit would it have? Only so that the administrators could take trips out of the country." He went on to explain the sense of reciprocity played out in the rituals: "We eat the mines and the mines eat us. For that reason, we have to give these rituals to the spirit of the hills so that he will continue to reveal the veins of metal to us so that we can live."

In the course of the sacrifice, the men call out to the Tío, the *awichas*, *machulas*, and *tiyulas* (the last two being attendants of the Tío and awichas), and throw the blood of the llama to all the danger points in the mine, the elevator, the winch, and the machines, while asking for work safety. The heart of the llama is buried near the image of Supay in a remote gallery of the mine, where he can eat it in peace. The llama used in the sacrifice I attended was pregnant, and the miners discovered the fetus when they butchered her. This was thrown on the pile of bones stripped clean by the diners in the banquet of baked flesh held on the following day. As the bones burned on a pile of faggots, surmounted by the fetus, a miner said to me:

> This is the luck of the working class. It is our offering because of our faith in the Tío Lucas [another name given to Supay]. He walks in the mine. We walk with him. He takes care of us, and we arrive with him. He is still owner of the mine. Before, we worked with greater strength and without accidents. It is the fault of the security engineers that we had this accident. They are in collusion with the administration. We make claims without any effect.

The multiplicity of understandings embodied in Supay are called into play in the mining community as they relate their present lives to his power. Through their lived relationship with Supay in the weekly *ch'allas* and the biannual *k'araku,* the miners overcome their own alienation in the mines. This enables them to generate an autonomous, liberating consciousness, though it does not ensure that this will be translated into an active movement. The force of this relationship can be coopted by the owners if, as Patiño chose to do, they enter into the rituals and reciprocate gifts. The unfortunate translation by the Spaniards of Supay into the devil, in their own version of a dichotomized moral universe, transmogrified a prehispanic vision of a power domain that contains good and evil in all the supernatural entities to which they relate. The recognition of Supay as the source of material abundance is only one aspect of his many powers. The miners feel that when they enter as a group to ask him to enrich the mines, they ensure the life of the community. It is only when they enter as individuals to seek his favor that they fall into a "pact with the devil." The wide range of attitudes and behaviors by which miners relate through Supay to their identification as an expropriated autochthonous group and as an exploited proletariat is far more complex than an interpretation that identifies the devil as a projection of commodity fetishism (Taussig 1980).

RITUAL, CLASS CONSCIOUSNESS, AND IDEOLOGY

Working-class consciousness among these Bolivian miners is founded in a strong identity as a common group, united by their collective work, in which they see themselves helped by these primordial sources of power. The rituals evoke this identity as workers discuss their problems and unite them against their oppressors. They are not so much a charter for behavior, as the early structural functionalists in the field of anthropology surmised, as a generative base motivating political action that might take many forms. These could underwrite reaction and even support for the military who have attacked them as well as adherence to revolutionary movements.

In order to understand how these rituals relate to the politicized ideologies of national parties, we must respond to questions on at least three different levels: (1) What happens with the people relating to one another in the scene? (2) How does the ritual unite these participants to other significant reference groups? (3) How has the significance of the ritual changed over time?

A simple Malinowskian functionalism helps us to answer the first question. The *ch'alla* integrates men within the work site and thus promotes the solidarity of the primary group. This is best expressed in the words of Manuel, a carpenter in the mine:

> This tradition inside the mine must be continued because there is no communication more intimate, more sincere, or more beautiful than the moment of the *ch'alla,* the moment when the workers chew coca together and it is offered to the Tío. There we give voice to our problems, we talk about our work problems, and there is born a generation so revolutionary that the workers begin thinking of making structural change. This is our university. The experience we have in the *ch'alla* is the best experience we have.

Manuel, who was one of the top leaders in the union before the Barrientos coup, was perhaps unusual in equating primary group solidarity with the basis for revolutionary action. Although it is a basic Marxist proposition about the beginning of class consciousness, many union leaders seem to negate it and often criticize traditional rituals. This negation may stem from the fear, on the part of leaders who wish to impose their plan of action, to independent sources of consciousness and self-determination that are not controlled by the party or trade union.

The second issue of how the ritual relates workers to other significant reference groups requires a historical perspective. In the days of the tin barons before nationalization of the mines in 1952, when the owners, especially Patiño, would come to the celebration and dance with the *palliris* and the men, they overcame a great deal of the rebelliousness of the miners. The exchange of the *t'inka* (management's gift to the workers) and the *achura* (the workers' gift of prize ore to the owners) symbolized reciprocity in the labor relationship. Although this reciprocity was not equal, it reinforced a set of paternalistic ties that gave the workers greater spirit to work and sacrifice themselves. It overcame, even if only momentarily, the rebelliousness of the work force. Furthermore, in the days of the tin barons, the workers within each work group were paid according to a contract figured on the basis of the mineral content of the ores they produced. Like piecework systems of payment in developed industrial countries, this promoted compliance with management and division among workers. There was a great deal of competition between work groups to secure the richest vein, and the hostility engendered was worked out in witchcraft. An old miner who had worked in most of the mines of Bolivia and a copper mine in Chile described these customs:

> The men in the mines who got high returns on their contracts were most often the targets of witchcraft. The miners used to go seek the shamans from among the campesinos who know more about this. These shamans have animal spirits. Here, and especially in Colquecharka, many miners use witchcraft to make their more fortunate companions lose the vein. They went into the mine with the shaman and they threw water with salt on the vein where their enemy was working and this made it disappear. Sometimes the miners knew they were being bewitched and they called on the Pachamama.

Other miners reported pouring the milk of a black burro mixed with garlic on the veins of their enemies to make them disappear. The miners also had to protect veins against the evil eye (*bankanowi*) of any workers entering their sector. When they struck a good vein, they sometimes slept in the mine to protect it. The miners never brought garlic into the mine because this could make their own vein disappear, since the Tío did not like it.

In short, hostile competition was intense, and the solidarity built up in the *ch'alla* was limited to the immediate group of men working on the same contract. Following the nationalization of the mines, the base pay was raised and equalized for all the mines, and the negotiation for the contract was carried out by the union agents in open bargaining procedures. Workers felt that one of the most important gains they made was to have the contracts figured openly with the superintendent of the mine, foremen, and the head of the work group witnessing the contract statement.

Yet these bureaucratic controls introduced after the revolution had another consequence. The contract was paid to work teams of two men rather than to a work gang, and it was based on total output measured in cubic feet regardless of mineral content. Thus the solidarity of the work group was weakened at the primary group level, but a larger unity was maintained in the work force as a whole. The union welded together not only the work units within the mine, but through the Federation of Mine Workers' Unions of Bolivia (FSTMB) created a massive political force of all miners and through the Bolivian Workers' Central (COB) linked miners to other industrial workers and organized campesinos.

Militant political action, of which there was a great deal prior to the revolution, was separate from ritual relations, which were often rejected by the leaders both before and after the MNR entered power. The force of these rituals was in part coopted by the private owners, although the currents of identity were not fully controlled by them. Only when the management forthrightly opposed them, as during the military occupation of the mines in Barrientos's presidency, did the reaction to domination become a subversive force realized in the rituals.

During the period of nationalist solidarity within the populist revolutionary government, the *ch'alla* in the mines served as a recreation more than as a point for mobilizing rebellion and focusing on dissatisfactions. This brief period of amicable labor-management relations came to an end in the early 1960s with the so-called Triangular Plan. This plan provided the Bolivian state with much-needed capital to modernize the mines, but the financiers made the loans conditional on the firing of hundreds of "excess" miners and the termination of workers' representation in the management of the mines. The foreign financiers in the process deprived miners of revolutionary gains. Labor-management relations deteriorated still further after the military occupation of the mines by Barrientos in 1965. The miners say that Barrientos suppressed the *ch'alla* because he was afraid of the solidarity promoted in these drinking sessions. The suppression of the *ch'alla* added to the resentment of the workers against both management and the government.

Along with the suppression of the *ch'alla* came a sharp drop in the production of high-quality ores. This was coincident with a falling off in exploration. Furthermore, the nationalized mining administration never succeeded in developing work incentives. The deterioration of wages, coupled with the rising salaries of administrators and army officers, has resulted in both alienation of the workers and stagnation in production. A brief respite came with the populist Torres regime in 1970, when wages were reinstated to the pre-1965 levels, but his presidency came to an end after ten months with the military coup of Colonel Hugo Banzer Suárez. Management rejection of the *ch'alla* reveals the complete transformation of the ritual from one in which worker-management solidarity was reinforced to one in which the ritual becomes the basis for communication of rebellion.

The miners finally regained worker control, with the right of veto and participation in management, during Siles Zuazo's second term of office in 1984. Although Siles had undermined the labor movement during his first term of office with the stabilization plan and the Triangular Plan, he returned to power three decades later with labor's support. This time he remained loyal to his electoral ally. This meant that he could not, as a consequence, obtain needed foreign financial assistance. Because the state was bankrupt, labor's gains proved to be an empty shell. Production reached a near standstill because tools and machinery were inadequate and mineral veins were depleted. As the director of labor relations in COMIBOL, the nationalized mining corporation, told me in 1985, the restoration of their earlier rights served to minimize worker hostility to management. Yet workers' rights had lost much of their historical significance as mine production, along with world prices, plunged.

We have partially answered our third question, how the ritual has evolved over time, in the course of analyzing the changing structure of relations. The ideology expressed through ritual has not been a one-way street from paternalism to revolution. When the conditions were ripe for revolt prior to 1952, especially in the early labor struggles of 1918 and during the Chaco War, the *ch'alla* became a point for mobilizing discontent. It did not come as a surprise when I learned that in 1918 the aggrieved workers of the San José mine chose the *ch'alla* on the night of 31 July to declare the first strike recorded for the mine. Again, when there was extreme discontent over the Chaco War, the shrine of the Sapo (toad) was chosen as an assembly point. Recognizing this, the general ordered that it be destroyed. These time and place mementos of primordial supernatural power enhance the determination of those who still bear that culture to resist the oppression in which they live. After the general died of the stroke that paralyzed him following his sacrilegious act, the people of Oruro symbolized this by sculpting a new statue of the toad, resurrected on this same spot.

The 1952 revolution, in turn, did not result in long-term worker identification with the state. Even once miners won their ritual rights back after Barrientos had suspended them, workers felt alienated from the management of the state-run mines. The failure of the supervisors to attend the ceremonies accentuated their distance from the work force. As one worker said, on the occasion of the *k'araku*, "The Tío is the real owner here. The administrators just sit in their offices and don't help us in our work." The failure of the administration to make the traditional exchange of gifts, and the impoverished nature of the celebration because of insufficient funds, minimized its impact. "The Tío is still hungry," another miner said on leaving the celebration, "and so are we."

Assumptions about traditional and modern systems of belief often fail to capture the complexity of selective changes in symbol systems. The Tío is more important now in reference to accidents than as a generator

of mineral wealth. This is tied to a contract system, established after nationalization, in which the payoff depends on the total tonnage of output
rather than the mineral content of the ore. The significance of rituals is
directly related to this changing reality. The Tío is an explanation for
the inexplicable, a rationale for the irrational destiny forced on the
miner. Their faith in him enriches a barren existence of unremitting toil.
In the colonial period, when he appeared before the workers, he had the
face and figure of the enemy of their enemy, the devil, red-faced, horned,
and dressed in the royal robes of a medieval underworld denizen. In the
period of private large-scale exploitation, he appeared as a gringo, wearing a cowboy hat, boots, red-faced, and larger than life. When one makes
a contract with him, one is assured of riches even at the price of one's
life, but he pays off with a greater certitude than government bureaucrats or officials. Supay transcends the medieval conception of the devil
imported by the Spaniards; he is the source of wealth and desired power
as well as the agent of evil. He is not only a projection of the fetishism of
commodity production in capitalism whereby all social relations are
transformed into those of the cash nexus, as one very imaginative an-
thropologist has claimed (Taussig 1980), but a means to satisfy communal goals when approached collectively. When a lone miner works with
the devil in solitude, it is believed that he will die within ninety days and
that his heirs will never enjoy the wealth he accumulates. In contrast,
when the devil is given an offering by the miners as a group in the
k'araku, he reveals to them veins that all can work to make it possible for
the mine to remain productive and sustain the people who live on it.

Supay is a multifaceted power, neither all good nor all bad. As the
central figure in Carnival, Supay is both an expression of the frustrations
and anxieties in the lives of these people and a projection of their desire
to overcome them.

RELIGIOUS BELIEF AND POLITICAL BEHAVIOR

The power of these preconquest beliefs reinforced by ritual observances
lies in their stimulus to collective identity and the sense of when that has
been violated. The ritual calendar becomes a schedule for acts of protest
that have frequently upset governments and disturbs a given covenant in
industry. These events and the political repercussions that follow become part of the collective memory of people as they draw upon their
indigenous traditions to resist exploitation.

Resistance may take many forms, but it is always strengthened by the
self-determination of a people who have not yet lost their self-identity.
Rituals and belief combine to reinforce the myths that encompass their
history, and the celebrations of Carnival, the *ch'alla,* and the earth-
warming ceremonials prepare the people for a time when they can shape

their own destiny. Sectarian political leaders and orthodox religious leaders usually reject ritual protest as deviance. However, if one thinks of it as a rehearsal that keeps alive the sentiment of rebellion until a historically appropriate moment, it may reinforce political movements.

REFERENCES

Alessandri, Arturo Z.
  1968   "Facetas de 'la morenada': Un ensayo." In *Ensayo de interpretación del Carnaval Orureno: Leyendas, tradiciones, costumbres.* Oruro: Instituto de Filosofía Indígena Oruro.
Beltrán Heredia, B. Augusto
  1962   *Carnaval de Oruro y proceso ideológico e historia de los grupos folklóricos.* Oruro: Edición del Comité Departmental de Folklore.
Buechler, Hans C.
  1980   *The Masked Media: Aymara Fiestas and Social Interaction in the Bolivian Highlands.* Hawthorne, N.Y.: Mouton.
Murillo Vacareza, Josermo
  1969   "El diablo de Oruro y la supervivencia de un anhelo." *Fraternidad Revista Cultural* [Oruro], pp. 7–9.
Nash, June
  1979   *We Eat the Mines and the Mines Eat Us: Dependency and Exploitation in Bolivian Tin Mines.* New York: Columbia University Press.
Reyes, Simón
  1967   *La masacre de San Juan.* Oruro: n.p.
Rojas, Juan, and June Nash
  1976   *He agotado mi vida en la mina.* Buenos Aires: Nueva Visión.
Taussig, Michael
  1980   *The Devil and Commodity Fetishism in South America.* Chapel Hill: University of North Carolina Press.

CHAPTER SIX

Religion and Popular Protest in Latin America: Contrasting Experiences

Daniel H. Levine and Scott Mainwaring

For centuries, religion stood as a bulwark of conservatism in Latin America. The Catholic church was allied to conservative elites opposed to change in the established order of things. Church leaders generally set themselves firmly against popular activism and protest. But over the past few decades, significant elements in the church have moved to promote change, empowering and legitimating popular protest across the region. Once seen as a cultural reservoir of apathy and fatalistic resignation, the Catholicism of the popular classes now commonly appears as synonymous with solidarity and resistance to injustice in cases otherwise as different as Brazil, Chile, and El Salvador.

This chapter is one of many current attempts to pay closer attention to popular patterns in the process of political and religious change.[1] We examine the relation between change in religion and popular protest in the widely contrasting cases of Brazil and Colombia. This general issue has lately become salient in Latin America (as in much of the world), where struggles within religion have intersected with deep social and po-

The authors wish to thank Thomas Bruneau, Caroline Domingo, Susan Eckstein, Michael Löwy, James Scott, and Alexander Wilde for comments and criticisms.

1. During the late 1960s and much of the 1970s, most theoretical work on Latin America focused on how elites dominated their societies. In particular, attention was devoted to dependency, the so-called "new authoritarianism," the state, and multinational corporations. Although there were some good studies on the popular classes and the ways they resisted domination, this theme was subordinate. While the analysis of popular subjects was somewhat neglected by Latin Americanists during the 1970s, elsewhere it burgeoned. The British school of "history from below" (Thompson 1964) and the works of Michel Foucault (1980) and Natalie Davis (1974, 1975) were highly influential. A major recent statement in this line is Scott 1986. In recent years there has been much new research on popular religion and politics across a wide range of regions, disciplines, and intellectual traditions. For detailed comment, see Levine 1986c.

litical transformations to create new legitimations and structures of protest. Much of the process hinges on what are essentially political issues. But note that more is at stake now than just the opposition of religion to political power. Latin American history provides many precedents of intense conflict between church and state, and of a wide range of partisan entanglements by ecclesiastical leaders.

The current scene differs because for the first time the locus of decision, conflict, and initiative has shifted to groups that poor people play a key role in establishing and maintaining. The centrality of such groups, known widely in Latin America as base communities, or CEBs (from their initials in Spanish or Portuguese, *comunidades eclesiales de base*), gives new depth to the link between religion and politics. As they press for greater equality and autonomy, CEBs and similar groups challenge established norms of power and authority *within* the churches. In addition to the familiar story of churches affirming or opposing states and regimes, we must now also analyze the way CEBs question and rework basic cultural categories like hierarchy, equality, activism, and passivity, or how the qualities making for legitimate authority are called into question and reworked in the routines of everyday life.

Although change has affected the church throughout Latin America, change is not everywhere the same, nor is it irreversible. The nature of these CEBs and of the churches varies considerably from country to country; one of our primary concerns is addressing these differences between popular groups. A few questions arise at once. Why do the churches, and religion in general, empower and legitimate protest in some cases and not in others? Why do activist popular groups find a welcome and support in some churches and not others? In what follows, we explore these and related issues through a close look at the nature of religious change (especially in CEBs) and its complex impact on protest.

Much writing on CEBs in Latin America is highly general and abstract. It fails to convey the sharp heterogeneity of CEBs in different settings and the complex nature of the linkages between CEBs and politics. To convey the richness and complexity of these relationships, our general discussion of CEBs is followed by detailed comparison of popular and institutional transformations in Brazil and Colombia.[2] These nations hold down the progressive and conservative ends, respectively, of the spectrum of Latin American Catholicism. They promote very different ideological and organizational agendas at home and also compete in regional and worldwide Catholic forums to advance the positions with which each has become identified. In the late 1960s and early 1970s, the

2. On Brazil, see Mainwaring 1986a; Bruneau 1974, 1982, 1986; Della Cava 1976 and forthcoming; and Souza Lima 1979. On Colombia, see Levine 1981, 1985b, 1986a; Wilde 1986; and Zamosc in this volume.

Brazilian church emerged as a progressive model in the region. But Colombians now dominate the leadership positions in the Latin American bishops' council (CELAM), and use them to advance the new Vatican line, devoted above all to reining in autonomous grass-roots activism.

Such national and international differences have shaped the possibilities of popular action and give a characteristic quality to popular religious attitudes, practices, and organizations in the two nations. To avoid the overgeneralization that plagues so much recent work on CEBs, we anchor analysis of Brazil and Colombia in a pair of life histories. On the basis of extensive field research in these countries, we have selected individuals who reflect trends and differences in the two churches and societies. Because they are broadly representative of lay leaders in the two churches, these contrasted lives provide rich contextual detail without the danger of either idiosyncracy or excessive generality. To set the stage for analysis, we begin with some theoretical comments on issues in the study of religion and politics that are relevant to the study of CEBs.

RELIGION AND POLITICS:
CONCEPTUAL AND THEORETICAL ISSUES

The study of religion requires attention to more than documents, formal positions, or the sermons heard in church on Sundays. Analysis must also consider the normal practice of religious life and the everyday activities and modes of discourse through which notions of power, authority, and commitment are worked out in practice. The point is important here because CEBs have encouraged new religious practices that embody more critical conceptions of authority.

While separated here for purposes of exposition, institutional and popular levels of action are closely linked in reality and shape and influence one another in many ways. Exclusive focus on either institutions or popular groups will not do. The case of CEBs points up the importance of this enduring tie. Although CEBs are often depicted as if they came directly "from the people," in fact they almost always begin as the result of some sponsorship by the institutional church. Moreover, as we shall see, the CEBs' ties to the church persist and are valued by ecclesiastical elites and grass-roots members alike.

These reflections suggest the need to rethink common ideas about both institutions and popular religion. Institutions are more than machines for grinding out documents and allocating roles and statuses. They are vital, changing structures that project ideas and resources, thus shaping the contexts in which everyday experience is lived. They provide members with elements of identity, material services, and links to a larger universe of moral significance that undergird perceptions, commitment, and action. At the same time, institutions are not wholly autonomous. They are influenced by their constituencies and adapt creatively to changing circumstances. Even the Catholic church, that most hierarchical of religious organizations, is affected by change at the base. In the next section, we show in detail how transformations at the popular level have been powerful motors for change in Catholicism over the past few decades. While the poor people who participate in CEBs value ties to the church, they bring their own changing agenda of urgent needs to the encounter with religious institutions. The working out of these needs can change the religious institutions that organized the groups in new and unexpected ways.

Popular religion, in turn, is no natural, "spontaneous" product. It is formed historically through the encounter of popular groups with institutions of power and meaning in their societies. As noted earlier, institutions reach out to shape popular beliefs and practices, and they are deeply affected themselves by the process. Since the mid 1960s, a profound reevaluation of popular religion, and of the role and status of popular groups generally, has been under way in the Latin American churches. Once taken without much question as the superstitions of the unenlightened and (it might be hoped) humble masses, waiting to be led and instructed by clergy, popular religion is now increasingly seen as a legitimate source of valid religious values and orientations (Levine 1985a, 1986b, 1986d; Kselman 1986).

The importance of analyzing the interaction between the institutional and popular dimensions is especially clear for the Catholic church, since both elites and rank-and-file Catholics value the institutional link and strive to remain within its bounds. This common commitment to the church sets limits to the likely scope of change, and poses problems for the long-term viability of radical projects of democratization within such a hierarchical organization. Although we emphasize the capacity of the grass roots to transform the church, in fact the Catholic church remains a very hierarchical institution, whose authority structure and universality are critical dimensions. Authority ultimately rests with the pope, who in recent years has bolstered the position of conservatives concerned with what they perceive as excessively autonomous and radical grass-roots practices. This authority structure underscores the importance of the international character of the church. Catholic practices in the remotest regions of the world are influenced by the Vatican.

Our perspective on politics and protest also cuts across conventional definitions limited to explicit vehicles of the "political" such as the state, parties, interest groups, rallies, elections, strikes, barricades, and demonstrations. Following Eckstein's introductory chapter, we look further, to the way religious practice in the CEBs encourages or inhibits new ways of thinking about and acting on the world. Religious change can reshape prevailing images of the self and patterns of intragroup relations, thus laying a foundation for new ideas about legitimacy and different cultural representations of authority. Such a perspective makes us dwell on matters that may at first blush seem wholly nonpolitical. But in our view, this apparent nonpolitical character stems more from the blinders of customary expectation than from a real appreciation of what is at issue to those involved.

How do institutional politics fit into this analysis? Clearly, institutional politics involve control over the ideological projections, resources, and action programs of big structures. Institutional politics set the context and possibilities of informal politics and popular action. They thus have an immediate impact on the organization and distribution of power in ways informal politics can rarely match.[3] What difference do cultural transformations and informal politics make if institutions themselves do not change, if there is no shift in the structure of power? First, participation in CEBs clearly matters to those involved. Even if collective action with explicitly "political" goals never develops, the search for meaning goes on in the spaces of ordinary life. The powerless work with the tools at hand. Regardless of their short-term political impact, CEBs fill critical religious and affective needs and can stimulate deep changes in personal as well as group life.

Further, religious change can nurture dissent and delegitimize established structures or leaders. Even if "power" is not "taken," the experience of discussion, organization, struggle, and action can nurture an independent popular consciousness and in this way make possible continued resistance to authority and sustained struggle for change. This is what lays down a cultural foundation for change, and undergirds long-term transformations in the meaning and possibilities "politics" holds for popular groups (Ileto 1979). Scholars have focused too much on the apparent political results of religious action, with little sense of why motives emerge or how they may stimulate and sustain action in the first place (Levine 1986c). Explicitly political vehicles and outcomes are, of course, important, but if analysis ends here, much of great value is missed. Most of the interest of recent Latin American struggles over religion and politics lies less in conventional political manipulations of religion (e.g., the use of shrines and symbols or processions, or the formation of religious political parties) than in the way changes within religion are associated with new kinds of social organization and with activities whose political meaning arises less from direct confrontations with authority (although these may occur) than from the legitimation of new ideas about activism, power, and governance in ordinary life.

People learn about politics and religion, not only through explicit

3. In this sense, while we agree with Foucault (1980) that there are multiple loci of power (and politics) in society, we believe that these are more concentrated than he suggests, and have a logic of domination that clearly favors some groups and classes over others. Institutions are critical, and while we center attention here on informal politics and popular groups, we stress the critical nature of their linkage to institutions.

messages, but also through the implicit models of good societies and proper behavior that they encounter in the contexts of daily routine. As these contexts change, legitimations of power and authority are reworked. Again, explicitly political change comes at the end of a long chain of events, not at its beginning. Stated otherwise, we look first to understand the religious content of religion. Without analyzing the powerful motivating capacity of religious ideals, it is impossible to understand the political significance of religious transformations. Generally speaking, the most important political consequences of religious change occur not in the realm of institutional politics but rather in ideas about power, authority, and justice—ideas that are shaped by religion.[4]

The renewed salience of religion in politics in the late twentieth century would surely have surprised many earlier thinkers. Since the nineteenth century many students of religion have seen it as an atavism likely to disappear with the advent of modernization. Despite otherwise radical differences of opinion, writers like Freud, Nietzsche, Marx, and Feuerbach agreed that religion was epiphenomenal, secondary to expressions of interests, desires, or processes that are somehow more "real." Until recently, much sociological analysis of religion has continued to make this assumption.

The importance of religion in the politics of Latin America, Africa, Asia, and increasingly in the United States underscores the need for theoretical reassessment. Far from declining, religion shows great import throughout the world. Moreover, analysis that makes religion epiphenomenal is hard pressed to grasp the central value of religious belief to those involved. Religion is clearly a powerful motivating force on its own. Religious ideas inspire and legitimate action while religious structures simultaneously produce enduring social bonds that make collective endeavors possible. External pressures create alternatives and opportunities, but prior transformations within religion have autonomous validity and an independent impact on politics and protest. Analysis that forgets the powerful motivating force of religious belief and looks only to concepts such as "elite manipulation" or "popular struggle" misses much of the reason why people join religious groups in the first place. It thus fails to see how religious motives and values undergird other aspects of group life. Religion provides enormous political energies, which

4. Of course, the centrality of religious motivation to political action does not apply exclusively to one side of the religious spectrum. Frequently, sympathizers of the "liberationist" church recognize the religious motives of Catholic radicals, but see the actions of conservative religious leaders as inspired by purely political considerations (e.g., defending the status quo). Conversely, conservative critics often charge that radicals use religion for political purposes, when generally the opposite is true, i.e., the radicals act politically out of religious conviction. Although there may be isolated cases of individuals who use religion for instrumental purposes, religious motivation must be taken seriously at both ends of the spectrum.

change expectations, challenge accepted notions of the legitimate, and refocus action on new areas and issues of conflict. Moreover, the current visibility of religion is not well understood as a fundamentalist or atavistic reaction—the last gasp of a dying worldview. Fundamentalists are not much in evidence in the Latin American cases we discuss.

The importance of understanding the religious motivations of actors holds in particular for the exaggerated radical expectations common in much writing on CEBs in Latin America. Most CEBs are not necessarily, or even usually, interested in revolution. CEB members generally have more urgent needs and more modest goals. To see them primarily as tools for political change (as the left often does with praise, and the right with condemnation) is to overstate their political involvement and to misread their religious nature. Where revolutionary commitment of CEBs occurs, as in Nicaragua and El Salvador, it is the product of external pressures that drive groups, in Berryman's apt phrase, "from evangelization to insurrection" (Berryman 1986). The next section looks closely at the origins and character of CEBs in Latin America, with special reference to the link between the religious and political dimensions of the CEBs.

THE NATURE OF BASE COMMUNITIES

Much has been written lately about CEBs, with particular stress on their supposed potential to stimulate and nurture a new sort of involvement by poor Catholics in society, culture, politics, and religion. Limitations of space make a detailed review impossible here,[5] but a few critical points may be noted. Despite the broad interest in CEBs, there is little agreement as to just what these groups are like. Widely varying kinds of organizations are lumped together and presented as CEBs. Even a cursory review of the evidence turns up major differences in CEBs between nations, and also among regions, dioceses, and localities in the same country. Thus, what passes for a base community in El Salvador or Brazil often bears little relation to groups of the same name encountered in Colombia or Argentina. Conversely, a group that meets all of the normal definitions of a CEB may not call itself a base community.

A common working definition of CEBs takes off from the three elements of the term *ecclesial base community*: a striving for community (small, homogeneous); a stress on the ecclesial (links to the church); and a sense in which the group constitutes a *base* (either the faithful at the base of the church's hierarchy or the poor at the base of the social pyra-

5. We discuss CEBs in detail in Levine 1984a, 1984b, and 1986d and Mainwaring 1986a, chaps. 5, 7–9, and 1987a. See also Azevedo 1987; Bruneau 1980; Betto 1981; C. Boff 1979; L. Boff 1977; Ferreira de Camargo et al. 1980; Hoornaert 1978; Ireland 1983; Souza Lima 1982.

mid). Most CEBs are small groups, involving ten to thirty people, usually relatively homogeneous in social composition. They gather regularly (usually once every week or two) to read and comment on the Bible. They are most often composed of poor people in a single neighborhood, village, or hamlet.

As noted earlier, CEBs are rarely spontaneous creations, springing full-blown and unbidden "from the people." They are born linked to the churches, specifically to initiatives by bishops, priests, nuns, or lay agents commissioned by the church. Links to the church are maintained through a regular routine of courses, visits by clergy, and especially sisters, and the distribution of mimeographed circulars, instructional material, and cassettes. All this means that while the CEBs are popular in social composition, they are not autonomous or isolated from the church. They are constantly influenced by the institutional church and often subject to its monitoring and control. This situation easily leads to conflict between the institution and the CEBs where the former is relentless in its demand for control or where the popular groups attempt to develop in a direction opposed by the clergy.

Why did CEBs develop as they did? Across the region, religious and political trends converged to give a specific character to emergent groups. Change in the Catholic church, encouraged by the Second Vatican Council (1962–65) and peaking at the 1968 meeting of the Latin American bishops' conference at Medellín, Colombia, set in motion a broad range of innovations, including stress on lay participation, more attention to the promotion of justice (and the denunciation of injustice), and more effective evangelization among the popular classes. These changes enhanced the status of popular action and expression within religion and formed part of a broad upsurge of grass-roots experiences all across Latin America.

Within the churches, these changes responded to growing secularization, urbanization, and (in many countries) the erosion of the Catholic religious monopoly and the growth of the left. Rapid social and cultural change in the post-1945 period also created new needs on the part of the popular sectors that established groups did not fulfill, including the need for more participatory experiences that would provide friendship, meaning, and structure as they faced the changing world around them. Thus, as the Catholic church opened its doors in new ways to the poor, the poor sought new answers and experiences in religion—whether through the Catholic church, the Pentecostal churches, or (as often was the case in Brazil) Afro-Brazilian sects. It is no accident that religious growth since the 1950s has affected a wide amalgam of faiths in Latin America. Growth has been particularly pronounced among religions and varieties of religious experience that offer a strong sense of community, friendship, and meaning, regardless of political content.

These religious and social changes intersected historically with the emergence of "national security" military regimes and a regional turn to "new," more repressive authoritarianism. The conjuncture was critical. In the late 1960s and early 1970s, as the Catholic church opened up more to popular groups, repression intensified in many countries, and popular religious groups became targets of official violence because any autonomous organization was suspect in the eyes of fearful elites. Because normal political channels (parties, unions, neighborhood associations) were closed, church-sponsored groups and activities inadvertently became the only available political outlets in some countries. The impact of political closure was mostly indirect. As noted, the initial impetus for most CEBs was religious, not political; they emerged as part of a broad church strategy designed to reach the popular sectors. The initial impact of the CEBs stemmed above all from the fact that the religious, social, and cultural experiences they offered found a ready clientele. But in all the cases where CEBs later became prominent, political closure was decisive in magnifying their impact as CEBs became the only available vehicles for popular organization. At the same time, repression radicalized many bishops and pastoral agents, who then intensified efforts to create and extend CEBs. Further, the national security states were so manifestly antipopular that they unwittingly encouraged the politicization of most CEBs by repressing just about any collective popular action, no matter how innocuous its initial goals.[6]

If we look at the actual process of grass-roots organization, a clear pattern emerges across the region. In most cases, the first step came as pastoral agents set about reworking the ties between churches and popular classes. In large numbers they went to live in popular communities and work alongside residents on a day-to-day basis. CEBs were typically formed after some such contact, and only after a few years of experience did a more elaborate and articulated vision begin to appear of what CEBs were supposed to be like. National and regional programs soon followed, dedicated to leadership training and group promotion, and to the general dissemination of these initiatives.

One of the characteristics of this intersection of grass-roots innovations and institutional changes was an emphasis on "the people." This emphasis was visible in heightened respect for the poor as sources of religiously valid insights. The very term "popular religion," once syn-

6. Of course, not all cases followed so stark and clear a path. The case studies of Brazil and Colombia, presented below, show how different the sources and pathways of religion and politics turn out to be in each case. Brazil is close to the trajectory just outlined; a progressive church became more progressive and more attuned to the popular classes because of political closure. In Colombia, on the other hand, a consistently conservative church fears and distrusts popular initiatives. The generally open and clientelistic character of Colombian politics reduces the opportunities and legitimation for popular action.

onymous with ignorance and superstition, became practically a code word for authenticity and for values like generosity, selflessness, and solidarity. Religious populism stressed the need to go to the people, share their conditions, and identify with their situation. Much like the *narodniki* of nineteenth-century Russia, sisters, priests, and middle-class activists throughout Latin America moved to seek the "wisdom of the people" (DeKadt 1970; Kselman 1986; Paiva 1984).

Much of this populism, and the accompanying adulation of "the popular" by progressive groups, is wrapped around an intense fight for power. An old-fashioned bitter political struggle rages all over Latin America to control popular groups, and especially to control programs that train pastoral agents and produce materials for group use. At issue is who will staff the institutes, run the mimeograph machines, record and distribute the cassettes, make the visits to the groups and coordinate their activities. In short, who will set the agenda of CEBs, and what will it contain? Will they stress spiritual matters to the exclusion of social and political issues, or will it be the reverse, or some combination of the two? The general trend in the Catholic church, reinforced strongly by Pope John Paul II and pushed with notable vigor after the 1979 meeting of Latin American bishops at Puebla, has clearly been to stress the former. As yet, the outcome is not uniform, but politically active CEBs are obviously under pressure.

We have argued that CEBs emerge primarily as the result of initiatives of pastoral agents to reach out to the popular sectors. But the CEBs involve a relationship between the church and the popular sectors, so it is also essential to explore the bases of popular receptivity. This receptivity is not unlimited; there are countless cases where clerics have attempted, but failed, to create CEBs. Interestingly, failure was more likely where the pastoral agents attempted to encourage highly politicized CEBs from the beginning. Conversely, success was more likely where religion and community were the main objectives. Popular receptivity was also greater where some traditional religious values (respect for images, processions, veneration of saints) were upheld, even as other aspects of popular religiosity changed.

Concern with the political impact of CEBs should not obscure their central religious character. If we ask what CEBs actually do every day, and how their ordinary routines converge with the pressures and opportunities of institutional politics, we must begin with ties to the church. In daily practice, CEBs are much more conventionally religious than is commonly realized. Members pray a lot, both individually and as a group; they also value and practice very traditional prayers and rites, such as rosaries, nocturnal vigils, and adorations, now disdained by some radical church activists. They place great stress on liturgies and traditional religious celebrations, including processions and pilgrimages. These are ex-

plicitly downplayed by those radicals who favor preaching and sociological discourse over liturgy. Indeed, the clash of popular desires for
liturgy with activist stress on "useful" collective action is a permanent
feature of much CEB life. As noted, CEB members value links to the
church and generally have great respect for church leaders like priests,
and especially bishops and the pope.[7] Radical clergy, sisters, and activist
laity all over Latin America have learned that attacking the hierarchy
drives the people away.

These explicitly and conventionally religious activities cut through
all aspects of group life. No matter what the social or political agenda
may be, in all instances there is great stress on prayer, Bible study, and
liturgy. Moreover, most of the groups' social and political agendas are
also quite conventional.[8] Typical activities include sewing, visiting the
sick, or "social action," which usually means collecting money, clothing,
or food for those in extreme need. There is often an attempt to found
cooperatives, which generally remain limited to very small-scale savings
and loan operations, or at most to collective marketing or common purchase arrangements.

Within this seemingly innocuous set of activities, CEB life represents a
sharp break from most previous religious practice. Members meet regularly to read and discuss the Bible, pray together, and celebrate liturgies
as a group. None of this occurred on any significant scale before the mid
1960s. Until recently, most popular religious life in Catholicism was sporadic, centered around celebrations of mass (especially on major holi-
days) or visits to church coinciding with key sacraments. Scarcity of
clergy meant that many people's only contact with the official church
(particularly in the countryside) came on isolated occasions. The promotion of CEB formation, Bible study, and the change to Spanish or Portuguese liturgy have significantly altered religious life. Group meetings
make religious life more regular and familiar. Moreover, access to the
Bible lessens the dependence of the poor on traditional authority figures
like priests. After getting under way, many groups continue on their
own, visited only occasionally by clergy or sisters.

The religious innovations of CEBs help explain why they have be-

7. The most visible exception to this generalized pattern has occurred in Nicaragua,
where much of the grass-roots church has expressed a rejection of the conservative bishops
and the pope. Even here the evidence is far from conclusive. Apart from the possible Nicaraguan example, the only exceptions have occurred in situations where an already well institutionalized network of grass-roots groups came into conflict with a new bishop who attempted to curtail CEB activities.

8. El Salvador and Nicaragua represent exceptions here. In both countries, the explosive political situation eventually led most grass-roots Catholic activists to engage in institutional politics. On CEBs in El Salvador, see Cáceres 1982 and also Berryman 1986. On
Nicaragua, see Dodson 1986; Crahan forthcoming; Williams forthcoming. On Central
America generally, see Opazo and Cáceres 1987.

come so controversial and are at the center of the current debate about the church. Conservatives believe CEBs have become too autonomous and form what Pope John Paul II terms "a popular church." This fear has triggered a series of efforts to control grass-roots religious activities more closely, as will be seen from the Colombian case. In reality, even self-consciously "progressive" groups may have less revolutionary impact than is often suggested. But because the normal practice of CEBs encourages critical discourse, egalitarianism, and experiments in self-governance within the groups, even the most "apolitical" CEBs can have long-term political consequences. They do so by stimulating and legitimating new kinds of leadership and commitment in the larger society. The next two sections describe how and explain why CEBs variously foment popular protest or fail to challenge entrenched authority patterns. The contrasting experiences of CEBs in Brazil and Colombia show how CEBs vary in their impact depending on the institutional and political context in which they are embedded.

BASE COMMUNITIES
EMPOWER POPULAR PROTEST: BRAZIL

Base communities emerged earlier in Brazil than elsewhere in Latin America; the first ones sprang up in the period immediately before the 1964 military coup. From this time on, the Brazilian church has served as a model for Catholic progressives throughout Latin America. By the mid 1970s the Brazilian church was probably the most progressive in the world. The hierarchy assumed strong positions in defense of human rights, trenchantly criticizing the military government on many occasions. Under the new democracy (1985–present), the church has continued to criticize elitist patterns of politics and egregious inequalities, as well as to call for agrarian reform, income distribution, and broad popular participation. Equally important is the fact that the Brazilian church has been the continental leader in grass-roots innovations, among which the CEBs are the most outstanding. Although it is difficult to rely on these numbers (which are probably somewhat exaggerated), spokespeople for the Brazilian church say that there are now approximately 100,000 CEBs in Brazil, with over two million participants. CEBs have clearly been a major pastoral priority of the Brazilian church.

CEBs have been heavily concentrated in dioceses where bishops have encouraged their promotion. The support of dozens of progressive bishops was a necessary condition for CEBs to assume such a central role in the church. Given its limited material resources and clergy, the Brazilian church has provided vast intellectual and human resources for grass-roots groups. Without exception, Brazil's most prominent progressive theologians have worked extensively with CEBs. CEBs are a leading priority of many dioceses and archdioceses. The National Conference of Brazilian Bishops (CNBB) has sponsored several book-length studies of CEBs and many studies on related subjects (CNBB 1977, 1979, 1982). In addition, many leading CNBB statements have addressed the issues that are vital in the life of CEBs. These include religious issues proper, such as popular religiosity and the saying of mass for popular groups; they also include socioeconomic questions of central importance to the popular classes. Although the CNBB did not officially endorse the five national encounters of CEBs, it did support them unofficially.

In Brazil, about 80 bishops (out of 350) have actively promoted CEBs, and most of these bishops have also encouraged CEB people to participate in institutional politics. Arguably the most distinctive feature of the Brazilian church has been the harmony between progressive grass-roots experiences and the hierarchy, a harmony made possible only because of the progressive character of many Brazilian bishops. Meanwhile, the openness of the Brazilian hierarchy to concerns originating among grass-roots pastoral agents has given a dialectical quality to change in the Brazilian church. Grass-roots pastoral agents pushed for change and were directly responsible for most of the innovations. The hierarchy legitimated and further encouraged these changes, and theologians (who generally had considerable contact with the grass roots) elaborated theologies that underpinned the innovations.

This concern of the Brazilian church's with promoting CEBs has been integrally connected to its desire to promote more effective and participatory church structures, and also to its view that a necessary component of the church's mission is promoting social justice. For example, the bishops have stated that the church should assume "its critical and prophetic mission of denouncing injustice and promoting the solidarity and legitimate hopes of people" (CNBB 1975:78–79).

The CEBs are one of the primary means of promoting social justice within the Brazilian church. The bishops, theologians, and social scientists who promote CEBs clearly believe that base communities should not form a church ghetto. On the contrary, they encourage CEB people to participate in the social movements and political parties to help transform the society's elitist political patterns and inegalitarian social structures. Typical of the discourse one finds in materials produced by the church for distribution in the CEBs was a highly publicized document issued by the archdiocese of São Paulo—the most populous archdiocese in the world and the most influential (although far from the most radical) in the country.

> Everyone should participate in politics, because everyone is a free and responsible citizen. The citizen has a right and an obligation to give an opinion, criticize what is wrong, suggest new paths, and indicate the real needs of the people. Politics cannot be limited to a group that knows every-

thing and manipulates the people, for the first subject of political action is the people, organized to make their rights as citizens count. (Comissão Pastoral 1981:82–83)

Often there is a gap between this participatory discourse and grassroots pastoral practices, which sometimes are more authoritarian, clerical, and conservative than the discourse would indicate. Moreover, where pastoral agents actively promote political involvement, the move from participation in CEBs to participation in progressive social movements and party politics is not an easy one for most CEB people. Brazilian politics has been so elitist that its structures discourage political participation. The slow, controlled, and conservative nature of the liberalization process (1974–85) blocked the kind of radicalization of CEBs that occurred in Nicaragua after 1976 and El Salvador after 1979. Nevertheless, the impact of grass-roots Catholic leaders on an amalgam of social movements that emerged in the 1970s is undeniable. Indeed, since the 1970s, one cannot understand popular movements in Brazil without reference to the political style and impact of grass-roots Catholic activists. All over the country, people who have participated in CEBs are among the leaders of neighborhood associations, labor unions, and peasant unions. Popular movements, in turn, were important actors in redefining the nature of the liberalization project initiated by the military government in 1974 (Cardoso 1983; Mainwaring 1987b). The impact of poor Catholics migrating from CEBs to partisan politics is particularly clear with the Workers' Party, the most progressive major party in this country where politics is thoroughly dominated by elite transactions. The popular presence in political life is still weak, but it has been strengthened considerably by the grass-roots church.

The life of one Brazilian woman who began to participate in a base community in 1974 helps show how and why CEBs have assumed political importance in Brazil. Azuleika Sampaio is a remarkable example of a person whose life changed dramatically because of her involvement in a base community.[9] In turn, this CEB experience enabled her to become an outstanding leader in her city's neighborhood movement and, to a lesser extent, in the women's movement. Although she is unusual in her leadership abilities, throughout the country thousands of individuals like her have influenced the grass-roots church and political life.

Azuleika was born in 1933 in Recreio, Minas Gerais, where she grew up as a practicing Catholic. Her religious practice as a child was typical of

9. This account is based on formal interviews Mainwaring did with Azuleika Sampaio on 27 March 1981, 6 June 1981, and 20 December 1985. Numerous informal discussions with Sampaio also provided some basis for reflection. Additional information came from other interviews Mainwaring conducted in Nova Iguaçu. For a detailed discussion of the church and the popular movement in Nova Iguaçu, see Mainwaring 1986a, chap. 8, and 1987a.

that of most poor rural Brazilians. She had a strong faith, instilled mostly by her father, but she rarely went to mass. The closest church was too far to make a regular practice of doing so. But her father prayed every night, and Azuleika did likewise.

In 1946 she and her family moved to Rio de Janeiro. From then until 1974, she lived in one of Rio's largest *favelas*. At thirteen she began to work as a domestic servant, and at fourteen as a factory worker. She became the only member of her family to frequent the local church. At sixteen Azuleika married. From then until 1974, her life revolved around her family and home, her paid jobs, and her religious practice. Shortly after marriage, she joined the Apostolado da Congregação, a church movement that focused on spiritual devotion, prayer, and charity. She notes that she "started in the church by tradition and continued because of devotion." She helped with catechism classes, cooked for the priests, and so forth. She retrospectively describes her faith as "traditional" and "pre-Conciliar." Religion was "an end in itself," with no sense of political commitment. Politics was an issue only during campaign periods, when the priest told the people how to vote. She herself voted for conservatives like Carlos Lacerda and Jânio Quadros. Charitable actions (such as hospital visits) marked the limit of her social commitment. As she says, "I later changed radically, like water to wine."

Always a hard worker, in 1967 Azuleika went to work at a sewing factory, where she became the head of a section, overseeing some minors who worked there. In 1970 she won a prize as the best worker in Rio de Janeiro. She also returned to school in 1967, having previously completed only two years of schooling. In 1973 she finished *ginásio*, the equivalent of ninth grade.

In 1974, along with her two sons and husband, she made the short move to Nova Iguaçu, a poor working-class city some twenty miles to the north of Rio. In this overgrown (1.5 million people by the mid 1980s) and rapidly expanding commuter city, she and her family were able to purchase a small lot, even though they remained very poor. It was at this point, at the end of the most repressive phase (1968–74) of the dictatorship, that she started participating in a base community that had been organized by the local priest. She also participated in a church-organized mothers' club, but eventually left because she considered the priest too authoritarian and conservative. However, this more independent assessment came only after exposure to other church activities had enhanced her personal confidence. She speaks of the sense of belonging that she found in her local CEB.

In 1975 Azuleika was elected social coordinator of the local community. Later that same year, because of her growing responsibilities in the local community she started to attend some discussions about health issues. These discussions became the basis for forming a more dynamic

218   DANIEL H. LEVINE AND SCOTT MAINWARING

neighborhood movement in Nova Iguaçu. From the outset, Azuleika was challenged and stimulated by the leaders of these health discussions, four doctors who were interested in organizing the local population to obtain better urban services. "When I entered the movement, I met people on the left engaged in popular health work," she relates. "My relationship with them was terribly important to me; they taught me a lot. Our friendship is very deep and meaningful. They are very capable and intelligent. We have been friends now for ten years."

Her evident skills made her an outstanding leader. After 1976 she began to move in more sophisticated political circles, with other popular leaders of the region. In 1977 Azuleika started a new neighborhood association in her community. That same year, a Maryknoll priest from the United States began to work with the CEBs in her region. This man also had a significant impact on her life. He supported her deepening involvement in political and religious issues in Nova Iguaçu. In 1979 she became part of the Justice and Peace Commission, and in 1980 she started to work for Cáritas, an international organization of the Catholic church that works for the poor. Nova Iguaçu's Cáritas was directed by a progressive priest, who also supported Azuleika in many ways.

In 1979 she was elected part of the first Coordinating Commission of the citywide neighborhood movement, which by then had become one of the most important neighborhood movements in Brazil. Her leadership in local politics led Azuleika to become the president of the Federation of Neighborhood Associations of Nova Iguaçu in 1983. Created in 1981 in response to the dramatic growth of the neighborhood movement of Nova Iguaçu, this federation now coordinates the activities of over 160 neighborhood associations and is known for its capacity to mobilize the popular sectors. In late 1985 she was reelected to this position.

Several points of Azuleika's story are particularly important for present purposes. Most obvious, yet most important, is the dramatic potential that religion has for transforming common people's lives. Azuleika's life was radically altered through her participation in a CEB. Her initial impulse for political involvement came from religious participation.

Yet religion was not simply a way station en route to developing a more advanced political consciousness. On the contrary, Azuleika remains profoundly marked by a religious vision of the world. Although she no longer participates in her local CEB on a regular basis, she continues to go to mass and remains friends with the individuals in the local CEB. Religion was not the only factor in her political transformation, but it was the motivating force behind the early stages of this transformation.

Given the living conditions that Azuleika and millions of Brazilians face, it takes very strong motivation to be as persistent as she is. She works a whole day; is absorbed by her family life, including taking care of a retarded son; and yet finds time to participate in countless activities, some of which are tied to the church, while others are strictly political.

Religious motivation alone does not explain this extraordinary dedication, but it has been the core of it.

Religion's political impact first came in the sphere of "informal politics." Azuleika emphasizes that it was the combination of developing personal confidence and a greater concern for community affairs, both results of her participation in the base community, that led her to get involved in the neighborhood and women's movements. Personal confidence need not lead to political involvement, but for many women and men it has been a necessary stepping stone to political participation. CEB life can stimulate new sources and types of leadership. The pervasive stress on self-expression and participation clearly works to elicit hitherto hidden capacities for leadership. We have observed countless meetings where once tongue-tied men and women step forward to speak and share experiences. Their capabilities are nurtured in the group, supported and drawn out by friends and neighbors, and then spill over to affect other issues—from agricultural practice to savings, from personal relations to marriage patterns, schools to politics. People who were once afraid to speak out, now do so with confidence and vigor. People who did not even have a rudimentary notion of their rights now stand up for them. The potential for a move from CEB activities to participation in larger political circles is clearly borne out in Azuleika's case.

How was such a change in religiosity and politics possible? Part of Azuleika's transformation resulted from her own talents and dedication, but an adequate explanation also involves broader institutional changes, both in the Catholic church and in local politics. The institutional church played a decisive role in her transformation, with the two local priests being the most important individuals. Although individual priests and nuns can and do sometimes encourage progressive change in conservative dioceses, such change is more likely in situations like that of Nova Iguaçu, where the bishop and a significant percentage of the clergy are progressive. Since 1966, when Dom Adriano Hypólito became bishop, the diocese of Nova Iguaçu has pioneered in promoting ecclesiastical innovations, with CEBs as a major priority. The diocese also created a wide network of mostly progressive religious institutions and groups. Particularly significant in Azuleika's case were the diocese's chapter of the Justice and Peace Commission, which deals with a wide range of human rights issues, especially for the poor; and the diocesan Cáritas, which originated as a relief organization and deals with material problems of the needy. Her involvement in both organizations helped change Azuleika's life; both organizations exist because of the initiatives of Dom Adriano and progressive clergy. All of this serves to reinforce our earlier point about the importance of pastoral agents; it particularly suggests the ongoing centrality of the bishop, notwithstanding the efforts to decentralize ecclesiastical authority.

Compared to what we shall see in Colombia, most CEBs in Nova

Iguaçu place great emphasis on lay leadership, participation, and even autonomy. At the annual assembly that establishes diocesan priorities, lay people are in the majority, and each one has a vote equal to sisters, priests, and Dom Adriano. One popular diocesan publication makes this sentiment clear: "We [the people] are the church, and it is descending from the clouds to be among us. At times, the church must restructure itself to correspond to what is expected of it" (Diocese de Nova Iguaçu 1983). This process is hard to imagine in Colombia. This emphasis on lay autonomy was particularly visible in the priests who so influenced Azuleika's life. Furthermore, these priests strongly encouraged lay involvement in politics. Indeed, within what is an exceptionally heterogeneous diocese in terms of pastoral and political positions, the bishop and most priests in leadership positions have actively promoted lay involvement in progressive political movements.

Changes in local politics, and in particular the emergence of a neighborhood movement, also formed an important springboard. From the beginning of her political involvement, she received the encouragement of secular activists. Azuleika herself is quick to point to the profound impact these secular activists had on her political development. In this sense, Azuleika's story reflects broad changes in Brazilian politics between 1974 and the present. The growth of popular movements after 1974 was made possible by the slow process of political liberalization. Popular movements contributed, in turn, to the demise of the military government in 1985.

The narrative also suggests the limits of the church's ability to promote political change. Azuleika's evaluation needs no comment: "The CEB was important for me because it gave me a chance to read the Bible, to get involved in the life of the neighborhood, to begin to sense the importance of politics. But few people in the CEB have a political vision. The CEBs discuss a lot, but they don't act. . . . I couldn't realize my objectives in the CEB. The CEB is concerned with the narrow world of the neighborhood and the community."

Finally, the story hints at the fragility of some changes in popular identity, as well as the central role priests and nuns usually have in encouraging base communities. When the progressive priests left Azuleika's neighborhood, the local CEB activity stagnated. Many grass-roots people participate partly because of the direct encouragement of priests and nuns and never acquire such an independent stance as Azuleika.

The point of Azuleika's story is not to suggest that involvement in base communities has transformed all individuals in similar ways. Azuleika is unusual in her intelligence, dedication, and courage, just as the Nova Iguaçu neighborhood movement has been unusually successful by comparative standards. Yet even within the diocese of Nova Iguaçu, dozens of popular leaders got involved in politics primarily because of their church connection.

In concluding this section on Brazil, we should call attention to the limits of the short-term political changes effected by CEBs. In the late 1970s, as popular organization and protest burgeoned, there was widespread optimism about the capacity of CEBs to promote broad political change in Brazilian society. Now, a decade later, this optimism appears to have been ill founded. The military and conservative political elites maintain dominant positions in Brazil. The new democracy (1985–) has been a sharp disappointment to grass-roots leaders, who hoped for deeper changes, and grass-roots movements have experienced cyclical processes of mobilization and demobilization. Moreover, the political involvement of CEB participants has been less influential than progressive church intellectuals hoped. Why? In part because political liberalization satisfied the demands of major groups in the interclass civilian opposition movement (see chapter 9 below) that surfaced in the late 1970s. Moreover, in contrast to the recent Argentine military regime (1976–83), politicians associated with the Brazilian dictatorship retained reasonable popularity and as a result were able to negotiate a transition to democracy that maintained intact the broad parameters of the political system.

In revolutionary Nicaragua and El Salvador, CEB participants believed that change was desirable and possible. The polarized nature of conflict in the two countries meant that political options were relatively straightforward: one fought for the revolution or not at all. But in Brazil, under conditions of divisions within the opposition and ongoing strength of conservative forces, political choices were greater. Whether to support a party, and which party to support, were divisive issues.

Thus, the conservative character of the political system discouraged and made complex the passage from small groups to institutional politics. Religion is not a constraining force. Rather, the nature of the political system in which the CEBs operate limits linkages between grass-roots groups and broad political movements. As Susan Eckstein argues in her introduction to this volume, elite politics shapes popular protest—even though popular behavior is, of course, not infinitely malleable.

Azuleika Sampaio herself is well aware that the efforts of thousands of other grass-roots leaders have had limited impact on macropolitical structures in Brazil. In an interview in December 1985, she expressed profound disappointment with the nature of Brazil's new democracy and called attention to the state's capacity to coopt popular organizations. Nevertheless, as chapter 9 suggests, without popular mobilization, it is doubtful that Brazil would have returned to democratic government in 1985, and religion helped bring about popular mobilization. Moreover, the reworking of perceptions of authority, justice, politics, and legitimacy that has taken place in CEBs helped redefine the cultural underpinnings of Brazilian democratic politics in small, but potentially significant, ways.

SUCCESSFUL ECCLESIASTICAL CONTROL
OVER POPULAR GROUPS: COLOMBIA

The Colombian experience differs in almost every respect. As pointed out earlier, in Colombia Catholic elites are hostile to the theory and practice of autonomous popular groups. In this regard, they are like the nation's social and political elites generally, whose ideologies and key institutions (e.g., political parties) encourage dependent vertical ties and clientelistic relations. When autonomous groups do arise, they are rejected. More important, prevailing ideological and structural patterns in Colombia make the emergence of such alternatives unlikely in the first place. Whatever grass-roots groups do exist are carefully nurtured along lines that preclude or inhibit autonomy and any hint of spillover to social or political concerns and alliances. Further, unlike in Brazil, where a substantial minority in the ecclesiastical elite has supported progressive movements, the Colombian hierarchy has been very unified and has faced only scattered and sporadic challenges from popular groups or progressive clergy or other pastoral agents.

This unity in the Colombian church is built on a vigorous conservative project, stressing the centrality of hierarchy, authority, and unity around core church institutions (bishops, priests, parishes, etc.). Rejection of popular groups rests on fear of their double-edged political potential. The bishops dislike and fear the possible political consequences of grassroots activism. They fear even more the challenge such groups pose to established relations of power and authority within the church. These fears reinforce one another, and together have shaped recent Colombian experience. The end result is that any kind of organization the church has sponsored, from massive Catholic Action movements to student groups, unions, and now base communities, has been marked by concern for ideological and structural reliability. These are to be ensured by continued, subordinate links to hierarchical authority and thorough control over the training and orientation of intermediaries (priests, sisters, pastoral agents in general).

Just as the orientation of the church has remained constant, so too the social and political order has seen little dramatic change. Unlike in Brazil, there has been no drastic imposition of authoritarianism, no dramatic restoration of democracy, no open clash of church and state, and no sudden, sharp escalation of social and political conflict. The churches have neither initiated activism nor been forced to adopt it by social pressures. Instead, since 1958 a contained competitive electoral political system has been the rule, even when guerrilla groups and peasant movements have challenged the status quo in selective regions of the country (see chapters 3 and 4 above). Under the circumstances, the church in Colombia has pursued an aggressively conservative line, reaching out to capture new groups and contain their social and political activity within sharply circumscribed limits.

Consistency of political rule and social organization has thus been matched by continuity in religious ideologies and structural norms. This is not a matter of survival alone: the Colombian church does more than just survive. It is vigorously creative, asserting and promoting its lines of action with great energy. All this suggests that a close look at popular groups and base communities in Colombia is likely to show a pattern whereby daily practice is held within relatively narrow limits, and also where any popular action or expression gets under way and operates with tight links to higher authorities.

Vertical control operates in two ways. First, initiatives and projects are monitored by reliable intermediaries and worked out in close coordination with official church structures and agents. "Dangerous" or suspect alliances, coalitions, or extensions of religiously inspired activism into undesirable terrain are strongly discouraged. Control is further ensured by screening the possible religious character and legitimation of change from the start, and by organizing group life so that its normal practice reaffirms hierarchy and vertical links to established authority. Recall our earlier comment about the bureaucratic and ideological struggles that underlie grass-roots experience. In Colombia the battles to train and orient leaders, to legitimize pastoral agents, to produce texts and discussion material, record cassettes, visit and monitor groups, and the like have all been won by central church institutions. Unreliable leaders and programs have been marginalized and "dangerous" tendencies to autonomy nipped in the bud.

New leaders are sought out and trained with an eye to reliability and loyalty. The ideal group is always portrayed in tight connection to the church (parish, priests, sisters, etc.) and painted as a seedbed for future clergy and sisters. The ideal member appears as a potential priest or sister, or more likely a lay minister or deacon in training (mini-clergy, if you will). In all these ways, the whole project of base groups is molded to fit existing parameters of church structures and lines of authority. The theory and practice of democratization, so prominent in discussions of CEBs in many Latin American countries, are carefully kept out of the Colombian scene.

Colombian Catholic elites see many dangers in uncontrolled popular groups, but at the same time they recognize that popular groups are very much in fashion in Latin American Catholicism today. To adapt to current trends without relinquishing security and control, the bishops themselves have sponsored group formation, often simply renaming existing groups "base communities." Wherever possible, the formation of new CEBs has been managed through highly controlled, very conservative organizations. Thus, official documents claim that thousands of CEBs exist, but a closer look reveals that what pass for base communities in Colombia most often arise out of movements like the *cursillos de cristiandad*, widely known for their stress on personal spirituality and deference to authority (Levine 1981 : 233–37).

In the larger ideological arena, the bishops have tried to capture the high ground, redefining concepts like "base" and "popular" in ways that underscore their subordinate role within larger hierarchical structures. Official visions of "ecclesial base communities" (in pastoral letters, training manuals, and the like) thus give place of preference to the *ecclesial* dimension, stressing loyalty to the church. Notions of *community* run a close second, with the emphasis on the virtues of solidarity in small groups. *Base* appears mainly in terms of the lowest level of hierarchical structure (here the church). Definitions of base in social class terms are absent, and the notion of a "popular church" composed mainly of the poor and identified with them in struggles for justice and liberation is violently rejected.

Despite these constraints, change does get under way in Colombia, but not surprisingly, its effects remain mostly localized, concentrated above all in the growing personal horizons and sense of dignity and self-worth of individual members. To grasp the possibilities and limitations of the process, consider the life and times of one very poor, very devout peasant, Patricio Alvarez.[10]

Patricio Alvarez was born on 17 March 1930 in the hamlet of Agua Fría, where he has lived all his life. His parents and grandparents also came from Agua Fría, a small agricultural settlement in the diocese of Facatativá, not far west of the capital city of Bogotá. About three hundred people live in Agua Fría (in approximately seventy-five dwellings), and all of them make a living in some way from agriculture.[11] There is a small, irregularly staffed school, but otherwise no services—no light, no electric power at all, no piped water, and of course no sewage or locally available medical care. Public transport exists only in the shape of a twice-a-day bus, which, on its run between two larger towns, will pick up and drop off Agua Fría's people on the road. From the "bus stop," it is about a twenty-minute uphill walk to the settlement. Residents go to church in the nearby town of Quebradanegra; they sell their produce and buy goods and services in larger regional centers, above all Villeta.

Like many peasants in this region, Patricio Alvarez came to his deep religious involvement through a three-day *cursillo de cristiandad* orga-

10. This account is based on three interviews Levine conducted with Patricio Alvarez on 19 November 1982, 6 January 1983, and 15 January 1983. Information also comes from other interviews Levine conducted in Agua Fría, in the region around it, and throughout the diocese of Facatativá.

11. Most residents engage in small-scale, labor-intensive farming. Major products are coffee, sugar cane, and a locally processed crude brown sugar known as *panela*.

nized in 1972 by a Spanish priest, P. Román Cortés. This priest served the diocese of Facatativá as a roving missionary, holding *cursillos*, motivating individuals, and establishing small base communities in a number of rural parishes. We shall have more to say about Román Cortés below. Here, it suffices to note his key role, and the very intense character of the *cursillos* he organized. If one asks Patricio and others in the initial groups about the *cursillo*, a common response brings up themes like these: we were bad, we became good; once full of vices, now we lead a moral life; we moved from darkness to light; now we know what it really means to be a good Christian.

Like Azuleika Sampaio, Patricio Alvarez has experienced great change through his participation in church-sponsored grass-roots communities. Involvement in the CEB opened doors for Patricio to a new world of meaning and contacts far beyond the confines of Agua Fría. The changes have been many. For example, Patricio's limited knowledge of religion, mostly instilled by his mother, was greatly deepened and broadened. He remembers learning religion as a child by rote: "You had to record [lit. "tape"] questions and answers in your memory. But later I learned that Catholicism isn't learning prayers by rote, but rather that we have to incarnate prayers in ourselves, and live in them our actions." Patricio has had only five months of formal schooling in his entire life. Illiterate as an adult, he learned to read and write as a result of the *cursillo* in order to be able to know the Bible and participate in the life of the community. All his education has come through some church-sponsored programs: "All the courses I have done have been Christian ones. My formation for entering society is owed entirely to the meetings in our hamlet. . . . My spelling is still not well developed, but I love to read, and I love to write, especially to read. Reading is a great thing!"

Raised in the closed environment typical of rural Colombia, over the past fifteen years Patricio Alvarez has traveled extensively to local and regional meetings and even to national church-sponsored encounters of base community leaders. He remains poor, ultimately dependent on very small-scale, labor-intensive, unproductive farming. Don Patricio has worked hard all his life, and although his economic situation is little changed, he has become a recognized local and regional leader. He founded the CEB in Agua Fría and helped establish a cooperative store to get around the high prices charged by local middlemen. He is an articulate, even eloquent, man, respected by his neighbors, and able to take on great responsibilities. He is one of the very few peasants in the diocese to become a lay minister.

Patricio is very devout. He reads the Bible every day, "if only a little bit," and reads and discusses it with others in the weekly meeting of Agua Fría's CEB. He goes to mass every Sunday, prays regularly, and has made a number of pilgrimages, promises, and missions in the past fif-

teen years. Patricio's vision of his ministry is humble and rests on a hierarchical, trickle-down theory of religious life. He knows that lay ministries were part of early Christianity, but then disappeared. The priests
were careless, and let them slip into disuse.[12]

> Later, during the pontificate of John XXIII, he convoked the Second
> Vatican Council, and in this council they discovered that there had to be
> lay participation in the things of religion, that they [laity] could help in
> their own religious education, in so many aspects of the family, evangeliz-
> ing in their own family. This is what we are called to. Later these docu-
> ments began to come out, and the bishops distributed the documents to
> the parish priests, the priests started distributing them to us, we began in-
> terpreting them, and in this way I started to become aware and I com-
> mitted myself.

Being a lay minister is important to Patricio Alvarez. "To me, this is a
work of great responsibility. I have to be careful to call people. I try to
know what is happening to them. I suffer to draw out the truth with
them." Patricio weighs the value of group meetings and activities above
all in terms of moral regeneration and self-help. In his eyes, Agua Fría
appears much improved morally, moving away from vices like alco-
holism to a sense of serious and sober community concerns. His personal
goals are focused above all on the church's specifically religious work:

> The apostolate, concretely this year. To make myself useful to the
> church, to be able to leave this hamlet for others and promote the Chris-
> tian movement. Thanks to this the church noticed me and gave me the
> ministry. And for the future?
> To prepare myself better for the apostolate. I want nothing else. I don't
> care about things connected with the cooperatives, communal action, or
> any of that. It isn't important. I am going to dedicate myself entirely to the
> apostolate.

Group activities are rooted in Bible study. Each meeting begins with a
Bible reading and discussion; then members move on to share experiences and to consider common problems and possible solutions. At first
it was difficult: people were accustomed to acting and working individually, or at best within a limited family circle. They could not get used to
the idea of acting as a group without outside help. Returning to Agua
Fría after the first *cursillo* with Román Cortés, they wondered: "How can

12. Patricio's account is reminiscent of Alberto Gruson's (1980:233) characterization of
conservative pastoral strategies: "There is a kind of catechism whose goal seems to be to
convince the student that he knows nothing, that the catechist knows more (but not much),
that in turn who really knows is the sister, who knows more than the sister is the priest; he
in turn is subject to the superior knowledge of the theologian controlled by the bishops;
and episcopal declarations frequently cite the pope. [There is] a practically static stratification, like a caste system, based on learning more in its transmission than in its elaboration."
On this point, see also Segundo 1978 and L. Boff 1986.

we get started? Who will move us for these meetings? Who will read, and what? We also faced the problem that those who had not gone to the *cursillo* were jealous and suspicious. They even thought we were not Catholics anymore, but had joined some [Protestant] sect."

As the group developed over time, the normal round of participation and discussion uncovered shared problems. This led to initiatives of mutual aid and self-help. There is a regular system of rotating voluntary labor, whereby members help one another (and especially poor residents of the area) in specific tasks like house building, harvest, provision for emergency medical bills, and the like. The agenda of group concerns arises in part from shared needs and experiences, and also from themes and programs circulated by the diocese. The diocese of Facatativá has an elaborate structure for reaching and monitoring the groups. There are regular visits, training sessions, and monthly meetings of group leaders in a regional center staffed by two sisters. The sisters play a critical mediating role. They interpret diocesan plans to the communities, facilitate contacts with higher levels, run the monthly meetings, and also visit the hamlets regularly to encourage leaders, and provide concrete advice on a wide range of topics. They are trusted completely by the communities. The sisters themselves see their work as all of a piece. In their view, any community action rests on prior spiritual regeneration and enhancement of the value of the family. According to Patricio, ties to the church are "through the priest and concretely with Sister Sara. The diocese's plans often don't arrive, and if they are very difficult, then Sister Sara is in charge of telling us how to carry them out."

In social terms, the group's main achievements to date have come by pooling labor to put up a small school and lay out playing fields, and through cooperative action to establish a community store. The need for a store became apparent through discussion in group meetings: "At first, we only got together to read the Bible. Later, we started talking about our own family problems. We began to see that one of the problems everyone in our hamlet had was buying things in the markets, which every day is harder and more costly. Finally, we got the idea of creating the cooperative." The cooperative began on a very small scale in 1975, with pooled resources to buy and sell at better prices in regional markets. Later the store was built, shelving put up, and a stock of merchandise laid in. Patricio and others from Agua Fría have also joined an existing cooperative in the local town of Quebradanegra and use their position to press for better prices and conditions.

If we ask about general social and political projections, and in particular about linkages to institutional politics, it is important to begin by noting the suspicion common throughout rural Colombia of "politics" and of explicitly political organization. This is partly a heritage of the well-known party-inspired violence that claimed hundreds of thousands of lives after 1948.[13] It also arises from active distrust of the motives of politicians and "big shots" generally. With rare exceptions, rural Colombia has little experience of political organization other than the traditional elite-led parties. Almost no one in Agua Fría has ever had contact with trade unions or with secondary associations of any kind apart from those sponsored by the church.

Patricio's vision of politics is complex. He knows about national and international events, and mentions them regularly in conversation. Indeed, he draws much of his model of a good society and of the possibilities of self-moved change from Israel, whose experience of self-improvement and cooperatives fills him with admiration. Patricio has little faith in politicians and their promises, but no aspiration to other kinds of collective action or to alternative links to power that might change the political landscape in some basic way. He knows that many in Colombia view elections as irrelevant; that there is great abstention. But he votes in good faith: "When there are elections, I always vote for the one I like the best, the one I prefer, who seems most committed, in spite of the fact that they have fooled us so often, that we have always been victims of trickery." In Patricio's eyes, people should struggle against exploitation and learn to help one another, but violence of any sort is ruled out.

> For ten or eleven years now, I have dedicated myself to studying the situation. This has led me to rebellion, but to a Christian rebellion, a peaceful rebellion, not rebellion like those groups who say: "No, I will not go along with the government any more. I will not go along with this group or with the other. I'll get a rifle or a revolver or even just a machete and go out to kill." No, no, this is not what we are called to do.

Patricio's goals are simple and local: to live a moral life, to serve the church and spread the Gospel, and to help his community where possible. He is aware of his poverty and lack of formal schooling, but no longer feels ashamed or ill at ease dealing with wealthy and powerful people. He has a strong sense of self-worth and dignity. Witness his account of the problems of sharing experiences with people from the larger towns. It is hard,

> because in Villeta they are businessmen, people with money. It is very difficult to share with a group from Quebradanegra, because we are peasants, with no more than a few months of primary school, and over there are very well prepared people, university graduates, doctors and all that. But no matter, this year we had a one-day get together with them, and they

13. On the violence, see Levine and Wilde 1977. For a detailed account of the precipitating incident, see the oral histories collected in Alape 1983. A useful account of the violence in towns and provinces is Sánchez 1983.

had to hang their heads before us. We bested them, we surpassed their level, and they were convinced. Economic resources don't matter at all. They have no effect on anything. Money is money, morals are morals.

There is little sign here of the traditional combination of personal passivity and public submission. Patricio has no awe of the wealthy and powerful; but he also has little drive to change the pattern of social relations. His energies go to moral regeneration and very small-scale collective enterprises. Despite great poverty (exacerbated lately by illness, especially arthritis), he has little sense of material deprivation. Patricio feels fulfilled. His world has changed, and he has a clear sense of himself as a person of dignity and realized potential. He wants above all to do his duty, to serve God, the church, his family, and his community.

How can we summarize the experience of Patricio Alvarez in ways that make sense for the issues being considered here? First, it is clear that his initial stimulus for change came from religion, specifically from the intense conversion experience of the *cursillo*. Second, the critical changes have been at the personal and small-group level, and are found above all in a growing sense of self-worth, dignity, and capacity for action. Third, any kind of collective action is undertaken in close connection with the institutional church (diocese, parish, and especially the sisters). Fourth, both "protest" and "politics" in any conventional sense are absent, or at best notably muted here. They are excluded from the initial structuring of experience, not represented in the discourse of the people, and not represented in their texts, discussion materials, and conversations. Moreover, any horizontal contact with possible allies in social or political groups is simply not there.

The sorts of change exemplified by Patricio Alvarez make sense in the context of broader institutional patterns in Colombia as a whole, and more specifically in the region where Patricio lives and works. We have already commented in general terms on the nature of prevailing ideological and structural patterns in Colombia. Consider now the impact of the diocese of Facatativá.

On the Colombian church scene, Facatativá is generally viewed as "progressive." The diocese is new (founded only in 1962), and its leaders have always stressed grass-roots organization. Religious innovation (seeking to teach and spread the Gospel in new ways, encouraging lay participation) has been joined from the outset to encouragement of social and economic reform, especially through self-help programs. The diocese has put great resources into grass-roots promotion.

In the early 1970s, along with two other dioceses, Facatativá was designated as a pilot experience in base community formation. Concretely this meant that local resources were channeled in this direction, in close coordination with the national programs and staff of the bishops' conference. Religious personnel (especially sisters) were concentrated in pilot parishes and communities, and charged with stimulating and encouraging groups there. Moreover, with financial help from U.S. Catholic Relief Services and from various European sources, the diocese has underwritten a team of specialists (educator, catechist, cooperative expert, agronomist, teachers) who encourage and evaluate requests for help, get projects under way, and ultimately help direct and coordinate small-scale self-help programs much like Agua Fría's community store.

All these efforts have been undergirded and knit together by a general stress on the formation of *communities*. Even before the general notion of CEBs was widely diffused, energies and resources in Facatativá were devoted to the formation of small groups of this kind throughout the peasant hamlets of the diocese. This is where the efforts of P. Román Cortés come in and help make sense of the whole. Let us consider his work in closer detail for a moment.

P. Román Cortés came to Facatativá from Spain in 1970 with the specific mission of stimulating base communities, and through them, spurring a general process of religious renovation and social change. He died of cancer in early 1982. In his memory, the diocese issued a book with his deathbed "messages" to clergy, pastoral agents, laity, and the like, and also with remembrances of him and his work by friends and collaborators (Cortés Tossal 1982). These documents give extraordinary insight into the kinds of base communities in Facatativá, and help us understand how the experiences of someone like Patricio Alvarez took on a recognizably and distinctively Colombian form even within the relatively "progressive" diocese of Facatativá.

Cortés's vision of base communities was firmly grounded in religious fundamentals. All communities were to begin through very intense religious renovation (hence, the *cursillos*) and operate subsequently in a way that made the sacraments, love of the church, and attention to family and community (in that order) central. The normal progression he foresaw thus took off from religious renovation, moved through a reorganization of family life and reinforcement of mutual support, and then evolved through concerns about ecology and community, ending with cooperatives and self-help projects. He stresses constantly that *cursillos* are only a means: "We do *cursillos* so that people will form groups and communities; we don't create communities so that people will go to *cursillos*. The community is the splendor of the garden whose gateway is the *cursillo*." (Cortés Tossal 1982:26–27)

Exactly what sort of community is stressed here? What does it mean to form a community, to live in a community? Cortés stressed commitment to Christ and to the community. He acknowledges how hard this can be; and he urges CEBs to seek help and guidance from the church. The

whole apparatus of personnel and structures carefully created in Facatativá is there precisely to ensure a successful and harmonious convergence of religious and social renovation in the towns and villages of
the diocese.

> Learning to live in a communitarian way in such an individualistic
> world is not a matter of a moment. Do not despair! Try and try again. Seek
> the help of the Diocese. Seek the help of your parish priests to live in com-
> munity. Try communitarian living. Learn to pray together, to love to-
> gether, to share together the Word, the Mass, food, money, life, every-
> thing. Share everything personal, everything we know is part of being a
> person. Learn to share as brothers and sisters, and to form yourselves and
> help yourselves and commit yourselves together. Those who are already
> living a communitarian life will give you the message: commitment, com-
> mitment, commitment. No one can be a good *cursillista* who is not living in
> community, no one is truly living in community without commitment.
> (Cortés Tossal 1982 : 27)

While the program of base communities covers much of the diocese,
the scale and scope of any particular program is limited. The typical
group agenda has clear boundaries. Once outside the immediate group
of friends and neighbors, all ties are vertical, managed through sisters
and clergy and reinforced by regular visits, training sessions, and the
promotion of lay ministries as the ideal outcome. In Colombia, then,
most religiously inspired grass-roots activity remains deliberately bound
to church structures and programs in a way that reinforces a hierarchical
vision of the world, in the process setting clear limits to the potential political impact of CEBs.

We do not mean to suggest that there is some normal progression
from the religious to the explicitly political that is thwarted in Colombia.
No sequence of any kind is inevitable, and none can be taken as "normal" by definition. Rather, our argument is that in Colombia (in contrast
to much recent Brazilian experience), the particular legitimation and
structuring of group activities makes such a progression unlikely. It does
so above all by maintaining and reinforcing the hierarchical expectations
so prominent elsewhere in the society. The church in Colombia will not
provide a source of new cultural orientations to authority. No matter
how critical its stance on a given issue may be, no matter how strongly
much injustice or inequality may be condemned, the process will always
be one in which messages, orientations, and legitimations flow from the
top down. This clearly fits the overall institutional and ideological pattern prevalent in Colombia and makes it hard for any effective alliances
or coalitions to form at the local level through which grass-roots religious
groups could join forces and ideas with others.

This does not mean that the groups have no importance. But it does suggest that their significance is to be found mostly at the level of personal growth and somewhat in the informal politics of group relations. Left to their own devices, members do talk, share experiences, and come up with solutions. But the point is that they are hardly ever left to their own devices for long. At a minimum, the groups provide some space and a sense of legitimacy in a hostile or indifferent environment. They also help overcome the distrust and mutual suspicion endemic in rural Colombia. When Román Cortés first came to many towns and hamlets, people hid. The *cursillos* he started opened the communities and their inhabitants to new horizons. One woman in a parish near Patricio's put it this way:

> People here lived in fear. Fear of the army, of the guerrillas. This hasn't gone away, but it is better now. Now people talk among themselves with more confidence.
> Why?
> It must be the meetings. Because as for the rest, what is there, what is there? We don't even have a schoolteacher. The only thing that functions is this. This is the only way people can meet others apart from those in their hamlet.

To this woman, the church is practically the only institution available, and certainly the only one worthy of trust. No other can be relied on for probity, moral rectitude, and caring about the interest of the people. This positive image rests in part on the diocese's active and innovative programs and on the lasting influence of P. Román Cortés. It also reflects the basic legitimacy religion gives to any undertaking in this milieu. But without denigrating the worth of these achievements, we can still note that links to institutional politics, to the possibility of enduring collective organization, and hence to power are at best a weak reed here, as among grass-roots groups generally in Colombia.

CONCLUSIONS

The lives of Azuleika Sampaio and Patricio Alvarez have much to say about the churches, polities, and societies they live in. Although these two lives differ in many ways, consider a few of the more noteworthy similarities. Both are poor and started life with few advantages and many problems. Both have become leaders in their communities. Religion is central to the daily experience of both, and it was in part through the church that both came to occupy their positions of leadership.

As noted earlier, progressives and conservatives both often question the authenticity of one another's religious motives. But the tremendous power of religion in the lives of Azuleika and Patricio suggests how shallow such arguments are. Different kinds of religious experience, with different political implications, not only *remain* central in the lives of hundreds of millions of Latin Americans; if anything, the vitality of religion is greater today than it was three decades ago. Religious institutions, and in particular the Catholic church, have clearly changed to meet the challenges of the time. Looking at Azuleika and Patricio together points up the great vitality of the Catholic church in many Latin American countries. This vitality is by no means uniform: the energies go in different directions. Thus, the churches in Brazil and Colombia are both exemplars of religiously based dynamism, but they are working with remarkably different models of the church. At the same time, each church does reach out in new ways to the poor, with kinds of grass-roots initiatives that have few precedents in the past. The result, particularly in these two countries, is an institution that has become more dynamic than it was during most of its past history.

Religion was the common source for change in the lives of Azuleika Sampaio and Patricio Alvarez. But the content of their religious experience differs sharply, as does the nature of the religious institutions that sponsored the grass-roots changes. Both individuals stress commitment to the local community, but the nature of this commitment and the conception of faith that underlies it are much at variance. Azuleika's faith demands an effort to fight for social justice. In the repressive context of the military regime of the 1970s, this effort required considerable courage. For Patricio, faith involves above all the search to better oneself and others in spiritual terms, and to help the local community. Azuleika's commitment to her community was expressed in her involvement in religious matters, but also through her leadership in popular movements. She perceives her political involvement as an expression of her faith; the neat analytical distinction between religion and politics thus dissolves somewhat in the unity of her thought and practice. Patricio, in contrast, finds his commitment to the community above all through his lay ministry.

These contrasting visions of faith have led to very different levels and directions of political activity. Azuleika has become one of the outstanding popular leaders in the seventh biggest Brazilian city; Patricio is not especially interested in politics. Azuleika's political life has involved her in a world of complex and sophisticated political debates, a world where the left holds considerable sway; Patricio's political references are more traditional, and in any case far less central to his life. These differences are not simply idiosyncratic details in the lives of two people, but rather reflect and illuminate broader patterns in the churches and societies. In the dozens of dioceses in Brazil where bishops have encouraged base communities, one encounters individuals like Azuleika. For the progressive clergy who have really let go of traditional clerical authority, she is something of a model lay leader. Patricio is also something of a model lay leader in Colombia, where traditional authority lines remain unchallenged even as the church has successfully incorporated greater mass involvement. Don Patricio represents what much of Colombia's hierarchy and clergy have sought: a stronger understanding of Catholic faith and a deeper commitment to the church than were common in the past, coupled with an unswerving loyalty to church leaders.

Each of these churches has shown great vitality in the past fifteen years, but for quite different reasons. Since the early 1970s, Brazil has had the most visible, intellectually forceful, and progressive Catholic church in the world. It stood out for its defense of human rights, its trenchant criticisms of the military regime, and its panoply of grass-roots innovations, most notably the CEBs. This was a traditionally weak church along many parameters: number of priests, influence among vast sectors of the population, institutional development. The church often was an object of state attempts to win support and legitimacy, but its pastoral work with the popular classes was particularly lacking. Through the CEBs, the Brazilian church changed this, acquiring not only a greater influence among the popular classes, but also international attention for its innovations.

The Colombian church was traditionally much stronger in its own society, but here the hierarchy has enhanced its own institutional strength in the years since the second Vatican Council, especially the late 1960s (Levine 1985b). The conservative nature of the predominant theology in the Colombian church can easily obscure the important changes that have been put into effect at the grass roots. While it is true that the church remains conservative, its conservatism is more assertive, and its institutions more dynamic, than in the past. It is precisely this combination of conservatism and dynamism that has made the Colombian church what one might term the "leading edge of the old wave." The political consequences of these changes are markedly more conservative and less salient in terms of popular mobilization, but the ecclesiastical and social implications of the new grass-roots groups are not less important for that reason.

The vitality of the Colombian church suggests a point generally overlooked by proponents of the popular church: conservatives can have popular appeal. In the past, conservative pastoral positions were associated with elitist stances that disdained the popular classes. But today there are many priests like Román Cortés in Latin America. These men are not political radicals, but they sympathize deeply with the poor and find great receptivity among them. Conservative ecclesiastical sectors clearly reject the politics and theology of radical Catholics, but have learned much from them about how to work with the poor. The result in many countries is escalating competition to control popular religious organizations.

In the late 1960s, the conservatives were ill prepared to compete in this terrain, but in current battles to win popular sympathies and control the church, conservatives and moderates have clearly gained the upper hand. As a result, throughout Latin America, progressive grass-roots innovations are under attack. Conservative bureaucracies in CELAM (the Latin American Conference of Bishops) and in the Vatican see the left as undermining lines of authority in the church and, furthermore, as interfering in politics in improper ways. These concerns are most visible in the Central American crisis, especially in Nicaragua, where conflict is very sharp (Dodson 1986; Crahan forthcoming). But the Brazilian CEBs are also objects of considerable suspicion. This has been clear in many Vatican edicts, including the veto of two masses proposed for use with popular groups; punishments of brothers Leonardo and Clodovis Boff, renowned liberation theologians who have worked extensively with CEBs; and consistent support for bishops who oppose the more autonomous and progressive CEBs.

We have shown that the way CEBs evolve depends in great part upon the pastoral agents who work directly with them and upon the bishops. These developments are also conditioned by the broader political context; here, too, we find differences between Brazil and Colombia. In both countries, popular organizations are peripheral to the main currents in political life. But in the late 1970s new challenges to the traditional elitist pattern of popular exclusion emerged in Brazil. A more dynamic and autonomous labor movement emerged; peasant unions were formed and grew rapidly all over the country; and neighborhood associations also sprang up in great numbers. In terms of partisan politics, the Workers' Party has captured the imagination of many grass-roots activists. Although it remains a small party, its presence represented a political alternative unknown in Colombia (Keck 1986). In the midst of many signs that the new democracy will be quite elitist (Mainwaring 1986a; Alves, this volume), this strengthening of popular initiatives is somewhat limited. But the point remains that in tandem with other grass-roots groups, CEBs became a prominent part of the political scene (Ireland 1983).

All this is hard to imagine in Colombia. Popular organizations there have shown less capacity to influence national politics, or even to forge enduring links to them. Moreover, there has been no shift in the pattern of political rule; no consistent transformation of religious ideologies or structures. Instead, older patterns are vigorously reinforced in all areas: traditional civilian leadership persists, as does a pervasive stress on hierarchically dominated, paternalistic organizations in politics, social life, and in the churches. Sporadic challenges erupt, but in recent decades they typically have been contained.[14] Like popular groups generally, CEBs sputter in Colombia. They have few consistent sponsors and no reliable or enduring allies, and they face more or less continuous harassment. At the same time, the extreme vertical structuring of Colombian programs effectively precludes much spillover to social or political arenas. Coalitions with other groups are restricted, all significant action is cleared with the parish, and independent initiatives of any kind are actively discouraged. It is not always possible to control all groups, but the effort is strong and consistent and fits well with the restrained and constraining ideological leadership the church provides on national and regional levels.

In contrast to Brazil, popular initiatives and protest with religious roots in Colombia faced steady opposition from church and political elites alike throughout the period. Most energies in this process went to promote control, not activism. For these reasons, as we have seen, popular groups in Colombia have rarely been able to accumulate a critical mass of moral and religious legitimacy for social action, not to mention practical experience, which together make for impact beyond the confines of the group itself.

Looking at Brazil and Colombia together highlights the central role institutional churches can play in stimulating, shaping, focusing, and often constraining popular initiatives. Bishops, priests, sisters, and pastoral agents of all kinds enjoy considerable prestige and legitimacy among popular groups. This popular acceptance gives them an edge in setting the agenda of such groups, and thereby giving a particular tone to the informal and implicit politics of popular practice. Moreover, even though progressive bishops are not always directly responsible for initiating grass-roots pastoral groups, their support for—or at least toleration of—these groups has been indispensable. Whether the bishop supports pastoral agents in creating and working with base communities and what kinds of resources and attention are allocated to the CEBs are critical issues in determining the role of grass-roots groups in the church and society.

---

14. Indeed, challenges may be more extreme in Colombia, given the tremendous weight of conservative domination. The well-known short and sad career of Camilo Torres is a case in point. While Torres remains a powerful symbol for radical political Catholicism in Latin America, it is important to recall that the politics he promoted had little in common with the grass-roots movements discussed here. Torres tried to fashion a broad political movement, using his image as a priest as a magnet for popular support. He attracted little effective support, and left no enduring legacy of organization after he left the priesthood, joined a guerrilla group, and was killed by the military. See Levine 1981: 41–44, and the sources cited there. See also Levine 1988.

REFERENCES

Alape, A.
1983   *El Bogotazo: Memorias del olvido.* Bogotá: Fundación Universidad Central.
Azevedo, M.
1987   *Basic Ecclesial Communities in Brazil.* Washington, D.C.: Georgetown University Press.
Berryman, P.
1984   *Religious Roots of Rebellion: Christians in the Central American Revolutions.* Maryknoll, N.Y.: Orbis Books.
1986   "El Salvador: From Evangelization to Insurrection." In *Religion and Political Conflict in Latin America,* edited by D. Levine, pp. 58–78. Chapel Hill: University of North Carolina Press.
Betto, F.
1981   *O que é comunidade eclesial de base.* São Paulo: Brasilense.
Boff, C.
1979   "A influência política das CEBs." *Religião e Sociedade* 4 (January–February):95–119.
Boff, L.
1977   *Eclesiogênese: As comunidades eclesiais de base reinventam a Igreja.* Petrópolis: Vozes.
1986   *Church, Charism, and Power: Liberation Theology and the Institutional Church.* Minneapolis: Winston Press.
Bruneau, T.
1974   *The Political Transformation of the Brazilian Catholic Church.* Cambridge: Cambridge University Press.
1980   "Basic Christian Communities in Latin America: Their Nature and Significance (Especially in Brazil)." In *Churches and Politics in Latin America,* edited by D. Levine, pp. 111–34. Beverly Hills, Calif.: SAGE.
1982   *The Church in Brazil: The Politics of Religion.* Austin: University of Texas Press.
1986   "Brazil: The Catholic Church and Basic Christian Communities." In *Religion and Political Conflict in Latin America,* edited by D. Levine, pp. 106–23. Chapel Hill: University of North Carolina Press.
Cáceres, J.
1982   "Radicalización política y pastoral popular en El Salvador, 1969–1979." *Estudios Sociales Centroamericanos* 33 (September–December):93–153.
Cardoso, R.
1983   "Movimentos sociais urbanos: Balanco crítico." In *Sociedade e Política no Brasil pós-64,* edited by B. Sorj and M. H. Tavares de Almeida, pp. 215–39. São Paulo: Brasiliense.
CNBB [National Council of Brazilian Bishops]
1975   "Diretrizes gerais da ação pastoral da Igreja no Brasil." Documentos da CNBB, 4.
1977   *Comunidades: Igreja na base.* São Paulo: Paulinas.

1979   *Comunidades: Igreja na base.* São Paulo: Paulinas.
1982   "As comunidades eclesiais de base na Igreja do Brasil." Documentos da CNBB, 25. São Paulo: Paulinas.
Comissão Pastoral dos Direitos Humanos e Marginalizados de São Paulo
1981   *Fé e política.* Petrópolis: Vozes.
Cortés Tossal, R.
1982   "Testimonio y mensajes del Padre Román Cortés Tossal." *Comunidad Diocesana* (Diocesis de Facatativã) 14, no. 115.
Crahan, M.
Forthcoming   "Religion and Politics in Revolutionary Nicaragua." In *Voice of the Voiceless: The Progressive Church in Latin America,* edited by A. Wilde and S. Mainwaring. Notre Dame, Ind.: University of Notre Dame Press.
Davis, N. Z.
1974   "Some Tasks and Some Themes in the Study of Popular Religion." In *The Pursuit of Holiness in Late Medieval and Early Renaissance Religion,* edited by Charles Trinkaus and Heíko Obermann, pp. 307–36. Leiden: E. J. Brill.
1975   *Society and Culture in Early Modern France.* Stanford, Calif.: Stanford University Press.
De Kadt, E.
1970   *Catholic Radicals in Brazil.* London: Oxford University Press.
Della Cava, R.
1976   "Catholicism and Society in Twentieth Century Brazil." *Latin American Research Review* 11 (Summer): 7–50.
Forthcoming   "The Church and The 'Abertura,' 1974–1985." In *Democratizing Brazil,* edited by A. Stepan. New York: Oxford University Press.
Diocese de Nova Iguaçu
1983   *O povo de Deus assume a caminhada.* Petrópolis: Vozes/IDAC.
Dodson, M.
1986   "Nicaragua: The Struggle for the Church." In *Religion and Political Conflict in Latin America,* edited by D. Levine, pp. 79–105. Chapel Hill: University of North Carolina Press.
Ferreira de Camargo, C. P.
1980   "Comunidades eclesiais de base." In *São Paulo: O povo em movimento,* edited by P. Singer and V. Caldeira Brant, pp. 59–81. Petrópolis: Vozes/CEBRAP.
Foucault, M.
1980   *Power/Knowledge.* New York: Pantheon.
Gruson, A.
1980   "Religiosidad y Pastoral." *Nuevo Mundo* [Caracas], May–June.
Hoornaert, E.
1978   "Comunidades de base: Dez anos de experiência." *Revista Eclesiástica Brasileira* 38: 474–502.
Ileto, R. C.
1979   *Pasyon and Revolution: Popular Movements in the Philippines, 1840–1910.* Quezon City: Ateneo de Manila University Press.

Ireland, R.
1983   *Catholic Base Communities, Spiritist Groups, and the Deepening of Democracy in Brazil.* Latin American Program, Woodrow Wilson Center, Working Paper no. 131. Washington, D.C.: Smithsonian Institution.
Keck, M.
1986   "From Movement to Politics: The Formation of the Workers' Party in Brazil." Ph.D. diss., Columbia University.
Kselman, T.
1986   "Ambivalence and Assumption in the Concept of Popular Religion." In *Religion and Political Conflict in Latin America,* edited by D. Levine, pp. 24–41. Chapel Hill: University of North Carolina Press.
Levine, Daniel H.
1980   *Churches and Politics in Latin America.* Beverly Hills, Calif.: SAGE.
1981   *Religion and Politics in Latin America: The Catholic Church in Venezuela and Colombia.* Princeton, N.J.: Princeton University Press.
1984a   "Popular Organizations and the Church: Thoughts from Colombia." *Journal of Inter-American Studies and World Affairs* 26, no. 1 : 137–42.
1984b   "Religion and Politics: Dimensions of Renewal." *Thought* 59, no. 233 : 117–42.
1985a   "Religion and Politics: Drawing Lines, Understanding Change." *Latin American Research Review* 20, no. 1 : 185–201.
1985b   "Continuities in Colombia." *Journal of Latin American Studies* 17, no. 2 : 295–317.
1986a   "Colombia: The Institutional Church and the Popular." In *Religion and Political Conflict in Latin America,* edited by D. H. Levine, pp. 187–217. Chapel Hill: University of North Carolina Press.
1986b   *Religion and Political Conflict in Latin America.* Chapel Hill: University of North Carolina Press.
1986c   "Religion and Politics in Comparative and Historical Perspective." *Comparative Politics* 19, no. 1 : 95–122.
1986d   "Religion, Politics, and the Poor in Latin America Today." In *Religion and Political Conflict in Latin America,* edited by D. H. Levine. Chapel Hill: University of North Carolina Press.
1988   "From Church and State to Religion and Politics and Back Again." *World Affairs.* Forthcoming.
Levine, Daniel, and A. Wilde
1977   "The Catholic Church, 'Politics,' and Violence: The Colombian Case." *Review of Politics* 39, no. 2 : 220–49.
Mainwaring, Scott
1986a   *The Catholic Church and Politics in Brazil, 1916–1985.* Stanford, Calif.: Stanford University Press.
1986b   "The Transition to Democracy in Brazil." *Journal of Inter-American Studies and World Affairs* 28, no. 1 : 149–79.
1987a   *Grass Roots Catholic Groups and Politics in Brazil, 1964–1985.* Notre Dame, Ind.: University of Notre Dame, Kellogg Institute Working Paper no. 98.
1987b   "Grass Roots Popular Movements and the Struggle for Democracy:

Nova Iguaçu." In *Democratizing Brazil,* edited by A. Stepan. New York: Oxford University Press, forthcoming.

Opazo, A., and Cáceres J.
1987   "La iglesia centroamericana: Aportes y limitaciones en la construcción de un sujeto político popular." Paper presented at Institute of the Americas conference, Church and Change, La Jolla, Calif.

Paiva, V.
1984   "Anotações para um estudo sobre o Catolicismo popular." In *Perspectivas e dilemas da eduacação popular,* edited by V. Paiva, pp. 227–65. Rio de Janeiro: Graal.

Sánchez, G.
1983   *Los días de la revolución: Gaitanismo y 9 de Abril en provincia.* Bogotá: Centro Cultural Jorge Eliécer Gaitán.

Scott, J.
1986   *Weapons of the Weak: Everyday Forms of Peasant Resistance.* New Haven, Conn.: Yale University Press.

Segundo, J. L.
1978   *The Hidden Motives of Pastoral Action: Latin American Reflections.* Maryknoll, N.Y.: Orbis Books.

Souza Lima, L. G. de
1979   *Evolucão política dos Católicos e da igreja no Brasil.* Petrópolis: Vozes.
1982   "Notas sobre as comunidades eclesiais de base e a organização política." In *Alternativas populares da democracia,* edited by J. A. Moíses, pp. 41–72. Petrópolis: Vozes/CEDEC.

Thompson, E. P.
1964   *The Making of the English Working Class.* New York: Pantheon.

Wilde, A.
1986   "Redemocratization, the Church, and Democracy in Colombia." In *Colombia beyond the National Front,* edited by Bruce Bagley. Boulder, Colo.: Westview Press.

Williams, P.
Forthcoming   "The Catholic Church in the Nicaraguan Revolution: Differing Responses and New Challenges." In *Voice of the Voiceless: The Progressive Church in Latin America,* edited by A. Wilde and S. Mainwaring. Notre Dame, Ind.: University of Notre Dame Press.

CHAPTER SEVEN

The Personal Is Political: Las Madres de Plaza de Mayo

Marysa Navarro

Las Madres de Plaza de Mayo, the Mothers of the Plaza de Mayo, is perhaps the most famous of all the mothers' organizations that have emerged in Latin America since the mid seventies. Las Madres first appeared as a distinct group on 30 April 1977, during the Proceso (Process), as Argentines call the repressive military regime that ruled their country from 1976 to 1983. In a society cowed into silence and where all the traditional means of public expression, dissent, or protest were closed or forbidden, fourteen women decided to stand near the pyramid of the Plaza de Mayo in downtown Buenos Aires to demand an answer to the question, "Where are our children?" Initially dismissed, then ridiculed, and later on brutally persecuted, they did not give up, stubbornly refusing to be silenced or to accept official explanations.

What transformed a group of mothers, most of them housewives without previous political experience, into political subjects and, ultimately, into the symbol of resistance to military dictatorship? The answer to this question lies on the one hand in the nature of the military regime created by the armed forces when they seized power on 24 March 1976 and on the other in the effect some of their policies had on women.

The March 1976 military coup deposed President María Estela Martínez de Perón (Isabel) who had succeeded her husband General Juan Domingo Perón after he died in office. It put an end to a period marked by economic and political chaos, with inflation rocketing to 335 percent

Research for this chapter was made possible by the Dartmouth College Faculty Research Program. A preliminary version was presented at the Latin American Studies Association's Thirteenth International Congress, Boston, October 1986, and at the Seventh Berkshire Conference on the History of Women, Wellesley, June 1987. I would like to thank the members of the Barnard Motherist Seminar for their support. This chapter is dedicated to Eunice Paiva.

in 1975, government inefficiency and corruption, bitter squabbling between the president and her own deeply divided Peronist supporters, and growing violence spurred by audacious guerrilla operations and her policies to counteract them.

To combat the guerrilla groups, the Montoneros and the People's Revolutionary Army (ERP), or "eradicate subversion," to use the official rhetoric, after she declared the state of siege in November 1974, Isabel Peron relied, not only on the police and the armed forces, but also on parapolice organizations, or so-called right-wing squads. The most active was the Argentine Anticommunist Alliance (AAA), which had connections with her own Social Welfare Ministry. It began to operate in December 1973 with an attempt on the life of Radical senator Hipólito Solari Yrigoyen, a well-known civil rights activist. This attack was followed by one on a priest, Carlos Mugica, who was shot on 12 May 1974. Prominent lawyers, rank-and-file trade unionists, politicians, labor leaders, intellectuals, journalists, students, and teachers were also targeted. Despite repeated denunciations and requests for investigations, no death squad member was arrested or brought to trial. Between July 1974 and June 1975, the number of victims attributed to the "Triple A" alone rose to 285 according to press accounts, although the real figure was probably higher. Some were known to have been killed, but others simply disappeared, establishing a pattern that would become prevalent during the Proceso.

The armed forces deposed Isabel and replaced her with a junta composed of the commanders in chief of the army, navy, and air force: General Jorge Rafael Videla, Admiral Emilio Massera, and Brigadier Orlando Agosti. The junta maintained the state of siege, banned all political activity, dismissed elected officials, closed down Congress, provincial legislatures, and municipal councils, relieved all Supreme Court judges and suspended the terms of all other judges, intervened in labor unions, the universities, and other public institutions, and established a rigid censorship of all media. It also outlawed five political parties, imprisoned leading Peronist politicians and trade unionists, enacted draconian repressive legislation, and replaced Congress with a Legislative Advisory Committee composed of nine military officers.

The junta headed by General Videla remained in power until March 1981, when it was succeeded by a second junta, composed of General Roberto Viola, Admiral Armando Lambruschini, and Brigadier Omar Graffigna, commanders in chief of the army, navy, and air force respectively. In 1982 they were replaced by three new commanders in chief of the armed forces, General Leopoldo F. Galtieri, Admiral Jorge Anaya, and Brigadier Basilio Lami Dozo, who presided over the Falklands/ Malvinas debacle. On 2 April 1982 the third junta sent an expeditionary force to occupy the Falklands/Malvinas, a group of windswept islands off the shore of southern Argentina. Ruled by Great Britain, they had long been claimed by Argentina. England responded to the attack by sending a major navy task force and promptly recapturing the islands. Argentina's defeat forced Galtieri's resignation and led to the withdrawal of the navy and the air force from the junta. On 2 July 1982 General Reynaldo Bignone became president and began to actively prepare the return to civilian rule. On 30 October 1983, after nearly eight years of military rule, Argentines went to the polls and elected Raúl Ricardo Alfonsín, the Unión Cívica Radical candidate.

From their first pronouncement, the armed forces made clear that they had not left their barracks once again merely to put an abrupt end to Isabel Peron's disastrous term in office. On 26 March the junta issued a document in which it explained that before returning to representative, republican democracy, Argentina would have to undergo a Process of National Reorganization that would promote economic development, "eradicate subversion," and "restore the values fundamental to the integral management of the state, emphasizing the sense of morality, fitness, and efficiency indispensable for the reconstitution of the nation" (*La Nación*, 26 March 1976).

The junta put the economy in the hands of José Martínez de Hoz, a prominent landowner, businessman, and ardent advocate of "neoliberalism," who was given carte blanche and took over the war against "subversion." It launched a massive attack against the guerrillas, which soon yielded results, and by mid 1977 both the ERP and Montoneros were effectively neutralized. On 28 September 1977 the military command in Tucumán province announced that the ERP guerrillas operating in that area had been wiped out, and ten days later, General Viola declared that ERP and Montoneros had lost 80 percent of their forces and no longer presented "a threat to national security."

THE REPRESSIVE STATE

The military called its "war against subversion" a "holy war" or a "dirty war," justified in all its aspects by the danger the guerrillas posed to the Argentine nation and the excesses of the guerrillas, especially their attacks against the armed forces. As a government official explained to an Amnesty International mission in November 1976, "Systematic subversion and terrorism have cost the lives of many police and military and have compromised the security of the Argentine people. . . . If anybody violates human rights in Argentina, murdering, torturing and bombing, it is undoubtedly the terrorists. These people use violence for its own sake or to create chaos and destruction. We understand that the state has the right to defend itself, using whatever force is necessary" (Amnesty International 1977 : 49).

The war was waged on two levels. On the one hand, there were conventional confrontations with guerrilla forces both in the cities and in the countryside; on the other, a long clandestine campaign carried out by special task forces, also known as *patotas* (gangs), the new name given to the right-wing death squads created during the Peronist administrations. No longer connected to the Social Welfare Ministry, and seemingly independent, they were brought under the control of the armed forces and made an integral part of their strategy to annihilate subversion. However, the junta did not officially acknowledge responsibility for either their existence or their activities, a position adopted by the successive juntas and maintained until the present. At best, when questioned about human rights abuses, the Argentine military admitted the existence of uncontrollable right-wing groups. On several occasions General Videla denied categorically that human rights were violated in Argentina. While visiting Washington for the signing of the Panama Canal treaties, however, he finally admitted that persons did disappear in his country, but he was careful to add that his government could not be blamed for the actions of groups that were an outgrowth of the "dirty war" and beyond the control of the junta. "We understand but do not justify the actions of groups that, perhaps with good intentions, want to do what they think the government is not doing" (*Facts on File,* 1977 : 922).

Using a sui generis definition of subversive, because it encompassed guerrillas, Marxists of varying persuasion, liberals, and reform-minded Catholics and Jews, as well as all those suspected of actively, remotely, or accidentally, willingly or unwillingly, aiding or abetting terrorists, tens of thousands were arrested. In January 1978 General Videla defined a terrorist as "not just someone with a gun or a bomb but also someone who spreads ideas that are contrary to Western and Christian civilization" (*The Times* [London], 4 January 1978). Some were formally arrested. They were known as *detenidos PEN,* those detained at the disposition of the National Executive Power. For almost two years, the junta refused to disclose the number or the identity of the *detenidos* officially, although in September 1977, General Albano Harguindeguy, minister of the interior, admitted that in May of that year 5,018 persons were being held. In January 1978 the junta finally stated that a total of 3,472 persons had been detained. On the eve of the arrival of the Inter-American Human Rights Commission, September 1979, there were only 1,438 left.

Many *detenidos* were eventually released, sometimes after being imprisoned for several years. They were held incommunicado in inhuman conditions and brutally tortured. Since they were not charged, they were never brought to trial. Others, however, were never released, and together with those who were not formally arrested, they are known as *desaparecidos* ("disappeared"), because they simply vanished. Some, like Senator Hipólito Solari Yrigoyen, were both *detenidos* and *desaparecidos.*

Solari Yrigoyen was kidnapped on 17 August 1976 together with Senator Mario Abel Amaya and taken to an army barracks in Bahía Blanca,
Buenos Aires province, where they were tortured. After the Inter-
American Human Rights Commission requested their release, on 30 August 1976, they were found by the roadside in another town in Buenos
Aires province. According to the government, the police rescued them
after an armed confrontation with the kidnappers, although both Amaya
and Solari Yrigoyen denied hearing shots. They then became *detenidos*
and were accused of having "connections with subversive activities."
They were taken to Rawson, a prison in southern Argentina. Upon arrival they were so badly beaten that Amaya had to be hospitalized. He
died on 19 October 1976. Solari Yrigoyen remained in Rawson for nine
months and then was allowed to go into exile, where he joined thousands
of his compatriots. Fleeing from the repression unleashed by the junta,
they had emigrated after the coup and would continue to do so in large
numbers throughout the Proceso.

The National Commission on the Disappearance of Persons (Conadep), created by President Raúl Alfonsín after Argentina returned to
democracy in December 1983, has been able to document the disappearance of 8,960 persons, a number that by no means represents all the
desaparecidos (Conadep 1985). Conadep points out that during the Proceso many families failed to report the disappearance of a relative because they were afraid to endanger his or her life. When the military dictatorship ended, they refused to testify, still afraid of the consequences.
In other cases, the whole family disappeared and did not have relatives
who could report the kidnappings.

The Conadep report shows that whereas 600 persons disappeared
prior to 24 March 1976, most of them during 1975 (that is to say, during
Isabel's administration), the numbers rose dramatically right after the
coup: 45 percent of all disappearances took place in 1976. The number
of the missing diminished slightly in 1977, dropped sharply in 1978, and
continued to decrease until 1982. Since most of the disappearances took
place during the period in which the campaign against the guerrillas was
most intense, these figures confirm the conventional as well as clandestine nature of "the war against subversion." The information provided by Conadep also reveals that the military seemed to view Argentina as an enemy territory whose population was by definition, actively,
potentially, or unwittingly subversive. Most of the *desaparecidos* were
young people between the ages of twenty and thirty. A significant number were in their thirties, but there were also teenagers, infants, children, and senior citizens in their seventies. Most were blue collar workers, followed by students and white collar workers. A substantial number
were professionals, especially lawyers and teachers. There were also
housewives, journalists, priests, nuns, and conscripts. The majority were

men (70 percent). Among the women, 3 percent were pregnant. While most of the disappeared were Argentines, there were also Uruguayans, Chileans, and Paraguayans. In fact, Amnesty International documented the disappearance of nationals from twenty-eight countries.

The *desaparecidos* were abducted in their homes, on the street, while at work, and even at school, following the same general pattern. Those who were kidnapped in their homes, for example, were taken away in the middle of the night or at dawn toward the end of the week by groups of five to ten heavily armed men dressed in civilian clothes or fatigues. They arrived in unmarked vehicles, frequently Ford Falcons, having previously received the "green light" from the local police precinct and often also protected by a blackout. Once inside, they brutalized all the members of the household, including children and old people, and ransacked the home. When they left, they often took away all the family members present, and even visitors, with their eyes taped. They also carried away whatever they pleased as "war booty."

With their departure, the process of disappearance began. The kidnappers took their victims to one of the 340 concentration camps or clandestine detention centers identified by Conadep, known as *chupaderos* ("suckers"). Once there, they were systematically subjected to various forms of psychological and physical torture either to obtain information or confessions or to terrorize them. The prisoners, pointedly called *chupados* (sucked or swallowed ones) by the kidnappers, were permanently hooded or blindfolded, handcuffed, and shackled. They were insulted, humiliated, and brutally beaten. Women were raped, including those who were pregnant. Some were forced to witness the torture of their own children. All prisoners were also periodically subjected to mock executions and electric shocks to the most sensitive parts of their bodies. An unknown number were killed, their bodies thrown into the sea from helicopters, burned, or mutilated and buried in unmarked graves.

Once the disappearance took place, the victims' relatives went to local police precincts, police headquarters, the ministries of the air force, the army, and the navy, the courts, and the Ministry of Interior to report the kidnapping and to seek information. They were usually told that no record could be found of any arrest. When they began legal proceedings, their writs of habeas corpus were systematically denied.

The French newspaperman Jean Pierre Bousquet recounts the story of a woman he calls Marta. In October 1976 she asked him to help her locate her son, who had been kidnapped in August as he was leaving the hospital where he worked as a pediatrician. Seeking to find out his whereabouts, she had first attempted to use family connections and had gotten nowhere. She then presented two writs of habeas corpus to the courts, but both were answered negatively. She went to the police, the army, and the Ministry of Interior, but no one knew anything about her son. She then decided to begin her own investigation, "interrogating Luis's colleagues, the neighbors, and merchants of the area where the abduction took place" (Bousquet 1983 : 17). Despite the resistance she encountered, she managed to get some fragments of information and presented a third writ of habeas corpus and also took her case to the press. Unable to obtain a response in the Argentine press, she contacted Bousquet, who worked for Agence France-Presse in Buenos Aires.

While the authorities disclaimed any knowledge or responsibility for the kidnappings, they nevertheless often advised the victims' relatives not to present writs of habeas corpus or to denounce the abductions because such steps would endanger the lives of the disappeared. Victims' relatives who persisted in seeking information, and anyone helping them to obtain it, were threatened with kidnapping, and some indeed disappeared. The Conadep report describes the case of a midwife and a nurse who disappeared because they contacted the relatives of a *desaparecida* who had given birth to a baby girl in the hospital where they worked. The mother, the child, and the two women are still missing (Conadep 1985 : 281).

The victims' relatives found themselves in a Kafkaesque situation. They had to prove that a son or a daughter had been kidnapped to authorities who denied that abductions occurred in Argentina. Furthermore, the detention centers were clandestine; the kidnappers could not be identified; the courts were under military control; the press was censored; and the police, like the armed forces, did not admit the existence of the task forces. The victims' relatives had nowhere to go.

While proclaiming its belief in "Christian and Western moral values," in the name of national security, the junta "eradicated terrorism" by creating a thorough and all-powerful form of state terrorism. It used the forced disappearance of men, women, and children not only to destroy the guerrillas and their sympathizers but also as a means of social control. Its purpose was to paralyze all possible opposition and instill fear, passivity, and compliance in the general population, a policy undoubtedly successful during the early stages of the dictatorship. Even the powerful Peronist labor movement was kept under control during much of the Proceso.

The Argentine military was not the first to use forced disappearance as a weapon to combat guerrillas and to achieve social control. The Brazilian armed forces had tried it out in a limited form a few years earlier, and it was also used in other countries, such as Guatemala and Chile. However, the Argentine military perfected the weapon, widened its scope, and in fact transformed it into a policy.

The existence of a parallel, but hidden, *aparato represivo*, a structure of repression that carried out actions not acknowledged by the government and for which it did not take responsibility, created a deep cleavage between the state and civil society. All legal recourses for redress available under normal circumstances vanished. Either shut or controlled by the armed forces, they were in any case impenetrable to civilians. For the first time in Argentine history, previous networks based on personal, familial, professional, or political contacts also proved useless. No one could bypass or penetrate the armed forces to reach the clandestine level. The impossibility of establishing contact with the *aparato represivo* even affected the military at times, as the case of Adriana Landaburu demonstrates. She was the daughter of Brigadier Major Jorge Landaburu, a former air force minister. Almost immediately after she was abducted in the street on 7 June 1977, her father had an interview with General Videla during which the latter personally called the three commanders in chief and requested them to initiate an investigation. Admiral Massera even called her house and assured her parents that the navy had nothing to do with her disappearance. In fact, according to Conadep, she was imprisoned in the infamous detention center of the Escuela Mecánica de la Armada (ESMA), the navy mechanics' school, and she was dumped into the sea (Conadep 1985:250–51).

The absence of mediating institutions or mechanisms was underscored by the ambiguous role of the Catholic church (see Mignone 1986). Some members of the hierarchy and many individual priests and nuns lent their support to those who requested it. The bishops' conference initially criticized the methods used by the armed forces in their struggle to eradicate "subversion," but the church never dissociated itself clearly from the junta. It did not become the voice of moral opposition to the military regime, as the Chilean church did under the leadership of Cardinal Raúl Silva Henríquez, although two bishops died under mysterious circumstances and are considered *desaparecidos,* and some seventeen priests and nuns were killed or kidnapped.

Gradually, the void created by the absence of mediating institutions was filled by human rights organizations. Some were old, like the Argentine League for the Rights of Man. The Liga, as it is known, was closely connected with the Communist Party, and as denunciations of disappearances increased, it created a committee to provide support and legal help to those who requested it, the Commission of Relatives of the Disappeared and Political Prisoners. Other human rights groups were more recent, like the Ecumenic Movement for Human Rights (MEDH), the Service for Peace and Justice (SERPAJ), whose founder, Adolfo Pérez Esquivel, received the Nobel Peace Prize in 1980, and the Permanent Assembly for Human Rights. The latter, which included prominent jurists, politicians, and churchmen, was presided over by Raúl Alfonsín and Monsignor Jaime F. de Nevares, bishop of Neuquén. Besides working with the relatives of persons who had disappeared or been detained and offering them legal counsel, the human rights groups provided information to Amnesty International and to all other organizations or individuals concerned with conditions in Argentina and willing to exert international pressure on the junta. They represented a new type of resistance to military dictatorship in Argentina, and their activities brought the repressive arm of the government down on them. Pérez Esquivel was jailed in 1977–78. In August 1979, on the eve of the arrival of the Inter-American Human Rights Commission, the offices of the Permanent Assembly, the Liga, the Ecumenic Movement, and the Commission of Relatives were raided. Files and a petition that had been drafted for the Inter-American Commission were seized. On 27 February 1981 the human rights activists Emilio Mignone, Augusto Conte MacDonell, and José Federico Westerkamp were detained and held incommunicado for several days. At the time of their arrest, records documenting the disappearance of more than 6,000 persons were also seized.

THE MOTHERS' RESISTANCE MOVEMENT

Las Madres was yet another mediating institution that emerged as a result of the conditions created by the Proceso. Though it came into existence on 30 April 1977, right after the fourteen women had first met in the Plaza de Mayo, it did not acquire a formal structure until 1979. That same year, it was joined by the Abuelas de Plaza de Mayo, the Grandmothers of Plaza de Mayo, founded by women whose grandchildren had disappeared, having either been abducted with their mothers or born in the clandestine detention centers. In contrast with other human rights organizations, Las Madres was composed exclusively of women, most of them mothers of children who had been kidnapped. Its other distinctive feature is that from the very beginning it was committed to a militancy shunned by the other groups.

The fourteen women who marched on 30 April had met in antechambers and public offices while attempting to obtain information about their children. Most of them were of working-class origin. A few had jobs, but they nevertheless saw themselves primarily as housewives. None had been politically active prior to the 1976 military coup. Many were Catholic, and that made them suspicious of human rights groups like the communist-linked Liga. Although Catholic organizations like MEDH and SERPAJ provided them with support, they felt frustrated because they did not see concrete results. Powerless, but also angry and unwilling to give up their search, they continued to make the rounds of all the offices where they might gather information. One of the offices where many waited for long hours was that of Monsignor Emilio Grasselli, general chaplain of the navy. María Adela Antokoletz, for example, went to see him after trying several other avenues. When her son Daniel disappeared on 10 November 1976, she presented a writ of habeas corpus, went to the police, and even approached the Amnesty International delegation that visited Argentina that month. She also sought the help of her parish priest. He directed her to his bishop, who in turn gave her a letter of introduction to the Curia. From there she was sent to see Monsignor Grasselli. While waiting in his crowded office, she met Azucena Villaflor de De Vicenti, a soft-spoken woman in her late fifties, mother of four children, one of whom had disappeared. As Antokoletz told me in July 1987, Azucena proposed: "We are wasting our time. This is not where we must look for our children. We have to go to the Plaza de Mayo and then speak with Videla, because he does not know what is happening." A small group of women agreed that this was a good idea, and they decided to meet in the Plaza de Mayo on 30 April at 11 o'clock in the morning to publicize the plight of their children so as to feel that they were doing something for them and to break the silence about the kidnappings.

The Plaza de Mayo is in the heart of downtown Buenos Aires. In its center is a small pyramid erected to commemorate the beginnings of the independence movement on 25 May 1810. The large rectangular space is dominated by the Casa Rosada, Argentina's White House and seat of the Interior Ministry. Other buildings surrounding the plaza are the Cabildo, the old colonial town meeting hall; the cathedral where Argentina's liberator, General José de San Martín, lies; and the National Bank and other government offices. It is usually crowded with tourists, strollers, and people either on their way to the nearby business district or sitting on its numerous benches, feeding pigeons or enjoying the well-tended flower beds.

Ready to confront the police, the fourteen women were sorely disappointed: 30 April was a Saturday, and the plaza was empty. They decided to return the following week, at the same hour, but on a Friday. This time, some twenty women came, and one of them proposed changing the hour to 3:30 in the afternoon. The following Friday, 13 May, the number of women had increased, and one of them proposed still another change: Friday being an unlucky day, they should meet on Thursdays at 3:30 P.M.

The idea of going to the Plaza de Mayo at a time when demonstrations of any kind were forbidden frightened many women. Their lives as wives and mothers had not prepared them to break the law and demonstrate right in front of the well-guarded Casa Rosada, where no demonstration had taken place since the military coup. They initially sat on the benches or huddled in groups, exchanging information or discussing the names of women who might be willing to join them. On one occasion, the police told them that they could not loiter in the plaza and had to move, so they decided to walk silently for half an hour around the pyramid.

Under normal circumstances, marching silently around the pyramid would have been an innocuous act, entirely devoid of political significance for Argentines. Since the mid forties, when Perón began addressing his supporters from the balcony of the Casa Rosada, political demonstrations in the Plaza de Mayo had meant massive, boisterous rallies. Under the conditions created by the military since 1976, however, marching silently around the pyramid was an extraordinary act of defiance that no human rights group or political organization had dared to undertake. While the marches initially had a limited and very personal objective and were not intended to be confrontational, they were the first demonstrations denouncing disappearances in Argentina. Furthermore, the marches had unforeseen consequences for their participants. By walking around the pyramid as mothers of children who had disappeared, they transformed their private, personal statement into a public and political act. Additionally, marching dissipated their misgivings and fears, gave them strength, and uncovered a new side to them. It transformed them into Las Madres, women committed to demonstrating every week for however long it took for their children to reappear and ready to do whatever else was necessary to attain their objective. Not being militants, marching was "a difficult step for us," recounted a participant at the time, "but now that we have dared, I am sure that many others will follow" (Bousquet 1983:49). Indeed, their example gave courage to many others, and by June 1977 the group marching every Thursday at 3:30 P.M. had grown to 100. As the repression subsided and the military regime weakened, the ranks of the organization swelled, and by 1982 the Madres claimed to have a membership of 2,500.

The Thursday marches soon became a ritual that could not be missed by any of the mothers who joined the movement. At times the police did not permit them to march and arrested several women for a few hours, but they returned the following week. At first, they used Catholic symbols—for example, a carpenter's nail on their backs, in memory of "Christ's sacrifice," one of the Mothers explained. "We too have our Christ, and we relive Mary's sorrow, but we are not even allowed to console him with our presence" (Bousquet 1983:47). Later they began to wear white handkerchiefs and to carry pictures of their kidnapped children around their necks or in their hands. They also wrote the names of their children and the dates of their disappearances on the white kerchiefs that they wore weekly at 3:30 P.M. Passersby looked at them uneasily, or with indifference, contempt, or fear, while the Casa Rosada guards kept a close watch on them.

The junta's initial response to the weekly marches was to ignore them and when pressed by an inquiring journalist, to ridicule the Mothers, calling them *las locas de Plaza de Mayo* (the madwomen of Plaza de Mayo). The junta did not recognize the political nature of the Madres' actions and did not attempt to suppress the group. This reaction was crucial for the evolution of the movement because it gave the women the necessary time to strengthen their resolve, contact other mothers, establish an informal organization, and engage in other activities. At the suggestion of Azucena Villaflor de De Vicenti, "a natural leader" and "a great organizer" (Fernández Meijide 1984), they planned a collective claim of habeas corpus, and on 28 June, a delegation presented writs on behalf of 159 persons. When Patricia Derian, the U.S. State Department's human rights coordinator, visited Argentina on 7 August, they requested an interview with her. A few days later, Terence Todman, assistant secretary of state for inter-American affairs, visited Buenos Aires. As he arrived to meet General Videla at the Casa Rosada, the Madres held a demonstration at which some 100 women were arrested. They began to work with other groups, such as the Movement of Relatives of the Disappeared, an organization that included both men and women searching for vanished relatives. On 14 October some 300 people, mostly women, gathered in front of the Congress building while a delegation presented a document addressed to the junta signed by 24,000 people, requesting the investigation of disappearances and the release of all PEN prisoners. The demonstrators were dispersed by the police with tear gas and shots in the air, and 150 were arrested. They were released the following day.

Finally, recognizing the political implications of the Madres' Thursday marches, petitions, and demonstrations, the military decided to strike. On 8 December a group of mothers met in a church with members of the Movement of Relatives of the Disappeared to work on a letter to be published on 10 December, Human Rights Day. As they left the meeting, nine women, including a French nun, Alice Domont, were abducted by a group of men who arrived in Ford Falcons. The kidnappers also took away all the money collected that day for the newspaper advertisement. Two days later Renée Duquet, another French nun, and Azucena Villaflor were kidnapped in their homes. The two nuns and Azucena Villaflor disappeared.

The blow was severe, but it did not destroy their determination. They managed to collect more money and publish the letter. They held their regular Thursday march, and the following day, they called a press conference right on the Plaza de Mayo. It was attended only by foreign correspondents and the *Buenos Aires Herald,* an English-language newspaper, whose editor, Robert J. Cox, still dared to write about the disappeared despite threats, arrests, and censorship. Their purpose was to set the record straight and correct the official version of the December events. According to the government, the abductions were the work of the "nihilist subversion."

Throughout much of 1978, the Madres continued their Thursday marches undisturbed, while the junta concerned itself with its preparations for the World Cup soccer championship. Argentina won the cup, and Argentines celebrated their victory with an explosion of jingoistic nationalism, which greatly satisfied the military junta. On 28 December, however, a thousand women were forcefully expelled from the Plaza de Mayo by the police and were prevented from returning the following two Thursdays. Continually harassed throughout 1979, they nevertheless held on to the plaza, but had to give it up for much of 1980.

Unable to demonstrate, the Madres began to meet in churches on Thursday afternoons. They decided to become a formal organization, electing Hebé Pastor de Bonafini as their first president. A stocky fifty-year-old woman who "was brought up to be a housewife" and had a limited education, Hebé Bonafini had had little preparation for the life she led after her two sons and a daughter-in-law disappeared. She was married at twenty to her first sweetheart, an auto mechanic, and they had three children, two sons and a daughter. When two of her sons and a daughter-in-law disappeared in 1976, she tried to locate them using every avenue she could think of, but ran into a blank wall. During her repeated visits to the Ministry of Interior, she met other mothers looking for their children and soon joined the Thursday marches. Her husband, who died in 1982 after a long illness, supported her activities with the Madres, although "he was scared at times." For her part, she lost her fears early on. She was not even afraid "when the police kicked us out of the Plaza with loaded submachine guns and one policeman shouted 'Ready?' and we shouted back 'Shoot!'" Nor did she become frightened when Azucena Villaflor disappeared or when she discovered a Ford Falcon following her at night when she went home, because "our desire to find our sons was stronger than our fright" and because "thinking about our children we don't think about our sufferings" (*Humor*, October 1982).

Under her courageous and vigorous leadership, the group joined other human rights organizations in their efforts to publicize the plight of the disappeared in Europe and the United States. The Madres established contacts with human rights organizations in other countries, lobbied for support among foreign congressmen, testified wherever they were invited to do so, and visited any president willing to receive them. Despite fears of reprisals against their abducted relatives or against themselves, they flocked to give testimony during the hearings held by the Inter-American Human Rights Commission, which visited Argentina in September 1979 for three weeks. The queues outside the OAS building in downtown Buenos Aires grew to up to 3,000 people at times. The six-member team took note of denunciations of disappearances from individuals and human rights organizations, visited prisoners, a detention camp, and graveyards. Unable to prevent the OAS visit, the junta published a book presenting its own version of events and plastered Buenos Aires with posters proclaiming "Somos derechos y humanos" ("We are right and human").

Vulnerable, isolated, and constantly threatened by the overwhelming power of the junta, the Madres nevertheless persisted in their struggle. On 12 March 1981, sixty-eight were arrested, held for several hours, and then released. On 7 July of that same year, Hebé Bonafini and the Madres' vice president, María Adela Antokoletz, were detained for two hours at Ezeiza airport when they returned from Houston, Texas, where they had received a human rights award. Their activities in the international arena and in Argentina, as well as those of other human rights organizations, had a significant impact on the military dictatorship. Their denunciations affected the junta's international standing, especially its relations with the United States. In February 1977 President Jimmy Carter cut off military aid to Argentina because of human rights abuses, and in mid 1978, the State Department blocked a $270 million Export-Import Bank loan. By 1980 the decline in disappearances and human rights violations in general forecast a change in U.S.–Argentine relations. However, while the junta could improve its standing in the international community by reducing its level of repression internally, it could not solve the problem of the *desaparecidos*. The "dirty war" had produced new political actors in Argentina—some informally connected with political parties, others, as in the case of the Madres, entirely outside of the traditional political party structure—for whom the issue of the disappeared was vital, paramount, and therefore not negotiable. The military government could boast of having "eradicated subversion," but it could not control human rights organizations and devise a solution to the problem of the *desaparecidos*, especially after the economic situation began to deteriorate and social unrest spread.

In August 1979 the armed forces thought they had found a solution to their predicament. In order to alleviate financial and legal hardships, the military government announced that it would promulgate a law permitting a relative of a missing person or the state to seek a ruling from a judge declaring a person who had disappeared between November 1975 and the date of the promulgation of the law to be dead. The enactment of the law proved implicitly that the Madres were not "mad" and that the human rights organizations had not invented their denunciations, as the junta often claimed. The law was rejected, not only by the Madres and all other human rights groups, but also by several governments as a ploy on the part of the junta to arbitrarily declare the disappeared dead.

To gain broader political support, the junta made some moves toward democratization. In the improved political environment, the Madres became increasingly militant. In December 1979 they were prevented from paying homage to General San Martín, so they turned around and organized an impromptu march through the busiest section of downtown Buenos Aires. They even demonstrated during the Falklands/Malvinas war, when opposition parties and labor unions rallied behind the flag. On Thursday, 10 December 1982, Human Rights Day, they held a special 24-hour march, even though the police refused to grant them the required permit. The march began on Thursday at 3.30 P.M. and lasted through the night until the following afternoon. The Madres were joined by hundreds of sympathizers, both men and women, who accompanied them for varying periods of time. The mothers, however, remained in the plaza, walking at a slow pace and leaving the circle from time to time to rest on the benches. The march ended the following day with a demonstration along the avenue that connects the Plaza de Mayo with the Congress building. The demonstrators carried a huge banner and large posters with the pictures of their children or grandchildren and had enough energy to chant "Liberty! Liberty!" "Where are the disappeared?" and "We want our children alive and the culprits punished!"

As the military gradually loosened their grip, especially after the Falklands/Malvinas war, the Madres' marches spearheaded the vast mobilizations that hastened the end of the Proceso. When the electoral campaign began, they had successfully transformed the *desaparecidos* into an issue that no political party could ignore or could afford to negotiate.

CONCLUSION

Like other human rights groups, individuals, and families affected by the abduction of relatives in Argentina or elsewhere, the Madres refused to accept that the disappearance of a person necessarily meant his or her death. Take the reaction of Eunice Paiva fifteen years after the disappearance of her husband, Rubens Paiva, in Rio de Janeiro, Brazil. Rubens Paiva, a former congressman, was kidnapped by six armed men in his home in Rio de Janeiro, on 20 January 1971. His wife Eunice and Eliana, one of their four children, were arrested the following day. The latter was released after twenty-four hours, while the former remained in jail for thirteen days, but Rubens disappeared.

On 1 September 1986 a military doctor declared that he had seen Rubens Paiva shortly before he died in a cell at Rio de Janeiro's military police headquarters. "His whole body [was] a bruise," the doctor said. Upon hearing the news, Eunice Paiva stated:

> Today I became a widow and my children became orphans. For the first time, after fifteen years, someone has said that he had seen Rubens in prison, tortured, dying. . . . Until today, although we knew the truth, my children and I still had fantasies. The description of Rubens' last moments destroyed these fantasies. We never saw him in a coffin. Maybe that is the reason we never imagined him dead, and as incredible as this may seem, we often spoke as if he were alive. (*Jornal do Brasil*, 2 September 1986)

What differentiated the Madres from other groups of relatives of disappeared, however, was their militancy. Obviously, the abductions and their aftermath affected deeply all the members of the victims' families. "The anguished pilgrimage in search of news in public offices, courts of justice, precincts, and military barracks, the hopeful wait for some information or rumor, the specter of a mourning that could not take place are factors that [played] a destabilizing role in the family group and in the personality of each of its members" (Conadep 1985:332). Indeed, after the kidnapping of a child, both parents were generally equally involved in the search for information. They were compelled to do so by the abduction itself. They had no reason to believe that the disappearance of, say, a daughter generally meant her death. They knew she had been taken away, sometimes under their very eyes, but death did not have tangible form because there was no corpse to prepare for burial, no wake to ease the pain, no grave to visit in the cemetery. Furthermore, since she had been taken away, it was logical to think that she had been put somewhere. She was only missing, and that meant that if one searched hard enough and long enough, she could be found. As long as they lacked any proof of her death and her body had not been recovered and accorded the proper ritual, parents could hope that she was still alive or that her death was somehow avoidable.

But the effect of the abductions on mothers was notably different from the impact they produced on fathers. The latter tended to accept the finality of the disappearances more readily than mothers. After a certain time, they realized that the wall erected by the military was indeed impenetrable and that it was useless to persist in wanting to know what had happened to a disappeared child. Having done everything humanly possible, individually or through one of the human rights organizations, and while perhaps still hoping for the impossible, they listened to reason and common sense and did not openly confront the military junta.

On the other hand, mothers simply refused to acquiesce in the loss of their children, even though they had been socialized to be passive and obedient. Instead of reinforcing acceptance and obedience in them, the disappearances had the precisely opposite effect. In fact, the abduction of a child was the catalyst that prompted a mother to act.

The kidnappings were brutal assaults on women, against their role as mothers. Suddenly deprived of their children, their lives as wives and mothers had lost meaning. They had to reconstruct their shattered lives, not only by searching for their children, as earlier they had cared for them, nursed them, educated them, and worried about them, but by attempting to do the impossible on their behalf. They were compelled to act not on moral or political grounds or out of concern for gross human rights violations, as in the case of other groups, but because they were mothers. Their refusal to acquiesce in the loss of their children was not an act out of character, but a coherent expression of their socialization, of their acceptance of the dominant sexual division of labor and of their own subordination within it. True to themselves, they had no other choice but to act, even if it meant confronting the junta.

They also had more time than men to search for their missing children, or at least they could find time more easily. Men could not spend endless hours making the rounds of ministries and precincts, waiting for an audience with yet another official who might provide information. They had to earn a living, and although they could take some time off, they could not risk losing their jobs, so they eventually had to return to work. On the other hand, after taking care of their housework, women could find the time to go once more to the Interior Ministry, follow a lead that might prove useful, get another writ of habeas corpus, collect money or signatures for an advertisement, contact women in the provinces whose children had also disappeared, help those who had been left destitute, and so forth.

Furthermore, while Buenos Aires was a city where men and especially young people could vanish without leaving a trace, older, matronly women could safely move about without too much fear for their own security—at least during the first year of the Proceso—because they were mothers. In a society that glorified motherhood and exalted women as domestic beings, they were implicitly excluded from the different groups defined as "subversives."

Since the junta concentrated its repression on young people between twenty and thirty, it created a critical mass of women who despite class divisions and differences in life experience or values had one crucial thing in common: they were mothers of children who had disappeared. Motherhood brought them together and gave them the opportunity to meet one another, commiserate together, and share their frustration, their pain, and their anger. Motherhood created the bond that allowed them to pool the information they obtained and the rumors they gathered and develop a sense of solidarity, from which they drew the strength to press for an answer to their questions.

Motherhood permitted them to stage the first public protests against the military government without facing jail or worse. They were conscious of the public acceptance of their role as mothers and used it as a shield, deciding to march alone, without men. "You have to leave," the women told those men who wanted to accompany them. "If there are only women [the police] will not dare to intervene, but if you come they won't hesitate to take you away" (Bousquet 1983:47).

Until December 1977 motherhood empowered them to continue marching at a time when no public expression of dissent was allowed and to engage in other activities without risking being kidnapped, because mothers were not perceived as political subjects. Their actions were therefore politically invisible. The junta's initial reaction to the Plaza de

Mayo marches is explained by the political invisibility of the mothers, reinforced by the view that while women might be politically active, they were not necessarily independent political actors. This belief was confirmed by the actions of such political women as Evita and Isabel Perón in the immediate past, albeit that the latter had achieved the highest office in her country.

Finally, motherhood also gave the Madres an additional advantage. Since most of the mothers lacked political experience, they were unburdened by ideological constraints or obedience to party directives or the need to replicate proven tactics. They were therefore free to use new symbols, devise appropriate tactics, and adopt actions, such as the Thursday marches, that had not been tried before in Argentina. In the terrorist state created by the military, motherhood in fact protected them and gave them a freedom and a power not available to traditional political actors, especially if they were male.

REFERENCES

Amnesty International
  1977   *Report of an Amnesty International Mission to Argentina, 6–13 November 1976.* New York: Amnesty International.
Bousquet, Jean Pierre
  1983   *Las locas de Plaza de Mayo.* Buenos Aires: El Cid Editor.
Conadep [National Commission on the Disappearance of Persons]
  1985   *Nunca Más: Informe de la Comisión Nacional sobre la desaparición de personas.* Barcelona: Seix-Barral.
Fernández Meijide, Graciela
  1984   Unpublished lecture, delivered to Lugar de Mujer, Buenos Aires, 14 December.
Mignone, Emilio F.
  1986   *Iglesia y dictadura.* Buenos Aires: Ediciones del Pensamiento Nacional.

CHAPTER EIGHT

Popular Mobilization and the Military Regime in Chile: The Complexities of the Invisible Transition

Manuel Antonio Garretón M.

In 1973 the democratically elected Chilean president, Salvador Allende, was overthrown in a coup d'état by the commanders in chief of the armed forces. General Augusto Pinochet has since ruled Chile. His repressive regime quickly ended the left coalition's efforts to promote a "Chilean road to socialism" and decades of democratic stability. For ten years civilian opposition to the regime was expressed "sectorally" (through economic groups), under the umbrella of the Catholic church, or through the underground activities of political parties and social organizations. It was almost impossible to organize public and massive expressions of dissent and opposition, and when such outbreaks occurred they were severely repressed. However, beginning in May 1983, some mass mobilizations occurred, which came to be known as national protests. This chapter addresses the significance of these challenges to the military's authoritarian rule.

What role can the protests play in restoring democracy? The opposition movement is divided on this matter. Some opponents see the protests as a means of wearing down the regime and forcing it to negotiate a democratic transition, while others believe that the mobilizations will in and of themselves destabilize the regime to the point where it will be forced to relinquish power. Social mobilizations have become ever more frequent in the years since the first protest, and some regime opponents remain committed to them as *the* strategy of opposition. Others attribute Pinochet's success in retaining power to the failure of this strategy (see Garretón 1985, 1986, and 1987).

This chapter was prepared at the Latin American Faculty of Social Sciences (FLACSO) in Santiago, Chile, and completed during the author's stay as visiting professor at the Ecole des Hautes Etudes en Sciences Sociales and the Centre d'Analyse et d'Intervention Sociologiques, Paris, in 1987. The author wishes to thank Federico Joannon for his bibliographical assistance. The chapter was translated by Philip Oxhorn and Susan Eckstein.

— plebiscito 1984

The political debate is connected to a more academic debate about the role of social mobilization in transitions from authoritarian to democratic regimes (see O'Donnell and Schmitter 1986). Is mobilization indispensable for redemocratization, or does it result in greater repression and greater consolidation of military power? How does it relate to other aspects of political transitions, such as regime decomposition, external influences, or internal mediations between regime and opposition? If mobilizations can play an instrumental role in the transition process, is the timing of the defiance consequential and are some types of mobilization better suited than others?

The political debate is also a debate over new social movements. It has been argued that structural and cultural change in industrial or postindustrial societies, as well as in less developed and dependent countries, including Latin America, are generating new types of expressions of defiance and mobilizations for change (see Touraine 1978, 1984, and 1987; Campero 1986; Garretón 1984). Do the social mobilizations in Chile constitute something more than mass discontent with authoritarian rule? Do they represent the seeds of a new breed of social movements involving new political actors, premised on a redefinition of the relationship between politics and society?

The "invisible transition" to democracy, entailing the recomposition and reorganization of civil society (see Garretón 1983 and 1986c), must be distinguished from the formal transition to democracy. The latter involves specific measures that are designed ultimately to end military rule. Since civilian groups mobilized much more in Chile than under repressive governments in other Latin American countries in the 1970s, and since the military remain in power in Chile, whereas they have returned to their barracks elsewhere in the region, the Chilean case raises the question of the potential and limits of "invisible transitions" to democracy.

In the first part of this chapter I discuss the general characteristics of social mobilization under military regimes. In the second part, I review the evolution of the mobilizations under the Chilean military government. In the third part, I present interpretative hypotheses to account for the effects of different types of mobilizations, their social bases, and the relationship between protest movements and opposition articulated through political parties.

SOCIAL MOBILIZATIONS AND MILITARY REGIMES

A review of the characteristics and evolution of the military regimes that emerged in the 1960s and 1970s in the Southern Cone of Latin America is not possible here (see Collier 1979; Garretón 1984 and 1986b). For present purposes, several features need only be noted.

First, the regimes were hostile to "popular" mobilizations. Having imposed themselves on highly politicized societies, they sought to demobilize the civilian populace. They did not even attempt to build up political bases of their own. Their concern with depoliticization led them not only to dismantle established forms of mobilization but also to prevent new forms and new social actors from arising. Under such conditions, the presence of social mobilizations represents an authoritarian regime's inability to rule through repression and the existence of pockets of space in civil society for the reconstitution of collective action.

Second, the likelihood and nature of mobilizations are partially contingent on the period of regime consolidation. When military regimes first come to power, they are especially repressive: if there is any civilian mobilization, it is minimal and limited to testimonials or defensive expressions by groups directly affected by the repression. Even such restricted mobilization generally occurs under the shelter of such powerful institutions as the Catholic church. However, once the regimes do not merely stake out their claims to power, but also try to transform the economic and social order and establish new bases of hegemony, sectors adversely affected by the transformations begin to mobilize in opposition. Should the regime's transformative project show itself not to work, mobilizations may become massive.

The first large-scale mobilizations reflect a loss of fear. However, these mobilizations and the demands that participating groups make do not alone produce a sufficient crisis to undermine the regime. To bring down the state and usher in a democratic transition, political leadership and coordination are also needed. The political leadership must address the multiple and varied expressions of discontent and the aspirations of protesters in a manner that unifies the groups opposing the regime.

Large-scale mobilizations can be found under the spectrum of regime types. However, under dictatorships and highly repressive governments, the movements are aimed, explicitly or implicitly, at the termination of the regimes, and they are shaped by the institutional context, which prohibits or constricts their activity. As a consequence, protests and mobilizations under dictatorships and authoritarian states have an emotional and "heroic" aspect, which contributes to their politicization. Moreover, social movements under military governments represent efforts of groups in civil society that were eliminated, weakened, and denied political expression to regroup and reassert themselves, and the mobilizations may exacerbate regime crises and unleash or accelerate the process of redemocratization. The latter two processes do not always coincide, and they may involve contradictory dynamics.

Third, social mobilizations may also assume a diversity of meanings and functions under military regimes. One type of mobilization is expressive and symbolic, with a strong ethical and emotional component.

Above all else, this type of mobilization affirms or defends an identity and community that has been threatened, and it involves rebellion for its own sake. Fasts and hunger strikes in defense of the right to live by families whose kin have "disappeared" under the military exemplify this type of mobilization. The other types of mobilizations are more instrumental and oriented toward specific ends. One centers on mobilization as a means of strengthening organizational identity, autonomy, and legitimacy, as illustrated by organizational elections. Another is the classical mobilization in which protesters assert demands to improve their level of well-being. Land seizures and strikes for higher wages exemplify this type. Still another type of mobilization is explicitly political and aimed directly at the termination and replacement of authoritarian regimes. The Brazilian movement for "direct elections" is illustrative of this type of mobilization.

The analytically distinguishable mobilizations in practice often exist in combination. The mixes, however, vary. One of the basic problems for an opposition movement is to combine the different types of mobilizations without having them identified with the particularistic concerns of any one participating group (or class). Another problem is to avoid excessive politicization, which may make mobilizations unappealing to many.

Finally, the political significance of the mobilizations depends on the effect they have on the state. This significance is not inherently determined either by the level or the type of mobilization. Social mobilizations do not in themselves bring about transitions from authoritarian to democratic rule. They can play a critical role in such a transition, but they are not *the* source of change. For the transition to be completed, the governing bloc must decompose. Some negotiation between power holders and opposition must occur, and normally some external mediation must effectively press for such negotiation. For such reasons, the opposition strategy must take the "state effect" of mobilizations into account. If it does not, the effect is likely to be determined by power holders. The relationship between civilian mobilizations and political negotiation is, therefore, of crucial significance (see Garretón 1986d).

SOCIAL MOBILIZATIONS AND CHANGING STATE/SOCIETAL RELATIONS IN CHILE BEFORE 1973

From the 1930s on, three processes occurred concomitantly in Chile. There was a process of political democratization involving progressive citizen participation, with a party system including the complete spectrum from the right to the left. Chile also experienced social democratization: the middle classes and, to a lesser extent, organized labor (workers in the so-called formal sector) were progressively extended social welfare benefits. The state played a crucial role in the extension of social

benefits. Until the 1960s the peasants and urban *marginales* (impoverished workers in the "informal sector" living in *poblaciones,* or shantytowns) were excluded from social welfare benefits. During the 1960s,
though, peasants were mobilized for an agrarian reform and were unionized by the state and political parties, while the urban *marginales* mobilized through state-linked local organizations for goods and services. In
the post–World War II period Chile also experienced capitalist import-
substitution industrialization, with a strong state presence in the economy. The country industrialized, while remaining dependent on copper
for trade revenue. Foreign capital dominated the copper industry (see
Garretón 1983 and 1986; Moulián 1983; Pinto 1971; Loveman 1979).

The three processes implied a gradual and institutionalized, but con-
flictual, basis for the integration of socioeconomic groups into the body
politic and highly politicized struggles for state benefits. While the political parties, including those on the left, accepted the political system,
their involvement in social and economic struggles made for an exceptionally politicized society. This gave a distinctive mark to the Chilean
integration process: a strong emphasis on social organization, with political party ties, and high value placed on demanding benefits of the state.
It also resulted in legal and quasi-legal mobilizations, with the state the
focus of the collective action.

In the 1960s the dynamics of dependent capitalist development came
into conflict with the process of democratization. The political parties
radicalized and the party system became highly polarized. The traditional right unified in the National Party, with increasingly authoritarian
and nationalistic tendencies. The center consolidated in the Christian
Democratic Party, which had a strong messianic and transformative content. The Christian Democrats believed that they were the only party
capable of ruling and promoting social change, and they accordingly
resisted political alliances. Their vision of politics was exceedingly ideological and nonpragmatic. Meanwhile, the two major parties of the left—
the Socialists and the Communists—formed an alliance, together with
some groups that splintered off from the center; they pressed for radical
socialist changes within the confines of democracy. The ideological climate was radicalized leftward by the Cuban revolution.

In 1964 President Eduardo Frei, a Christian Democrat, initiated a
process of capitalist modernization and democratization that incorporated previously excluded peasants and urban *marginales.*[1] His government promulgated an agrarian reform and partially nationalized the
copper industry. Midway through his government, though, the reform
process bogged down. The state failed to respond adequately to the demands of the highly politicized civilian population. There were wide-

1. On the Frei period, see Moulián 1983; Stallings 1978; Molina 1972; Loveman 1979.

spread illegal strikes and urban land seizures, which the government sometimes severely repressed. The increasing isolation of the Christian Democrats from both the right and the left, in a social and ideological context that legitimated social change, helped the left win the 1970 election.

Salvador Allende's government of the left (Unidad Popular) tried to implement reforms that benefited the "popular" sectors at the expense both of foreign capital and large-scale Chilean capital. From the inception of his administration, the vast "popular" sectors, the government, and the parties of the left were, as a consequence, in conflict with the right and the upper classes. The confrontations drove the center, and, most important, the middle classes into militant opposition to the Allende government. Little by little, the middle and upper classes abandoned institutional politics, culminating in their support of a coup d'état. Massive mobilizations ensued among all groups, and the society became progressively polarized politically. Although Allende's Unidad Popular received 44 percent of the vote in the March 1973 parliamentary elections, once the middle sectors and the Christian Democrats sided with the right, the government was left isolated. Allende's problems were further compounded by the U.S. government's refusal to continue to extend much-needed economic aid and by its strategy of so-called political destabilization. In the context of polarization and deinstitutionalization, the armed forces, under the leadership of General Pinochet, usurped power, on 11 September 1973. They did so under the pretext of "restoring the broken institutional system."[2]

The military regime had to address the crisis of Chilean capitalism as well as the highly politicized Unidad Popular, and the socioeconomic sectors it represented. It promoted a technocratic free-market economic restructuring, relying on the "Chicago boys," close associates of Milton Friedman. It accordingly retracted state programs that favored the "popular" sectors. Politically, it relied heavily on repression and confronted the church, which denounced human rights violations and protected political victims. It eliminated all channels of collective political expression. The parties of the left were outlawed, and the activities of other parties were highly restricted as well. Power, including within the armed forces, was personalized in the hands of Pinochet. However, Pinochet gradually began a process of political institutionalization, resulting in a new constitution in 1980. The constitution allows for a transition from the military dictatorship to an authoritarian regime, under the presidency of General Pinochet until 1989. The period until 1989 is officially called a period of "transition," during which time the governing

2. On the Allende period and the military coup, see Valenzuela 1978; Garretón and Moulián 1983; Garcés 1976; Prats 1985.

junta has legislative power and no political activity is permitted. In 1989 the junta must propose one name for the next presidential period, which extends until 1997; Pinochet is making all efforts to be the designated nominee. The candidate is to run in a single-candidate plebiscite. In 1989 the new constitution is to take full effect. The constitution lays the basis for a strong executive and a weak parliament; it excludes parties of the left from the political party system; and it gives the armed forces veto power. The stipulations of the document make constitutional revisions nearly impossible.

Beginning in 1981 the military's economic and political programs ran into difficulty. Many domestic businesses were hard hit once the laissez-faire economy made them exceptionally vulnerable to a global economic recession. The living standards of the middle classes plunged, while the livelihood of the "popular" sectors deteriorated even further than during the first years of Pinochet's rule. The regime's civilian bloc of support began to wither, in turn, to the point where the military was increasingly isolated politically. Meanwhile, "popular" expressions of protest and pre-coup political parties—which had never been inactive but were necessarily limited in their public actions—reasserted themselves. In 1983 massive political and social protests began. The discontented middle classes supported the demonstrations and other forms of mobilizations. The regime responded with repression, although it allowed for limited, informal channels of political articulation (*aperturas*). It enforced the institutionalization designated in the 1980 constitution, which was designed to assure authoritarian rule after 1989.

Although the opposition has become increasingly outspoken, it remains very fragmented. Various efforts to establish alliances among the reconstituted political parties have been short-lived, and they have failed to bring about a common strategy of transition. The social mobilizations described below, must be understood in this political and economic context.

PROTEST UNDER THE CHILEAN MILITARY REGIME, 1973–83

Until 1983 antiregime activity was rarely expressed through large mass mobilizations. When social mobilizations occurred, they addressed either government abuses or the specific concerns of individual socioeconomic sectors. The mobilizations included defensive protests against assassinations, detentions, torture, and "disappearances." These protests took the form of fasts, hunger strikes, and quick, limited public rallies.

When the populace mobilized around economic issues, concerns varied. In low-income neighborhoods, people organized for subsistence needs: they set up soup kitchens and their own employment agencies, and they pressed local authorities for land and housing. Workers and university students, in turn, pressed their own sets of claims. Workers pressed for higher wages and changes in labor legislation through slowdowns and other work disruptions. Students began to mobilize through cultural activities, and they held short rallies to protest high education fees, the presence of repressive agents in the universities, and, more generally, military intervention in academic life. There were also some mobilizations of a more explicitly political nature. There were rallies, for example, to celebrate the International Day of Labor (1 May) and to protest the 1980 plebiscite on the constitution proposed by the military.

The diverse mobilizations between 1973 and 1983 had certain features in common. First, they were isolated incidences, erratic, and generally brief in duration. The size, irregularity, and brevity of the demonstrations reflected people's fears of government reprisals. Second, the mobilizations were rarely directed at anyone in particular in the expectation that demands would be satisfied. Instead, they reflected the efforts of groups to assert themselves. When groups attempted to press specific claims and their efforts were repressed, the mobilizations ended (see Baño 1985). Third, many of these mobilizations occurred under the institutional protection of the Catholic church. This protective environment helped social organizations to reconstitute themselves gradually as autonomous entities. Fourth, some militants and activists associated with the political parties, human rights groups, and church organizations gave a certain degree of continuity to the mobilizations during this period. They operated somewhat autonomously of their respective institutions, and they were always more radicalized than rank-and-file members. This emergent intermediate political class, linked with groups in civil society, helped lay the groundwork for the massive 1983 protest.

THE CYCLE OF PROTESTS AND STRIKES SINCE 1983

The first so-called national protest occurred in May 1983. The Copper Workers' Confederation (CTC) had initially called for a national strike. However, a few days beforehand, it decided to call instead for a broadbased protest, inasmuch as important union locals refused to support the strike and the union felt it could capitalize on the growing discontent among the population at large. The CTC was well situated to lead such a mobilization because it is centered in a crucial sector of the Chilean economy. Since Chile is dependent on copper for foreign exchange earnings, the CTC's political importance has always been far greater than the size of its membership would suggest.

On the day that the CTC called for the national protest, there were strikes, high rates of absenteeism, work slowdowns, and demonstrations at work centers. At the universities, there were assemblies and demonstrations. Younger children stayed away from school. In the city center and on main thoroughfares drivers honked their horns and people staged brief demonstrations. In middle- and lower-class neighborhoods alike, residents boycotted stores; at night they turned out their lights and banged their pots and pans. The middle classes, who had used their kitchen utensils to express their opposition to Allende, now used them to symbolize their opposition to the very regime they had helped bring to power. Some shantytowns, in addition, erected barricades. Although the government had sought to ignore the protest, it responded with force once it became apparent that the mobilization had broad support and was politically threatening: two died, fifty were injured, and three hundred people were detained.[3]

Subsequent national protests were called almost monthly. As of July 1983, the mobilizations also began to involve cities other than Santiago. They varied in their success and the groups who joined in. More barricades were set up, and electrical blackouts became increasingly frequent. The government responded, in turn, with greater use of force. For example, Pinochet announced the presence of 18,000 soldiers in the streets of Santiago during the fourth protest in August 1983. A large number of the troops were sent into low-income neighborhoods, and hundreds of protesters were either detained or sent into internal exile.

The opposition movement during this period did not merely involve the monthly protests. There were also political rallies, marches, and campaigns for human rights and "the right to live."

The eleventh protest, in October 1984, turned into a kind of general strike. The government responded by imposing a state of siege, which nearly ended the cycle of protests. While there were new calls for protests after the government lifted the state of siege half a year later, the mobilizations were smaller than in 1983 and generally involved only limited sectors of the opposition. However, at the end of 1985 a big mass rally was convoked by the Democratic Alliance (Alianza Democrática), a political bloc including the Christian Democrats, some small parties of the right, a socialist party, and other socialist groups. The Popular Democratic Movement, which included the other socialist party, the Communist Party, the Left Revolutionary Movement (MIR), and other groups of the left, also supported the rally.

In autumn 1986 steps were taken to strengthen the protest movement under the aegis of a newly formed group with ties to the political parties, the Civic Assembly (Asamblea de la Civilidad). The new group organized a politically effective two-day national strike. The regime responded, as in the past, with repression. This time, though, the burning of two youths gained international as well as national attention. Nonetheless,

3. For general descriptions and analyses of the Protest cycles, see de la Maza and Garcés 1985; Martínez 1986; Campero 1986; Agurto, Canales, and de la Maza 1985.

the detention of the protest leaders, division within the opposition over the role such protests should assume as a political strategy, the discovery of arsenals among pro-insurrectional groups, and the imposition once again of a state of siege following an attempted assassination of Pinochet, undermined the protest movement.

What accounts for the emergence of the protest movement on the one hand and for its inability to sustain itself on the other? The surprising success of the initial protest can be traced to three factors: its multiclass base, the involvement of Chile's most powerful union, and stress on broadly based defiance rather than more limited work-based strikes. Since the Pinochet regime is more reluctant to use force against the middle classes than against the working and lower classes, middle-class participation reduced fears that the protest would end in a massacre. The 1983 protest marked the first time in decades that the middle and "popular" classes had allied themselves; under Allende, in particular, they militantly opposed one another. The involvement of the Copper Workers' Confederation, in turn, was important, not only because the union is very influential, but also because it includes representatives of diverse opposition parties. For all these reasons it could mobilize large-scale support, which further minimized participants' fear of government reprisal (see Martínez 1986). The call for a mass protest, rather than for more limited and traditional expressions of defiance (such as strikes), moreover, created a feeling of autonomy among participants.

The three elements were not equally present in the subsequent protests. The CTC, for example, later assumed a less activist role, because the government severely repressed it for involvement in the first protest. A broader-based organization, the National Workers' Command, instead sought to mobilize organized labor. While it incorporated unions in diverse economic sectors, including peasants, salaried white collar employees, and small businessmen, and workers in both the state and private sectors, unions at the time lacked their former ability to mobilize the rank and file. Moreover, the National Workers' Command had to share leadership of the opposition movement with political parties, which became increasingly influential in subsequent mobilizations. As the political parties gained force, massive mobilizations could only occur when convoked by the entire spectrum of parties. The parties, meanwhile, came to assign different meanings to the social mobilizations. The more centrist parties increasingly viewed the protests as a means of forcing the armed forces to negotiate democratization. The left parties, by contrast, believed that mobilizations in themselves could destabilize the regime to the point where it would collapse. In addition, groups within the opposition movement were not equally committed to militant mobilizations, and their styles of activism differed. As the party blocs distanced themselves from one another, it became more difficult to mobilize support for the protests.

The formation of the Asamblea de la Civilidad was an effort to overcome differences within the opposition movement. Though dominated by middle-class groups, the Asamblea included representatives of a wide variety of socioeconomic groups and political parties, among them the National Workers' Command, groups of *pobladores* and university students, professional organizations, truckdrivers, women's associations, human rights organizations, and the Study Group for an Alternative Constitution.

Most of the organizations in the Asamblea were committed to pluralism. Moreover, all the opposition parties participated in the Asamblea, although the Christian Democrats dominated it. With such a broad base, there was support for a two-day protest in July 1986. But the protest movement had undergone change between 1983 and 1986. The middle class, for one, became increasingly reluctant to support mobilizations. The combination of government repression, some concessions to middle-class *gremios* (unions), and expectations that the government would negotiate with the opposition made the middle class increasingly disinclined to oppose the regime openly. Labor remained more favorably predisposed toward the protests, but government repression undermined its capacity to mobilize. As a consequence, over time, students and, especially, young urban *pobladores* came to constitute the core of the protest movement. They tended to express themselves more aggressively than had the middle and organized working classes, and they were distrustful of political negotiation and coordination. Shantytown dwellers were also radicalized by groups such as the Frente Patriótico Manuel Rodríguez and Milicias Rodriguistas (both linked to the Communist Party) and the MIR, which began to organize in their neighborhoods. These groups pressed for violent confrontation and insurrection. They viewed the protests as heroic moments of confrontation and liberation, but their tactics served to isolate them from the rest of society.

The limits of the protests notwithstanding, their impact has been substantial. They enlarged the field of collective action in a highly repressive environment. As a result of the mobilizations, people became less fearful of the military, and the relationship between civil society and the state changed. Moreover, the protests compelled the military to make some economic concessions, above all to the middle classes in order to coopt them. Pressures from civil society forced the government to modify certain labor practices and aspects of its laissez-faire economic model. The protests resulted in some political changes as well. After the fourth protest the regime began to combine a political logic with its military strategy. The government appointed an old politician of the right as minister of the interior. The new minister initiated a partial "opening" (*apertura*) to mobilize civilian support for the regime and to institutionalize its rule, but he concomitantly limited the political options of the opposition. Although this political "project" did not have its intended effect, the government granted certain political concessions, for example, allowing some exiles to return and some opposition journals to be published.

From the viewpoint of the opposition, the protests allowed for the public appearance and revitalization of political parties and the grouping of parties into larger political blocs (such as the Democratic Alliance and the Popular Democratic Movement). However, once the parties assumed leadership of the protests, differences in goals and strategies adversely affected the fate of the mobilizations. None of the parties provided a basis for consensus among the opposition. Although all the parties attached considerable importance to the mobilizations, none offered a coherent opposition strategy to put an end to the military regime. In the absence of any consensus among the party-dominated opposition, such general goals as "Democracy Now" helped the civilian population overcome their fears and isolation. But such general goals did not provide a basis for transforming the mobilization of the civilian population into a more stable political force.

Thus, the mass mobilizations since 1983 changed the face of the society. They allowed people to overcome fear. They revealed the military's failure to dissolve collective identities and inhibit collective action, and they reintroduced political "space" for civil society. They also forced some concessions from the regime. However, they have failed, to date, to bring about the widely desired transition to democracy.

SECTORAL MOBILIZATIONS AND THEIR LIMITS

A full understanding of the dynamics of the protest movement requires a more detailed analysis of the role of specific socioeconomic sectors (see Campero 1986). The leadership of organized labor (see Campero and Valenzuela 1984; Barrera 1986; Ruiz-Tagle 1985) played a central role in the convocation of the protest movement. However, rank-and-file workers did not play a very forceful role in the mobilizations. Their relatively weak presence is rooted in the military regime's impact on the labor movement. The economic crisis brought about by the laissez-faire economy of the "Chicago boys" cost many workers their jobs, and the military drastically restricted labor's capacity to organize and defend its own interests. The unionized labor force declined by 54 percent between 1972 and 1981, leaving only about 9 percent of the labor force unionized after a decade of military rule (Ruiz-Tagle 1985). No doubt many of the workers who were fortunate enough to hold on to their jobs feared that they might be fired if they defied the government. Political divisions at the union leadership level also had the effect, if not the intent, of undercutting labor's capacity to organize. Labor leadership was divided even on whether to organize into a single labor confederation. The Democratic Workers' Central associated with the Christian Democrats advocated independent, ideologically distinct *centrales* (national labor associations), while the National Union Coordinating Organization associated with the left (but including the more progressive sectors of the Christian Democrats) sought a unitary labor organization. Such division among the labor leadership affected labor relations at the base level.

The critical role that the urban *pobladores* came to assume has had great bearing on the dynamics and impact of the protest movement. The core group to mobilize tended to be young *pobladores*, perhaps the sector most adversely affected by government repression and educational, employment, and housing policies. The mobilizations gave the socially and economically marginalized poor a sense of participation and belonging and affirmed their individual and social identities. The protests were of expressive and symbolic significance to the young *pobladores*, whose style was aggressive and, on occasion, violent. They set up barricades, burned tires, and engaged in rock throwing. Their style, however, served to isolate them from other socioeconomic groups.

As important as their participation came to be to the protest movement, most *pobladores* mobilized for specific demands, such as land and housing. Their participation tended to be short-term, whether or not their demands were satisfied, and their demands did not provide a base on which the protests could build. Moreover, the sector is so large that efforts to unify it have failed. The political parties added to the problem of mobilizing shantytown dwellers. The Christian Democrats, the Christian left, the Communist Party, and the MIR all tried to build up their own political bases in low-income neighborhoods; in so doing they created divisions among the poor. The competing activity of the political parties contributed to the failure of such efforts as that of the Unitary Congress of Urban Pobladores to organize the shantytown dwellers collectively in 1986. The *pobladores* therefore remain without a broad-based organization of their own through which their activities are coordinated and their interests collectively articulated.

Within the middle class, at least three sectors must be distinguished:

(1) *Small and medium-sized businesses, including independent truck drivers, and petit bourgeois shopowners.* This sector was hard-hit by the "Chicago" economic model. Yet it has tended to support mobilizations, through individual *gremios*, only when the groups felt they could thereby negotiate concessions for themselves from the regime. They have never supported sustained antiregime activity, and coordinated their efforts with other socioeconomic sectors (see Campero 1984).

(2) *Professional groups.* Professional *gremios* have mobilized in defense of their own interests. They have accordingly organized against regime legislation constricting professional association activities and against repression that their membership has suffered. They have pressed for association rights, including the right to select their own association leadership; in so doing they have strengthened their organizations and

their autonomy from the state on the one hand, and politicized their groups on the other. Candidates linked to the opposition movement have won *gremio* elections in nearly all associations affiliated with the Federation of Professional Associations. The impact of the opposition has not, however, been confined to the internal affairs of the *gremios*. Professional associations have, for example, been active in the Civic Assembly, through which they have issued declarations and called rallies in opposition to specific military legislation or abuses.

(3) *University students.* Student federations most approximate a sustained social movement through which specific interests of the group's social base are linked with more general goals of democratization (see Valenzuela and Silva 1985; Agurto, Canales, and de la Maza 1985). In recent years the student federations associated with anti-Pinochet political parties have successfully consolidated in all the universities. In 1985, for example, twenty-two of the twenty-four student federations had as their heads democratically elected opposition leaders. Within the university system the student groups have pressed for reduced tuition fees, as well as for more radical changes, such as a revision of the system of rectorship appointments. Student activities have not, however, been confined to the universities. Students have played an important role in the protests. They have seized campuses, and in so doing brought university activity to a halt, and they have organized street meetings. Linkages with national political parties have, however, had the same adverse effect on students as on other mobilized sectors: they have divided the student movement and consequently weakened it. For example, whereas the first democratic university elections under Pinochet, in 1984 and 1985, centered around alignments with the government or the opposition, in 1986 the opposition split. Electoral lists represented the diverse national political blocs. Tactics as well as party loyalties divide students. The nonpoliticized mass of students oppose disruptive activity. Also, many academic faculty and researchers oppose disruption of their work. In creating the sense that the university is ungovernable, student activists may alienate academic faculty and researchers, whose support is necessary for any substantial university change.

Women have also emerged as a distinctive social force in the opposition movement, and they have mobilized differently than the other social and economic groups (see Kirkwood 1986; Meza 1986). They have become active participants in "popular" organizations and the protests, although surveys show many of them still to be conservative in their visions and opinions. The failure of the "Chicago" economic model has also strengthened the presence of women in the informal sector. As men have lost their jobs or experienced a decline in their earning power, many women have been forced to take on low-paid jobs.

Women's mobilization strategy has been particularly effective. They have mobilized more independently of political parties than have other social sectors. They have stressed unity over partisan fragmentation. A good example is the Mujeres por la Vida (Women for Life) movement.

In December 1983 this group convoked the most unified massive protest against the regime. The group involved women of different socioeconomic classes and diverse opposition parties. Whether women's demands and participation will be marginalized in the future and whether they will be able to resist partisan ties remains, of course, to be seen.

In sum, different groups have mobilized separately for their own sets of concerns and collectively in the protests. Participation in the protests has been impressive, but how widespread is support for the anti-regime activity? Public opinion surveys indicate that most Chileans support peaceful defiance that calls for negotiations to end the military regime. However, most Chileans reject violent and disruptive activity (see FLACSO 1986; Huneuus 1987). In essence, there is widespread approval of strikes, petitioning of authorities, marches, and *caceroleos* (opposition shown by banging pots and pans at designated times). There is little support, by contrast, for bombings, blackouts, land seizures, and traffic blockages.

CONCLUSIONS

The military has tried to eliminate collective identities, collective organization, and collective action, but has failed, although it has successfully reduced, weakened, and atomized the collective capacities of groups. The government has restricted the impact of protests through the use of force, but the defiance won some concessions for many groups. Civil society has reasserted itself to the point where it has room to organize and express itself. The recomposition of civil society constitutes what I have called the invisible transition to democracy.

This invisible transition has largely involved groups that were active and politicized prior to the coup. The principal new social forces to have emerged are women, youth, and social, cultural, and religious groups born in direct response to subsistence needs and human rights violations and other government abuses.

The limits of the protest movement notwithstanding, some important lessons can be extrapolated from the experience of the Chilean opposition movement. First, the structural and institutional transformations introduced by the military reduced, weakened, and atomized the organizational "space" of economic and social groups. Under the Brazilian military regime (see chapter 9), by contrast, there was much more room for organization (albeit of a corporatist nature). The contraction of the formal sector and rising unemployment, in particular, undermined the capacity of previously organized groups to mobilize against the regime in Chile. The percentage of wage earners in the economically active population declined from 53 percent in 1971 to 45 percent in 1980 and 38 percent in 1982 (Martínez and Tironi 1985), and the percentage of the economically active population who were either unemployed or employed in jobs paying less than the minimum wage, and offering no stable employment or social security, rose from 14 percent in 1971 to 25 percent in 1980 and 36 percent in 1982. The younger generation and women were especially hard hit by the economic contraction. The percentage of the economically active young population (15–24 years old) in the formal sector dropped from 80 percent in 1971 to 61 percent in 1980 and 49 percent in 1982, while the percentage of economically active women in the formal sector dropped from 68 percent in 1971 to 60 percent in 1980 and 50 percent in 1982 (Martínez and Tironi 1985). Thus, the labor force has become more atomized and disarticulated.

Second, the economic dislocations shifted the bases of mobilization somewhat from the "classes" to the "masses": that is, from the more organized and formal sectors of society to the more amorphous or marginalized ones. Women and youth, for example, who have been so adversely affected by the military regime's economic policies, have become active in the opposition movement; however, they have mobilized through neighborhood and women's groups, not through work-based groups, which historically have been the loci of economic struggles in Chile.

Third, because the society has become so fragmented, each sector has assigned its own meaning to mobilizations and promoted its own forms of mobilizations, at times in conflict with other sectors. The call for a generic goal with broad appeal such as "Democracy Now" was an effort to overcome fragmentation. However, when the goal was not attained, the opposition movement was debilitated. Moreover, the repressive environment has encouraged highly expressive and emotional mobilizations, not instrumental mobilizations designed to attain specific and negotiable demands.

Military rule has taken its toll on society. It has modified relations between the state, the political party system, and social movements (see Garretón 1983 and 1986a). Even if the military regime has been unable to create the political system it intended, it has disarticulated the previous system. The political forces that have surfaced under the military maintain some continuity with the past, but they have great difficulty in political negotiations. The newly politicized "popular" sectors and emerging social forces are poorly represented. While some activists and militants have gained preeminence, they remain isolated from both the more established party leadership and the social bases of the "popular" organizations. Moreover, ideological and organizational differences among the "political class" make the formation of a strong, unified opposition movement that transcends the particularistic concerns of diverse social and economic groups difficult.

Finally, the Chilean experience highlights both the strengths and the weaknesses of mobilization as a strategy for bringing about a transition from dictatorship to democracy. Social mobilization is undoubtedly indispensable for such a transition. However, in the absence of a consensual and coherent political strategy for change, ideological and expressive differences fragment groups similarly committed to democracy, and in so doing limit the impact of mobilization as *the* political strategy. Mobilization must be combined with other political processes, such as negotiation and regime decomposition, before redemocratization is likely. Social mobilizations by themselves help to reconstitute civil society and they help to transform military regimes. They can "deepen" the "invisible transition" and result in some political concessions. But in themselves they will not bring about the array of institutional changes necessary for the restoration of full democracy. Political direction and coordination are also essential.

REFERENCES

Agurto, Irene, Manuel Canales, and Gonzalo de la Maza, eds.
   1985   *Juventud chilena: Razones y subversiones.* Santiago: ECO [Educación y Comunicación]–FOLICO [Formación de Líderes Cristianos Obreros]–SEPADE [Servicio Evangélico para el Desarrollo].

Baño, Rodrigo
   1985   *Lo social y lo político.* Santiago: FLACSO [Facultad Latinoamericana de Ciencias Sociales].

Barrera, Manuel
   1986   *La demanda democrática de los trabajadores.* Santiago: CES [Centro de Estudios Sociales].

Campero, Guillermo
   1984   *El sindicalismo internacional y la redemocratización de Chile.* Santiago: CED [Centro de Estudios del Desarrollo].

Campero, Guillermo, ed.
   1986   *Los movimientos sociales en Chile y la lucha democrática.* Santiago: ILET [Instituto Latinoamericano de Estudios Transnacionales]–CLACSO [Consejo Latinoamericano de Ciencias Sociales].

Campero, Guillermo, and José Antonio Valenzuela
   1984   *El movimiento sindical en el régimen militar chileno.* Santiago: ILET [Instituto Latinoamericano de Estudios Transnacionales].

Chateau, Jorge, et al.
   1987   *Espacio y poder: Los pobladores.* Santiago: FLACSO.

Collier, David, ed.
   1979   *The New Authoritarianism in Latin America.* Princeton, N.J.: Princeton University Press.

De la Maza, Gonzalo, and Mario Garcés
   1985   *La explosión de las mayorías: Protesta nacional, 1983–1984.* Santiago: ECO.

Facultad Latinoamericana de Ciencias Sociales
   1986   "Encuesta sobre la realidad socio-política chilena: Resultados preliminares." Documento de Trabajo no. 81 (May). Santiago: FLACSO.

Foxley, Alejandro
    1983   *Latin American Experiments in Neo-Conservative Economics.* Berkeley and Los Angeles: University of California Press.
Fruhling, Hugo
    1984   "Repressive Policies and Legal Dissent in Authoritarian Regimes: Chile, 1973–1981." *International Journal of the Sociology of Law,* no. 12.
Garcés, Joan
    1976   *Allende y la experiencia chilena.* Barcelona: Ariel.
Garretón M., Manuel Antonio
    1983   *El proceso político chileno.* Santiago: FLACSO.
    1984   *Dictaduras y democratización.* Santiago: FLACSO.
    1985   *Escenarios e itinerarios para la transición.* Cuadernos ESIN 4. Santiago: Instituto para el Nuevo Chile.
    1986a   "Chile: In Search of Lost Democracy." In *Latin American Political Economy: Financial Crisis and Political Change,* edited by Jonathan Hartlyn and Samuel Morley, pp. 197–216. Boulder, Colo.: Westview Press.
    1986b   "The Failure of Dictatorships in the Southern Cone." *TELOS,* no. 68 (Summer):71–78.
    1986c   "The Political Evolution of the Chilean Military Regime and Problems in the Transition to Democracy." In *Transitions from Authoritarian Rule: Prospects for Democracy,* edited by Guillermo O'Donnell, Philippe Schmitter, and Laurence Whitehead, pp. 95–122. Baltimore: Johns Hopkins University Press.
    1986d   "Seis tesis sobre democratización en Chile." *Convergencia,* no. 10 (December):15–20.
    1986e   "Transición a la democracia en Chile: Avances, obstáculos y dilemas." *Mensaje* 35 (January–February):29–32.
    1987   "Balance y perspectivas de la transición a la democracia en Chile." *Análisis,* no. 158 (20–26 January):34–37.
Garretón M., Manuel Antonio, and Tomás Moulián
    1983   *La unidad popular y el conflicto político en Chile.* Santiago: Ediciones Minga.
Huneeus, C.
    1987   *Cambios en la opinión pública: Una aproximación al estudio de la cultura política en Chile.* Santiago: CERC [Centro de Estudios de la Realidad Contemporánea], Academia de Humanismo Cristiano.
Kirkwood, J.
    1986   *Ser política en Chile: Las feministas y los partidos.* Santiago: FLACSO.
Loveman, Brian
    1979   *Chile: The Legacy of Hispanic Capitalism.* Oxford: Oxford University Press.
Martínez, Javier
    1986   "Miedo al estado, miedo a la sociedad." *Proposiciones,* no. 12 (October–December 1986):34–42.
Martínez, Javier, and Eugenio Tironi
    1985   *Las clases sociales en Chile: Cambio y estratificación, 1970–1980.* Santiago: SUR.

Meza, M. A., ed.
1986   *La otra mitad de Chile.* Santiago: Ediciones CESOC, Instituto para el Nuevo Chile.
Molina, Sergio
1972   *El proceso de cambio en Chile: La experiencia 1965–1970.* Santiago: Editorial Universitaria.
Moulián, Tomás
1983   *Democracia y Socialismo en Chile.* Santiago, FLACSO.
O'Donnell, Guillermo, and Philippe Schmitter
1986   "Tentative Conclusions about Uncertain Democracies." In *Transitions from Authoritarian Rule: Prospects for Democracy,* edited by Guillermo O'Donnell, Philippe Schmitter, and Laurence Whitehead, part 4. Baltimore: Johns Hopkins University Press.
Pinto, Aníbal
1971   *Tres ensayos sobre Chile y América Latina.* Buenos Aires: Ediciones Solar.
Prats, Carlos
1985   *Memorias de un soldado.* Santiago: Pehuén.
Rodríguez, Alfredo
1983   *Por una ciudad democrática.* Santiago: SUR.
Ruiz-Tagle, Jaime
1985   *El sindicalismo chileno despues del plan laboral.* Santiago: PET [Programa de Economía del Trabajo].
Stallings, Barbara
1978   *Class Conflict and Economic Development in Chile, 1958–1973.* Stanford, Calif.: Stanford University Press.
Touraine, Alain
1978   *La Voix et le regard.* Paris: Seuil.
1984   "Les Mouvements sociaux: Objet particulier ou problème central de l'analyse sociologique." *Revue Française de Sociologie* 25.
1987   *Actores sociales y sistemas políticos en América Latina.* Santiago: PREALC [Programa Regional del Empleo para América Latina y el Caribe]–OIT [Organización Internacional del Trabajo].
Valenzuela, Arturo
1978   *The Breakdown of Democratic Regimes: Chile.* Baltimore: Johns Hopkins University Press.
Valenzuela, Arturo, and Samuel Valenzuela, eds.
1985   *Military Rule in Chile: Dictatorship and Opposition.* Baltimore: Johns Hopkins University Press.
Valenzuela, Esteban, and Eduardo Silva
1985   "El movimiento estudiantil: Un actor social relevante." *Mensaje* 34 (December): 508–10.

CHAPTER NINE

Interclass Alliances in the Opposition to the Military in Brazil: Consequences for the Transition Period

Maria Helena Moreira Alves

The movements of opposition to the military governments in Brazil after the 1964 coup d'état involved interclass alliances. At each particular point the hegemonic control of the overall alliance was held by elite groups. Working-class interests were systematically bypassed and laid aside in the interest of maintaining unity on the more important issue of defeating the military governments.

There are some important historical preconditions to the development of an opposition movement characterized by periodic alliances between social classes. Unlike in Chile, Argentina, and Uruguay, working-class movements in Brazil, prior to the military takeover of 1964, lacked a strongly rooted autonomous base of organization. The trade union movement, for example, was tied directly to the state through a legal mechanism of control that provided for a corporative institutional framework. The legislation that controlled trade unions was passed in 1944. Therefore, during the entire populist period of democratic governments, the working class was prevented from developing an autonomous organization. The peasant leagues in the northeast of Brazil were perhaps the only major example of a serious attempt to organize independently of state control prior to 1964, when the military seized power. As a result of the lack of autonomous organization, working-class movements tended to become vehicles of political support for populist governments, rather than institutional conduits for working-class pressure. Hence, relations between social movements and the state during the populist period preceding the 1964 coup were characterized by negotiations "from above" with little effective effort on the part of working-class leadership to develop an independent base of operation.

During the populist period the process of industrialization in Brazil was based on import-substitution. The growth of national industry during this period also allowed for a degree of political flexibility, so that working-class pressures could be accommodated to a degree. This economic model of development reached a bottleneck by the end of the fifties. In spite of their institutional ties to the state, working-class movements began to increase pressure for structural economic reforms. At the same time, the continuation of the capital accumulation process required the development of state structures capable of ensuring a high rate of exploitation. An economic and political crisis ensued, paving the way for the military takeover of 1964 (Dreyfus 1980).[1]

Even though the national bourgeoisie fully supported the military takeover of state power, contradictory economic interests soon began to foment dissatisfaction. The economic model pursued by the military became increasingly beneficial to multinational corporations. A system of tax incentives to attract foreign capital facilitated multinational takeovers of nationally owned companies. It became apparent in time that the interests of different sectors of the bourgeoisie conflicted. Those sectors of the national bourgeoisie less intrinsically tied to foreign capital began to develop a political opposition to the military government based on a nationalist platform. This was particularly true after the period of the "economic miracle," when the overall domination of foreign capital in key sectors of the economy became apparent. In essence, the interests of the national bourgeoisie demanded a greater share of political influence in economic decisions.

During the same historical period, from 1964 to 1974, the working class suffered tremendous repression, with the arrest and/or exile of hundreds of leaders of the "popular" sectors. The continuous military takeover of trade unions hampered the reorganization of a strong labor movement. After 1974, however, albeit debilitated, workers began to develop alternative forms of organization clandestinely within the trade unions and inside the plants. The working class organized not only in the traditional manner, through trade unions, but increasingly also through new community-oriented organizational strategies. By 1978 it became apparent that a new kind of working-class movement was emerging with ties to other classes opposed to military governance.

What were the historical conditions that allowed for the formation of interclass alliances in the opposition to the military governments? Which political issues provided the necessary rallying point for the building of such alliances? What have the political consequences of this history of interclass alliances in the opposition been for the transition to democracy in Brazil?

In this chapter I examine the development of interclass alliances in

---

1. An analysis of the role of the associated dependent sector of the national bourgeoisie in the conspiracy to overthrow the government of Goulart may be found in Dreyfus 1980.

order to analyze, within a historical perspective, the consequences for political and economic policy in the present government of transition to democracy.

THE CHANGING ROLE OF THE STATE

When the civil-military coalition took power in 1964, there was an explicit design to institutionalize a new state. The structures determining the formation of the national security state in Brazil were, however, set up in time through a constant dialectical interplay between the state and opposition forces (Moreira Alves 1986). A dynamic relationship was established whereby the tactical and strategic advances of the opposition led the state to modify specific mechanisms of social control in an attempt to curb opposing forces. The modifications in turn prompted new groups to counter the power of the national security state. Hence, a dialectical relation was established between the regime and its opponents, whereby each modified the other.

A primary goal of the civil-military coalition in power was to lay the structural roots of a state capable of enforcing a particular model of economic development. The model of economic development was formed by a tripartite association of state capital, local private capital, and foreign private capital (Evans 1979). The military rulers accepted capitalist development, though, unlike their Chilean counterparts, they did not believe in laissez-faire capitalism. Their national security doctrine allowed for state regulation and investment in the process of capital accumulation. They encouraged foreign investment by using political means to minimize labor troubles and allow large profits. The economic model of rapid capitalist accumulation with high profit returns required significant state input in the shape of infrastructural investments and control of social dissent to regulate labor disputes.

To assure the success of the economic model, specific legislation and regulations were introduced (executive-initiated decree-laws and institutional acts). One of the first new regulations established a policy whereby salaries would no longer be determined by collective bargaining between employees and their employers but would be decreed by the state, at first once a year and later, after 1979, twice a year, according to a predetermined formula of indexing tied to rates of inflation. The salary legislation, collectively known during the period of military rule as the "belt-tightening laws," greatly reduced the purchasing power of workers and, at the same time, promoted a drastic concentration of income.

Incentives to foreign investment were established by a generous legislation of repatriation of profits and tax deductions for investment in areas considered of developmental priority. The profit-rate of invested capital would also be guaranteed by an ambitious program of infrastructural improvements, too costly for private capital, which was almost exclusively shouldered by state investment. Dams, roads, highways, electrical facilities, airports, ports, and waterway systems were built by the state—and financed by and large by foreign bank loans—so as to facilitate multinational corporation access to difficult mining regions of the Amazon basin and the installation of modern factories.

Opposition to the economic policies of the civil-military national security state was almost immediate. To control the level of dissent the foundations of a system of social and political control were laid.

The Serviço Nacional de Informações (SNI), or national information service, was established by Decree Law Number 4,341 of 13 June 1964. The SNI was to be responsible for the collection of information on citizens and for careful control of opposition organizations in civil society, in the state bureaucracy, and even in the military. A vast network of internal espionage, the SNI proved efficient in keeping tabs on pressure points that develop against the state. The work of the SNI was linked to direct coercion by military and paramilitary organizations controlled by local military police and the army. Repression was therefore not the work of the intelligence organization, but of interlocking police and military apparatuses (Moreira Alves 1983). A sophisticated system of high-tech political and social control was developed.

The legality of the system of control was established by a series of institutional acts and decree laws. Perhaps the most important of all of these was the Institutional Act Number 5 (AI-5), enacted in December 1968, which eliminated the right of habeas corpus, allowed direct censorship of the press, of correspondence, of the theater, cinema, literature, music, and all cultural activities, severely curtailed the prerogatives of the legislature, canceled the electoral mandates of elected representatives, and established military trials for crimes judged under the National Security Law. Together with the 1969 National Security Law, which defined opposition activities to be tried as crimes against the state, AI-5 formed the basis for far-reaching control of political dissent.

All other legislation of social control was designed to target specific sectors of opposition. For example, legislation was passed to control information flows, limit the autonomy of universities and other centers of learning, prevent free organizing of trade unions, prohibit strikes, suppress political parties, and control the legislative branches of government at federal, state, and municipal levels. The state elaborated such a vast body of legislation that it institutionalized a system of parallel legality.

Growing sectors of the population began to rebel against the repressive power of the national security state. In terms of class and political strategy, the composition of the opposition differed over the years as groups sought to deal with specific state measures.

THE HISTORY OF THE INTERCLASS ALLIANCE

By 1965 allegations of the torture of political prisoners were so numerous that the major daily newspapers began an educational campaign to denounce torture in prisons and army headquarters and demand an investigation of the conditions under which prisoners were being held. The impact of the coordinated press campaign eventually succeeded in forcing then President Castello Branco to send in a special investigator. Although the investigation itself was watered down, the continuation of press pressure, as well as the organized activity of human rights groups, eventually succeeded in temporarily halting the use of torture during the rest of Castello Branco's term. The torture of political prisoners had been the political issue that provided a rallying point for the building of a specific movement to pressure the state into lessening the repression.

At the end of 1965 Castello Branco signed Institutional Act Number 2. This abolished all hitherto existing political parties and allowed the development of only two legal parties, one to represent the government and the other for the opposition. After the enactment of Institutional Act Number 2 there was a renewed period of purges, trials, and cancellation of electoral mandates. Another law followed immediately to provide for the indirect election of state governors through the vote of state assemblies. The military believed that local state assemblies were more easily controlled and susceptible to pressure.

In reaction to this new wave of repressive measures, opposition groups sought to deepen their organizational structure by developing an interclass alliance composed of underground political parties, urban and rural trade unions, human rights groups, and other civic organizations.

This alliance between organized sectors of different classes was intended to strengthen the pressure upon the state and force liberalization measures. At that time, trade unions and peasant organizations felt the weight of the controls most heavily. They were often disbanded, broken up, or forcibly merged. Working-class organizations struggled to survive in spite of widespread fear among the rank and file. The military government, making use of article 5 of the Consolidation of Labor Laws, allowed the Ministry of Labor to intervene in trade unions, remove elected officials from office, cancel union elections, and control the budgets of unions and regulate their growth and territorial representation. The government dissolved opposition trade unions and created others that were more malleable. In addition, the effect of the wage/salary legislation was to weaken the position of unions by eliminating both the right to collective bargaining and the right to strike. Working-class sectors accepted an interclass alliance to diminish the level of violence.

The first efforts to institutionalize the national security state increased the political influence of the economic sectors of the bourgeoisie connected to international capitalism. Other segments of the upper classes resented the depth of the repression and the ferocity of the military's centralization of political power. Many who had originally supported the coup began to have second thoughts. They saw their parties abolished and their elected representatives removed from office, and many also felt personally threatened by the military's aggressivity against university and student movements. The repression of members of the working class and of university students had been particularly severe. It should be noted particularly that university students came largely from middle- and upper-class families, many of whom had originally supported the military coup in the belief that it would "save them from communism." The shock of now having members of their own families persecuted by the government slowly changed the perceptions of members of the upper classes and spurred them to engage in opposition activities.

Against this background, the first concrete attempt to build an inter-class alliance was formalized in a movement termed the Frente Ampla (Broad Front), which was responsible for the coordination of all opposition activities. The nature of the broad front alliance can be demonstrated by a brief look at the groups that formed it. First of all, two of the most important state governors—who had played a key role in the conspiracy to overthrow President João Goulart in 1964—now led the Frente Ampla: Magalhaesa Pinto, at the time governor of Minas Gerais, and Carlos Lacerda, who was an influential leader and former governor of the state of Guanabara. Lacerda had his political rights cancelled in order to keep him from ever being able to become a conservative civilian alternative president. Both of these conservative leaders were particularly critical of the measures that curtailed the power of the congress and limited the freedom of the judiciary. They began a movement called "Defense of Democracy," which exercised considerable influence among middle- and upper-class sectors. Lacerda and Magalhaesa Pinto were eventually joined by former President Juscelino Kubitschek, whose enduring influence had been shown in the victory of candidates supported by him in the local elections of 1965. Kubitschek, who was a senator at the time of the coup, also had his political rights cancelled for ten years so as to eliminate him as a possible presidential contender. In September 1967 the main leaders of the Frente Ampla moved one step further toward the establishment of an interclass alliance. During a visit to deposed President João Goulart—at the time exiled in Uruguay—a formal agreement was signed to establish the grounds of the alliance. The document, known as the Pact of Montevideo, became the official program of the Frente Ampla. The fact that it was possible to unite different ideological sectors in an interclass movement clearly defined the scope of the alliance. The Pacto de Montevideo was not a party program, but rather established the "fight for the return of democracy" as a common program. The state was identified as the prime enemy, and the main joint commitment was to representative forms of government. Partisan politics were avoided and ideological debates on the relations of production carefully ignored. The conflicting interests of the working class and the bourgeoisie were pushed aside in an effort to develop a political platform that could serve to unite different organizations.

Goulart brought to the movement significant labor and working-class support. Street demonstrations were organized, union meetings were held to educate the rank and file, and debates were arranged at universities. The press dedicated most available space to the coverage of activities connected to the Frente Ampla. In fact, the movement grew so rapidly that one observer of the time commented that "within one year in this country there will only be the Frente Ampla and the government."[2] The influence of the movement caused an explosion of activity in labor unions, in middle-class circles, and even among sectors of the military itself. The threat to the national security state was thus established in a matter of a few months. The state was obliged to resort to an act of overt coercion. Early in April 1968 the Frente Ampla was formally prohibited by a decree law of the government. Its records were seized, and the press was strictly censored and prevented from publishing any comments about the movement. The most militant members were persecuted and tried.

Throughout 1968, however, the interclass alliances established by the defunct Frente Ampla took root and developed into a mass movement of significant proportions. Marches, demonstrations, and rallies were organized by students, middle-class politicians, and workers. The streets of the major cities filled with dissenters. The largest demonstration of this period, in Rio de Janeiro, received the official support of the Catholic church through a widely publicized pastoral letter of the bishops. Two major strikes, in the industrial cities of Contagem (Minas Gerais) and Osasco (São Paulo), added a strong working-class presence to the opposition movement during 1968.

In the case of the Frente Ampla, the basis for the interclass alliance was avoidance of specific grievances so that conflicting groups could gather around a common banner of "democracy." In the demonstrations that followed in 1968, the movement tended to become more specifically tied to class interests and issues. Workers in Contagem and Osasco demanded the right to form free trade union organizations. They also organized to pressure for the repeal of the wage-control legislation. University students organized around their own specific grievances, particularly against the governmental controls of university life and the infringement of university freedom. Underground parties representing middle-

2. Comment by Congressman Oswaldo Lima Filho, at the time vice president of the opposition party, MDB (*Jornal do Brasil,* 12 October 1967), p. 4.

class sectors demanded the right to elect government representatives and sought to increase their influence in the government decision-making process.

The experience of the Frente Ampla had made members of the opposition aware that forceful pressure could best be exercised if organized sectors of different classes could temporarily ignore specific contradictions to concentrate upon the appeal of issues that were widely shared by all classes. This effort did not eliminate the contradictions of inherent interclass conflict, though a temporary degree of cohesion was obtained for the larger goal of lessening the power of the repressive forces of the state.

In 1968 the opposition achieved sufficient strength to challenge the state, but was not, however, really able to deeply affect the basis of its power. The ruling civil-military coalition could muster significant levels of coercive force to crush challenges. The state could also still count upon the largely passive support of many members of the middle and upper classes. Nonetheless, those in power realized that if the movement of political opposition was allowed to continue, this support base would perhaps be eroded. The national security state therefore utilized its still vast reserves of coercive power to strike a blow against the burgeoning interclass movement of opposition.

In December 1968, after months of congressional crisis, the military president signed Institutional Act Number 5. Congress was closed for almost a full year. During this period, the executive ruled by decree. In this way the National Security Law of 1969 was enacted. It broadly treated any form of organized opposition as a crime against the state. The repressive potential of the National Security Law, together with the extensive powers granted to the executive by clauses of AI-5, succeeded in silencing those engaged in political resistance for years.

At that point many opposition groups, including university students, turned to armed struggle in the belief that only violent rebellion could defeat the violence perpetrated by the state. The majority of the population, however, remained fearfully passive, silently awaiting an opportunity to manifest dissenting opinions in alternative ways. By 1973 it had become clear that the strategy of violent revolutionary resistance was failing. Isolated in their hideouts, with almost no public repercussion to their armed actions, the guerrilla groups slowly abandoned efforts to establish a focus of revolutionary activity in the countryside and increasingly turned to armed actions in the cities. These were confined to bank robberies to finance their organizational efforts and the kidnapping of foreign diplomats to force the state to exchange them for political prisoners. Although the population by and large did not disagree with the strategy of exchanging kidnapped persons for political prisoners, active support for the guerrillas was limited.

The armed actions provided a justification for the national security state to implement the most violent policy of repression in the history of the country. The press was silenced by severe censorship, and armed guards were posted in newspaper offices and at radio and television stations. The universities were either closed or repressed, with military invasions of premises, troop occupations, faculty purges, and intolerance of student dissent. Working-class neighborhoods, both in urban and rural areas, were devastated by coordinated military police blitzes that spread fear and confusion among the unarmed population. Torture was institutionalized as a method not just of eliciting information on the activities of guerrillas but especially for explicit intimidation of the population. The guerrilla groups eventually suffered tremendous losses and were crushed in the cities. The strategy of armed rebellion was largely defeated by 1972 or 1973.

The year 1973 was a turning point in the history of the Brazilian opposition. Guerrilla groups disappeared and other groups in opposition recognized that armed actions were allowing the state to justify a violent policy of repression against the population as a whole. Sectors of the opposition committed to nonviolent means of resistance slowly regained a measure of confidence, questioned the tactic of armed struggle, and began to reorganize. At this point two important institutions were utilized as vehicles to begin anew a slow process of nonviolent resistance: the Catholic church and the only legal opposition party, the Movimento Democrático Brasileiro (MDB), or Brazilian Democratic Movement.

The Catholic church had already by that time gone through a significant process of internal transformation. This process was influenced by the decisions of Vatican II and the Latin American bishops' conference in Medellín, Colombia, which established a pastoral guideline with an "option for the poor." The social, economic, and political context of the time spurred Christians to engage in political action in conformity with pastoral and theological teachings that encouraged Christians to participate in both secular and religious grass-roots organizations. The church organized justice and peace committees, set up legal advisory groups to defend political prisoners, and backed and protected members who opposed torture and arbitrary arrests. The importance of the Catholic church's power of organization among working-class people, both rural and urban, cannot be overestimated. It is in the small groups organized under church auspices that one may find the seeds of the vast grass-roots movement of ecclesial base communities, or CEBs (see chapter 6 above); of rural and urban trade union renewal; and of neighborhood and other community organizations.

The Catholic church's activities were also extremely influential in convincing upper- and middle-class people to join the opposition. Many of the same people who had originally helped to bring down Goulart's populist government in 1964 out of a firm belief that it was communist

were now actively organizing middle- and upper-class groups to study
the policies of the national security state, read the gospel in the light of
liberation theology, and analyze the duty of Christians to actively participate directly in opposition to a government widely considered oppressive and violent. This process politicized groups associated with the
interclass alliance against the military government. By its very nature,
the Catholic church served as an organizational umbrella for political action and aided the articulation of political movements of different social
classes.

The MDB, the only legal opposition party, began to play a major role
in the channeling of political interests after 1973. The military were considering the next stage in the transfer of central power. The system of
political control was explicitly not tied to a single strongman, and it had
been important for the state to transfer power every few years. This both
allowed for the accommodation of different ambitions within the military itself and prevented the development of a one-man dictatorship,
which was seen by the Brazilian military as highly vulnerable to rebellion. Since the intent of the civil-military coalition in power was to form
an effective state system of institutionalized structures of control, it was
important to avoid the establishment of a one-man regime. For those in
power, the major problem in 1973 was to develop new mechanisms for
regular transfer of executive power. It was decided that the next president should be chosen by an electoral college composed in such a manner as to enable tight control by the power holders but sufficiently flexible to provide an institutionalized framework. At this point, however,
the opposition groups also saw an opportunity. They launched a presidential campaign. Congressman Ulisses Guimarães, president of the
MDB, was chosen as the candidate for president of Brazil. Barbosa Lima
Sobrinho, a respected journalist and a founder of the Brazilian Press Association, was chosen as the vice-presidential candidate. An impressive
symbolic campaign was organized, which the opposition named the
"anti-candidacy campaign." The MDB organized rallies, demonstrations, debates, and other political events, with the support of large sectors of the middle and working classes. For the first time since the enactment of AI-5, people could muster together the strength to defy the
National Security Law and meet peacefully in the open squares of the
cities to hear the two "anti-candidates" of the opposition discuss the electoral system and denounce the repression and the economic policies pursued by the government. The immediate result of the "anti-candidacy"
presidential campaign of 1973 was to increase the legitimacy of the MDB
and reestablish channels for active resistance to the government, as was
demonstrated by the victory of the MDB in the congressional elections of
1974. Its long-term result was to establish the validity of alternative techniques of nonviolent organization as a form of active resistance.

With the end of the period of armed struggle and the impact of the "anti-candidacy campaign," a new phase of opposition began. Workers in industrial areas organized in groups inside the factories to discuss working conditions and low salaries. In their unions they met regularly to study the legislation controlling trade union activities and develop ways of countering the prohibitions. In some of the most important unions—in particular, among the metalworkers of the industrialized areas of São Paulo—the process of organization from the base was well advanced by 1977. Peasant groups similarly studied the existing legislation on land distribution and organized rural unions to defend the economic rights of rural workers and squatters. In the working-class areas of the cities, where urban infrastructural improvements such as running water, light, and sewage were summarily ignored, neighborhood associations sought to improve living conditions.

It is interesting to note, at this point, that the nascent working-class organizations—in both urban and rural areas—developed with an increasing determination to build organizational structures autonomous of the state. There was strong criticism of state controls over labor under populist governments prior to the 1964 coup. Efforts to build strong, independent working-class organizations were constrained, however, by state repression and state-enforced legal controls. Under the circumstances, working-class leaders sought ways to diminish the repression.

At the same time middle-class professional groups that had been alienated from the state by the force of the repression began to actively engage in political action within their professional associations. Lawyers demanded respect for legality through the Bar Association (Ordem dos Advogados do Brasil, or OAB). The explicit educational tool of the OAB was to make a sharp distinction between the definition of "legitimate legality"—laws enacted by a freely elected congress—and "parallel, or illegitimate legality"—the laws enacted under coercion or summarily imposed by the executive. In the course of the educational campaign spearheaded by the OAB, the question of legal rights and individual freedoms became central. The effectiveness of the OAB derived from its ability to focus on individual rights—specifically the right of habeas corpus, a major concern of the opposition.

After 1977, led by the OAB, a second major attempt was made to establish an interclass alliance of the opposition. The success of the campaign rested on a clear set of demands: the end of AI-5 and the restoration of habeas corpus. It was understood by opposition groups in all classes that their specific demands could not be met if the highly repressive controls of AI-5 remained in effect. Without habeas corpus, people could be arrested without charge and be held incommunicado. There was no mechanism to force authorities to give the cause of arrest or admit to having the person. This situation, common in Latin American dictatorships, allowed people to simply "disappear." The centrality of the fight to regain the right of habeas corpus was thus due to an understanding that the possibility of arrest without charges, followed by possible torture and even disappearance, was a powerful element in a policy of social control through intimidation and terror.

The campaign was conducted in a unified manner, utilizing the organizational vehicle of the OAB, the Press Association (ABI), the Brazilian Conference of Bishops (CNBB), and the opposition party, MDB. Because of the widespread interclass involvement, it was possible to keep the main issues of individual guarantees in the limelight so as to secure the unity of sectors that were not disposed to political action connected to the parties. Working-class people also recognized that the fight for union organizational freedom and better salaries was also linked to the regaining of institutionalized legal guarantees. Without habeas corpus, intimidation of the rank and file could be so severe as to completely discourage active participation in other struggles. The Catholic church connected the issue of regaining individual rights to a more general human rights campaign it was waging on behalf of the persecuted, tortured, and oppressed. The press, involved in its own struggle against censorship, saw in the campaign an opportunity to advance the cause of press freedom. In short, all class sectors of the opposition came to understand the primacy of regaining political and individual freedoms as a necessary step to redemocratization. Accordingly, until 1979—when AI-5 was finally repealed by the government—the opposition drew its strength from an alliance of groups whose membership came from all classes.

In 1980 the opposition began a third effort to achieve a united interclass alliance. The movement centered on a large-scale campaign to regain the right to elect state governors directly by secret ballot. The different class sectors also sought to gain power at the municipal and state levels of government and win a majority control of congress so as to enable major reforms to be implemented. This strategy was designed to force the national security state to share power. Opposition leaders believed that it was necessary to move piecemeal in order to gain further political space for organization. Winning local power could also give the opposition parties a chance to demonstrate an alternative model of social and economic development.

In 1980 and 1981 all efforts were concentrated on forcing the government to change the electoral laws and allow direct gubernatorial elections in November 1982. The campaign was organized on the basis of a vast network of interlocking entities: the grass-roots organizations, the trade unions (both rural and urban), the student movement, the OAB, the Press Association, and the Catholic church. All activities were further coordinated by the political parties, which were by then already fully formed. The political parties served as conduits through which the single-issue demand for direct election of governors could reach all parts of the country.

The opposition did not entirely succeed in winning free election of members of congress and the governors of states. The policy makers of the national security state devised a series of mechanisms to subvert the electoral strategy. Already in 1977 they decreed that one-third of the senate be indirectly elected by the state assemblies.[3] This meant that bills could effectively be stopped through the government's hold upon the indirectly elected senators. The policy was designed to diffuse dissent while maintaining tight control of political and economic initiatives. Most ordinary bills could be passed even if the opposition won a majority in the house of representatives. One major problem remained for the government: prior to 1977 a constitutional amendment required a simple majority vote of both houses of congress. It was, therefore, possible that the opposition's expected gains in the 1982 House elections would permit reform of the Constitution in spite of the indirectly elected senators. Thus, before allowing elections in 1982, the executive enacted a provision changing the rules regulating the approval of constitutional amendments. Under the new rules all amendments would require two-thirds approval of both houses of Congress.

The election of November 1982 showed significant gains for the opposition parties. Together they elected 246 members, as against the government's 234, gaining a small majority in the house of representatives. In the senate, however, because of the indirect election clause, the government won 46 seats and the opposition only 23. The clause thereby prevented the opposition from gaining congressional control. However, out of the twenty-two states that held elections for governor, opposition parties won in the ten most important and modernized ones. With victory in the gubernatorial races of São Paulo, Paraná, Minas Gerais, Espírito Santo, Mato Grosso do Sul, Goiás, Acre, Amazonas, Pará, and Rio de Janeiro, the opposition parties not only gained power in the industrial heart of Brazil but also won access to the country's crucial mineral resources. The states that passed into the control of the opposition generated 80 percent of the gross national product and represented 60 percent of the territory, where 58 percent of the population lived (*Veja*, 1 December 1982).

LOCAL VERSUS CENTRAL POWER: NEW DILEMMAS FOR THE OPPOSITION

The opposition had followed some distinct strategies of organization. First, local groups, in every class segment of society, created grass-roots

---

3. A complete legal analysis of the changes contained in Constitutional Amendments 7, 8, and 9 may be found in Jacques 1977.

organizations actively seeking specific benefits. If there was already an association or corporatist institution in existence, the opposition would work within the existing structures to activate and organize dissent. Hence, the strategy was one of organizing from the base, creating a widespread network of active civic entities. This strategy allowed for the building of alliances between multiclass groups to pressure the state for larger institutional reforms of interest to all. Second, the opposition's strategy aimed at controlling increasing levels of representation in congress, the state assemblies, and the municipal councils. The strategy developed by the interclass alliance was to parcel out power and build upon local political influence to slowly compel the state to grant larger concessions. In this way, it was argued, it would be possible to negotiate piecemeal reforms and to exercise moderate levels of political power. It should be noted that this strategy was a direct reaction to the state's policy of repression.

However, with the opposition victories in key states and municipalities throughout the country in 1982, the opposition's political perspective changed. Once in posts of administrative responsibility, opposition leaders found that the built-in economic, bureaucratic, and military constraints at the federal level neutralized their local efforts to implement alternative policies of development and welfare. In Brazil the distribution of tax revenue is extremely centralized in the federal government. Taxes are collected directly, and small percentages are then redistributed to the states and municipalities, with little or no possibility of local flexibility in financial resources and taxation. Local administrations, strangled by previous debts both to the federal government and to foreign creditors, were trapped by having to cave in to central government demands to avoid being starved financially. In addition, major economic decisions, which would have a direct and dramatic impact upon local state and municipal populations, were all made by the controlling groups at the national level. For example, once Brazil agreed to the established orthodox program of the International Monetary Fund at the end of 1982, policies were implemented that caused the growth rate to fall from 8 percent in 1980 to zero in 1981 and 4 percent in 1982. Unemployment, particularly in the opposition-governed industrial states, soared to unprecedented heights. The central government also implemented a new salary policy, in October 1983, that cut deeply into the income of the middle classes. Widespread hunger, social dissent, and increased misery ensued. Immediately upon taking office, opposition governors were faced with large-scale riots in the major cities, increasing violence, wildcat strikes, and systematic ransacking of supermarkets by hungry mobs.

Opposition governments also discovered that their control over state police forces was greatly impaired by federal mechanisms. In July 1983, after the major food riots in São Paulo, the federal government enacted a decree that allowed the army to take over the local military police force "in case of civil disturbance and when the local government proves itself unable to effectively deal with the situation." In essence, the decree removed from opposition leadership the choice of how to handle dissent in their own states and municipalities. As a result, opposition governors and mayors were placed in the uncomfortable position of watching violent police repression of strikes, protests, and demonstrations. It was difficult, after that, to explain to voters who had chosen their "alternative political and economic model of government" in the election of 1982 that they effectively held little power. They were blamed for the economic crisis and for the continuing unemployment as well as for the violent repression. Their legitimacy plummeted with alarming rapidity in public opinion polls. One demonstration in São Paulo against Franco Montoro, who had been elected with 54 percent of the vote just a year before, brought together fifty thousand people, who cried, "The people now have the vote but have already regretted their choice." The opposition leadership clearly began to be perceived as partners of the federal government and co-administrators of a growing economic and social crisis.

In such an unfavorable economic and political context, a reconsideration of strategies began to be debated. The limitations of local political power under a centralized authoritarian government became clear. Hence, the mechanism for the succession to President Figueiredo through the indirect electoral college became a focus of the opposition's attention. By the middle of 1983, groups of all classes within the opposition began to concentrate their fire on criticism of the indirect method of choosing the president through a highly unrepresentative and illegitimate electoral college. A broad-based educational campaign, simultaneously conducted through debates in the grass-roots organizations, trade unions, universities, and churches, was organized. The opposition parties also spoke out through their representation in government and congress.

In November 1983 the first formal attempt to institutionalize another interclass organization to press for the direct election of the president gave rise to the "Inter-Party Committee for Direct Elections." At first the campaign was a network of opposition political parties; it then was broadened by the participation of trade unions, neighborhood committees, Catholic lay organizers, the Bar Association, and a group of dissenting members of the government's own party, the Partido Democratico Social (Social Democratic Party, or PDS).

An opposition congressman of the Partido do Movimento Democratico Brasileiro (Party of the Brazilian Democratic Movement, or PMDB), Dante de Oliveira, presented an amendment to the Constitution aimed at establishing the principle of direct elections for president as early as in 1984. This amendment was to come to a floor vote on 25 April 1984. All efforts were geared to showing popular support for the amendment so as to convince recalcitrant members of Congress to vote in its favor. An agenda of events to mobilize public support for the demand for direct elections for president was drawn up. "Inter-Party Committees for Direct Elections" were quickly set up in all states, coordinated by a National Committee for Direct Elections. The first major rally, on 16 January 1984, was held in Curitiba (Paraná) and drew over 30,000 people. The campaign began to acquire a symbolism of its own. Yellow became the official color of those who supported direct elections. Artists, musicians, television actors, and sports announcers were called on to perform at rallies and to organize events that alternated music, sports commentary, and performances with speeches by top opposition leaders. Such rallies always began with the singing of "Menestrel das Alagoas" in tribute to the deceased opposition leader Senator Teotonio Villela by a top popular singer, Fafa' de Belem. White doves were then released by the thousands. People were told to bring both Brazilian flags and yellow flowers or banners to add color to the crowd. Finally, the national anthem was played, while all present held hands and raised their arms. All rallies were organized in the same manner.

The second rally, on 25 January in São Paulo, drew 400,000 people in pouring rain. This was followed by a larger event at the end of February in Belo Horizonte (Minas Gerais), which attracted an estimated 800,000 people. The "Inter-Party National Coordination Committee for Direct Elections" planned a "Caravan for Direct Elections" and scheduled rallies in every major city of the country over the next two months. Demonstrations were held in a series of large and small towns, including the northeast, the Amazon basin regions, and the central states. All were organized by a tight, unified coalition of political parties, grass-roots organizations, and trade unions. Everywhere the demand for the right to elect the president directly mobilized the largest demonstrations in the history of each place.

The response of the population increased with each successive demonstration: in Goiânia (Goiás), 30 percent of the local population attended the public rally.[4] In Pôrto Alegre (Rio Grande do Sul), 200,000 people were in attendance. On 10 April in Rio de Janeiro, a million people filled the downtown area with flags, music, yellow shirts, flowers, and the participation of the major samba school groups. Finally, on 16 April the largest demonstration was held in São Paulo. Over a million and a half people filled the downtown streets of the metropolis in a long march for the right to elect the president of the republic directly.

According to all press accounts, between 16 January and 16 April

4. The press gave a complete coverage of the campaign. See, for example, *Folha de São Paulo*, 6 April 1984, p. 2; 11 April 1984, p. 2; 13 April 1984, pp. 3–4; 14 April 1984, p. 2; and *Jornal de Tarde*, 17 April 1984, pp. 1, 7, 22. For an extensive coverage of the entire campaign, see also *Isto E*, 18 April 1984, pp. 28–36.

1984, close to six million people took to the squares of the nation to show their support for direct elections. Never in the history of the country had the population achieved such unity on a single issue. Public opinion polls showed that 97 percent of the population favored a system of direct election for president. All of the demonstrations were completely peaceful. Not a single incident or disturbance occurred. The cities were taken over by a disciplined and joyful mass of citizens, politically conscious of their rights and aware of their own collective power of organization. The unity of opposition forces during the demonstrations was enhanced by the participation of representatives of all Brazil's different cultural, political and social groups. The symbolic impact of the presence of local samba schools, soccer stars, circus artists, TV, radio, and movie stars, and other celebrities was enhanced by the rallies being run by Osmar Santos, a nationally known soccer sports announcer, and by their ending with the local symphony orchestra playing the national anthem.

What allowed such unprecedented mobilization? At least five important conditions fueled the campaign for direct election for president. First, the chaos of the economy, which was entirely geared to paying the foreign debt, contributed to disillusionment with the regime. Agreements with the IMF had resulted in salary cuts, unemployment, and a growing recession. Inflation rates, notwithstanding monetarist policies, rose to an unprecedented 200 percent, with basic foodstuff prices rising between 400 and 800 percent in 1983. The consequent social crisis could not be dealt with at the local level, and opposition groups became more convinced of the need to redefine their political strategy to gain access to federal power. The various public opinion polls showed an increased awareness that the economic crisis was caused by incorrect economic policies and commitments to foreign creditors. The campaign for direct elections was therefore tied to a desire for a change in the social and economic policies of the central government. The campaign for the right to elect the president directly reflected a desire for deep structural and policy changes in the country. This explains the vast working-class support for the campaign.

A second condition underlying the take-off of the campaign was the instability and total lack of legitimacy of the federal government. This lack of legitimacy was exacerbated by the confusion of the process of presidential succession. After twenty years of military rule, the question of the nature of state power became a focal point. It was argued that an illegitimate government, chosen by unrepresentative means through an unrecognized electoral college, could not have a base of support sufficient to provide any measure of long-term stability to face the crucial economic and social decisions urgently needed. Hence, the question of legitimation of government was perceived as important.

Third, people felt a new sense of empowerment. The grass-roots movements and major strikes in 1978, 1979, and 1980 had laid the basis for a growing network of politically effective organizations. Coming from the base, organized in a myriad institutions, the working people learned to press for demands, to negotiate solutions, and to acquire confidence in their rights as citizens. Collectively, people began to lose their fear of the military government.

Fourth, the elite organizations in the opposition had also gone through a learning process: the campaign for habeas corpus, for amnesty, for freedom of the press, for the repeal of AI-5, and for the right to elect the governors of states directly succeeded in cementing an alliance between groups. Their effectiveness increased their legitimacy, which allowed them to be spokesmen of civil society. Their presence in the campaign for direct elections for president won support for the movement.

Finally, the interclass alliance, uniting political parties, community groups, trade unions, peasant organizations, elite groups, and political representatives, was effective because it centered on a single issue with broad appeal. The focus of the campaign was simple: tens of millions of voters demanded their right as citizens to elect the president of the republic directly. The movement avoided potentially divisive subjects, such as party and individual candidacies.

To maintain a strong interclass alliance, it was necessary to circumvent the conflicting interests that would naturally be reflected in specific election platforms. A simple program was devised to mobilize public support: mass demonstrations to educate the public about the proposed constitutional amendment for direct elections and rally pressure against recalcitrant members of congress. Hence, the amendment served as a rallying point for the mobilization of public opinion and the forging of the interclass alliance. It was defeated by only twenty-two votes in congress. The defeat left much of the population disappointed. Thousands wept in the streets and gave up on politics.

ELITE HEGEMONY
AND THE LIMITS OF "POPULAR" DEMOCRACY

Almost immediately after the defeat in congress, top leaders of the elite opposition began a series of negotiations with groups within the military government. Within less than a month they initiated a movement to persuade the public to support the choosing of Tancredo Neves, a senator of the PMDB party, as president through the indirect electoral college. The same leaders who had so recently sharply criticized the system of choosing the president by indirect vote in the electoral college now equally strongly defended the position that the only alternative left to the opposition was to participate in the indirect election process. What had happened?

At this point it is important to understand the distribution of political power within the interclass alliances. As already pointed out, at each moment in history where an interclass movement coalesced around specific political issues, the interests most closely connected to the working class (i.e., socioeconomic structural reforms connected to the distribution of income and ownership of capital and land) were pushed aside so as to enable a unified program to be developed. Specific working-class concerns, such as the right to organize and the right to strike, were included in the various joint documents but never actually made into major political issues. On each occasion hegemony over the movement remained in the hands of elite groups.

Two main reasons may be mentioned to account for this phenomenon: first, the historical weakness of autonomous working-class organizations. As pointed out, it was not until the end of the 1960s that grassroots organizations independent of state structures were developed. Even the new trade union movement after 1978—both urban and rural—was hampered by direct control by the state. Hence, the nascent working-class organizations lacked the experience and political clout necessary to enforce equal status in the interclass coalition. Second, the policy of political liberalization initiated by the various military governments in response to the challenges presented by the overall opposition movement allowed sufficient space for negotiations with key elite groups. Cognizant of the fact that growing sectors of the Brazilian national bourgeoisie were alienated from the state, the military took the initiative in opening larger arenas of political participation for elite, but not working-class, groups. For the civil-military coalition in power, the experience of shared government at the local level carried with it the lesson that limited sharing of power with key elite opposition groups was not a threat. In the process, elite groups became more influential within the opposition movement, and their hostility toward the military leadership waned as they were, in essence, coopted.

With the Campaign for Direct Elections for President, however, another element in the analysis must be considered. The vastness of the movement and the sheer size of the public demonstrations frightened the elite groups within the opposition almost as much as they frightened the military government. The potential of losing hegemonic control of the interclass alliance was, for the first time, openly acknowledged.

Once the threat to the common interests of the bourgeoisie surfaced, a new political alliance was formed among elites that had until then differed in their stance toward the military regime. In a show of sudden opposition, the "official" party (PDS) broke with the military government to form a Democratic Alliance with elite sectors of the opposition. Though eliciting the support of working-class groups, it maintained extremely tight control of power. The new Democratic Alliance included almost all civilian elites formerly associated with the national security state and provided the unified base necessary to accomplish a conservative transition from military rule. The working-class sectors of the opposition were marginalized in the process.

The history of the interclass alliances in the opposition to the military governments, therefore, determined the makeup and composition of the forces that eventually carried out the transition. The profoundly conservative socioeconomic program of the elected postmilitary "New Republic" is partly attributable to the marginalization of the working classes. Labor's willingness to set aside its own specific class interests to support the multiclass concern with civil liberties proved, with time, to contribute to its marginalization. Deeper structural and economic issues were not addressed as the opposition pressed for political liberalization.

What were the consequences of the elite-dominated shift to civilian rule for the "popular" classes? The most important effect has been an inability, to date, to carry out a deeper transformation of Brazilian society. Civil libertarian concerns get greater attention than the pressing economic needs of the laboring classes. As a result of postponing pursuit of their own class interests, the organizations of the working class have emerged from the military period weakened in their capacity to impose and implement a more radical program of political transformation during the period of transition to postmilitary government.

Multiclass coalitions for political rights are, of course, important. Such alliances should, however, ideally be built upon a stronger working-class organizational base to avoid the hegemony of elite groups within the opposition. In the context of Brazilian history, such an organized base had difficulty establishing itself because of the fragility of the nascent "popular" movement. The experiences of interclass alliances in other countries show, though, that labor can impose its class interests on interclass opposition movements to military rule. This has been true in Chile, as elaborated in chapter 8.

REFERENCES

Dreyfus, Rene
    1980   *A conquista do estado: Acao politica e golpe de classe.* Rio de Janeiro: Editora Vozes.
Evans, Peter
    1979   *Dependent Development: The Alliance of Multinational, State, and Local Capital in Brazil.* Princeton, N.J.: Princeton University Press.
Jacques, Paulino
    1977   *As emendas constitucionais n. 7, 8, e 9: Explicadas.* Rio de Janeiro: Companhia Editora Forense.
Moreira Alves, Maria Helena
    1983   "Mechanisms of Social Control of the Military Governments in Brazil

(1964–1980)." In *Latin American Prospects for the Eighties: What Kinds of Development?* edited by David Pollock and A. R. M. Ritter, pp. 103–51. New York: Praeger.

1986   *State and Opposition in Military Brazil.* Austin: University of Texas Press.

CHAPTER TEN

Debt, Protest, and the State in Latin America

John Walton

Speaking to the United Nations in the fall of 1985, Peru's recently elected president, Alan García Pérez, described the plight of Latin American states in blunt alternatives: "We are faced with a dramatic choice; it is either debt or democracy." The options were scarcely García's invention. In the preceding five years, Peru and half the countries of Latin America had experienced a singular and unprecedented wave of social unrest in response to the domestic policies of their governments for dealing with a redoubling foreign debt. Riots, political demonstrations, and general strikes presented the alternatives as a choice between a new and desperate form of working-class poverty, self-imposed in the interests of foreign creditors, or the right to a living wage for shantytown residents, labor, and the middle classes. The *barriadas* of Lima faced the bankers of London as mediators on both sides scrambled for ground safe from the opening chasm.

The uprisings in Latin America simplified García's rhetorical choice. Indeed, in the previous summer's political campaign, he had chosen a course that resonated with voters and governments around the continent: "We will pay, but not at the time they want. First we'll pay off our debt to the people by providing food and jobs. It's not fifty foreign bankers who pick the president of Peru." The call that won voters in Peru was raised by militant crowds elsewhere. In September 1985 hundreds of Panamanian workers invaded their legislature chanting: "I won't pay that debt! Let the ones who stole the money pay!"

Panamanian insurgents and a youthful Peruvian president alone have little effect on the direction of continental politics and international finance. But these scenes were repeated throughout Latin America in the early 1980s. Brazil's debt, the world's largest, is eight times Peru's and the former's hemispheric influence may be proportionately larger. Prior to congressional selection of the ill-fated president-elect Tancredo Neves (who died before taking office) in January 1985, half a million marchers on the boulevards of Rio de Janeiro demanded "Out with the IMF!" At the United Nations, José Sarney, Tancredo Neves's successor, followed García to the podium and echoed his mood: "Crushed under the weight of an enormous foreign debt, the countries of the region are living through a scenario of severe difficulties with domestic repercussions resulting in recession, unemployment, inflation, increased poverty and violence. . . . Brazil will not pay its foreign debt with recession, not with unemployment, nor with hunger" (*New York Times*, 24 September 1985). More rhetoric, to be sure, but rhetoric with a purpose.

Latin America is presently undergoing a profound political transformation. On one hand bedrock poverty has worsened under the combined assault of inflation, debt, and austerity. On the other hand the very urgency of such acute underdevelopment has energized democratic aspirations and economic nationalism. Bureaucratic and authoritarian state structures have unraveled, although their successors are as yet unformed (O'Donnell 1979). Political struggles have converged in the debt crisis, suggesting that its resolution will play a central part in shaping the next era of development. This chapter attempts to assay the significance and direction of recent political change. First, I briefly describe the debt crisis, with particular attention to the meaning of its timing and magnitude. Second, I situate the economic condition of Latin America in the context of interacting states and international actors. Third, I analyze popular protest in response to the crisis—the motives, forms, perpetrators, and effects of class action aimed at austerity policies; this is the principal task of the chapter. Finally, I argue that the significance of popular protest is not understood as a singular determinant of change, but must be sought within a field of forces that converge on the state.

THE CRISIS

The debt crisis came to world attention in August 1982 when Mexico announced that its foreign exchange reserves were exhausted and it was unable to continue external debt payments. Mexico was broke by international standards and technically a nation in default, a circumstance unknown internationally since the 1920s. Mexico's trouble was particularly alarming to international banks and lending agencies. Under the prevailing theory, a petroleum exporter and model of Latin American hospitality to foreign investment should have been immune to such problems. The realization that similar foreign exchange deficits were common in debtor countries around the world gave still greater significance to Mexico's plight. Indeed, although the debt crisis was imminent in all Latin America, awareness of the crisis had been obfuscated by the tendency to consider Latin debt as a problem of individually misguided countries such as Peru and Jamaica, which were in de facto default as early as 1976 (Girvan, Bernal, and Hughes 1980; Honeywell 1983). Moreover, the problem extended far beyond Latin America and the Third World. Scores of countries, from Egypt and Korea to Poland and Israel, now appeared to be in as much danger as Mexico.

Albert Hirschman (1986:56) has observed that the Latin American debt "is a very large subject on which almost everything has been said." From detailed studies of the international economic crisis (e.g., Block 1977; Brett 1983; Moffitt 1983), just two features need be recalled for present purposes. First, the vital link between international creditors and the Third World that was forged in the 1970s began with trade deficits run up by the United States as it contended with the rising costs of the Vietnam War and stronger economic competition from Europe and Japan. The U.S. deficit, benignly known as a "dollar overhang," was temporarily redressed when the Nixon administration abrogated the Bretton Woods agreement by ending the limited gold standard that had been in effect for decades and floating the dollar against strong international currencies. In effect, the dollar was devalued. As the dollar fell with respect to its value in gold, the U.S. debt owed in dollars to other countries was reduced. The United States exported its debt.

Equally important was the related growth of international banking. Beginning in the 1960s, the United States had attempted a series of capital control programs aimed at the domestic side of the dollar overhang. Banks responded by creating international affiliates unfettered by national regulations. In 1964 just eleven U.S. banks operated abroad from 181 locations. A decade later 129 banks were doing business out of 737 branches (Moffitt 1983). This trend intersected with huge increases in world petroleum prices that produced bulging Eurodollar accounts in the international banking system. Up to their ledgers in petrodollars, the banks were eager to find new creditors and, driven by competitive pressures, to reinvest in the seemingly secure future of developing countries. Nations, conventional wisdom held, never go bankrupt. As commodity prices rose on the petroleum tide, there appeared no reason to doubt this wisdom. Between 1970 and 1983 the total debt of developing countries grew from $64 to $810 billion, with the fraction of that debt held by private banks increasing from one-third to over one-half.

Latin America absorbed nearly half of these loans, or $350 billion, distributed as shown in table 10.1. (The table excludes Belize, Cuba, and Guyana, where data are unavailable. The addition of these would contribute most of the balance of the $350 billion and a universe of twenty-four countries. The latter figure ignores eight "mini-states" such as Suriname and Saint Lucia.) Several features of the table are remarkable. One is the great *magnitude* of the debt, ranging from $200 to over $2,000 per

TABLE 10.1 Latin American Debt by Country

| | Mid 1984 Total external debt (U.S.$bn) | Mid 1984 External per capita debt (U.S.$) | Mid 1984 medium- & long-term external debt service as % of export earnings | Mid 1984 total external debt service as % of export earnings | External public debt | | | | Interest payments on external public debt (Millions U.S.$) | | Public debt service as a percentage of exports | |
| | | | | | Millions U.S.$ | | As a % of GNP | | | | | |
					1970	1983	1970	1983	1970	1983	1970	1983
1. Argentina[a]	45.3	1,554	58.1	199.5	1,878	24,593	8.6	32.1	121	1,343	21.5	24.0
2. Bolivia[a]	2.9	612	52.7	72.3	479	2,969	33.8	77.7	6	165	11.3	30.5
3. Brazil[a]	95.0	734	51.7	113.5	3,234	58,068	7.7	29.3	133	5,004	12.5	28.7
4. Chile[a]	18.6	1,619	55.9	140.4	2,066	6,827	25.8	39.2	78	557	18.9	18.3
5. Colombia	10.2	427	38.8	118.9	1,293	6,899	18.4	18.3	44	516	12.0	21.3
6. Costa Rica	4.1	1,635	51.4	106.4	134	3,315	13.8	126.3	7	504	10.0	50.6
7. Dominican Republic[a]	1.9	418	29.4	58.8	226	2,202	15.5	26.7	5	110	4.7	22.7
8. Ecuador[a]	6.9	794	39.9	118.6	217	6,239	13.2	63.0	7	365	9.1	32.5

9. El Salvador	1.2	218	—	—	88	1,065	8.6	29.2	4	37	3.6	6.4
10. Guatemala[a]	2.0	234	16.2	29.2	106	1,405	5.7	15.8	6	76	7.4	11.7
11. Haiti[a]	—	—	—	—	40	433	10.3	26.8	—	7	7.7	5.0
12. Honduras	1.5	531	32.9	55.3	90	1,570	12.9	56.3	3	83	2.8	14.9
13. Jamaica[a]	3.4	1,527	43.5	49.0	160	1,950	11.8	65.2	9	101	2.7	15.4
14. Mexico	89.8	1,230	56.7	146.5	3,206	66,732	9.1	49.1	216	6,850	23.6	35.9
15. Nicaragua	3.4	1,133	—	—	156	3,417	15.7	133.3	7	37	11.1	18.3
16. Panama[a]	3.3	1,712	6.8	9.6	194	2,986	19.5	73.6	7	283	7.7	6.8
17. Paraguay	1.4	424	—	—	112	1,161	13.1	28.6	4	45	11.9	14.9
18. Peru[a]	12.5	686	35.2	109.7	856	7,932	12.6	48.1	44	406	11.6	19.6
19. Trinidad/ Tobago	1.3	1,203	12.4	20.5	101	887	12.2	10.7	6	101	4.4	2.8
20. Uruguay	4.3	1,527	25.3	159.6	269	2,523	11.1	48.4	16	198	21.6	19.8
21. Venezuela	34.0	2,372	18.8	106.9	728	12,911	6.6	19.8	40	1,658	2.9	15.0
Total/ Average	343.0	1,030	36.8	95.0	15,633	216,084	13.6	48.5	763	18,446	10.4	19.8

SOURCES: *Wall Street Journal*, 22 June 1984; *Latin America Weekly Report*, 20 July 1984; *World Development Report, 1985* (Oxford: Oxford University Press for the World Bank, 1985).

[a]Countries experiencing political protest of austerity policies.

capita in countries whose annual per capita income is in the same range. Second is the rapid *rate of increase*. Between 1970 and 1983 the external public debt, for example, increased fourteenfold (from $15 to $216 billion). Third, the *debt burden* and its increase are striking. Latin American countries owe medium- and long-term debts that average one-third of their annual export earnings for debt service alone, and the figure increases to 95 percent if short-term debt is considered. Since exports are the principal source of the foreign exchange needed for payment, the debt-to-export ratio is, of course, crucial. Public debt as a percentage of GNP increased nearly four times in the thirteen-year period, and it almost doubled as a percentage of exports.

By the mid 1980s, debt had become the central political issue confronting Latin American states domestically and suffusing their relations with the rest of the world. Although the repercussions of the debt crisis now spell domestic turmoil, its origins lay at the intersection of global patterns of accumulation and the developmental ambitions of dependent states.

DEBT AND THE DILEMMA
OF DEPENDENT STATES

Developing countries were not forced to take the loans that came so easily in the 1970s. Aggressive bankers needed upright borrowers, and they found them in eager governments, state corporations, and large firms around the world. Certainly, these borrowers were short-sighted— or so it appears now. But they were also subject to potent pressures at the time. First, they had palpable needs. Although the 1960s witnessed impressive growth rates in the Third World, development was uneven, leaving the poor, especially the burgeoning urban poor, relatively worse off. Second, external funding provided states and dominant classes with the means to industrialize on a scale that matched the transnational corporations. At the same time, infrastructural projects and new state-owned corporations made it possible for the state to respond to popular pressures with jobs. "The lack of local private investment potential, the political need to prevent multinational corporations from single-handedly appropriating the most strategic sectors of the economy and their most dynamic branches . . . has led local states, despite the capitalist ideology they defend, to expand their functions and thereby to create a national basis from which to bargain with the multinationals" (Cardoso and Faletto 1979:205).

Beneath these strategies, however, was a more fundamental explanation for the debt expansion. The state in Latin America was predicated on growth within the norms of dependent capitalism. Above all, that meant uneven development: prosperity for comprador classes, agri-business, industry, and services linked to transnational corporations; relative impoverishment for workers, independent producers, peasants, and tenants; and precarious gains for the middle classes in between. International loans, particularly those channeled through governments and state corporations, provided a solution, or at least an emollient, for the hardships entailed by uneven development. They enabled states to create the *appearance of development,* a set of debt-financed programs that provided national enterprises and enhanced the social wage.

This was no illusion. Loans made it possible for governments to sub-sidize the costs to consumers of necessities such as food, cooking oil, gasoline, and public transportation. The elevated social wage, in turn, enhanced the perceived performance of governments. Foreign credits made it possible for states to build heavy industry and its elaborate infra-structure, often under the aegis of state-owned corporations. Alongside these *developmental effects* were equally important *appearances:* the ap-pearance of a strong government as reflected in a stable currency, the appearance of affluence in imported consumer goods, the appearance of a living wage in what substandard wages could purchase in subsidized goods and services. Mexico and Venezuela, for example, borrowed heav-ily to sustain overvalued currencies and foreign imports. Brazil con-structed huge mining, hydroelectric, and industrial projects. Economi-cally flawed states could deliver on a set of class interests and enjoy the political returns. Finally, since much of the borrowing took place in highly inflationary periods, interest rates were negative in the short run. Loans were free money with a multitude of state-building uses.

The Latin American countries used their billions in new money for astute political purposes. They bought some of the fruits of develop-ment on credit. Doubtless, too, they bought a good deal of corruption, many an economic albatross, numerous white elephants, and some pro-ductive apparatus. Judged by the unpreparedness for hard times that would follow, little of the borrowed money was invested in sound devel-opmental ventures. The significance of these purchases, however, was less in their economic sense or nonsense than in their political intent. They provided social mobility for the middle classes, particularly those dependent on expanding public expenditures. They ensured subsis-tence for some of the poor. They awarded mobility and profit to classes linked to the international economy and to those who managed the state, not least the political officials who engineered the debt. The summary result was a state mechanism for achieving uneven growth and legiti-macy by apparent development—a strategy of statecraft that united Latin American regimes of sundry political description that boasted the effects of development as a legitimizing principle.

RECESSION, AUSTERITY, AND THE IMF

The global recession that began in 1973 initiated the gradual end of debt-financed apparent development. The quadrupling of oil prices in that year delivered a serious, but not catastrophic, blow, as commodity prices enjoyed a short related boom. Nevertheless, by 1975–76 weaker economies such as Jamaica and Peru experienced the first bona fide debt crises. Conditions worsened in the late seventies and dramatically so with the second oil price shock of 1979–80. In the first two years of the new decade, "world commodity prices dropped by 35 per cent to their lowest levels for 30 years" (Honeywell 1983:5). International trade slumped and interest rates rose rapidly, an especially vexing circumstance since so much of the new debt was held by private banks that employed floating interest rates. Foreign exchange flowed out from Latin America in accelerating debt service and needed or contracted imports, while less came in.

The banks profited handsomely as countries tried to pay their outstanding debt. "Citicorp, one of the largest US banking companies, increased its profits from its Brazilian lendings by 46 per cent in one year and that country now generates 20 per cent of Citicorp's world-wide profits. . . . Lloyds Bank International, on announcing quadrupled profits in the half-year beginning in September 1982, noted that a major boost to its profits came from countries such as Mexico which were rescheduling their debts" (Honeywell 1983:10). But the profits were chimerical from the standpoint of the international system. As countries exhausted their reserves, debt service was paid with new loans. The only options for debtors were now default or fresh money and renegotiated payment schedules.

The debt crisis signaled an expanded role for the International Monetary Fund. Since 1946 this weaker sister of the World Bank had confined itself to the problem of periodic trade deficits and relatively small loans aimed at restoring balances. Beginning in the 1960s, however, the IMF was not only lending large sums itself, it was prescribing conditions for economic stabilization to debtor countries that other international agencies and banks adopted as requirements for their own new loans and debt renegotiations. In effect, the IMF became a credit-rating service for the banks and a domestic policy maker for indebted states.

Guided by the potent combination of neoclassical economic orthodoxy and the interests of the advanced nations, the IMF prescribed a clear and remarkably uniform adjustment policy aimed at promoting market economies geared to export production. As debt renegotiations became common, borrowers were expected to introduce domestic reforms, including some combination of devaluation, reduced public spending, elimination of subsidies for food and necessities such as cooking oil and gasoline, wage restraint despite inflation, increased interest rates, taxes related to demand restraint, elimination of state-owned enterprises, greater access for foreign investment, reduced protection for local industry, import curbs, export expansion, and, at bottom, the application of new foreign exchange to debt service.

The IMF policy carried forceful implications. First, the poor, and specifically the urban poor, bore the greatest relative burden for repaying the bankers, since the most typical cuts came in publicly subsidized consumption (Frenkel and O'Donnell 1979; Sheahan 1980; Foxley 1981). The poor were not alone, of course, since reduced government spending affected middle-class state employees, import restrictions hurt some business and national industries, and the sale or closure of state corporations affected a broad employment spectrum. Second, economic growth was discouraged by measures that shifted public revenues from domestic investment to external debt payment. Austerity was the emphatic means of adjustment. Third, although reforms were doubtless needed in some of the countries, their indiscriminate recommendation suggests that repaying the creditors was the essential aim. Fourth, by implication, the policy was unrealistic. Not only was it unlikely that countries could revitalize their economies through austerity alone, it was impossible that eighty debtor countries around the world could all simultaneously reduce imports and improve their export performance, particularly as protectionism reasserted itself in recessionary advanced nations.

Since the IMF could not systematically impose its will on the world, the international austerity policy had other limitations. On one hand, political considerations temporized policy. Large nonperforming loans to diplomatically key states such as Korea, Israel, and Poland drew no stern reaction, while Nicaragua was subjected to sanctions despite its modest efforts at repayment. Exceptions were allowed for the Philippines, but cold theory recommended for the Dominican Republic. On the other hand, the IMF had no ultimate recourse for dealing with countries that resisted compliance or simply failed to meet negotiated targets. The latter, as it turned out, included most countries. Mexico endeavored to cut public spending, but failed to reduce inflation as much as prescribed. Brazil let its money supply grow more than the IMF desired. Argentina under its new civilian government initially insisted on wage increases to compensate for inflation. Yet, despite being "out of compliance," these states suffered no grave sanctions, since that would only jeopardize the banks' interests. The result was a series of renegotiations, more conditions, and more frustrated efforts.

Austerity policies have nevertheless had extensive and deleterious effects on Latin American development. Obviously, these countries suffer from global and domestic difficulties, but the new policies fail to reverse those and contribute in their own right to deterioration. The Latin American gross domestic product grew at an annual average of 5.5 per-

308   JOHN WALTON

cent from 1973 to 1980, but became negative in 1982 and stood at minus
3.3 percent in 1983; on a per capita basis, the same index went from 3.2
to − 5.6 percent (Stallings 1985).

Beyond these aggregate statistics, a few examples typify the general
situation and show the specific contribution of austerity policies to rever-
sals in the standard of living. In Mexico, where the IMF program has
been applied with some alacrity, real wages reached "their lowest level in
recent years, below their purchasing power in October 1976, and well below their level in December 1981" (*Latin America Weekly Report*, 1 June
1984). The real income of Mexican workers was reduced by 40 percent
between 1984 and 1986. Reduced public spending produced massive
layoffs in the construction industry. As a result of import restrictions,
"automobile union officials say that more than 30,000 workers had been
laid off . . . Diesel National, a state-owned firm, said that half its 6,000
workers will be laid off" (*Los Angeles Times*, 23 October 1983). For Brazil,
1983 was "the third year in a row in which per-capita income has declined, surpassing even the worst years of the Great Depression" (Fishlow 1983). Real wage declines were the lot of those who kept their jobs,
but "many did not, particularly those working for small and medium-
sized businesses. . . . Unemployment has risen sharply in Brazil's towns
and cities since 1980. The official statistics show the jobless rate is now
above 9%; nobody doubts that the real figure is higher" (*Economist*,
12 March 1983). In Peru, sociologist Julio Cotler explained, workers
"are desperate. The debt has blocked any progress. Average income is as
low as it was twenty years ago. All this has produced a high degree of
social unrest" (*Wall Street Journal*, 13 July 1984).

The special significance of these depredations is that they have undermined the whole mechanism by which states cultivated legitimacy with
apparent development. The crisis has been experienced as something
more than hard times, more than a failure of the economy. The states
that prospered until the mid 1970s on a binge of apparent development,
and consolidated their political support by distributing the effects of borrowed development, were held accountable on the austere morning
after. The economic debt crisis became a social crisis as the same mechanism that had once engendered state legitimacy was turned on its popular head to legitimate protest against the state and its international
patrons.

THE ANATOMY OF SOCIAL UNREST

From mid 1976 through 1986, more than half of the major countries of
Latin America and the Caribbean experienced social upheavals in direct
response to austerity measures. Thirteen of twenty-four nations in the
region (excluding the mini-states) produced fifty separate protest events.

In most cases protests were precipitated by economic policies urged by the International Monetary Fund operating in collaboration with other lending agencies such as the World Bank, the U.S. government, and consortia of private banks. In a telling phrase, the protests came to be known as "IMF riots," and Latin America came to be regarded as the seedbed of this recusancy. Both notions are oversimplifications.

In the first place, the austerity protests of the decade were but one symptom of a worldwide recession that also engendered economic nationalism, capital retrenchment, and labor struggles. Second, the IMF was not the only exponent of austerity, and protest was directed at additional institutions both within and outside the realm of public policy. The IMF had a heavy hand in global policy making, but it also provided a convenient symbol that exaggerated its responsibility. Third, austerity policies were not unilaterally dictated or imposed by the IMF, the banks, or by the U.S. government. Strong pressures were applied to debtor countries, but some resisted and others, in varying degrees of agreement, implemented unpopular austerity measures while attempting to diffuse responsibility by citing external coercion. Fourth, the protests took other forms in addition to riots. Finally, austerity protests were a worldwide phenomenon, erupting in a dozen more nations from Poland to the Sudan and Turkey to the Philippines. Latin America led other world regions in what, nevertheless, was an unprecedented wave of international protest; unprecedented in the scope and essentially singular cause of a global protest analogous to earlier national strike waves. In frequency and vigor, the Latin American protests are distinct and provide the richest material for focused analysis of a global phenomenon. Table 10.2 summarizes these events in a set of descriptive categories.

Table 10.2 is intended as a summary of the universe of Latin American austerity protests defined as large collective actions in opposition to state economic policies that stem from international pressures and aim at domestic reforms to reduce foreign debt. Circumstances surrounding the protests are summarized in a set of categories covering factual details (dates, places, severity), proximate causes (economic conditions, policies), and short-run consequences. The evidence comprising the body of the table is drawn from a variety of journalistic sources. Obviously, these data are less desirable than firsthand accounts or sociological analyses of protest events. Where observer accounts exist, relevant data are incorporated in the table and subsequent discussion. The data are sometimes incomplete, and they may reflect reporting biases. Events that escaped the attention of news-gathering services are not included, which may rule out not only minor and rural events but also significant events in countries, like Mexico, where the press is discouraged from publishing accounts of antigovernment action. Attention from the news media does not define the occurrence of protest but, conversely, events about which

TABLE 10.2 Summary by Country of Latin American Austerity Protests, 1976–87

Country/Cities	Date	Action/Duration	Severity	Precipitating Events	General Policies and Their Source	Consequences
1. *Peru* Lima Sicuani Ayacucho Trujillo Urubamba Cuzco Arequipa Huancayo Puno Chiclayo Piura Chimbote	July 1976, June– July 1977, May 1978, Jan. 1981, Mar. 1983, Sept. 1983, Feb. 1984, June 1984, Nov. 1984, May 1985	Initially, street demonstrations and riots in Lima. Protest spreads to other cities and to strikes. General strikes by labor unions, students, teachers, civil servants. Persistent one-to-three-day strikes. Demonstrations by students and in shanty towns; 10,000 march on government palace. General strike of public employees and industrial unions.	Initially, 5 killed, then 6. 200 union officials arrested. Approximately 10 killed. "Dozens" injured. 300–800 arrests.	Price increases in basic foods and gasoline, elimination of government subsidies, inflation, unemployment, cuts in university funding.	Reductions in public spending and devaluation ordered by IMF and World Bank as conditions for new loans and debt rescheduling.	Martial law, price increases reduced, price freeze on basic foods, devaluation halted. Return to civilian government. Government resistance to IMF, especially wheat and gas price increases. Protracted negotiations on rescheduling. Alternately austerity measures imposed and ameliorated. State of siege finally called to end strikes.
2. *Jamaica* Kingston Montego Bay Ochos Rios Negril May Pen	Jan. 1979, Jan. 1985	Three days each of street demonstrations, barricades, looting of stores, protest marches on government house.	5 killed (1979). 10 killed and 20 arrested (1985).	Price increases in gasoline, food.	Government elimination of subsidies and devaluation in response to IMF recommendations.	Government held firm on austerity measures, contained disorder.

	Dates	Protests	Consequences	Causes	IMF role	Outcome
3. *Argentina* Buenos Aires Mendoza	Mar. 1982, Oct. 1983, June 1984, Sept. 1984, May 1985, Aug. 1985	Demonstrations by labor unions, series of 24-hour strikes, general strike, some looting.	Hundreds arrested.	Price increases, inflation, policies on foreign debt.	Austerity measures by military and, later, Alfonsin government in negotiation with IMF.	Economic problems contribute to military withdrawal from government. Alfonsin administration first resists IMF, granting wage increases, then implements its own comprehensive austerity program with broad acceptance.
4. *Ecuador* Quito Guayaquil	Oct. 1982, Mar. 1983, Jan. 1985, Mar. 1987	General strikes, one and two days. Demonstrations, street violence.	Schools and universities closed. 7 killed, 50 wounded, 500 arrested.	Price increases and elimination of government subsidies on flour, gasoline. Price increases in milk and fuel oil.	Devaluation and subsidy cuts required by IMF as condition for refinancing debt.	Approval of rescheduling and new IMF special drawing rights. Agreement to delay debt repayments. Compensatory wage increases.
5. *Bolivia* La Paz Cochabamba	Mar. 1983, Nov. 1983, Dec. 1983, Apr.–May 1984, Nov. 1984, Feb.–Mar. 1985, Sept. 1985, Aug. 1986, Mar. 1987	General strikes, one to four days. Strike of bank employees responsible for implementing austerity measures. Demonstrations, street violence, looting, protest marches.	Approximately 10 killed, 1,500 arrested. Industry, mines, banks, shops and universities shut.	Proposed austerity measures that would have increased basic food prices and gasoline and a proposed devaluation. Unemployment, inflation, devaluation.	Devaluation and subsidies elimination urged by IMF as a condition for new loan.	Replacement of cabinet and key ministers. Government-labor agreement not to implement austerity measures, wage increases to partly offset inflation, postponement of debt payments. Renewed austerity with elected government and state of siege to end general strike.

TABLE 10.2 (continued)

Country/Cities	Date	Action/Duration	Severity	Precipitating Events	General Policies and Their Source	Consequences
6. *Chile* Santiago Valparaiso	Mar.–May, 1983. June 1983. Aug. 1983, Sept. 1983, Oct. 1983, Nov. 1983, Sept. 1985	Near-monthly political protests over unemployment, inflation, and Pinochet government. Many one-day protests. Demonstrations, "National Social Protest," general strikes, looting.	30–60 killed. 1,000 + arrests. Several thousand detained.	Pinochet dictatorship and unemployment, devaluation, price increases.	Devaluation, end to state subsidies and enterprises, and free market system urged by monetarist advisors and IMF.	Emergency public works projects and jobs. Mass detentions of protestors and poor neighborhood residents. Debt rescheduling.
7. *Brazil* São Paulo Rio de Janeiro Santos Campinas Fortaleza Ribeirão Prêto Brasília Major Cities	Apr. 1983, Oct. 1983	Political demonstrations, riots over food prices and unemployment, looting of supermarkets. Three days + persistent looting.	2 killed. 130 injured. 566 arrests.	Price increases, devaluation, elimination of subsidies, inflation and unemployment.	Devaluation and austerity measures adopted in order to meet IMF conditions for new loans.	Emergency job program promised for 170,000. New loans and debt rescheduling agreed with IMF. Food stamps, incentives to small and medium firms.
	Nov. 1986, Dec. 1986, July 1987	Violence, looting of shops, vandalizing of banks and government buildings. Peaceful general strike.	Tens of people injures, 30 arrested.	Renewed austerity, tax & price increases following state and congressional elections.	Efforts to revive the deteriorating Cruzado Plan and stem returning inflation.	No concessions.

					Recommended by IMF and world bank.	
8. *Panama* Panama City Colón	Oct. 1983, Sept. 1985	General strike, demonstrations, national legislature occupied, strikes, protest marches.		Proposed freeze on wages of public employees, reduced subsidies to business.		President resigns under pressure from labor, business, and military (and other mysterious military intrigue). No austerity measures implemented.
9. *Dominican Republic* Santo Domingo Santiago San Francisco de Macoris San Cristobal	Apr. 1984, Feb. 1985, July 1987	Food price riots. Organized protest by church, business, and labor. Strikes. Three days. Protests and strikes by shopkeepers, transit workers, and middle-class neighborhoods.	60 killed. 150–300 injured. 1,000 arrests. Schools, university, and radio station closed. Two killed (1985).	Government announced price increases on food staples, all imports including medicine, and gasoline. New price increases, devaluation.	Elimination of government-subsidized prices part of an agreement with the IMF for a $600 million loan. Measures urged by IMF and creditors in 1984, but rescinded, imposed again.	Some basic food and medicine prices moderated, but not gas and most imports. Labor leaders jailed to prevent further protest. New IMF agreement. Some renewed price increases moderated and wage increases proposed.
10. *Haiti* Cap Haitien Gonaives Bombardopolis	May 1985	Riot, attack on local barracks, looting of food stores and warehouse.	3 killed. Several hundred riot.	Food shortages, corruption in government distribution of food aid, restriction of emigration, police brutality.	Government crackdowns. IMF austerity measures and suspended public works employment.	Replacement of cabinet and local government officials. Government distribution of food and money.
11. *Guatemala* Guatemala City	Sept. 1985	Protest, riot, looting, demonstrations, job actions, strikes one week. Strikes by teachers and public employee job actions in support.	2–10 killed, 1,000 arrested. Troops invade university.	Government announced increases in bus fares, bread, and milk.	IMF urging reduced government deficit, increased taxes, and cuts in public spending.	Government agreed to freeze prices of basic goods and rescind bus fare increase. Agreed to raise salaries of public employees and to urge same from private employers.

TABLE 10.2 (continued)

Country/Cities	Date	Action/Duration	Severity	Precipitating Events	General Policies and Their Source	Consequences
12. *El Salvador* San Salvador	May–July, 1985, Feb. 1986	Demonstrations by 30,000 workers for salary increases (May), by 50,000 students and teachers for university budget (July), by 15–50,000 workers and public employees protesting economic policies (Feb.).	Work stoppages, hospital takeover. Armed forces occupied hospital. Fifteen union, teacher and student leaders arrested.	Initially, price rises and inadequate university budget. Later, January 1986 austerity program and devaluation.	Devaluation and sharp increases in gasoline prices with moderate wage increases and price freeze. Economic policy influenced by U.S. advisors.	Growing opposition to Duarte administration from once-supportive moderate unions and from business groups and coffee exporters.
13. *Mexico* Mexico City	Feb., May, 1986	Demonstrations by 20–50,000 people from various labor unions and left-wing parties demanding moratorium on debt payments and housing for earthquake victims (Feb.). May Day protest march.	Unknown number injured in clashes with police.	Three years of declining real income, public spending cuts, and Sept. 1985 earthquake.	Broad set of austerity policies (spending and subsidy cuts, devaluation, privatization) adopted with U.S. and IMF encouragement as a condition for renegotiated and new loans.	Social tensions and opposition to official party (PRI) electoral practices in several regions (e.g., Chihuahua, San Luis Potosi). Rare public disapproval of president. Cabinet splits and replacement of finance minister. Tougher negotiating stance with IMF.

SOURCES: *New York Times, Wall Street Journal, Economist, Latin American Weekly Report, Time, Newsweek, Business Week, Veja,* 1976–87.

there are no accounts cannot be included in the analysis. Suffice it to say that the table provides a first approximation of the frequency and nature of austerity protest and invites empirical and interpretive refinements.

What explains the incidence of social unrest? A comparison of the countries and features of protest in table 10.2 with all of Latin America and the Caribbean suggests some tentative answers. First, the question is simplified by eliminating plausible explanations that do not find supporting evidence. The level of economic development bears no clear relation to the incidence of protest. Brazil and Haiti experience unrest, for example, while Venezuela and Honduras do not. In a related vein, dependent ties to the world economy based on mining and export agriculture do not discriminate protest from nonprotest countries. Finally, there is no consistent association between unrest and the type of political regime. Austerity protests were mounted in both democratic (e.g., Jamaica) and authoritarian (e.g., Chile) states, yet no protest occurred in some of their counterparts (e.g., Costa Rica and Paraguay). In Brazil, Argentina, and other countries, protests spanned the transition from military to elected regimes.

A pattern of positive associations can be derived from a close inspection of the table. The major debtor countries, on an absolute or per capita basis, have experienced protest. Debt burden is a factor, operating directly and through the consumer price index. Urbanization is another feature of protest countries and, particularly, the level of collective action organized in networks of cities. Finally, the strength of organized labor is associated with the frequency and the substance of protest activity. The evidence suggests a working hypothesis: the incidence of austerity protest is associated with a combination of hardship and the potential for mobilization (i.e., urbanization, unionization), but not with conventional political and economic variables. That is, protest derives from an interaction of the pains of austerity and the capacity for mobilization, rather than from singular or conventional causes. The hypothesis is not pursued in this chapter, but awaits more rigorous statistical treatment based on worldwide comparisons.

If the preceding analysis helps explain the locus of austerity protest, its forms still require elaboration. From a descriptive standpoint, the protests are mainly urban events and frequently involve networks of cities. The generalization deserves some qualification. Rural and small-town protests have occurred, for example in Bolivia, Mexico, and Peru. Reporting bias may restrict our knowledge of such actions. According to what we know about these events, however, they often involve indirect expressions of economic discontent (e.g., electoral strife in the northeastern Mexican states) or local support for urban-centered protests (e.g., sympathy strikes in Peruvian mines). Typically, the capital city is the focus, but unrest does not always begin or end there. The first instances of social unrest explicitly prompted by government austerity measures appeared in Lima in July 1976. Eleven months later, following renewed price hikes, street demonstrations erupted in Arequipa, Sicuani, Ayacucho, Trujillo, and Urubamba. Food riots that began in São Paulo (1983) and Santo Domingo (1984 and 1985) spread to other cities. This pattern suggests the pervasiveness of urban grievances and, in cases of coordinated general strikes, some intercity organization of protest, usually by labor confederations. Finally, the unrest is often recurrent. Peru, once more, stands out, with ten years of nearly continuous protest, but the majority of countries have experienced repeated instances.

The austerity measures prompting mass demonstrations are relatively uniform. Typically, they come in a set that cuts deeply into the subsistence capacity of low-income groups: rescinded government subsidies of food, basic necessities, and gasoline, meaning price rises; cuts in subsidized services, leading to fare increases in public transportation, for example; public spending reductions that eliminate jobs in government and government-contract work (e.g., construction). In short, rapid reductions in the standard of living by visible government action is the most common precipitant of protest. Other circumstances that mobilize collective action are devaluations that soon show up in domestic price increases, inflation, unemployment, and wage freezes.

The forms of unrest exhibit more variety and some specificity by country. The three general types of protest are food riots, political demonstrations, and general strikes. Countries tend to have a modal pattern: riots in Jamaica and other Caribbean nations; demonstrations in Chile and Central America; strikes in Argentina and the Andean countries. Doubtless, these are related to political styles, trade union strength, and the opportunities afforded by particular regimes. Strikes flourish in countries with independent labor unions, national labor confederations, and relatively tolerant regimes (e.g., Peru, Bolivia, Alfonsín's Argentina). Demonstrations are associated with active left-wing political parties and regimes that may draw the line at general strikes (e.g., Chile, Mexico). Riots occur where organized groups are absent or fail to control the protest (Haiti and the Dominican Republic respectively) and where factional violence is cultivated by parties (e.g., Jamaica).

Protest forms are highly mutable. They change with regimes and the likelihood of repression, but they also change with the circumstances of unfolding collective action. Protests that begin in one form often evolve to another. The riots and looting in São Paulo began as a demonstration for jobs; Bolivian strikes turned violent in response to police zeal; a tentative and successful "national social protest" demonstration in Chile emboldened labor to call illegal strikes.

As nearly as the scope and severity of these events can be measured, they are serious protests. People are killed in police and army responses.

Fatalities range from none or a handful to scores in Chile and the Dominican Republic. Many more are injured. Hundreds are jailed. Thousands stand up to high-risk expressions of their political views, particularly in the large strikes. In most countries, moreover, unrest is recurrent despite these hazards. The average number of separate national protest events is nearly four, although countries that began early (e.g., Peru) and those with an organizational capacity for mass mobilization (e.g., Argentina's unions or Chile's suppressed parties) account for much of the repetition.

Who are these protesting masses? Are they, indeed, masses or social classes? The evidence provides a clear and consistent answer. The largest category are the urban poor: the shantytown residents of Lima, Santiago, and Santo Domingo who stage mass demonstrations in city centers and resort to looting when their rallies are disrupted by troops. Equally important is organized labor, particularly in its role in coordinating and mobilizing sustained strikes. Labor union confederations have led the anti-austerity movement in Argentina, Bolivia, the Dominican Republic, Ecuador, and Peru. In many instances students or left-wing political parties have enlisted in the demonstrations organized by labor unions (e.g., in Guatemala and Peru).

If there is some coincidence of class situation among the preceding participants, a distinct set of protestors comes from the middle classes. Public employees are the largest subcategory here: white collar workers in ministries of finance and public works, health and hospital staffs, school teachers, and transportation operators. Middle-class neighborhoods have demonstrated in their own fashion: Chile's legendary pot-bangers and horn-honking traffic tie-ups in the Dominican Republic. Shopkeepers and businesses have joined in this middle-class protest, particularly in mobilizations sponsored by an alliance of left and center political parties and the church (e.g., Chile, Peru).

If austerity protests mobilize participants from varied class situations, they also encourage deliberate alliances. The degree of organization must not be exaggerated. Protests frequently begin with poor neighborhoods or labor unions and only subsequently gain the support of state employees or opportunistic political parties. In cases of sustained opposition, however, lower-class neighborhood organizations and labor confederations enlist allies for premeditated actions such as mass demonstrations and general strikes. Poor neighborhoods coordinate with students and public employees (e.g., Guatemala), miners and church groups join forces (Bolivia), and general strikes mobilize across class boundaries (Argentina, Peru, Chile). So far there is no evidence that these protest coalitions lend themselves to longer-range political action.

The symbols and strategy of protest suggest an energizing sense of legitimacy, a right to redress abuse. In cases of riot, for example, the targets of attack are selective and meaningful: affluent supermarkets in Rio, clothing and appliance stores in São Paulo, private automobiles and gas stations in Kingston, government offices in Chile, public buildings such as the Treasury and national lottery offices in Peru, banks in Brasília, a CARE warehouse in Haiti, and police stations in Haiti and the Dominican Republic. As in collective violence from European bread riots (Thompson 1971) to ghetto revolts in the United States (Berk and Aldrich 1972), the targets of the crowd define its apprehension of the culprits. Latin American class consciousness interprets austerity as the work of national governments, implemented by banks and international agencies and enforced by the police in the interests of commercial enterprises. However valid the analysis, it reflects a structuralist appreciation of institutional relations. Equally accessible institutions such as public markets and factories were not targets.

Political demonstrations express the same moral sense in strategic actions: a twenty-mile march from Lima's shantytowns converged on the national palace; Jamaican demonstrators rallied in front of Government House; in Panama they invaded a legislative session and left the chamber's marble walls decorated in red spray paint spelling "IMF get out." The connection between international agencies and their own plight was not lost on the protestors. In Bolivia, central bank employees joined a general strike with the expressed intent of preventing the administrative introduction of austerity measures. In Thompson's (1971) phrase, Latin American austerity protest has its own moral economy. It claims a right to dissent, expressing it through popular organizations, public channels, appeals to authority, and a palpable sense of injustice. Governments that had promised development were seen by protestors as accountable for their failures.

The character of this moral economy emerges in accounts that shift from aggregate comparison to detailed description. Protest emanates from contradictions and class action, but these analytic notions are expressed in the behavior of members of urban communities. Organized community action mediates the causal influence of structural conditions. Two brief case studies provide the flavor of protest as well as some of its intervening causes.

During the week after Easter 1984, unrest in the Dominican Republic climaxed in the most violent single episode of austerity protest. At least sixty people were killed, hundreds injured, and one thousand arrested in just three days of rioting. But much more than a food riot took place. Following the government's announcement of immediate and substantial price increases for basic foods, medicines, and imported goods pursuant to the conditions of a new IMF loan agreement, a mood of unrest came over the cities. In the Santo Domingo suburb of Capotillo, a citizens' committee hastily planned a twelve-hour strike for 23 April, attracting the support of three other neighborhoods. "The main influence in the strike committee [the Comité de Lucha Popular de Barrio Capotillo y Zonas Aledañas] came . . . from local *communidades de base* of the Catholic Church. . . . The organizers of the original protest in Capotillo were thus well-prepared. The mass meeting that decided to declare the strike appointed groups to contact the media, collect money and carry out door-to-door canvassing for support. The strike in Capotillo was totally successful, but it rapidly ran out of control of the organizers" (*Latin America Weekly Report*, 11 May 1984).

The riot that ensued surprised community organizers by the depth of its anger. The cosponsoring Frente de la Izquierda Dominicana "had no idea what was happening." The affair shocked President Salvador Jorge Blanco, his ruling Revolutionary Democratic Party, and Juan Bosch's opposition Dominican Liberation Party. Both parties scrambled for advantage by publicly rehearsing the speeches they would have delivered to the IMF loan negotiators. The Dominican National Workers' Union also endeavored to capture the energies of popular mobilization by calling for a general strike, but the result was only the arrest of labor leaders. The government retreated on the price increases and, in a habit of political opportunism that became common in other countries, blamed the IMF for policies in which it was a willing participant. In July the same government announced new price increases following the arrest of three hundred members of "leftist" organizations as a "preventive measure." Austerity prevailed, but the base community initiative transformed the national political agenda by providing labor and opposition parties with a new basis for challenging the party in government.

The Brazilian demonstrations that began in São Paulo in April 1983 posed new problems for the credibility of adjustment policies. The Mexican shock was just being absorbed when another pillar of Latin American industrialization and economic orthodoxy began to shake. Failing economies in Peru and the Dominican Republic were easily explained; riots that spread to Rio were puzzling at least. The locus of protest, once again, was a working-class community. The São Paulo barrio of Santo Amaro houses one million people, including 100,000 shantytown residents and 80,000 unemployed. Santo Amaro had experienced prior unrest. In 1981 squatters had invaded a state farm, and just one month earlier protestors had destroyed twenty-seven buses belonging to a private transportation company that locked out riders to pressure the government for a rate hike. In February, moreover, a thirty percent devaluation began to press meager incomes below subsistence levels. Within Santo Amaro, the number of employed steel workers had dropped from 100,000 to 80,000 and the local Telefunken factory had moved to a tax-free zone in Manáos, taking 6,000 jobs with it. Unemployment and austerity were thus the daily concerns of the barrio's ninety-three neighborhood improvement organizations, the active union movement, and political groups ranging from the Brazilian Communist Party and the Workers' Party to the center-left Party of the Brazilian Democratic Movement.

On 4 April a demonstration was called by the coalitional Committee Fighting against Unemployment, unified under the slogan "We won't die of hunger and be quiet about it." Two hundred demonstrators gathered in front of a popsicle factory that had recently attracted throngs of applicants for five job openings. As the demonstrators moved to a nearby square for speeches, their numbers swelled to two thousand, many of whom picked up oranges from a delivery truck along their route. Sometime during the perorations, the oranges took flight, bombarding the surrounding commercial zone. A thirty-hour riot was under way that drew 3,500 protestors and alleged "popular sector" opportunists, who looted two hundred stores, invaded forty homes, and destroyed one hundred twenty-five cars and buses.

On the third day, organizers of the initial demonstration sought to refocus action on their complaints about unemployment and rallied a new march of 3,000 to the state governor's palace. When the governor sent the labor secretary out to meet the peaceful assembly, and palace guards tried to lure it within water cannon range, more mischief followed. Symbolically, perhaps, the iron fence around the palace was torn down. Eventually, the governor did meet representatives of the crowd, but to no one's satisfaction. The protestors smashed buses provided by the governor for their return home, and police were finally set on the crowd.

The Dominican and Brazilian events exhibit similarities that may be generalized based on other accounts and the tabular summary. Far from being mere spasmodic eruptions by marginal masses, such protests are launched by organized working-class communities through their associations. They involve planning, clear objectives, and political strategy— although discipline may lapse as their following grows. Most distinctively, they articulate and dramatize the public mood in ways that have escaped political leaders, economic experts, and institutional attention. Popular sector mobilization shows an unexpected potential for political unrest and has forced that worry into the calculations of governments and the IMF. The protestors have made it clear that austerity is not a socially workable, much less a just, program. In that, they anticipated and contributed to the position that has since emerged in many national leadership circles.

CONSEQUENCES

What have the protests accomplished? This is a fair question with an inconclusive answer, at least for the moment. Some answers are available and straightforward, others are forming, and both kinds are important.

The short-run effects of the protests are clear and varied. First and most common, insurgents won the day, if not much more. Stunned governments frequently rescinded or ameliorated the policy. Subsidies were restored, rate hikes canceled, and compensatory wage increases granted. Sometimes relief was only temporary, as in the Dominican Republic, where another devaluation led to a new round of price rises. But reinstituted exactions were also followed by renewed protest. Second, in some cases the new policies were maintained in the face of unrest, but other compensations were provided: promised jobs and even food stamps in Brazil; wage increases in Ecuador and the Dominican Republic. Ironically, these benefits often flowed from new loans following debt renegotiations with the IMF. Third, some governments held firm and repressed the unrest, reluctantly in Jamaica, and aggressively in Chile, where working-class barrios were invaded (although even in this extreme case the Pinochet regime created a palliative jobs program).

Fourth, the protests sometimes initiated a successful movement to depose ruling governments or added a push to regimes that were teetering (e.g., Peru in 1980 and 1984, Argentina in 1983, Brazil in 1984, Panama in 1985). The fall of Haiti's Duvalier in February 1986 illustrates the point. In 1981 the Duvalier regime implemented austerity measures at the urging of the IMF. "Public Works and irrigation programs were suspended, causing further unemployment and the loss of arable ground" (*Latin America Weekly Report*, 8 June 1984). The United States increased food aid, typically distributed through private charities. "The country is suffering from serious food shortages, but government employees and military officials are selling on the black market food sent by international organizations to ease the famine" (ibid.). Unemployment, hunger, and corruption combined with the bleak circumstances of austerity to produce a series of food riots in May 1984. Duvalier shuffled his cabinet and replaced local officials in the affected areas to quiet unrest. In November 1985, however, revolt was rekindled on a broader scale. Student protestors were killed, the urban poor took to looting again, and middle-class teachers and shopkeepers joined the growing demand for Duvalier's removal. The following three months of continuous mayhem convinced the U.S. State Department that human rights were not improving (as it had previously claimed). A week after direct foreign aid to the Haitian government was reduced, Duvalier boarded a U.S. Air Force transport for unwelcome exile in France. Austerity policies were not the sole or even the principal cause of Duvalier's fall (Nicholls 1985), but protests stemming from the effects of austerity played a key role in initiating the expanded rebellion.

Finally, protest underscored the urgency of negotiated concessions that were provided by the IMF and the banks in many cases. From a political standpoint, the policies were not working and, as the *Wall Street Journal* observed, "now the bankers are beginning to face that reality—

and they are scared. It's one thing, they say, to deal with inflation, balance of payments and capital flows. But politics are a wild card that most bankers don't understand" (7 October 1983). Threatened and actual social unrest is only one of a set of inducements to renegotiate. Others include the financial exposure of international banks in particular countries, the strategic importance of the nation (e.g., Brazil), potential repercussions of growing poverty for creditor countries (e.g., Mexico in relation to the United States), and special political circumstances (tolerance for new democracies like Argentina, but discipline for Manley's Jamaica). The unique contribution of protest cannot be separated from so many confounded causes, yet creditors worry about it and policy makers testify to its influence (Silva Herzog 1987).

Despite the tangible character of these effects, some were transitory and others acquire significance mainly for what they portend in long-term political transformations. A case for fundamental change requires a deeper reading of these events—one that shifts from questions about the causes, forms, and direct effects of protest to an interpretation of the connection between social unrest, the state, and the international system.

Broadly, the debt crisis has generated three changes in the relations of state and society. Resistance is the first, and resistance not only by the urban poor, working, and middle classes, as we have seen, but also by states vis-à-vis the international order represented by the banks and IMF. The initial stage of this state resistance occurred in Peru, Nicaragua, and, particularly, Michael Manley's Jamaica, which defied IMF recommendations on wage increases, deficits, and monetary expansion. In January 1977, following his reelection, Manley explained to the nation:

> "We are now facing a situation in which some of the people who could lend us money will apparently do so only on the condition that they should be able to tell us how to conduct our affairs. . . . The International Monetary Fund, which is the central banking agency for the international capitalist system, has a history of laying down conditions for countries seeking loans. . . . This government, on behalf of our people, will not accept anybody anywhere in the world telling us what to do in our country. We are the masters in our house and in our house there shall be no masters but ourselves. Above all, we are not for sale." (quoted in Girvan, Bernal, and Hughes 1980:122)

Although desperate conditions soon forced Manley to acquiesce, the resistance was picked up elsewhere: in Ecuador and, more vigorously, in Alfonsín's Argentina and García's Peru. By far the most consequential act of resistance was Brazil's year-long suspension of interest payments to foreign banks that were running at $2 billion per year in 1987, when foreign exchange reserves had dropped from $11 to $4 billion over the preceding year.

The resistance gathered political significance with the unification of

Latin American countries on efforts to find a coordinated means for dealing with their creditors. Talk of a "debtors' cartel" was overblown, but a series of meetings took place (Panama in March 1983, Caracas in September 1983, Quito in January 1984, Cartagena in June 1984, Mar del Plata in September 1984, Santo Domingo in February 1985, Oaxtepec in July 1985, Havana in July–August 1985, and Acapulco in November 1987) aimed at a united front on equitable rescheduling of payments. By contrast to cartel hyperbole and Fidel Castro's ambitions, this was a "weak response to the crisis" (Stallings 1985:16). But the Cartagena Group is a rare and sometimes unified response, challenging conceptions of the crisis that blamed the victims and treated them as isolated economic bunglers.

The second change is a steady policy shift on the part of the U.S. government and the IMF. At the annual IMF–World Bank meeting held in Seoul, South Korea, during October 1985, U.S. Treasury Secretary James Baker indicated that "Washington now accepted the Latin American argument that growth-oriented policies would enable the region to meet its huge debt obligations more effectively than the austerity programs demanded until now by the International Monetary Fund" (Riding 1985b). In this aspect the policy shift should not be exaggerated. Growth was also the hope of the Carter administration. Yet other changes are afoot. A new Mexican agreement with creditor banks announced in October 1986 calls for additional guaranteed loans if national economic performance droops. Although this falls short of Mexico's proposal to link debt payments to oil revenues, it is nevertheless an important concession— one that Argentina is already seeking. In January 1987, after a long struggle, Brazil succeeded in gaining new loan approval without IMF conditions. At the same time banks have reduced their relative exposure in Latin America and cultivated a small discounted secondary loan market. Finally, late in 1987 the U.S. government proposed an arrangement for discounting Mexico's debt through the use of Treasury Bonds. In perceptible ways there is a retreat from austerity policies, at least for the large-debt nations.

What produced the shift? Although policy makers are reluctant to explain their change of mind, plausible surmise points to several inseparable considerations. Austerity did not work, and it produced social unrest. The unrest acquired a special significance as "political instability" in a host of new democracies traditionally allied with the United States. Hemispheric political hegemony was threatened, mildly by the Havana conference, but more seriously by the growing precedent of leaders, from Manley to Alfonsín, Sarney, and García, calling for collective resistance.

Third, the Baker plan did not work with the banks, which were soon hit by more sobering policy shifts. Although the Baker plan was significant as a more flexible approach to debt servicing, it assumed or cajoled new money from the increasingly skeptical banks. Normally sympathetic to some kind of temporary fix, the banks were stunned by Brazil's suspension of interest payments in early 1987. Within weeks, the major banks began to reclassify large Brazilian loans to nonaccrual status and to absorb heavy losses in shareholder equity and net income. The "write downs" that began with Republic Bank in March 1987 spread in two months to many others, including such giants as Chase Manhattan, Bank of America, Chemical Bank, J. P. Morgan, Mellon Bank, and, in the largest single "hit," Citicorp. These changes suggest the continuing urgency of the crisis. Lending of new money has declined substantially and is now mainly confined to international agencies. Without new money, Latin American governments must resort to de facto suspensions of payments or negotiate some form of permanent debt relief—as even the U.S. Treasury now seems to realize.

In general, it is the sheer failure of austerity policies to reduce the debt burden that urges change. "The most important single factor in feeding the upsurge of resistance to austerity has been Mexico, which dutifully carried out its IMF program only to find itself in new financial straits this year" (Riding 1985a). Economists and administration advisors have publicly criticized austerity policies for several years (e.g., Fishlow 1983; Lever 1984). Prepossessing policy makers such as Henry Kissinger and Felix Rohatyn have proposed alternatives that would shift portions of the debt burden to banks and governments in the developed nations. All of these critics, moreover, understand the problem as a practical and a political matter. There is a growing recognition of the need for new alternatives at the international level.

More decisive are changes in the relations of the state and social classes in Latin America. The debt crisis pits rebellious working and middle classes against international financiers and their allies in the domestic economy (e.g., exporters). The state is caught between powerful class interests, forced to concede a decisive role in social policy to its international patrons in exchange for survival loans with which to appease domestic antagonists. In a deeper sense, however, states are actors in this relationship with interests and conflicts of their own—interests in legitimacy and maintaining power, conflicts in their own ranks between public employees and state corporations on one hand and proponents of austerity on the other. The state, therefore, incorporates the debt crisis in a special way, absorbing the tensions of its political environment and endeavoring to mediate them according to its own capacities—themselves affected by how the mediation is conducted.

The social crisis plays itself out differently in each country as a result of class mobilization and the distinctive features of states. Since they enjoy less tolerance from their creditors and constituents, small democratic states are most vulnerable to crises. After some initial defiance, Manley

and the People's National Party were pressed by the IMF to adopt an un-
popular austerity program that helped lose the next election to Edward
Seaga and the Jamaican Labor Party (Girvan, Bernal, and Hughes 1980).
Panama and Ecuador experienced similar political turmoil, and in the
Dominican Republic the disturbances split the Dominican Revolutionary
Party.

Large authoritarian and corporatist states have been more successful
at implementing austerity policies (e.g., Mexico), but as some of these return to democratic ways, they gain another, popular base of support for
autonomous state action. Domestic class mobilization comes into play
here. The Bolivian government rejected IMF loans and conditions out
of respect for its powerful labor supporters. The Peronist movement in
Argentina is strong enough to persuade any democratic regime to oppose austerity programs, and in 1984 Alfonsín was all the more disposed
to do so given his need for support in the struggle with the retired, but
uncontrite, military. Self-imposed austerity in the Austral Program was
possible in June 1985 because it addressed a new hyperinflation, included price controls, and partook of Alfonsín's popularity for bringing
the former military dictators to trial. Peru was in an analogous situation
in 1985 when García was elected with strong labor support. There is no
functionalist formula for these developments. In each case states worked
out positions that responded to the conditions of government, international pressure, and domestic class mobilization.

It is in this context of political strategy that the mediated effects of
social unrest are best demonstrated. Latin American urban risings did
not single-handedly bring bankers to their knees, or their senses. But the
protests clearly influenced international agencies and states. The debt
crisis is still with us and moves by international actors are aimed primarily at relieving its destabilizing aspects, not least in the interests of the
banks. The role of the Latin American state in these moves is twofold.
On one hand, states are palpably threatened by class mobilizations that
demand an end to debt exploitation and the machinations of apparent
development. Governments have been deposed, retired, and seriously
weakened by popular insurgencies. Opposition to the IMF in some form
is often a political necessity. On the other hand, states have *used* the crisis
in their own struggles for survival and consolidation. The failures of apparent development are conveniently blamed on the opprobrious IMF.
Wandering constituencies are courted with tough talk during a crisis or
election campaign. New governments lay a broader foundation for state
reorganization with real and internationally risky resistance such as the
insistence on wage increases in Brazil and Argentina, Peru's limit on debt
service payments to 10 percent of export revenues, and Brazil's recent
moratorium on interest payments and refusal to enter into an IMF-
arranged agreement on rescheduling. The significance of social unrest

lies in how its varying potency articulates with the constraints and political alternatives of states. The state is the fulcrum, and the changing role of the state in Latin America is the most immediate general consequence of the crisis.

CONCLUSIONS

This chapter has focused on social unrest in relation to the state and the international political economy. Broad as that topic is, the chapter only glances at other forces that are reshaping state and society—cultural changes, for example, and the more direct role of national capital in the struggle for state power. Inferences about the nature of state reorganization must be qualified accordingly. "Any practical appraisal of where the current crisis is leading would require a careful analysis of the political composition of these movements [of international capital, national capital, and popular mobilizations], as well as an examination of the particular conditions of the elite forces in various Latin American countries" (MacEwan 1985: 12).

From the standpoint of popular movements, the debt crisis has generated an unprecedented wave of protest around the world. In Latin America, the protest was virulent precisely because governments had borrowed from the fund of world overaccumulation to support a "politicized economy" (Fishlow 1985) that granted to a few the benefits of development and to most its mere appearance. These ephemeral effects were real enough as long as they lasted, but short-lived, since they were bought on credit and loans were not employed in development that would generate the ability to repay. Much of the lending took place in highly inflationary times with negative interest rates, and the "free money" was susceptible to profligate use. The 1982 crisis caught nearly everyone by surprise.

Nations that combine economic hardship and a capacity for mobilization are more disposed to social unrest. The protest is expressed, according to the political contours of particular societies, in riots, demonstrations, and general strikes, but these intermix and generally engage coalescing elements of the urban poor, labor, and the middle classes. Protests prompted by austerity programs have frequently succeeded in reversing those policies in the short run and registering more durable changes in the state.

In the face of this crisis, states have perforce reorganized—democratized, moved perceptibly to the left, taken on the colors of economic nationalism, and experimented with continental unity. States have won temporary relief from mounting debt service and grudging acceptance of the necessity of growth. In the long run, the banks and lending countries will accept the inevitable—namely, that the debt cannot be paid and must either be absorbed by the developed economies, converted to equity, or expunged through some combination of the many available plans. In the short run, however, austerity pressures will be maintained to ensure debt servicing and to provide an eligibility test for new loans. As long as the debt service continues to roll in, international banks and the developed economies will benefit from the mounting net transfer of capital. But those profits depend on new and renegotiated loans, which recent events seem to have halted. The economic crisis is undiminished.

The Latin American social crisis has supplanted bureaucratic authoritarian regimes and helped to create a democratic austerity state that fuses the popular response to inequality with modest, pragmatic methods for confronting the pains of underdevelopment. Whether the reorganized democracies prove to be more than a means for getting through the lean years—whether they will find the political formula for equitable development—depends on how the forces analyzed here, particularly the popular movements, fare in the continuing struggle.

REFERENCES

Berk, Richard, and Howard Aldrich
    1972   "Patterns of Vandalism during Civil Disorders as an Indicator of Selection of Targets." *American Sociological Review* 37:533–47.
Block, Fred
    1977   *The Origins of International Economic Disorder: A Study of United States International Monetary Policy from World War II to the Present.* Berkeley and Los Angeles: University of California Press.
Brett, E. A.
    1983   *International Money and Capitalist Crisis: The Anatomy of Global Disintegration.* London: Heinemann.
Cardoso, Fernando, and Enzo Faletto
    1979   *Dependency and Development in Latin America.* Berkeley and Los Angeles: University of California Press.
Fishlow, Albert
    1983   "Brazil Gets Bad Medicine for Its Ailment." *Los Angeles Times,* 11 December.
    1985   "State and Economy in Latin America: New Models for the 1980s." Paper prepared for conference, The Impact of the Current Economic Crisis on the Social and Political Structure of the Newly Industrializing Countries, São Paulo, February.
Foxley, Alejandro
    1981   "Stabilization Policies and Their Effects on Employment and Income Distribution: A Latin American Perspective." In *Economic Stabilization in Developing Countries,* edited by William Cline and Sidney Weintraub, pp. 191–225. Washington, D.C.: Brookings Institution.
Frenkel, Roberto, and Guillermo O'Donnell
    1979   "The 'Stabilization' Programs of the Internationl Monetary Fund

328   JOHN WALTON

and Their Implications." In *Capitalism and the State in U.S.-Latin American Relations,* edited by Richard Fagen, pp. 171–216. Stanford, Calif.: Stanford University Press.

Girvan, Norman, Richard Bernal, and Wesley Hughes
  1980   "The IMF and the Third World: The Case of Jamaica, 1974–80." *Development Dialogue* 2:113–55.

Hirschman, Albert
  1986   "Out of Phase Again." *New York Review of Books,* 18 December.

Honeywell, Martin
  1983   *The Poverty Brokers: The IMF and Latin America.* London: Latin American Bureau.

Lever, Harold
  1984   "The Debt Won't Be Paid." *New York Review of Books,* 28 June.

MacEwan, Arthur
  1985   "The Current Crisis in Latin America and the International Economy." *Monthly Review* 36 (March):1–18.

Moffitt, Michael
  1983   *The World's Money: International Banking from Bretton Woods to the Brink of Insolvency.* New York: Simon & Schuster.

Nicholls, David
  1985   *Haiti in Caribbean Context: Ethnicity, Economy, and Revolt.* New York: St. Martin's Press.

O'Donnell, Guillermo
  1979   "Reflecting on Change in the Bureaucratic-Authoritarian State." *Latin American Research Review* 13, no. 1:3–38.

Riding, Alan
  1985a   "Latin American Debt Plan Is Assessed." *New York Times,* 7 October.
  1985b   "The U.S. Policy Shift is Seen as Key to Easing Latin Debt Crisis." *New York Times,* 3 October.

Sheahan, John
  1980   "Market-Oriented Economic Policies and Political Repression in Latin America." *Economic Development and Cultural Change* 28 (January):267–91.

Silva Herzog, Jesus
  1987   "The Mexican Debt Crisis: Lessons for the Americas." Public Address, University of California, Davis, 4 February.

Stallings, Barbara
  1985   "The Debt Crisis: Back to the Dependency Syndrome?" Paper presented at conference, The Impact of the Current Economic Crisis on the Social and Political Structure of the Newly Industrializing Countries, São Paulo, February.

Thompson, E. P.
  1971   "The Moral Economy of the English Crowd in the Eighteenth Century." *Past and Present* 50 (February):76–136.

CHAPTER ELEVEN

Poor People versus the State and Capital: Anatomy of a Successful Community Mobilization for Housing in Mexico City

Susan Eckstein

Studies of social movements typically focus on their origins. Much less is known about conditions that shape movement outcomes. This chapter addresses the empirical and analytic void. It focuses on a successful housing movement in downtown Mexico City, from a community perspective. People in the area pressured the government to build them affordable housing in place of run-down tenements. The community was a classic slum, located just blocks away from the central plaza, the center of governance and commerce in Mexico's capital city. Liberal and Marxist urbanologists, as well as planners, for different reasons had believed that such areas were doomed for demolition, to make room for more profitable commercial use (see, e.g., Turner 1968; Portes 1972; Burgess 1978). But the inner-city residents defied the presumed "forces of history."

The government's decision to respond to "popular sector" pressure for housing was especially noteworthy in that it occurred in the midst of a severe fiscal crisis, when authorities dramatically cut back social expenditures and implemented austerity measures that cut deeply into poor people's living standards. Moreover, it occurred in an area that the government had been trying to gentrify for middle-class habitation.

My analysis is based on extensive research in the inner-city area in 1967–68 and 1971–72 and on follow-up work in 1987 and again in 1997. It is based primarily on approximately sixty-five in-depth, open-ended interviews with local organization and institution officeholders and "influentials" in the four time periods. Some of the interviews lasted four to eight hours and took place on multiple occasions. Interviewees were asked

This chapter is a revised and updated version of an article that appeared initially in the *International Journal of Urban and Regional Research* 14, no. 2 (1990): 274–96.

about the activities of their groups, the history of their community, and their personal backgrounds. The earlier research also included formal interviews with one hundred residents and some fifteen institutionally based functionaries about political, economic, and social beliefs and practices; detailed interviews with a smaller sample of male residents about their work experiences; and a survey of local businesses. I also attended group meetings, talked informally with many community residents, and consulted documents, available surveys, and other relevant publications.[1]

Drawing on these diverse sources of information, my analysis elucidates conditions under which poor people's movements may succeed even when participants have few material resources and limited formal political power. First, a framework for understanding factors shaping movement dynamics is briefly summarized. It builds on my analysis in chapter 1. Then I shift to the case study. I provide a brief history of the community and the mobilization for housing, after which I examine factors accounting for the rise, success, and ultimate demise of the social movement.

THE PATTERNING OF "POPULAR" PROTEST: A CONTEXTUAL APPROACH

Building on the structural frame outlined in chapter 1, it is my contention that deteriorating economic conditions generate dissatisfaction but alone rarely prompt protest. Collective mobilizations for change are typically contingent on the support of well-placed individuals and groups, local institutional and cultural bonds, cross-class ties, limited state support through formal political channels, and the lack of alternative options or options perceived as attractive. Protest is more probable when groups have cultural repertoires, including repertoires of resistance, on which to build. The impact of mobilizations for change, in turn, hinges to a large extent on elite responses.

Economic Bases of Defiance

Much of the urban labor force in Latin America is either self-employed or employed in small businesses not covered by labor laws. People so employed experience tensions rooted more in market than in production relations. With competition stiff, collective energies in the so-called informal sector tend to center on restricting access to such work (so as to minimize competition), on minimizing work-related (e.g., taxes) and consumer costs, and on improving access to goods and services.

Residents of the urban squatter settlements that mushroomed on the periphery of Latin American cities during the years of import substitu-

---

1. For a more detailed discussion of my methodology, see Eckstein 1988: Appendixes A, B; Eckstein 1999: postscript.

tion typically were portrayed as politically quiescent because they generally supported incumbent governments and rarely parties of the left (except where, as in Allende's Chile, the left organized squatter invasions).[2] However, squatters' electoral support for mainstream parties should not obscure the fact that the illegal land seizures were an expression of consumer defiance: a form of protest against the high cost and low supply of shelter in the formal housing market.

Much less attention has been paid to inner-city Latin American slum dwellers. This is partly explained by the declining statistical significance of slums in the region once squatter settlements expanded on city peripheries. But the few urbanologists who analyzed such areas inaccurately understood what life there was like. They alleged that permanent slum dwellers (in contrast to residents of squatter settlements) were trapped in a "culture of poverty." The slum dwellers were portrayed at best as apathetic, hopeless, and disinclined to organize and participate in communal problem solving, at worst as ne'er-do-wells, violent, and crime-prone.[3] Economically mobile migrants who settled in the inner city supposedly moved away as soon as they could consolidate their status. The slum dwellers also purportedly had little sense of community and consequently were not likely to organize to improve their lot or to defend their neighborhood from demolition. This interpretation, as I argue in detail elsewhere (Eckstein 1990), was based on an ideal-typical (negative) conception of the inner city that had little empirical foundation. Not only did few students of the urban poor venture into the inner city, but those who did failed to modify their conceptions of inner-city residents in light of what they observed. They found slum dwellers to organize in opposition to discriminatory housing policies (e.g., in Lima in the 1970s), rent hikes (e.g., in Montevideo in the late 1970s and the 1980s and in São Paulo in 1987), and slum demolition (e.g., in Mexico). There is no a priori reason why residents of the inner city inherently passively accept state and market forces that drive up the cost of their subsistence while squatters on the periphery mobilize in self-defense. Responses of dwellers in both types of areas are contingent on contextual factors.

Contextual Factors Shaping Responses to Economically Rooted Grievances

Protest movements do not inevitably emerge out of contradictions in structural arrangements, even when subordinate groups perceive their situation to be unsatisfactory and unjust. As I argued in chapter 1, when institutions bring people together in similarly structured situations, indi-

2. See, e.g., Perlman 1975; Cornelius 1975; Dietz 1980.
3. On contrasting characterizations of slums and shantytown dwellers, see Mangin 1967; Turner 1968; Portes 1972; Dietz 1980. These authors portray shantytown dwellers, unlike inner-city residents, as entrepreneurial, community oriented, and efficacious. For a critique of these characterizations, see Eckstein 1990.

viduals are likely to feel that their private grievances are collectively shared and collectively soluble.

Mutually reinforcing neighborhood and work ties are especially likely to incline neighbors to organize on the basis of shared consumer concerns. And common involvements in community-based rituals that build on cultural repertoires of resistance make collective opposition to shared concerns more probable.

Macro economic policies introduced by debt-ridden governments in Latin America in the 1980s stirred new types of neighborhood-based movements. Austerity policies caused living costs to rise and income opportunities for the popular sector to contract. Religious and other nongovernmental organizations (NGOs) sought to address poor people's plight that formal political institutions did not.

Options poor people have, or perceive themselves to have, in turn influence how they respond to felt injustices. The stronger the kinship, community, cultural, and other ties, the more inclined aggrieved individuals are to seek collective solutions to their plight. The support of "better-situated people" with leadership skills and material resources may make collective protest more probable. Well-placed individuals may induce humble folk to consider as unacceptable conditions that they otherwise might tolerate. And the very involvement of better-situated people increases the chances that the government will respond to protest with reform rather than repression.

State institutional arrangements and the stance of people in authoritative positions similarly influence the likelihood and patterning of protest. Since democratically elected governments must regularly hold elections, they must be somewhat responsive to movements for change or risk electoral defeat. Otherwise, the electorate may shift its political loyalty. Independent of regime type, however, responses of authorities are contingent on the material and symbolic resources they command and on their priorities. And the way that authorities respond, not merely the resources they allocate, may affect movement dynamism. In the process of allocating goods and services, elites may defuse collective mobilizations.

If I am correct in arguing that the patterning and impact of protest are shaped by the above factors, their importance should be illustrated in the mobilization for housing in the inner city I studied. And the movement should dispel prevailing conceptions of Latin American slum dwellers as apathetic, hopeless, downtrodden, and disinclined to organize and partake in communal problem solving.

El Centro

El Centro, as I euphemistically call the inner-city area I studied, was an infamous slum of some sixty blocks. Along with neighboring *tugurios*, as such inner-city neighborhoods are called, El Centro housed most low-income families in the capital and about one-third of the city's total population through World War II. While the relative importance of *tugurios* declined as the city's population mushroomed after the war, and as the growing population of poor people settled in shantytowns on the city's periphery, in the mid-1980s El Centro still had about one hundred thousand inhabitants.

El Centro has a rich history that dates back to the pre-Conquest period. Spaniards then settled locally, imposing their own economic, political, and religious order on the indigenous population. And in the century and a half following independence, the area became home to nascent industries. Canned goods, chocolate, and mattress factories are representative of early Mexican industrialization. Most important, however, the area increasingly became home to thousands of artisans, especially shoemakers and metalworkers, and vendors and hawkers.

The quality of housing deteriorated over the years. Following the typical settlement pattern in Latin America, El Centro once was home to the rich. After modern transportation made suburban living feasible and attractive, the well-to-do moved away. Afterward, the area gradually became blighted. The former houses of the rich were subdivided into small apartments, and in the early twentieth century new dwellings were constructed with similarly small apartment units. The one-room, one- and two-story tenements, known as *vecindades,* were built inward from the street around courtyards. Absentee owned for the most part, they were poorly ventilated and rarely had interior plumbing. Tenement dwellers often had to rely on shared courtyards for cooking, washing, and toilet facilities (Lewis 1959).

Long-term residents at least paid little for their poorly serviced, dilapidated housing. Their rents were regulated by a law that had been enacted during World War II. However, more recent tenants had to pay either substantial money "under the table" to get access to apartments or the market value if the landlord found a way to circumvent the Rent Control Law. In essence, demand for housing in this well-situated area far exceeded the supply, the quality of the housing stock notwithstanding. As a result, rents of similarly run-down units varied substantially.

In the 1970s the government sought to upgrade El Centro: to replace tenements with modern multistory apartment complexes. The urban renewal project was consistent with the national government's pro-business bias and with urban analyses contending that capitalist class interests in commercially valuable inner-city land make slum demolition likely (see Turner 1968; Burgess 1978). Absentee landlords supported the neighborhood slum clearance plan. They wished to drive tenants out to benefit from the true market value of their properties. The government did not succeed, however, in implementing much of the urban renewal project. A tenants' movement, described below, and then the debt crisis put a halt to it.

In 1985 the area was hit by an earthquake that cost thousands of lives throughout the city. Few local residents perished in the rubble, but nature appeared to do what the government could not: force people to move and thereby clear the area for "development." The government's initial postearthquake policy was one of inaction. The Ministry of Urban Development and Ecology announced that the city's housing stock was sufficient to absorb people whose domiciles the earthquake made uninhabitable.

Who lived in this seemingly ill-fated area? At the time of the earthquake El Centro did house social outcasts and ne'er-do-wells, as previously noted characterizations of inner-city slums would predict. However, it also housed many more families who did quite well, relative to shantytown dwellers on the outskirts of the city. Most El Centro residents were hardworking "petty" (and some not so "petty") entrepreneurs or formal sector workers (including 12 percent who held "white-collar" jobs).[4] Heads of households earned on average twice the minimum wage.

In the 1980s, moreover, El Centro contained a flourishing informal economy, significantly more dynamic than the local economies of outlying shantytowns. Street activity then was also more vibrant than when I had been there in the late 1960s and early 1970s—partly because of, not despite, the country's debt crisis-linked economic downturn. As employment opportunities contracted in the productive and state service sectors, and as the purchasing power of salary and wage work plunged, increasing numbers of people turned to street commerce in this well-situated, traditional market area. Local families often took advantage of neighborhood market opportunities even when heads of households held formal sector jobs. The head of household could help out in the evenings and on weekends, while other family members maintained one or more stalls the rest of the time.

Merchants here are not dependent merely on local clientele. People come from the provinces and other low-income urban neighborhoods for produce, secondhand stolen and recycled items, and new consumer goods. Merchandise sells for less here than in outlying districts. Although once considered too dangerous to enter, in recent decades even middle-class people living elsewhere have come to include a visit to the area as a weekend outing. They come for bargain-priced designer clothing and high-tech equipment.

A section of El Centro became a flourishing center of contraband trade. The stiff import taxes that the government imposed during the import-substitution era to protect local industry here were circumvented. Thus, in the midst of the debt crisis, El Centro was bustling. Famous for its

---

4. Other countries have the equivalent of *vecindades*, for example, the *callejones* of Peru, the *conventillos* of Chile, and the *avenidas* or *vilas* of Brazil.

cut-rate prices, El Centro commerce continued to flourish even once neoliberal tariff roll-backs made previously illegal local trade legal.

Not only did economic life and employment patterns defy conceptions of slums, so too did living patterns. Many residents with the earning power to move opted to stay. At the time of the earthquake heads of households had lived in the district, on average, thirty years.[5] Those who could afford to move tolerated cramped living quarters in dilapidated buildings partly because housing was so inexpensive. In 1985, 97 percent of tenants paid, on average, 9 percent of the minimum wage in rent and more than 50 percent of the tenants paid no more than 4 percent of the minimum wage in rent. The Rent Control Law, which some landlords abused, kept rents well within the means of the typical tenant.

Residents tolerated the physical decay not merely because the price was right. They liked the area's central location and the informal sector opportunities it provided. Many of them also were fond of the community. Whereas outsiders viewed El Centro as a hard-core, crime-ridden slum, long-term residents, especially in the oldest section, took pride in their neighborhood. They viewed it as authentic, representing the "soul" of Mexico City. Since the 1970s the area even experienced a cultural renaissance, which included a muralist movement inspired by Mexico's early-twentieth-century revolutionary art. Commitment to the area was strengthened by local friendship, kinship, and work ties and reinforced through community-based rituals, festivities, and pilgrimages.

El Centro had its own subculture but not, in the main, one of despair. Although Oscar Lewis (1959, 1961) based his "culture of poverty" thesis on research he conducted locally, the subculture was vibrant and a source of pride. Its subculture included *modismos* (slang) and distinctive norms and values. The core of residents who were born and raised in the *barrio* had their own local heroes and "natural leaders." Among the prestigious and influential local leaders were informal sector vendors. They did not include industrialists who worked locally while living in more elegant neighborhoods, or state functionaries, with greater national standing, assigned to jobs in the area. *Comerciante* leaders could hold their positions for life, as long as rank-and-file members of their associations were satisfied with their work. In contrast, occupants of formal positions of power typically changed every three to six years, with changes at higher administrative and political levels.[6]

The local subculture was, in part, a "culture of resistance." Local

5. Unless indicated otherwise, statistical data on earnings, employment, and housing in the mid-1980s come from a survey conducted by SEDUE (1987). The data refer to neighboring areas in addition to El Centro.

6. The political system has been premised on the principle of "no re-election" since the consolidation of the 1910 revolution. This principle is strictly enforced.

pilgrimages to the Basilica of Guadelupe, the church of Mexico's patron saint, as well as to other shrines of favored Mexican saints and to rural communities from which families migrated reflect resistance to orthodox Catholicism and the Catholicism of the well-to-do. Similarly, local leaders were revered in part because they reflected community as distinct from elite values. The low residential turnover and large number of people who both lived and worked locally helped to keep community identification and the subculture alive.

In sum, El Centro proved the conventional image of Latin American slums ill founded. In the main, the area did not house a transient population, and the stable population was not composed of downwardly mobile social outcasts. Committed to the area, many residents engaged in locally based, informally organized social and cultural activities. And the slum dwellers were not always passive and quiescent.

Community Mobilization for Housing

Groups in El Centro mobilized for housing concerns in both the 1970s and the 1980s. However, their objectives changed after the 1985 earthquake. Initially seeking merely to defend their rights as tenants, after the earthquake they pressed for expropriation of absentee-owned properties and then for new housing.

Landlords' efforts to force tenants out of the *vecindades,* so that they could replace dilapidated buildings with new higher-rent units or more lucrative condominiums, increased in the 1970s. The value of the centrally located land rose with inflation tied to the country's mid-1970s oil boom. The increase in land value had been an impetus for the urban renewal project, which called for slum clearance.

The government's promulgation of a redevelopment plan made residents realize that their collective right to remain in the area was in jeopardy. Consequently, they sought creative ways to keep absentee landlords as well as authorities from forcing them to move. They organized with some outside assistance and set off firecrackers to create an atmosphere of disorder.[7] They were assisted by students and faculty from the national university who had been politicized and radicalized by state repression of demonstrators at the Plaza de las Tres Culturas in 1968, when officials fired on hundreds of student protesters. The repression had led some university affiliates to feel that change could best come about at the grassroots level by organizing outside official channels. Slum dwellers also were assisted by catechist groups inspired by liberation theology, and by the Coordinadora Nacional de Movimientos Urbanos Populares or CONAMUP. CONAMUP was a national "front" composed of neigh-

7. On tenant mobilizations in the area, see Rosales Ayala 1987. On CONAMUP, see *Estudios políticos* (1985–86).

borhood groups deliberately resisting state affiliation, a "new social move-ment" group that reflected disenchantment with state institutions and state authorities. Residents did not turn to the Institutionalized Revolu-tion Party (PRI), which authorities at the time referred to as the official party, or to government groups for redress, because state policy called for the bulldozing of the community.

The tenants' movement was partially effective—in a defensive man-ner. It helped to stop slum clearance. However, the quality of local hous-ing remained substandard.

After the earthquake a new grass-roots movement emerged when the government refused to address tenants' housing concerns. Residents or-ganized on a *vecindad* basis: on their own, with earthquake victims in other parts of the city, and with the support of parties of the left, univer-sity students and faculty, and "socially conscious" priests, architects, engi-neers, and other professionals. Each *vecindad* organization typically affiliated with a supra-*vecindad* group. The movement built on the rich informal social life of the community and on the "social infrastructure" of the tenants' movement of the 1970s.

Unable to contain the protest movement, the national government conceded and expropriated earthquake-damaged *vecindades* one month after the disaster. Expropriation reduced abuse by landlords, who tried to profit from the crisis by forcing tenants to leave and then raising rents, ostensibly to cover building repair costs. But mere expropriation did nothing to improve housing quality.

With housing in disrepair, earthquake victims—called *damnificados*—continued to mobilize. The *damnificados* of El Centro took their de-mands, en masse, to the central plaza, to the house of the president, and to government offices. One day, for example, residents of about two hun-dred *vecindades* marched from their earthquake-damaged quarters to the Plaza of the Constitution to make public their demands and present pe-titions to the mayor. And in March 1986 some fifty thousand earthquake victims, from El Centro and elsewhere, threatened to camp out in Aztec Stadium, where a world soccer tournament was scheduled to begin two months later, should the government not tend to their housing needs. Some groups in El Centro coordinated their defiance with earthquake victims from other areas through the Sole Coordinating Committee of Earthquake Victims, or CUD. The CUD was a middle-class-led multiclass movement organized at the neighborhood level. Like CONAMUP, it de-liberately formed independent of the state.

The community was not, however, unified in its response to the crisis. Groups differed in the strategies they advocated, their objectives, and their political leanings. Some *vecindad* groups had close links to the left. Some supported solidarity activity with Central American guerrilla groups and pressed for "proletarian justice." The left-leaning activists

presented themselves as a cultural vanguard and sought to form a unified front. They pressed for new housing, but they wanted the right to
build it themselves so as to minimize state intervention and thereby avoid
co-optation. Some such activists had been inspired by "ecclesial base
community" (CEB) activity initiated by a foreign priest who had lived in
the area until he was reassigned to a remote rural community (according
to locals, he was reassigned to dampen his political influence).

Another set of groups, by contrast, built on the values of the *barrio*.
They emphasized the cultural roots of the community, including its arti-
san roots. Their approach was more restorative: to preserve the *barrio*
and its traditions. They resisted both affiliation with the citywide organization of *damnificados* (the CUD) and formal ties with the left, because
they believed that either affiliation would compromise their interests
and values. They saw the CUD as primarily a middle-class organization
whose concerns differed from theirs.[8] But they agreed to work closely
with members of the intelligentsia, including left-leaning university students and faculty, "popular sector" activists, and a painter involved in the
local muralist movement. Whereas the more politicized groups appealed
to the younger generation, the more restorative groups appealed to the
middle-aged residents in the oldest part of the neighborhood.

Most significant, both sets of groups rejected working with the PRI. Although the PRI, in keeping with official policy, initially was indifferent to
local demands for housing, in the politicized context it also began to organize *vecindades* and sponsor marches. PRI otherwise risked losing political control in the area. Under the circumstances, some *vecindad*
associations opted to affiliate with the party, less out of political commitment than opportunism. They felt that their prospects of getting state assistance would thereby be improved, given the close ties between the
party and the government.

The earthquake-generated social turmoil shook the political system at
the highest levels, not merely in the affected neighborhoods. High-level
authorities had no tolerance for political disorder. As a consequence, in
Spring 1986, both cabinet-level and locally based municipal functionaries who were blamed for the disorder were replaced. Typically, such a
changing of the guards gives the appearance of government responsive-
ness to citizen concerns while leaving policies unaltered. However, this
time the change in leadership resulted in the construction of some
forty-eight thousand housing units in a little over a year in El Centro and
other inner-city areas damaged by the earthquake. In El Centro the proj-

---

8. The middle-class *damnificados* who dominated the CUD lived in high-rise condominium apartments. Many of them had property title problems and no strong commitment to their place of residence. By contrast, the people of El Centro were tenants in
rent-controlled buildings and had strong ties to their community.

ect consisted of low-cost, low-rise (two- to three-story) prefabricated units, forty square meters in size, on the sites of the old *vecindades*. The new buildings were painted in exquisite pastel colors, blue and green, purple and pink, yellow and orange.

Unlike the urban renewal plan of the 1970s (and earlier urban renewal projects elsewhere in the city), this one respected community traditions and community wants. The new apartment complexes had interior courtyards, like the *vecindades* they replaced. Moreover, earthquake victims were allowed to relocate on their old rental sites. Decades-old neighbors thus were able to stay in close proximity, and artisans and *comerciantes* could retain their clientele and marketing networks. Some well-organized *vecindades* pressured the government to build only the number of units that would accommodate former neighbors when, by government criteria, there was space for more. The new housing, implemented reluctantly in response to pressure from below, was such a success that it won national and international acclaim, including planning and architectural awards.

Former tenants were to become condominium owners after approximately eight years of monthly payments (although the government offered apartment recipients the option to speed up payments). Apartment dwellers were charged only the direct building costs. The monthly outlays were set at 20 to 30 percent of the minimum wage, which most El Centro households earned. Only about 13 percent of household heads in the district earned less than the minimum wage, and the government claimed that those who were slow to pay would not be forced to move.[9]

For most residents, the new housing was an improvement. Only about 14 percent of all households had larger apartments, in terms of square footage, in their old *vecindades*.[10] Moreover, all the new units had private bathrooms and kitchens, whereas only about one-third of the old rental units had private bathrooms and only two-thirds had private kitchens.

Reflecting newly found strength in collective mobilization, residents managed to pressure the government to build them provisional quarters locally to house them while the neighborhood was being rebuilt. When they considered the temporary housing inadequate, they set it ablaze. To restore order, the government gave in to neighborhood demands.

Some two-thirds of former tenants relocated in the new housing. Although not all *vecindades* damaged by the earthquake were rebuilt, and some tenements undamaged by the disaster were left in disrepair, the

9. It should be remembered that the monthly obligations were considerably higher than most former rents and that the cost of living in general had risen markedly in the 1980s after the peso devaluation. Before the earthquake more than half of the tenants paid no more than 4 percent of the minimum wage in rent.

10. Because many tenants had constructed mezzanine lofts in their high-ceilinged *vecindades*, their former *usable* floor space was greater than square-footage figures convey.

government physically upgraded the inner-city slum. And it did so in a manner that left much of the vibrant informal social and economic life of the community in tact.

Factors Accounting for the Success of the Housing Movement

Why did a government that in the past had promoted an urban renewal program favoring middle-class commercial and real estate interests reverse its stance and rebuild a humble neighborhood in a manner respecting local traditions, values, and wants? And why did it do so in the midst of a severe fiscal crisis, when it was restricting most social expenditures and implementing austerity policies that cut deeply into poor people's living standards? Several factors help to explain the community mobilization, on the one hand, and the state's response, on the other hand.

Shared Economic (Housing) Deprivation and Limited Alternatives. That there was a need and a demand for improved housing in El Centro is indisputable. But housing conditions were already bad before the earthquake. Indeed, in the 1970s the government used the area's physical disrepair as a pretext for its urban renewal project: for slum removal, not neighborhood reconstruction for its inhabitants. Had its plan been implemented, the area would have been gentrified, the local populace would have been squeezed out by high rents, and community traditions and lifestyles would have been lost in the name of "development."

The even more urgent need for improved housing after the earthquake, moreover, did not immediately persuade the government to rush to assist tenants. Officials instead argued that the city's housing stock was sufficient to accommodate El Centro dwellers left homeless by the disaster. Even once the government made the decision to address tenants' housing concerns, it might have built new accommodations for residents—as have other Latin American governments, including Mexico's, in the past—on the periphery of the city, where the commercial value of real estate was much lower.[11]

El Centro tenants, in turn, might have opted to move rather than to fight for affordable housing locally. Over the years some residents had left, to settle especially in outlying squatter settlements where they could afford their own homes and more living space. But the squatter option became less viable by the 1980s. Affordable housing in new settlements was hours away by public transportation, and prospects for urban amenities had dwindled. The fiscally strapped government had cut back expenditures on schools, roads, electricity, health facilities, and police

---

11. The military governments in Brazil and Chile, for example, forced the urban poor who resided in commercially valued land to relocate on the outskirts of Rio de Janeiro and Santiago, respectively. The Mexican government did the same in the mid-1960s when building a large middle-class modern housing complex near El Centro.

protection that it had provided in the 1960s and 1970s. With viable options limited, El Centro dwellers had reason to want to stay.

Community Dynamics.   Both the tenants' movement in the 1970s and the postearthquake housing movement in the 1980s in El Centro built on local social networks, organizations, and commitments. Collective efforts to address individual housing needs had economic, social, and cultural roots.

People who worked in El Centro had economic reasons for fighting the demolition of the area. Among those who both lived and worked in El Centro social and economic networks reinforced each other. Artisans and *comerciantes* (including *ambulantes,* who set up shop daily) were enmeshed in dense work, kinship, and friendship ties locally. Moreover, for decades local *comerciantes* had been organized, and their groups served as springboards for mobilization after the earthquake. While their associations were tied to the state's and the party's corporatist structure, their influence hinged on their informal power, including that of their natural leaders. Although the corporatist associations were conceived as instruments of co-optation and control, leaders of the largest and wealthiest vendor associations wielded considerable political clout.

Moreover, the crisis brought about by the earthquake strengthened community solidarity and resistance to both landlord abuse and government indifference. Locally based social networks, and the local subculture embedded in those networks, contributed to feelings that deprivations were commonly shared and that they could be collectively redressed.

Indicative of the vibrancy of informal social ties, shared traditions and beliefs, and neighbor solidarity, earthquake victims were quick to put up small shrines not only in the courtyards of their new condominiums but also in the communal areas of the temporary barracks set up during the period of housing construction. The shrines resembled ones they had in their old *vecindades.* Also, neighbors typically celebrated the inauguration of their new housing with ribbon-cutting ceremonies blessed by the priest. (Priests participated even though, according to the law at the time, outdoor religious activity was illegal.)

Ironically, the government's effort in the 1970s to bulldoze the area for "development" had the unintended effect of strengthening community resistance a decade later. Tenants' groups that had organized against the government's earlier urban renewal effort had experience and a social infrastructure on which to build after the earthquake.

Accordingly, the community's distinctive economic base, informal social networks, and experience in resisting state policies all help to explain why residents collectively mobilized to pressure the government to rebuild their community after the earthquake. The economic vitality of the area made earthquake victims all the more determined to band together for community restoration.

Support of "Better-situated" Individuals and Groups.   Over the years the corporatist structure of the polity led groups to deal dyadically with the state. After the earthquake, however, cross-class linkages formed that made it more difficult for authorities to ignore *damnificado* housing demands, in El Centro and elsewhere in the city.

Middle-class individuals and groups provided useful leadership and technical skills. Their very involvement contributed to the state's decision to be responsive to defiant *damnificados.* Sympathetic members of the middle class had been a force behind the 1970s tenants' movement, but in the 1980s middle-class support was much greater. Immediately after the earthquake the people of El Centro received material and social assistance from NGOs. Foreign aid agencies and privileged Mexicans provided food, clothing, and technical skills. Engineers and architects offered ideas about how to rebuild the community, and psychologists helped victims deal with the trauma of the disaster.

Not only did concerned middle-class individuals help and advise the people of El Centro. A cross-class alliance was formed through the CUD, the citywide organization of *damnificados.* Although some local groups refused to affiliate with the CUD, the multiclass base of the highly politicized CUD made it difficult for the government to ignore the demands of *damnificados* or to accommodate to the more politically influential middle-class CUD affiliates and not to lower class affiliates as well. Indeed, a leading architect of the redevelopment project admitted to me in an interview four years after the earthquake that officials had thought the CUD was more influential than proved to be the case.

In addition, the media helped the *damnificado* cause. Although for decades uncritical of the state, owing to government allocation of news print and payoffs to sympathetic journalists, the media began to exercise greater independence in the 1980s. Sympathetic coverage of the plight of the *damnificados* put additional pressure on the government to be responsive to their demands. A superman-type figure, known as Superbarrio, the Blue Demon, added to the publicity given to the *damnificados.* He appeared in public places calling attention to *damnificado* concerns.

That moneyed and politically powerful groups did not *oppose* the housing movement was also of consequence. Empathy, the specter of growing disorder, and foreign support all served to contain opposition from the economic and political elite who disapproved of government social expenditures at the time.

State Structures and Restructuring.   Government populist claims influenced how authorities responded to the mass mobilization for housing. While such claims had not kept officials from repressing popular sector movements in the past, the unpopularity of the 1968 student massacre at the Plaza de las Tres Culturas made authorities more sensitive to *damnificado* demands. Nonetheless, these political conditions did not make reform inevitable. Housing reconstruction came about only after individual and institutional changes occurred within the state apparatus itself.

The housing reconstruction project was contingent on personnel changes in early 1986. Most important, the president appointed a new minister of urban development and ecology, Manuel Camacho Solís, who initiated a novel strategy to deal with the crisis. All groups that had sympathized with the earthquake victims and championed their cause were required to agree to the terms specified in the accord he set forth before construction of new housing would begin. After consulting with defiant groups, Camacho Solís proposed the *Convenio de concertación democrática para la reconstrucción de vivienda.* The document specified technical, social, and financial aspects of the housing program.[12] One hundred six groups signed the pact in May 1986. Signatories included not only some dozen local groups based in El Centro and other groups of *damnificados* but also university and other educational groups and technical and professional associations. The *damnificados* did not need to belong to a group that signed the *Convenio* to get housing, but all of the *damnificado* advocacy groups were required to comply with the accord. In so doing, the groups agreed, in effect, to work with and not against the state. The accord cleverly brought groups into line and reined in social protest. Only after all groups within an area were compliant did construction begin. Indeed, building was delayed somewhat in El Centro because of lingering noncompliance with the state-imposed rules of the game.

The *Convenio* marked a turning point in state-community relations and in state-societal relations as well. It was consistent with long-standing state strategies of co-optation and inclusionary corporatist group relations, but it relied on a new means of conflict resolution where old mechanisms no longer worked. It involved a public pact between the state and social groups that did not necessarily affiliate with official associations, and it centered on binding negotiations between parties with disparate interests.

The *damnificado* pact, in essence, involved housing concessions in exchange for political quiescence. Satisfied with the depoliticizing effects of the *Convenio* vis-à-vis *damnificados,* the government initiated similar pacts, involving labor, business, and the government, in conjunction with

---

12. The document specified the following guidelines: dwellings were to be reconstructed on the same plots and for the original tenants of the damaged buidings; safe provisional housing was to be provided for families during the reconstruction period, close to their original homes, or families were to receive economic assistance if they found their own temporary accommodations; all the new dwellings would be forty square meters and include a living-dining room, two bedrooms, a bathroom, a kitchenette, and a space for washing; beneficiaries would have to repay only the direct building costs; and a committee, composed of representatives of the organizations participating in the agreement, would evaluate proposed alternative projects in terms of the norms of the agreement and existing building codes.

subsequent neoliberal austerity initiatives. In the process organized labor agreed to reforms that cut deeply into rank-and-file earning power. And authorities considered the *Convenio* such a success that Camacho Solís was named secretary-general of the trouble-ridden PRI, following its poor electoral showing in 1988. Then, on assuming the presidency, Carlos Salinas appointed the hero of the earthquake crisis mayor of Mexico City (where the PRI had lost, for the first time, the presidential election).

While responsive government leadership contributed to the success of the housing movement, several structural factors help to explain why leadership intervened on behalf of the popular sector in the midst of a severe fiscal crisis. First, the timing of the disaster was crucial. The government's international credibility was low owing to its enormous foreign debt and inability to repay it. Making matters worse, concomitantly there were disclosures of major corruption among high-ranking functionaries and allegations of state ties to the drug trade. Moreover, the World Cup brought the foreign media to Mexico. Under the circumstances, government action, or inaction, would be known to the world. Such visibility did not make housing reform inevitable, especially one respecting community lifestyles and traditions, but it put pressure on the state to act, and to act responsibly.

Second, the physical disaster removed the government somewhat from routine debt crisis-based budgetary constraints. Since 1982 the government had been closely monitored by international creditors, limited in its fiscal options, and cut off from new lines of foreign credit. Yet after the earthquake foreign assistance was forthcoming, following an international tradition of disaster relief provisioning. The World Bank financed the direct building costs of the housing program (U.S. $15,264.2 million), amounting to 57 percent of the program's total cost.

The success of the housing program is rooted in the government's determination to put the funding to good use and not in the foreign funding per se. The Mexican government used the relief funds differently than had other Latin American governments in the recent past. Neither President Anastasio Somoza Debayle in Nicaragua in the early 1970s nor President José Napoleón Duarte in El Salvador in the mid-1980s did anything comparable to Mexico's housing program with foreign relief funds after their countries experienced earthquakes. Somoza's misappropriation of international relief moneys was a precipitating factor in his overthrow; it turned the middle class against him, swelling the ranks of the mass-based Sandinista movement. Duarte's meager reconstruction effort did not result in comparable middle-class political "defection"; however, it confirmed widespread dissatisfaction with the government and fueled the continuation of the country's civil war.

To minimize bureaucratic resistance to reform and private appropriation of relief funds and to dampen demand for housing, the Mexican government created a special parastatal agency for overseeing the reconstruction program. As an independent agency of limited duration, with its own sources of financing, it was not subject to typical bureaucratic and political constraints—including red tape, corruption, and employee opposition or indifference to change. The semiautonomous agency had the capacity to implement a large housing program rapidly and could contract with private firms to do the construction. Moreover, the newly created agency was overseen by the Ministry of Urban Development and Ecology, where many progressive social scientists were employed.

The government, nonetheless, manipulated the reconstruction program in a manner that contained the demands of inner-city *damnificados*. In addressing the needs of different housing constituencies separately, the different groups of *damnificados* were delinked, which undermined the collective strength of the initially highly politicized multiclass alliance.

Accordingly, government authorities accommodated to *damnificado* demands both because the earthquake created such a political crisis that they felt pressured to respond and because the crisis removed them from routine constraints. Once inaction, or benign neglect, proved politically unfeasible, the powers that be responded to the crisis in an exemplary fashion.

Political Consequences of Material Concessions: Demobilization of the Housing Movement

Many *damnificados* in El Centro (and neighboring areas) attained relatively affordable housing as a result of their persistence. Yet the recipients of new condominiums were not the only victors of the housing movement. The government and the PRI, and to a certain extent real estate interests, emerged victorious as well.

That *damnificados* gained from their defiance is indisputable. The housing program in El Centro respected much of the social, cultural, and economic lifestyle of Mexico's most infamous slum. This preservation of a community has little precedent in urban renewal programs anywhere, including in the United States, where both resources and community power are greater.

Though financially costly, the government handled the program in a manner that strengthened it politically. Internationally, it demonstrated its ability to put foreign funds to good use. Domestically, it showed itself to be responsive and responsible. It also "tested," with the *Convenio de concertación,* a new strategy of conflict resolution, at a time when old strategies were proving increasingly ineffective. And within El Centro it established new channels of political control and political influence.

Both the government and the PRI manipulated housing allocations to strengthen their influence locally. The government insisted that each condominium complex be organized, that the organizations have a specific structure, that the leadership represent residents in their respective buildings vis-à-vis the state (rather than tenement dwellers coming en masse), and that the association heads be people who had not previously been active in tenants' groups. The government, that is, sought to bypass and undermine groups that had deliberately formed independently of the state and to deprive the housing movement leadership of its social base.

Gratitude for the condominiums made the residents of El Centro positively predisposed toward the PRI, especially in the old *barrio* section where the restorative movement was strongest and the left weakest. To fuse (or confuse) gratitude to the government with gratitude to the ruling party, the PRI offered residents a free tank of gas when they moved into their new condominiums. But the new condominium dwellers were instructed to petition the party for the gas. The "favor" was granted, less than a year before a presidential election. The head of the ministry in charge of the housing, who subsequently was appointed mayor of the city, used the program, in turn, to build up a following locally (as well as in other areas affected by the earthquake). Thus housing and house resources were allotted in a personalistic fashion that reinforced paternalistic government-party, state-societal relations. The style contrasts markedly with the impersonal manner in which public housing is allotted in the United States. From the state's vantage point, the strategy paid off. In 1988 most voters in El Centro, especially in the old barrio section, supported the PRI, while the lower-class electorate elsewhere in the city defected in large numbers to the opposition.[13]

The housing crisis was resolved in a manner that even met with minimum landlord opposition. Slum landlords did not entirely lose out, because the government compensated them for holdings it expropriated. Also, they had the right to contest any expropriation they considered unjust. Since the Rent Control Law limited landlord rent income, most El Centro *vecindad* proprietors did not oppose the urban reform.[14] They might have preferred to develop El Centro for greater personal gain, but community resistance foreclosed that option.

CONCLUSION

Low-income center-city neighborhoods in Third World cities have been presumed to be places of despair, disorganization, and apathy, destined to be bulldozed for "development." Because these slums were seen as crime-ridden and populated by social outcasts, few scholars or planners argued for their preservation. But the experience of El Centro suggests that the inner city is worthy of preservation and that, under certain conditions, people who live and work there will fight for their right to their community.

13. According to a leading architect of the *Convenio,* 85 percent of earthquake housing recipients voted for the PRI in 1988.

14. Landlord resistance was greater in middle-class neighborhoods. Opposition to the expropriation decree in these neighborhoods led to some rapid modifications in the law.

The successful mobilization for housing in El Centro gives credence to the thesis that protest movements among the economically and politically weak are especially likely to occur when a community of people with social and cultural bonds experience sudden material deprivation, when they lack attractive alternatives to exit and seek individual solutions to their plight, and when they have the support of better-situated individuals and groups. The experience of El Centro also suggests that movements are likely to succeed under such circumstances if the state claims to rule in the name of democracy, if it is biased toward reform rather than repression, and if the protest challenges regime legitimacy and regime norms.

The generalizability of this thesis ultimately rests, of course, on additional research. However, as this model of protest movements and their impact is extrapolated from the experiences of a broad range of Latin American social movements, there is reason to believe that the success of the inner-city movement was not contingent on a unique set of circumstances.

The impact of the social movement was not a zero-sum affair. The government and PRI, as well as the slum dwellers, benefited from the housing reform. To get housing, protest groups had to agree to quiescence and to accept the terms authorities imposed.

Depoliticization of the grassroots movement was not an inevitable outcome of material gain. The movement might, for example, have gone on to press for more housing for earthquake victims who failed to receive housing in conjunction with the initial reconstruction program. Or it might have pressed for new housing for tenement dwellers whose buildings were undamaged by the earthquake. Alternatively, it might have transformed the housing movement into a movement addressing other widely felt grievances: for example, into a movement in opposition to the austerity policies that drove locals' cost of living up and their earning power down (see chapter 10 for an analysis of such movements).

Government handling of the housing movement helped to keep collective mobilization at bay when the area (and the country) experienced another devastating economic recession in the mid-1990s. By then, however, the government's stance cost it the political loyalty of residents. In 1997 El Centro dwellers joined others in the capital to defeat the PRI in mayoral and other municipal as well as congressional contests. For the first time, they turned in significant numbers to pursue electoral channels of resistance.[15]

State undermining of community mobilization had the effect, if not

15. Voting for opposition parties, that is, not for the government-defined official party, reflected a changed concept of citizenship as well. On this changed concept and its relationsip to social movements of the 1980s, see Tamayo 1989, 1997; Foweraker 1989; Foweraker and Craig 1990; Davis 1994; and my discussion in the epilogue.

the intent, of also increasing the intrusion of market forces, market forces—consistent with the government's neoliberal restructuring—that eroded the social base of the community. For example, by 1997 it was estimated that 70 percent of local *comerciantes* lived elsewhere. Moneyed people with no community claims paid locals to give up their vending rights (Eckstein 1999: postscript). Residents were not compelled to sell their informal vending claims, but they were enticed by the opportunity to make a quick profit. The transfer price for the best locations went for $12,500, up from $5,000 ten years earlier. Most residents without stalls who wished to take advantage of local commercial opportunities could no longer afford to buy in.

In addition, outsiders began to rent or buy local condominium units. In 1997 about 25 percent of the units were estimated to no longer be used by the original housing recipients. New occupants typically used the apartments to store their merchandise, not for living, since they had to disassemble their street stalls and pack their wares daily. The market value of the units had risen to $15,000 by the late 1990s. Within ten years residents had attained an asset of considerable worth through their mobilization for community reconstruction.

Illegal market activity also became profitable, which further eroded the community. The growth in Mexico's drug economy, tied to rising U.S. demand, contributed to a secondary domestic market, especially for the cheapest drugs, marijuana, and industrial cement. A niche developed in El Centro for the cheaper drugs. Residents were caught up in this economy, both as consumers and as distributors, especially the younger generation who had difficulty finding work. By the late 1990s as many as one-third of local youth were believed to be involved in narcotrafficking.

The expanding drug economy generated violence and eroded the social order of El Centro. There came to be, on average, three drug-related homicides per week. The intrusion of drugs had such a corrosive effect that families who had been committed to the community and who had overseen its renaissance in the 1980s moved to more peripheral areas, to provide a safer haven for their children. The community thereby lost some of its most influential local leadership.

Accordingly, market dynamics were quietly transforming the area, although not in the manner envisioned by the government in the 1970s when it introduced its development plan. Market forces, which residents so effectively staved off by pressuring the government to continue to honor the Rent Control Law in the 1970s and then to sell them new housing at cost in the 1980s, may prove to be the community's undoing. By the late 1990s the inner-city area had come to serve the middle class as never before, albeit middle class *comerciantes* who had a comparative advantage within the informal economy, not the real estate interests that the government had fostered in the 1970s. The area was in the process of transformation without the government subjecting itself to criticism for siding with the middle class against the popular sector, at a time when austerity policies cut deeply into the living standards of the latter. For a community of people of modest means that so effectively resisted state and market pressures not to its liking, middle-class intrusion and the drug trade were unfortunate turns of events. Individual residents benefited from the material asset they acquired through their housing mobilization, but the community as a collectivity had disintegrated.

REFERENCES

Burgess, R.
1978   "Petty Commodity Housing or Dweller Control? A Critique of John Turner's View on Housing Policy." *World Development* 6: 1105–33.

Cornelius, Wayne
1975   *Politics and the Migrant Poor in Mexico City.* Stanford: Stanford University Press.

Davis, Diane
1994   "Failed Democratic Reform in Contemporary Mexico: From Social Movements to the State and Back Again." *Journal of Latin American Studies* 26: 375–408.

Dietz, Henry
1980   *Poverty and Problem-solving under Military Rule: The Urban Poor in Lima, Peru.* Austin: University of Texas Press.

Eckstein, Susan
1988   *The Poverty of Revolution: The State and Urban Poor in Mexico.* Princeton: Princeton University Press.
1990   "Urbanization Revisited: Inner City Slum of Hope and Squatter Settlement of Despair." *World Development* 18 (2): 274–96.
1999   *El estado y la pobreza urbana en México.* Mexico City: Siglo XXI.

Foweraker, Joe
1989   "Los movimientos populares y la transformación del sistema político mexicano." *Revista Mexicana de Sociología* 51 (4): 93–113.

Foweraker, Joe, and Anne Craig, eds.
1990   *Popular Movements and Political Change in Mexico.* Boulder, Colo: Westview Press.

Lewis, Oscar
1959   *Five Families: Mexican Case Studies in the Culture of Poverty.* New York: Random House.
1961   *The Children of Sanchez: Autobiography of a Mexican Family.* New York: Random House.

Mangin, William
1967   "Latin American Squatter Settlements: A Problem and a Solution." *Latin American Research Review* 2: 65–98.

Perlman, Janice
1975   *The Myth of Marginality: Urban Poverty and Politics in Rio de Janeiro.* Berkeley: University of California Press.

Portes, Alejandro
    1972   "The Urban Slum in Chile: Types and Correlates," *Ekistics* 202: 175–80.
Rosales, Ayala, and Silvano Héctor
    1987   *Tepito arte acá.* Cuernavaca: Universidad Nacional Autónoma de México, Centro Regional de Investigaciones Multidisciplinarias.
Secretaría de Desarrollo Urbano y Ecología (SEDUE)
    1987   *Housing Reconstruction Program in Mexico City.* Mexico City: SEDUE.
Tamayo, Sergio
    1989   *Vida digna en las ciudades: El movimiento urbano popular en México, 1980–1985.* Mexico: Gernika & Universidad Autonoma Metropolitana-A.
    1997   "La participación ciudadana: Un proceso." *Revista Mexicana de Sociología* 59 (4): 155–85.
Turner, John
    1968   "Housing Priorities, Settlement Patterns, and Urban Development in Modernizing Countries." *Journal of the American Institute of Planners* 34: 354–63.

EPILOGUE

Where Have All the Movements Gone?
Latin American Social Movements
at the New Millennium

Born of both hope for a better future and despair over conditions past and present, the Latin American social movements described in this volume had experienced different life histories by the start of the new millennium. Some movements accomplished part, if not all, of their goals, and others were more influential than most participants dreamed possible. But some movements were less fortunate; they failed to bring about change, and their members lost their lives or were imprisoned. What accounts for such diverse fates?

This epilogue gives me a unique opportunity to reflect on the long-term effects of social movements and to compare older movements with those that emerged on their heels. It also allows for an analysis of the effects of macro economic, political, and social conditions on mobilizations for change, including macro changes the movements themselves helped to usher in. In particular, it highlights the impact of deepening U.S.- and International Monetary Fund (IMF)-backed market reforms, democratization rooted both in the demise of the Cold War and in domestic opposition to military rule, and increased transnational cultural and social ties. The new structures generated new grievances and new bases of movements for change at the same time that they addressed problems and grievances of the past. This epilogue also affords an opportunity to elucidate how Latin American social movements and the changes they helped to bring about modified the efforts of even such powerful institutions as those associated with the so-called Washington

I benefited from comments on earlier drafts of this chapter by Diane Davis, Manuel Antonio Garretón M., Daniel Levine, Scott Mainwaring, Cynthia McClintock, June Nash, Maryssa Navarro, John Walton, and Leon Zamosc, as well as from reading recent works of theirs. They also kindly provided me with information specifically for this chapter. In addition, I benefited from discussions with Eduardo Gamarra, Daniel Mato, Peter Ward, Kay Warren, and Deborah Yashar, among others.

consensus—the U.S. government, the IMF, and the World Bank—to re-make Latin America in its own image.

Global trends rooted in a restructuring of production, consumption, and capital accumulation on a world scale affected all regions of the Third World. Yet conditions distinctive to Latin America influenced the speed, scale, and nature of changes there. The debt crisis of the 1980s brought import substitution, the Latin American development model of choice since World War II, to a precipitous halt. It discredited the model and weakened the negotiating position of governments in the region vis-à-vis foreign banks. Neoliberalism arose on its ashes. Premised on the prioritization of unfettered market activity, neoliberalism contributed to privatization of economic activity, removal of state subsidies and price controls, liberalization of prices, export promotion, and the reduction of barriers to trade and foreign investment. Economists helped to legiti-mate the new economic model. They argued that it fostered maximum efficiency, growth, trade, and repayment of foreign debt.

By the dawn of the new millennium, the new economic schema bene-fited most those domestic sectors and firms best able to compete in a globalized free trade economy. It benefited large-scale foreign businesses above all, insofar as the restructuring increased their access to local mar-kets. Latin American governments nonetheless saw the restructuring as a means to make their economies more competitive, to generate hard cur-rency for debt repayments and imports, and to make their economies more attractive to investors. But what may be good for banks, investors, and, in certain respects, governments has not been uniformly and consis-tently good for many in the lower, working, and even middle class, at least in the short run. For this reason, the deepening of the neoliberal reform process has continued to spark resistance, although the new insti-tutional changes shifted the social bases and concerns of movements.

Somewhat independently but in tandem, democratization took the re-gion by storm. Latin America joined the global democratizing trend. Once Latin America became safe both for democracy and for business and the Cold War ended with the collapse of the Soviet bloc and then the Soviet Union, Washington withdrew its support of the military dicta-torships it had backed from the 1960s through the 1980s. But democra-tization also had widespread domestic support in the region. Indeed, movements of the 1980s, several of which are analyzed in this book, helped to usher in the political transformations.

Civilian rule and competitive elections became pillars of the new democracies. In most countries the political transformations put an end to the deplorable human rights abuses of the former regimes and opened up institutional channels of representation and demand making. Yet the depth and meaning of democratization has varied across borders in the region. The deepening of democracy has been uneven and in some in-stances contentious.

The global political and economic structural homogenization has cultural underpinnings as well. Values and norms sanctioned from above and abroad, that is, backed by dominant elites, foreign governments, and multilateral powers, have legitimated the changes. Yet Latin American responses to structural reforms have been filtered by local beliefs, customs, and mores and shaped by people's positions in institutional hierarchies and social involvements. Individuals, groups, and communities have in certain respects resisted cultural homogenization and pressured for respect for local particularities.

Just as people's views toward reforms have varied with their lived experiences and values, so too have social scientists' analyses been contingent on the conceptual lenses through which they view society. What social scientists see, highlight, and prioritize depends on their a priori assumptions and analytic frames. At one extreme are neoliberal economists and others who attach primacy to global modernization dynamics and point to transnational homogenizing tendencies and international policy makers and political analysts who point to a correlation and natural affinity between democratization and market reforms.[1] They perceive the homogenization to be good and political institutions to be the basis for channeling concerns. Their frame of analysis does not point them to social movements, which they would see as fetters obstructing the full play of market forces and democratic institutional practices.

At the other extreme are postmodernists, who focus on local resistance and local variability, which they attribute to disparately held beliefs and norms. From their perspective, Third World people do not automatically accept the views and practices imposed from above and abroad, and there is no unilinear path of development. In place of global universal structures, processes, and values, postmodernists highlight what they call "decentered" particularities, rooted not merely or mainly in institutional relations but in individual and group perceptions and beliefs. Paradoxically, the two extreme perspectives gained currency in the 1990s.

Meanwhile, Marxists and neo-marxists continue to attribute primacy to class dynamics on the national and international level, and they see social change as driven first and foremost by class interests. To the extent that they focus on resistance to change, they highlight economically rooted social movements, above all, movements rooted in relations of production. State-centric analysts, in turn, highlight how the state, institutionally and ideologically, mediates between globalization tendencies, on the one hand, and civil society, on the other. Social movements

---

1. They contribute to an inaccurate reinterpretation of history. In their efforts to discredit import substitution, they ignore the internationally impressive growth rates that some Latin American countries experienced under military rule and under protectionist "inwardly oriented" economies. The key problem with import substitution in Latin America was that exports were not prioritized along with production for the domestic market.

accordingly are seen not merely as responses to globally grounded tendencies, class dynamics, or "decentered" local beliefs, customs, and norms, as neoliberal/modernization, Marxist, and postmodern analysts emphasize, but to state institutional structures, practices, and discourse.

In essence, each of the different perspectives focuses on distinctive features of a world that in the concrete is complex. Each frame of analysis highlights certain tendencies while leaving others unnoticed, undocumented, and unanalyzed. While a specific frame of analysis may reveal more, and more accurately account for what indeed transpires, precisely because different frames privilege different information each is more illuminating in certain contexts than others.

I use a historically grounded institutional approach, so ably drawn on by the authors in this volume, to explore below the conditions under which features identified with the different perspectives highlight and explain social movement dynamics of the 1990s. This textured approach can capture the interplay between macro political, social, cultural, and economic dynamics, on the one hand, and the social relations in which deprivations are experienced, on the other. Institutionally based activity provides a window through which to illuminate the relationship between structure and agency, structure and culture. Historically rooted conditions and cultural practices will be shown to continue to shape but not predetermine when and how Latin Americans have collectively resisted the established order and pressed for change.

But to fully understand the social movements, we need to capture the role of human agency as well. Marx remains correct in his argument that men make history but not under conditions of their choosing. Even when common features are found in different settings to pattern protest, they alone do not explain when movements arise, the form they take, the range of issues they address, and the effects they have. And the more sustained movements are not single-issue based. They might respond to grievances rooted in specific neoliberal policies but to other concerns as well. The very multiplicity of concerns may make mobilization against any unpopular reform more probable.

A contextualized approach thus best explains both the generalizable and the specific features of social movements. It can best explain diverse local responses to similar macro changes and commonalties among localized responses. Deploying this frame of analysis, I first summarize the repertoire of protest and resistance in the 1990s and then analyze movements in terms of their social bases.

VARIED FORMS OF PROTEST

Large-scale rebellions and revolutions were less visible on the Latin American political map at the turn of the century than in the 1960s through mid-1980s. The end of the Cold War eroded the appeal of Marxism for pragmatic, if not ideological, reasons. The Soviet Union and its regional ally Cuba could no longer be counted on for economic assistance. And a wave of redemocratization brought to power more flexible and decentralized governments that undermined the principal political, if not social and economic base, for revolution. The change in macro political conditions, however, neither eliminated old guerrilla movements nor prevented new ones from emerging. But the change kept many guerrilla movements from expanding their base of support, a prerequisite—elaborated by Wickham-Crowley in chapter 4—for a revolutionary seizure of power.

The military return to the barracks defused large-scale human rights as well as most guerrilla movements. The multiclass movements in Chile, Brazil, and Argentina, described in this volume by Garretón, Alves, and Navarro, respectively, for all intents and purposes died quiet deaths with transitions to civilian rule. Meanwhile, after a brief efflorescence of strike activity during redemocratization, most tensions between labor and capital ceased to be channeled through work disruptions. The "invisible market," as concretely experienced with stepped-up global competition, made the risks of job loss too great. Under the circumstances private sector workers accepted, however grudgingly, material setbacks at work while turning to strategies to lower their living and other costs and supplement their incomes. Remaining strike activity centered in the more politically vulnerable public sector, which underwent extensive downsizing with the new economic model.

At the same time, the repertoire of social movements expanded. Latin America became even more of a living museum of mobilization activity in the 1990s than in previous decades. Older movements continued, though often in modified form, while new movements, born of new concerns, new identities, and new resources, arose.

Reflecting the persistence of movements rooted in conditions of the past, residues of the human rights movements against the military regimes remained. New civilian authorities, their own power precarious, granted immunity to officers of the repressive regimes they replaced. They put their own concern with governance above justice. Against this backdrop, a core of activists continued to press for military accountability for former crimes against humanity. This was especially true in Argentina, where more civilians were killed than in any other Latin American country besides Guatemala; there, opposition to the military also was grounded in a cohesive single-issue movement, and the armed forces left office discredited militarily (after the failed Malvinas War) as well as economically and morally. Meanwhile, a decade after the return to civilian rule, Chilean memories of Pinochet's atrocities resurfaced and stirred protests when a Spanish judge sought to extradite and bring to trial the then eighty-two-year-old former dictator. The Spanish issued an arrest warrant when Pinochet was hospitalized in London. They issued an arrest warrant when Pinochet was hospitalized in London. The manner in which Pinochet orchestrated the Chilean democratic transition, described below in more detail, prevented Chileans from pressing charges on their own. Until then the prohibition had forced Chileans to privatize their longing for military accountability. Even after Pinochet's arrest government disapproval tempered collective pressure for justice. We see here how new regime institutional practices shape but alone do not determine what transpires with movements rooted in the past.

The macro political and economic changes of the 1990s, moreover, stirred new movements policy makers had not intended and often did not want. Whatever the logic of the economic restructuring, the deepening of the reform process eliminated jobs, generated new inequities, and, in most countries, also reduced income opportunities for the urban and rural poor. Reforms also made the populace more vulnerable to market vicissitudes. The new conditions generated new grievances, among new categories of people, and, in turn, new collective efforts for change. The squeezed middle class became more defiant. And indigenous peoples, in countries where they were still numerically significant, became more assertive and they developed new identities in the process. No longer did they unequivocally embrace assimilation and acculturation.

The range of economically grounded movements, much less other movements, are not understandable independent of politics, societal relations, and culture. First, Latin American governments were responsible for implementing the new economic policies. Market fetters did not simply disappear on their own. Defiance accordingly varied, in part, with how lean and mean and how populist the new democracies were. Also, the new democracies typically tolerated citizen claims more than their military predecessors had, which made grievance-based collective demand making less risky and sometimes therefore more likely. The less repressive milieu also brought previously submerged identities, such as ethnicities, to the fore, which generated new social movements for new rights. Second, citizen responses varied with the social context in which reforms were embedded. The weaker and more politicized a regime and the greater the number of people experiencing new deprivations, the more probable the opposition to unpopular policies. Similarly, state-labor relations patterned protest. Defiance against neoliberal reforms was most frequent in the countries where civil society was highly politicized through trade unions and not allied in cross-class government-orchestrated "pacts."

The very "thickening" of civil society that redemocratization allowed generated new bases of collective action. The thickening eroded the *relative* power, authority, and influence of dominant and ruling classes. Subaltern cultures were thereby strengthened, to the point that assimilation, acculturation, and acquiescence fell somewhat out of favor. Under the changed conditions, groups pressed for respect for their differences and new citizenship claims.[2]

The repertoire of movements was also influenced by new involvements of nongovernmental organizations, NGOs. Directly and indirectly, NGOs contributed to social movement formation and to new types of collective efforts to bring about reform. In providing human and material resources, NGOs sparked new collective identities and new collective efforts to resolve problems previously addressed and redressed individually, if at all (see Chalmers et al. 1996; Jelin 1994). They also framed issues in ways that brought attention and resources to local groups.

Typically, the more meager the state provisioning, the greater the impact of NGOs. The NGOs of consequence were both national and international in origin and reach. National NGOs often relied on international networks, international sources of communication, and international funding, and they appealed to international norms. Many of them also depended, their formal status notwithstanding, on domestic and foreign government support (Keck and Sikkink 1998).

New NGO-fostered activity was partly the ripple effect of a shift in U.S. foreign policy. Beginning with the Reagan administration (1980–88), Washington cut back bilateral assistance and favored the private sector, voluntary aid, and contracting to independent groups responsibility for carrying out government-funded missions. After the demise of the Cold War, U.S. aid shrank further, rooted as bilateral aid had been in political more than humanitarian considerations. In the changed international context, the relative and not merely absolute importance of NGOs increased.

But NGO influence picked up in the 1980s also, because new insecurities made people open to assistance. The Catholic church, itself in crisis, through ecclesial base communities (CEBs) and the preferential option for the poor they espoused, championed NGO-fueled secular as well as religious movements for change. The changed influence of CEBs by the turn of the twenty-first century is detailed below.

While NGOs filled an important social vacuum under the dictatorships, their focus shifted somewhat with redemocratization—from defensive claims against injustices to proactive initiatives for new rights. They contributed to a modification in how civil society organized and for what ends. In part by expanding domains of mobilization, NGOs created pockets in which new relationships took shape and new types of demands found voice. NGOs induced women in particular to become less passive and accepting of their fate. Yet with the return to democracy and

2. For a more pessimistic analysis of civil society vibrancy under redemocratization, see Oxhorn 1998. His pessimism derives, in part, from his focus on activity in the political domain.

the initiation of government-backed targeted anti-poverty programs (meager as they were), NGO-nurtured poor people's movements, especially neighborhood-based movements, lost momentum. Governments used the programs to win support and undermine movements that challenged their authority.

Some, though not all, NGOs themselves changed in the 1990s. As bilateral and multilateral donors cut back their NGO funding after the Cold War, NGOs became more dependent on private money. They became, in turn, more subject to market logic[3] and, accordingly, less accountable to those they claimed to represent.

Subject to similar macro economic, political, and social trends, Latin American countries experienced a certain pan-regional movement homogenization. The homogenization was partially rooted in groups and governments learning from each other. Latin American governments mimicked each other in ways that unwittingly stirred similar types of movements. And groups emulated each other across national borders. Las Madres de Plaza de Mayo, for example, became a model for women's struggles for women's rights and basic human rights. Meanwhile, modern means of communication brought messages to and from the remotest areas of the continent. Accordingly, indigenous movements, such as the Zapatistas in Mexico's poorest region, disseminated information electronically that sparked other Latin American movements. By the 1990s the Internet influenced social movements.

Some movements rooted in global trends nonetheless took on a distinctive regional character. The "IMF protests" described by Walton in chapter 10, for example, became implanted in the Latin American repertoire even when protests remained localized and short-lived. No other region experienced as many. And in Latin America such protests were more gendered, that is, more female based, and, in comparison especially to North Africa and the Middle East, more secular in orientation. In the latter regions, mushrooming fundamentalist movements channeled outrage against neoliberal reforms (Walton 1998).

No Latin American country, however, experienced the impact of IMF protests that Indonesia did in 1998. There, anger over newly imposed austerity measures sparked a movement that forced the notoriously corrupt long-standing autocratic ruler Suharto from power and paved the way for democratization. The political opening quickly fueled a successful independence movement in East Timor, colonized by Indonesia as well. Comparable rulers in Latin America, such as Batista, Somoza, and Stroesner, in Cuba, Nicaragua, and Paraguay, respectively, had been ousted by mass movements in preceding decades. Of less political significance, mass opposition to austerity measures, however, on occasion

3. Multilateral banks, to varying degrees depending on their mission, were themselves subject to a market logic. See Reilley 1996.

drove even democratically elected governments in Latin America from power. This occurred, for example, in Ecuador.

Similar macro experiences notwithstanding, countries *within* Latin America had somewhat distinctive movement repertoires in the 1990s, as in the preceding decades, owing to distinctive traditions and distinctive local conditions. Protest movements in Colombia, for example, continued to build on a long-standing tradition of violence. And protests were most prevalent in countries where governments were discredited and weak, where the populace was politicized, and where government reforms made people feel collectively vulnerable—in, for example, Venezuela, Argentina, and Bolivia as well as Colombia.

SOCIAL BASES OF DEFIANCE

In chapter 1, I argued that social movements typically varied with their social base, although not in a mechanistic, predetermined way. People respond not to macro reforms in the abstract but to the manner in which they experience them concretely.

Contextual factors—namely, culture, institutional structures, interclass ties, and real or perceived options—as well as elite responses, class alliances, and global economic and political forces were shown in the 1960s through 1980s to shape movements and their outcomes. Resources and leadership, internal to groups, also influenced what movements did and with what effect. Below I show how these factors continued to influence social movements in the 1990s, with respect to both movements that have been analyzed in this book and new ones.

I do not pretend to discuss all movements of the 1990s. Rather, I focus on a sampling, and only in terms of their social bases.[4] The social bases delineated below should be seen as analytically, but not necessarily empirically, distinguishable. In the everyday world people who come together in a single movement have certain shared identities, experiences, and concerns. But they typically come with different bundles of experiences, expectations, and values that may, in turn, influence movement dynamics.

Movements Rooted in Economic Relations

In response to advice and pressure from Washington, international banks, and foreign advisers, Latin American governments in the 1990s embraced neoliberalism as a set of policies and an economic philosophy.

---

4. An issue-oriented approach, by contrast, would privilege, for example, environmental movements. Environmental movements gained momentum by the 1990s. They did so not merely because pollution, soil erosion, and other problems worsened but also because such concerns complemented other group concerns, because NGOs supported such preoccupations, and because they resonated with overseas environmental concerns and movements. Some environmental movements are analyzed in this chapter, in the context of movement bases.

They sought to restructure their economies accordingly. Yet the depth of the reform process they set in place varied. Electoral politics, as well as social movements, tempered what they did.

Reforms advisable from a macro economic perspective often generated new inequalities and new felt injustices in a region that already suffered profound economic inequality. Although most Latin Americans responded with passivity or hidden resistance to newly experienced deprivations, on a range of occasions they openly opposed aspects of the reforms they found especially egregious. But protests came to focus less on directly experienced tensions between labor and capital, because in the age of globalization the risks to private sector laborers were too great. Instead, economic protests focused on government policies, as people experienced them: for example, on official price and tax increases, currency devaluations, and agrarian reforms that deprived peasants of their historical claims to land. These policies centered on the removal of market fetters to improve market competition and export earnings and on budgetary considerations. How people responded hinged not merely on their objective experiences but also on the work of political parties, unions, and other groups, as well as assessments of risks and gains.

Peasant-based Movements. Trade and price liberalization, plus the new export emphasis, subjected peasant producers to more competition from domestic and foreign agribusiness and to world market commodity price fluctuations than during the import-substitution era. And in countries where governments rescinded agrarian reforms that had protected peasant land rights, as part of their drive to remove market fetters, small-scale agriculturalists were made even more vulnerable to global market dynamics. Large farmers, with access to more capital and technology as well as land and to better marketing networks, were best placed to compete in the new economic order.

Growing land concentration and capitalization of production, combined with demographic pressures, left *campesinos* increasingly landless and impoverished. Perceiving that rural options were inadequate, they typically opted for migration, in Albert Hirschman's (1970) terminology, for "exit" versus "voice." The number of Latin Americans living in the countryside plunged from about 60 percent in 1960 to less than 30 percent in the 1990s. Urbanization rates in Latin America resemble those of the United States and Western Europe, not those of other Third World regions. There are several reasons for Latin Americans' individuated response to the agrarian crisis since the mid-1980s. First, mass migration had been decades in the making, increasing the likelihood that additional *campesinos* would "opt out"; it began during the era of import substitution, when government policies were urban biased. Migrants during that period came to feel that cities offered the best opportunities, especially for their children. Thus, when opting for migration in the 1990s, peasants built on long-standing urban family and community networks, even as urban opportunities contracted. Second, owing to the extreme concentration of land ownership in Latin America, more than in other poor regions of the world, rural opportunities were objectively meager. Third, the rural power structure made collective *campesino* resistance difficult. Landlords were powerful. They could hire their own militia, and they had government, police, and juridical allies. Meanwhile, peasants often farmed independently, so that they experienced their hardships individually, not collectively.

Workers seeking individual solutions to their plight increasingly also turned to emigration. It is noteworthy that neoliberalism in the Western Hemisphere does not allow for the free legal mobility of labor across national borders. Although transnational migration occurs among Latin American countries, on both a seasonal and a more permanent basis, the United States is the main magnet of immigration. Many Latin Americans come illegally to the United States because they cannot enter legally, given U.S. immigration restrictions. The inability of neoliberalism to address domestic Latin American labor force needs accordingly has had the unintended effect of stirring international illegal activity.

The migration across borders reflects a growing disparity in opportunities between the weakest and strongest economies in the region and, most of all, between all Latin American countries and the United States, the core economy in the hemisphere. In some countries, especially El Salvador, Guatemala, Nicaragua, and Peru in the 1980s and Colombia up to the present, political violence, only partially explained by neoliberal-linked economic dislocations and blocked economic opportunities, further contributed to uprooting. Immigration is politically as well as economically driven.

Were exit not an option, agrarian tensions undoubtedly would have fueled more rural protests. Indeed, among *campesinos* who have not opted out, some have turned to collective efforts to improve their lot. Even when grounded in neoliberal-linked dislocations and deprivations, the movements of significance reflect an interplay among cultural, social, and political, as well as economic, forces. For this reason, the key movements, described below, have taken different forms in different countries.

Variants of Marxism inspired guerrilla movements between the 1960s and the 1980s, as Wickham-Crowley described. The collapse of the Soviet bloc and the Soviet Union and the crisis Cuba suffered as a consequence eroded most external Latin American sources of guerrilla training, funding, and inspiration by the end of the twentieth-century. The fate of guerrilla movements as of the 1990s, nonetheless, was only partially rooted in the changed international context, because the movements always were rooted largely in domestic conditions. Since market reforms caused peasants to experience new dislocations and new immiseration, and since state structures and civil society remained weak in most rural regions, a potential base for guerrilla activity continued (Degregori 1986; Degregori et al. 1996). What did change, with significant ramifications, was the source of guerrilla funding. Rebels turned increasingly to kidnappings and drug trafficking for money.

Sendero Luminoso—whose earlier history Cynthia McClintock detailed in chapter 2—expanded its social base in the early 1990s in the sprawling shantytowns of Lima, the country's capital, as well as in the countryside. The combination of the state's inability to provide elemental public services, to rein in drug activity, and to prevent a drastic economic downturn at the time (as evidenced by negative growth rates, hyperinflation, and mounting poverty) provided fertile terrain for Sendero to recruit supporters through "carrot" and "stick" tactics. President Alan García's mid-1980s government was quickly discredited once its ability to deliver, economically and politically, collapsed. When García tried to resist neoliberalism, most notably, debt service payments, Peru was isolated by the Reagan and Bush administrations and the international financial community. This isolation contributed to economic disaster.

Under the circumstances, support for García's party, APRA, eroded, and tensions among political parties of the left undermined the capacity of the party system to serve a mediating role between state and society (Burt 1998; Burt and Espejo 1995). Sendero took advantage of the situation to weaken the remaining legitimacy of the government and the party system. While defending squatters' land claims and offering limited material supports, it simultaneously deployed terrorist tactics, in the countryside and then also in Lima. Sendero members engaged in assassinations, armed strikes, and acts of sabotage. By the early 1990s Sendero claimed some twenty-five thousand militants and controlled about one-fourth of all municipalities, but more significantly, it undermined the moral, social, and political order.

A turnabout in Sendero's fate came when García's successor, Alberto Fujimori, deployed an aggressive two-pronged strategy: stepped-up repression, combined with anti-Sendero community mobilizations. His government expanded *rondas*, anti-Sendero civilian peasant defense units known as Comités de Autodefensa Civil. As of mid-1993 there were more than four thousand such *rondas* involving some three hundred thousand *campesinos*. The counterguerrilla initiative built on community solidarities, in a manner that combined an extension of benefits with a strengthening of protective capabilities. The Fujimori government provided *rondas* with food, medicine, and arms, while the military extended civic action programs to the communities involved (McClintock 1997).

The *rondas* represent a state-generated movement. Movements need not be anti-state (as Zamosc also illustrated with ANUP in the context of Colombia), and the battle indeed came to be between peasant communities that did and did not have state assistance, not between the state and the peasantry. Openness to *ronda* formation, and the impact *rondas* had, varied by community. Peasants were most receptive where they wished Sendero brutality and the Sendero collectivist agrarian model brought down (Degregori et al. 1996).

The coup de grâce to Sendero (as well as to the more urban based Túpac Amarus guerrilla movement) came, however, with a stepped-up government campaign to hunt down the guerrilla leadership. With the decapitation and imprisonment of Sendero's top ranks the movement floundered, although on a much-reduced scale the guerrilla group retains support in some regions. With 85 percent of the labor force lacking full-time work and half the population living in poverty in the mid-1990s (up from 38 percent in 1985), the social and economic problems that initially fueled the movement remained. Yet the Peruvian example suggests that at least in the short run repression may undermine the vibrancy of a guerrilla movement, if deftly exercised and supported by civilians. The capture of Abimael Guzmán, Sendero's leader, diffused the movement. Guzmán was revered as a deity by his disciples. Had leadership been less hierarchical and more decentralized, Guzmán's capture would have been less consequential to the movement. In fostering reverence, Guzmán unwittingly contributed to the very conditions that eroded movement support.

Peasant-based guerrilla movements also appeared to reach their twilight in Central America at the century's end, although not before some three hundred thousand people were killed and some two million were forced to flee their communities. One out of every one hundred and fifty or so Central Americans lost their lives during the decades of civil strife, with Nicaragua, El Salvador, and especially Guatemala suffering most. As in Peru, the taming of the guerrilla movements came with shifts in state rule and state policies, but also with a shift in U.S. foreign policy. The U.S. government had provided much of the financing and training for the anti-guerrilla state repressive forces. In Guatemala, for example, U.S.-trained and financed military personnel were responsible for 97 percent of the two hundred thousand civilian war-related deaths. Yet in Central America, unlike in Peru, government and guerrilla willingness to *negotiate* peace defused the tumult. In agreeing to elections and honoring their results, the civil wars in Nicaragua, El Salvador, and Guatemala died quiet deaths.

In El Salvador and Guatemala government authorities signed peace accords with the major left-leaning guerrilla groups. Able to destabilize the regimes but not to seize the state and transform society, the leader-

ship of the erstwhile guerrilla forces in the two countries agreed to dis-
arm, to organize as political parties, and to contest electorally for the
right to rule, compromises that involved a muting of their social and economic ambitions. Concomitantly, the political right in the respective
countries, allied with the landed elite, pulled back their paramilitary
forces. Under the circumstances, guerrillas-turned-democrats won control of a number of municipalities and congressional seats in El Salvador.
In Guatemala the right, as well as the military, remained stronger, more
violent, and less committed to political compromise. While it tolerated a
political opening that allowed a voice for both popular sector and indigenous groups, it continued to blatantly violate citizen rights. In both
countries, as in Peru, the long-term prospects for peace rest on resolution of "underlying" socioeconomic inequities. The peace accords call,
for example, for agrarian reform, but implementation on any scale had
not occurred by the dawn of the twenty-first century (Paige 1996).

In Colombia, by contrast, guerrilla activity stepped up in the 1990s.
Civil strife then was more pervasive and violent than at any point in the
preceding thirty years. There, FARC, Latin America's largest surviving
1960s-style guerrilla group, pressed for increased government social
spending, nationalization of key industries, and a temporary moratorium on foreign debt payments. A peace accord proved less effective in
Colombia than in the Central American countries. The seventeen thou-
sand-member FARC controlled an area the size of Switzerland, which the
government ceded, in 1998, in exchange for opening peace talks. The
accord notwithstanding, by the turn of the century paramilitary forces
and local private armies had entered the war previously fought between
guerrillas and the military (Chernick 1997). Although the M-19, the
April 19th Movement, by then had laid down its arms and begun to participate as a political party in electoral politics, FARC, the principal guerrilla movement, did not follow suit.

Violence and other human rights abuses exploded. Under a veneer of
democracy, the rule of law disintegrated. In 1996 Colombia had one of
the highest homicide rates in the world, and the highest rate identified
as politically motivated. There were more than 26,000 murders in the
country that year and an estimated total of 35,000 between 1988 and
1998, several times more than under any of the notoriously repressive
South American military regimes of the 1960s through 1980s. Some 62,
27, and 11 percent of the Colombian deaths in the mid-1990s were attributed, respectively, to paramilitaries, guerrillas, and the military. The
struggle also left more than a million Colombians refugees in their own
country. The conflict increasingly centered around cocaine, not merely
ideology.

Why did guerrilla activity become more widespread and violent in
Colombia when it diminished in neighboring countries? First, in Colom-

bia the most important guerrilla groups never agreed to lay down their arms. Second, Colombia has a culture of violence on which the feuding groups built. That culture does not itself explain the explosion of violence, but it provides a cultural frame that makes violence more likely. Third, formal democracy at the national level obscured the violence and in so doing tempered domestic and international efforts to bring the abuses to an end. Fourth, state authority withered as the illegal drug economy became more entrenched. Guerrillas stepped up kidnappings, murders, and extortion, and they defended coca producers in return for a "cocaine tax." In 1997 they purportedly collected $60 million a month.

Growing international demand for cocaine is at the root of the problem. Colombia, the world's largest cocaine paste producer, has a comparative advantage in production of the commodity. And no other economic activity in Colombia is as lucrative. Consequently, the stakes in Colombia are high, and drug interests are well organized. Under the circumstances, the government has been weakened to the point that it has difficulty imposing order, through either "carrot" or "stick" measures. It could no longer implement a populist movement like ANUP, as it had a quarter century earlier (see Zamosc's chapter), or pursue a strategy that combined well-targeted repression with reform, as Fujimori did in Peru.

Meanwhile, the U.S. government became part of the problem, in the very process of attempting to be its solution. U.S. intervention had the effect, if not the intent, of exacerbating violence and the breakdown of the rule of law. In conjunction with its "War on Drugs," Washington stepped up military aid to fight the drug problem "at its source." As military aid increased, so too did military brutality. And in its "War on Drugs" the U.S. backed coca crop eradication projects, which angered coca farmers and led them to mobilize in protest and side with the guerrillas. With their means of livelihood threatened, some 241,000 coca-growing *campesinos*, for example, staged a protest march in 1996. Concerned with its own claims to rule, the Colombian government stopped the eradication project. Forced to choose between terminating coca production and threats to its claims to rule, it opted for its immediate institutional political interests over reigning in production of the drug.

On a more reduced and less violent scale, and without ties to a guerrilla movement, world demand for coca stirred unrest in Bolivia as well. Under U.S. pressure and with U.S. assistance, the government there too sought to eradicate illegal coca growing. And there too coca growers did not acquiesce. In the Chapare, where one-fourth of the world's cocaine supply originates, crop eradication projects stirred coca growers to organize, blockade crucial roads, and fight security forces. Only when the government moved massive military cadres to the region, out of fear of losing U.S. certification and aid, and after paying peasants thousands of dollars to destroy their bushes, did peasants cut back their yields.

Nonetheless, with coca commanding four times as much income as other crops, production moved to less heavily policed areas (and to Colombia). Income-deprived peasants soon protested increased consumer costs, e.g. of water.

At the same time, new armed peasant movements arose in Mexico. The Zapatistas, members of the Ejército Zapatista de Liberación Nacional or EZLN, were the most politically important. Building on a growing pan-village indigenous identity, the EZLN appeared in the public arena on January 1, 1994, in Chiapas, Mexico's poorest state. For both symbolic and strategic reasons, they timed their appearance with the inauguration of the North American Free Trade Agreement (NAFTA). The accord formalized free trade, a key feature of neoliberalism. Although the implementation of the accord was not the cause of the new movement, it provided a context around which Zapatistas channeled grievances, including grievances about conditions antedating and unrelated to neoliberalism. And in timing their emergence from the jungle, where they had trained, with the initiation of the historic accord, they could readily bring their cause to the attention of the world. The international media was in Mexico to cover the event.

It is worth noting here that from the onset Zapatistas combined guerrilla with populist and electoral tactics, and they framed the movement in terms of indigenous rights than a variant of Marxist class discourse or drug-related pragmatism. While never pressing for revolution, they took their name from the peasant hero of the country's early-twentieth-century social transformation and they wore masks resembling those used by earlier Zapatistas.

The Mexican government, in turn, responded differently than other governments in the region to their respective guerrilla mobilizations. Already at the eve of the Zapatista uprising, undoubtedly aware of brewing unrest, President Carlos Salinas de Gortari (1988–94) channeled antipoverty funds through his famed Solidarity program. But Solidarity focused on showpiece projects, not peasant desires for land titles and cash crop assistance, and its initiatives were too little too late (Nash n.d.). Then, after the January 1 uprising, the government sought immediately to negotiate with the masked guerrillas. After that effort failed it combined stepped-up reform with stepped-up repression. The authorities initiated development projects on a scale previously unknown in the region. And they gave food handouts to villagers who collaborated with them, to build a loyal local base and drive a wedge between them and Zapatistas. The authorities also succeeded in dividing the Zapatistas. Some came to side with the government, including its neoliberal agrarian reform. But when these efforts also failed to bring the Zapatista movement to its heels, the government turned to low-intensity repression. It increased the military presence in the region and allowed soldiers to attack armed EZLN. It also encouraged civilian loyalists to attack unarmed Zapatista sympathizers and arrested and harassed Zapatistas while hemming rebels in to isolated areas of the state. Then, in 1997 officials oversaw an infamous village massacre and the following year they launched a campaign against foreign human rights "infiltrators." Low-intensity state repression stepped up not because the EZLN posed a growing guerrilla threat but because it fueled electoral opposition to the PRI, nationally as well as locally, and questioned state legitimacy.

The Mexican government's initial flexible and "carrot"-type strategy reflects learning from past mistakes. The beginning of the erosion of the government's and the so-called official party's (the Institutionalized Revolution Party, PRI) political hegemony dates to the brutal 1968 student massacre in Mexico City. Brutality again on a large scale might have done in the PRI-led government. Moreover, involvements of new internationally linked NGO human rights groups, as well as the presence of the international media, pressed the government to be more accountable for its actions than in years past. The changed global and national context, in essence, influenced the evolution of an indigenous movement grounded in local concerns.

While the Zapatistas never defeated government forces militarily or established political domination in Chiapas, they sparked a growing countrywide critique of PRI politics, especially once the Mexican "miracle" turned bust after the peso devaluation in December 1994. Zapatistas challenged the neoliberal economic model as no other group had, and they inspired a range of social movements and electoral challenges to the PRI. But as electoral options opened in the course of the decade, general public patience with and sympathy for the Zapatistas waned.

Not all rural mobilizations for change were channeled through guerrilla movements. In Brazil, for example, rural unions mobilized small farmers and the agricultural proletariat. Nearly three thousand trade unions representing eight million laborers established themselves already under the 1964 to 1985 military governments (Maybury-Lewis 1994). The authoritarian governments cultivated the unionization not because they were pro-labor but because they sought to co-opt labor and thereby undermine the appeal of the independent, politicized peasant *ligas* (leagues) that Francisco Julião had mobilized in the early 1960s. Although the impact of the rural labor movement varied regionally, and by farm crop, unions managed to negotiate health benefits in return for their moderation. Union impact was partly contingent on local interclass alliances. With democratization rural unions remained active and somewhat of a counterweight to politically powerful large farmers. However, they were unable to stop increased land concentration even after the promulgation of an official land reform. In a country that had one of the world's most unequal distributions of land, the number of small farms dropped from over three million to under one million in the 1990s (Langevin and Rosset 1997: 2). Agribusiness became more entrenched in the process.

With small farmer marginalization and growing landlessness, the ranks of the Landless Workers Movement (Movimento dos Sem Terra, or MST) more than unions swelled. The MST appealed to rural laborers' desire both for land and for social welfare. Between the mid-1980s, when it was first formed, and the mid-1990s the MST successfully helped to negotiate land claims for 146,000 families involving nearly five million hectares. Its de facto land reform from below proved of greater significance than the government's de jure land reform from above. Emphasizing community building within and solidarity among encampments, the MST also successfully pressed for additional health care, education, and agricultural extension services. To further its cause it organized invasions of idle land, blocked highways, and organized a two-month thousand-kilometer march to the country's capital in 1997. The most dynamic and influential Brazilian political movement of the 1990s, it was structurally innovative. It was collectively organized. In lieu of a president, vice president, treasurer, and the like, it had collectives based on themes such as organization, land occupation, land use, education, and health. It benefited from trade union and especially church group support, and from a government—under Fernando Henrique Cardoso—publicly committed to reform and not repression. But the movement experienced losses as well as gains. Some one thousand activists and landless MST sympathizers reportedly were assassinated or injured during the first ten years of the movement's existence. Military police troops that sided with landowners were responsible for most of the fatalities (Hammond 1999; Langevin and Rosset 1997).

Labor Protests. Under import substitution workers in medium and large enterprises unionized in both the public and the private sectors. But unions were not sufficiently forceful to shield members from neoliberal reforms that eroded economic and social rights won during import substitution, including rights to employment, a minimum wage, health and other benefits, and even the right to unionize. Although democratization in principle restored labor rights that the military governments had revoked, the new neoliberal regimes in practice contained workers' efforts to exercise those rights.

Indeed, by the 1990s more Latin American countries experienced decreases than increases on the three standard indicators of workplace disruption: number of strikes, number of workers involved, and workdays not worked. Only El Salvador and Panama experienced increases on all three measures; Costa Rica and Chile experienced increases on two indicators and Bolivia on one (see table E.1). Immediately following the

TABLE E.1 Latin American Strike Activity, 1990–1995
(in countries with available information)

	Increase	*Decrease*
Number of strikes	Bolivia Chile El Salvador Panama	Brazil Colombia Costa Rica Ecuador Guatemala Honduras Mexico Nicaragua Peru
Number of strikers	Costa Rica El Salvador Panama	Brazil Chile Colombia Ecuador Mexico Nicaragua Peru
Workdays not worked	Chile Costa Rica El Slvador Panama	Brazil Ecuador Mexico Nicaragua Peru

SOURCE: ILO 1998: 1204–11, 1229–36, 1255–61.

restoration of democracy strike activity *had* picked up in many countries, in both the private and the state sectors, but more for politically- than economically-grounded reasons rather than economic factors. With the lifting of repression, labor successfully pressed for pent-up demands. Soon thereafter, however, protest tapered off, above all in the private sector. It declined even though work conditions deteriorated.

Why did protest taper off as work conditions deteriorated with the deepening of neoliberalism in the new, more politically hospitable milieu? Although the reasons vary by country and within country over time, labor's increasing quiescence in the private sector can be traced to the increased globalization of production. Under the circumstances, labor was pressured to tolerate unattractive conditions or risk their firms either being wiped out of the market or moving to where workers willingly worked for lower wages. It also can be traced to new state-engineered cross-class "pacts" through which labor officially became a partner in worker-unfriendly policies. As a result, workers could not readily use their primary negotiating weapon: the power to disrupt production. Conditions in the public sector differed somewhat. Under neoliberalism, governments engaged in a twofold attack. They sought to curb employee unions to make state-owned enterprises that had proliferated under import substitution more attractive to potential private investors. And they slashed employment and wages in the rest of the public sector to reduce fiscal expenditures and maximize efficiency.

Whereas private sector wage workers buckled under as work conditions deteriorated, public sector employees were less accepting. The strike activity of the 1990s centered mainly in the public sector. Governments were less immune than business to protest. First, in providing services public sector activity was shielded to some extent from global market dynamics; this gave labor certain leverage. Second, by their very nature states are politically vulnerable, especially in a democracy where they are dependent on the backing of the electorate. This vulnerability works to the advantage of public sector employees as well. Third, downsizing in the public sector hurt many workers simultaneously.

Exemplifying worker resistance to public sector downsizing, miners in Bolivia, who had won political and economic rights through their participation in the nationalist-populist revolution of 1952, and for a time had even co-managed the mines in return for their support, suffered the coup de grâce in the mid-1980s. Paz Estenssoro, the leader of the revolution, by then had returned to power as a born-again neoliberal. His new government, with U.S. and IMF backing, shut the tin mines that he had nationalized during his first term.

Miners did not passively acquiesce to the elimination of their means of livelihood. Miners—who live in relative geographic isolation, are fairly homogeneous economically, and work under difficult conditions—have been notorious worldwide for their militancy. In Bolivia they were no exception, in the latter 1980s as earlier. They organized a hunger strike and a march from the mines through the countryside to the nation's capital, La Paz. They were joined by some ten thousand peasants, teachers, shop owners, students, and religious leaders who depended on the mining communities for work, who sympathized with the miners, and who opposed, for their own reasons, other neoliberal economic reforms (e.g., IMF-proposed taxes). As June Nash so vividly describes in her chapter in this book, miners never entirely broke with their agrarian roots, socially or culturally. Continued peasant-miner ties lent strength to the interclass resistance to new reforms.

The protests proved of no avail. Fiscally strapped and dependent on international financial support, the government deferred to foreign financiers and their demand to close the mines that had long been globally uncompetitive. In the process, miners lost their jobs and more: their communities were destroyed, and their families were dislocated and often torn apart. With few or no alternative employment options in their communities many dismissed miners migrated. They exited once the government refused to respond to their voice. Former miners did best economically by going to the Chapare and joining the booming coca economy there. Although the U.S. government disapproved of this livelihood as well, its antinarcotics funds, training, and equipment (as in Colombia) drove employment underground and fueled corruption. It did not put an end to commercial coca growing (although production slowed when the government, with U.S. funds, stepped up law enforcement and payoffs for plant eradication). In destroying community and family, the closing of the mines generated other social problems and changes as well. Nash, who went back in 1994 to investigate the effects of the mine closings, found that drinking, addiction, and theft had increased. Some former miners sought solace in religious conversion, above all, to the Latter Day Saints, which had proselytized in the region.

Protest in Bolivia was not confined to the mines and the surrounding countryside. Public sector workers in La Paz shut down the transportation system and looted stores when reforms cost them their jobs and caused consumer prices to rise. Fiscally strapped, the government was not well positioned to contain protest either with carrot or stick measures.

Victims of neoliberal reforms protested in stronger states as well. With economic restructuring and redemocratization, strike activity in Argentina picked up and its loci shifted, from the private to the public and mixed-ownership sectors, from the working to the middle class, and from Buenos Aires, the nation's capital and historic epicenter of labor militancy, to the provinces. Public sector wage cutbacks and withholding of wage payments under both the Peronista president Carlos Saul Menem and his Radical Party predecessor, President Raul Alfonsín (1983–89), for example, fueled protests (McGuire 1996). The two governments prioritized their own institutional concerns by placing fiscal deficit reduction over workers' rights to a livelihood, including the right to payment for services rendered. Confrontations became especially violent when authorities withheld paychecks. Automobiles were set aflame and buildings were sacked.

Strikes in Argentina, however, reveal no mechanistic relationship between economic deprivation and protest. The number of strikes, strikers, and days lost to strikes were lower under Menem, especially in the first half of the 1990s, than under Alfonsín during the preceding decade, even though Menem's aggressive restructuring involved greater layoffs and deprivations. In Argentina, as elsewhere, government taming of inflation initially was politically popular, even when associated with a decline in earnings and employment. Workers, moreover, increasingly became preoccupied with holding on to their jobs, threatened not merely by globalization but also by government emphasis on "labor flexibility," a euphemism for reduced employment security.

Strike activity in Brazil as well was a political and not merely economic matter. There too the number of strikes and strikers and the duration of strikes rose substantially immediately following the restoration of democratic rule. Strike activity picked up even as labor conditions improved, because the risks of rebellion subsided with the political transition (Noronha, Gebria, and Elias 1998) and because the union movement gained momentum with redemocratization and encouragement from church groups. Yet in Brazil, as in Argentina, labor strife tapered off with the routinization of democratic rule. The number of annual strikes dropped from a peak of more than two thousand to under one thousand in the course of the 1990s, although work conditions by then had begun to deteriorate again with a substantial deepening of neoliberalism and then a currency devaluation. And, as in Argentina, strike activity came to center mainly in the state sector.

Meanwhile, state-crafted labor-business pacts defused opposition to labor-unfriendly neoliberal stabilization policies in Mexico, but more so in the private than public sector. Teachers, angry with falling purchasing power, demanded better wages, and health workers pressed not merely for more take-home pay but also for improved work conditions. In 1997 in Mexico City, for example, nurses upset with shortages of medicines for state-supported hospitals dramatized their outrage in postmodern-esque ways, drawing blood from their arms with syringes and squirting it at the front doors of the hospital administration (*New York Times*, 21 January 1997: 10). Even publicly employed street sweepers in the provincial capital of Tabasco staged a hunger strike, raided Congress and peeled off their clothes in its chambers, and marched to Mexico City. They demanded compensation for the extra private services politicians demanded of them and employment reinstatement when austerity policies cost them their jobs.

In Chile more than in any other Latin American country, labor militancy became a shadow of its former self. The Chilean case highlights the significance of the timing of reforms. There the most painful reforms occurred under the repressive rule of Pinochet, when protest was risky, not under democratic rule. The center-left pact, *Concertación de partidos por la democracia*, formed at the time of redemocratization, contained without repressing labor politicization. Parties to the pact, including socialists who before the coup had championed worker militancy, placed a high priority on governance and macro economic stability. Meanwhile, labor gradually won back wage losses from the Pinochet period, although in a context of mounting income inequality. Prosperity and expectations of gains contributed to labor quietude.

A comparative study of Argentina, Mexico, and Venezuela suggests that labor strife varies with political party and union institutional dynamics, somewhat independently of macro political and economic conditions (Murillo 1998). Labor militancy varied sectorally within and among the countries, with union and party competition. It was greatest when political parties competed for the labor vote, while union competition was minimal. Even Costa Rica, with its long democratic and social welfare tradition, experienced protests when authorities there joined the neoliberal restructuring bandwagon. There too privatization of public enterprises instigated clashes with police.

Civil society responses to downsizing in the public as well as private formal sector must be understood, in turn, in the context of opportunities to exit—to other jobs as well as to other places domestically or abroad—and to supplement declining state sector earnings with informal sector work. As a result of restructuring, the portion of the labor force in jobs protected by labor codes decreased. In the absence of public welfare, city dwellers have had to turn increasingly to the informal economy; so much so that it became the main source of employment. Although earnings for most in the informal sector are low, precarious, and declining, conditions are not conducive to unionization or to work stoppages to press for work-related improvements. Surplus labor has a negative effect on earnings, and competition makes organization difficult. Moreover, many in the sector are self-employed. Nonetheless, the opportunity to exit makes for less protest to formal sector downsizing than would otherwise be likely. People's reactions must be understood in the context of the total labor market in which the formal sector downsizing is embedded.

Non-Union-based Urban Movements.   Throughout Latin America economically rooted urban protests were not confined to the workplace. Indeed, as neoliberalism contributed to formal sector downsizing, the loci of economic resistance shifted to the informal sector and to collective strategies to minimize living costs.

Neoliberal government measures to reduce import substitution-initiated consumer subsidies became especially contentious, for they drove living costs up while earnings stagnated or declined. Most Latin American countries experienced what have been dubbed "IMF protests," consumer protests against austerity measures that increased the cost of subsistence. The protests were sparked by government efforts to reduce fiscal expenditures and remove market obstacles and sometimes also to increase revenue (in the case of government-provided goods and services).

While consumer revolts are shaped by the social, cultural, and political context in which consumption is embedded, data on price increases of basic goods give a sense of why such revolts mushroomed under neoliberalism. Between 1990 and 1997, for example, only two countries, Costa Rica and Panama, experienced less than a 200 percent rise in food prices (see table E.2). Brazil, Ecuador, Peru, Uruguay, and Venezuela experienced increases of over 500 percent. And of the ten countries for

TABLE 11.2 Consumer Price Increases:
Food and Fuel/Electricity (1990=100)

	Food		Fuel/Electricity	
	1995	1997	1995	1997
200% or less	Bolivia Chile Costa Rica Dominican Republic Nicaragua Panama	Costa Rica Panama	Argentina Bolivia Costa Rica El Salvador Mexico Panama	Argentina Bolivia Costa Rica El Salvador Panama
201–500%	Argentina Colombia Ecuador El Salvador Guatemala Haiti Honduras Mexico Paraguay	Argentina Bolivia Chile Colombia Dominican Republic El Salvador Guatemala Honduras Mexico Paraguay	Ecuador Honduras	Ecuador Honduras
501+%	Brazil Peru Uruguay Venezuela	Brazil Ecuador Peru Uruguay Venezuela	Uruguay Venezuela	Uruguay Venezuela

NOTE: No information for Haiti and Nicaragua for 1997.
SOURCE: ILO 1998: 1036, 1037, 1044, 1045.

which information on fuel and electricity prices is available, four—Ecuador, Honduras, Uruguay, and Venezuela—experienced increases of over two hundred percent.

There appears to be little relation between consumer price increases and strike activity, that is, worker efforts to press for better wages to offset cost of living increases. In 1995, for example, none of the countries that experienced more than a 500 percent increase in food and oil prices saw an increase in strikes. And three of the four countries where the number of strikes rose experienced the lowest consumer price increases (see table E.1). Workers turned to strategies outside formal sector employment to cope.

Official food and gasoline price hikes made commerce especially contentious. Latin Americans perceived the government, not the "invisible market," as the source of their rage. While the poor were hurt most by consumer price increases, labor, the middle classes, indigenous groups, and students typically joined them in the streets. Price hikes stirred different combinations of demonstrations—riots, strikes, looting, attacks on official buildings—depending not only on the severity of the austerity measures but also on different national repertoires of resistance, different macro political-economic conditions, and different popular sector alliances. They evoked riots in Jamaica, Argentina, and Venezuela, street demonstrations in Chile, and strikes and roadblocks in the Andean nations. The consumer revolts were most prevalent in countries that were politicized, where power struggles prepared the ground, where governments were weak and discredited, and where unions maintained some modicum of strength, militancy, and independence. The seemingly spontaneous eruptions typically involved some degree of organization and occurred especially when backed by unions. In Brazil and Ecuador they were coordinated by the Catholic church as well. In Brazil in 1999, for example, the national bishops' organization in coordination with unions and parties of the left and the MST, sponsored demonstrations in opposition to neoliberal policies, called the Cry of the Excluded Ones.

While governments typically acquiesced to insurgents' demands to retract price hikes, so as to reestablish order and their own claims to rule, on occasion they have collapsed under the weight of resistance to their own reform initiatives. In Ecuador, in particular, trade union and indigenous groups prepared the ground, stirred by earlier church concern with injustices. They left governments between a rock and a hard place. In attempting to appease the populace, authorities defaulted on foreign loans and in desperation turned to hyper-inflationary policies that made them yet more unpopular. Resistance to oil price hikes, in the context of a dramatic drop in the value of the national currency, contributed to the deposing of two elected presidents, in 1997 and 2000.

Students protested the cost of studies, in addition to the cost of subsistence, sometimes in collaboration with labor groups. Their defiance became less explicitly political and more economically driven than in previous years. In 1997, for example, Venezuelan students rioted against cuts in school and transportation subsidies. In Argentina the same year, tens of thousands of students joined street vendors, plus angry current and dismissed public and sugar sector workers, in blocking roads and government buildings, hurling stones, and setting up barricades in cities in nine provinces. Meanwhile, in the Dominican Republic blackouts along with price hikes sparked protests in more than a dozen towns, at the instigation of students and unions. Protesters burned tires and cars, threw stones and homemade bombs at the police, and staged a general strike. And in Nicaragua students who protested over university funding were joined by shantytown dwellers.

Mexican students were among the most ambitious. Their protests eroded the legitimacy of the state and paralyzed universities. In 1988 hundreds of thousands of students marched in protest against government efforts to impose fees and entrance exams at a time when a major peso devaluation and austerity measures drove up living costs dramatically; the government raised the cost of public university education to address its dire fiscal crisis at the time. But the students captured the imagination of the capital and won (Castañeda 1993: 204). The government retracted the newly imposed fees. History repeated itself a decade later when students closed down the campus of the main university, the largest in Latin America. Begun again as a protest against a newly sanctioned university tuition policy, which would have raised the annual fee from a few cents to $140, this time strike organizers refused to back down when the government offered to make the new tuition a voluntary expense for students who could afford it. Instead, they broadened their list of demands and their critique. They framed their protest as part of a struggle against free market economic policies and for university democratization. They called for the resignation of the rector and increased student involvement in university decision making. Yet as the paralysis of university education dragged on, the movement fragmented; some students organized against the strike, and public sympathy for the defiant students waned, especially as strikers conducted frequent marches along the main thoroughfares of the capital city, clogging rush-hour traffic and angering motorists. The government had been reluctant to use force to bring the university shutdown to an end, in order not to repeat the experience of 1968, when it fired on hundreds of students. It never fully recuperated its legitimacy. When President Ernesto Zedillo de la Ponce finally ordered the police to raid the occupied campus, nearly ten months after the strike began, the protest became embroiled in the country's increasingly competitive political system and the turmoil spilled onto other campuses in the capital city. Yet Zedillo, learning from past government mistakes, ordered the police to go into the campus unarmed, and he had the operation conducted under the supervision of official human rights observers. We see here how historical memory influences both protest activity and state response.

Movements related to so-called collective consumption, such as movements for housing rights and services, took a somewhat different turn. By the 1990s squatter movements in the major cities of the region had declined, even though affordable housing needs remained unmet. Squatter invasions tapered off, first, because government tolerance, predicated on macro political-economic conditions that no longer prevailed, subsided. During import substitution, authorities accommodated urban land, to keep labor costs down for industry and to consolidate a populist base of support. Under the circumstances, political parties in and out of power defended illegal collective land claims in exchange for political loyalty. But by the 1990s governments were less populist. Feeling less pressed to respond to housing and other neighborhood demands, they cut back provisioning of city services that were essential for new settlements.[5]

Second, governments, already under import substitution, only tolerated squatters who occupied public land (or property of politically weak peasants). By the century's end claims had already been made to most such land. In addition, the neoliberal governments were biased toward market, not political, processes. Consistent with their bias, they favored informal commercial dealings over land invasions to address pent-up demand for affordable housing (Durand-Lasserve 1998: 236). Meanwhile, landowners became more aggressive in defending their holdings, while real estate developers who previously backed irregular settlements acquired access to more profitable alternatives. And, third, the neoliberal emphasis on decentralization placed a greater onus on local governments to reduce demands on the central government, including demands for urban services.

In the changed milieu squatter movements did not disappear but ceased to be a fundamental feature of the social movement repertoire of key Latin American cities. Venezuela was an exception. Portraying himself as a populist, Hugo Chavez, on assuming the presidency, sought to consolidate his political base among the urban poor by overseeing a boom in land invasions. Costa Rica, on a more reduced scale and for dif-

5. In Argentina, where the government initiated *Plan de Arraigo* in 1991, its first effort to regularize squatter settlements on state-owned land, social provisioning received little attention. The program concentrated on the sale of publicly owned land, in line with the financial reorganization of the state. Thus a program that appeared to be populist was both designed and implemented in a manner that was largely market and fiscally driven, consistent with governmental institutional interests. The program concentrated merely on property transfers, and only in areas where invasions had occurred on government-owned land. See Martinez Nogueira 1995: 61–66.

ferent reasons, was another exception, but in the 1980s. A strong squatter movement emerged in San José, the capital city, in response to neoliberal cutbacks in government provisioning of neighborhood services. Given the country's long history of social welfare programs, Costa Ricans had become accustomed to state support. The movement may also be grounded in unrelenting demographic pressures. New export processing zones on the outskirts of San José became a magnet for migration, bad as work conditions in the zones were (see Lungo 1996).

An important non-squatter-based housing movement, described in chapter 11, emerged in Mexico, but only after independent grass-roots groups paved the way and contributed to a more assertive conception of citizenship (Davis 1994); Foweraker 1989; Foweraker and Craig 1990; Tamayo 1989, 1997; Zermeno 1997) and after an earthquake left tens of thousands of Mexico City residents homeless. The housing movement was especially interesting in that it involved inner-city residents whom urbanists had dismissed as apathetic, incapable of organizing, and weighed down by a "culture of despair." Government manipulation through its first official *concertación*, or pact, initiative defused neighborhood mobilizations before all earthquake victims received housing and before the mobilizations evolved into a new, broader urban strategy for housing.

Conditions in Brazil gave rise to yet another type of housing movement in the 1990s. There, the Roofless People Movement, composed of very poor people who live in slums or in the streets, organized the seizure of unoccupied urban buildings. By the beginning of the twenty-first century, it was one of the strongest movements in urban Brazil, especially in Rio de Janeiro and São Paolo but also in the states of Bahia and Rio Grande do Sul. Though protective of their independence, the Roofless People had the support of the Workers Party and the left-wing labor confederation, CUT, and especially of the progressive wing of the Catholic Church. Aside from obtaining housing, in São Paolo, where they worked closely with the mayor, Luiza Erundina, they succeeded in getting legislation changed pertaining to such urban issues as land tenure and housing. Although still in its infancy, with limited unoccupied buildings to seize, the movement cannot be expected to become a twenty-first-century alternative to squatter mobilizations that claimed vacant land in the past.

At the same time, *economic*-based neighborhood movements gained momentum, despite and because of the informalization of the economy. While hard in principle to organize people who are independently employed, vendors have a history of joining together to fight for rights to street space. Such mobilizations were especially contentious where vending was lucrative, all the more so with the retrenchment of formal sector employment options and the decline in formal sector earnings. Their success, like that of squatter invasions, typically was contingent on ties to influential politicians and on savvy manipulation of the political system

(Cross 1998). Indeed, would-be vendors borrowed squatter tactics to lay claim to street locations, as I discuss in chapter 11. Offering next to no assistance to the unemployed, governments, however reluctantly, gave in to pressure for expanded informal sector work rights. Authorities understood that widespread unemployment can be politically explosive.

Neoliberal-linked currency devaluations designed partly to strengthen export competitiveness also hurt people across the socioeconomic and rural-urban divide in ways that sparked protest movements. Devaluations drove up business costs to repay outstanding hard currency loans and to import inputs and merchandise. For the first time in the 1990s, debtors banded together to protest precipitous increases in their loan costs. One of the most interesting debtor movements was El Barson in Mexico. Beginning in 1993 with a few thousand farmers angered about state termination of subsidies, the movement spread to urban settings and came to include tens of thousands of under- and unemployed, middle- and working-class housewives, retailers, taxi drivers, and businessmen. What unified El Barson supporters was a tripling of bank interest rates, combined with a sudden plunge in living standards after the 1994 devaluation.

The debtors' alliance combined new strategies of defiance and new postmodern cultural expressions with old ones. Supporters staged raucous street theater and parades, sometimes featuring effigies of corrupt judges and, like other grass-roots groups in Mexico, masked superheroes. Similar to Superbarrio, who rose from the rubble of the earthquake, and Superecologist, Chupacabras emerged as a bloodsucking creature who represented the banking system to debtors. Also, to capture the popular imagination, some Barsonistas hauled tools to street corners and set them aflame. In August 1996 debtors all but halted trading on the Mexican stock exchange, as they rode an elephant to the doors of the Central Bank to dramatize their cause. Comical as their initiatives appeared, they were designed to draw media coverage to deeply felt grievances and to press for redress. Indeed, debtors simultaneously organized collective defenses against moneylenders and police who confiscated their properties when forced to default on loans. Defiant Barsonistas sometimes successfully reclaimed their tractors, cars, and farms and convinced bank officials both to restructure outstanding loans and to extend new lines of credit. They also convinced the government to initiate debt-relief programs. The multiclass base of the movement, and its range of strategies of resistance, induced banks and authorities to be responsive. Meanwhile, in selectively responding to El Barson concerns, the government defused movement support.

A debtors' movement arose in Brazil as well, in response to macro economic policies that had caused interest rates to soar and the value of the national currency to fall. Formed in 1997, within two years the debtors' rights movement claimed ten thousand members in two dozen Brazilian cities (*Wall Street Journal,* 6 January 1999: 1). The Brazilians deployed a strategy different from that of their Mexican counterparts. They deliberately clogged the courts with lawsuits, thereby giving debtors leverage. As legal cases in Brazil can drag on for years, creditors would settle for debt rescheduling or partial debt forgiveness.

Taxes also came to be a source of contention in the 1990s. As governments privatized and lowered tariffs, their revenue base declined. To generate needed revenue they decreed new taxes. With Latin Americans historically resistant to taxation, governments met with collective as well as individual resistance. And sometimes public protests followed announcements of new taxes, with authorities caving in under the political pressure. When forced to choose, we see here too how officials prioritized politics over fiscal needs. Shared anger over newly imposed taxes sometimes brought together groups that otherwise saw their interests as disparate. Such was the case in Cuzco, Peru, in 1993 when Fujimori announced that all businesses would be subject to an 18 percent tax. Tensions among wholesalers, retailers, truck drivers, and groups of market vendors were put aside as they all took to the streets to oppose the tax (Seligmann 1998: 76).

By the 1990s anger and disillusionment contributed to stepped-up antisocial activity. Crime, including violent crime, took cities in the region by storm. Rates of theft, pilfering, looting, illicit dealings, kidnappings, and homicides rose to unprecedented levels. The region became the most violent in the world. Crime generated more crime as a culture of illegality became entrenched and the likelihood of punishment diminished. People broke with the law both individually and collectively (through gangs, crime rings, and coordinated corrupt dealings). Poverty and unemployment, the drug trade, and police corruption were at the root of the problem. In many countries law enforcement agents became part of the problem, not its solution. They joined the ranks of the criminals and operated with impunity.

The breakdown of public safety sparked movements to restore order. In Rio de Janeiro in 1995, for example, a civic group, Viva Rio, oversaw a massive demonstration for a cleanup in the police department and improved urban services. Hundreds of thousands of rich and poor and old and young, cloaked in white, joined the demonstration, React Rio. The demonstration combined elements of a political rally, a religious revival, and Carnival. Similarly, in Mexico City two years later tens of thousands of frustrated and frightened residents of all social classes, but especially the middle class, paraded, with white ribbons and blue flags, in outrage over a mounting wave of violent crime there. Like the Brazilians, they demanded an end to police corruption and violence as well as to common crime.

Before the Peruvian government reined in Sendero Luminoso, Lima was a city under siege. There the breakdown of social order was politically induced. Sendero activists staged acts of sabotage against banks, government offices, and basic infrastructure, set off car bombs, and committed political assassinations. They deliberately sought to undermine civil society.

Had city dwellers not increasingly turned to emigration as domestic opportunities diminished, Latin American cities would have experienced even greater disarray. Rates of out-migration, both legal and illegal, rose dramatically after the 1980s—especially from Central America, the Caribbean, and Mexico but from other countries as well. Émigrés opted for exit rather than voice, and the remittances they sent to families left behind helped to defuse social pressure.

The case of Cuba highlights how state regulation of economic activity drives activity "underground," not out of existence, when it diverges from what people want and when legal options are limited. It also highlights the symbiotic relationship between what governments and people do. In response to scarcities caused by cutbacks in Soviet (and Soviet bloc) aid and trade, Fidel Castro's government reintroduced rationing in the 1990s. Although it was designed with the best intentions—to "equalize sacrifice" and make food affordable to everyone—because scarcities drove up the "real" market value of goods, a runaway black market evolved. The black market was highly coordinated and rooted in informal networks, including networks spanning from the city where food was consumed to the countryside where it was produced. By 1993 the value of black market commerce was estimated to have exceeded the value of official retail trade. Nearly everyone participated in illicit dealings, as buyer if not also seller. Participation varied more with economic resources than morality. And fueling the black market in goods was a runaway black market in dollars. The dollar became the islanders' currency of choice. In its effort to reverse the collapse of the official economy, the government legalized urban markets, self-employment, and the dollar. And because of its own fiscal needs, it imposed taxes on the newly sanctioned, formerly covert activity. But because vendors wanted profits for themselves, taxation drove a portion of the activity back underground. Scarcities at the same time contributed to record rates of theft, pilfering, bribery, and corruption. People thereby gained access to goods that they could sell in turn, legally or illegally, depending on state policy at the time. The Cuban experience thus demonstrates not only how state structures and policies pattern defiance but also how covert disobedience may induce institutional change (Eckstein 1994).

Gender-based Resistance

While the political and economic crises of the 1980s fueled women's involvement in human rights and neighborhood subsistence groups, by the 1990s democratization eliminated most human rights abuses that had brought them into the public arena (Colombia and Guatemala were notable exceptions). And while poverty remained rampant, in the changed political context women turned to new institutional sources of help or relied on their personal resources. To the extent that women engaged on their own in social movements, they focused on specific gender issues. But most noteworthy, women's concerns came to be incorporated into the new institutional life. Earlier movements had helped to transform societal expectations and practices.

Paradoxically, the military governments that clamped down on mass politics created the very conditions that had brought women into the public arena in novel ways. Navarro and Garretón described how the repressive military regimes in Argentina and Chile unwittingly politicized the personal while depoliticizing institutional politics. The women's human rights movement in Argentina, in particular, became internationally renowned and the inspiration for multiclass rural and urban women's movements throughout the region (e.g., in El Salvador as well as in Chile) (Stephen 1997). But these were movements to reestablish women's rights to motherhood, not to transform or transcend women's place in the home.

The gendered movements of the 1980s, in bringing women into the public arena, generated consequences participants had not intended. Not only did the movements help to discredit the military regimes, and in so doing help to usher in democratic transitions, they also influenced political discourse, political strategies, and official policies under the new regimes. In addition, they opened up opportunities for women. The women's movements did not alone induce the changes, but they were central to the remaking of gender relations and gender expectations.

The dialectic between changing *political* conditions and women's responses to them is illustrated in Argentina. There, Raul Alfonsín's election in 1983 appeared to be a victory for Las Madres de Plaza de Mayo and other human rights groups. Alfonsín ran for office on a human rights platform, he promised to prosecute all those who had sown "terror, pain, and death," he ordered the trial of members of the juntas, and he created the National Commission on the Disappearance of Persons (Conadep) to investigate the disappearances. Yet Conadep was only an advisory panel. Military rather than civilian courts handled Dirty War cases, and none of the military were brought to trial. Alfonsín's successor, Menem, moreover, pardoned members of the former juntas who had been incarcerated. While Las Madres had helped to pave the way for redemocratization by exposing military atrocities to the world, the civilian governments secured the upper hand in defining how lingering human rights issues were addressed under their rule. They prioritized their own institutional concern with governance over military accountability for crimes against humanity.

Redemocratization defused the influence of Las Madres also because the compromising policies of the civilian governments divided women's groups. One faction became more militant, while another reconstituted itself as a human rights NGO more willing to forgive and forget.

Yet the question of disappearances refused to go away. The media continued to disclose abuses. Some members of the military and the police publicly confessed to misdeeds. The church publicly admitted its support of the military regimes. And in 1998 Las Abuelas de Plaza de Mayo (the Grandmothers of the Plaza de Mayo), a splinter group of the Madres, obtained the arrest of General Jorge Rafael Videla, one of the junta heads of state. The Madres managed to keep past military abuses part of the national memory, so that culprits continued to be publicly shamed and society reminded that such human rights violations were intolerable. Indeed, between the latter half of 1998 and early 1999, fifteen years after the Dirty War ended, eight other military officials were arrested. The new arrests included the last military president, Reynaldo Bignone, for the theft of babies. Death squads had run a secret maternity ward, where pregnant women were induced into labor or forced into cesarean births and then killed. In essence, the remains of the internationally renowned women's movement, along with the work of other human rights NGOs, deepened the democratization process outside the political party system, even as the movement became internally divided and defused.

With a large indigenous and peasant population and an even more repressive state, the women's movement evolved somewhat differently in Guatemala than in Argentina. There the government destroyed approximately 440 villages, killed some 200,000 citizens, and left more than 100,000 children orphaned, 150,000 refugees in camps in Mexico, and an estimated one million people displaced internally. Against this backdrop women organized across class and ethnic lines to defend their rights as mothers, wives, and daughters. For example, Coordinadora Nacional de Viudas de Guatemala (CONAVIGUA) became an organization of ten thousand middle-class, working-class, and indigenous widows of the civil war. The group provided psychological, political, and material support (Warren 1998: 180). Yet here too redemocratization transformed protest. The group's focus broadened, its priorities shifted, and certain concerns came to be addressed through formal political channels. Leaders such as Rosalina Tuyac won congressional office, unthinkable in the past.

Fueled by the movements of the 1980s and the groundwork laid by new feminist groups, gender came to be defined as sufficiently important to have Argentina, Guatemala, and other new democracies incorporate women's rights into their constitutions and to establish women's agencies. Official preoccupation with gender equity was without precedent in the region. Reflecting the new preoccupation, a number of countries introduced gender quotas on party electoral lists. As a consequence, the number of women in the Argentinian House of Representatives rose from 4 percent in 1991 to 28 percent four years later. In Brazil the number of women legislators in 1997, when quotas began, increased nearly 40 percent over the preceding election. Meanwhile, in Mexico the PRI and its leftist opposition, the PRD, adopted quotas to appeal to women voters, although the parties were not required to do so by law. And other countries in the region debated gender quota systems by the century's end (Jaquette 1997). Women had come to be recognized as a politically important constituency independent of men, and regimes became more inclusionary as a result.

At the same time, redemocratization divided and depoliticized women. In putting an end to government and military torture, killings, and rape, the new governments stamped out the human rights conditions that had driven women to the streets. With the opening of formal representation, along with the termination of abuses central to women's identities, the gendered political roots of protest dissipated.

Meanwhile, economic opportunities opened up for women, especially women of the middle class. They entered the labor force in record numbers. Their concerns came to vary with their social class and in some instances also with their race and ethnicity.

As new concerns came to the fore women's movements became smaller in scale, less intense, and less visible in the streets. Some women's movements (often with NGO assistance) focused on new gender issues, such as domestic violence, health, psychological and legal services for women, and reproductive rights. And in some countries gays pressed for their own issues. Women's groups became more proactive, less confrontational, and more institutionalized.

Poor women remained preoccupied with subsistence. As under military rule, when they organized they tended to do so in the neighborhoods where they lived—typically with the support of political parties of the left, church groups, and other NGOs. But their mobilizations became less frequent and less participatory as well, even when their livelihood became more precarious. Through targeted (minimal) poverty alleviation programs new governments—for example, in Mexico, Chile, and Peru—co-opted subsistence concerns, while NGOs withdrew and modified their involvements.

The experience of Lima shantytowns is telling. There austerity policies and not merely repression prompted creative and empowering collective community initiatives by poor women (Burt and Espejo 1995). While Villa El Salvador was famous for its politicization, it was far from the only Lima shantytown where women organized (Schonwalder 1998). Women's responses were contextually contingent, varying with the interplay between conditions at the macro and neighborhood levels and grass-roots work of church groups and other NGOs. They did not emanate from material deprivations alone.

Women in Villa El Salvador organized block-level cleanup committees to deal with lack of garbage collection, tree committees to beautify the area, local crime prevention watch groups, preschool *animadores* (preschool teachers' organizations), and soup kitchens to address family nutritional needs. And in 1983 FEPOMUVES, the Popular Federation of Women of Villa El Salvador, was formed with help from parties of the left. It centralized and coordinated the various local women's organizations, and took responsibility for coordinating "Glass of Milk" Committees, linked to a mayoral program to improve child nutrition.[6] City government, then in the hands of the left, strengthened and deepened such collective community efforts to combat poverty. Through neighborhood groups thousands of women gained experience in administration, leadership, and involvement in the public arena, and not merely around "women's issues" as traditionally defined. A co-founder of FEPOMOVES, Maria Elena Moyano, for example, served as vice-mayor of Villa after it became an independent municipality (until assassinated by Sendero Luminoso in 1992).

Evidence from Santiago, Chile, also suggests that such collective initiatives thrived when women had both informal neighborhood social networks on which to build and outside NGO support (Schneider 1995). When governments took over administration of soup kitchens in conjunction with official targeted antipoverty programs, the food dispensaries came to operate as handouts that appealed to women individually. We see here how governments regulated antipoverty programs to their own institutional advantage, most of all to depoliticize poverty.

In essence, by the 1990s women's public involvement became more institutionally based and legitimated. Gender concerns were codified in law and incorporated into public discourse and practice. Women's movements of the 1980s laid the groundwork for bringing women into the public arena and for making government and society more accommodating to them. In the process exclusively women's movements became less broad based, smaller, and more limited in their goals.

Racial, Ethnic, and Indigenous-based Movements

Ethnicity, according to development and modernization theory, was to wither away as Third World peoples were exposed to modern ideas and culture, as they became versed in Western language (in the case of Latin America, Spanish and Portuguese), and as they became educated.

---

6. The municipal milk program organized one hundred thousand women to distribute milk in 1986. In 1988 it was estimated that six hundred communal dining halls had been organized by poor women (Barrig 1989: 134).

But those very conditions became linked to an ethnic resurgence in the 1990s. And as with ethnicity, so too with movements rooted in racial identity. Movements pressed for ethno-national rights, including the right to be collectively and selectively different.

These movements must be understood in the context of changes at the global level. A growing global consensus concerning minority rights helped to legitimate movements. This international aspect represents an instance in which evolving universal values contributed paradoxically to movements premised on the right to be distinctive. But these movements must be understood in the context of changes experienced at the national and local levels as well: democratization, market reforms, improved means of communication, and new NGO-provided human and material resources.

The ethnic solidarities of the 1990s were premised in part on an articulation of previously latent and repressed identities—on identities elites in the past had compelled subaltern groups either to conceal or to articulate in tolerated transmuted forms such as *indigenismo*. *Indigenismo* had previously allowed indigenous groups symbolic national representation but no institutionalized collective rights. The new movements reveal that elites had previously obscured, repressed, and manipulated subaltern identities but never successfully eliminated them. They forced ethnicity underground, not out of existence.

While indigenous people had over the years individually opted out to assimilate into the mainstream national societies and cultures as mestizos, the new movements were premised on the right to be different. But the movements also entailed new ethnic identities, new objectives, and new bases of organization and communication along with the old ones. They were not merely revivals of ethnicity as previously conceived. Indeed, movements combined premodern with modern and postmodern features. In different ways neoliberal reforms and democratization unwittingly contributed to the new ethnic movements, as well as to their politicization, just as they contributed to other social mobilizations. Economic reforms sparked indigenous movements when governments stripped communities of long-standing land claims, when they retracted social supports, and when they promulgated new laws attracting investments that dislocated indigenous peoples and eroded their means of livelihood.

At the same time, indigenous peoples faced fewer risks in asserting claims under the new democracies than under the previous authoritarian regimes. More inclusionary, the new governments were more tolerant of indigenous movements: if for no other reason than their opportunistic interest in the ethnic vote. Indeed, in countries with large Indian populations political parties sought to champion the concerns of the newly politicized indigenous communities. And NGOs provided ethnic groups with material resources, skills, and encouragement both to organize defensively and to assert new claims. They also helped to frame local movements in ways that attracted international support. In response both to changing international views on the rights of indigenous peoples and to nascent domestic ethnic pressures channeled by NGOs, many of the new democracies established a legal framework for indigenous rights in their new constitutions. This was true, for example, in Guatemala, Bolivia, Ecuador, and Brazil. And countries that had remained nominally democratic in the 1960s through 1980s, such as Colombia and Mexico, amended their constitutions to include indigenous rights.

Although they were typically fueled by newly experienced and newly perceived economic injustices, racial, ethnic, and indigenous movements had political and cultural agendas. They demanded respect for indigenous legal autonomy, for the right to rule within their communities according to their own customary laws and their own system of authority. They also pressed for a community-based concept of citizenship premised on collective rights as Indians, along with citizenship based on individual rights. Their vision of citizenship differed from the Western concept grounded in equal rights and responsibilities as individuals. And consistent with their community claims, they pressed for bilingualism and other cultural features grounded in respect for their ethnic heritage.

Most important, movements took on ethnic expression because by the 1990s indigenous communities had produced some leaders with the social capital to function in the national and international as well as indigenous arena. Experiencing partial but blocked additional socioeconomic mobility, the new educated leaders maintained ties with their roots. With the capacity to articulate and disseminate ideas about indigenous peoples bilingually, they helped to re-create, remake, and reprioritize indigenous culture. And they did so in a manner that built bridges among indigenous communities (which did not always speak the same Indian language) as well as between them and other lower-, working-, and middle-class people nationally.

This combination of factors helps to explain the emergence and patterning of nationally significant indigenous movements in Mexico, Bolivia, Ecuador, and Guatemala. Together with Peru, these countries are home to 90 percent of Latin America's indigenous peoples (Yashar 1998: 24–25).

The Zapatista movement in Chiapas, Mexico, became the most internationally renowned of the new indigenous movements, but not because it was the largest or entirely under the influence of indigenous leadership. Rather, its leadership and main nonindigenous spokesperson, whose nom de guerre was Subcomandante Marcos, astutely used the media and the Internet and allied with human rights groups and other NGOS willing to defend the Zapatista cause. The Zapatistas combined violent with nonviolent tactics, demands for local change with demands for national change, and the use of historical symbolism, including the movement's name, with state-of-the-art cyberspace technology.[7]

The Zapatistas fused a shared sense of socioeconomic deprivation with ethnic identity and combined economic and political with cultural demands. They pressed for respect for cultural and political autonomy, dignity, and justice for indigenous groups and for greater democratization. The movement quickly combined a concern about ethnic justice with broader-based concerns, no doubt because Mexico's indigenous population was small, because its top leader himself was not Indian, and probably also because conditions were ripe, given the national economic crisis following the 1994 peso devaluation, for a broader-based challenge to government and PRI hegemony.

From its inception, the Zapatista movement challenged neoliberalism and official claims of democratization. Timing its emergence from the jungle with the initiation of NAFTA, it demystified government claims to bringing Mexico First World status, economically and politically. Under the guise of democracy, Chiapas had long been ruled autocratically. The Zapatistas opposed neoliberalism not in the abstract but in the concrete. They called for the repeal of NAFTA, for the protection of communal lands threatened by President Salinas de Gortari's agrarian reform, and for the restoration of farm price subsidies that neoliberal governments since the 1980s had cut back.

Recognizing the limits of an armed strategy, the Zapatistas turned to coalition building: to a multiethnic, multiclass, transterritorial alliance. As part of a "centering" strategy—in opposition to postmodernists' emphasis on "decentering"—the Zapatistas invited civic groups and opposition party members from all over the country to discuss ways to democratize the state, to form the Frente Zapatista de Liberación Nacional (FZLN), and to collaborate with the PRD, the left-leaning party that gained regional and national influence following the deep 1994–95 economic recession. The founding congress of the FZLM culminated with a highly publicized caravan of 1,111 unarmed Zapatista guerrillas and fellow supporters who marched from Chiapas to Mexico City. They timed their arrival in the capital with the annual celebration of Mexico's independence. The timing once again reflected the Zapatistas' masterful use of historical symbolism.

In challenging the political and economic order, the Zapatistas succeeded in unleashing a wave of protest movements nationwide. Al-

---

7. Reflecting Zapatista use of the Internet, its leadership halted an impending military attack by publicizing electronically the news through national and international solidarity networks. Mexican government electronic mailboxes were flooded with messages of protest. Publicly exposed, the government halted its repressive clamp-down (Yudice 1998: 344).

though unassociated with any specific movement, a character with a mask resembling the former president, Salinas de Gortari, who was responsible for mustering Mexican support for NAFTA, surfaced in the congested streets of the capital with a toy machine gun that he aimed at cars. Such presidential mockery was unheard of in previous decades. Concomitantly, the Zapatistas inspired several non-Zapatista peaceful indigenous community rebellions for equal rights under the law and cultural autonomy, as well as a more traditional small guerrilla movement in the state of Guerrero, which (like Colombia) has a history of guerrilla defiance on which the new movement built.

Indigenous movements in Bolivia, in turn, need be understood in the context of the country's revolution. Before the 1952 upheaval Indians had no nationally recognized political rights. With the revolution they gained electoral and other rights,[8] and their identities were reframed as *campesinos*. At the local level, ethnicity, nonetheless, remained an important socially and culturally important basis of identity, for the weak state only minimally penetrated remote communities (even if more than in the prerevolutionary period). A Katarista movement, to which I alluded in chapter 1 had gained momentum after the country fell under military rule in the 1960s. Named after an eighteenth-century Aymaran hero, the Kataristas challenged a government-initiated military-*campesino* pact (Rivera Cusicanqui 1984). The military had tried to use the peasantry in a Bonapartist manner to build a civilian support base so as to offset the power of militant labor and middle-class civilian democrats. But also reflecting their collective solidarity, the Kataristas refused to subordinate themselves to the national labor federation. Organized labor, part of the 1952 revolutionary coalition, had similarly tried to manipulate newly defined *campesinos* for their own political ends.

The peasant movement, which took on an indigenous cast, protested neoliberal reforms in the 1980s and reforms of the Gonzálo Sánchez de Lozada government (1993–97) a decade later which participants also labeled neoliberal. Although the Katarista movement by then had lost momentum, the indigenous vote and indigenous identities were considered of such significance that the prerevolutionary *latifundista* Sánchez de Losado selected the Katarista Victor Hugo Cárdenas as his vice presidential running mate. Indeed, this symbolic co-optation contributed to the taming of the Katarista movement, although not necessarily as the president had intended. The Kataristas, already factionalized at the time, almost uniformly rejected Cárdenas for being co-opted. Cárdenas was more successful in establishing ties with a new indigenous movement

---

8. However, their right to vote was rescinded early in the 1960s when the military ousted the democratically elected MNR (Movimiento Nacionalista Revolucionaria) revolutionary-based coalition. Civilian rule did not return until the 1980s.

evolving in the Amazon region. Yet, in exchange for political support, the Sánchez de Losado government addressed certain indigenous demands, such as the desire for bilingual education. And at the start of the twenty-first century, Sánchez de Losado's successor sanctioned a new penal code that incorporated into the country's legal system the customary law of the Quechua and Aymara peoples.

The newer indigenous movement in the Amazon took a different stance toward the government. They viewed its more inclusionary stance as an opportunity to press for territorial autonomy, land reform, and political participation (Yashar 1998: 25, 35). Stirred in part by neoliberal restructuring, Indians there also protested reforms that encouraged foreign investment, investments perceived as causing environmental damage and impeding their livelihood in turn.

Meanwhile, in Ecuador tens of thousands of Indian peasants staged the Levantamiento Nacional Indígena in 1990, a weeklong indigenous civic strike. In conjunction with the Levantamiento, peasants stopped delivering farm products to the towns, blocked the main highways and cut off commerce, and marched en masse to regional capitals. In some places demonstrators occupied government offices. Support for the Levantamiento was greatest in the central highlands and the Amazon, under the aegis of the Confederación de Nacionalidades Indígenas del Ecuador, CONAIE (Zamosc 1994; Trujillo 1994). CONAIE built on two regional federations, one in the Andes, the other in the Amazon. The Levantamiento in particular, and CONAIE in general, served to channel localized ethnic solidarities into a pan-ethnic movement through which a new Indian identity was socially constructed. However, there too local ethnic identities did not disappear in the process.

Building on earlier regional organizations, CONAIE demanded a redefinition of citizenship that recognized indigenous rights to cultural distinctiveness and political autonomy. Formed in the 1980s, the Confederation came to demand a redefinition of Ecuador as a plurinational country, autonomy for Amazonian groups, bilingual education, and legalization of Indian medicine (Zamosc 1994). Then, in 1996, it entered the electoral arena as part of a larger coalition. Through the coalition it successfully fielded Andean and Amazon legislative candidates. And during the next few years CONAIE played a critical role in the countrywide protests, fueled by official increases in oil prices and a substantial drop in the value of the country's currency, that deposed two democratically elected presidents. At the same time that the pan-Indian movement gained social and political force Amazonian organizations within CONAIE became more assertive. Amazonian Indians organized marches, demanded territorial autonomy, and negotiated terms of oil exploration in their region. They were hostile to the expansion of environmentally damaging oil exploration that came with the liberalization of foreign investment rules.

Similarly, in Guatemala newly founded Maya organizations committed to strengthening indigenous identities, indigenous cultural revitalization, and indigenous rights gained strength in the 1990s. The movement, however, has roots in the 1960s, when Catholic groups introduced egalitarian notions and this-world social action. At the time some indigenous people enjoyed new educational opportunities but blocked economic mobility, the latter of which they attributed to racism. Then, in the 1980s, genocidal repression linked to a military-backed counterinsurgency war politicized indigenous people. A class analysis framed the politicization, but at the grass-roots level people were frustrated with the sidelining of ethnicity (and racism). By the 1990s neoliberal pressures and the human rights language that also accompanied the transitions to democracy left Mayas frustrated with the pace of change, as well as with a growing inequality in the distribution of wealth, and with their exclusion from full participation in the country's institutional life. The result of these accumulating pressures contributed to the Mayan movement.

Led by educated Mayas employed by development NGOs and state bureaucracies (as teachers, extension service workers, and researchers in government centers), a pan-Mayan movement evolved that built on a multiclass social base, on a combination of professionals, businessmen, students, development workers, rural shopkeepers, and cultivators. Though living economically modest lives, the leadership had command of rich and diverse cultural resources that ranged from bilingualism (i.e., knowledge of indigenous languages as well as Spanish) to the use of the Internet. Thus they could readily communicate across rural communities, between the city and the countryside, and internationally with global solidarity networks (and members of their groups abroad).

And, as in the other countries with new indigenous movements, in Guatemala the Maya movement politicized and transformed how Indians responded to both old and new grievances. The peace accord that ended the country's violent civil war proved crucial to the vitality of the movement. The participation of indigenous organizations in the peace negotiations served to strengthen the Maya movement, in legitimating indigenous groups and indigenous rights and in creating a political opening. But the very coming together of indigenous groups in a pan-Maya movement can be traced back to the brutality of military repression in the early 1980s and to new economic vulnerability rooted in austerity policies at the time. With the return to civilian rule indigenous groups found themselves with the political "space" to press for shared concerns that until then had no legal means of expression. In addition, the emergent post-Cold War international human rights discourse provided a language of rights on which the emergent movement could and did build (see Warren 1998). While Maya groups pressed for autonomy, land reform, better wages, and better prices for crops they grew, they never experienced a contraction of state support that incensed indigenous peoples elsewhere in the region. Conservatives ruled the country for some forty years, with almost no populist concessions.

Culturally, Maya intellectuals produced new school texts that critiqued the racism of official national histories, promoted the preservation of the Maya language, disseminated information on indigenous rights, and promoted community councils of elders premised on Maya leadership norms. Not surprisingly, they criticized the Western development model, which prioritized assimilation over ethnic and indigenous claims. Yet, in forging a broad-based Maya identity that united peoples across language groups and communities, the Guatemalan, like the Ecuadorean, movement built a new identity, a new social formation: one that built on but transcended local ethnic differences. The movement did not merely call for respect of traditions that national and local elites previously denied. In 1992, the five hundredth anniversary of the Conquest, the indigenous Guatemalan activist Rigoberta Menchú received the Nobel Peace Prize, giving added legitimacy to ethnic concerns. Indigenous groups gained a new international voice.

On the political front, the pan-Maya movement convinced the new democratic government to sign an accord that recognized the rights of indigenous peoples. It also participated in an electoral coalition, Nukuj Ajpop, that won some municipal and legislative seats and allied with popular sector groups in the New Guatemala Democratic Front (FDNG, or el Frente). Nonetheless, in 1999 the Maya movement suffered a political setback. That year a national referendum on linguistic and other indigenous reforms was defeated.

Only one country with a sizable Indian population experienced no indigenous movement of significance in the 1990s: Peru. Sendero Luminoso, anti-Sendero state-promoted *rondas,* and the militarization of the countryside combined to politicize the countryside in a manner that submerged ethnic identities. Only in the Amazon region, removed from Sendero/anti-Sendero tensions, did some Indians organize qua Indians, to defend local land claims and press for local autonomous governance. Peruvian exceptionalism suggests that when both an influential agrarian movement and government machinations polarize a populace along nonethnic lines, formal democratization is unlikely to stir indigenous movements—even when economic conditions are ripe.

In the Brazilian Amazon indigenous movements also arose, but of a different sort. Accounting for a smaller portion of the national population and reflecting a different ethnic-social organization, Indians there focused initially on rights to their traditional means of livelihood. The expansion of agribusiness, under the military and then under democratic governments, occurred at the expense of local people. Under the circumstances, Amazonian groups associated with national and international movements that championed their concerns. The rubber tappers and other Amazon indigenous peoples thereby gained international as well as national attention and support. But the support came with a reframing of their movement, as an effort to save the rain forest, and the movement came with costs similar to those experienced by the Landless Workers Movement. Large farmers, seeking to appropriate Amazonian land for themselves, violently attacked, with their own hired militia, indigenous people in the area. Some thousand people were murdered, the famed leader of the rubber tappers, Francisco (Chico) Mendes, among them (Keck 1995). Assassins operated with impunity, reflecting the close ties between large landowners and juridical and other authorities.

Meanwhile, in countries with a black population movements were racialized. They built simultaneously on traditions brought from Africa and on contemporary global black culture. The nature and demands of race-based movements varied with local conditions, including class-based experiences. But they also varied with local social constructions of race, as in the case of indigenous movements. In Brazil, for example, movements were contingent on leadership inventing "flattened," simplified, and polarized racial identities and discourse. Brazil is officially a racial democracy. A multiplicity of socially defined racial categories typically divide people of color there. To break down racial divides and politicize race-based movements, some movement leaders appealed to shared cultural motifs (Gomes da Cunha 1998).

Brazilian race-based movements had difficulty transcending class divisions, however. Middle-class mulattoes and lower-class black and mixed-race populations tend to have different concerns and different identities. Lower-class movements in the country's Northeast, the region with the greatest concentration of poor blacks, focused on issues of poverty and demands for government services, and they fused their energies with African-Brazilian religious movements. Though race-based, race was typically not the most salient feature around which they mobilized.

While Colombia was one of the few countries that never formally fell under military rule in the 1960s through 1980s, a new constitution that went into effect in 1991 extended collective rights to black communities there and advanced the goal of a pluriethnic and multicultural nation (Grueso, Rosero, and Escobar 1998):[9] in line with the new international

9. An important grass-roots coalition, the Civic Movement (Movimiento Cívico), combined with the breakdown of the traditional elite two-party system, paved the way to the drafting of the new constitution. Movimiento Cívico involved urban dwellers who pressed for municipal services, municipal democratization, resources, housing, land, and security. Perhaps the most powerful urban movement in Latin America in the 1980s, urban strikes that it supported paralyzed the nation. The new constitution that the Movimiento Cívico backed provided for direct elections of municipal authorities as well as a multicultural society. Accordingly, the indigenous movement must be understood in the context of nonindigenous movements and broader political processes.

norms respecting the right to be different. The new national vision con-
secrated in the constitution served as the basis for incipient black community mobilizing for cultural, ethnic, and territorial demands in the
Pacific portion of the country. Leaders framed the movement in terms of
the government's redefinition of citizenship rights, but also in terms of
environmental issues. In the context of increased international concern
with tropical rain forests, as seen in Brazil, scientists and NGOs encouraged blacks in the area to emphasize biodiversity conservation and natural resource control. Indeed, it was economic marginalization linked
to ecological deterioration that drew blacks in the region to the movement. As in Brazil, however, in Columbia the race-based movement
tended not to cut across the class divide. Most black elites in the area did
not identify with the movement; they wished not to be singled out as an
ethnic minority.

In sum, race as well as ethnicity became a basis of collective identity
and collective mobilization for change in the 1990s. However, most typically the race-based movements were class specific, owing to the continued significance of class, objectively and subjectively. And for such
reasons race-based movements did not necessarily focus primarily or exclusively on matters of race.

Religious Movements

Although modernization theory also predicted that secularism would
erode religiosity and that the two were poles apart, religion gained new
currency and meaning in the late 1900s. New religions and new religious
interpretations captured the popular imagination in ways that influenced
social movements and inspired change. As Islamic fundamentalism spread
in other regions of the developing world, in Latin America evangelical
Protestantism, especially Pentecostalism, did. Liberation theology and
base communities, as described by Levine and Mainwaring in chapter 6,
by the 1990s were losing out in the "struggle for the spirit," both in numbers and in their ability to invoke the populace and speak in its name.

The "theology of liberation" lost out for several reasons. Among them,
the Vatican intervened to marginalize religiously inspired activism.
Fewer priests, as a consequence, engaged in activity that captivated
parishioners. Also, liberation theology never evoked the nonrational appeal that evangelical Protestantism did.

In Brazil, the CEB movement accordingly lost much of its dynamism.
The Vatican imposed conservative ecclesiastical appointments, sanctioned the leaders of the progressive base, most notably Leonardo Boff,
and exerted other pressures to cripple the base community movement.
The main growth within Catholicism shifted to the conservative charis-
matics. Moderates favored social justice and sided with the MST, the
Landless Workers Movement, as well as other populist concerns, but they

preferred a hierarchical church. The conservative turn notwithstanding, Catholic leadership continued to stir movements for justice, even if not through CEBs. In 1999, for example, the national bishops' organization sponsored a series of nationwide demonstrations, the Cry of the Excluded Ones, in opposition to official neoliberal policies. And they did so with some effect. The Cardoso government announced an ambitious social spending program as unions and political parties of the left, and the MST, along with the bishops, coordinated strikes and protest marches.

And the CEB setback notwithstanding, liberation theology continued to inspire people outside as well as within the church. It inspired people to side with the subaltern stratum and to address the most egregious social effects of structural adjustment policies. It also influenced electoral and NGO development activity. Individuals who had participated in the CEB movement came to occupy prominent positions in unions, the Workers Party, and social movements. CEB values, in essence, had been internalized and routinized.

Populist church initiatives failed, nonetheless, to stop religious defections and the erosion of centuries of Catholic religious hegemony in the region. The regional religious transformation was of such magnitude that it was compared to the sixteenth-century Reformation (Stoll and Garrard-Burnett 1993). One-third of the twenty principal Latin American countries experienced an increase of more than 600 percent in Protestantism between the 1960s and 1990s, with evangelical fundamentalist and charismatic groups gaining the most followers. Brazil, the largest Catholic country in the world, was one of those that experienced dramatic rates of conversion. Missionaries initially made inroads by providing food, health care, and community services along with religious solace (Stoll 1990), but subsequently they were able to attract converts with minimal direct material offerings.

Evangelism became a social movement of sorts, with significance, like liberation theology, extending beyond the religious domain. But in contrast to the new Catholicism, it inculcated a servile attitude to the culture of the popular classes, at the same time that it attacked many of its central elements (Lehmann 1996). Affecting nearly every aspect of daily life, the religious-induced cultural change had particular appeal to the poor.[10]

While Pentecostals claim disinterest in ideology, apart from an aversion to communism, and doctrinal separation between religion and politics, the impulse behind evangelism in the region could be traced in part to the rise of the religious right and its political mission in the United States. Conservative U.S. political activists supported missionary efforts in Latin America, especially but not only in countries where revolutionary movements had gained a footing in the 1980s, such as Guatemala

10. On the different Protestant currents, see Stoll 1990 and Sarmandu 1990.

and Nicaragua. Evangelicals sided with counterrevolutionary forces. But whether directly active in politics or not, throughout the region they were politically conservative.

In applying their quasi-magical language to financial success and acquisitiveness, the message of Pentecostals resonated with neoliberalism (Lehmann 1996). Pentecostalism is suited to the more individualistic and less statist political-economic order associated with economic restructuring. Religion and economic change thereby were mutually reinforcing, just as religion and politics were.

Meanwhile, in former slave countries syncretic cults that built on the populace's African heritage continued to gain popularity. This was especially true in the northeast of Brazil and the Caribbean. Even in Cuba religion, which had fallen out of favor after Castro took power, experienced a revival after the 1980s. Afro-Cuban syncretic religions, evangelical Protestantism, and Catholicism, in descending order, attracted new adherents. In 1994 one in five Cubans surveyed (by Gallup) acknowledged attending church the preceding month (*Miami Herald,* 18 December 1994: 39A). Indicative of the emergent significance of religion, in the 1990s hundreds of thousands of islanders turned out for annual once-small church celebrations, often with *santería* amulets (Oppenheimer 1992: 341), and the pope was greeted with mass turnouts as he toured the island in 1998. In welcoming the pope and appearing with him in public, Castro himself tacitly sanctioned religion. Religion, in turn, began to redefine the political-moral order. It eroded the legitimacy of the Marxist-Leninist atheistic state at the same time that it deflected popular discontent with the regime. Its impact in Cuba, as elsewhere in the region, came to extend to the secular domain.

In sum, in the 1990s religions new to the region and revivals of old syncretic religions (which historically involved resistance to the Catholicism imposed by the *conquistadores*) eroded Catholic religious hegemony as never before. And they had the effect, if not the intent, of challenging the broader cultural and institutional order.

Politically Grounded Movements

The repressive political regimes of the 1960s through 1980s, which had as their mission the obliteration of radical political movements, paradoxically generated some of the largest and most broad-based protest movements in modern times in the region, involving men as well as women. In closing down institutional bases for channeling demands, military governments compelled those opposed to the political order either to deploy extrainstitutional means to make their wants known or to settle for covert noncompliance and internalization of grievances. While rebellion was risky, in focusing on fundamental human rights, movements evolved that helped to usher in democratic transitions. The interclass movements for political rights in Brazil, Chile, and Argentina, examined in this book, contributed to the restoration of civilian rule. They even stirred a contagion. With the exception of Cuba, all the countries of Latin America returned to civilian rule by the 1990s. Countries such as Paraguay and Haiti, long under autocratic rule, joined the pro-democracy bandwagon (with limited success).

Austerity policies following the 1980s debt crises unwittingly contributed to the erosion of regime authority. Angry with the loss of political rights, people became even angrier at the devastating declines in their living standards. Meanwhile, NGOs that exposed the human rights atrocities through international networks helped to turn world opinion against the dictatorships. They even influenced the United States' decision to stop supporting the regimes, a critical turn of events (Keck and Sikkink 1998).

In Chile the economy had been on an upswing when General Pinochet lost a crucial plebiscite. However, the roots of the pro-democracy movement had been established earlier, during an economic downturn, as Garretón highlights in his chapter. Opposition movements took hold especially where informal networks provided a bedrock for collective resistance. Such conditions were found, for example, in Chilean shantytowns that had been Communist Party strongholds and where parish priests brought residents together in soup kitchens, *talleres* (workshops) for the unemployed, and other collective undertakings. Such conditions also were found among university students who had solidary networks along with a tradition of activism on which to build (Schneider 1995).

In principle, the restoration of democracy eliminated the need for extrainstitutional political movements. The transitions ushered in relatively free and fair elections. And political parties, especially of the left, appealed to the popular sectors and the movements with which they had been associated. Parties of the left won municipal, though not national, elections. This was true in Brazil, Mexico, Peru, Paraguay, Uruguay, Argentina, the Dominican Republic, and El Salvador. In the process institutional politics defused social movement activity.

But politically inspired mobilizations dissipated for other reasons as well. First, people wished to avoid the risks of a new wave of violence, repression, and military usurpation of power. Accordingly, they subordinated their particular grievances to a widely shared interest in political stability. Second, the democratization movements themselves, as the chapters in this book indicate, were composed of groups with disparate interests; only a shared concern with the restoration of political and human rights had united them. Third, some of the new civilian governments, as already noted in the context of labor and urban movements, turned to pact-like strategies to defuse political pressure from civil society. And fourth, both movement leaders and rank and file shifted their support to institutional politics. The organizational logic of the political parties and government agencies with which movements, their leadership, and their membership bases established ties was grounded in order, bureaucratization, and institutionalization, not mobilization.

The Workers Party (Partido dos Trabalhadores, PT) in Brazil, the Izquierda Unida in Peru, and the Frente Amplio in Uruguay are examples of left-wing parties that built their political bases on the remains of grass-roots and labor movements from the period of military rule. And in Mexico the Revolutionary Democratic Party, the PRD, under Cárdenas built its base on the grass-roots groups that proliferated in the 1980s, especially after the earthquake; then, in the 1990s it built on the Zapatista movement and the movements it inspired as well. Accordingly, social movements not only helped to redemocratize the region, they strengthened and broadened the institutional base of the new regimes, including at their own expense. Countries that experienced no such movement-based political party vitalization experienced crises. Their traditional parties responded to elite but not mass concerns. Venezuela and Colombia are cases in point (Colombia's guerrilla groups, in the main, opposed rather than engaged in electoral politics). By the year 2000 both countries' party systems had effectively collapsed.

Municipal victories of the left on occasion also enabled the residues of social movements to gain new voice in government and to reform governance "from within." This occurred, for example, in Porto Alegre, Brazil (Baierle 1998) and in some contexts political parties and social movements were mutually reinforcing. The experience of Juchitán, Oaxaca, illustrates how electoral and collective resistance strategies may be effectively combined. Juchitecos staged roadblocks and hunger strikes (in addition to appropriating indigenous cultural traditions and symbols) in opposition to the PRI (Rubin 1997). It was in Juchitán that the left, in the early 1980s, first obtained local power in Mexico. And in Guatemala peace accords fueled both a political coalition of the left and indigenous and other social movements.

The relationship between democratization and social movements is, in essence, historically contingent. If and when political parties get the upper hand, social movements tend to lose their vitality; however, if they do not or before they do, political parties and social movements may nurture each other.

Democratization itself may stir new social movements, even though it in principle establishes the institutional means for interest articulation. First, democratization may generate discontent if elected governments prove incapable of or unwilling to address the principal concerns of their citizenry (Oxhorn 1998; Garretón 1999). For example, in Mexico antifraud movements emerged after the 1988 elections. Supporters argued that the "official party" stole the election. Base communities, though opposed by the Hierarchy, played an important role in the movement. And in Brazil disclosures of widespread corruption identified with the first elected president in the postmilitary period, Fernando Collor de Melo, stirred a mass movement for impeachment. The movement resulted in the world's first removal from office of an impeached president and soon thereafter inspired impeachments elsewhere in the region. In the 1990s presidents were impeached or seriously threatened with impeachment in Paraguay, Colombia, Venezuela, and Ecuador. The success of the Brazilian impeachment movement came from its moral appeal and the support it ultimately garnered from well-placed professionals, businessmen, and conservative politicians, along with labor unions, political parties of the left, students, NGOs, Catholic organizations, and the remains of earlier social movements. The impeachment movement also built up momentum by appealing to the country's popular carnevalesque repertoire and to patriotism. Impeachment supporters appeared in mass rallies in numerous cities with their faces painted the colors of the national flag. Framed as a pro-democracy movement, for ethics in politics, the movement was seen as an effort to strengthen, not weaken, the fledgling democracy.

Second, democratization may evoke unrest by providing opposition groups with democratic pillars around which to organize. This was especially true in Colombia. Rebels there kidnapped election officials, burned ballots, and threatened prospective voters in local elections in October 1997 and in congressional elections the following March. The deepening of formal democracy, which had included a shift from an appointed to an elected mayoral system, had the effect but not intent of strengthening local-level political disruption. The Colombia Revolutionary Armed Forces (FARC), the country's oldest and largest guerrilla group, spearheaded election boycotts. They cited government and political party corruption and attacks on local candidates of the left as reasons for voter protest. But the political mobilizations backfired on FARC. Tensions rose to the point that military and paramilitary forces killed some five thousand members and leaders of the Patriotic Union, the political party launched by FARC. The brutality succeeded in destroying the party by 1999. Rather than strengthen democracy, party disintegration had the opposite effect. Patriotic Union loyalists reemphasized their ties to FARC, the guerrilla wing of the movement.

Third, administrative, fiscal, and political decentralization, emphasized both by neoliberalism and democratization, may generate conditions conducive to local resistance. Reduced central state control can make local governance more contentious. Precisely for this reason the conservative president of Nicaragua clamped down on newly elected local governments after massive hurricane destruction in 1998. Fearing that elected Sandinista mayors would use relief funds to mobilize constituencies for their party's own political advantage, he sent federal authorities to assume municipal control.

Fourth, a *rescinding* of political rights in newly restored democracies may stir unrest. In Peru, for example, Fujimori faced thousands of pro-democracy protesters in June 1997 when he dismantled the constitutional court, and more protesters in 2000 after allegedly manipulating electoral results. Peruvians saw formal political channels as inadequate for defending their perceived rights.

Under other circumstances, however, democratization was politicizing. The center-left political pact in Chile, *Concertación de partidos por la democracia*, for example, contributed to cross-party, cross-class collaboration, demobilization, and pragmatic politics, at the same time that an "authoritarian enclave" remained. (Garretón 1995).

In Cuba, the one remaining nonmultiparty regime in the region, people mainly channeled their political discontent covertly. In the 1990s approximately one-fifth of the electorate, according to official sources, defied government voting orders—by spoiling their ballots casting blank ballots, or refusing to comply with authorities' call for a "show of unity" (involving voting for the entire state slate of candidates). In August of 1994, however, some one thousand to two thousand Havana residents, angered about a subsistence crisis as well as Castro's continued rule, took the risk of publically rioting. It was the largest protest since Castro's consolidation of power. When the government responded by allowing islanders to leave, to exit rather than to have voice, some thirty-three thousand took advantage of the opportunity before the U.S. and Cuban governments signed an accord that restricted and regulated emigration. Dissident and other groups, in addition, organized informally and illegally, in opposition to specific state-imposed conditions they disliked. Through the formation of Concilio Cubano they tried to coordinate their opposition. However, authorities restricted what the umbrella group could do. Accordingly, state functionaries drove most challenges to the regime underground, even if they failed to repress them out of existence.

In sum, most democracies opened up to previously excluded groups. Yet at the dawn of the new millennium democratization proved no panacea to regional problems. Politics on occasion became contentious, but more significantly the new democracies left yearnings of many lower-, working-, and middle-class people, the numerical majority, unmet.

CONCLUSION

Latin Americans viewed the key structural changes of the 1990s, redemocratization and market reforms, as resolving certain problems while creating others. The changes defused earlier movements by correcting the most egregious conditions, by expanding rights, and by opening up institutional channels to previously excluded groups. But new structural conditions also generated new deprivations for some, and new feelings of injustice. Whatever the natural affinity between democracy and unfettered market capitalism, individually and in combination the two sets of reforms generated conflicts and new extrainstitutional movements for change. Simultaneously, the neoliberal democratic state brought previously submerged identities to the fore and provided the formal bases for mobilizations for new rights and claims.

Meanwhile, the structural changes contained some earlier social movements. In particular, as the risks of rebelling against capital increased, strike activity tapered off. Under the circumstances workers internalized their grievances or directed them toward the state, toward policies that they potentially could change. Work identities were not relegated to the dustbin of history. Rather, workers channeled their grievances to venues where, in the new economic order, there was a chance they would be addressed.

As bases of movements for change broadened, so too did mobilization strategies. Groups turned to new mechanisms of communication, such as the Internet, and to the media once state censorship softened under democratization. As postmodernesque as the movements on occasion appeared in their symbolism and public displays, and as localized as movements often were, they responded to shared underlying conditions, were inspired by one another, and sometimes also coordinated protests.

An institutionally grounded historical approach accounts for the generalizable as well as the particularistic features of Latin American social movements. It accounts both for localized responses that modernization-based analyses overlook and for translocal features that local-centric postmodern analyses neglect and about which they do not theorize. The institutionally based analysis also best explains the shifts in the Latin American repertoire of resistance.

Theoretical efforts at explanation aside, injustices that persist in the twenty-first century, and changing conceptions of injustices, are likely to continue to stir new social movements and new constructions of movements born from conditions of the past. Latin Americans can be expected to continue to press the limits of the art of the possible, as they did in the past. They are their own best hope for a more humane and just future.

REFERENCES

Baierle, Sergio Gregorio

1998   "The Explosion of Experience: The Emergence of a New Ethical-Political Principle in Popular Movements in Porto Alegre, Brazil." In *Cultures of Politics/Politics of Cultures*, edited by Sonia Alvarez, Evelina Dagnino, and Arturo Escobar, pp. 118–40. Boulder, Colo.: Westview Press.

Barrig, Maruja

1989   "The Difficult Equilibrium between Bread and Roses: Women's Organizations and the Transition from Dictatorship to Democracy in Peru." In *The Women's Movement in Latin America: Feminism and the Transition to Democracy*, edited by Jane Jaquette, pp. 104–24. Boston: Unwin Hyman.

Burt, Jo-Marie

1998   "Shining Path and the 'Decisive Battle' in Lima's Barriadas: The Case of Villa El Salvador." In *Shining and Other Paths: War and Society in Peru, 1980–1995*, edited by Steve Stern. Durham, N.C.: Duke University Press.

Burt, Jo-Marie, and Cesar Espejo

1995   "The Struggles of a Self-Built Community." *NACLA Report on the Americas* 28 (4): 19–25.

Castañeda, Jorge

1993   *Utopia Unarmed: The Latin American Left after the Cold War.* New York: Alfred Knopf.

Chalmers, Douglas, and Carlos Vilas et al., eds.

1996   *The New Politics of Inequality in Latin America: Rethinking Participation and Representation.* London: Oxford University Press.

Chernick, Marc

1997   "The Crisis of Human Rights in Colombia." *Latin American Studies Association Forum* (3): 20–22.

Cross, John C.

1998   *Informal Politics: Street Vendors and the State in Mexico City.* Stanford: Stanford University Press.

Davis, Diane

1994   "Failed Democratic Reform in Contemporary Mexico: From Social Movements to the State and Back Again." *Journal of Latin American Studies* 26: 375–408.

Degregori, Carlos Ivan

1986   *Ayacucho: Raices de una crisis.* Ayachucho: Instituto de Estudios Regionales José María Arguedas.

Degregori, Carlos Iván, et al., eds.

1996   *La rondas campesinas y la derrota de Sendero Luminoso.* Lima: Instituto de Estudios Peruanos.

Durand-Lasserve, Alain

1998   "Law and Urban Change in Developing Countries: Trends and Issues." In *Illegal Cities: Law and Urban Change in Developing Countries* edited by Edésio Fernandes and Ann Varley, pp. 233–57. London: Zed Books.

Eckstein, Susan
1994 *Back from the Future: Cuba under Castro.* Princeton: Princeton University Press.

Foweraker, Joe
1989 "Los movimientos populares y la transformación del sistema político mexicano." *Revista Mexicana de Sociología* 51 (4): 93–113.

Foweraker, Joe, and Anne Craig, eds.
1990 *Popular Movements and Political Change in Mexico.* Boulder, Colo: Westview Press.

Garretón M., Manuel Antonio
1993 "La renovación ideologica en Chile." In *Renovación ideologica en Chile: Los partidos y su nueva visión estratégica.* Santiago: Instituto de Ciencia Politica, Universidad de Chile.
1995 *Hacia una nueva era política: Estudio sobre las democratizaciones.* Mexico: Fondo de Cultura Economica.
1999 "Social and Economic Transformations in Latin America: The Emergence of a New Political Matrix?" In *Markets and Democracy in Latin America: Conflict or Convergence?* edited by Philip Oxhorn and Pamela Starr, pp. 61–78. Boulder, Colo.: Lynne Rienner.

Gomes da Cunha, Olivia Maria
1998 "Black Movements and the 'Politics of Identity' in Brazil." In *Cultures of Politics/Politics of Cultures,* edited by Sonia Alvarez, Evelina Dagnino, and Arturo Escobar, pp. 220–51. Boulder, Colo: Westview Press.

Grueso, Libia, Carlos Rosero, and Arturo Escobar
1998 "The Process of Black Community Organizing in the Southern Pacific Coast Region of Colombia." In *Cultures of Politics/Politics of Cultures,* edited by Sonia Alvarez, Evelina Dagnino, and Arturo Escobar, pp. 196–219. Boulder, Colo: Westview Press, 1998.

Hammond, Jack
1999 "Law and Disorder: The Brazilian Landless Farmworkers' Movement." *Bulletin of Latin American Research* 18 (4): 469–89.

Hirschman, Albert
1970 *Exit, Voice, and Loyalty.* Cambridge, Mass.: Harvard University Press.

ILO [International Labour Office]
1990–98 *Yearbook of Labour Statistics.* Geneva: ILO.

Jaquette, Jane
1997 "Women in Power: From Tokenism to Critical Mass." *Foreign Policy* 108 (Fall): 23–27.

Jelin, Elizabeth, ed.
1990 *Women and Social Change in Latin America.* London: Zed Books.
1994 ¿Ciudadania emergente o exclusión? Movimientos sociales y ONGs e los años noventa." *Revista Mexicana de Sociología* 94, no. 4 (October–December):

Keck, Margaret
1995 "Social Equity and Environmental Politics in Brazil: Lessons from the Rubber Tappers of Acre." *Comparative Politics* (July): 409–24.

Keck, Margaret, and Kathryn Sikkink
1998 *Activists Beyond Borders.* Ithaca, N.Y.: Cornell University Press.

Langevin, Mark, and Peter Rosset
  1997   "Land Reform from Below: The Landless Workers Movement in
          Brazil." *Backgrounder* (Institute for Food and Development Policy)
          4, no. 3 (Fall): 1–3.
Lehmann, David
  1996   *Struggle for the Spirit: Religious Transformation and Popular Culture in
          Brazil and Latin America.* Cambridge: Polity Press.
Lungo, Mario
  1996   "La ciudad y la nación, la organización barrial y el estado: Los dile-
          mas de la urbanización en Costa Rica a principios de los años
          noventa." In *Ciudades del Caribe en el umbral del nuevo siglo,* edited by
          Alejandro Portes and Carlos Dore Cabral, pp. 65–94. Caracas:
          Nueva Sociedad.
Martinez Nogueira, Roberto
  1995   "Devising New Approaches to Poverty in Argentina." In S*trategies to
          Combat Poverty in Latin America,* edited by Dagmar Raczynski, pp.
          33–38. Washington, D.C.: Inter-American Development Bank.
Maybury-Lewis, Biorn
  1994   *The Politics of the Possible: The Brazilian Rural Workers' Trade Union
          Movement, 1964–1985.* Philadelphia: Temple University Press.
McClintock, Cynthia
  1997   "The Decimation of Peru's Sendero Luminoso." Paper presented at
          the conference on Comparative Peace Processes in Latin America,
          Woodrow Wilson Center, Washington, D.C., March.
McGuire, James
  1996   "Strikes in Argentina." *Latin American Research Review* 31 (3): 127–50.
Murillo, Maria Victoria
  1997   *From Populism to Neoliberalism: Labor Unions and Market-Oriented Reforms
          in Argentina, Mexico, and Venezuela.* Cambridge: Doctoral Disserta-
          tion, Harvard University.
Nash, June
  1991   "The Reassertion of Indigenous Identity: Mayan Responses to State
          Intervention in Chiapas." *Latin American Research Review* 30 (3): 7–42.
  N.d.   *Re-Envisioning Mayas: Contesting Strategies of Globalization in Chiapas,
          Mexico.*
Noronha, Eduardo Garuti, Vera Gebrin, and Jorge Elias, Jr.
  1998   "Explicaçoes para um ciclo excepcional de greves: O caso brasile-
          iro." Paper presented at the Latin American Studies Association,
          Chicago, September.
Oppenheimer, Andres
  1992   *Castro's Final Hour: The Secret Story Behind the Coming Downfall of Com-
          munist Cuba.* New York: Simon & Schuster.
Oxhorn, Philip
  1998   "Social Inequality, Civic Society and the Limits of Citizenship in
          Latin America." Paper delivered at the Latin American Studies As-
          sociation, Chicago, September.
Paige, Jeffery
  1996   "Land Reform and Agrarian Revolution in El Salvador: Comment on
          Seligson and Diskin." *Latin American Research Review* 31 (2): 127–39.

Reilley, Charles
 1996   "Complementing States and Markets: The Inter-American Develop-
          ment Bank and Civil Society." Paper presented at Multilateral Ap-
          proaches to Peacemaking and Democratization in the Hemisphere,
          North-South Center Conference, April.
Rivera Cusicanqui, Silvia
 1984   *Oprimidos pero no vencidos: Luchas del campesinado aymara y qhechwa de
          Bolivia, 1900–1980.* La Paz: HISBOL-CUSTCB.
Rubin, Jeffrey
 1997   *Decentering the Regime: Ethnicity, Radicalism, and Democracy in Juchitán,
          Mexico.* Durham, N.C.: Duke University Press.
Sarmandu, Luis, ed.
 1990   *Protestantismos y procesos sociales en Centroamerica.* San José: Editorial
          Universitaria Centroamericana.
Schneider, Cathy
 1995   *Shantytown Protest in Pinochet's Chile.* Philadelphia: Temple University
          Press.
Schonwalder, Gerd
 1998   "Local Politics and the Peruvian Left: The Case of El Agustino."
          Latin American Research Review 33 (2): 73–102.
Seligmann, Linda
 1998   "Survival Politics and the Movements of Market Women in Peru in
          the Age of Neoliberalism." In *In the Third Wave of Modernization in
          Latin America,* edited by Lynne Phillips, pp. 65–82. Wilmington,
          Del.: Scholarly Resources.
Stephen, Lynn
 1997   *Women and Social Movements in Latin America.* Austin: University of
          Texas Press.
Stoll, David
 1990   *Is Latin America Turning Protestant?* Berkeley: University of California
          Press.
Stoll, David, and Virginia Garrard-Burnett
 1993   *Rethinking Protestantism in Latin America.* Philadelphia: Temple Uni-
          versity Press.
Tamayo, Sergio
 1989   *Vida digna en las ciudades: El movimiento urbano popular en México,
          1980–1985.* México: Gernika & Universidad Autónoma Metropoli-
          tana-A.
 1997   "La participación ciudadana: Un proceso." *Revista Mexicana de Soci-
          ología* 59 (4): 155–85.
Trujillo, Jorge León
 1994   *De campesinos a ciudadanos diferentes: El levantamiento indígena.* Quito:
          Cedime and Abya-Yala.
Walton, John
 1998   "Urban Conflict and Social Movements in Poor Countries: Theory
          and Evidence of Collective Action." *International Journal of Urban
          and Regional Research* 22 (3): 460–81.
Warren, Kay
 1998   "Indigenous Movements as a Challenge to the Unified Social Move-

ment Paradigm for Guatemala." In *Cultures of Politics/Politics of Cultures,* edited by Sonia Alvarez, Evelina Dagnino, and Arturo Escobar, pp. 165–95. Boulder, Colo: Westview Press.

Yashar, Deborah
    1998   "Contesting Citizenship: Indigenous Movements and Democracy in Latin America." *Comparative Politics* (October): 23–42.

Yudice, George
    1998   "The Globalization of Culture and the New Civil Society." In *Cultures of Politics/Politics of Cultures,* edited by Sonia Alvarez, Evelina Dagnino, and Arturo Escobar, pp. 353–79. Boulder, Colo: Westview Press.

Zamosc, León
    1994   "Agrarian Protest and the Indian Movement in the Ecuadorian Highlands." *Latin American Research Review* 29 (3): 37–68.

Zermeno, Sergio
    1997   *Movimientos sociales e identidades colectivas en México.* México, D.F.: La Jornada Ediciones.

INDEX

Las Abuelas de Plaza de Mayo, 383
Agosti, Orlando, 242
Agrarian reform, 18–19; in Bolivia, 135,
140, 167, 172; in Brazil, 214, 367, 368;
in Chile, 263; in Colombia, 102–4, 107,
111–16, 120, 123; in El Salvador, 167,
364; in Guatemala, 139, 168, 364; in
Peru, 72–75, 80, 92–93, 153, 172; in
Venezuela, 134, 153, 167
Agriculture: in Bolivia, 19, 50; and capitalism, 12, 16, 33–34, 84, 102, 105, 108,
111, 113, 116, 120–21, 124, 147; in
Colombia, 105, 108–9, 111, 120–21,
124, 224–25; and economic development, 92–93; and economic structure,
16–17, 51, 120; in El Salvador, 152;
globalization's impact on, 360; government intervention in, 17, 19; laborers in,
10, 15–18, 34, 48, 70, 108, 111, 121,
146–47, 149–50, 152; and market relations, 17–19, 80, 92, 146–47; in Mexico,
12; in Peru, 51, 67–70, 72–75, 80–81;
and rituals, 184–85, 195
Alfonsín, Raul, 41, 243, 245, 248, 322–23,
325, 371, 382
Allende Gossens, Salvador, 11, 22, 37, 177,
259, 264, 267–68, 331
Alvarado, Velasco, 51
Alves, Maria Helena Moreira, 355
Amaya, Mario, 245
Amazon region, indigenous movements in,
390–91, 392–93
Amnesty International, 243, 246, 249–50
Anaya, Jorge, 242

Anthropology, 3; structural, 197
ANUC (National Peasant Association of
Colombia), 38, 40, 55–56, 158; and
agrarian capitalism, 102–3; bureaucracy
in, 122–23, 125; and class alliance, 103,
114, 117, 123–25, 127; and demonstrations, 118; disaffection from, 121–22,
125; and economic development,
102–3; factionalism in, 119, 121;
government repression of, 102, 117–18,
120–21; and land tenancy, 102–3, 116,
118, 120, 124; leadership of, 45,
119–20, 122; and Maoism, 117–19, 122,
124–25; membership of, 114; political
oscillation of, 103, 123, 127; pro-govern-
ment, 117–18, 121–23; radical, 102–3,
116, 118–23; rightist turn in, 103,
122–23; and state, 102–3, 113–14, 116,
121–23; and strikes, 118
April 19th Movement (Colombia), 364
Arbenz, Jacobo, 134
Argentina: absence of mediating institutions in, 241, 248; austerity measures
in, 315, 317, 325; class alliance in, 317;
Communist Party in, 248; coup d'état
in, 241–42; death squads in, 242, 244;
democratization in, 243, 245, 254, 322,
355; demonstrations in, 250–55,
257–58; "disappeared" persons in, 26,
52, 242, 244–49, 252–57, 382–83; economic crisis in, 242–43; economic development in, 243; elections in, 28, 243,
255; foreign debt in, 322–23; gender
equity codified in, 384; guerrilla move-

ments in, 242–45, 247; human rights movements in, 248–49, 355; intelligentsia in, 242; Marxists in, 244; military government in, 25–26, 221, 241–44, 254, 325, 382; nationalism in, 253; political parties in, 254, 397; protest movements in, 315, 322, 375, 376; religion in, 52–53, 209, 244, 248–49, 251; repression in, 241–49, 252–54, 257; squatter settlement program in, 377n; strikes in, 316–17, 371; trade unions in, 242, 247, 317; and U.S. relations, 254; violence in, 242–43; and war with Britain, 26, 242–43, 254–55; women's movement in, 26, 35, 382–83; working class in, 54, 249, 278

Austerity measures, 6, 11, 20, 41, 47, 52, 55, 300, 307; in Argentina, 315, 317, 325; and authoritarianism, 325, 327; in Bolivia, 315, 317–18, 325; in Brazil, 315, 319–20; and class alliance, 317; and class consciousness, 318; in Colombia, 126; in Costa Rica, 315; and democracy, 326–27; in Dominican Republic, 30, 318–19, 321; in Ecuador, 317; in Guatemala, 317; in Haiti, 315, 318, 321; in Honduras, 315; and housing movement, 329; in Indonesia, 358; in Jamaica, 315, 325; in Mexico, 315, 329, 344; and middle class, 317; in Panama, 318; in Paraguay, 315; in Peru, 315–18, 325; and poor women's initiatives, 384–85; and protest movements, 308–9, 315–21, 323, 326–27, 373, 375, 397; and trade unions, 317; and urban poor, 317; and U.S. policy, 323; in Venezuela, 134, 139, 315; and working class, 320

Authoritarianism, 1, 3, 39, 104, 203n; and austerity measures, 325, 327; in Brazil, 292; in Chile, 259–60, 263, 315; in Colombia, 222, 235–36; in Guatemala, 134; in Haiti, 140; and military government, 261–62; and psychology, 4; and religion, 216; shift between democracy and, 11, 27, 260, 262; and state structure, 300, 327. *See also* Repression

Baker, James, 323
Baloyra, Enrique, 164
Banks, 13, 69, 92, 281, 318; and debt crisis, 300–301, 304, 306–9, 321–24, 326–27
Banzer Suárez, Hugo, 184, 199
Barco, Virgilio, 126

Barrientos, René, 165, 167, 172, 183, 188, 193, 195, 199
El Barson movement (Mexico), 379
Batista, Fulgencio, 133, 158, 161–64, 166, 168, 358
Behavioralism, 2–3
Béjar, Hector, 135, 155
Belaúnde Terry, Fernando, 72, 79–80, 90–92, 96–97, 166–67, 172
Bermúdez, Francisco Morales, 80
Berryman, P., 209
Betancourt, Rómulo, 133–34, 139, 167
Betancur, Belisario, 125–26, 135, 166, 172
Bignone, Reynaldo, 243, 383
Blanco, Hugo, 157
Boff, Clodovis, 235
Boff, Leonardo, 235, 394–95
Bolivia: agrarian reform in, 135, 140, 167, 172; agriculture in, 19, 50; austerity measures in, 315, 317–18, 325; Aymaran movement in, 24, 34–35; capitalism in, 183; class alliance in, 49–50, 317, 370; class struggle in, 183; coca production in, 45, 70, 365–66; Communist Party in, 135; consumption in, 183; coup d'état in, 165, 167, 184, 199; democracy in, 24, 40; demonstrations in, 40; elections in, 27–28, 166; guerrilla movements in, 133, 135, 139–41, 143, 147, 149, 153–54, 158–59, 165, 170, 172, 189; indigenous peoples in, 190–91, 389–90; indigenous rights codified in, 387; intelligentsia in, 24; labor disputes in, 187–89, 198–200, 368; landlords in, 153; land seizures in, 153; land tenancy in, 169; Marxists in, 182; middle class in, 49, 184; migratory labor in, 45; military government in, 24; mine closings in, 370–71; mine workers in, 6, 9, 36, 52–53, 182–89, 192–93, 195–201; mining industry in, 182–84, 198–200; peasants in, 24, 27–28, 34, 45, 135, 140, 149–50, 153–54, 158, 167, 169, 172, 183; political parties in, 183–84, 197, 199–200; protest movements in, 154, 182–83, 189, 315; railroad workers in, 192; recession in, 24; reform movements in, 153; religion in, 182; repression in, 36, 183–84, 188–89, 193, 195, 199; revolutionary movements in, 15, 19, 43, 49–50, 183, 197, 200; Siles Zuaso government in, 24, 43; socialism in, 183; squatters in, 147; strikes in, 40, 187–89,

200, 316, 318, 370–71; sugar production in, 147; trade unions in, 183–84, 187–89, 197–99, 317; village life in, 34–35, 45; violence in, 316; working class in, 183. *See also* Rituals, Bolivian Bourgeoisie. *See* Middle class

Bousquet, Jean-Pierre, 246–47

Brazil: agrarian reform in, 214; austerity measures in, 315, 319–20; authoritarianism in, 292; bureaucracy in, 281; capitalism in, 279–81; class alliance in, 278–79, 283–85, 287–89, 291, 295–97; Communist Party in, 320; consumer price increases in, 373, 374 fig., 375; coup d'état in, 278, 283; debtors' alliance in, 380; democratization in, 24, 29–30, 214, 221, 235, 278–80, 283–84, 297, 355; demonstrations in, 284, 287, 291, 293–95, 297, 316, 319–20; "disappeared" persons in, 289; economic development in, 278–80, 289; economic structure in, 279–81, 291, 294, 321; elections in, 177n, 262, 282–83, 287, 290, 292–95; elites in, 221, 235, 278, 295–97; foreign debt in, 299–300, 305, 307–8, 322–25; guerrilla movements in, 285–86; housing movement in, 378; impeachment movement in, 399; indigenous movements in, 392–93; indigenous rights codified in, 387; industrialization in, 278, 319; labor disputes in, 280; liberation theology in, 30; middle class in, 29, 279, 282–84, 287–88, 291, 296; military government in, 24, 38, 216, 220, 233, 273, 278–81, 283, 287, 294–97; nationalism in, 279; neighborhood groups in, 23; peasants in, 235, 278, 282, 288, 295; political parties in, 38, 216, 221, 235, 281–83, 286–87, 289–90, 292–93, 295–97, 319, 397, 398; protest movements in, 280–82, 284, 290–97, 315, 319–20, 375; race-based movements in, 393, 394; racial conflict in, 24; religion in, 30, 32, 203–5, 209–10, 214–21, 233–36, 286–87, 289, 292; religious transformation in, 394–95; repression in, 31, 233, 279, 281–83, 285–88, 291–92; revolutionary movements in, 285; riots in, 291, 316, 319–20; squatters in, 288, 319, 340n; state structure in, 278–80, 287–88, 290–92; strikes in, 291–92, 295, 371–72; student activism in,

283–85; trade unions in, 235, 278–79, 281–82, 284, 288–89, 292–93, 295–96, 367–68; unequal distribution in, 214, 367–68; upper class in, 24n; violence in, 282, 285–86, 292, 300, 380; working class in, 38, 217, 278–79, 282–84, 286–89, 294, 296–97, 319–20

Buechler, Hans, 192

Bureaucracy, 10, 17, 21, 41, 48, 104, 300, 327; and Colombian peasant organization, 122–23

Bush, George, 362

Camacho Solís, Manuel, 343, 344

Capitalism, 13–14, 17; agrarian, 12, 16, 18, 33–34, 84, 102, 105, 108, 111, 113, 116, 120–21, 124, 147; in Bolivia, 183; in Brazil, 279–81; in Chile, 264, 280; in Colombia, 102, 104–5, 108, 111, 113, 116–17, 119–21, 123–24, 126; and international banking, 301; in Mexico, 12, 333; and state structure, 280–81; urban renewal bias of, 333. *See also* Market relations; Neoliberalism

Cárdenas, Victor Hugo, 389–90, 398

Cardoso, Fernando Henrique, 368, 395

Cartagena Group, 323

Carter, Jimmy, 254, 323

Castello Branco, Humberto, 282

Castro, Fidel, 21, 34, 42, 51, 133, 139, 141, 156, 161, 163–65, 168–70, 176, 323, 381, 396, 400

Catholic church, 10, 30–32, 37, 52–53, 158–59, 172–73, 185–86, 203–4; in Argentina, 244, 248–49, 251; in Brazil, 204–5, 214–21, 233–36, 286, 289, 292; in Chile, 259, 266; in Colombia, 204–5, 222–36; and conservatism, 203, 206, 208n, 213n, 216–17, 219, 221–23, 226n, 232, 234–36, 394–95; and consumer protests, 375; hierarchy of, 206, 212, 214, 219, 222–23, 226, 231, 234–35, 248; and Mayan movement, 391; and NGO-fostered activities, 357; in Peru, 71, 95; and populism, 210–17, 220, 224, 229–30, 233–34, 236, 286–87; resistance to, by slum dwellers, 336; and U.S. aid, 230

CEBs (ecclesial base communities), 30–31, 37, 55, 158–59, 204–7, 209–25, 230–31, 234–36, 286; diminished dynamism of, 394–95; and housing movements, 338; and NGOs, 357

Central Intelligence Agency (CIA), 134

Chavez, Hugo, 377–78
Chile: agrarian reform in, 263; Allende government in, 11, 22, 177, 259, 264; austerity measures in, 11; authoritarianism in, 259–60, 263, 315; capitalism in, 263–64, 280; class alliance in, 268–69, 297, 317; class structure in, 11, 15; class struggle in, 264; Communist Party in, 263, 267, 269, 271; copper production in, 263, 266; coup d'état in, 259, 264; democratization in, 11, 29–30, 259–60, 262–63, 270, 273, 355, 397, 400; demonstrations in, 11, 265–67, 273, 316–17; "disappeared" persons in, 26, 265; economic structure in, 263–65, 269–70, 273–74; education in, 266, 272; elections in, 11, 39, 259, 264; human rights movements in, 355–56; industrialization in, 263; land seizures in, 264, 273; liberation theology in, 30; middle class in, 11, 29, 38, 262, 264–65, 267–68, 271–72; military government in, 25–26, 38, 259–60, 264–75, 382; nationalism in, 52, 263; neighborhood groups in, 23; peasants in, 263, 268; Pinochet regime in, 11, 15, 38, 259, 264–65, 267–68, 321, 355–56; political parties in, 23, 259, 262–72, 274, 317; protest movements in, 259–60, 265–75, 368, 375; reform movements in, 263–64; religion in, 30, 203, 248, 259, 264, 266; repression in, 11, 31, 38, 259–60, 264–69, 271, 274, 321; socialism in, 259; squatters in, 37, 331, 340n; state structure in, 262–63; strikes in, 39, 264, 266–68, 273, 316–17, 372; student activism in, 266, 269, 272; trade unions in, 15, 263, 266, 268–71; urban poor in, 23, 263, 269, 271, 317; and U.S. relations, 51, 264; violence in, 273; women's movements in, 385; working class in, 38–39, 54, 262, 266, 268–70, 278, 321
CIA (Central Intelligence Agency), 134
Citizenship: community-based concept of, 387, 390; and voting patterns, 348n
Civic Movement (Movimiento Cívico, Colombia), 393–94n
Class alliances: in Argentina, 317; and austerity measures, 317; in Bolivia, 49–50, 317, 370; in Brazil, 278–79, 283–85, 287–89, 291, 295–97; in Chile, 268–69, 297, 317; in Colombia, 103, 114–15, 117, 123–25, 172; in consumer protest

movements, 375; in Cuba, 162–65; in El Salvador, 164; and forms of defiance, 51; in Guatemala, 172, 317; and guerrilla movements, 162–65, 168, 171, 173; in impeachment movements, 399; in indigenous movements, 388, 391; in Mexican trade unions, 367; in Mexico, 49, 336–37, 342, 345; in Nicaragua, 162–65; in Peru, 172, 317; and power sharing, 296–97; in protest movements, 57, 268–69, 278–79, 282–85, 287, 289, 291, 295–97, 317, 331–32; in revolutionary movements, 49–50, 162–63; in Venezuela, 157; in women's movements, 383
Class consciousness: and austerity measures, 317; and Bolivian rituals, 187, 190–94, 196–98; and history, 12; and peasants, 122; and revolutionary movements, 197
Class structure: and austerity measures, 20; in Chile, 11, 15; in Colombia, 45, 103, 106, 113–14; and family, 25, 33; and forms of defiance, 33, 51; and hegemony, 2; and ideology, 3; and market relations, 17–18; and peasants, 102–3, 109, 112, 121, 123; and political activism, 1–5, 10; and political rights, 27–29, 38; and protest movements, 45; and racial conflict, 25, 53; and religion, 228–29; and revolution, 48–50; and rural population, 45; and social solidarity, 33; and women, 25, 257
Class struggle: in Bolivia, 183; in Chile, 264; in Colombia, 38, 40, 107, 113, 116–17, 125; and competition within elites, 40; in El Salvador, 164; in Mexico, 37; and political activism, 177; and racial conflict, 25
Cloward, Richard, 6–7
Coca production, 45; in Bolivia, 45, 70, 365–66, 371; in Colombia, 365; in Peru, 65, 67, 70, 84, 87–88; U.S. opposition to, 365, 371
Coffee production: in Colombia, 105–6, 108, 120, 151–52, 154; in El Salvador, 150, 155; in Guatemala, 150; and guerrilla movements, 146, 150
Collor de Melo, Fernando, 399
Colombia: agrarian reform in, 102–4, 107, 111–16, 120, 123; agriculture in, 105, 108–9, 111, 120–21, 124, 224–25; austerity measures in, 126; authoritarianism

in, 222, 235–36; capitalism in, 102, 104–5, 108, 111, 113, 116–17, 119–21, 123–24, 126; class alliance in, 114–15, 117, 123–25, 172; class structure in, 45, 103, 106, 113–14; class struggle in, 38, 40, 107, 113, 116–17, 125; coca production in, 365; coffee production in, 105–6, 108, 120, 151–52, 154; Communist Party in, 105, 112, 115, 117, 124, 134, 157; consumption in, 112; democratization in, 104, 125–26, 222; demonstrations in, 115, 118; economic crisis in, 29, 112–13, 125–26; economic development in, 102–3, 105, 108, 117, 119; economic structure in, l05–6, 108, 112–13; elections in, 114–15, 119, 122, 125, 135, 141, 166, 172, 228, 399; elites in, 222; and exports, 102, 105; guerrilla movements in, 112, 114, 125–26, 132–35, 139–42, 143–46, 149–50, 152, 154, 157, 159, 161–62, 165–68, 170–72, 177–78, 222, 232, 364–65; homicides in, 1988–1998, 364; indigenous rights codified in, 387; industrialization in, 102–3, 106; intelligentsia in, 124; landlords in, 103, 106, 108–9, 111, 113, 115–17, 121, 123; land tenancy in, 102–3, 111, 113, 116, 118, 120, 124, 152; marijuana production in, 121; middle class in, 50, 117, 122; migration in, 109, 117, 120–21, 124; military government in, 107; peasants in, 6, 29, 38, 40, 55–56, 102–27, 134, 140, 146, 150, 153, 157, 171, 222, 224–29; political parties in, 104, 106–7, 112, 115–16, 125–26, 134, 141, 158–59, 222, 227–28, 398; protest movements in, 125, 236; race-based movements in, 393–94; reform movements in, 111–13, 115–16, 120, 123, 126; religion in, 158, 172, 203–5, 209, 214, 222–36; repression in, 102, 104, 106, 117–21, 125; rural population in, 105, 108–9, 121, 125; sharecroppers in, 150; socialism in, 103; squatters in, 150; state structure in, 104–7; strikes in, 118; trade unions in, 105–6, 112, 119, 122, 125, 228; urban population in, 117; U.S. influence in, 114; La Violencia in, 29, 40, 104, 106–7, 111–12, 134–35, 139, 146, 149, 151–52, 157, 227–28; working class in, 105, 117, 124–25

Colombia Revolutionary Armed Forces (FARC), 364, 399
Colonialism, 3
Comités de Autodefensa Civil (Peru), 362
Communist Manifesto (Marx and Engels), 164
Communist Party: in Argentina, 248; in Bolivia, 135; in Brazil, 320; in Chile, 263, 267, 269, 271; in Colombia, 105, 112, 115, 117, 124, 134, 157; in El Salvador, 138; in Guatemala, 157; in Peru, 77, 135; in Venezuela, 134, 157
Conadep (National Commission on the Disappearance of Persons), 382
CONAIE (Confederación de Nacionalidades Indígenas del Ecuador), 390
CONAMUP (Coordinadora Nacional de Movimientos Urbanos Populares, Mexico), 336–37
CONAVIGUA (Coordinadora Nacional de Viudas de Guatemala), 383
Concertación de partidos por la democracia (Chilean pact), 372
Confederación de Nacionalidades Indígenas del Ecuador (CONAIE), 390
Consumer prices, 1990s' increase in, 373, 374 fig., 375
Consumer protest movements: class/union alliances of, 375; against food/fuel prices, 373, 374 fig., 375; by squatters, 330–31; by students, 376–77
Consumption: in Bolivia, 183; in Colombia, 112; domestic, 13; and neighborhood groups, 23; in socialist countries, 21; and urban population, 20; and women's organizations, 25
Convenio de concertación democrática para la reconstrucción de vivienda, 343n, 343–44, 345
Coordinadora Nacional de Movimientos Urbanos Populares (CONAMUP, Mexico), 336–37
Coordinadora Nacional de Viudas de Guatemala (CONAVIGUA), 383
Copper production, in Chile, 263, 266
Costa Rica: austerity measures in, 315; guerrilla movements in, 47; labor protests in, 368, 373; squatter movement in, 378
Cotton production, in El Salvador, 150
Counterinsurgency, 50; in Cuba, 133; in El Salvador, 160–61, 167–68; in Guatemala, 134, 160, 170; in Peru, 64,

76, 79–80, 83, 88–91, 94, 96; and United States, 134, 160–61; in Venezuela, 160

Coups d'état, 12, 27, 29; in Argentina, 241–42; in Bolivia, 165, 167, 184, 199; in Brazil, 278, 283; in Chile, 259, 264; in Cuba, 133; in Venezuela, 133

Cry of the Excluded Ones (Brazil), 395

Cuba: and aid to insurgents, 160, 169; Batista regime in, 161–65; class alliance in, 162–65; consumer prices in, 21; counterinsurgency in, 133; coup d'état in, 133; democracy in, 165; discontent in, 34n, 42; elections in, 133, 400; guerrilla movements in, 34, 133, 138, 143, 146, 150, 156, 159, 161–65, 168–71, 173, 176; landlords in, 151; land tenancy in, 151; market relations in, 19, 44–45; nationalism in, 51; peasants in, 34, 146–47, 150, 153; political parties in, 159, 163; protest movements in, 154; reform movements in, 165; religion in, 32, 164, 396; repression in, 165; revolution in, 15, 18, 32, 49, 54, 77, 132, 138–39, 161–65, 168–69, 263; sharecroppers in, 150; socialism in, 14, 49, 133, 168; squatters in, 147, 150–51, 156; state structure in, 42, 49; sugar production in, 34, 133, 151; underground economy in, in 1990s, 381; and U.S. relations, 51, 133, 139; village life in, 34; working class in, 54

CUD (Sole Coordinating Committee of Earthquake Victims, Mexico), 337, 338, 342

Culture: and colonialism, 3; and economic structure, 4–5, 7; and ethnic identity, 23–24, 387, 390, 392; and group solidarity, 4–5; and patriarchy, 25; of peasants, 81–82; popular, 7; and racial conflict, 53; and religion, 206–7; of resistance, 7, 33, 35–36, 38, 81–82, 141, 154–55, 201, 330, 335–36; and social structure, 56

Currency devaluations, 379, 388

Damnificados (earthquake victims): class alliances of, 342, 345; and *Convenio* accord, 343–44; housing movement of, 337–38; social status of, 338n. *See also* Housing movements (Mexico)

Davis, Natalie Zemon, 203n

Death squads, 170, 244; in Argentina, 242; in El Salvador, 29, 167–68, 176

Debray, Régis, 165, 168, 170

Debt crisis: in Argentina, 322–23; and austerity measures, 300, 306–9, 315–25, 327, 332; in Brazil, 299–300, 305, 307–8, 322–25; and Cartagena Group, 323; in Dominican Republic, 307; and economic development, 304–6, 315, 325; in Ecuador, 322; and exports, 301, 304, 306; and IMF, 306, 308, 321–24; in Jamaica, 301, 306, 322; in Mexico, 300–301, 305–6, 308, 322, 323, 344; and middle class, 324; Neoliberal response to, 352; in Nicaragua, 307, 322; in Peru, 299, 301, 306, 308, 322, 325; and protest movements, 300, 308–9, 315–22, 324–26; and public spending, 316; and slum economy of Mexico City, 334–35; and state structure, 300, 324–27; and unionization, 315; and urbanization, 315; in Venezuela, 305; and working class, 324; and World Bank, 306

Debtors' rights movement: in Brazil, 380; in Mexico, 379

de Hoz, José Martínez, 243

Democratization: in Argentina, 243, 245, 254, 322, 355; and austerity measures, 326–27; in Bolivia, 24, 40; in Brazil, 24, 29–30, 214, 221, 235, 278–80, 283–84, 297, 355; in Chile, 11, 29–30, 259–60, 262–63, 270, 273, 355, 397, 400; in Colombia, 104, 125–26, 222; in Cuba, 165; in El Salvador, 29; and ethnic groups, 356–57, 386–87; in Europe, 10–11; in Guatemala, 166; and guerrilla movements, 355; in Haiti, 30; international/domestic support of, 352; and labor protests, 368–69, 372; and market reform, 353; and middle class, 29; and nation state, 10; and NGOs' role, 357–58; in Nicaragua, 165, 400; in Peru, 61, 72, 77, 91–92, 299; and political demobilization, 397–98; and political mobilization, 398–400; and religion, 30; shift between authoritarianism and, 11, 27, 260, 262; and state structure, 39; in Uruguay, 47; in Venezuela, 133; and Western values, 2; and women's movements, 382–83, 384. *See also* Elections

Demonstrations, 9–10, 20, 326; in Argentina, 250–55, 257–58; in Bolivia, 40; in Brazil, 284, 287, 292–96, 316, 319–20; in Chile, 11, 265–67, 273,

316–17; in Colombia, 115, 118; in Jamaica, 318; in Mexico, 42, 316; non-violent, 26; in Panama, 318; in Peru, 299, 317–18
de Nevares, Jaime, 248
"Disappeared" persons, 26, 52, 90, 242, 247–49, 252–57, 262, 265, 288; investigation of, 26, 245–46, 382–83
Dominican Republic: austerity measures in, 30, 307, 316–21, 325; consumer protests in, 376; political party ties in, 397; religion in, 30
Dozo, Basilio, 242
Drugs. See Coca production
Duarte, José Napoléon, 138, 172, 176, 344
Duvalier, François, 140n
Duvalier, Jean-Claude, 140n, 321
Earthquake (1985, Mexico), 334, 336, 337, 340, 342, 344
Ecclesial base communities. See CEBs
Economic development: and agriculture, 92–93; in Argentina, 243; in Brazil, 278–80, 289; in Colombia, 102–3, 105, 108, 117, 119; and debt crisis, 315, 325; and dependency, 3, 10, 54; and foreign debt, 304–6; and ideology, 182; and modernization theory, 3; in Peru, 92–94; and Western values, 2
Economic structure: and agriculture, 16–17, 51, 120; in Brazil, 279–81, 291, 294, 321; in Chile, 263–65, 269–70, 273–74; in Colombia, 105–6, 108, 112–13; and culture, 4–5, 7; and dependency, 52; and foreign debt, 306; government intervention in, 17–18; international, 50–52, 300–301, 304, 306, 309, 326; and state structure, 113; and U.S. trade deficit, 301
Ecuador, 317, 322; codified indigenous rights in, 387; consumer price increases in, 373, 374 fig., 375
Education: in Chile, 266, 272; in Peru, 70–72, 96, 142; and protest movements, 141–43
Ejército Zapatista de Liberación (EZLN, Mexico), 366–67
El Centro. See Slum (Mexico City)
Elections: in Argentina, 28, 243, 255; in Bolivia, 27–28, 166; in Brazil, 177n, 262, 282–83, 287, 290, 292–95; in Chile, 11, 39, 259, 264; in Colombia, 114–15, 119, 122, 125, 135, 141, 165, 172, 228, 399; in Cuba, 133, 400; in El

Salvador, 138, 166, 172; and everyday forms of resistance, 9–10; fraudulent, 27–28; and gender equity, 384; in Guatemala, 134, 166, 172; and guerrilla movements, 28, 165–66, 169, 177; in Mexico, 28, 43, 166; in Nicaragua, 166; noncompliance with, 27–29, 62, 399, 400; "no re-election" principle of, 335; in Peru, 9, 28, 62, 75, 85, 87, 172, 299; in Philippines, 166; and state structure, 39; in Venezuela, 133–34, 165; and violence, 28, 62; and working class, 39
Eliécer Gaitán, Jorge, 134
Elites: agrarian, 48; in Brazil, 221, 235, 278, 295–97; in Colombia, 222; competition within, 40; in Guatemala, 151; in Peru, 70–71; and political rights, 27–29; and reform movements, 8, 46, 332; and religion, 203, 206, 211, 222–23, 234; and repression, 2, 46–47, 386
El Salvador: agrarian reform in, 167; agriculture in, 152; class alliance in, 164; class struggle in, 164; coffee production in, 150, 155; Communist Party in, 138; cotton production in, 150; counterinsurgency in, 160–61, 167–68; death squads in, 29, 167–68, 176; democracy in, 29; "disappeared" persons in, 26; Duarte government in, 138, 172, 176, 344; elections in, 138, 166, 172; foreign relief funds in, 344; guerrilla movements in, 29, 49n, 132–33, 138–40, 142, 150, 152, 155, 160–62, 164, 166–68, 171–73, 176–77; guerrilla-state negotiations in, 363–64; labor protests in, 368; landlords in, 164; land reform in, 40n; middle class in, 29, 164; migration in, 150; military government in, 25–26, 138, 140, 158; peasants in, 150, 152–53, 155, 158–59, 164; political parties in, 23, 141, 397; proletarianization in, 152; protest movements in, 138; reform movements in, 138, 164, 167; religion in, 30, 158, 173, 203, 209, 213n, 221; repression in, 31, 155; revolutionary movements in, 30; Romero government in, 138; sugar production in, 150; urban poor in, 23; and U.S. relations, 160–61, 176; violence in, 176; working class in, 164
Environmental movements, 359, 391, 394
Erundina, Luiza, 378
Ethnic groups, 4, 7, 12, 23–24, 33–35, 53; in Bolivia, 190–91; codified indigenous

rights of, 387, 390; elites' repression of, 386; in Guatemala, 134, 150, 157, 159; and guerrilla movements, 156–57, 159, 167; in Peru, 81–82, 154, 159, 167; re-democratization's tolerance of, 356–57, 386–87; and religion, 32. *See also* Indigenous movements

Exports, 13, 18, 21; and coca production, 84; Colombian, 102, 105, 108, 117, 120, 123; and debt crisis, 301, 304, 306

EZLN (Ejército Zapatista de Liberación, Mexico), 366–67

Falcoff, Mark, 177

FARC (Colombia Revolutionary Armed Forces), 364, 399

FDNG (New Guatemala Democratic Front), 392

FEPOMUVES (Popular Federation of Women of Villa El Salvador), 385

Food prices, 1990s' increase in, 373, 374 fig., 375

Foreign aid: to El Salvador, 344; and guerrilla movements, 160, 169; to Mexico, 344, 345; to Nicaragua, 344

Foucault, Michel, 203n

France, 41, 48, 159

Frei, Eduardo, 263

Frente Amplio (Uruguay), 398

Frente Zapatista de Liberación Nacional (FZLN, Mexico), 388–89

Friedman, Milton, 264

Fuel prices, 1990s' increase in, 373, 374 fig., 375

Fujimori, Alberto, 362–63, 380, 400

FZLN (Frente Zapatista de Liberación Nacional, Mexico), 388–89

Galbadón, Argimiro, 154

Galbadón, José, 154

Galtieri, Leopoldo, 242–43

García Pérez, Alan, 17, 28, 41, 47, 85, 89–94, 97, 168, 172, 299, 322–23, 362

Garretón M., Manuel Antonio, 11, 15, 38, 355, 382, 397

Gender, 4, 7, 12, 25–26; codified equity of, 384, 385. *See also* Women

"Glass of Milk" Committees (Villa El Salvador, Lima), 385

Goulart, João, 283–84, 286

Graffigna, Omar, 242

Gramsci, Antonio, 9

Gruson, Alberto, 226n

Guatemala: agrarian reform in, 139, 168; austerity measures in, 317; authoritari-anism in, 134; class alliance in, 172, 317; codified gender equity in, 384; codified indigenous rights in, 387; coffee production in, 150; Communist Party in, 157; counterinsurgency in, 134, 160, 170, 363; democracy in, 166; "disappeared" persons in, 26; elections in, 134, 166, 172; elites in, 151; ethnic groups in, 134, 150, 157, 159; guerrilla movements in, 132–34, 139–42, 146, 149–51, 155, 157, 159–62, 165, 167–68, 170–71, 177–78; guerrilla-state negotiations in, 363–64; land tenancy in, 151; Mayan movement in, 391–92; migration in, 150; military government in, 25–26, 140, 158; mineral resources in, 151; peasants in, 139, 146, 149, 151, 153, 155, 157–59, 172; political parties in, 141, 159, 317; racial conflict in, 24; reform movements in, 134, 168, 172; religion in, 32, 158–59, 173; repression in, 31, 151, 172–73; sharecroppers in, 149; United Fruit Company in, 151; and U.S. relations, 134, 160; women's movement in, 383–84

Guerrilla movements: in Argentina, 242–45, 247; in Bolivia, 133, 135, 139–41, 143, 147, 149, 153–54, 158–59, 165, 170, 172, 189; in Brazil, 285–86; and class alliance, 49n, 162–65, 168, 171, 173; in Colombia, 112, 114, 125–26, 132–35, 139–42, 149–50, 152, 154, 157, 159, 161–62, 165–68, 170–72, 177–78, 222, 232, 364–65; in Costa Rica, 47; in Cuba, 34, 133, 138, 143, 146, 150, 156, 159, 161–65, 168–71, 173, 176; and Cuban model, 139; and culture of resistance, 36; deaths tied to, 363, 364; democratization's impact on, 355; drug economy of, 362, 365–66; and elections, 28, 165–66, 168, 177; in El Salvador, 29, 49n, 132–33, 138–40, 142, 150, 152, 155, 160–62, 164, 166–68, 171–73, 176–77; and ethnic groups, 156–57, 159, 167; factionalism in, 134, 138, 161–62, 169, 171; failure of, 133, 139, 141, 143, 149, 153, 160–61, 165–66, 173; and foreign aid, 160, 169; in Guatemala, 132–34, 139, 141–42, 146, 149–51, 155, 157, 159–61, 165, 167–68, 170–71, 177–78; history of, 133–35, 138; in Honduras, 47; and ideology, 135, 139, 155, 162,

165, 168–69; and intelligentsia, 141–43, 155–56; leadership of, 38, 139, 141, 143, 155–57; and linguistic barriers, 158–59; and Maoism, 61, 77, 83, 94, 117–19, 135, 141; and market relations, 18–19, 146, 151–52; and Marxism, 168–69; and mass media, 163, 169–70; and migratory labor, 146, 150; military strength of, 160–62, 176; and nationalism, 139; in Nicaragua, 132–33, 135, 138–40, 142–43, 146, 149, 162–65, 168–71, 173, 176; and peasants, 16, 18–19, 28, 38, 72, 82, 96, 132, 135, 139, 143–46, 147, 149–50, 153, 155–60, 164, 166–69, 171–73, 176–77; in Peru, 35–36, 132–33, 135, 139–43, 149, 153–55, 157–58, 161, 165–66, 167–68, 170–72, 177, 362–63; and political parties, 156, 159; popular support for, 143–59, 171–76; and reform movements, 165–68, 173, 176; and religion, 82, 156, 158–59, 164, 172–73; repression of, 140, 155, 158, 170, 242–44, 247, 286, 363; seizure of power by, 132–33, 138–39, 146, 162, 165, 168, 173, 176; and sharecroppers, 146–47, 149–50; social base of, 47, 55, 76–79, 85, 87, 92, 156–57; and socialism, 173; and squatters, 146–47, 149–50, 156; state's negotiation with, in Central America, 363–64; success of, 132–33, 139, 143, 160, 162, 173; supported by privileged groups, 76–78, 141–43, 155, 164; and trade unions, 189; and university students, 16, 38, 63, 71–72, 77–78, 118, 135, 141–43, 156, 164, 168, 171, 189; and urban insurrection, 170–71; in Uruguay, 47, 170; in Venezuela, 133–34, 139, 141, 146–47, 150, 153–54, 156–57, 159, 161, 162, 165–67, 170–72; and violence, 9, 176, 242–43; of Zapatistas in 1990s, 366–67, 387–89. *See also* Revolutionary movements; Sendero Luminoso

Guevara, Ernesto ("Che"), 133, 135, 139–41, 147, 154, 158, 165, 168, 176–77, 189

Guimarães, Ulisses, 287

Guzmán, Abimael, 77–78, 81, 83, 96, 363

Haiti: austerity measures in, 315, 318, 321; authoritarianism in, 140; democracy in, 30; Duvalier regime in, 321; economic crisis in, 321; peasants in, 140n; protest movements in, 315; religion in, 30; riots in, 140n, 316, 321; and U.S. relations, 321; violence in, 316

Harguindeguy, Albano, 244

Hirschman, Albert, 301, 360

History: and class consciousness, 12; and domination theory, 203n; of guerrilla movements, 133–35, 138; and ideology, 139; and methodology, 3–5

Honduras, 47, 315, 375

Housing movements (Mexico): class/political alliances of, 42, 336–38, 342; community dynamics of, 341, 345–46; *Convenio* accord on, 343–44; and foreign funding, 344, 345; government's response to, 329, 338, 340–41, 342–45, 347, 378; landlords' response to, 346; media support of, 342; new units from, 339–40, 348; success model of, 341. *See also* Slum (Mexico City)

Human rights movements: against former military regimes, 355–56; of women in Argentina, 25–26, 248–58, 382–83

Ideology: and class structure, 3; and economic development, 182; and guerrilla movements, 135, 139, 155, 162, 165, 168–69; and history, 139; and peasants, 1, 15; and political parties, 41, 197; populist, 41; and protest movements, 53; and racial conflict, 24; and religion, 53, 82, 182, 207, 222–24, 231, 235–36; and repression, 47; and revolutionary movements, 48, 139; and social base, 1; and state structure, 41–42

IMF (International Monetary Fund), 20, 41, 126, 291, 294, 300; and austerity measures, 306–9, 318, 321–25, 358; and protests, 309, 318–21, 358–59, 373

Impeachment movements, 399

Import substitution, xv–xvi, 352, 353n

Indigenous movements: of Brazilian Amazonians, 392–93; class alliances with, 388, 391; for cultural identity, 23–24, 387, 390, 392; democratization's tolerance of, 356–57, 386–87; of Ecuadorean Amazonians, 390–91; of Kataristas, 389–90; of Mayas, 391–92; for rights to livelihood, 392–93; of Zapatistas in 1990s, 366–67, 387–89, 388n. *See also* Ethnic groups

Indonesia, IMF protests in, 358

Industrialization, 10–11, 13, 22, 54; in Brazil, 278, 319; in Chile, 263; in

Colombia, 102–3, 106; in Mexico City slum, 333

Institutionalized Revolution Party. See PRI

Institutions: and agrarian reform, 74; democratic, 10; hierarchical, 12; local, 7; participation crisis in, 140; religious, 30–32, 158–59, 205–7, 219, 222–24, 231–34, 332; and social structure, 12

Intelligentsia: in Argentina, 242; in Bolivia, 24; in Colombia, 124; and housing movements, 336; in Peru, 76–78; and revolutionary movements, 38, 139, 141–43, 155–56

Inter-American Human Rights Commission, 244–45, 249, 253

International Monetary Fund. See IMF

Izquierda Unida (Peru), 398

Jamaica: austerity measures in, 315, 325; demonstrations in, 11, 318; foreign debt in, 301, 306, 321–22; protest movements in, 375

Juchitán (Oaxaca, Mexico), 398

Julião, Francisco, 367

Katarista movement (Bolivia), 389–90

Kelley, Jonathan, 48

Khmer Rouge, 61

Kissinger, Henry, 324

Klein, Herbert, 48

Kornhauser, William, 36

Kubitschek, Juscelino, 283

Labor: agricultural, 10, 15–16, 17–18, 34, 44, 48, 70, 108, 111, 121, 146–47, 149–50, 152, 367–68; and collective bargaining, 48; exploitation of, 12–13, 17–18; industrial, 10, 13–15, 48, 54, 119, 183; migratory, 16, 33–34, 44, 54, 72, 121, 146, 150, 360–61, 370–71, 373; neoliberalism's impact on, 368–73; organization of, 13–15; relations with state, 39–40, 54; in small businesses, 10; and surplus value, 12; and urban population, 20; and wages, 12–13, 16–17, 70, 119–20, 288. See also Strikes; Trade unions

Lacerda, Carlos, 283

Lamberg, Robert F., 172

Lambruschini, Armando, 242

Landaburu, Jorge, 248

Landless Workers Movement (Movimiento dos Sem Terra, or MST), 368, 375, 393, 395

Landlords, 48; in Bolivia, 153; in Colombia, 103, 106, 108–9, 111, 113, 115–17,

121, 123; in Cuba, 151; in El Salvador, 164; and labor relations, 146–47; of Mexico City slum, 333, 336, 346; in Peru, 71, 78, 140, 153–54; rural power structure of, 361; in Venezuela, 157

Land reform. See Agrarian reform

Land seizures, 9–10, 15, 22, 40, 115–17, 120–21, 262, 330–31; in Bolivia, 153; in Chile, 264, 273; in Peru, 140, 157, 167

Land tenancy, 16–19, 34, 150–51; in Bolivia, 169; in Colombia, 102–3, 111, 113, 116, 118, 120, 124, 152; in Cuba, 151; in Guatemala, 151; in Mexico, 151; in Peru, 73, 169; in Venezuela, 169

Leadership, 31, 37–38; of Argentine women's organization, 252–53; of Bolivian trade unions, 183, 197; Catholic, 205, 234, 236; of Colombian peasant organization, 119–20, 122; of guerrilla movements, 139, 141, 143, 155–57; of Mexico City slum, 335–36, 348; of political parties, 40; of protest movements, 261, 270, 292, 295–96; of Sendero Luminoso, 38, 61, 63, 65, 77–79, 83; of trade unions, 270–71; and transition to democracy, 261

Levantamiento Nacional Indígena (Ecuador), 390

Levine, Daniel, 1, 9, 30, 55, 394

Lewis, Oscar, 335

Liberation theology, 2, 30, 55, 158, 160, 208n, 235, 287, 336; diminished appeal of, 394–95

Lima shantytowns, women's groups of, 384–85

Lleras Restrepo, Carlos, 112–14, 117

López Michelsen, Alfonso, 119–20

McClintock, Cynthia, 1, 9, 16, 35, 38, 362

MacDonnell, Augusto Conte, 249

Las Madres de Plaza de Mayo, 241, 249–58, 358, 382–83

Mainwaring, Scott, 1, 9, 30, 55, 394

Malinowski, Bronislaw, 197

Manley, Michael, 232, 322, 324

Maoism, 61, 77, 83, 94, 117–19, 122, 124–25, 135, 141

Marcos, Subcomandante, 388

Marijuana production in Colombia, 121

Market relations: and agriculture, 80, 92, 146–47; and class structure, 17–18; and community demobilization, 348–49; in Cuba, 44–45; global versus local, 18, 20; and government policy, 17–18; and guerrilla movements, 146, 151–52; and small businesses, 17–18, 330; and socialism, 19, 21; and social solidarity, 33. *See also* Capitalism; Neoliberalism

Marx and Marxism, 26, 53, 132, 353; and analysis of racial conflict, 25; in Argentina, 244; in Bolivia, 182; and guerrilla movements, 168–69; and industrial labor, 13; and methodology, 5; in Nicaragua, 163; and peasants, 15; in Peru, 61–62, 65, 71, 75–78, 82–83, 85, 96

The Masked Media (Buechler), 192

Massera, Emilio, 242, 248

Matthews, Herbert, 169

Mayan movement, 391–92

Media coverage, 35, 163, 169–70, 342, 379

Menchú, Rigoberta, 392

Mendes, Francisco, 393

Menem, Carlos Saul, 371, 382

Mercier Vega, Luis, 171

Merton, Robert, 8

Mexican Ministry of Urban Development and Ecology, 334

Mexico: agrarian capitalism in, 12; austerity measures in, 315, 329, 344; Catholicism in, 53, 336; class alliances in, 42, 49, 336–38, 342; class struggle in, 37; codified indigenous rights in, 387; corruption in, 42–43; debtors' alliance in, 379; demonstrations in, 42, 316; earthquake in, 42, 334, 336, 337, 340, 342, 344; economic crisis in, 28, 42–43, 308; elections in, 28, 43, 166; foreign debt in, 300–301, 305–6, 308, 322–23; housing movement in, 329, 336–40; land tenancy in, 151; middle class in, 28, 41–42, 49, 349; neighborhood groups in, 23; peasants in, 34–35, 49, 51; political parties in, 39–41, 43, 74, 397, 398; poor in, 28; protest movements in, 309, 315, 366–67; public safety problem in, 380–81; revolution in, 12, 15, 34, 41–42, 53; squatters in, 340; state structure in, 42; strikes in, 39, 372; student activism in, 376–77; urban renewal projects in, 333, 336; and U.S. relations, 51, 322; village life in, 34–35; Zapatista movement in, 358, 366–67, 387–89, 388n. *See also* Housing movements (Mexico); Slum (Mexico City)

Middle class, 17, 20; and austerity measures, 317; in Bolivia, 49–50, 184; in

Brazil, 29, 279, 282–84, 287–88, 291, 296; in Chile, 11, 29, 38, 262, 264–65, 267–68, 271–72; in Colombia, 50, 117, 122; and debt crisis, 324; in El Salvador, 29, 164; and guerrilla movements, 164; in Haiti, 321; and mass media, 163; in Mexico, 28, 41–42, 49, 349; in Nicaragua, 135; in Peru, 299; and political parties, 141; and political rights, 28–29; and protest movements, 55, 267–72, 284, 317, 322, 324, 326; and repression, 37, 49; and revolutionary movements, 49; and state employment, 20n

Mignone, Emilio, 249

Migratory labor, 16, 33–34, 44–46, 54, 121; from Bolivian mines, 370–71; and guerrilla movements, 146, 150; in Peru, 72; reasons for, in 1990s, 360–61

Military government: in Argentina, 25–26, 221, 241–44, 254, 325, 382; and authoritarianism, 261–62; in Bolivia, 24; in Brazil, 24, 38, 216, 220, 233, 273, 278–81, 283, 287, 294–97; in Chile, 25–26, 38, 259–60, 264–75, 382; in Colombia, 107; and depoliticization, 261; in El Salvador, 25–26, 138, 140, 158; exposed atrocities of, by Las Madres, 382–83; extrainstitutional opposition to, 396–97; factionalism in, 74; in Guatemala, 25–26, 140, 158; and mass media, 35; in Nicaragua, 140; in Peru, 51, 72–75, 80, 96, 153; and protest movements, 261–62; and repression, 46, 261; and state structure, 39; in Venezuela, 133

Mills, C. Wright, 12n

Miranda, Rogelio, 189

MNR (Movimiento Nacionalista Revolucionaria, Bolivia), 389n

Modernization, 263; and religion, 30; theory of, 2–3, 24; and village life, 55

Montgomery, Tommie Sue, 177

Montt, Efraín Rios, 134, 159, 168

Moore, Barrington, Jr., 132

Mothers of the Plaza de Mayo. *See* Las Madres de Plaza de Mayo

Movimiento Cívico (Civic Movement, Colombia), 393–94n

Movimiento dos Sem Terra (MST). *See* Landless Workers Movement

Movimiento Nacionalista Revolucionaria (MNR, Bolivia), 389n

Moyano, Maria Elena, 385

Mugica, Carlos, 242

NAFTA (North American Free Trade Agreement), 366, 388

Nash, June, 1, 9, 12, 32, 36, 53, 370, 371

National Commission on the Disappearance of Persons (Conadep), 382

Nationalism, 51; in Argentina, 253; in Brazil, 279; in Chile, 263; and guerrilla movements, 139; and state structure, 300

Nationalization: of Bolivian mines, 182–84, 198, 200, 370; of Chilean copper industry, 263; of Cuban sugar production, 133

National Peasant Association of Colombia. See ANUC

Navarro, Marysa, 355, 382

Neoliberalism: and community demobilization, 348–49; consumer revolts against, 373, 375–77; debtors' protest of, 379–80; exit response to, 360–61, 373; homogenization tendencies of, 353; intent/impact of, xv–xvi, 352, 359–60; Kataristas' opposition to, 389–90; labor rights under, 368–73; Mayan reaction to, 391; and Pentecostalism, 396; in redemocratized environments, 356; squatter claims under, 377–78; and tax increases, 380; Zapatistas' opposition to, 366–67, 388

Neves, Tancredo, 295, 300

New Guatemala Democratic Front (FDNG), 392

NGOs (nongovernmental organizations), 332, 342, 367; domestic/international influence of, 357–58, 397; and ethnic groups, 387; private money funding of, 358; and women's groups, 384–85

Nicaragua: cattle ranching in, 153; class alliance in, 162–65; consumer protests in, 376; democratization in, 165, 400; earthquake in, 138; elections in, 166; foreign debt in, 307, 322; foreign relief funds in, 344; guerrilla movements in, 132–33, 135, 138–40, 142–43, 146, 149, 162–65, 168–71, 173, 176; guerrilla-state negotiations in, 363; market relations in, 21–22; Marxists in, 163; middle class in, 135; military government in, 140; nationalism in, 51; peasants in, 135, 146, 153, 159; political parties in, 23, 141, 163; reform movements in, 165; religion in, 30–31, 52–53, 158–59, 164, 173, 209, 213n,

221, 235; repression in, 165; revolutionary movements in, 30, 49, 162–65; Sandinistas in, 21, 52–53, 61, 149, 152–55, 161–63, 165, 170; socialism in, 49; Somoza regime in, 135, 138, 158, 162–65, 169, 344; squatters in, 149–50; trade unions in, 22; urban poor in, 23; and U.S. foreign policy, 51; working class in, 163

Nixon, Richard, 301

Nongovernmental organizations. See NGOs

Nonviolence, 9, 11, 26, 28, 286–87, 294

North American Free Trade Agreement (NAFTA), 366, 388

Olson, Mancur, 4

Organizations: hierarchical, 14; for human rights, 248–58, 355–56, 382–83; of peasants, 1, 74–76, 82, 102–27, 158, 278, 282, 295; religious, 30–31; and social structure, 12; of urban poor, 23; of women, 25, 241, 249–58, 272–73

Ovando Candia, Alfredo, 184, 189

Oxhorn, Philip, 357n

Paige, Jeffery, 16, 18, 48, 146, 150

Panama, 299, 318, 368

Pan-Maya movement, 391–92

Paraguay, 140, 315, 397

Partido dos Trabalhadores (PT, Brazil), 398

Pastrana, Misael, 115, 117, 119

Patronage, 33, 41, 156–57

Paz Estenssoro, Víctor, 183–84, 370

Peasants: in Bolivia, 24, 27–28, 34, 45, 135, 140, 149–50, 153–54, 158, 167, 169, 172, 183; in Brazil, 235, 278, 282, 288, 295; in Chile, 263, 267; and class consciousness, 122; and class structure, 1–2, 102–3, 109, 112, 121, 123; collectivization of, 169; in Colombia, 6, 29, 38, 40, 55–56, 102–27, 134, 140, 146, 150, 153, 157, 171, 222, 224–29; in Cuba, 34, 146–47, 150, 153; culture of, 81–82; dislocation of, 84, 150–54; in El Salvador, 150, 152, 155, 158–59, 164; in Guatemala, 139, 146, 149, 151, 153, 155, 157–59, 172; and guerrilla movements, 16, 18–19, 28, 38, 72, 82, 96, 132, 135, 139, 143–46, 147, 149–50, 153, 155–60, 164, 166–69, 171–73, 176–77, 361–67; in Haiti, 140n; and ideology, 1, 15; and illiteracy, 225; in Katarista movement, 389–90; in labor movements, 367–68; and land tenancy,

16–19, 24, 34, 73, 111, 113, 120, 124, 150–52, 169; Marx on, 15; in Mexico, 34–35, 49, 51; and migratory labor, 34, 45–46, 360–61; in Nicaragua, 135, 146, 153, 159; organizations of, 1, 74–76, 82, 102–27, 158, 278, 282, 295; in Peru, 62–63, 65, 67–71, 74–76, 78, 81–84, 96, 140–41, 149–50, 153–54, 157, 167, 169, 172; and protest movements, 81–82; and reform movements, 102–3; and religion, 82; and revolutionary movements, 15–16, 34, 38, 48, 72, 103, 151; and Sendero Luminoso, 75–76, 78, 82–83, 94–96, 135, 141, 150; in Venezuela, 133, 146, 150, 157, 167, 169, 171–72; and village life, 33–35, 45–46

Pentecostals, 395–96
People's Republic of China, 41, 48, 61, 169
Pérez, Crescencio, 156
Pérez Esquivel, Adolfo, 248–49
Pérez Jiménez, Marcos, 133, 139
Perón, Evita, 258
Perón, Isabel, 241–43, 258
Perón, Juan, 54, 107, 241, 251
Peru: agrarian reform in, 72–75, 80, 85, 92–93, 95, 153, 172; agriculture in, 51, 67–70, 80; austerity measures in, 315–18, 325; Belaunde government in, 72, 79–80, 90–92, 96–97, 166–67, 172; Catholicism in, 71, 95; class alliance in, 172, 317; coca production in, 65, 67, 70, 84, 87–88; Communist Party in, 77, 135; consumer price increases in, 373, 374 fig., 375; counterinsurgency in, 64, 76, 79–80, 83, 88–91, 94, 96; democratization in, 61, 72, 77, 91–92, 299; demonstrations in, 299, 317–18; depoliticization in, 400; "disappeared" persons in, 90; economic crisis in, 67–70, 72, 74, 88, 91, 308, 319; economic development in, 92–94; education in, 70–72, 96, 142; elections in, 9, 28, 62, 75, 85, 87, 172, 299; elites in, 70–71; ethnic groups in, 81–82, 154, 159, 167; foreign debt in, 299, 301, 306, 308, 322, 325; Fujimori's counterguerrilla initiatives in, 362–63; Garcia government in, 89–94, 97, 172, 325; guerrilla movements in, 9, 16, 35–36, 132–33, 135, 139–43, 149, 153–55, 157–58, 161–62, 165–66, 167–68, 170–72, 177, 362–63; illiteracy in, 70,

72; intelligentsia in, 76–78; landlords in, 71, 78, 140, 153–54; land seizures in, 140, 157, 167; land tenancy in, 73, 169; living standards in, 67–70; Marxists in, 61–62, 65, 71, 75–78, 82–83, 85, 96; mass media in, 35; middle class in, 299; migration in, 72, 82; military government in, 51, 72–75, 80, 96, 153; natural disasters in, 69; nonethnic polarization in, 392; peasants in, 62–63, 65, 67–71, 74–76, 78, 81–84, 96, 140–41, 149–50, 153–54, 157, 167, 169, 172; political parties in, 23, 61–62, 71–72, 74–75, 77, 82, 91–93, 317, 397, 398; protest movements in, 81–82, 322, 380; reform movements in, 47, 167; religion in, 82, 158, 172; repression in, 47, 64, 89–91; riots in, 299; socialism in, 87; strikes in, 316–17; tourism in, 68; trade unions in, 71, 317; urban poor in, 23, 299, 317; and U.S. military aid, 89; Velasco regime in, 72–74; violence in, 89–91, 135, 380, 381; women's groups in, 384–85; working class in, 299

Pinochet Ugarte, Augusto, 11, 15, 38, 259, 264–65, 267–68, 321, 372, 397; military accountability of, 355–56
Pinto, Magalhaesa, 283
Piven, Frances, 6–7
Plan de Arraigo (squatter settlement program), 377n
Plaza de las Tres Culturas massacre (1968, Mexico), 336, 343
Political activism: and austerity measures, 2; and class structure, 3–5, 10; and class struggle, 177; democratization's impact on, 397–400; extrainstitutional resources of, 396–97; global versus local, 3, 12; historical forms of, 10–11; and nonviolence, 9; and religion, 203–4, 207–9, 211–12, 214–18, 222–23, 227–29, 231–33, 235–36, 292; and social base, 1–2; and university students, 266, 269, 272; and women, 2, 216, 219, 249–58, 272–74, 382
Political parties: in Argentina, 254, 397; in Bolivia, 183–84, 197, 199–200; in Brazil, 38, 216, 221, 235, 281–83, 286–87, 289–90, 292–93, 295–97, 319, 397; in Chile, 23, 259, 262–72, 274, 317; in Colombia, 104, 106–7, 112, 115–16, 125–26, 134, 141, 158–59, 222, 227–28; and competition within elites,

40; in Cuba, 159, 163; in Dominican Republic, 319, 325, 397; in El Salvador, 23, 141, 397; generating political activism, 398–400; grass-roots ties of, 397, 398; in Guatemala, 141, 159, 317; and guerrilla movements, 156, 159; and ideology, 41, 197; in Jamaica, 325; leadership of, 40; in Mexico, 39–41, 43, 74, 397, 398; and middle class, 141; in Nicaragua, 23, 141, 163; in Paraguay, 397; in Peru, 23, 61–62, 71–72, 74–75, 77, 82, 91–93, 317, 397; and religion, 216; in Uruguay, 397; in Venezuela, 74, 133, 158–59

Political rights: and class structure, 28–29, 38; and forms of defiance, 27–30

Popular Federation of Women of Villa El Salvador (FEPOMOVES), 385

PRD (Revolutionary Democratic Party, Mexico), 384, 388, 398

PRI (Institutionalized Revolution Party, Mexico): gender quotas of, 384; Juchitán's opposition to, 398; and slum housing movement, 337, 338, 345–46, 347–48; Zapatista opposition to, 366–67

Production relations, 12–17, 20–22; in private versus public sector, 369–70; women's position in, 25–26

Proletarianization, 10, 18, 34, 54, 111, 152

Protestantism, 31–32, 158–59, 227; increase in, 395–96

Protest movements: in Argentina, 315, 322; and austerity measures, 308–9, 315–21, 323, 326–27, 373, 375, 397; in Bolivia, 154, 182–83, 189, 315, 370–71; in Brazil, 280–82, 284, 290–97, 315, 319–20, 367–68; in Chile, 259–60, 265–75; and class alliance, 57, 268–69, 278–79, 282–85, 287, 289, 291, 295–97, 317, 331–32; and class structure, 45; in Colombia, 125, 236; consumer, 373, 375–77; contextualized approach to, 354, 359; in Cuba, 154; deaths tied to, 363, 364, 368; and debt crisis, 300, 321–22, 324–26; by debtors, 379–80; democratization's impact on, 355, 356–58, 372; in Dominican Republic, 325; economic/political perspectives on, 353–54; in El Salvador, 138; fragmentation of, 273–75; in Haiti, 315; and ideology, 53; in inner cities, 346–47; leadership of, 261, 270, 292, 295–96; and mass media, 33; in Mexico, 309,

315, 336–40, 379–80; and middle class, 55, 267–72, 284, 317, 322, 324, 326; and military government, 261–62; NGOs' role in, 357–59, 384–85, 387; nonpolitical, 53; and nonviolence, 286–87, 294; pan-regional homogenization of, 358–59; patterning of, 12, 43, 54–56, 330–32; and peasants, 81–82; in Peru, 81–82, 322; and racial conflict, 23; and religion, 52–53, 203–4, 208, 236, 248, 259, 261, 264, 266, 286–87, 289; and social structure, 5; and state structure, 262, 332; by street vendors, 378–79; against taxes, 380; and unequal distribution, 54; and university students, 266, 269, 272, 283–85, 376–77; and urbanization, 315–16; and urban poor, 271, 317, 322, 326; in Venezuela, 133, 154; and women, 272–73; and working class, 266–71, 284, 320, 322, 324, 326

Psychology, 4–5, 56

PT (Partido dos Trabalhadores, Brazil), 398

Racial conflict, 23–24, 53; and race-based movements, 393–94

Rational-choice theory, 4, 6, 13–14, 19, 30, 39

Reagan, Ronald, 357, 362

Reform movements, 6, 8; in Bolivia, 153; in Chile, 263–64; in Colombia, 111–13, 115–16, 120, 123, 126; in Cuba, 165; and elites, 46, 332; in El Salvador, 40n, 138, 164, 167; global versus local views of, 352–53; in Guatemala, 134, 168, 172; and guerrilla movements, 165–68, 173, 177; in Nicaragua, 165; and peasants, 102–3; in Peru, 47, 167; and repression, 46; in Venezuela, 167. *See also* Agrarian reform; Neoliberalism

Religion, 4, 9; in Argentina, 209, 244, 248–49, 251; and authoritarianism, 216–17; in Bolivia, 182; in Brazil, 30, 32, 203–5, 209–10, 214–21, 233–36, 286–87, 289, 292; in Chile, 30, 203, 248, 259, 264, 266; and church-state relations, 30, 204, 222; and class structure, 228–29; in Colombia, 158, 172, 203–5, 209, 214, 222–36; and conservatism, 31–32, 203, 206, 208n, 213n, 216–17, 219, 221–23, 226n, 232, 234–35; in Cuba, 32, 158, 164; and culture, 206–7; and democracy, 30; in Dominican Republic, 30; and ecclesial base communities (CEBs), 30–31, 37, 55, 158–59, 204–7, 209–25, 230–31, 234–36; and elites, 203, 206, 211, 221–23, 234; in El Salvador, 30, 158, 173, 203, 209, 213n, 221; and ethnic groups, 32; and forms of defiance, 32, 52–53; in Guatemala, 32, 158–59, 173; and guerrilla movements, 82, 156, 158–59, 164, 172–73; in Haiti, 30; and ideology, 53, 82, 182, 207, 222–24, 231, 235–36; institutional, 205–8, 219, 222–24, 231–34; and latitudinarianism, 52–53; and modernization, 30; in Nicaragua, 30–31, 109, 158–59, 164, 173, 213n, 221, 235; and peasants, 82; in Peru, 82, 158, 172; and political activism, 203–4, 207–9, 211–12, 214–18, 220, 222–23, 227–29, 231–33, 235–36, 292; and political parties, 216; and populism, 204–6, 210–15, 219–20, 224, 229–30, 233–34, 236, 286–87; and protest movements, 52–53, 203–4, 208, 236, 248, 259, 261, 264, 266, 286–87, 289; regional transformation of, 394–96; and repression, 31, 211; and revolutionary movements, 30, 158–59, 209, 221; and U.S. influence, 32; and violence, 158. *See also* Catholic church; Liberation theology; Protestantism

Rent Control Law (Mexico City), 333, 335, 346

Repertoire of protest, 9–11, 19, 139–41, 149, 330, 331–32; in the 1990s, 354–59. *See also* Protest movements

Repression, 11, 316–17; in Argentina, 241–49, 252–54, 257, 383; in Bolivia, 36, 183–84, 188–89, 193, 195, 199; in Brazil, 31, 233, 279, 281–83, 285–88, 291–92; in Chile, 11, 31, 38, 259–60, 264–69, 271, 274, 321; in Colombia, 102, 104, 106, 117–21, 125; and counterinsurgency, 64; in Cuba, 165; and elites, 2, 46–47; in El Salvador, 31, 155; of ethnicity, 386; extrainstitutional response to, 396–97; in Guatemala, 31, 151, 172–73, 383; of guerrilla movements, 140, 155, 158, 170, 242–44, 247, 286, 363; and ideology, 47; in Jamaica, 321; in Mexico, 336, 366–67; and middle class, 37, 49; and military government, 46, 261; in Nicaragua, 165; in Peru, 47, 64, 89–91; and reform movements, 46; and religion, 31, 211; and

state structure, 42; and strikes, 13–14; of trade unions, 119, 125, 188–89, 269; and urban poor, 23; in Venezuela, 134, 139, 170; and violence, 9; of Zapatistas in 1990s, 366–67

Resistance: culture of, 7, 33, 35–36, 38, 81–82, 141, 154–55, 182, 201, 335–36; everyday forms of, 1, 8–10, 13–15; supported by privileged groups, 37–38

Resource-mobilization theory, 6, 43, 155

Revolution: agrarian, 15–16, 34–35; in Bolivia, 15, 19, 43, 49–50, 200; in China, 41, 48; and class structure, 48–50; in Cuba, 15, 18, 32, 54, 77, 132, 138–39, 161–65, 168–69, 263; French, 41, 48; and ideology, 48; in Mexico, 12, 15, 34, 41–42, 53; and military desertion, 48; in Nicaragua, 162–65; outcomes of, 48; rareness of, 8; Russian, 41, 48; and state structure, 48; and student militants, 37; supported by privileged groups, 37–38, 49–50

Revolutionary Democratic Party (PRD, Mexico), 384, 388, 398

Revolutionary movements, 1, 6, 8, 12; in Bolivia, 49, 183, 197; in Brazil, 285; and class alliance, 49–50, 162–63; and class consciousness, 197; in Cuba, 49; and Cuban model, 139; in El Salvador, 30; and ideology, 139; and intelligentsia, 38, 139, 141–43, 155–56; leadership of, 37–38; in Mexico, 49; and middle class, 49; and modernization theory, 2–3; nationalist, 16; in Nicaragua, 30, 49; and peasants, 15–16, 34, 38, 48, 72, 103, 151; and religion, 30, 158–59, 209, 221; and socialism, 16, 49, 173; and social science, 64–65; and state structure, 41–43, 48–49; supported by privileged groups, 49–50, 76–78, 155, 164; and trade unions, 183; and university students, 285; urban, 170–71, 285–86; in Venezuela, 161; and village life, 34; and working class, 54. *See also* Guerrilla movements; Sendero Luminoso

Riots, 9–11, 20, 291, 299, 309, 316, 318, 326; in Brazil, 316, 319–20; in Dominican Republic, 319; in Haiti, 140n, 321

Rituals, Bolivian, 6, 9, 32, 36, 182; and agriculture, 184–85, 195; and Carnival, 185–87, 190–95, 201; and Christianity, 185–88, 190–91, 194, 196, 201; and class consciousness, 187, 190–94,

196–98; and commodity fetishism, 193, 196, 201; and dance, 188, 190–93; and ideology, 197, 200; and Pachamama spirit, 184–86, 189, 192, 194–95, 198; repression of, 185, 188–89, 193, 195, 199; and sacrifice, 184–85, 187, 192, 195–96; and Supay spirit, 185–87, 190, 192, 195–96, 201

Rohatyn, Felix, 324

Rojas Pinilla, Gustavo, 107, 112, 115, 134

Romero, Archbishop, 31, 158, 172

Rondas (anti-Sendero defense units), 362–63

Roofless People movement (Brazil), 378

Rural population, 17, 33–34; and class structure, 45; in Colombia, 105, 108–9, 121, 125; and migratory labor, 44–45

Russell, Diana, 161

Salinas de Gortari, Carlos, 344, 366–67, 388

Sánchez de Losado, Gonzálo, 389–90

Sandinistas, 52–53, 61, 135, 149, 152–55, 161–63, 165, 170

Sandino, Augusto, 154

Sarney, José, 300, 323

Scott, James, 8

Seaga, Edward, 325

Sendero Luminoso: assassinations by, 61, 78–79, 87, 94–95; clandestine structure of, 79, 91, 96; and coca production, 84, 87–88; and competition with MRTA, 87–88, 95–96; and elections, 28; and ethnic groups, 159, 392; and everyday forms of resistance, 9; Fujimori's strategy against, 362–63; government repression of, 62, 64, 79–80, 89–91, 96; and highlands culture, 81–83; initiation of armed struggle by, 61, 76, 78; and intellectuals, 76–78; leadership of, 38, 61, 63, 65, 77–79, 83; and Maoism, 61, 77, 83, 94, 141; and media coverage, 170; and peasants, 62–63, 65, 75–76, 78, 82–83, 94–96, 135, 141, 150; popular support for, 62–65, 81–85, 87, 94–95, 97, 135, 155, 172; recruitment tactics of, 362; social base of, 9, 16, 36, 38, 47, 76–79, 85, 87–88, 95; and students, 63, 65, 76–78, 83, 96, 135, 142, 159; and urban insurrection, 94, 171; and violence, 61, 63–64, 78–79, 83, 85, 87–88, 95, 135, 176, 381

Siles Zuaso, Hernán, 24, 43, 183–84, 200

Silva Henríquez, Raúl, 248

Skocpol, Theda, 7, 41–42, 48

Slum (Mexico City): community demobilization in, 347–49; and *Convenio* accord, 343–44; economic/social base of, 334–36, 341–42; housing movement in, 336–40; inhabitants of, 331, 332–33, 334; rents for housing in, 333, 335, 339; squatter alternative to, 340–41; urban renewal plans for, 333, 336, 340. *See also* Housing movements (Mexico City)

Smelser, Neil, 5–6

Socarrás, Carlos Prío, 163

Socialism: in Bolivia, 183; in Chile, 11, 259; in Colombia, 103; in Cuba, 14, 49, 133, 168; and guerrilla movements, 173; and market relations, 19, 21; in Nicaragua, 49; in Peru, 87; and revolutionary movements, 49; and social structure, 12; and unequal distribution, 14, 21

Social science: and analysis of insurgency, 64–65; and behaviorism, 2–3; and dependency theory, 3; and functionalism, 197; and historical-structural approach, 4–7; and methodology, 2–3; and modernization theory, 2–3, 24; and psychology, 4, 56; and rational-choice theory, 4, 6, 13–14, 30, 39; and resource-mobilization theory, 6, 43, 155

Social structure: analysis of, 5–7; and culture, 56; and forms of defiance, 5, 7; global versus local, 3, 12; and institutions, 12; patriarchal, 25; and protest movements, 5; and socialism, 12; and unequal distribution, 3, 12; and village life, 33–35

Sole Coordinating Committee of Earthquake Victims (CUD, Mexico), 337, 338, 342

Solidarity program (Mexico), 366

Somoza Debayle, Anastasio, 31, 53, 132, 135, 138, 155, 158, 162–66, 168–69, 344, 358

Somoza Debayle, Luis, 135

Somoza García, Anastasio, 135

Soviet Union, 41, 48, 61, 169

Squatters, 16, 22–23, 25, 34; Argentina's settlement program for, 377n; in Bolivia, 147; in Brazil, 288, 319, 340n; in Chile, 37, 340n; in Colombia, 150; consumer defiance by, 330–31; in Costa Rica, 378; in Cuba, 147, 150–51, 156; and guerrilla movements, 146–47, 149–50, 156;

in Mexico, 340; in neoliberal environment, 377–78; in Nicaragua, 149–50; slum dwellers versus, 331, 331n, 334; in Venezuela, 150, 377–78

State structures, 2–4, 7; authoritarian, 39–41, 104, 140, 300, 327; in Brazil, 278–80, 287–88, 290–92; and bureaucracy, 41–43, 48, 52–54, 104, 281, 300, 327; and capitalism, 280–81; in Chile, 262–63; and church-state relations, 30, 204, 222; in Colombia, 104–7; and community-state relations, 342–45, 346; and corruption, 42; in Cuba, 42, 49; and debt crisis, 324–27; and economic structure, 41, 113; and elections, 39; and employment, 20n; and foreign debt, 300; and forms of defiance, 51, 381; and hegemony, 42; and ideology, 41–42; and labor relations, 39–40, 54; in Mexico, 42; and military government, 39; and nationalism, 300; and participation crisis, 140; and protest movements, 262, 332; and repression, 42; revolutionary, 41–43, 48–49; and unequal distribution, 39, 41, 48–49

Strikes, 1, 8, 10–11, 326; in Argentina, 316–17, 371; in Bolivia, 40, 187–89, 200, 316, 318, 370–71; in Brazil, 291–92, 295, 371–72; in Chile, 39, 264, 266–68, 273, 316–17, 372; in Colombia, 118; decrease in, in 1990s, 368–70, 369 fig., 372; in Dominican Republic, 318–19; globalization's impact on, 355, 360, 369–70; illegal, 13–14; in Mexico, 39, 372; in Peru, 316–17; political dynamics of, 371–73; in private versus public sector, 369–70. *See also* Trade unions

Stroessner, Alfredo, 140n, 358

Student activists: in Brazil, 283–85; in Chile, 266, 269, 272; in consumer protest movements, 376–77; in guerrilla movements, 16, 18, 63, 71–72, 77–78, 118, 135, 141–43, 156, 164, 168, 171, 189; in Mexico, 376–77; and Sendero Luminoso, 63, 65, 76–78, 83, 96, 135, 142, 159

Sugar production: in Bolivia, 147; in Cuba, 133, 151; in El Salvador, 150

Suharto, 358

Tax resistance, 380

Tilly, Charles, 10–11, 27, 143, 145, 159

Torres, Camilo, 172, 236n

Torres, Juan, 184, 189, 199

Trade unions: in Argentina, 242, 247, 317; and austerity measures, 315–17; in Bolivia, 183–84, 187–89, 197–99, 317; in Brazil, 235, 278–79, 281–82, 284, 288–89, 292–93, 295–96, 367–68; in Chile, 15, 263, 266, 268–71; in Colombia, 105–6, 112, 119, 122, 125, 228; and consumer protests, 375; and debt crisis, 315; in Dominican Republic, 317, 319; in Ecuador, 317; and guerrilla movements, 189; leadership of, 183, 270–71; under neoliberal reform, 368–70; in Nicaragua, 22; in Peru, 71, 317; repression of, 119, 125, 188–89, 269; and revolutionary movements, 183; and strikes, 13–14. *See also* Strikes

Trotskyism, 115, 117, 124, 157, 182

Túpac Amaru guerrilla movement, 363

Tuyac, Rosalina, 383

United Fruit Company, 151

United States: anticommunist foreign policy of, 51, 169; and Argentina, 254; and Chile, 264; coca eradication projects of, 365, 371; and Colombia, 114; and counterinsurgency, 134, 160–61, 363; and Cuba, 133, 139, 163; and debt repayment, 47; and El Salvador, 160–61, 176; and Guatemala, 134, 160; and Haiti, 321; and hegemony, 2; immigration restrictions of, 361; and Mexico, 322; and military aid, 89; NGO contracts with, 357; religious right in, 396; support for Somoza regime by, 163; support of democratization by, 352; and Third World debt, 323–24; trade deficits in, 301; and Venezuela, 160

Urbanization, 2, 22, 315; of peasants, in 1990s, 360–61

Urban population, 17–18, 20; in Colombia, 117; and neoliberal reform, xvi, 371–73; and organization of poor, 23; squatter movements of, 330–31, 377–78

Uruguay: consumer price increases in, 373, 374 fig., 375; democracy in, 47; guerrilla movements in, 47, 171; political party ties in, 397, 398; working class in, 278

Vecindades (tenements), 333, 334n, 336, 339

Vecindad organizations (Mexico), 337–38

Velasco Alvarado, Juan, 72, 74

Véliz, Claudio, 52

Venezuela: agrarian reform in, 134, 153, 167; austerity measures in, 134, 139,

315; class alliance in, 157; Communist Party in, 133–34, 157; consumer price increases in, 373, 374 fig., 375; counterinsurgency in, 160; coup d'état in, 133; democracy in, 133; elections in, 133–34, 165; foreign debt in, 305; guerrilla movements in, 133–34, 139, 141, 146–47, 150, 153–54, 156–57, 159, 162, 165–67, 170–72; landlords in, 157; land tenancy in, 169; military government in, 133; peasants in, 133, 146, 150, 157, 167, 169, 171–72; political parties in, 74, 133, 158–59, 398; protest movements in, 133, 154, 375, 376; reform movements in, 167; repression in, 134, 139, 170; revolutionary movements in, 161; sharecroppers in, 147, 150; squatters in, 150, 377–78; and U.S. relations, 160; violence in, 134; working class in, 171–72

Videla, Jorge Rafael, 242, 244, 248, 383
Villa El Salvador (Lima shantytown), 385
Village life, 33–35, 45–46, 54–55, 224
Villalobos, Joaquín, 161
Viola, Roberto, 242–43
Violence, 9, 20, 25; in Argentina, 242–43; in Bolivia, 316; in Brazil, 282, 285–86, 292, 300; in Chile, 273; in Colombia, 29, 40, 106–7, 111–12, 134–35, 139, 146, 149, 151–52, 157, 227–28; in Dominican Republic, 318; in El Salvador, 176; and guerrilla movements, 176, 242–43; in Haiti, 316; and land tenancy, 151–52; in Peru, 89–91, 135, 380; public response to, in 1990s, 380–81; and religion, 158; and Sendero Luminoso, 61, 63–64, 78–79, 83, 85, 87–88, 95, 176, 381; in Venezuela, 134
Wages, 12–13, 16–18, 20, 53, 70; in Brazil, 288; in Chile, 262, 266; in Colombia, 119–20; and debt crisis, 308, 321
Wagley, Charles, 24

Walton, John, 6–7, 11, 20, 40–41, 47, 55, 358
War on Drugs (United States), 365
Weber, Max, 32, 139
Westerkamp, José Federico, 249
Wickham-Crowley, Timothy, 1, 16, 18, 36, 38, 46–47, 55, 355, 361
Wolf, Eric, 16, 34, 84
Women: and class structure, 25, 257; "disappeared persons" investigation by, 26, 382–83; and family, 25; gender equity for, 384; institutionalized programs of, 384–85; marginalization of, 25–26; and Marianismo, 26; organizations of, 25, 241, 249–58, 272–73; in pan-regional movements, 358; and political activism, 2, 216, 219, 249–58, 272–74, 382; and rights of motherhood, 25–26, 382; and sexual division of labor, 256–57
Workers Party (Partido dos Trabalhadores, Brazil), 398
Working class: in Argentina, 54, 249, 278; in Bolivia, 183; in Brazil, 38, 217, 278–79, 282–84, 286–89, 294, 296–97, 319–20; in Chile, 38–39, 54, 262, 266, 268–70, 278, 321; in Colombia, 105, 117, 124–25; in Cuba, 54; and debt crisis, 320, 324; and elections, 39; in El Salvador, 164; in Nicaragua, 163; in Peru, 299; and protest movements, 44, 266–71, 284, 320, 322, 324, 326; and revolutionary movements, 54; and state structure, 54; in Uruguay, 278; in Venezuela, 171–72
World Bank, 69–70, 306, 323, 344
Yrigoyen, Hipólito, 242, 244–45
Zamosc, León, 1, 6, 38, 50, 55, 363
Zapata, Emiliano, 12, 34, 151
Zapatista movement, 358, 398; PRI's response to, 366–67; tactics/strategy of, 366, 387–89
Zedillo de la Ponce, Ernesto, 376–77

Compositor: G&S Typesetters, Inc.
Text: 10/12 Baskerville
Display: Baskerville
Printer: Maple-Vail Book Manufacturing Group
Binder: Maple-Vail Book Manufacturing Group